HASIDISM

SUNY Series in Judaica:
Hermeneutics, Mysticism, and Religion

Michael Fishbane, Robert Goldenberg, and Elliot Wolfson, editors

HASIDISM

Between Ecstasy and Magic

by MOSHE IDEL

STATE UNIVERSITY OF NEW YORK PRESS

Published by
State University of New York Press, Albany

Printed in the United States of America

For information, address State University of New York Press,
State University Plaza, Albany, NY 12246

Production by Christine Lynch
Marketing by Theresa Abad Swierzowski

Library Of Congress Cataloging-in-publication Data

Idel, Moshe, 1947–
Hasidism : between ecstasy and magic / by Moshe Idel.
p. cm.—(SUNY series in Judaica)
Includes bibliographical references and index.
ISBN 0–7914–1733–6 (CH acid-free).—ISBN 0–7914–1734–4 (PB acid
-free)
1. Hasidism—History. 2. Mysticism—Judaism—History. 3. Cabala-
-History. I. Title. II. Series.
BM198.I32 1995
296.8'09—dc2093- 92-47504
CIP

10 9 8 7 6 5 4 3 2 1

To J.N.
in friendship

"Put your shoes [*na ᶜaleikha*] off of your feet [*rageleikha*]." This means that you should put off the enclosure [*Ferschlissung*] of your routine [*regilut*].

Rabbi Moshe of Kobrin, *ʾAmarot Tehorot*

Every advance in a science takes us farther away from the crude uniformities which are first observed, into greater differentiation of antecedent and consequent, and into a continually wider circle of antecedents as relevant.

Bertrand Russell, *Mysticism and Logic*

Contents

Preface

The present book emerged from the gradual evolution of some ideas presented in a number of articles and lectures prepared during the last decade. Most decisive was a lecture delivered in 1984 at a symposium on the eighteenth-century Jewish thought organized by Professor Isadore Twersky, at Harvard University, printed in German in 1987 and more recently in English 1991.[1] Its content forms most of chapters 1 and 4. A conference on Hasidism at the University College of London in 1988, which will soon be available in print in the proceedings of the symposium, served as a catalyst for ideas presented, in more elaborate manner, in parts of the introduction. Another, unpublished lecture, delivered at the first anniversary of the death of Professor Shmuel Ettinger, organized by the Shazar Center for Jewish History in 1989 at the Van Leer Institute in Jerusalem, provided the core of chapter 2. The material collected and analyzed in a series of articles printed during the last decade, dealing mainly with ecstatic Kabbalah and magical interpretations of Kabbalah, convinced me that the resistance, sometimes rather sharp, to some of the views presented in these lectures apparently stems more from the fact that there are some scholars who are not sufficiently acquainted with some aspects of Jewish mysticism, rather than from a superior understanding of Hasidism. From those exchanges I learned, nevertheless, that the scholars' tendency to minimize the impact of speculative corpora, neglected by modern scholarship, might be somehow attenuated, if at all, by adducing tens of quotes in order to make a point that, in a less inertial entourage, would be understood much easier.[2] Therefore, all the lectures have been expanded and much more material has been introduced than a neutral reader would expect. This material, sometimes still in manuscripts, may help not only to understand better some aspects of Hasidism, but also to contribute to another view of Kabbalah in general. In the present form of my exposition an attempt has been made to approach the Hasidic and Kabbalistic material as part of an inner development, that will propose a certain answer to the question what is the relationship between these two lores.

---

1. See *The Journal of Jewish Thought and Philosophy* I (1990): 53–114.
2. With the exception of Miles Krasen's Ph.D. thesis, the above discussions of magic and Hasidism have been ignored by all the studies and books on Hasidism printed in the last years.

A first draft of the book, completed at the end of 1992, has been read by some colleagues, who have contributed very helpful remarks. Thanks are due to Professor Ithamar Gruenwald, Dr. Moshe Halbertal, and Professor Yehuda Liebes. Conversations with Dr. Michael Silber, Dr. Elhanan Reiner, Professor Isadore Twersky, and Dr. Beracha Sack contributed to formulations of some of the issues treated below. A penetrating perusal of the book has been very kindly undertaken by Professor Arthur Green, whose many suggestions and corrections have been integrated, improving the book. Both his critique and encouragement have been very constructive. Professor Elliot R. Wolfson has read carefully the whole manuscript and proposed several helpful suggestions, for which I am very grateful. I would like to express also my thanks to Dr. Daniel Abrams and Ephraim Jacob, who have been very helpful in preparing the various stages of the manuscript. Last but not least: the book has been written while a member of the Shalom Hartman Institute for Advanced Studies in Judaica in Jerusalem, which provided an encouraging ambiance. The Center for Research on History and Culture of Polish Jewry of the Hebrew University has been helpful in the preparation of the final form of the book. For any mistakes still remaining in the book, I am solely responsible.

Special thanks are due to Jeffrey Neuman, whose friendship and generosity have been decisive in completing this manuscript.

Introduction

Ecstasy and magic stand at the opposite extremes of most modern religious modalities. The spiritualization of the contact with the divine in Western mysticism, radically different from the more materialist propensities of magic, invites detachment from the body—and from corporeality in general—in order to be able to enjoy communion with the divine. Magic has been conceived of as a phenomenon drastically different from ecstasy. However, the founder of eighteenth-century Hasidism has been described as both a mystic and a magician. Rabbi Yisrael ben Eliezer, better known as the Ba^{c}al Shem Tov, literally, "the Master of the Good Name," combines in his praxis these two ways of relating to reality, which were so characteristic of archaic modes of religion. Were they independent activities, unrelated moments in his spiritual life? Did they create a tension in Hasidic religiosity? Does magic preclude an intense mystical life, or vice versa? From the phenomenological point of view, what does the nexus between these two ideals mean? Does Hasidism in the eighteenth and nineteenth centuries preserve this dual nature of its found? Is the link between mysticism and magic new with Hasidism or can we find precedents for it in earlier forms of Jewish literature? Are the answers to these questions available in the framework of the existing historical and phenomenological descriptions of Hasidism?

These questions have apparently been marginal in academic surveys of this mystical lore; they move at the center of the present study. Rather than portraying Hasidic literature as reflecting disparate religious moments, the ecstatic and the magical modes, we shall propose here a more complex religious model, one that sees these two aspects as phases of a more comprehensive scheme. The gist of this argument is that in many instances the Hasidic "righteous men," the *ẓaddiqim,* did not conceive of ecstasy as their ultimate goal; rather, they had an additional spiritual aim: the drawing down of the divine effluence for the benefit of the community. This latter movement, described here as magic, shows that mysticism and leadership are part of a more coherent way of life, one that incorporates the sublime experience of the *perfecti* into a large ideal, and that strives to contribute to the more ordinary well-being of the *Ẓaddiq*'s humble adherents. It is the return of the Hasidic mystic from his ecstatic experience as a powerful master who is, consequently, conceived as the pillar of his community, that will concern us in the following discussions.

In depicting various Hasidic phenomena as mystical and magical, I do not intend to imply any negative valuation. Indeed, in line with the modern concern with religious issues—issues that were once conceived as pernicious—I am inclined to see the two extremes of the Hasidic experiences as attempts to deal, on one hand, with the contact with the divine, and on the other, with the role of the mystic in his community and his attitude to corporeality. By emphasizing the role of magic, and that of the theory of magic, I hope a more comprehensive picture will emerge, one that does justice to the experiential aspects in all their diversity and that takes into account more sources than the prevailing scholarship has done.

However, before addressing these matters in detail, a survey of the two main attempts to describe Hasidism as a mystical phenomenon in modern times, that of Martin Buber and that of Gershom Scholem, will prepare the ground for some methodological proposals. It is only by standing on the shoulders of these two giants that another vision of Hasidism is possible.

1. HASIDISM AND TWENTIETH-CENTURY APPROACHES

Twentieth-century interest in Jewish mysticism started as early as 1906, with Martin Buber's very successful expositions of Hasidic tales to the general public. A drastic departure from nineteenth-century scholarly descriptions, which were concerned with Kabbalah but very rarely with Hasidism, Buber's project was from the very beginning different from his *Wissenschaft des Judentums*' predecessors in Germany and elsewhere in central Europe. Buber was little concerned with the history of the movement, even less with the philological analyses of texts, and still less with tracing their precise ancient or medieval sources. He described Hasidism in a positive light, as being a form of mysticism sui generis, one that had nourished the spiritual life of communities for many decades. Buber's emphasis on the experiential side of Hasidism is related to his interest in the legendary aspects of Hasidic literature, rather than the more theoretical aspects of Hasidic homiletics. It is the popular tales, much more than the "sublime" but at the same time abstract thought of the masters, that, already at the beginning of our century, fascinated Buber, and with him many readers.[1]

However, the course of interest in Jewish mysticism changed dramatically in one generation with the emergence of the scholarship of Gershom Scholem and his school. Following, to a certain degree, the more historical-philological avenue opened by nineteenth-century Jewish scholars, they undertook an extensive and solid examination of the numerous Jewish mystical texts, their historical development and leading ideas. By using classical tools of textual analysis, by relating ideas to their background, and above all by attempting to locate Hasidism within the larger scheme of Jewish mystical and messianic trends, Scholem and his students made possible the emergence of a much more detailed and accurate picture of Hasidic thought. In what may be the most interesting intellectual debate in twentieth-century Jewish studies, the more impressionistic descriptions of Buber came under the fire of the historical-philological school. On one side of this debate was Buber, attempting to answer queries asked from perspectives he was not interested in; on the other side were Scholem and Schatz-Uffemheimer, who took Buber to task on a number of important issues, among them his neglect of the more theoretical aspects of Hasidism, as well as his existential and subjective readings of the sources.[2]

Since then, the Scholemian approach has been accepted as the standard method by modern scholars, and only very rarely are academic disagreements with the founder of modern scholarship in the field of Jewish mysticism discernible.[3] The historical problems that were marginal to Buber moved, in most cases, to the center of the research of Scholem's school.[4] Outside its perimeter, various other disciplines, like sociology[5] and psychology, have been used sporadically to study Hasidism.[6] Consequently, some more general explanations concerning the emergence of Hasidism, all of them concerned with historical factors, have been proposed here.

What are the important differences between the approaches of Buber and Scholem? According to Buber, Hasidism represents, in essence, a departure from the major form of Jewish mysticism that preceded its emergence, namely Lurianic Kabbalah; the originality of Hasidism as a mystical phenomenon lies, according to Buber, in the introduction of a unique type of religiosity, which has hardly any parallel in the history of mysticism.[7] Buber presents Hasidism not so much as a continuation of, or even a reaction to the dominant type of Kabbalah, namely Lurianism, but *sui generis,* as a phenomenon that is unique not only in comparison to other kinds of Jewish mystical literature, but even when compared to any other form of mysticism. For Buber, Hasidism represents the transformation into a mystical ethos of two earlier forms of Judaism, Halakhic Judaism and the Kabbalah, conceived of mainly, or even completely, as Lurianic mysticism, a lore that was regarded as a type of Gnostic thought.[8] According to the explanation proposed by Gershom Scholem, however, Hasidism constitutes a reaction to the Sabbatean movement, which was regarded by the early masters of Hasidism as a heresy, although some of the concepts of Sabbateanism, and most of the view of Lurianism, were adopted by the nascent, Hasidic type of mysticism. Let me start with an especially significant statement that illustrates Scholem's stand.

> Lurianic Kabbalism, Sabbateanism and Hasidism are after all stages of the same process . . . a proselytizing tendency which was already inherent in the first. The distinguishing feature of Lurianic Kabbalism was the important part played by the Messianic element . . . In the Sabbatean movement this urge for redemption "in our time" became the cause of aberrations. Great as was the influence of Sabbateanism . . . [i]ts extravagant paradoxicalness,

> which overstressed the fundamental paradox inherent in every form of mysticism, remained an affair of comparatively small groups. Hasidism . . . represents an attempt to make the world of Kabbalism, through a certain transformation or re-interpretation, accessible to the masses of the people. Here, [in Hasidism] the Kabbalah did not renounce its proselytizing mission . . . Hasidism represents an attempt to preserve those elements of Kabbalism which were capable of evoking a popular response, but stripped of their Messianic flavor to which they owed their chief successes during the preceding period. That seems to me the main point.[9]

In other words, Hasidism is considered a reaction to Sabbateanism through its neutralization of the messianic elements (which, Scholem says, had already characterized Lurianism) without, however, combating Kabbalah as such. It is obvious that in Scholem's view Sabbateanism and Hasidism are only two different types of reactions to the dissemination of what he conceived to be the messianic nature of Lurianism; Sabbateanism actualized the messianic elements to a point that they came to the fore on the historical arena in the form of a mass movement, while Hasidism neutralized those apocalyptic elements, whose explosion on the public scene had created a heretical type of Jewish mysticism.

An important contribution to the problem of the sources of Hasidism, which does not attempt to offer a large-scale theory of its emergence, was proposed by Isaiah Tishby. He pointed out the relationship between the Kabbalah and the ritual practices of R. Moshe Ḥayyim Luzzatto, who flourished shortly before the appearance of Hasidism as a mystical movement.[10] Tishby even indicated that it is possible Hasidism emerged from circles of Sabbateans.[11] Much more than his effort to find in the rituals of Luzzatto the origins of certain practices of the Hasidic masters, his argument that Hasidism may have originated among former Sabbateans is the most outspoken form of what I propose to call "proximism."[12]

The latest view, though not the least important, is the explanation offered by Mendel Piekarz, who emphasized as a motive for the emergence of Hasidism the dissemination and influence of the moralistic and ethical literature written under the profound influence of Safedian Kabbalah. Piekarz's minimizes the impace of Sabbateanism, although he implicitly agrees with the deep contribution of Lurianic Kabbalah to the formation of the new mysticism.[13]

Though conspicuously different from each other, all these explanations share an important common denominator, which was not openly articulated, as far as I am aware, by these scholars: they all explained the mid-eighteenth-century mystical movement as the continuation of the religious phenomenon that immediately preceded it. Alhough to Buber it was a minor point, he nevertheless considered Hasidism to be a reaction to Kabbalah, though he did not totally ignore the reaction to Sabbateanism; for Scholem it was obviously the attempt to offer a religious alternative to the Sabbatean crisis that motivated the formation of the Hasidic teachings. Tishby was even more inclined to see the continuation of Sabbateanism in Hasidism.[14] For Piekarz, however, the ethical literature was the closest body of literature, both in time and space, to Hasidism, and as such was considered a major source of basic Hasidic concepts. The divergences among these explanations may be attributed to a preceding spiritual event that, in each case, motivated—even in a reactive manner—the emergence of Hasidism. In one way or another, these explanations accept another basic assumption, reasonable in itself, that the closer two or more religious events are to each other in space and time, the greater the chance that they are related to one another in a significant way. Before turning to an examination of the problems involved in this explanation, let me address briefly some divergences between Buber and Scholem on other issues.

a) Buber's basic approach is phenomenological; he is interested primarily in the religious characteristics of a certain type of mysticism, and only secondarily in its historical genesis.[15] His discussion centers on the spiritual parameters of Hasidic mysticism and touches only tangentially on historical points.[16] By contrast, Scholem's interest in Hasidism is primarily historical, since he regards this brand of mystical literature as the most recent expression of a larger phenomenon, Jewish mysticism, whose complete history he attempts to describe. Thus, the relationship between Hasidic ideas and earlier mystical literature—in this case, almost exclusively the literatures of the Lurianic and the Sabbatean schools—is crucial to an understanding of Scholem's approach to Hasidism.[17]

b) Buber was concerned from the very beginning with mysticism in general, as his *Ecstatic Confessions* would testify. His enterprise in the field of Hasidism was an integral part of his philosophical-experiential orientation, which gravitated toward the Orient in the nineteenth-century, *fin de siècle*, fashion of his time.[18] Scholem's frame of mind was different: the continuum of Jewish mysticism and its particular dynamic had formed the starting point of his considerations, which centered upon the historical and philological questions.[19]

c) In moving from the realm of textology to that of phenomenological understanding, Scholem was more concerned with the theological problems posed by Hasidism, such as the importance of the ideal of *devequt* and the place of pantheism,[20] while Buber, in his early mystical phase, was more concerned with experiential issues,[21] turning later to the dialogical approach.[22]

d) These divergent approaches directed the two scholars to two different types of Hasidic sources. For Scholem, concerned with describing Hasidic theology, the pertinent body of texts was the theoretical, homiletic writings of the masters of Hasidism.[23] Buber, on the other hand, interested in the living expression of the Hasidic phenomena, in the realization of the Hasidic experience in daily life and popular literature, focused on the legendary accounts of the lives of the Hasidic masters, and it was this type of literature that became the basis for his interpretation of Hasidism.[24]

e) Guided by his phenomenological approach, Buber ultimately reached the view that Hasidism expressed the quintessence of Judaism, excluding other types of Jewish spirituality such as the Kabbalah and apocalypticism from what he considered to be the essential components of the Jewish religion.[25] In principle, Buber was looking for the perennial element in Hasidism that could nourish his own religiosity. Scholem, on the other hand, was guided by historical and critical considerations that he translated into a theological stance, accepting most of the various expressions of Jewish mysticism as authentic Jewish phenomena, in line with his pluralistic vision of Judaism. Buber's romantic posture is conspicuously different from Scholem's critical approach; indeed, Scholem himself pointed out that Buber had ignored some of the less attractive aspects of Hasidism, most strikingly its magical components.[26]

Notwithstanding the crucial divergences discussed above, it is possible to identify some important common ground shared by these two great scholars. Both not only aspired to understand the essence of Hasidism, they also considered Jewish mysticism as a possible bridge between Jewish tradition and the Judaism of the present. Thus, their presentation of the writings of the past is not only a scholarly endeavor, but a creative cultural act intended to generate a new relationship to Jewish tradition, to coexist with if not to replace traditional orthodoxy. From this point of view Buber, an exponent of Hasidism, and Scholem, a scholar in the field of Jewish mysticism in general, share a similar basic orientation: their reevaluation of Jewish mysticism is a crucial aspect of their literary activities, an integral part of their respective visions of national revival.

Though differing from these two scholars in many ways, Abraham J. Heschel also emphasized the vital role of Hasidism for modern Judaism and portrayed it, sometimes in a way reminiscent of Buber, as representing the essence of Judaism. Less concerned than Scholem was with the historical aspects of the emergence of Hasidism, Heschel was more interested in it as a spiritual, rather than a mystical phenomenon; his expositions of Hasidism reflect a deep affinity both with the literary texts and with the Hasidic lived experience.[27]

2. PROXIMISM

Let us turn to the major points of agreement between Buber and Scholem.[28] These are a) what one could call proximism; b) the assumption that the Kabbalah is a gnostic type of mystical lore; and c) reductionism. Let me start with proximism, which seems to be the most important.

a) Buber and Scholem are in agreement that Hasidism has to be understood as part of a greater development whose turning point was the diffusion of Lurianism and its messianic explosion in Sabbateanism and Frankism. In order to understand the Hasidic phenomenon historically, each looked at the peculiar spiritual situation of the Jews in Poland before the emergence of Hasidism, and thus each was guided by the assumption that a great spiritual upheaval had found expression in the formation of Hasidism. The nexus between messianic Lurianism in its heretical forms and Hasidism is essential to the understanding of the historical explanations advanced by both scholars.[29] Proximism may evolve in two different forms. The first is reactive, asserting that a later phenomenon is related to one immediately preceding it by virtue of the fact that the later phenomenon is a reaction to the former one. On the other hand, proximism may point to a relation of partial continuity between two consecutive phenomena; thus Hasidism could be seen not only as the reaction to some elements in the heretical form in which Lurianism was presented in Sabbateanism, but also its continuation with respect to other elements. Scholem espoused both forms of proximism,[30] whereas Buber was more sympathetic to reactive proximism.[31]

b) Scholem, and under his influence Buber,[32] considered the Kabbalah as a gnostic phenomenon.[33] For Buber, primarily in the later phase of his thought, the characterization of the whole of Kabbalistic tradition as gnostic had a negative connotation, because it was this quality, he felt, that caused the estrangement of the mystic from the real world.[34] In the case of Scholem, too, it is possible to detect a certain derogatory note in his exposition of the emanative structure in the Kabbalah, though this is marginal to his vast scholarly enterprise. According to Scholem, the emanative system of theosophical Kabbalah was detrimental to the mystical nature of Kabbalah.[35] Although in evaluating the great abyss between man and God the respective religious concerns of Scholem and Buber were quite different, it seems that both agreed on the uniqueness in Judaism of the median structure of emanation, and it is this that accounts for their characterization of the Kabbalah as gnostic. Scholem had stamped the Kabbalah with the mark of gnosticism at the very beginning of his scholarly career, drawing on what was then the modern vocabulary of the field.[36] Buber, who was critical of the Kabbalah for its schematization of the mystery, conceived this lore as a peculiar, antidualistic form of gnosticism. The underlying assumption of Buber and Scholem with regard to the gnostic structure of the Kabbalah is one of the cardinal (and in my opinion the most problematic) hypotheses related to Jewish mysticism ever formulated by Jewish scholarship. If it should prove erroneous, and for the time being I do not see any historical or philological reason for accepting it, then the entire exposition of the relationship between Kabbalah and Hasidism would need to be set out afresh, with a new set of concepts and criteria.

c) Buber's characterization of the whole of the Kabbalah as gnostic, and his frequent references to this characterization when comparing Hasidism and Kabbalah, render his approach to this mystical lore monolithic, and consequently reductionist; this can be demonstrated by his presentation of Hasidism as a single unified phenomenon.[37] Buber's comparison between the two huge literary corpora of Hasidism and the Kabbalah was a daring spiritual enterprise that, curiously enough, was never challenged by Scholem. Buber contrasted Hasidic devotion with its gnostic "core," which he implicitly identified with Lurianism,[38] entirely overlooking the diversity of each of these two brands of literature. Scholem, who was acquainted with the diverse literature of the Kabbalah, was uncritical of this omission because he himself was convinced that the only Kabbalistic school to be taken into serious consideration when attempting to explain the emergence of Hasidism was the Lurianic one.[39] Although he was well aware that the Kabbalah could not be reduced to mere Lurianism, Lurianism alone was featured in his own analysis of Hasidism.

d) Last but not least, Buber and Scholem were in disagreement over the type of Hasidic literature that was most likely to reveal Hasidism's true essence. According to Buber, the legendary literary corpus was more representative of what he considered to be essential Hasidism,[40] whereas Scholem gave preference to the speculative literature of the movement.[41] Moveover, *ex silentio,* we learn that Buber and Scholem never acknowledged each other's preferred literary corpora as in any way capable of yielding an authentic characterization of Hasidism. Each argued that "his" type of literature alone could expose its true nature. Thus, the implicit assumption of both was that Hasidism must be seen as a unilateral type of mysticism, legendary and dialogical according to Buber, or pantheistic and speculative as claimed by Scholem.

As far as I am aware, neither Buber nor Scholem was ready to offer a more complex picture that would include both aspects of this richly variegated religious phenomenon. The simplistic assumption that the truth was to be found mainly in the books in which each was interested, but not in those preferred by the other, is problematic; but it was clearly shared by these two giants of the modern exposition of Jewish mysticism. Dialogical as Buber's view was, it could not enter into a fruitful dialogue with the more historical presentation of Scholem; pluralistic and liberal as Scholem's view of Judaism was in general, it was not pluralistic enough to take into account some of the findings of Buber's phenomenological approach, which are pertinent to the last phase of Jewish mysticism. A more moderate approach, less concerned with the importance of one type of literature over another, might attempt to find the common denominators of these types of literature, without entering a harmonistic frame of mind. Great as the two authors were as religious thinkers, they often used terminology that was too grandiloquent to define a phenomenon as multifaceted as Hasidism in their efforts to conform its various aspects to the particular concerns of their minds.

It seems reasonable to argue, though I cannot elaborate here on this proposal, that the theoretical literature reflects mainly the mystical relationship between the *Ẓaddiq* and the divine, whereas the narrative part of the Hasidic writings reflects the social dimension of Hasidism, namely the relationship to his community of the mystic who returns to this sphere in order to contribute to its improvement. Thus, the question of what particular type of Hasidic literature is more representative of its essence may be solved by the proposition that different topics are dealt with in different types of literature.[42] Buber, who described Hasidism as capable of living with paradoxes without resolving them, nevertheless did not imagine that Hasidism might have been transmitting on more than one wavelength.

3. THE PANORAMIC APPROACH

In lieu of and to a certain extent in addition to the above explanations, which are so strongly historically oriented, I would like to propose an explanation that may appear prima facie to be less historical, and which nonetheless differs drastically from both Buber's existentialistic approach and Scholem's historicism. Its basic assumption is that, notwithstanding the fact that Lurianism, Sabbateanism, and the ethical-Kabbalistic literature all display a certain affinity in their religiosity and genre and were closest in time and space to Hasidism, the alternatives that faced Hasidic masters in the construction of their own peculiar spiritual configurations were more numerous and diverse than these three particular bodies of literature. In print at that time were more Kabbalistic works than Sabbatean ones, more pre-Lurianic Kabbalistic writings than Lurianic ones; as for the *Musar* literature, its popularity and immense influence must be placed in a larger context, which will permit a fuller acknowledgement of the parallel influence of purely theological works, all of which, available in print, had opened up Kabbalistic doctrines to a wider public.[43]

Let me state at the outset that I do not envisage the emergence of Hasidism as a battle of books, ancient versus modern, in the manner of eighteenth-century English literary debates. The dissemination of a particular book or group of books does not produce, in itself, a major spiritual phenomenon. Such an explanation of the rise of Hasidism is simplistic, and no less blinkered than the explanations we are presently trying to modify. My assumption is that not only were the Hasidic masters exposed to a more multifaceted, mystical literature than it is assumed in modern scholarship, but that most of the available texts in matters of Jewish mysticism belong to the pre-Lurianic type of Kabbalah. The quantitative criterion is meaningful only if it is corroborated by evidence of the dissemination of qualitatively different concepts. In other words, I would consider the impact of one set of works decisive by comparison with that of another only if they presented two distinct types of ideology or theology. Consequently, the difference between the presentation of a mystical paradigm in an ethical treatise and the same idea in a theological work seems only secondary. The real issue, which goes beyond the sheer variety of available sources, is that the founders of the nascent Hasidic movement had access to a long series of written mystical materials that stemmed from periods recognized as equally decisive in the formation of Hasidiam, notwithstanding the historical gap that separated their time of composition from the time when the first Hasidic masters began their activity. Theoretically, in fact, the whole range of Jewish cultural traditions was available to the early Hasidic masters, from the Bible to the most recent Sabbatean and Frankist innovations. Since I do not see why anyone would have preferred a more recent, heretical series of texts and concepts to earlier and more authoritative material, the emphasis of both Buber and Scholem on the crucial relevance of the "modern" Sabbateans as against "ancient" authorities must be seen as derived, at least to a certain degree, from a historiosophical model that neither of them ever set out in a systematic way. In order to be free of such an historiosophical model of thought when attempting to pinpoint the most important factors that contributed to the formation of Hasidism, we must allow for the widest range of possibilities before selecting any as the most influential.

Such an approach results in a broader view of the relevance of the history of Jewish mysticism on the understanding of Hasidic mystical thought. The central question in the development of Jewish mysticism does not seem to be the links between the various Kabbalistic schools within a historical continuum, with the *Zohar* necessarily preceding the expulsion from Spain, the expulsion preceding (and thus explaining) Lurianism, and Lurianism preceding Sabbateanism, which in turn is "logically" followed by Hasidism. Instead of this developmental model, one may observe in each of the manifestations of Jewish mysticism, including Hasidism, a series of choices made from a variety of existing alternatives.

Divergent mystical paradigms had been available since the earliest stages of Jewish tradition in Talmudic-Midrashic times; these were enriched by the medieval Jewish mystics.[44] In the thirteenth century, a variety of these mystical paradigms crystallized into several articulated mystical schools, which can be defined phenomenologically, historically, and geographically. The Kabbalah, for example, appeared at the end of the twelfth century, in several distinct formulations that are still extant.[45] None of the variegated developments of thirteenth-century Kabbalah had disappeared completely, at least not as literary documents that could surface and fructify the spiritual lives of later Kabbalists. The assumption that Lurianism alone, or any other particular type of Kabbalistic thought, was the single major impetus behind all subsequent developments in Jewish mysticism, including Sabbateanism, is an oversimplification that would become all too prevalent in the literature of modern scholarship. Only the coexistence in Jewish mysticism of a variety of mystical paradigms can explain how Hasidism was able to put back in circulation a whole range of key mystical concepts that were either marginal or absent from both Lurianism and Sabbateanism. How can anyone explain, for example, the centrality in Hasidism of the concepts of *hitbodedut, hishtawwut, hitpashshetut ha-gashmiut, bittul ha-yesh,* and *hitkallelut,* or the extreme formulations of *unio mystica,* as merely a continuation of or reaction to Lurianism and Sabbateanism, in which these mystical ideas are negligible or even nonexistent?

What are the major speculative paradigms, in addition to Lurianism and Sabbateanism, that were available to the Hasidic masters before the middle of the eighteenth century? They are (a) the Heikhalot literature; (b) early Kabbalah, which consisted mostly of Castilian treatises written in the thirteenth century, in the generation of the composition of the *Zohar;* and the *Zohar* itself. Let me quote in this connection a pertinent passage from R. Meshullam Phoebus of Zbarazh's *Yosher Divrei ʾEmet.*

> On the issue of the study of the writings of Luria, blessed be his memory, I know that you yourself will not study it without a [master] greater than you are, and you cannot find someone. But you shall study *Sefer Shaʿarei ʾOrah* and *Ginnat ʾEgoz* and, mostly, the book of the *Zohar* and the *Tiqqunim.*[46]

As we shall see below, fifteenth-century Kabbalistic treatises, like R. Shem Tov ben Shem Tov's *Sefer ha-ʾEmmunot,* also left an imprint on Hasidism, directly or indirectly.

c) Cordoverian Kabbalah. Besides the Lurianic Kabbalah, whose importance has been recognized by Hasidic masters and modern scholars, the Cordoverian Kabbalah was highly influential. In print, it was no less available than the Lurianic corpus, and it was circulated in wider circles than the doctrines of Luria. It penetrated Eastern Europe through two channels: the theoretical works of Cordovero and the popular expositions of his views that appeared in the Musar literature.[47]

d) The mystical theories of the Maharal of Prague, which had been available in print for several decades, drew on the authority of this highly respectable author and offered a less technical *Weltanschauung* than that of all the Kabbalistic treatises. Recently, two scholars have pointed to the deep affinity between some of the Maharal's concepts and certain Hasidic doctrines, and there is no doubt that his is a fertile field for future research on the emergence of Hasidic mysticism.[48] In this context it should be mentioned also that a biblical commentary composed by a disciple of the Maharal, R. Shelomo Ephraim of Luenitz's *Keli Yaqar,* was widely quoted by the Hasidic masters.

e) Renaissance Kabbalah. This is a combination of Spanish Kabbalah and various philosophical schools, from medieval Aristotelianism and Neoplatonism to Hermeticism and Renaissance Neoplatonism.[49] Although the impact of this type of Kabbalah on further developments in Jewish mysticism has not been investigated closely, its influence was apparently considerable. This was mostly an indirect influence, through the integration by Cordovero of some features of Renaissance Kabbalah,[50] but possibly there was also a direct influence on eighteenth-century Kabbalistic authors by Kabbalists like R. Matatiahu Delacrut, who had studied in Italy during the sixteenth century and whose works were in print for almost two centuries before the emergence of Hasidism. This, too, must be pursued in future studies of the emergence of Hasidism. For the time being, it seems obvious that the amalgam of Kabbalah, philosophy, and magic, characteristic of some Renaissance figures, can be detected also during the period of the crystallization of Hasidism in the manuscript writings of Salomon Maimon, who lived in the same areas of Eastern Europe where Hasidism flourished.[51]

f) The earlier Ashkenazi Hasidism of the twelfth to thirteenth centuries;[52]

g) The Polish Kabbalah of the first half of the seventeenth century, written by Kabbalists such as R. Sampson of Ostropoler, R. Nathan Netaᶜ Shapira of Cracow, and R. Arieh Leib Pryluk.[53]

h) The Kabbalistic writings of R. Joseph ben Shalom Ashkenazi, especially his *Commentary on Sefer Yeẓirah,* printed and quoted by the Hasidim under the name of Rabad. The depth of influence of this book has not yet been recognized in modern scholarship. That influence is both direct, through quotes and from the printed edition, and indirect, as the result of its impact—along with other writings of this Kabbalist—on *Sefer ha-Peliyʾah,* Cordovero, and Luria.[54]

i) The ecstatic Kabbalah of the thirteenth and fourteenth centuries, written in Italy and the East. These manuscripts were still available in and were circulated in eighteenth-century Poland. In this way this school influenced Hasidism directly, as well as indirectly through its earlier influence on the Kabbalah of Safed.[55] Some of the mystical concepts related to Hasidism stem, ultimately, from the interest of ecstatic Kabbalah in methods for reaching the mystical experience. It is also possible to detect some structural affinities between Hasidic hermeneutics and the hermeneutics characteristic of ecstatic Kabbalah, all of which have been ignored by modern scholarship.[56]

j) Medieval philosophy, mostly as formulated by Maimonides, but also the more Neoplatonically inclined variety, such as that found in the works of R. Abraham ibn Ezra, R. Yehudah ha-Levi, or R. Yiẓḥaq Abravanel.

We have enumerated here only the major bodies of medieval and post-medieval speculative literature that were available, in more than one way, to the early Polish Hasidism. There is no question that they were also acquainted with the Heikhalot mysticism and at least some of the pietistic theology of the twelfth and thirteenth centuries formulated in the Rhineland.[57] Important Kabbalistic books, like *Sefer Berit Menuḥah,* or *Sefer ha-Peliyʾah,* should also be counted among the books that shaped some Hasidic views. Only when we take into account the entire range of paradigms—what I call the mystical panorama—and the possible interplay of all its elements with one another, shall we arrive at a sounder understanding of the more complex phenomenon of Hasidic mysticism.

Provided that these sources were available to the emerging Hasidism, such a panoramic approach would see Hasidism not as a reaction to a crisis but, primarily, as the result of the interaction of a long series of spiritual concepts and paradigms and social factors. The basic assumption of this approach is the existence of the regular curriculum of the Jews, who were supposed to study the Bible and later on the basic halakhic texts, but only rarely—at the very end of the ideal Jewish curriculum—mystical sources. Access to mystical ideas was not only achieved directly, through the major *chef d'oeuvres* of the Kabbalists, but also through the more popular presentations of Kabbalistic ideas as they appeared in ethical and moral literature, saturated as it was by Cordoverian Kabbalistic concepts.[58] In principle, the study of complex Kabbalistic texts, either in print or in manuscript, was the prerogative of a small elite. One can only assume that access to the heretical Kabbalah—Sabbatean or Frankist—was extremely limited, not only because of theological inhibitions but also because of the limited diffusion of such texts.

The necessity for giving greater importance to the non-Lurianic forms of Jewish mysticism can be easily demonstrated by a short survey of some key concepts of Hasidic mysticism that are either marginal or completely absent in Lurianism in all its forms. For example, *devequt* cannot be found as a crucial mystical requirement in the religiosity of Luria or the Lurianic texts. This deemphasis, though not rejection, of *devequt* as the main ideal represents a retreat even from the peculiar structure of the mystical religiosity of the *Zohar,* whose impact on Lurianism was overwhelming. Thus, the increase in the importance of *devequt* has nothing to do either with Lurianism or Sabbateanism, or with anti-Lurianism or anti-Sabbateanism.[59] I would argue that basically, the retreat from theosophy and theurgy, with their messianic implications in Sabbateanism, is not a neutralization of either one of them. Every neutralization is, after all, a reaction. Essentially, Hasidism is a choice between, rather than a reaction to, already existing mystical values, numerous and often diverging speculative themes, and religious models in Judaism—a selection emphasizing topics that were active and effective in the earlier stages of Jewish mysticism and were still propagated in some forms of ethical literature.

We may take as an example the practice of *hitbodedut,* the seclusion or isolation from society as part of the mystical path of the ideal Hasid. Though Luria himself practiced *hitbodedut,* it does not become an organic element in Lurianic Kabbalah; this Kabbalah was rooted in group study and emphasized the importance of ritual deeds, the *miẓwot,* which are accomplished ideally in the community. *Hitbodedut* was thus marginal to the spirit of Luria's Kabbalah.[60] Nevertheless, the influence of this concept, with all its nuances, is visible in the major versions of Hasidism, a fact that cannot be explained either as a reaction to or a continuation of Lurianic and Sabbatean Kabbalah.[61] Such examples are numerous and concern not marginal concepts but, on the contrary, vital components of Hasidic mysticism. If this diagnosis is correct, it attenuates the importance of analyzing Hasidic mysticism in terms of its relationship to those mystical phenomena that are closest to it historically. Linear historiosophies engage only one set of problems, while evading, as in the case of the origin of Hasidic mysticism, other central types of problems.

The interest of the Hasidic masters in Kabbalah seems to be much broader and more variegated than that of Buber, for example. This we can easily learn from the fact that among those Kabbalistic writings Hasidim chose to print at the end of the eighteenth century, only a few are Lurianic treatises. Indifferent to the linear concept of history as advocated by modern scholarship, and apparently rejecting the Lurianic assumption that Kabbalistic works written after Naḥmanides are to be ignored as the result of the human intellect—that is, as too human a creation in comparison to Luria's revealed Kabbalah—Hasidim embarked on a fervent campaign of printing that included classics of Kabbalah from the thirteenth to fifteenth centuries, like *Sefer Temunah, Sefer Qanah,* and *Peliyʾah,* and *Sefer Shoshan Sodot* by R. Moses of Kiev, and his *Commentary to Sefer Yeẓirah,*[62] or *Liqqutei R. Hai Gaon.*[63]

The preoccupation with these writings and other similar early Kabbalistic texts testifies to a profound interest in several versions of Kabbalah, basically different from the Lurianic one. The interest in these non-Lurianic books can be seen by examining the texts on which the Hasidic masters commented. In comparison to the variety of the earlier literary genres cultivated by the Kabbalists, Hasidism was much more limited in its literary expression. Most of the literary creations of Hasidism are based either on commentaries on the Pentateuch or on ethical literature; nevertheless, there are also various attempts to comment on Kabbalistic texts, particularly the *Zohar,* about which Hasidism produced an impressive body of literature that has been ignored by modern scholars of both Kabbalah and Hasidism. Though this is the most important genre of Hasidic commentaries on Kabbalah, surpassing their interpretive interest in Lurianic literature, there are several commentaries on early Kabbalistic texts, such as the numerous glosses of R. Yisrael of Kuznitz on some Kabbalistic works like *Sefer ha-Temunah* and *Liqqutei Rav Hai Gaon,* as well as short observations on *Peri ʿEẓ Ḥayyim* and *Siddur ha-ʾAri.*[64]

The need for a panoramic approach to the sources that molded the mystical ideas of Hasidism is thus readily apparent. The proximist approach, whether reactive or continuative, was based upon the assumption that the texts that had the most decisive influence on the Hasidic masters were the Lurianic ones, or the Sabbatean versions of them. Thus, the scholars who advocated this approach implicitly excluded the possibility of any interplay between different strands of Kabbalah, the only notable exception being Mendel Piekarz, who introduced the ethical-mystical literature on a large scale into the academic discussion. However, even he did not point out that some of the important "Hasidic" ideas that he traced back to the *Musar* literature originated ultimately from one peculiar type of Kabbalah, the Cordoverian one.[65] No serious scholar acquainted with Hasidic texts would argue that because Lurianic Kabbalah was based upon Zoharic ideas and was transmitted as a more profound interpretation of these ideas, Hasidim ignored the *Zohar*. Even when aware of the importance of Luria for understanding the *Zohar,* Hasidic masters nevertheless did not refrain from composing their own original commentaries to the *Zohar*. Beginning with the disciples of the Great Maggid of Miedzyrec, the literary genre of Zohar commentaries flourished and infiltrated a whole body of Hasidic writings, almost all of which have been ignored by the modern study of Hasidism.[66] This genre constitutes only one obvious demonstration of the coexistence of different strata of Kabbalistic literature, despite the fact that the Hasidic masters themselves did consider the latest developments in matters of Kabbalah as the most profound.

The question may be asked. Is it possible to reconstruct the mystical panoramas that lay before the individual Hasidic masters? Along the lines of earlier remarks, we should stress that the mystical panorama of the Besht does not appear to have been identical, or even similar, to that of the Great Maggid. We must assume the existence of a whole range of panoramic views, each characteristic of the curriculum of a Hasidic master and of his spiritual idiosyncracy. There is no way to portray one basic panorama, and it would be reasonable, in order to avoid an extreme atomization of the academic discourse on the source of Hasidism, to outline a broader landscape, whose crucial components were either fully or partially shared by some or all of the Hasidic masters.

As in viewing a physical landscape, the process of observing this spiritual landscape entails not only comprehensive, or holistic, perceptions but also linear connections between one point and another, the shift from one to the other affecting the unique perspective of the observer. So, for example, if one became acquainted first with the Cordoverian Kabbalah and only then with the Lurianic Kabbalah, this could well affect one's understanding of the nature of Lurianic Kabbalah;[67] the opposite is also true. At times, the fascination with or fixation on an attractive idea or cluster of ideas found in one Kabbalistic school could well nourish a Hasidic master for years, while all other points on the landscape would linger in view without affecting his perception, however important or daring these ideas might be in themselves. Surely, the eighteenth-century Hasidic masters were not able to take in each and every detail of this vast landscape; no doubt there were numerous blind spots, areas that escaped their attention altogether. Moreover, an idiosyncratic perspective would yield an idiosyncratic view, and some of the masters had clearly misunderstood or distorted the "real" spiritual concerns of the original sources. Despite these limitations, there is no reason why we should exclude from their field of vision all but those developments in Jewish mysticism that were nearest to their own time. The plurality of the mystical and non-mystical sources, the panoramic landscape, is one of the reasons for the diversity of Hasidic mystical phenomena.

4. "NEUTRALIZING" MESSIANISM?

Let me offer one example of the difference between the panoramic and proximist approaches: the central and highly disputed subject of the status of messianism in Hasidism. According to both Buber and Scholem, Hasidism had neutralized the messianic elements inherent in Lurianic Kabbalah as a reaction to the fateful events connected to Sabbateanism. Thus, according to both Buber and Scholem, Lurianism had to lose its putative vital messianic character in order to function effectively in the new "critical" conditions of mid-eighteenth-century Poland.[68] Scholem suggested, therefore, that *devequt,* essentially confined to the inner process of individual redemption, had come to replace the collective messianism of the "Lurianic" school.[69] In principle, I am inclined to accept Scholem's phenomenological diagnosis of what was most highly valued in Hasidism,[70] although I strongly disagree with his historical explanation for it. Moreover, I am not sure we must assume an acute messianism in Lurianism in general;[71] I am not aware of a specific example provided by Scholem where a messianic discussion stemming from Lurianic circles was interpreted so as to neutralize its alleged acute messianism. Indeed, it can be easily demonstrated that not only was collective messianism put aside or neglected by the leading masters of early Hasidism, this happened also with the messianically charged concepts of *ʾEreẓ Yisrael* and even the Temple, which were interpreted to point to personal perfection. Even the sacrosanct ten *sefirot* of the theosophical Kabbalah became, according to most Hasidic masters, allegories of inner psychological states.[72]

Thus it would be better, even from Scholem's point of view, to conceive of the neutralization of messianism in general—rather than of Lurianic messianism alone—not as a special case of the struggle with the quandary of Sabbateanism, but as part of a larger scheme or religious paradigm for constructing a devotional, ahistorical mysticism, free from any concrete geographical ties.[73] While some aspects of this scheme had also served polemical purposes, as did the attempt to counteract Sabbatean and Frankist heretical messianism, their significance should not be reduced merely to their having solved these quandaries. *Devequt,* as a way of personal redemption and a vital mystical value that was conceived as replacing the Lurianic *tiqqun,* with its messianic overtones, is not a new mystical value at all; it existed in thirteenth-century Jewish philosophy[74] and in the contemporary ecstatic Kabbalah of Abraham Abulafia.[75] However, it would be very difficult indeed to ascribe to these thirteenth-century Kabbalistic sources the tendency to neutralize an ideal of active messianism; this is highly improbable in the case of the philosophers, and it would not seem reasonable to envision Abulafia as someone who neutralized messianism or even acute messianic trends in Judaism. He in fact considered himself to be a messiah and acted in the public arena as such.[76] However, this does not detract from his presentation of the union with God, or the Active

Intellect, as a redemptive act, able to be achieved before the arrival of the messianic aeon.[77]

We may learn from this example that the neutralization of messianism in Jewish mysticism is not new, at least not on the phenomenological level, and thus we may assume, at least in principle, that part of the spiritual panorama of the masters of Hasidism also included an arena where *devequt* was considered to be an eschatological endeavor. To assume this, it is not necessary to prove that the whole paradigm of ecstatic Kabbalah was known to the Hasidim and used as an alternative for "messianic" Lurianism. It would be sufficient to show that the importance of *devequt* as the paramount mystical value was accepted by the Hasidim, even without showing its connection to Lurianism or Sabbateanism. By way of an inner and organic development, this might have shaped their consciousness, while external factors—historical, geographical, or theosophical—became marginal by comparison with their spiritual attainment at the moment of the mystical experience. Thus, according to this second assumption, it is possible to envision a situation in which *devequt* moved to the center of mystical life; this resulted in a complete restructuring of mystical thought along the lines of the ecstatic Kabbalah, despite the fact that the details of this type of mysticism may not have been entirely known. The shift of focus to the spiritual value of *devequt* automatically reduces the importance of the external factors in religion, including the dimension of historical time in connection with the eschaton.

5. IMMANENTISM

A similar approach may be taken in connection with the ideal of pantheism or, according to some scholars, immanentism—another important and controversial issue in Hasidic theology. According to Scholem, pantheism is characteristic of Hasidic thought;[78] another scholar has recently proposed to consider immanentism as one of its unique features.[79] However, despite the frequent use of immanentist imagery and concepts, this theological conceptions was not an innovation of Hasidic masters, but had been formulated long before them in older strands of the Kabbalah; as the Hasidim themselves acknowledged, and as Scholem has correctly pointed out,[80] Hasidic pantheistic and panentheistic formulations were drawn from R. Moshe Crodovero.[81] Moreover, it is possible to show evidence for a theory of immanence that was practically identical with that of the Hasidic masters in a teaching of a contemporary of the Besht, R. Menaḥem Mendel, the Maggid of Bar. He is reported to have explained why he looked down when he prayed by saying that "he is looking for a very low place, because there also is Divinity and His vitality,[82] and there is no place void of Him,[83] because in everything there is His vitality, even in the lowest degree."[84] The terms used here betray a view that is hardly distinguishable from any classical Hasidic formulation of immanence. If the quote is authentic, and for the time being I see no reason to doubt it, we may conclude that the immanentistic turn is not a specific development in Hasidism but was shared by a contemporary of the Besht and is to be seen in the larger context of the resurgence of Cordoverian thought in the eighteenth century.[85]

Thus, Hasidism does not constitute a dramatic departure from the universally accepted view of God's transcendence; the Hasidic masters simply preferred one available theological paradigm to another, in this case the more theistic Lurianic theosophy. Moreover, one of the crucial illustrations of immanentist perception in Hasidic literature, the vision of God when contemplating a woman, was clearly extracted from the work of R. Elijah de Vidas, a disciple of Cordovero, who quotes it from a lost treatise of R. Yiẓḥaq of Acre, who was profoundly influenced by ecstatic Kabbalah.[86] Although there is room for further discussion on the problem of Hasidic pantheism or immanentism, the question of sources lies beyond the scope of this study; these sources should be analyzed in detail in order to point out what is old and what is new before deciding that this shift departed dramatically from existing theological paradigms.

Finally, it is important to note that it is no accident that Hasidism as a mystical phenomenon was concerned with *devequt,* understood in some sources as *unio mystica,* and that, theologically, pantheism was preferred by this type of mystical thought. These two concepts had already been integrated in the paradigm of ecstatic Kabbalah as two correlative concepts.[87] It is possible to unite with God because He permeates all of existence, and this continuous diffusion of the divine facilitates the mystical encounter.[88]

6. HASIDISM: BETWEEN HARMONIZATION AND ATOMIZATION

The present proposal calls for a greater integration of the study of Hasidic mysticism within the framework of Jewish mysticism through the examination, in this context, of the various mystical and magical possibilities inherent in certain forms of Jewish mysticism that preceded Hasidism. Such an approach has been almost totally ignored by modern scholarship.[89] On the other hand, there is a need to adopt more phenomenological and comparative approaches to deal with Hasidism as a movement initiated and propagated by mystics, as a mystical paradigm in itself beside the other Jewish or non-Jewish mystical paradigms, at the expense of an historically oriented approach that emphasizes Hasidic mysticism as a solution for a crisis[90] or as a source of the revitalization of Judaism. Important as the concerns of Buber and Scholem may be, they tend to minimize the independent stature of Hasidism. Hasidism can be understood not so much as a reaction or solution to, but rather as a synthesis of diverse mythical elements and paradigms present in earlier types of Jewish mysticism.[91] Its vitality derives not so much from the fact that it provided an effective answer to a certain historical situation, but from its ability to exploit the achievements of previous generations of Jewish mystics, who had supplied the stones out of which a new mystical edifice could be built. The precise nature of this edifice still awaits a more nuanced phenomenological description, one that can identify those of its features that were most relevant to the spiritual demands of Eastern European Jews and their descendants for several generations. Without such a description, the reason why the response to the mid-eighteenth-century crisis has been a viable alternative for other forms of Judaism in the last two centuries will remain an enigma.

One avenue for this kind of evaluation is a hermeneutical approach. Hasidic literature of the eighteenth and nineteenth centuries is paramountly exegetical, even more than Kabbalistic literature. Whoever attempts to fathom the content of these writings is faced with a hermeneutical problem: should the scholar make an effort to reconstruct a coherent intellectual scheme or a consistent type of experience from pieces of information and hints spread alongside lengthy exegetical texts; or should he focus his efforts on interpretation, along with its methods and contents, as an attempt to illuminate the text rather than the commentator. There is no easy answer, if one can speak of an answer at all to such a quandary. Much more complex is the situation that arises when the corpus under discussion consists not of the writings of one author alone but, as in the case of Hasidism, of hundreds of authors spread over two centuries of intense religious and literary activity, and divided not only by geographical borders but also by dynastic struggles and individual predilections. In fact, Hasidism is a perfect case of the proliferation of small sects that differ from each other on relatively unimportant issues.

The question arises whether a comprehensive approach that attempts to discuss Hasidic thought as such is appropriate, or whether it is more advisable to study each school in itself, in order to "exhaust" its specific views, before adopting a more synthetic attitude. Undoubtedly, there are strong arguments in favor of both approaches, and in fact it would be better to follow both. Any attempt to overemphasize the differences between Hasidic schools tends, by itself, to result in an atomization that obscures the sense of continuity within this type of mysticism, a continuity that seems, in my opinion, to be undeniable; indeed, the proposal of some scholars to emphasize the differences among various kinds of Jewish literature, mystical and nonmystical, can contribute to a sensitive understanding of each of them; yet it fails to appreciate much of the hermeneutical pattern of Jewish culture. On the other hand, a harmonizing approach, which tends to attenuate the substantial divergences between various kinds of mystical literature, obliterates the distinctions between the sources or authors of the speculative structures and impoverishes the panoramic landscape of Hasidism—and of Jewish mysticism—in general. We must be aware of the paradoxical situation of the existence of both a stable core, or cores, or "minimum-essence" (or even models, as we shall see below) and fluid aspects of the same religious structures.

Using a theory of models, I shall propose a methodology that addresses the common denominators of several important forms of Jewish mysticism and describe their interactions and integrations, yet at the same time allows enough room for historical changes, which may be substantial or contingent. It seems to me that the Hasidic movement, which traces its pedigree from one founding figure, and has been dramatically shaped by the mysticism of his successor, the Great Maggid, should be examined to determine what spiritual common denominators exist beyond the differences we observe on the surface. The Hasidic masters explicitly subscribed to the message of the founder and attempted, in different ways, to disseminate it in homiletic forms. The models to be analyzed here are modes of organizing the huge, disparate Hasidic corpus into a more significant religious metalanguage. Beyond—and in my opinion despite—the individual, and sometimes scholastic divergences between the Hasidic masters, one can see a basic message, which posits the ideal of the extreme mystic and magician as the bridge between the Jewish people and God. The *Ẓaddiq*, a pontifical figure, serves qua mystic, the needs of the community, to which he is expected to supply spiritual and material assistance.

7. ESSENCES, HISTORY, MODELS

One of the basic assumptions of philosophical phenomenology as understood by Husserl is the concept of the "invariance of sense." This view, that a certain objective content transcends the contingent aspect of a phenomenon, is crucial to his methodology. This approach is no longer exceptional. Indeed, I found a suggestive formulation of the paradox of essence and change in one of Eugene Ionesco's autobiographical fragments.

> I agree with the idea that structures are, that they change, fall apart, and are reconstituted; structures, or models, or ideas, or archetypes are present, and are invariable in their essence.[92]

In line with his worldview, the playwright asserts that structures both change and are invariable. That is, a certain essence is stable but the structure representing this essence is nevertheless changing. This view is also expressed in modern psychoanalytic thought; a contemporary follower of Jung states, when attempting to account for the nature of the archetypes:

> Archetypal metaphors do change with the passing of each generation; this does not imply changes in the archetype as such. New metaphors do receive cultural acknowledgement and each subsequent generation has a different store of images on which to draw.[93]

Another phenomenologist, the contemporary philosopher Jean-Francois Lyotard, similarly asserts that "each thinking is a rethinking and that there is nothing the presentation of which could be said to be the 'premiere.' Every emergence of something reiterates something else, every occurrence is a recurrence."[94]

This dilemma concerning the interpretation of older elements in later corpora, oral and written, is a major problem in modern scholarship; it emerged, in my opinion, as the result of the collapse of the historically oriented attitude, which regarded later phenomena both as a transformation of earlier ones and, sometimes, their improvement. The Hegelian scheme, which has dramatically informed the history of ideas approach, seems to leave some unanswered questions, making a simplistic adherence to it problematic for anyone who is aware of modern methodological debates.[95] What we discover by resorting to the "history of ideas" method is more an earlier antecedent for a certain idea than a "premiere," to use Lyotard's term; more a repetition of an idea with a lesser or greater change from the first instance of its invention ex nihilo.[96]

This is one of the methodological reasons for the proposal, to be advanced in detail in chapters 2 and 5, that we must presuppose certain models to better understand the variegated phenomena that constitute both Kabbalah and Hasidism. Theoretically, it is easier to understand the changes happening within history than it is to analyze what one could call the "minimum-essence." Logically, however, the success of analyzing historical change is radically dependent upon the sometimes implicit assumption of scholars concerning the existence of a relatively stable minimum-essence, which may be said to represent the Husserlian "invariance of sense." Without assuming the inertial nature of language and thought, the idea of change becomes very vague: why not speak about disconnected concepts that use the same vocabulary, if major breaks are assumed to take place in each and every generation? Historical approaches, with their emphasis on change, must be complemented by phenomenological ones that deal with relatively stable essences. Although this approach has its own difficulties, it is nevertheless less problematic than the purely historical one.

It is not easy to explain why certain essences recur in historical and cultural circumstances that seem to invite dramatic changes in their expression. As we have learned from recent scholarship, mentalities are rather inertial, and only rarely is it possible to relate these changes convincingly to historical factors. However, in the case of the history of Jewish mysticism, one major factor that triggered many of the changes was rather neglected: that is, the interaction between different types of religious interests, models, and schools. The study of various kinds of Kabbalistic literature lead me to the conclusion that "pure" mystical schools are very rare. In most cases we can detect interactions between different types of mystical and nonmystical schools. Classical Jewish *mythologoumena* interacted with Neoplatonism at the beginning of Kabbalah; Ashkenazi mystical techniques interacted with Maimonidean proclivities in Abraham Abulafia's ecstatic Kabbalah; Abulafia's Kabbalah interacted with Sufi mysticism; the ancient magical concept of *golem* has interacted with a variety of speculative systems. R. Yoḥanan Alemanno's thought shows that nothing philosophical or occult in Judaism and Christianity was alien to him, he interpreted Kabbalah both magically and Neoplatonically; his thought represents an interaction between the Italian mystical traditions and those arriving from Spain after the expulsion. Likewise, I propose to see in the different types of interactions clues for understanding the development of Kabbalah in the wake of the expulsion. Later on, in Cordovero, the various theosophies of the different Zoharic layers were in fact harmonized, but at the same time, the ecstatic Kabbalah and magical concepts were widely absorbed. The following analysis attempts to apply this same "interactional" approach to the processes that were influential in the emergence of Hasidism.

Important forms of Jewish spirituality emerged not so much as the result of the confrontation between history, historical crises, or other socioeconomic circumstances with mysticism, but from syntheses between religious aspirations, personalities, ideals, nomenclatures, and fears, and various mystical models. Neglecting this methodological assumption of interactions between a variety of experiential and speculative models, many of the prevailing studies of historical development in Jewish mysticism have relied upon the belief that any explanation of a new type of mysticism must start with an examination of its historical circumstances. The latter are deemed to offer the answers to the quandaries posed by the new form of thought under examination. This presupposition, which assumes that we understand better and know more about "history" than about the speculative systems we choose to examine, is highly questionable. It presupposes that the historian of Jewish mysticism believes that the "plain" historians are able to produce a historical picture that is widely acceptable to other historians, a result that seems to occur only in rather exceptional cases. In very few cases do scholars of Jewish mysticism conduct historical research by themselves. Rather they rely, as a rule, on the findings of scholars in fields as diverse as thirteenth-century Provence or nineteenth-century Poland. By asserting the priority of historical circumstance, the historian of Jewish mysticism often falls prey not to the fallacies of his own research, but to that of others, which, given the special nature of his academic focus, he is unable to correct.

In lieu of relying on the findings of others, the student of Jewish mysticism might better investigate in depth the kinds of material that we may reasonably assume were seen, quoted, and though sometimes misunderstood by the mystics, were nevertheless formative with regard to their religious worldview. Without a thorough acquaintance with the main stages of Jewish mysticism that predate Hasidism, for example, it is hazardous to speak of novelties conditioned by "historical" circumstances. Hasidism is part of a larger whole—the variety of canonical and noncanonical mystical writings in Judaism—and the very existence and understanding of this movement as a mystical, though not as a social, movement, is contingent upon this whole. I propose that the historian of Hasidism, when dealing with this movement as a mystical phenomenon, might better operate in that area in which he has a qualitative superiority, namely the knowledge of the texts of Hasidism and their sources. It is only after a more exhaustive inspection of mystical sources and spiritual models, and we are very far from such exhaustive analyses, that recourse to corroborating material from other types of sources—historical, economic or otherwise—can be fruitful. Generalizations regarding historical and economic crises can help with our understanding of a particular thinker in a certain period, as much as the assumption that by an economic crisis the situation of all the people in a certain period were affected. As in many cases, at times of economic crisis there were many wealthy people, just as in times of prosperity, there were pessimistic thinkers. The implicit assumption that a thinker, or in our case a mystic, reflects the plight of his generation is as good as the assumption that his thought was formative for that generation.

These statements notwithstanding, our methodological assumption is that there are historical data that can be ascertained; biographical studies and bibliographical descriptions may clarify the contents of the teaching of a certain master, and historical circumstances may effect the flowering of one mystical model or the rejection of another. There can be no doubt that ideological clashes shaped many of the important aspects of Jewish mysticism, and interactions within the Jewish community and with the forces outside it should be carefully examined. Nevertheless, one must remain skeptical of proposals regarding the religious mentality of Hasidism that attempt to learn too easily from "history." In many cases "history" stands for the shaky picture accepted by one scholar on the basis of the writings of another, or for the construction of a picture out of selected pieces of information, collected sometimes according to a preconceived theory about the social, political, or economic situation. believers. By overemphasizing the impact of external history on inner developments, the modern scholarship of Jewish mysticism has adopted an evolutionary, almost materialist-dialectic, or Neo-Marxist type of explanation, which can be designated as proximism.[97]

One more observation regarding models: Throughout the text the word *model* is used in a rather explicit manner in order to point to patterns that can be discerned in the studied texts. This fact is important for my approach, which I would like to consider phenomenological. As is well known, phenomenological approaches are in general reticent insofar as model theories are concerned, since in many cases they require the imposition of an external, preconceived structure onto the process of observing the phenomena. The models I am concerned with here, however, are the result of observations of the Hasidic material; they are not artificial constructs introduced for the sake of a better understanding of that type of mysticism, but what I believe were existing ways of thought in pre-Hasidic Jewish mysticism. The term *model* is used rather than the term *system* because a given system of thought, like Hasidism, can be described, as we shall see below, by more than one mystical, or magical, model. From this point of view, a system is not always a systematic corpus, namely a body of writing that expouses a logically coherent way of thought. In some cases, of course, a certain comprehensive type of mystical corpus expressing a certain system, like Lurianic Kabbalah, or Abraham Abulafia's writings, is basically informed by one model alone. On the other hand, I use the term *model* as distinguished from the term *structure,* which may stand for a more limited concept than a model, and which is not a matter of imitation. So, for example, the anthropomorphic apprehension of the Torah, or of the world of the angels, belongs to a structure that unifies the concept of man and God. From this point of view, Lovejoy's "Great Chain of Being" represents a structure, since it presents reality more than it inspires a certain way of life. Structures, unlike models, are modes of thought that—to paraphrase Ricoeur's view of the symbol—invite thought but only rarely action. Structures may enter in the constitution of models.

In other words, the models proposed in the following chapters are similar to Buber's "primary words," which in his thought mean combinations among different entities, as well as intimate relations among them. Like primary words, models are related to the whole being. More than a *modus cognescendi,* like structures, models combine both a *modus operandi* and a *modus vivendi.* The emphasis in the following discussions will be on concepts like *kavvanah, devequt, ʿaliyat ha-neshamah, hamshakhah, horadat ha-ruḥaniyyut, sheʾiy-vah,* talismanic performance of the ritual combinations of letters—terms that convey a very dynamic relation between man and God and between man and his community. Our intention is to inspect Jewish mysticism more from the point of view of the syntax of the mystical language than it is an attempt at clarification of its morphology. This is why theological views like immanent-ism, transcendence, dialectical coincidence of oppositions, and the like serve as theological background for the religious activity of the eighteenth-century mystics and magicians more than as catalysts for their emergence; they are *points of reference,* which present the frame of an outburst of enthusiastic and ecstatic mood rather than the triggers of such moods. There can be no doubt that Hasidism, like many other forms of mysticism, was—as Hans Jonas[98] once put it—in search of validation by adopting a variety of theological stands, which contributed to the emergence of a more comprehensive worldview.

8. HASIDISM AND OTHER LITERARY CORPORA

In many fields in the humanities, the analyses of a significant literary corpus in relation to another body of literature contributes substantially to a different interpretation of the latter, both because of the novelty of the material and the concepts and because of the types of affinities between them. This is also the case with the scholarship on Hasidism. Its evolving understandings were deeply affected by various developments in the scholarship of Jewish mysticism, especially by the attention paid to underanalyzed works of mystical literature. So, for example, the emphasis on Sabbateanism that characterizes the scholarship of Gershom Scholem, Isaiah Tishby, and Yehuda Liebes has brought special attention to the affinities between Sabbatean ideas and Hasidic ones.[99] When the study of mystical thought in the circle of R. Moshe Ḥayyim Luzzato was undertaken by I. Tishby, one of its results was the theory—already adumbrated by E. Zweifel and H. N. Bialik—of the contribution of this messianic Kabbalist, who was at the same time a hidden Sabbatean figure, to the emergence of some Hasidic ideals.[100] When the study of the ethical Kabbalistic literature beginning with the Safedian period up to the emergence of Hasidism was advanced in the studies of Mordekhai Pachter and Mendel Pierkaz, one of their major findings was the affinity between certain Hasidic ideas, often conceived as radical and Sabbatean, and ethical Kabbalistic treatises, replacing a previous assumption that their background was Sabbatean.[101] The development of the inquiry into R. Moshe Cordovero's Kabbalistic thought, most recently advanced by the studies of Bracha Sack, has contributed significantly to a greater awareness of the sources in this Safedian Kabbalist's writings of certain Hasidic views.[102] Last but not least: the inquiry into the *hanhagot* literature undertaken by Ze᾿ev Gries has illuminated the details of the relationship between the pre-Hasidic spiritual guidance literature and its Hasidic counterparts.[103] These spadework studies are a major area that should be cultivated in order not only to understand Hasidism against its literary sources, but also to clarify both the details and the more general spiritual physiognomy of the various strains of Hasidic thought. These macro-analyses, the term used here to designate studies that deal with relationships among different forms of Jewish religiosity,[104] help us place Hasidic thought in its larger Jewish religious context, by disclosing the unspecified affinities between the earlier and the latter sources.

The present study strives to specify certain details of the influence of motifs found in Cordovero, who, from our point of view, is one of the main tradents of two other types of Kabbalistic thought: ecstatic Kabbalah and the so-called hermetical type of magic; from this vantage point it is also part of a macro-analysis. In line with the panoramic approach proposed above, it seems that these additional types of thought not only allow for a better understanding of aspects of Hasidism previously neglected by scholars, but may also affect the understanding of processes that have significantly shaped Hasidic mysticism in areas that have already been analyzed by scholars in other ways. The addition of these models of thought, to be discussed in the following pages, does not—at least not automatically—detract from the findings of previous scholars of Hasidism.[105] In some cases the issues discussed here have not been treated by other scholars; in others qualifications to the already existing analyses have been proposed.

What seems crucial, however, is not only textual findings but methodological attempts to study Jewish mysticism and, in our case, Hasidism, in a manner different from that accepted by modern scholarship. By entering into a discussion of a theory of models, we hope to contribute toward a more comprehensive view of the systemic factors active in Jewish mysticism in general.[106] Beyond these macro-analytical considerations, which will constitute the main part of this study, we shall propose, and hope to substantiate, more systemic observations that will take into consideration the macro-analytical, but will strive to illuminate the phenomenological structures of Hasidic mysticism. The proposed theory of models in pre-Hasidic Jewish mysticism, as well as the question of their interactions and the resulting new, and more comprehensive models, transcend the macro-analytic approach described above and should be understood as part of a larger attempt to understand the underlying structures of Jewish mysticism. This issue is the focus of the second chapter of the present study.

Before approaching the influences of the mystical and magical models, it is important to deal with the claim that underlies the proximistic theory of Scholem and Buber: Should we consider Lurianic Kabbalah—and in Scholem's case Sabbateanism was understood to be the amplification of Lurianic messianism and its realization on the historical scene—to be the single most important mystical trend of concern to the scholar of Hasidism? Is Sabbateanism so crucial[107] and Lurianism so indispensable for understanding the major religious changes that have originated in Hasidism?[108]

In the following pages we shall present a picture of Hasidic historical sources and phenomenology that differs substantially from the conventional descriptions of this type of Jewish mysticism. We shall pay much more attention to types of literature that reflect two of the central spiritual concerns of Hasidism: the mystical experience and magical practices. Without an examination of the spiritual possibilities contained in previous Jewish literature, the conclusions that link Hasidism to only some of the mystical paradigms are conjectural. The attempt to introduce neglected material into the discourse of Hasidic spirituality demands close study, and minute philological analysis, of texts written centuries before Hasidism appeared. However, in establishing a much more panoramic perspective on Hasidism as a mystical movement, these surveys are crucial, for they correct the present overemphasis on Lurianism as the only basic source of Hasidic spirituality.

Despite the fact that I frequently refer to Kabbalistic and magical types of literature from the beginning of Kabbalah to the seventeenth century, the major emphasis of this study is the Hasidic sources. Nevertheless, it is inevitable that a project attempting to establish affinities among several types of literature should quote extensively from all of them. In our case this need is much more pressing, as these bodies of literature that informed Hasidism are not always in the purview of those scholars who focus their academic attention on the late mystical literature. I have attempted to peruse the writings of the first four generations of Hasidism and pay special attention to some of the writings of the fifth generation.[109]

The core of the Hasidic writings quoted below was written from 1750 to 1850. However, we have also looked at the works of non-Hasidic contemporary authors like Shelomo Maimon, R. Pinḥas Eliyahu Hurwitz, R. Ḥayyim of Volozhin, and others. This amounts to a vast corpus of writings; however most of it was written in a small geographical area and is a relatively homogenous type of mystical thought in basically one language (though in some cases the Hebrew texts were initially delivered as sermons in Yiddish). We may therefore speak of different versions of Jewish mysticism emphasizing various aspects of the already existing paradigms and models. The geographical area is the greater part of Eastern Europe, bounded by Slovakia in the west, the Ukraine in the east, Belorussia in the north, and Moldavia in the south. It is important to note that this area includes only a small percentage of the countries the Jews inhabited in the middle of the eighteenth century. Hasidism was unable to go beyond these areas, with the exception of some small groups of Hasidim who emigrated to the Galilee. As a mystical phenomenon, Hasidism is the creation of part of the Ashkenazi world, which rejected Sabbateanism and Frankism on one hand, and the Enlightenment on the other. With the exception of some forms of Sabbateanism still active in the Ottoman Empire, all these spiritual phenomena flourished in eighteenth-century Europe. When comparing Hasidic thought to other forms of Jewish mysticism in the area (excluding most of the forms of Sabbateanism), we can see a certain homogeneity, which distinguishes Jewish from Christian and Muslim mysticism (though it is closer to the latter than to the former) as well as from the mystical traditions of the East. Most of the Jewish mystics agree about the theosophical structure of divinity, about the centrality of ritual, and about the impact of this ritual on the divine structure, an influence referred to here as "theurgy." Likewise, they agree on the possibility of reaching extraordinary spiritual experiences; revelations of angelic mentors, ascents of the soul, and even prophetic experience were conceived as positive.

Although there are different emphases on the centrality of these spiritual factors, we might compare the various versions of Jewish mysticism to a number of nets of different patterns all woven from identical threads. In fact, those threads are found in all the major centers of Jewish life: all these centers were acquainted with Kabbalah, including Cordoverianism and Lurianism; and even ethical Kabbalistic literature and Sabbateanism were known in several corners of the Jewish world. The question is, why did Eastern Europe generate its unique syntheses of these factors. The accepted scholarly answer, that Hasidism is a response to the Sabbatean challenge and to the despair that arose in the aftermath of its failure, does not address the question why only part of Eastern Europe produced the pecular version of Kabbalah known as Hasidism. Was the despair greater there than it was in the Middle East, North Africa, or Central Europe?

The relative homogeneity of these eighteenth-century writings is much more apparent after reading studies like those of Carlo Ginsburg, Lawrence Sullivan, and Bruce Lincoln on one hand, and those of Weinstein and Bell and Valerie Flint on the other. The work of the first three scholars, who analyze material spread over continents, deals with phenomena that developed over a period of several thousands of years; and several hundred years the second group of scholars, who deal with saints and magic in the Christian Middle Ages in Western Europe, take up phenomena that developed over several centuries. The inclusion here of these types of studies, which are not representative of existing works on Jewish mysticism and magic, may perhaps persuade younger scholars to adopt a much broader perspective for the study of both Hasidism and Jewish mysticism in general. We should not hesitate to relate eighteenth-century Hasidism to Arabic magic or to thirteenth-century ecstatic Kabbalah because of prejudices about the special status of certain phenomena that were a central academic concern of the older generation of scholars in the field of Jewish mysticism. The minute examination of detail found in texts, important as this is in itself, cannot take the place of the analysis of mysticism and magic as phenomena by means of the appropriate critical tools. Phenomenology, psychology, anthropology and the comparative study of religions,[110] intellectual history, and cultural history[111] should all supplement the textology and historiography that reign supreme in modern Hasidic studies.

The present study has benefited from modern scholarship in the field of Jewish mysticism in general and that of Hasidism in particular. The great achievements of Gershom Scholem and his school opened an avenue that ensured a far more sensitive approach to historical and conceptual aspects of this mystical lore. Most of their research focused upon the writings of the first generations of Hasidic masters. The major developments in the last generation of scholars, who turned their attention from analysis of the writings of earlier generations of Hasidic masters to those of later (the third and the fourth generations), have facilitated the present study to a large extent; the analyses of the thought of Habad Hasidism by Rachel Elior,[112] or of R. Naḥman of Braslav by Arthur Green,[113] to give only two examples, have contributed to a more profound understanding of these later layers of Hasidic mysticism. Moreover, some recent developments in the historical and social descriptions of Hasidism in the first generation, like those of Emanuel Etkes,[114] Ada Rapoport-Albert,[115] and Moshe Rosman,[116] have started to pave the way to a new understanding of the origin of this type of Jewish mysticism, presenting it as neither a protest nor a mass-movement in its inception. This more elitist understanding of the first two generations of Hasidic masters, dominant in the studies of Etkes and Rapoport-Albert, allows for a dynamic of historical explanation less concerned with the nexus between the masses and their charismatic leaders and more focused upon the first Hasidic masters as part of the general spiritual framework of Jewish mysticism.[117] The present study takes into account the conclusions reached by these as well as many other scholars in this area, especially those of Mendel Piekarz.

Most recently, two extreme formulations of the nature of Hasidic mysticism were expressed by two leading scholars in the field: Piekarz has argued that there is nothing new from the speculative point of view in Hasidism and it should therefore be regarded as a socioreligious movement that does not offer anything novel in comparison to Kabbalistic thought.[118] Conversely, Elior has emphasized the divergence between the Kabbalistic tradition and Hasidism, minimizing the continuity between them.[119] In my opinion, each of these positions, because of its extreme nature, reflects the actual situation only in a very partial way. Like Buber and Scholem, these scholars have approached Kabbalah as a relatively homogenous lore, and different as their answers are, they share a monolithic picture of what is in fact a more diversified Kabbalah. The answer seems to be oscillating somewhere between these two poles. One may see a certain continuity between some forms of Kabbalah and Hasidism, but even when such continuity is perceptible, significant changes—some of them a matter of structural shiftings—can also be detected.

9. ECSTASY AND MAGIC: DEFINITIONS

Through the study of models that inform the various forms of Hasidism, it will be easier to integrate Hasidism into the history of Jewish mysticism, and of mysticism in general, while at the same time acquiring a better understanding of its ecstatic and magical components. In the following discussion we shall use the term ecstasy to mean the temporary effacement of one's own personality, during which time one is possessed by the divine power or presence or divine spirit. This experience is sought after in Hasidism, but it is also one that does not occur, in general, without prior preparation. Mysticism may be understood as the experience of direct contact with the divine, expressed either by the Hebrew term *devequt* or related words. Like other scholars of Hasidism, I assume that the groups of pneumatics active at the inception of Hasidism exercised a formative influence on its spiritual physiognomy. However, we must also look into the wider mystical contexts that may help us understand the mystical and magical background to the activities of the Hasidim.

According to Flint, "Magic may be said to be the exercise of a preternatural control over nature by human beings, with the assistance of forces more powerful than they."[120] With its emphasis on control over nature, this definition makes a clear distinction between magic and theurgy, the latter understood as attempts by the Kabbalist or Hasidic master to induce a change within the divine intrastructure itself.[121] In general, we shall distinguish too easily or too strongly between magic and religion in the pages that follow. There is ample support for the view that, in some forms of the religious mentality, magic plays a central role.[122]

Part I
Models in Kabbalah and Hasidism

Three basic models can be seen competing throughout the history of Jewish mysticism: the theosophical-theurgical one, represented most eminently by Zoharic literature and the Safedian Kabbalah; the ecstatic, expressed in the writings of R. Abraham Abulafia, R. Yiẓḥaq of Acre, and some ecstatic Kabbalists; and the magical model, which is not expressed in a distinct body of Jewish mystical literature, but is present in certain writings of the other two models. The theosophical-theurgical and ecstatic models were already articulated by the thirteenth century; the magic model entered Kabbalah relatively early, at the end of the same century, though more elaborate examples of it are found in Kabbalistic literature after the fifteenth century. This model, as well as the ecstatic one, became more prominent in the writings of R. Moshe Cordovero, and certain of his followers, and came to the attention of the founders of Hasidism. Openness toward the magical and ecstatic aspects of Jewish mysticism emerged in a period when the most widespread version of the theosophical-theurgical model, Lurianic Kabbalah, was thought by some Jewish mystics and by some of the first Hasidic masters to be problematic. Far from constituting a repudiation of Lurianism, held to be the most sacrosanct body of mystical literature among Jewish mystics, this weakening accompanied a reorientation of spiritual concerns that gave rise to the inclusion of an elaboration upon elements from the other forms of Jewish mysticism: the ecstatic and the magical.

1

The Weakening of the Lurianic Kabbalah in the Eighteenth Century

Modern scholars have regarded Lurianic Kabbalah as the most crucial form of Kabbalistic literature to have influenced Hasidism. Lurianic concepts, either in their classical form or in their Sabbatean metamorphosis, were conceived as formative for the new type of mysticism, or at least as provoking new interpretations. As it has already been pointed out, it is necessary to adopt a more panoramic approach to the sources that have nurtured Hasidism; here we must draw attention to a phenomenon that apparently has passed unnoticed; namely, that during the formative decades of the nascent Hasidism, Lurianism did not always go unchallenged, as a form of Kabbalah that must either be accepted or interpreted. In fact, there is evidence for a weakening of the supremacy of Lurianic Kabbalah. This weakening opened the door for the surfacing of other forms of Kabbalah that, together with Lurianism, contributed to the physiognomy of Hasidism.

1. KABBALAH IN THE EIGHTEENTH-CENTURY CONTROVERSY

The second half of the eighteenth century was a period of bitter controversies between various Jewish groups in Eastern and Central Europe. The battle against the Sabbatean movement and its later metamorphosis into Frankism became famous through the polemical disputes between R. Jacob Emden and R. Yonathan Eibeschuetz; the emergence of Hasidism in several centers of Polish Jewry aroused the opposition of famous rabbis in Vilna and Brody. Toward the end of the century, the first representatives of the Jewish Enlightenment were bitterly fought by the rabbinic establishments of Central and Eastern Europe. The first two controversies focused upon two differing versions of Kabbalah: the Sabbatean version, stemming from further complications of Lurianic theosophy, which was mainly interested in the various maneuvers of the pretended Messiah Shabbetai Ẓevi, in his eschatological fight with evil; and the Hasidic version of Kabbalah, pointing the way to a new mystical modus vivendi to be achieved through enthusiastic prayer, various types of mystical union, and communion with God. The great opponents of these two brands of Kabbalah, like R. Jacob Emden and R. Eliyahu, the Gaon of Vilna, were themselves well-known Kabbalists. Therefore, Kabbalah itself was never the subject of a comprehensive criticism, but only its "heretical" interpretation, which was felt to have dangerous theological and social implications. With respect to the third important controversy, over the Enlightenment, Kabbalah was never a main issue: the majority of the opponents of the Enlightenment were Kabbalists or figures whose attitude toward Kabbalah was positive or reserved, but not totally critical.[1] In this tense atmosphere, where so many groups were critical, or at least suspicious of one another, Kabbalah enjoyed a peculiar status: it was almost universally accepted as the sacrosanct Jewish esoteric theology. Nevertheless, we do find occasional critical remarks regarding the nature of this lore, remarks that stem from unequivocally Kabbalistic authorities.[2]

2. THE STANDS OF THE CONSERVATIVES

The best-known instance of the orthodox criticism of Kabbalah in the eighteenth century was the incisive reexamination of Zoharic texts by R. Jacob Emden. The centrality of the *Zohar* for both Sabbateans and Frankists pushed their fervent adversary to a new and close perusal of this pivotal text. His conclusions were far from orthodox; according to his erudite inquiries, the *Zohar* was formed of at least three layers: an ancient one, authored by R. Shimeon bar Yoḥai; another layer, including *Ra ᶜya ᵓ Meheimna ᵓ* and *Tiqqunei Zohar;* and an even later part, the *Midrash ha-Ne ᶜelam.*[3] Moreover, he argued that later glosses had been incorporated into the original Zoharic text. Even though some of Emden's conclusions concerning the layers of the *Zohar* have not been accepted by modern scholarship of Kabbalah,[4] some of his textual analyses, when viewed from the perspective of literary criticism of the *Zohar,* are interesting achievements. In Emden's view, however, the problems Kabbalah posed went much further than the quandaries connected with parts of the *Zohar* or its glosses, and the ways they were misused or abused by heretical Jewish "sectarians." In Emden's period, the whole Kabbalistic body of literature became problematic. A highly significant passage from his *Mitpaḥat Sefarim* illustrates the confusion one faces when learning Kabbalistic works:

> Let no student imagine that he can study *Zohar* only from written texts,[5] since some persons "looked and were smitten,"[6] as we have heard and has been demonstrated by our sins - the sect of . . . Shabbatai Ẓevi . . . and we must be careful not to fail to recognize the real nature of the works of Shabbatai Ẓevi and his accursed disciples, which mixed together with the authentic Kabbalistic books, especially the works of the ARI, which were falsified by those abominable persons[7] . . . who all their days study only the esoteric lore, as I

> have heard regarding the new custom which became widespread in the Eastern countries.[8] They do not intend to study the knowledge of the performance of the commandments, but only look for the mystery of the Torah by the exclusive study of *Zohar* and Luria's works. Due to our sins it became a sinful obstacle and it [the study of Kabbalah] caused a large disruption in Israel's camp since by it [i.e. the study] they throw away the fulfillment of the Torah. . . .[9]

For Emden, the dangers of Kabbalah are implicit not only in its distortion and fabrication of pseudo-Lurianic books of a Sabbatean provenance; the very predominance of Kabbalistic studies imperiled, he believed, the integrity of the Jewish way of life, based principally upon the observance of the commandments.[10] Although his criticism was directed mainly toward the Sabbatean attachment to, and abuse of, Kabbalah, similar statements directed toward Hasidism may be found shortly after the above passage was written, in which the author also attacked the Hasidic way of prayer.[11] Therefore, not only is the text of the *Zohar* problematic, but all Lurianic texts, and the uncoordinated study of Kabbalah in general. Moreover, it seems that the quandary was even greater than this; according to Emden, who was, we must remember, a Kabbalist himself,[12]

> ... all the teachings of R. Yiẓḥaq Luria, may his memory be blessed, in *ᶜEẓ Ḥayyim* and his other books on these matters, are true from one point of view, and not true from another. They are true as understood by R. Yiẓḥaq Luria and others like him, but not true at all, in the way we understand them, since all that is stated in books and [other] works is the plain sense of the Kabbalah, which is not true, but the esoteric sense of the Kabbalah alone is true, and it cannot be written in any book.[13]

Although the importance of the inner sense of Kabbalah is not disputed by Emden, this lore is seen as distorted by the literal dimension of Kabbalistic literature: by committing Kabbalah to writing, its real meaning is lost. This is why Emden firmly recommends the oral study of the *Zohar*. As far as Lurianic Kabbalah is concerned, Emden believed its true meaning was ignored in his own time. A similar stand was taken by an illustrious synthesizer of Lurianic Kabbalah, R. Shelomo Eliashov, who maintained that

> all the teachings of Ari . . . are like the teachings of the Torah, which include the *Pardes*, and whatever was discussed here is only the plain sense, the esoteric one being very elusive.[14]

Another authority in Kabbalistic lore made interesting observations about the pernicious effects of the dissemination of Kabbalah in his time; Emden's deadly enemy, R. Yonathan Eibeschuetz, remarks in his approbation, or *haskamah*, of the printing of the book *ᵓAspaqlariah ha-Meᵓirah*, a commentary on the book of the *Zohar*, by R. Ẓevi Horowitz:

> I don't agree at all to the printing of Kabbalistic books, since the secret things belong unto the Lord our God [Deut. 29:28] and we are not permitted to expound the work of the [divine] chariot publicly. Whoever published something, his printing is tantamount to its exposition to large masses, and the text is equally available to everyone, worthy or unworthy. . . . On account of our great sins, they [i.e. the printed books] were pernicious for us, and some damage occurred because of the printing and their silence was more worthwhile than their speech. However, these booklets do not deal with the emanational chain according to ARI, blessed be his memory, like the teachings on the restorations of the worlds and the divine anthropomorphic configurations, concerning which it was said: it is the glory of God to conceal a thing [Prov. 25:2].[15]

The confession of an outstanding Kabbalist like Eibeschuetz that Lurianic teachings are dangerous when published is highly significant. These dangers are commonly viewed as connected with the Sabbatean anthropomorphic interpretations of them. However, even Eibeschuetz, whose links to the sect are by now better known,[16] is sensitive to the distortions that may result from Lurianic books. Having examined the Lurianic attitude to Kabbalah among eighteenth-century masters, let us now inspect various approaches of Hasidic masters to Luria's mystical thought.

3. HASIDIC MASTERS' QUANDARIES CONCERNING LURIANIC KABBALAH

One of the younger contemporaries of R. Yonathan Eibeschuetz, R. Abraham ha-Mal1akh, the son of R. Dov Baer of Miedzyrec, deplores the plight of Kabbalah:

> The true Torah, called Kabbalah, became corporeal, and it is indeed the true Torah, but it became very obscure and corporeal, because of our sins.[17]

An important disciple of the Great Maggid proposed an explanation for this plight. In the introduction to his *Dibrat Shelomo,* R. Shelomo of Lutzk indicates that the Lurianic teachings are focused upon anthropomorphic subjects, since they were intended for Luria's disciples, who had already studied the Cordoverian Kabbalah,[18] "wherein the real spiritual significance of anthropomorphism was exposed."[19] Only the deterioriation of the generations caused, according to this author, the simplistic understanding of Lurianic Kabbalah; the actual role of Hasidism is to restore the real spiritual Kabbalah.[20] R. Shelomo of Lutzk tacitly implies that such a reversal means, *inter alia,* the restoration to prominence of Cordovero, whose work, as we shall later see, was of utmost importance for Hasidic thought.[21] A similar stand may be discerned in a work by R. Meshullam Phoebus of Zbarazh, *Yosher Divrei ʾEmet.* He restricted the study of the *Zohar* and Lurianic works to a limited elite who have experienced supreme spiritual states; and this author approvingly quotes R. Menaḥem de Lonzano,[22] who asserts that these works were written for persons who are able to leave behind the corporeal world and attain a high spiritual status. R. Meshullam Phoebus and others like him imagine interpretations of these works that are totally different from the original intention of the texts.[23] The main mentor of R. Meshullam, R. Menaḥem Mendel of Premislany, is quoted as asserting that only those who have attained "cleaving with God" can truly understand the *Zohar* and Luria's writings.[24] Even the illustrious Kabbalist R. Eliyahu, the Gaon of Vilna, is reported to have been uneasy with the authoritative Kabbalah of Luria; R. Shneor Zalman of Liady maintained that[25]

> it is known to us for sure that the pious Gaon (the Hasid) does not believe in the Kabbalah of R. Yiẓḥaq Luria . . . in its entirety, that it was [received] from the mouth of Elijah . . . but only a small part of it was [received] from the mouth of Elijah . . . and the remaining part was from his [Luria's] great wisdom, and [therefore] we are not obliged to believe in it[26] . . . and [the Lurianic] writings are very corrupt.[27]

The aforecited passages present a very curious situation: though Kabbalah *per se* was not attacked in the major polemics of the eighteenth century, the greatest authorities in matters of Kabbalah were uncomfortable with some of its major facets—its diffusion by print, the acceptance of Luria's authority as a divinely inspired Kabbalist, and his peculiar method of prayer by *kavvanot*.[28]

This uneasiness was prominent among the Kabbalists themselves, though they never openly intended to undermine the centrality or importance of Kabbalah in matters of theology. However, certain steps were taken to reduce the possible pernicious effects of the premature study of Kabbalah; Luzzatto, for instance, was compelled to sign in Frankfurt a declaration in which he agreed not to study the works of Luria except under the guidance of, or in the company of, a worthy scholar, and only when both were over the age of forty.[29] At Brody, an assembly of rabbis declared in its excommunication of the Frankists that no one was permitted to study even reliable Lurianic texts before the age of forty, and that only the *Zohar* and some "simple" Kabbalistic works could be studied after the age of thirty.[30] These restrictions were not eighteenth-century innovations;[31] they had been in existence for centuries, but had never received the patronage and authority of a rabbinic assembly. Furthermore, at Frankfurt am Main, an interdiction against printing Kabbalistic works, including Lurianic ones, was issued after the crisis connected with Luzzatto's Kabbalistic books.[32]

4. THE VIEW OF SHELOMO MAIMON

In the background of these reservations to certain aspects of Kabbalah is the specter of sectarian interpretation of the esoteric lore. However, two similar positions regarding the nature of Kabbalah may also be found among Jewish philosophers in the late eighteenth century. In his autobiography, Shelomo Maimon asserts that originally, the Kabbalah was nothing but psychology, physics, morals, politics, and such sciences represented by means of symbols and hieroglyphics[33] in fables and allegories, the occult meaning of which was disclosed only to those who were competent to understand it. By and by, however, perhaps as the result of many revolutions, this occult meaning was lost, and the signs were taken for the things signified. But as it was easy to perceive that these signs necessarily had meant something, it was left to the imagination to invent an occult meaning that had long been lost. The remotest analogies between signs and things were seized, till at last the Kabbalah degenerated into an art of madness according to method, or a systematic science resting on conceits.[34]

Maimon apparently applies Maimonides' view on the "secrets of Torah" to Kabbalah. The medieval master indicated that in the Bible and Midrashic literature there are hints of esoteric tenets that were lost during the hard times of dispersion. In Maimon's view, the Kabbalah consisted of a body of truths that were transmitted in a ciphered way; however, the Jews lost the cipher, and the written form of the Kabbalah was misunderstood by imaginary interpretations.[35] We may therefore suppose that, according to Maimon, there is a core of true and valid knowledge that was the original and authentic Kabbalah, whereas its later common forms are degenerations of this core. Maimon believed that he was able to reconstruct the archaic meaning of Jewish esotericism by an adequate interpretation of Kabbalistic books and concepts; we shall therefore try to describe Maimon's attempt. However, it is worthwhile to note the obvious critical implication of his thinking toward the Kabbalah and toward Kabbalists of his time, who in his view deal only with a degenerate science far removed from its pristine value.[36] Moreover, in Maimon's autobiography we read:

Unsatisfied with the literary knowledge of this science, [i.e. Kabbalah], I sought to penetrate into its spirit; and as I perceived that the whole science [again, "the Kabbalah"], if it deserves this name, can contain nothing but the secrets of nature concealed in fables and allegories, I labored to find out these secrets, and thereby to raise my merely literary knowledge to a rational knowledge. This, however, I could accomplish only in a very imperfect manner at the time, because I had yet very few ideas of the sciences in general. Still, by independent reflection, I hit upon many applications of this kind.[37]

Maimon then goes on to indicate how he interpreted the Lurianic doctrine of withdrawal (*ẓimẓum*); for now it is enough to observe that he was confident in the possibility of decoding the real message of the Kabbalistic lore even in its "degenerate" form. This is the background of another passage in the autobiography:[38]

Shaʿarei Qedushah, or The Gates of Holiness, was the title of this book; and leaving out of account what was visionary and exaggerated, it contained the principal doctrines of psychology. I did with it, therefore, as the talmudic rabbis say that Rabbi Meir did, who had a heretic for his teacher:[39] "He found a pomegranate—he ate the fruit and threw away the peel."

Maimon, then, maintains that in his early youth he read Kabbalah in a very peculiar way, trying to penetrate to the undistorted truth of the source. By unearthing this truth, he discovered the true ancient Jewish lore, which for him seems to coincide with the sciences—the secrets of nature and psychology that can serve as important tools for the restoration of the original meaning of texts. We may infer that a comprehensive understanding of natural sciences and human psychology would be considered by Maimon as important preconditions for the proper study of Kabbalah. It appears that philosophy should also be added to these sciences; according to Maimon's early work, entitled *Ḥesheq Shelomo,*

whoever has not studied the books of the divine philosophers, especially the *Guide* of Maimonides, in order to comprehend the issue of rejection of all attributes, changes, and passions from God, has no way to enter the chambers of Kabbalah whatsoever. This gate should be closed, and not open [Ezek. 44:20].[40]

Philosophy, therefore, may well serve as a useful servant of its lady, the Kabbalah, and save the Kabbalists from theosophical errors. Moreover, we learn from another discussion found in *Ḥesheq Shelomo* that philosophy or philosophically oriented speculations are keys for the decoding of the "sealed" books of Kabbalah, which[41] are otherwise meaningless. Maimon reacts to the attacks that R. Nissim Gerondi (HaRaN)[42] and some Kabbalists[43] launched against Maimonides' identification of *Ma ͨaseh Merkavah* with metaphysics and of *Ma ͨaseh Bereshit* with physics by saying that[44]

according to their [i.e. Kabbalists'] opinion, *Ma ͨaseh Bereshit* and *Ma ͨaseh Merkavah* are secrets [belonging to] the lore of Kabbalah . . . that if Maimonides' intention was that *Ma ͨaseh Bereshit* and *Ma ͨaseh Merkavah* are solely what is explained in the Book of Physics and in philosophy, and no more, then all the deriders [of Maimonides] were certainly right. However, since he speaks of physics and metaphysics, his view includes all that was explained in those books, together with what remained still unexplained, namely everything that is possible to be comprehended by human reason. Hence there is no reason to deride him at all . . . and let us say that the opinions of the Kabbalists are certainly true regarding *Ma ͨaseh Bereshit* and *Ma ͨaseh Merkavah,* as secrets more profound and marvelous than those that were conceived by the philosophers dealing with natural science. They [the secrets] are really the Kabbalistic secrets. However, what can we do, for in spite of the fact that the table and meat are here, we cannot eat, since their [the Kabbalists'] words are sealed and are like the words of sealed books, of which a literate person, when presented with them will say: I cannot [understand] since it is a sealed [book], and they are like a dream that is not

> decoded. And if you will ask me and say, "It is because you have not comprehended anything concerning the lore of Kabbalah that you assert that there is no way to comprehend it, and look, we find out and see that in all the dispersion of Israel there are hundreds and thousands who study the lore of Kabbalah," my answer is, I am an intelligent man too, like the others, knowing the plain meaning of the [Kabbalistic] things and the significance of the words, as well as they do, and I am not inferior to them in any respect as regards this lore. However, what is the profit of the knowledge of these things that *ʾAbbaʾ* and *ʾImmaʾ* enclose the *ʾArikh* [*ʾAnpin*] under the beard[45] . . . and of other similar subjects, since their knowledge cannot be considered to be understanding or comprehension, but hearing or sight or tradition or tale [and] it is possible to teach the plain meaning of these things to a five-year-old child who is neither wise nor stupid.

Kabbalah is, therefore, a sealed book; it can be understood using two approaches: the content of classical philosophy, i.e., physics and metaphysics, which nevertheless do not exhaust the larger area of Kabbalistic lore; and human speculation, which is able to complement the already acquired body of knowledge. Only in this way will the Kabbalistic mythology become meaningful. We may, perhaps, put the matter in another way: Kabbalah can be partially identified with Maimonidean philosophy, though the former includes other subjects. This perception of Kabbalah as Maimonidean philosophy together with achievements of the human mind seems to be related to Maimon's qualification of Kabbalah; later, in his autobiography, he asserts:

> In fact the Kabbalah is nothing but an expanded Spinozism, in which not only is the origin of the world explained by the limitation of the divine being, but also the origin of every kind of being and its relation to the rest, are derived from a separate attribute of God.[46]

The general structure of this passage reminds one of Maimon's stand in *Ḥesheq Shelomo:* for the understanding of Kabbalah the framework of some speculative system is required, be it Spinozism,[47] Maimonides' philosophy,[48] or astral magic.[49] However, no system is sufficient for an exhaustive understanding of the Kabbalah; each has to be complemented by independent speculation, which may elucidate particular aspects of Kabbalah. No wonder Maimon irritated his contemporary Kabbalists, who considered Kabbalah a "divine science," i.e., a lore having no reasonable meaning.[50] Moses Mendelssohn described Kabbalah in a manner similar to Maimon: according to Friedrich Nicolai's testimony,[51] Mendelssohn conceived the Kabbalah as having a "consequent meaning," which was "dressed"; that is, which is rendered confusing by oriental metaphors. Moreover, the lack of philosophical terminology in ancient, "uncultivated" Hebrew resulted in frequent use of allegory. The specific content of this "consequent meaning" remains vague; however, since Mendelssohn uses the expressions *"orientalischen Philosophen"*[52] and

"Kabbalistik Philosophie," we may suppose that this meaning was connected with philosophical concepts or, at least, with philosophically expressible concepts. Since Mendelssohn and Maimon were—for a significant period in the latter's life—in close contact, it seems highly probable that the affinity between their conceptions of the degeneration of the Kabbalah is the result of the influence the two philosophers exercised on each other: Maimon had written his *Autobiography* in 1792, several years after Mendelssohn's death, but he indicated that he still viewed the Kabbalah as he had described it in his youth. His assertion is seemingly corroborated by the passages from *Ḥesheq Shelomo* that we discussed beforehand; therefore it is plausible that Maimon's view might have influenced Mendelssohn's appreciation of Kabbalah.

5. REORGANIZATION OF KABBALAH

For some of the more orthodox Kabbalists, then, the ultimate meaning of Lurianic Kabbalah was to some extent elusive; there was a feeling that its real message had escaped them. Others were overtly discontent with the way Kabbalah was studied and understood, although they assumed that a coherent significance underlay the distorted form in which Kabbalah reached them. This feeling of uneasiness regarding classical Kabbalah also found indirect expression in the second part of the eighteenth century in at least two closely related forms:

a) in the reorganization of older Kabbalistic values, i.e., in a reconstruction of Kabbalistic lore as Hasidism, focusing now upon the centrality of its mystical and magical as opposed to its theurgic aspects.[53]

b) in the reinterpretation of the classical texts, again in Hasidism, emphasizing now their psychological elements. Although there is an obvious affinity between these two "reconstructions," historically they may represent the interests and influences of different groups. A Kabbalist like R. Pinḥas Eliyahu Hurwitz may stress the importance of *devequt,*[54] combatting at the same time the psychologization of Kabbalah,[55] while a scholar like Maimon could be interested in the psychological aspects of the Kabbalah[56] without even discussing the problem of *devequt.* The mystical trend might be interested solely in developing a psychological system and technique that make mystical experience possible, whether the *unio mystica* or Maggidic revelation, neglecting discussions of a more theosophic nature.

6. BETWEEN LURIA AND CORDOVERO

The evidence presented above suggests that the status of Lurianic Kabbalah became problematic around the middle of the eighteenth century. While it still remained the apex of Jewish mysticism in the eyes of Kabbalists, its restriction to an elite, the prohibition against studying it before the age of forty, and the plight of the Lurianic texts, which reached Europe in at least two substantial versions[57] and were interpreted in at least two different ways[58] (together with Sabbatean works attributed to Luria),[59] rendered Lurianic Kabbalah suspect in the eyes of some, while to others it was too sublime. This situation permitted other forms of Kabbalah, whose importance was secondary and even marginal, to gain more prominence in the seventeenth and early eighteenth centuries. It was primarily Cordovero's system that gained from the weakness of Luria's Kabbalah. Several facts support the thesis that Cordoverian thought became more central in the period during which Hasidism emerged.[60]

(a) By the middle of the eighteenth century some of Cordovero's works had already been in print for more than a century,[61] some in more than one edition.

(b) Cordovero's followers propagated his Kabbalistic thought in their works. For example, R. Elijah de Vidas's *Reshit Ḥokhmah,*[62] R. Abraham Azulai's *Ḥesed le-ʾAvraham,* and R. Isaiah Horowitz's *Shene Luḥot ha-Berit* are to a great extent popularizations of the teachings of Cordovero.[63] We need not describe the extent of the influence of these works on Jewish culture in general and on Hasidism in particular.[64]

(c) Cordovero's books, unlike those of Luria, were studied and printed without restriction.[65]

(d) Some authors even preferred Cordovero's Kabbalah to the Lurianic texts; see, for example, Maimon's classification of Kabbalah:[66]

> There are two main systems of the Kabbalah: the system of Rabbi Moses Cordovero, and that of Rabbi Yiẓḥaq Luria. The former is more real, that is, it approximates more closely to reason. The latter, on the other hand, is more formal, that is, it is more complete in the structure of its system. The modern Kabbalists prefer the latter, because they hold that alone to be genuine Kabbalah in which there is no rational meaning.[67] The principal work of Rabbi Moses Cordovero is the *Pardes.* Of Rabbi Yiẓḥaq Luria himself we have some disconnected writings; but his pupil, Rabbi Ḥayyim Vital, wrote a large work under the title *ʿEẓ Ḥayyim* (The Tree of Life), in which the whole system of his master is contained. This work is held by the Jews to be so sacred that they do not allow it to be committed to print.[68] Naturally, I have more taste for the Kabbalah of Rabbi Moses than for that of Rabbi Yiẓḥaq, but durst not give utterance to my opinion on this point.[69]

This passage deals only with the preference of one person, Maimon, for Cordoverian Kabbalah; this fact is presented by Maimon himself as an exception. However, it remains true that Luria's writings are described as "disconnected," whereas the most important systematic Lurianic work, *ʿEẓ Ḥayyim,* remained in manuscript.

(e) Last but not least, Cordovero's thought was considered a necessary introduction to Lurianic Kabbalah. See, for example, the opinion of R. Shelomo of Lutzk quoted above.[70] Moreover, when certain Hasidic doctrines were criticized, the Besht and the Great Maggid indicated Cordovero as their source.[71]

In the next few chapters we will look at "reconstruction" in the realm of prayer and Torah study and discuss additional forms of criticism directed at Lurianism, more precisely the Lurianic mystical way of prayer.[72] An attempt will be made to show that views about prayer, the study of Torah, and the notion of the *Ẓaddiq,* as presented in Cordovero's own writings and in those of his followers were based on magical sources and were preferred by Hasidic masters, whereas the Lurianic *kavvanot* and other related issues did not attract most of the Hasidic masters. In fact, in some legends, we find evidence of a certain tension between Luria and the Besht;[73] however, I prefer to address here the more theoretical interpretations of the issues.

2

Models in Jewish Mysticism

1. MODELS IN JEWISH MYSTICISM: AN APPRAISAL

As mentioned above, the prevailing attitude toward the conceptual infrastructure of Hasidism assumes that the basic mystical system by which it is informed is Lurianic Kabbalah. This main form of classical Kabbalah was indeed well known and influential in the great majority of Hasidic writings. Witness to this are the numerous key concepts that the Hasidic masters borrowed from Lurianic texts, concepts such as *Yiḥudim, kavvanot, ẓimẓum, shevirah, ha ʿalaʾat niẓẓoẓot, mittuq ha-dinim, gadelut* and *qatenut,* or *tiqqun.* These are only a few of the many examples of the deep influence of this form of Kabbalah. Though some of these concepts were well known long before the emergence of Lurianism, it seems that their acceptance—and the depth of their impact—in this classical mystical literature since the sixteenth century contributed greatly to their later dissemination in Hasidic literature. However, while explicitly acknowledging the contribution of Lurianism to Hasidism, there are two questions of concern in any attempt to trace the genesis of Hasidic mystical religiosity.

The first is the ostensible centrality in Hasidism of numerous mystical concepts that are absent in the Lurianic corpus, or are at most marginal to its mystical physiognomy: the ideals of *devequt* and *hitkallelut;* the mystical states of *hishtawwut, hitbodedut,* and *hitpashshetut ha-gashmiut* and the concepts of *ruḥaniyyut, keli,*[1] *behirut,* and *ḥiyyut* cannot be derived easily, if at all, from the Lurianic corpus. There can be no doubt that they did not emerge as the result of a hermeneutical effort; neither are they synonyms for Lurianic concepts that were rendered in a different key. The assumption that Hasidism is a psychologization or neutralization of Lurianic concepts does not apply to these crucial terms. One may rightfully claim that they serve the processes of neutralization and psychologization, but even this instrumental role cannot explain their emergence. On the contrary, their presence may explain why these processes took place—why, that is, Lurianism could not be accepted by the Hasidim according to its classical interpretations.

The plausible sources of these cardinal concepts predate and substantially differ from Lurianic Kabbalah. As I have attempted to show above,[2] there is no reason to restrict the range of the literary sources that were available and acceptable to the Hasidic masters to the Lurianic corpus. Moreover, the types of spirituality reflected by these terms are sometimes dramatically different from the Lurianic one. Therefore, the occurrence of terms that represent neither Lurianic nomenclature nor its mystical axiology challenges scholarly assumptions about the crucial role of Lurianism in the genesis of Hasidism.

Provided that we can establish that a much greater variety of sources nourished Hasidic mysticism, the second question is whether these non-Lurianic sources contributed disparate motifs, random themes, and marginal types of thought and experience, or were consistent and coherent schemes that could substantially inform the nascent Hasidism. Or, to formulate the issue differently: Lurianism, despite its great complexity, is nevertheless a relatively consistent system, whose main concepts were indeed adapted by the Hasidic masters. The cohesiveness of this system, and of any system in general, is a significant factor in its ability to have a profound impact on other mystics. Hence, when discussing the relative influence on Hasidism of Lurianic mystical thought and practice and that of the other sources, we must determine whether there were distinct and consistent mystical systems that could have served as alternatives to Lurianic thought and literature. As we have mentioned in the Introduction, the answer to this question, while very complex, is that such systems did exist. However, let us first address the question of why the Lurianic terms were understood in a new way.

Even among scholars who consistently opt for the centrality of the Lurianic system in Hasidic thought, there is no doubt that almost all of the basic Lurianic concepts were not adopted by Hasidism as they existed in their original contexts. Different terms have been used to describe the shifts that can often be discerned between the original Lurianic and Hasidic understandings of these concepts: Scholem used the term "neutralization" to describe the marginalization of the Lurianic *tiqqun*;[3] he spoke about the "psychologization" of Kabbalistic theosophy, which includes a new understanding of the concepts of the *Sefirot, parẓufim, ẓimẓum,* and *shevirah*.[4] Buber referred to the shift between Kabbalistic gnosis and Hasidic ethos.[5] However, these dramatic changes were only rarely explained by scholars in detail;[6] neither were the hermeneutical processes involved in these conceptual shifts properly analyzed. Only in the case of the neutralization of messianism was an historical explanation offered: fear of the consequences of the acute messianic implications of the Lurianic concept were responsible for its being supplanted by the more personal concept of *devequt*.[7] Though this historical explanation can, at least in principle, account for the emergence of the centrality of *devequt,* it is very unlikely that more radical shifts in the meaning of many other Lurianic concepts can be attributed to an alleged apprehension of a popular messianism.

As more recent scholarship has shown, in its beginning stages the Hasidic movement was not inclined to impart its insight to the masses.[8] Moreover, psychologizations of other important religious concepts that have nothing to do with Lurianism or with Kabbalah in general, such as the Temple or the Land of Israel, cannot reasonably be attributed to the historical crisis provoked by Sabbateanism. After all, these concepts did not play an important role in Sabbatean eschatology.[9] Moreover, the existence of psychologizations in various forms of medieval Kabbalah invalidates any simplistic attribution of this hermeneutics to the peculiar circumstances of eighteenth-century Hasidism.[10]

Thus, instead of fragmenting the answer to this process, it would perhaps be more reasonable to offer more comprehensive solutions, which attempt to make sense of the direction of those changes that affected a whole series of religious concepts. In other words, by focusing our attention upon the non-Lurianic terms that were important for the Hasidic master, we may not only discover other Kabbalistic sources that had an impact on Hasidism, but also relate the appearance of these non-Lurianic terms to changes in the understanding of both Lurianic and non-Lurianic themes. This approach emphasizes the existence of mystical and magical models in Jewish thought that predate Hasidism and whose interaction can explain the emergence of certain speculative developments that have been attributed by modern scholars to the impact of the historical circumstances.

In principle, I do not deny the possibility that historical circumstance contributed to the religious physiognomy of Hasidism. However, this factor is to a great extent a matter of academic speculation, based upon the implicit, and sometimes explicit, modern assumption that certain crucial Hasidic processes, such as "neutralization" and "psychologization," are novelties, and should therefore be explained as innovations induced by historical circumstance and crises. This kind of explanation is not unique to Hasidism; it is an instance of the "crisical historiography" of Gershom Scholem and his followers. As in the case of the expulsion of the Jews from Spain, which produced a "new Kabbalah,"[11] the Sabbatean crisis produced a new form of Jewish mysticism. Indeed, as in the case of the expulsion, it is rather difficult to pinpoint the crisis in the writings of the authors discussed, not to mention direct references to such crises. These crises are introduced because of the intuition of the modern historian that certain kinds of events must inevitably produce traumatic effects, which are implicitly addressed by the subsequent thinkers. The main way of verifying these conceptual reactions is by the presence of new concepts that articulate the new trends.

Though such a hypothesis may sometimes be plausible, its strength depends to a large degree upon the innovative nature of these concepts whose emergence demands explanation. However, at least in the case of those concepts that were not significant in the Lurianic scheme, the historical explanation does not hold, for they may be traced, as we shall see in the following pages, to much earlier layers in Jewish writings. Whatever role historical factors may have played in their surfacing, it was probably not a dominant one. The same argument may also be made in the case of the new interpretations of the Lurianic terms. In some cases, which have already been examined by scholars,[12] philosophical interpretations of Lurianic thought directly contributed to the Hasidic understanding of those terms; in these instances, at least, it would be foolish to invoke historical explanations as pertinent to the Hasidic *condition humaine*. At the same time, however, it cannot be denied that some new interpretations of Lurianism were offered by the early Hasidic masters. It is the nature of the sources of these "innovative" interpretations that concerns us here. The major assumption that will inform our analyses is that the mystical and magical models to be discussed below, which provided most of the important concepts that distinguish Hasidism from Lurianism, also inspired many of the new interpretations.

To a great extent, we face a situation that assumes that changes in one system, the Lurianic one, are to be understood as the result of its penetration by concepts that belong to other mystical and nonmystical systems, at which we shall look more closely below. The nexus between the restructuring of a mystical type of thought by dint of other mystical models, as well as by historical circumstances, is of particular interest. There are at least three different possibilities for explaining significant changes in Hasidic mysticism other than through Lurianism. The first, espoused by Scholem and accepted by many other scholars,[13] emphasizes the role played by historical traumas in the nature and direction of the change. A second possibility is that those mystical concepts that have moved to the center of Hasidic mysticism were more consonant with the religious needs and sensibilities of eighteenth-century Eastern European Jewry. According to this view, although historical circumstances may inform the needs and expectations of individuals belonging to a certain generation, the patterns that provide the answer to those needs were already in existence and are consciously selected and adapted, as they were in this case by the Hasidic masters. This alternative attempts to combine some parameters of the historical situation with the complexities of the history of Jewish mysticism according to the panoramic approach that we have proposed above. A third alternative would be to deny the importance of history altogether and attempt to explain development along systemic lines alone, namely to regard Hasidism as the development of a more complex mystical model out of a variety of preexistent models. I am inclined to prefer the second alternative, without, however, disregarding the third, which offers inspiring explanations in certain instances.

Having enumerated above the kinds of literature that reflect the types of thought that were available to the Hasidic masters, either in print or manuscript form, let us focus the discussion on two different religious patterns, or models, that are found in some of the literary texts mentioned above and that had a deep impact on Hasidism. By using the term *model* I intend to describe not the canonized behavior of an exemplary figure,[14] but a cluster of concepts that constitute a relatively consistent religious structure, and which is either explicit in the sources or reasonably detectable by a scholarly effort of reconstruction from those sources. Let me emphasize that such a model involves, on the one hand, more than one central concept or theme and, on the other, presupposes coherent relations between certain of its constituent concepts. We might describe the models that will be discussed below as consisting of a major religious ideal and the mystical or magical techniques employed to achieve it; moreover, these constitutive elements of the various models are often presented in distinct nomenclatures. The models should therefore differ from each other both in their mystical or magical axiology and in their terminology.

Historically speaking, the two models, the mystical and the magical, stem from distinct religious sources; each was expressed in an independent literature with different constitutive assumptions concerning important religious issues. Nevertheless there are from time to time speculative convergences between these models, and since they were employed in the course of their history by Jewish mystics before the emergence of Hasidism, we cannot assume that they reached the attention of the Hasidic masters in their "pure" forms. For a conceptual analysis of Hasidic thought and praxis, the awareness of the meaning of both the individual concepts—what I have called the microanalysis—and the larger systemic contexts, the macroanalysis or the "Gestalt contextures," to use Aron Gurwitsch's term,[15] is essential.

Another methodological assumption of the present study is the crucial importance of the detection of models in Jewish mysticism, their description, and the various results arising from the different forms of interaction among these models. By using the term "model" for spiritual structures found in different versions in Kabbalah and Hasidism, I would like to distinguish the present approach from discussions of simple "influences," which are concerned mainly with tracing the vestiges of the impact of one author or text on the thought of another. Indeed, when direct and detectable influences are apparent, detailed analysis is important in order to establish the historical and conceptual relations betwen two authors. However, even when such a historical link can be established, the most important part of the analytical approach still remains: namely, to establish whether it is a formative influence or merely a quotation used as an authoritative prooftext for advancing an idea that stems from another source. The use of a quotation does not necessarily signify acceptance, but may reflect an attempt to rely on authorities whose thought was interpreted freely. Thus, establishing the influence of Lurianism on Hasidism amounts, in many cases, to finding out the source or sources of a quote whose content was substantially adapted to Hasidic spiritual goals. In other words, influence can be formative if the content of a quotation or series of quotations, or of terms derived from a certain system, reflect a meaningful transmission of content from the quoted source to the one quoting it; this formativeness does not imply servile acceptance of the earlier source and may include a fertile interpretation of it. A model will therefore become significant for a certain later type of literature not simply if it was quoted, but if it was fecund. One difficulty lies in defining the character of each of the mystical literary corpora in order to establish the transmission of content from one text to another. Here, either the systemic approach or that of models may be helpful. However, before describing these models, another methodological warning is in order.

In some cases, especially in those related to Hasidism, it is rare to find the sources of inspiration consisting of coherent bodies of thought. For example, R. Moshe Cordovero, aspects of whose thought will concern us in the following discussions, is considered by modern scholars to be one of the most systematic thinkers in the history of Kabbalah, yet he is, in fact, a very speculative Kabbalist.[16] Nevertheless, as we shall see below, in many instances that are directly relevant to Hasidic mysticism, Cordovero often drew from differing systems of thought with regard to the same idea.[17] The present approach assumes, and this discussion is not the place to elaborate in detail upon this assumption, that only in very rare cases—Lurianism being one of them—were Kabbalists very concerned about comprehensive systematic consistency. We should also bear in mind that we are dealing with mystical and mythical sources, which are by definition less inclined toward building systematic structures than their Jewish philosophical counterparts. Since it is rare that even the philosophers are able to present a totally consistent scheme, the search for such consistency among the Kabbalists, and a fortiori, the Hasidic masters, may at times seem a rather misguided enterprise. However, I would like to emphasize that the relative indifference of many Kabbalists toward strict consistency is the result of more than one cause. The eclectic nature of many Kabbalistic writings, particularly the later ones, is obvious to any knowledgeable student. There are many reasons for the variety of views found within a single Kabbalistic system:

a) the different philosophical sources that informed earlier and later Kabbalah: Neoplatonism, hermeticism, Aristotelianism, and later on, even Atomism. In different degrees, some of these sources were adopted by many Kabbalists.

b) the various types of Kabbalistic thought that were combined as early as the last third of the thirteenth century becoming part of the Kabbalistic tradition.

c) changes in the orientation of the Kabbalists from one kind of Kabbalah to another; the cases of R. Moshe de Leon and R. Joseph Giqatilla are well known. Sometimes the shift was from philosophy, especially the study of the *Guide of the Perplexed,* to Kabbalah, as in the case of Abraham Abulafia. Their previous orientation affected the Kabbalists' thought.

The sharp awareness of this situation is absent in many of the modern studies of Kabbalah. Most of them are guided by the search for the systematic cohesiveness of a certain Kabbalist, as in the case of Joseph ben Shelomo's analysis of Cordovero's view of theology[18] or Isaiah Tishby's attempt to offer a harmonious solution to diverging views in the Lurianic school regarding the source of evil.[19] These tendencies are characterized by a strong emphasis on the alleged preoccupation of these Kabbalists with systematic theology, or theosophy, in a way reminiscent of that of the philosophers.[20] Our concern here is less with the theological starting points but more with the experiential one: what kind of explanations were offered for the commandments and what mystical techniques were practiced or espoused by the Kabbalists or Hasidic masters? Or, to put it differently, while the dominant academic approach would start with the nature of the upper world and address only later the mystical and spiritual aspects of the literature and mode of life, here we shall start by focusing on the way of life, the existential dimension, and less (though I do not exclude the need to examine it, too) on the theological one.[21]

But let us return to the question of influences and models. To disclose the direct or indirect impact of a Kabbalistic text, one of Cordovero's, for example, we must proceed by examining the content of the passage being quoted, as well as its context, to see what eidetic contribution it may have made to the quoted text. Since two or more different modes of thought concerning the same idea are discernible and coexist in the same system, it would be reasonable to distinguish, whenever possible, the speculative models that informed Cordovero's thought and could have affected, in different ways, Hasidic mysticism. In other cases, the various Kabbalists share common *topoi,* and the tracing of direct sources does not add anything substantial to the discussion; the theosophical-theurgical Kabbalah, so influential in the book of the *Zohar,* in Cordovero and Luria, underwent several changes in those writings, but in some cases it does not matter whether a certain theme was quoted from the writings of one Kabbalist or another.

While establishing the existence of such models, we should nevertheless not deny the probability of shifts in the meaning of terms, either because of semantic developments or systemic changes. However, the major assumption of the present study, and in my opinion it is the implicit assumption in any comprehensive study of the history of ideas over a long period of time, is that not only change, but a certain amount of semantic inertia, is inevitable. In the case of the existence of models, namely webs of concepts that maintain similar types of relationships among them, we may assume that the relations among the concepts may be instrumental in preserving a greater degree of stability for the meaning of each of them. Thus, for example, the nature of mystical techniques, which are naturally adapted to the spiritual ideal the mystic is striving to attain, will change only rarely if the mystical ideal itself does not change. On the other hand, the fact that a mystical ideal is presented not only as an abstract value or a separate concept, but as the culmination of a mystical life that is described in detail, may serve as an indication that this ideal has actually been cultivated. Moreover, the existence of the two components of the model, the technical and the ideal, allows for a much more solid understanding of the texts as reflections of a mystical way of life, rather than as figments of the imagination. This point, whose central importance to the understanding of Jewish mysticism cannot be overestimated, shows that a more comprehensive approach to the texts is necessary in order to decide whether these texts merely reflect repetitions of revered religious content or represent a more intense spiritual life.

To take one important example: the status of *devequt* is, in my opinion, different in an exegetical text, where it is part of an attempt to explain the meaning of a biblical verse, than it is when elaborated in a book that proposes a specific way, nomian or anomian, to attain it. The presence of the technique, which together with the ideal constitutes the mystical model, can change our reading of the role or status of this ideal.[22]

One of these models has already been mentioned above: the Lurianic one. Characteristic of this model is a stable nomenclature, which occurs in a very definite type of text, stemming from Luria and his followers, who espoused, despite the existence of different versions, a rather coherent Kabbalistic system. Since details of this mystical model have been the subject of many other studies,[23] I shall present here briefly what seems to me the relevant aspects of this type of Kabbalah. Systemically, what characterizes Lurianic Kabbalah is the concentration of Jewish ritual around the mystical goal of restructuring reality and the Godhead in order to reconstitute the shattered unifying entity: *ʾAdam Qadmon*.[24] The detailed theogony and the less developed cosmology are speculative frames that provide the parameters of the ritual life. In other words, a very complex mythical theosophy supplies the meaning for the mystical performance of the ritual. It is an ascending ritual, as it intends to elevate the divided divine, as found in the lower realms, to its source and place on high, within the anthropomorphic structure. My emphasis on ritual, as well as the experiential aspects of Kabbalah in general, and in particular Lurianism, assumes that certain aspects of what may be called "Kabbalistic events" are documented only rarely, as they belong to the realm of transient experience. In other words, though Lurianism is indeed preoccupied with directives, rituals, theosophies, and occult powers, we may assume that the living experience originated within the compass of this system and was, for the Kabbalists themselves, as important, or even more important than the mental absorption of the mystical directives. In other words, there were psychological facets to the transformation of the abstract theosophy into mystical life, which may still be analyzed. This observation should open again the question formulated by Buber,[25] that Hasidism is Kabbalah that became ethos. Only by assuming that

Kabbalah, in fact Lurianism, is eminently gnosis, can one define the next stage in Jewish mysticism in such stark contrast to these earlier ones.

Before addressing the two models that will occupy us here, I would like to express my doubt as to whether Sabbateanism can be considered, systemically, a model in itself, because of the profound similarity between the speculative writings of this messianic movement and those of Luria. According to the description above, if the model consists of a technique, and an ideal that is achieved by means of the technique, Sabbateanism is a model of one person, Sabbatai Ẓevi. This is why, though Sabbateen themes might have been influential in later types of Jewish mysticism, as a system its influence was minimal.

2. THE MYSTICAL-ECSTATIC MODEL

"Mysticism" and "mystic," like "magic" and "magical," are generic terms that cover a wide range of phenomena. In the following, however, we shall use these terms to point to relatively well-defined types of corpora. In the case of the terms *mysticism* and *mystic,* we shall restrict our discussion to one of the many forms of Jewish mysticism that were, in my opinion, constitutive of Hasidic mysticism: the ecstatic one as it was formulated by Abraham Abulafia and his followers, including the Safedian Kabbalists. Therefore, while I openly acknowledge the mystical character of other types of literature in Judaism, including Lurianism, for heuristic reasons I will use this term in a relatively limited sense. Hasidism is conceived, like other major phenomena in Judaism, as the result of an act of revelation: this is the case of the Heikhalot literature, of the early Kabbalah, of Abraham Abulafia's special type of Kabbalah, and of Lurianism and Sabbateanism. The recurrence of revelatory experiences in the foundation myths of those brands of Jewish mysticism does not imply an automatic imitation of the earlier revelatory event in the later mystical development. Mysticism changes and with it the techniques and content of the experiences.

However, while in certain cases the revelation is connected to events, backgrounds, and persons to whom our access is difficult given the scant evidence available, in the case of Hasidism there are good reasons to accept the formative impact of a mystical group that served as the background of the articulation of Hasidic experience and thought. This is because one specific form of mysticism was cultivated in the circle of the Besht, the founder of Hasidism: ecstasy.

There can be little doubt that ecstasy is a constant of human religious experience. The wide dissemination of this type of experience in so many cultures[26] is evidence of its centrality. In our specific context, it should be noted that ecstatic experiences become more and more evident in the written documents of Jewish mysticism since the thirteenth century. It seems that a process of adoption and accommodation with paranormal experiences is characteristic of medieval and early modern Jewish thought, which addresses paranormal experiences with a growing seriousness as legitimate events. The concomitant spread of the Maggidic experiences,[27] Luria's claims of paranormal revelations,[28] and the discussions of the Dibbuq cases[29] that appeared may bear testimony not to the emergence of new forms of experience, but to the legitimation of their discussion in public.[30] However, it seems that no movement in Judaism has ever emphasized the importance of pneumatic experience, in its most intense and extreme forms, as much as Hasidism.[31] Here I would like to draw attention to some descriptions of the paranormal experiences of the founding fathers of this movement. Though some of them may well be exaggerations, the fact that they were expressed in such strong language constitutes in itself a very significant phenomenon. The founder of Hasidism was described repeatedly as someone who enjoyed a variety of mystical experiences.[32] However, even later, this emphasis on trances, ascents to heaven, cataleptic experiences, and so forth recurs widely in hagiographical sources. So, for example, the Great Maggid compares the experience of praying in a unitive mood to prophecy.[33] The grandson of the Besht, R. Moshe Ḥayyim Ephraim of Sudylkov, describes topics revealed to him in dreams.[34] R. Moshe Eliaqum Beri᾽ah reports the paranormal experiences of his teachers,[35] including some remarks about his father's listening to the "supernal ear," a euphemism for revelation.[36] R. Yiẓḥaq Aiziq Safrin of Komarno, a master who was immersed in an intense and extremely mystical life, testifies that he studied with masters who were

> Ẓaddiqim, the disciples of our master R. Elimelekh . . . and the disciples of R. Yeḥiel, and the disciples of the Besht; [these disciples are ones] who performed miracles, who possessed the divine spirit, who enjoyed the revelation of supernal lights[37] and worlds, who gazed upon the *Merkavah* like R. ᶜAqiva and his companions.[38]

These examples and numerous others testify to the self-awareness of the Hasidic masters that the highest form of religious experience is preeminently mystical, and sometimes ecstatic.[39] What, therefore, are the links between this self-perception (and, in my opinion actual experience) in the eighteenth and nineteenth centuries, and mystical experiences and mystical systems or models in Judaism in prior generations? Any attempt to restrict a late phenomenon to a specific mystical theory in the past would be both reductive and simplistic. However, while assuming that we must allow the influence of a variety of paranormal experiences, there is no reason not to attempt to survey one major possible source for some of these extraordinary experiences. Let me attempt to describe a model that informed, in its different stages, some of the later phenomena.

The mystical-ecstatic model gravitates around the ideal of *devequt,* an ideal that was understood in more than one manner, as indicating moderate or extreme types of union with the Godhead. The other important aspects of this model are techniques to ensure the attainment of this ideal. *Hitbodedut,* meaning both solitude and mental concentration,[40] *hishtawwut* or equanimity,[41] and linguistic techniques of combining Hebrew letters or contemplating divine names[42] are integral constituents of the mystical-ecstatic model. Paranormal experiences, such as revelations and prophecies, are also integral to this type of mystical model, more consonant with it than they are with theosophical-theurgical Kabbalah. The connection between these concepts and practices is rather obvious: there is an organic continuum between strong mystical techniques and extreme mystical experiences. Significant in this model is the anomian feature of the techniques and the paranormal states attained by them, though it would be very difficult to discern antinomian trends in these writings. The paramount importance of the linguistic components of these techniques must also be emphasized, especially because of their possible contribution to similar phenomena in Hasidism. Also conspicuous are the strong individualistic proclivities of this kind of mysticism and the deep influence of philosophy, especially Aristotelianism in the case of Abraham Abulafia, and the tendency toward Neoplatonism among his followers.

Although all of the aforementioned concepts, with the exception of *hishtawwut,*[43] are found in the writings of Abulafia, which are crucial both for the crystallization and the dissemination of this model, the presence of various elements of the ecstatic model are easily detectable in Neoplatonic philosophy and in Geronese Kabbalah. However, in a much more crystallized form, and under the influence of Abraham Abulafia's thought, the ecstatic model is visible at the end of the thirteenth and beginning of the fourteenth centuries in the writings of certain Kabbalists, such as R. Yiẓḥaq ben Shemuel of Acre, the anonymous authors of *Sha ͨarei Ẓedeq, Ner ᵓElohim,* and *Sefer ha-Ẓeruf,* and in the sixteenth century in the works of R. Yehudah Albotini, R. Moshe Cordovero, and R. Ḥayyim Vital, to mention the most important exponents of this model. Many of the concepts associated with the ecstatic model were disseminated by means of the widespread writings of Cordovero's disciples, though some folios of Abraham Abulafia's Kabbalah were in print as early as the sixteenth century. As we shall demonstrate elsewhere, there are good reasons to assume that some of Abulafia's manuscripts were well known in Eastern Europe in the eighteenth century.[44]

For the sake of a better understanding of the dynamics of Jewish mysticism in general and that of Hasidism in particular, I would like to emphasize that this model, though formulated in a systematic way by a Spanich Kabbalist, was not accepted by the Spanish Kabbalists in the Iberian Peninsula and was even sharply criticized, both in Abulafia's lifetime and after the expulsion of the Jews from Spain. Though Cordovero and his students were positively predisposed toward this type of mysticism, apparently the mystical model was not meaningful for Lurianic Kabbalah, as we can easily see from the writings of Luria and his disciples.[45] (A notable exception is R. Ḥayyim Vital, who was apparently influenced by the Cordoverian attitude to ecstatic Kabbalah.) Therefore, the resurgence of concepts that constitute the ecstatic model in Hasidism is, apparently, not a process of inner development within the Lurianic system, but one that runs against the basic approach of this type of nomian Kabbalah.

Two examples may indicate the possibility of an affinity between the teachings of the Besht and ecstatic Kabbalah. In a collection of R. Yeḥiel Mikhal of Zlotchov's teachings, the Besht is quoted as saying:

> If he is strongly united to the holiness, he is able to elevate profane things to [the level of] holiness by means of the lore of combinations of letters which is known to the holy and divine Besht, blessed be his memory, and to his disciples, who possess the divine spirit . . . we must recognize that there is such a lore, because there are some topics in legends of the *Gemara* that seem to be futile things. But the Tannaim were in the possession of the divine spirit and they possessed this wisdom in a perfect manner, [namely] the combinations of the letters, and they spoke in accordance to the divine spirit, and they [the topics] are secrets of the Torah, and they werre all worthy on account of their cleaving to the supernal holiness.[46]

Let me start with the remark that "the lore of the combinations of letters" was known to the ancient sages. A probable version of this concept is found in the *Zohar*. There the ancient generations, in contrast to later ones, were described as experts in combining letters. The earlier generations were Moses and his contemporaries,[47] in whose time, it is said, even sinners were acquainted with this lore. In later generations, this knowledge was the prerogative of only a small group.[48] Though the Zoharic view is conceptually similar to the claim of the Hasidic text, an alternative source seems even more plausible. A similar statement occurs in a passage found in *Sefer ha-Peliy'ah:* "Our sages, blessed be their memory, were experts in the combinations of letters."[49] Indeed, immediately before this assessment, there occurs a Talmudic discussion that interprets a biblical sentence in accordance with combinations of letters.[50] This text seems to be closer to the Hasidic one, because both of them speak about the sages and not about Moses, and both are written in Hebrew, without referring to the *Zohar*.

The precise source copies by the anonymous author of *Sefer ha-Peliy'ah* cannot, for the time being, be detected; however, by comparing the entire discussion in folio 17ab with numerous parallels in the work of Abraham Abulafia, it seems very plausible that Abulafia was the source of this passage.[51] In any case, this Kabbalist does maintain, like the author of *Sefer ha-Peliy'ah,* that the sages were acquainted with the combinations of letters, and he presents the same prooftext, the verse from Daniel, in order to make this point.[52] Since *Sefer ha-Peliy'ah* is a well-known Kabbalistic text, there is no reason not to assume that the Besht was acquainted with it, and that it served in this particular case as an intermediary between Abulafia's theory of the combination of letters and that of the early Hasidic masters. In any case, this Kabbalistic classic is replete with lengthy passages copied verbatim from Abulafia's books, and the possible contribution of those quotes to the Hasidic theory of language still awaits a detailed investigation.

The phrase *"Ḥokhmat Ẓerufei ha-'Otiyot"* is a very central concept in the passage related to the Besht, and it reflects a practice common in Hasidic thought and hermeneutics in general; here it refers to the knowledge of how to improve the fallen or to purify the impure by manipulating the letters of the entity to be changed.[53] Changing the order of the letters that expresses a deleterious state in such a way that they form a noun will have the effect of transforming reality in a positive way. According to Abulafia, the combination of letters is a way to transform the human psyche through separating it from its ties with the corporeal human faculties. Here, changing the structure of the psyche is done not by inducing change externally, as in Hasidism, but through spiritual attainment. Despite this difference, however, the very occurrence of the phrase suggests a source related to ecstatic Kabbalah. Moreover, the use of the phrase in the above passage is also significant: those who know the lore of the combination of letters are divinely inspired and united with God. Such spiritual states are strongly reminiscent of ecstatic Kabbalah; but whereas in this type of Kabbalah altered states of consciousness are commonly caused by means of the combinations of letters, in the Hasidic text the combinations of letters is possible and meaningful because of the prior cleaving of the mystic to God. Nevertheless, there are at least two instances of a Hasidic master attributing a paranormal experience to the combinations of letters. R. Menaḥem Mendel of Vitebsk indicates that

> In order to attain a total union with God, blessed be He, it is necessary to leave aside the attributes . . . and reach a state higher than these attributes by the letters of the combinations of [those] attributes themselves . . . [T]hose attributes are revealed by the combinations of letters.[54]

His contemporary, R. Abraham the Angel, states that "by the prayers and the combinations of letters the good revelation arrives."[55] This Hasidic master mentions the combinations of letters by intellectuals, which parallel the divine creative activity.[56] Moreover, it is only in the ecstatic Kabbalah that the cleaving to God enables someone to change the course of nature, which occurs in the context of manipulating language. Abulafia describes the last stage of interpreting the Bible by atomizing the canonical text into separate letters, which represent divine names; he defines this technique as the path of the prophets, saying, "It is proper for those who walk on this path to produce on her behalf a new universe, a language and an understanding."

Elsewhere, Abulafia speaks about the necessity to create new "words and confer onto them a meaning."[58] By combining the letters of the text one is not only able to achieve a prophetic state but also to confer another meaning upon the text, and perform powerful changes—"to produce . . . a new universe." Some of the sources of this practice of atomizing predate the emergence of ecstatic Kabbalah;[59] however, Abulafia presented it as a basic hermeneutical approach. Such an attitude is reflected also in Hasidism: R. Ze᾿ev Wolf of Zhitomir writes that it is possible to transform the stories in the Bible into nouns, adjectives, and appellations of the Holy, and cause the return of the Torah to its pristine luminosity, by combining its letters.[60]

b) That ecstatic texts did reach the Besht, who is the first Hasidic authority described as a source of the lore of combining letters, seems to be evident from another text attributed to him. R. Moshe Ḥayyim Ephraim of Sudylkov reports in the name of his grandfather, the Besht, a tradition that there are five pronunciations of the *᾿Alef.*[61] As R. Simeon Menahem Mendel, the author of the collection of the Beshtian traditions *Sefer Ba ʿal Shem Tov* has observed,[62] this tradition is to be traced either to a discussion in the *Shelah* or to Cordovero's *Pardes Rimmonim,* which is the undeniable source of the *Shelah.* However, the passage in Cordovero's compendium is a *verbatim* quote from Abulafia's *᾿Or ha-Sekhel,* where the five types of combinations of the ᾿Alef with letters of the Tetragrammaton and the five vowels are described by means of detailed tables.[63] The aim of this long quote from Abulafia is, according to Abulafia and Cordovero, to describe how to attain "the knowledge of God." Apparently, the same text of Abulafia, as copied by Cordovero, informs a statement found in R. Qalonimus Qalman Epstein's *Ma᾿or va-Shemesh,* where the creation of the world by means of the twenty-two letters and combinations of divine names is related to the notion that the Tetragrammaton is combined with each and every letter, forward and backward, together with the vowels.[64] This is, in fact, a description of the tables found in Abulafia's *᾿Or ha-Sekhel* and Cordovero's *Pardes Rimmonim.* Thus, we have at least one example of the direct acquaintance of the Besht with a crucial discussion of Abulafia's combination of letters as presented in classical Jewish sources that nevertheless do not mention Abulafia.[65]

c) Another topic, one that recurs several times in early Hasidism, is the acronym of the Hebrew term for mystery, *SeTeR,* derived from *Sof* (end), *Tokh* (middle), and *Rosh* (beginning). This device, which is characteristic of Abulafia's writings,[66] occurs in many Hasidic writings,[67] and may signify Abulafia's influence.[68] Though this is a minor example, it should be added to the former one, as well as to others to be adduced below,[69] in order to show that thirteenth-century Kabbalistic material may have shaped an important area of Hasidic speculations: the mystical view of language.[70]

d) An important issue in Hasidism, to which we shall return later in some detail, is the cleaving to letters.[71] This view was presented by Scholem as follows: "This definition of *devekut* as man's binding himself to the core of the letters, the Torah, and the commandments, instead of to their external aspects alone, seems to be a new point made by the Baal Shem."[72] However, it seems reasonable that this is also a reverberation of the ecstatic Kabbalah. R. Joseph Giqatilla has written, apparently under the influence of Abulafian thought,[73] that

> the letters of the Tetragrammaton, blessed be He, are all of them intellectual, not sensuous letters, and they point to the matter of existence and endurance, and to every entity in the world, and this is the secret meaning of "and thou who cleave to the Lord, your God, shall be alive today" [Deut. 4:4], that is, that those who cleave to the letters of the Tetragrammaton, shall exist and last forever.

e) Finally, in an early collection from the Hasidic tradition, compiled shortly before the end of the eighteenth century by R. Aharon Kohen of Apta, who was apparently in the entourage of the Ḥabad school, I found what seems to me to be an unmistakable example of Abulafian influence in early Hasidism. In Kohen's commentary on the Pentateuch, *ᵓOr ha-Ganuz,* we read as follows:

> The issue of prophecy is [as follows]: it is impossible, by and large, to prophesy suddenly, without a certain preparation and holiness, but if the person who wants to prepare himself to prophesy santicifes and purifies himself and concentrates mentally and utterly separates himself from the delights of this world, and he serves the sages, [including] his Rabbi, the prophet—and the disciples that follow the way of prophecy are called the sons of the prophets—and when his Rabbi, [who is] the prophet, understands that this disciple is already prepared for [the state of] prophecy, then his Rabbi gives him the topic of the recitations of the holy names, which are keys for the supernal gates.[74]

The terminological and conceptual correspondences between Abulafia's thought and this text are quite remarkable; prophecy is an experience that can be achieved in one's own time, by specific techniques taught by a master, described as a prophet, to his disciple. The most important element of these techniques, beside the cathartic preparations, is the pronunciation of divine names.

The first step of bringing together ancient and medieval Jewish practices of combining letters with certain forms of talismatics sometimes found in Abraham Abulafia became a blueprint for some later developments of Jewish mysticism, both in the immediate followers of this Kabbalist, like R. Yiẓḥaq of Acre and some other anonymous sources, to be discussed in the following pages, as well as in the work of R. Moshe Cordovero and his followers and, ultimately, for Hasidism. Together with the monadic view of language and its technical use, and the emphasis on the ideal of *devequt,* these factors made a distinct contribution toward a more variegated picture of subsequent forms of Jewish mysticism. It should be mentioned that thought most of Abulafia's writings remained in manuscript, at least two major Kabbalistic writings, the anonymous *Sefer ha-Peliy ᵓah* and Cordovero's *Pardes Rimmonim* copied significant passages and even whole books belonging to the ecstatic Kabbalist, contributing more to the dissemination of his ideas and practices than the numerous manuscripts of Abulafia himself.

Abulafia's possible direct and indirect influence on Hasidism is an issue that cannot be exhausted by the above observations. A study of his manuscripts, especially those of *Ḥayyei ha- ᶜOlam ha-Ba ᵓ,* copied in eighteenth-century Poland, will contribute to a better knowledge of the dissemination of his Kabbalah. However, even before such a study is published, I see no reason to ignore or reject the possible effect on the Hasidic masters of his view of the combination of letters and his ideal of *devequt.*

If the impact of the founder of ecstatic Kabbalah on Hasidism awaits further elucidation, that of R. Yiẓḥaq ben Shmuel of Acre, another important figure of this Kabbalistic trend, appears to be much more obvious. Like Abulafia, he practiced mystical techniques based on combinations of letters in order to receive revelations.[75] Also like his predecessor, he was attracted to unitive experiences.[76] In his book *Me ᵓirat ᶜEinayyim,* he wrote,

> He who merits the secret of communion [with the divine] will merit the secret of equanimity,[77] and if he receives this secret, then he will also know the secret of *hitbodedut,*[78] and once he has known the secret of *hitbodedut,* he will receive the divine Spirit, and from that prophecy, he will continue until he shall prophesy and tell future things.[79]

In another discussion in the same book, this Kabbalist quotes a different view in the name of a certain figure, the acronym of whose name forms the word "R. Abner":

> R. Abner said to me[80] that a man who was a lover of wisdom came to one of the practitioners of concentration,[81] and asked to be received as one of them. They replied: "My son, may you be blessed from heaven, for your intention is a good one. But please inform me, have you achieved equanimity[82] or not?" He said to him: "Master, explain your words." He said to him: "My son, if there are two people, one who honors you and one of whom despises you, are they the same in your eyes or not?" He replied: "By the life of my soul, master, I derive pleasure and satisfaction from the one who honors me and pain from the one who despises me, but I do not take vengeance or bear a grudge." He said to him: "My son, go in peace, for so long as you have not achieved equanimity, so that your soul feels the contempt done to you, you are not yet ready to link your thoughts on High, that you may come and con-

centrate. But go, and subdue your heart still more in truth, until you shall be equanimous, and then you may concentrate." And the cause of his equanimity is the attachment of his thoughts to God, for cleaving and attachment of the thought to God cause man to feel neither the honor nor the contempt that people show him.[83]

The occurrence of concepts like *hitbodedut, hishtawwut,* and *devequt* as part of a *via mystica* is crucial for the mystical model of R. Yiẓḥaw, but also for some of the sixteenth-century Safedian Kabbalists, whose influence on Hasidism is obvious.[84] It is possible to find each of these terms occurring separately in many sources. However, it can be shown that the Safedian Kabbalists like Cordovero, de Vidas, and Vital, who served as mediators between the ecstatic Kabbalists of the thirteenth and fourteenth centuries and eighteenth-century Hasidism, were aware of the writings of the ecstatic Kabbalists, and their use of the above concepts is not a matter of theoretical discussion, but arises out of a genuine mystical life.[85] Again, though scholars have already pointed out the affinities between some of these notions and Hasidic practices,[86] it seems probable that the impact of ecstatic Kabbalah was not only through disparate concepts that were absorbed separately, but also through acceptance of a larger scheme, a mystical model, by the eighteenth-century masters via the Safedian Kabbalists and others. One interesting example is a text of R. Yiẓḥaq of Acre, whose impact on Hasidism was undeniable and formative. The ecstatic Kabbalist is quoted in the book *Reshit Ḥokhmah* by R. Elijah de Vidas.

> Thus we learn from one incident, recorded by R. Yiẓḥaq of Acre, of blessed memory, who said that one day the princess came out of the bathhouse, and one of the idle people saw her and sighed a deep sigh and said: "Who would give me my wish, that I could do with her as I like!" And the princess answered and said: "That shall come to pass in the graveyard, but not here." When he heard these words he rejoiced, for he thought that she meant for him to go to the graveyard to wait for her there, and that she would come and he would do with her as he wished. But she did not mean this, but wished to say that only there[87] are great and small, young and old, despised and honored all equal, but not here, so that it is not possible that one of the masses should approach a princess. So that man rose and went to the graveyard and sat there, and devoted all his thoughts to her, and always thought of her form. And because of his great longing for her, he removed his thoughts from everything sensual, but put them continually on the form of that woman and her beauty. Day and night he sat there in the graveyard, there he ate and drank, and there he slept, for he said to himself, "If she does not come today, she'll come tomorrow." This he did for many days, and because of his separation from the objects of sensations, and the exclusive attachment of his thought to one object and his concentration[88] and his total longing, he soul was separated from the sensual things and attached itself only to the intelligibles, until it was separated from all sensual things, including that woman herself, and

> he communed with God. And after a short time he cast off all sensual things and he desired only the Divine Intellect, and he became a perfect servant and holy man of God, until his prayer was heard and his blessing was beneficial to all passersby, so that all the merchants and horsemen and foot-soldiers who passed by came to him to receive his blessing, until his fame spread far about. . . .

The passage goes on to discuss at length the high spiritual level of this ascetic, with R. Yiẓḥaq of Acre commenting that "he who does not desire a woman is like a donkey, or even less than one, the point being that from the objects of sensation one may apprehend the worship of God."[89]

A detailed analysis of this interesting parable has been offered elsewhere.[90] However, certain issues relevant to its later reverberations and to our theory of models are relevant here. Of Platonic origin,[91] this parable apparently reached R. Yiẓḥaq of Acre from a Sufi source.[92] Unfortunately it was preserved in a truncated form, as de Vidas indicates: "Thus far is the quotation as far as it concerns us and he went on at length." Our attempts to understand the significance of the parable depend upon what the Safedian Kabbalist selected as relevant.

Prima facie, the erotic opening underwent a transformation—one might even speak of a sublimation—according to which the corporeal eroticism was fastened to devotion to God. However, details from other writings of R. Yiẓḥaq[93] allow a more precise reading: the devotion to the "intelligibles," a term betraying the Aristotelian source, may be understood as devotion to the *Shekhinah,* conceived as the last divine manifestation. Indeed, there can be no doubt that this term, as well as the phrase "divine intellect," are additions to the story as it was learned from an alien source; they reflect the standard terminology of R. Yiẓḥaq in all his extant writings, where the theosophical-theurgical Kabbalah was combined on one hand with philosophical terminology and on the other with ecstatic elements. The occurrence of philosophical terms, the ideal of *devequt,* the issue of *hitbodedut* as mental concentration, as well as Sufi elements like the contemplation of beauty as a mystical technique, point to a synthesis between Sufi and other ecstatic types of mysticism. Although it is possible to determine that this synthesis took place by the end of the thirteenth century, some of the texts that reflect this encounter are apparently lost, including the source from which R. Elijah de Vidas quoted the parable. It is interesting to observe that this encounter, which in all probability took place in the Land of Israel,[94] was influential on later Safedian Kabbalah, which was in turn instrumental in preserving and transmitting this story to the Hasidic masters.

However, let us return to the parable; the non-encounter with the princess has nevertheless alerted the idle man that he should search for the source of her beauty, or the beauty in her source, the supernal feminine; ultimately this is not a story of frustration but of a substitution of spiritual for material beauty; the encounter was purposely postponed in time by divine providence, but was at the same time elevated to a more sublime level. However low the starting point of the spiritual journey may be, it is nevertheless indispensable; the lower beauty is, as R. Yiẓḥaq of Acre says elsewhere,[95] the stimulus for the religious search. Since, as we have noted, a detailed analysis of the peculiar formulations used by this Kabbalist has shown that the princess was no less than the *Shekhinah,* the divine presence,[96] it is clear that a certain immanentism is present, with profound implications for the way the Hasidic masters understood the story.

Although the name of R. Yiẓḥaq is only rarely mentioned in the Hasidic writings that were influenced by this parable, there can be no doubt as to its influence. Its impact on R. Jacob Joseph of Polonoy and other Hasidic masters has already been pointed out by Piekarz,[97] Pachter,[98] and Gries.[99] Indeed, R. Jacob Joseph of Polonoy explicitly mentions his source, "[R. Yiẓḥaq] of Acre," in a context that implies that the Besht himself concurred with the view of the ecstatic Kabbalist.[100] However, beyond the direct quotations, which show how the anomian way of life of the solitary sage brought him to the highest religious attainment, Hasidic masters have adopted and developed the attitude of R. Yiẓḥaq as a directive for their own life. According to a tradition of R. Aharon Kohen of Apta.

> the righteous is able to apprehend the innerness, which is the holiness and the Being,[101] the presence and the *ruḥaniyyut* that maintain everything. In every place that he looks, he sees only the divine and the Being, even etc.[102]

In my opinion, the "et cetera" stands for the contemplation of a woman, who can be conceived as enveiling the divinity, the presence, and spiritual force. The immanence of spiritual force is here obvious, as it is in the case of other terms like divine presence and *ḥiyyut* in other contexts.[103] Elsewhere, in the same writing, we learn that

> The intention of Sarah in all her adornments and embellishments [was] only for the sake of Heaven, as someone who embellishes the image of the King. Namely, there is a connection between the supernal vitality, which is the spark of the *Shekhinah,* and man. Therefore, if someone adorns himself, he does it in order to hint at the adornment of the *Shekhinah,* and his beauty is from the splendor of the *Shekhinah.* So also he must think of the case where someone sees a beautiful and adorned person. [He must think] that this person is in the image of God, and he shall think that he sees the beauty and the adornment of the image of the King. And this was the intention of Sarah when she embellished herself. Namely, as it is said: "Go out and see, daughters of Zion" [Song of Songs 3:11], namely, go out of your corporeality and see the *Ruḥaniyyut* of a thing, since the corporeality of a certain thing is only a sign [*Ẓiyun*] and a hint of the supernal Beauty.[104] Here, a spark of beauty

> out of the beauty of the world of *Tiferet* dwells below. And it is incumbent to reflect [*lekavven*] that this beauty is annihilated [*battel*] as a candle at noon, in comparison to the supernal beauty and splendor.[105]

What concerns us here is the fact that the immanentist theory of R. Yiẓḥaq of Acre[106] was developed in Hasidic discussions that emphasize precisely this practice of contemplating the beauty of a woman in order to reach out to the supernal source of beauty. Second, and even more important from our vantage point, is the assumption that the synthesis between ecstatic Kabbalah and the philosophical term *intelligibles* was accepted by R. Jacob Joseph in his elaboration on R. Yiẓḥaq's story.[107] Thus, in addition to mystical language, the ecstatic descriptions sometimes adopted philosophical terms, a fact that adds another dimension to the phenomenological affinities between Hasidism and ecstatic Kabbalah.[108]

Despite the differences between the mystical ways of Abulafia and R. Yiẓḥaq of Acre, both come under the rubric of the mystical-ecstatic model for several reasons: they share basic concepts which are anomian, such as combination of letters, mental concentration, and *devequt,* though the relation between them is not stable; and there seems to be a common assumption that these mystical practices are not only a matter of exegesis of ancient texts or utopian ideals, but constitute a practical path to be cultivated in the present.

Another seminal text for the ecstatic model in Hasidism is a short, highly influential passage found in an early legalistic compendium, the *Tur* of R. Yaᶜaqov ben Asher. When describing the preconditions for ideal prayer, this fourteenth-century author introduces several terms that betray the influence of Geronese Kabbalah.

> It is incumbent to direct own's thought, because for Him thought is tantamount to speech . . . and the pious ones and the men of [good] deeds were concentrated their thought and directing their prayer to such an extent that they reached a [state of] divestment of their corporeality and the strengthening of their intellective spirit, so that they verged on the state of prophecy.[109]

Unlike the anomian ecstatic Kabbalah, this passage presents another, nomian type of spirituality. The inner concentration of thought and the intensive channeling of the attention during the act of prayer may culminate in a paranormal state of consciousness that resembles ecstasy, described here as prophecy. What is important here is the fact that, following the Geronese Kabbalists, this passage uses terms like *hitbodedut, nevuʾah,* and *kavvanah* as pointing to spiritual states. Unlike the texts of the Geronese Kabbalists, this passage considers prayer to be part of a mystical technique that also includes the undoing of disturbing thoughts, *maḥashavot toredot,* and divestment of corporeality. Therefore, the Hasidic masters were aware of at least two major alternative ways to reach paranormal experiences, both designated by their sources as prophecy.[110] Despite the huge influence, direct as well as indirect, of this fascinating text on Hasidism, this is unique, and atypical, even for the book in which it occurs. Although it is reiterated in numerous sources, no larger context that consistently elaborates upon the content of this passage can be found. The ideal of this passage is nomian, the mystical prayer, and the technique is mentioned, but no detailed mystical way is proposed, such as we find in the ecstatic handbooks of Abulafia or the detailed techniques of visualizing letters in the school of R. Joseph ben Shalom Ashkenazi.

3. THE MAGICAL-TALISMANIC MODEL

The extent of the magical influence on Jewish mysticism is an issue that still awaits detailed treatment. However, there can be no doubt as to the importance of various forms of magic in several major forms of Jewish mysticism, beginning with the *Heikhalot* literature.[111] We cannot embark here on a general survey of this issue; instead we shall limit our remarks to an overview of one particular type of magic that was influential on certain forms of medieval and Renaissance Kabbalah, as well as on Hasidism.

Jewish literature contains various explanations of how magic works. Some of these explanations, including relatively ancient ones, assume that the Hebrew language possesses special traits, which account for the influence of masters using combinations of letters that form the divine names. No elaborate cosmology has ever been articulated in order to justify this assertion, yet this magical view of the Hebrew language is crucial for most of the forms of magic in Judaism, and it has remained influential in numerous texts, especially in Kabbalah. On the other hand, in the Middle Ages, under the influence of philosophical views found among the Arabs, another explanation appears; according to this belief, it is by cleaving to the spiritual source that rules this world—the universal soul—that the mystic or philosopher is able to affect the events in the sublunar world. This explanation of magic contains strong Neoplatonic elements; with regard to its availability to eighteenth-century authors, there were a number of sources already in print.[112] One of them is found in one of the major sources of Hasidism, R. Abraham Azulai's *Ḥesed le-ʾAvraham:*

> Know that the cleaving to the supernal light[113] cannot be attained but because of spiritual faculty, namely desire and love. By the effect of these qualities the soul overcomes the body and man cleaves to his Creator, and the whole world is under his feet, and he is elevated above everything and operates in the world as he likes, because he is the source of the supernal influx, which [comes] from his cause to the cause of the world . . . and everything is subdued to his will . . . and this is a plausible thing and a right explanation for the miracles.[114]

There is nothing Kabbalistic in this text; indeed it reflects a common medieval topos of the magical powers of the cleaving *perfecti*. Influential as these two types of explanations were, a third type of magic and magical worldview has competed with them since the twelfth century.

In ancient Hellenistic magic and in Arabic and Jewish medieval magic the dominant view asserted is that it is possible to attract downward the spiritual forces of the celestial bodies. It was believed that these spiritual forces—named *pneumata* in Greek, *Ruḥaniyyat* in Arabic, and *Ruḥaniyyut* in Hebrew—could be attracted and captured here below by means of special types of objects and rituals, whose natures are consonant with the features of the corresponding celestial bodies. These bodies were called in Arabic *hayakhal,* meaning palaces.[115] Recently, a very important study on this issue was published by S. Pines, along with detailed documentation of the history of this type of magic.[116] The major writings on this astromagical type of thought in Judaism are found in the descriptions of idolatry in Maimonides,[117] in certain authors who were more sympathetic than he was to this sort of activity, such as R. Yehudah ha-Levi and R. Abraham ibn Ezra,[118] and in the work of some of the fourteenth-century Jewish Castilian thinkers, who combined magic with philosophy and, at times, with Kabbalah.[119]

In fifteenth-century Kabbalah the use of the Hebrew language to draw down the spiritual force became explicit.[120] We also find, during this and succeeding centuries assumptions that each and every *sefirah* has a spiritual force of its own.[121] Thus, the astrological structure of this model was projected onto the "higher" theosophical structure, thereby diminishing the potential criticism that a strong astrological stand could arouse. While not totally obliterating the astral meaning of the term *ruḥaniyyut,* some Kabbalists attributed to the sefirotic realm a structure that they adopted from astrological thought: on high, a distinction should be made between the more material and spiritual aspects of reality. Moreover, it is possible to detect some translation of aspects of the astral bodies to the corresponding divine powers, the *sefirot.*[122] While the Arab astrologers differentiated between *haikhalat,* "supernal palaces," and *ruḥaniyyat,* "spiritual forces," the Kabbalists introduced this distinction in the realm of the intradivine: the *sefirot* have an external aspect, the vessels named *kelim,* and the more inner component, the spirituality of each *sefirah.* Though this division has also served other theological goals, such as attempts to offer a synthesis between two competing views of *sefirot* (conceived sometimes as the essence of God, and at other times as the vessel of the divine influx or the instruments of the divine activity), the terms used by R. Yoḥanan Alemanno[123] and R. Moshe Cordovero[124] in this context betray their sources. Especially important for our discussion is the emergence of the term *ruḥaniyyut ha-sefirot,* the spiritual force of the *sefirot.* This phrase still retains the concept of multiplicity in the spiritual world: each *sefirah* possesses a distinct inner power that reflects the specific quality of the respective divine power. Again, this elevation of the term *ruḥaniyyut* to the rank of the plurality of the divine essence did not supersede the magical use of the term in the writings of those

Kabbalists who adopted this projection. Therefore, while accepted by the Kabbalists, the magical model was changed in two major aspects: the theological—actually, the theosophical plane—supplanted the celestial-astrological one, while the magical practices were replaced, to a great extent, by the Jewish rites and especially by the ritualistic use of the Hebrew language in prayer and study.[125] This is a pivotal change, which took place in a conspicuous way in the writings of Alemanno, Alqabetz, and Cordovero, and is part of an attempt to offer an explanation of the efficacy of the commandments, in addition to or as an alternative to the more common theurgical rationales in Kabbalistic literature. In adopting Jewish ritual for the sake of magical attainments, or by considering these rites to be magically effective, the more problematic aspects of magic—consisting of acts that are not part of the normal behavior—was attenuated to a great extent. It is by fulfilling the divine will that the material and spiritual attainments are drawn down and not by attempts to force that will or short-circuit the order of nature.

Although, as we shall see, the term *ruḥaniyyut* preserves in many cases overtones from its magical sources, in many others, both in Cordoverian Kabbalah and Hasidism, this term designates the ideal spiritual realm, without maintaining any of its astral-magical meanings. It is this sense of the term that penetrated modern Hebrew, where *ruḥaniyyut* means spirituality, a fact that was instrumental in the neglect of the magical meaning of this term in some classical mystical texts.

Let me present here some examples for this adoption of the magical model in Kabbalistic sources (many more will be cited in the following discussions).[126] Although astral magic is indeed crucial for the writings of the fifteenth-century Italian Jewish Kabbalist R. Yoḥanan Alemanno, we have had the opportunity to explore his thought elsewhere;[127] here our main concern will be with the magical views that reverberate in the writings of the sixteenth-century Safedian Kabbalist R. Moshe Cordovero. It seems reasonable to assume that the emergence of astro-sefirotic magic in Safed was not the result of the influence of the works of the Italian Kabbalist but of his sources, which emerged from fourteenth-century Spain. If Alemanno's books influenced Cordovero at all, it seems they did so in a very limited manner. Yet I should like to point to one instructive example of hermetic magic as it was expressed in a classic of Safedian Kabbalah, Cordovero's *Pardes Rimmonim:*

> There is no doubt that the colors can introduce you to the operations of the *sefirot* and the drawing down of their overflow. Thus, when a person needs to draw down the overflow of Mercy from the attribute to Grace, let him imagine the name of the *sefirah* with the color that is appropriate to what he needs, in front of him. If he [applies to] Supreme *Ḥesed,* [let him imagine] the outermost white. . . . Likewise, when he undertakes a certain operation and is in need of the overflow of [the attribute on Judgment], let him then dress in red clothes and imagine the form [of the letters of] the Tetragramm-

> aton in red, and so on in the case of all the operations causing the descent of the overflows. . . . Certainly in this manner [we may explain] the meaning of the amulets. When a person prepares an amulet for the *[Sefirah* of] *Ḥesed,* let him imagine the [divine] name in a bright white, since then the operation of that name will be augmented.[128]

This passage is highly significant, for in it the sefirotic system is conceived as instrumental to the efficacy of magical activity. However, in lieu of the common spiritual forces that are appointed over the planets and manipulated by the use of colors and clothes, here the magical Kabbalist addresses the *sefirot.* The astral spiritual forces were projected onto the divine inner realm and manifested by the use of magical categories. The basic technique in this type of magic is the drawing down of divine powers, or the overflow of the *sefirot,* in accordance with the needs of the magician. Cordovero was very well aware of the affinity of his conception to that of astral magic. Immediately following the above passage, he wrote:

> All these topics are known and apparent to those who write amulets, and we have no part in their labor. But we have seen someone who designed amulets that refer to the [attribute] of [stern] judgment using the color red, and those that refer to Grace in white and those which refer to Mercy in green, and everything [was done] in accordance with what [was revealed] by true [angelic] mentors, who taught to him the preparation of the amulets. All this [was done] in order to introduce him to the subject of the colors and the operations that derive from above.[129]

Cordovero was aware of the similarity between the type of Kabbalah he was proposing and pagan magical practices. Moreover, he considers the knowledge of the preparation of amulets or talismans as a revealed gnosis, which serves as an introduction to the knowledge of the Kabbalah. Notwithstanding his reservations regarding magical practice, it is obvious that he was in contact with someone who indulged in these practices, and Cordovero even considered that person's knowledge to have come from above. In any case, his reluctance to acknowledge it more openly, while understandable, does not detract from the profound similarity and historical links of his Kabbalah to a certain type of magic. Moreover, magical activity is compared by Cordovero to the rituals performed by the priests and Levites in the service of the temple:

> When he becomes interested in [the influence of the attributes] of *Ḥesed* and *Raḥamim,* let him dress [in] white [clothes]. And we have clear evidence from the priests, whose overflow is from the part of ḥesed, and their clothes were white in order to point to peace. And this is the reason that the great priest on the Day of Atonement was put off the golden [clothes][130] and put on white ones, since the worship of that day was [to be performed] in white clothes.[131]

The principle behind religious ritual is the same, according to Cordovero, as that regulating magical activity. As in the case of the natural magic of Yoḥanan Alemanno, Cordovero did not intend to disrupt the natural order by appealing to demonic forces that could destroy it. Instead, he proposed to complement natural activity by adding a dimension of praxis based on laws already in existence but hidden from the eyes of the uninformed. Kabbalistic activity was supernatural not because it intruded into the regular order of events, but because it was of a superior order.

In another passage in *Pardes Rimmonim,* Cordovero quotes an already existing concept of drawing down the supernal influx, again by using the divine names:

> Some of the ancients commented that by the combination and permutation of the Name of 72 [letters][132] or other [divine] names, after a great concentration [of mind],[133] the righteous man, who is worthy and enlightened[134] in such matters, will have a portion of the divine voice[135] revealed to him, in the sense of "The spirit of God spoke to me, and his words were on my lips" [II Samuel, 23:2]. For he combines the forces and unites them and arouses desires in them, each to his brother as the membrum virile of man and his companion [i.e. the female] until there is poured upon him a great influx, with the condition that he who deals with this will be a well-prepared vessel and worthy of receiving the spiritual force. For if it is not the case, it will become cruel[136] to be turned into a "degenerate wild vine."[137]

Bringing the supernal influx down upon the righteous by the combination of the letters of the divine names is similar to causing the descent of the overflow of the *Sefirot* by employing the color technique, as described above. However, whereas the names may sometimes be conceived as static talismans, here we have a dynamic process inducing the spiritual force from above, and we may assume also that this dynamic descent is incited by the combination of letters. In other words, the talismanic implications of Abulafia's techniques were enhanced by some of his anonymous disciples, who vigorously introduced the talismatic view of language. The human body was thereby conceived as the locus where the divine influx is received and as a vessel to hold the descending influx. Interestingly enough, it is the mystico-magical technique that may induce an experience of the divine, present in and working through the human body, a view reminiscent of what is called the "quietistic" attitude in Hasidism.

We witness a certain shift from the theurgical ideal, which was so central in the classical Spanish Kabbalah (referred to by Cordovero's source, above, as the unification of supernal forces), toward a more magical view, represented by the ideal of drawing down the divine influx.[138] As in the case of the acculturation of the hermetic type of magic into Jewish ritual in the above passage, similarly the Kabbalist performing the practice of concentration and pronunciation of the combinations of letters is presented as a righteous—that is, as an ideal—religious type. Although not part of the regular ritual, the above technique is nevertheless considered to be a legitimate practice, as it is attributed to an ancient source, and the practitioner is described as a righteous man.

Moreover, according to yet another passage from the same book, the highest domain of study, which transcends even the study of the *Zohar,* the most important text of Kabbalah, is knowledge of the "spiritual force of the letters and their existence and their combination with each other," for this knowledge enables the Kabbalist "to create worlds."[139] This assertion is indeed noteworthy; the spiritual forces of the letters seem to be omnipotent, and this gnosis is, according to Cordovero, very rare. For our purpose it is enough to mention the obvious magical implications of the manipulation of the spiritual forces of the letters, an issue to which we shall return later.[140]

In his treatise on the angelic powers, R. Moshe Cordovero asserts that

> everything depends upon the spiritual force, the influx, that flows by means of the Ẓaddiq and of his proper deeds . . . The world is blessed by the spiritual force flowing because of the merit [of the Ẓaddiqim] . . . and all of the worlds and things are subject[141] to the Ẓaddiq . . . and everything depends upon the secret of the Torah that is transmitted to him.[142]

This short sentence contains, *in nuce,* the most important elements of the magical model: the world depends upon the higher powers, the spiritual force that is attracted below by the very body of the *Ẓaddiq* and by his religious acts, as well as by his knowledge of the secrets of the Torah.[143] It is a magical universe that is described by Cordovero: the *Ẓaddiq* is not only able to change the mundane realm; he is also conceived as governing the celestial world, *Ẓevaʾ Marom.*[144] By virtue of the divine soul that dwells in a human being, the righteous man, since he is cleaving to the world of emanation, rules over the world. This expansion downward of the divine influx depends on religious behavior, which is instrumental in attracting the "light of the world of emanation"[145] onto all the worlds, this being the reason that all of them obey him and are compelled by his will.[146] Here we have already an adumbration of the transition from magic to mysticism: while in magical sources the drawing downward of spiritual forces is deeply related to objects, rituals, and propitious times and less with the inner essence of the ritual's performer, Cordovero emphasizes—following Kabbalistic anthropology—the divine nature of man; he cleaves to the divine world by virtue of the highest soul, which enables him to rule over the extradivine universes. The Safedian Kabbalist uses, time and again, the term *Ẓaddiq* to refer to the extraordinary individual who is able to perform ritual in a manner that changes the course of nature.[147]

Cordovero takes pains to distinguish between this type of influence on the world, which is for him, as for his Renaissance contemporaries in Italy, a type of natural magic[148] and the drastically different and more radical forms of Jewish magic that operate by virtue of the divine names, and which should be avoided as much as possible.[149] Indeed, Cordovero is also eager to forbid the use of the astral-magical model as it was practiced by the gentiles[150] though in some cases he describes devices for preparing amulets using astromagic.

Let me present another example pertinent to the magical model, this time doncerning the realm of ritual. According to Cordovero, the blessing, *berakhah,* means the "drawing down," *hamshakhah,* namely,

> the drawing down of spiritual force and influx from the top of the degrees [namely, the *sefirot*] to *malkhut,* the reservoir where the influx is gathered, . . . and from there it comes down to the lower [entities], though we are incumbent to draw only until her [*malkhut*] . . . When there is a blessing after a commandment or an act . . . that act is a vessel and a bucket,[151] by means of which the waters of the influx[152] are drawn.[153]

The "drawing down" consists of two stages: the intradivine, from the peak to the last *sefirah, malkhut,* a stage that can be designated as theurgical; and drawing the influx from the last *sefirah* toward the lower entities, which can be called magic.[154] What is significant for the present study is that a ritualistic term and a ritual act are involved in the process of attracting spiritual power downward. The use of the term *hamshakhah* reflects a magical component that may indeed be a return to a more ancient layer of thought, a Jewish adoption of the idea of drawing down astral influences by using a "traditional," that is, well-established, Kabbalistic term. In fact, Cordovero is an inheritor of a tradition found in a long series of Kabbalists who connected the concept and practice of blessing, *berakhah,* and the drawing down, *hamshakhah.* Let me briefly describe the main phases of this nexus in the Kabbalah prior to Cordovero.

The term *hamshakhah,* a derivation from the root *MShKh,* assumed a great variety of meanings in medieval speculative literature. On the simplest level, it means the act of drawing something toward a certain point. It also means concentration of thought, and in philosophical writings is used to refer to semimystical experience.[155] However, *hamshakhah* is most frequently used for the drawing down of the divine influx. We may distinguish between two main types of drawing down: the theurgical, within the sefirotic realm, that is to say from the divine infinity toward its finite divine manifestations; and the magical, which describes the pulling of the influx from the divine source to the extradivine realms, either cosmic or human. The theurgical *hamshakhah* depends upon the theosophical system, though even in such a theology the magical drawing down can follow the theurgical stage. In other words, it is possible to assume that the theurgical drawing may open the way for the magical one, by supplying the energy within the sefirotic world that will subsequently be drawn into the nondivine realms. Let me start with a short survey of the theosophical-theurgical *hamshakhah.*

The relation between the *hamshakhah* and the commandments occurs by the beginning of Kabbalah in the thirteenth century: according to R. Yiẓḥaq Sagi Nahor and his disciple, R. Abraham ben Yiẓḥaq, a Geronese cantor, it is possible by means of the words of a prayer to draw essences from one *sefirah* to another, lower one.[156] However, this drawing forth takes place, at least according to one passage, "when he will elevate, at the end of each and every blessing, his thought to the *Teshuvah*[157] . . . he will draw until the Great Name."[158]

Therefore, the drawing forth follows the mental ascent to the source of power or influx. According to this text, the main goal of the ascent is solely the intradivine process. However, elsewhere, R. Yiẓḥaq Sagi Nahor is reported to have said that after drawing the "blessing" to the sixth *sefirah*, the influx is distributed to "the whole world."[159] The meaning of this phrase is far from clear; it could stand for the six lower *sefirot* that receive their power from the *sefirah* of *Tiferet*, and if so, it is again a theosophical system that informs this type of theurgy. However, if the world is to be understood literally and not symbolically, we have here a sequel of theurgy and magic.

A more magical turn of the meaning of the term *hamshakhah* is discernible in R. Joseph Giqatilla's *Ginnat ᵓEgoz*. Less interested in the theosophical structure of the divine world, this early work of Giqatilla's betrays in its use of this term a more philosophical, and perhaps esoteric, magical propensity.[160] In the middle of the sixteenth century two eminent Kabbalists embraced the wide use of the term *hamshakhah*—R. Shimeon Lavi[161] and Cordovero, whose Kabbalah is replete with the link between blessing and *hamshakhah*[162].

However, we should also be aware that other term occurring together with *hamshakhah*, namely *berakhah*, may also reflect a magical view. In other types of literature, for example Islamic literature, *baraka* means a "paraphysical force, a kind of spiritual electricity. . . . Like the notion of the exemplary center, it is a conception of the mode in which the divine reaches into the world."[163] The ritual and the acts related to it are instrumental in attracting and collecting the divine power here below.

In regard to the relation between blessing and drawing down, which had already appeared in R. Yiẓḥaq Sagi Nahor's Kabbalistic thought, we find a collection of traditions from the school of the Great Maggid that any blessing that does not involve *hamshakhah* is not a blessing, drawing down being related to the process of contraction for the sake of revelation.[164] *Berakhah* is conceived here in magical terms as a way to attract the infinite divine as energy here below in a contracted form.

The views related to the magical model that draw their inspiration from hermetic literature remained part of Jewish culture after the period of Cordovero and his disciples. Abraham Yagel in Italy was well acquainted with the magic of causing the descent;[165] the very printing of the Safedian books, which followed Cordovero, contributed to the dissemination of these views in larger circles, albeit in a rather fragmented manner. Nevertheless, in various ways we can still find a familiarity with talismatic astral magic in the generation of the Great Maggid, in his geographical area, and, in fact, the writings of someone who met him: Shelomo Maimon, in his still unedited *Sefer Ḥesheq Shelomo,* describes the astral magic that is the origin of the magical model as follows:[166]

> It is well known in the science of the planets[167] that when someone makes a particular image from a particular matter connected with a peculiar planet—as they [the ancestors] said: "There is no [blade of] grass on earth, etc.,[168]—and he places it under the power of the above-mentioned planet when the latter is at its ascendant and in the house of its glory. Then will the power of the star pour upon that image, and it [the image] will speak[169] and perform certain operations, and they are the *Teraphim,*[170] which are mentioned in the Book of the Prophets.[171] Likewise when a person prepares himself for that, for example, to receive the power and spiritual force of the planet Saturn, he dresses in black and wraps himself in black [clothes] and covers the place he stands upon with black clothes and eats things that increase the dark bile, which is under the dominion of Saturn. . . .[172] Then the power and the spiritual force of the above-mentioned planet will pour upon the person, and this is the essence of the prophecy of the Baʾal and the prophets or Ashtoret and similar [phenomena].[173]

As a superficial reading of this passage shows, astral magic, as presented by many medieval and Renaissance thinkers, was well known to the young Maimon. Although his attitude toward this discipline was negative, he affirmed, as R. Moshe Cordovero had already done before him,[174] that there is a structural affinity between the praxis of the magicians, which is viewed as negative, and that of the Kabbalists who follow the halakhic prescriptions. Nevertheless, the very comparison between the two types of lore and the highlighting of the similarities show that Renaissance and early modern Jewish thinkers did not ignore the common structure, though none of them would agree to see in astral magic the source of corresponding Kabbalistic views. One example of the magical interpretation of the Midrashic dictum interpreted by Maimon may be found in the Hasidic camp; R. Yehudah Leib ha-Kohen of Hanipoly mentions in his *Ve-Zot li-Yihudah* that there is nothing in the world, including minerals, that does not have "vitality, spiritual forces, a zodiac sign and a decan that is governing it."[175] The fact that the terms vitality and spiritual force occur together with the astrological terms shows that the affinity between them persisted into the second half of the eighteenth century.

An interesting Hasidic attempt to differentiate between the various meanings of the term *hamshakhah* is found in the work of R. Eliezer Lippa of Lisansk; he describes the primordial *hamshakhah,* namely the constant drawing down stemming from the days of creation, and the active *hamshakhah,* which depends upon the deeds of the children of Israel.[176]

The passages from Cordovero quoted and analyzed above were printed and disseminated as part of the commonly accepted Kabbalah and did not meet any resistance or criticism. It would be no exaggeration to assert that they were also included in the most influential Kabbalistic collections. No wonder that the Hasidic type of magic and mysticism follows the pattern proposed in Cordovero's thought, which reached Hasidism in numerous ways.

Let us elaborate, in the context of this type of magic, on the most powerful magical entity in Judaism. As we shall see later,[177] the strongest talisman is the divine name. Indeed, since the founder of Hasidism is called the Master of the Good Name, it would be pertinent here to survey some stages of the history of the nexus between the concept of names and spiritual forces. In the famous magical text *Picatrix,* known in Hebrew as *Takhlit he-Ḥakham,* it is said that, according to Aristotle, "in ancient times, divine names had a certain ability to bring spiritual force to earth. At times, these forces descend below."[178]

R. Menaḥem Azariah of Fano, a late sixteenth- and early seventeenth-century Italian Kabbalist and a fervent admirer of Cordovero, indicates that

> there is a great preparation inherent in the names of the righteous [which enables] the dwelling of the divine overflow on them, as it is written: "See, I have called you by name" and only afterward [is it written] "I shall fill him with the spirit of God."[179]

The name of the righteous one, in our case Beẓalel, was given as the reason for the dwelling of the divine spirit upon that person; the precise meaning of the preparation inherent in the name is not clear, but it seems reasonable to assume that it is similar to that indicated by Cordovero when he referred to the drawing down of the overflow by means of the divine names. It is important to emphasize the fact that the righteous ones, in Hebrew the *ẓaddiqim,* are referred to by the Kabbalist, for this is the term that will designate the leaders of the new mystical trend in Judaism, Hasidism. Interestingly, the passage of R. Menaḥem Azariah of Fano was indeed quoted by a Hasidic master, R. David Moshe of Cherkov.[180] Under both the direct and indirect influence of Cordovero's conception of prayer, the early Hasidic masters understood prayer in terms of the attraction of spiritual force from above onto the letters—or more precisely onto the sounds—of the prayer. In one case, the magical implication of this theory still remained perceptible. R. Jacob Joseph of Polonoy, the disciple of the founder of Hasidism, wrote:

> The quintessance of the [mystical] intention [of the prayer] is that the person who prays should direct his intention to cause the descent of the spiritual force from the supernal degrees to the letters that he pronounces, so that these letters will be able to ascend to the supernal degree, in order to perform his request.[181]

According to this passage, the attraction of the supernal forces is understood as a prerequisite for the ascent of the letters to the divine world, a process that ensures the divine response to prayer. In contrast to the usual understanding of mystical prayer as causing the descent of the divine in order to enable an encounter—namely, a union with the divine[182]—here the more practical, magical possibility is alluded to. Prayer, and the divine names in the prayers, are conceived of as not just mystical ritual but as vehicles for the attainment of one's request.

Perhaps the most influential figure in Jewish mysticism, designated a magician even by his name, was R. Yisrael ben Eliezer, the Besht, or Ba^{c}al Shem Tov, namely "the Master of the Good Name." A mystic of wide influence, he practiced healing, using names as a means for his healing. This perception of the Besht was expressed explicitly by Shelomo Maimon, who in his autobiography stressed the magical side of the Besht's activity, especially his magical healing, accomplished with the help of the divine name. According to Maimon, some of the Besht's disciples were also renowned for their successful healing.[183] Moreover, in a series of legends, the Besht's power of shamanistic clairvoyance is reported—that is to say, his ability to see things happening at a remote distance when looking into the Torah, or more precisely into the light hidden in the letters of the Torah.[184] This light, similar to the ether that pervades everything, was the medium that enabled him to see events taking place at a distance.[185]

Although the activity of the Besht has been analyzed on several planes by scholars, who have tried to present a detailed picture of this founder of a new sort of mysticism, it is strange that their academic analyses give no detailed account of magic. I would suggest that the theory of magic employed by the Besht was consonant with and influenced by the magical model described above. It should be emphasized that while the following discussion gravitates around the theory of magic, which is fully consonant with some forms of Beshtian mysticism, the details of his practical magic, his use of clairvoyance, amulets, and healings, are beyond the scope of this work. Then omission should be understood neither as a rejection of the Besht's involvement in practical magic nor as an assumption that this is not an important domain of investigation. However, given the scant evidence in our possession, it is doubtful whether a very fruitful discussion is possible at this stage. Nevertheless, though we may assume that some of these practices were inherited by the Besht from an older source, one that apparently had nothing to do with talismatic magic, it seems plausible that the Besht understood his practice of magic, or at least some part of it, within the framework of the theory described above.

Although different in nature, the two kinds of magical activities engaged in by the Besht that are mentioned above, healing and clairvoyance, share a common concern. Like most other Jewish magicians, he used linguistic techniques, and according to the Hasidic sources, it was these techniques that enabled him to perform his magic. In Hasidic literature, there appears to be no direct and detailed reference extant to the magical theory of the Besht. However, I should like to propose here a certain way of understanding this magic based on inference from two important facts.

1. First, there is the peculiar nature of the mysticism introduced by the Besht, which served as the basis for Hasidic mysticism. According to the Besht and his disciples, mystical prayer consists of concentration and the pronunciation of the letters of the words of the prayer as if these sounds were the "palaces," or containers, of the divine influx, which enters these sounds and permits the mystic to unite with it. This understanding of prayer is not a new one; as we shall see below, in chapter four, it is a continuation of the Cordoverian theory regarding Kabbalistic prayer.[186] According to Cordovero and his sources, mystical activity is achieved when the divine spiritual force descends into the words of prayer. The sources of this Kabbalistic view are magical, "hermetic" views that penetrated Kabbalah in the fourteenth century and were understood in a more mystical way than they were in their Arabic sources. As we have seen above, in the passage from the work of R. Jacob Joseph of Polonoy, the magical implications of this conception were still perceptible in his formulation of the Cordoverian view of Kabbalistic prayer. Let us look briefly at an important legend dealing with the content of the amulets prepared by the Besht:

> When R. Isaac of Drohobyz heard of the remarkable powers of the Baʾal Shem's amulets, it occurred to him that this was most certainly accomplished by means of the sacred Names written in them. So he decreed, "Because of the improper use of the Name of God, the power of the amulets must pass away." And that, indeed, is what happened. The talismans issued by the Baʿal Shem were now unavailing, having lost their special potency. . . . When the Baʿal Shem finally realized that his amulets were no longer providing any benefits, he sought the reason. It was eventually revealed to him that it was because of the pronouncement of the *ẓaddiq* R. Yiẓḥaq. The Baʿal Shem thereupon wrought a remarkable feat by means of a Kabbalistic combination of the words of the prayer *ʾAnaʾ Bakoaḥ*. As a result of the Baʿal Shem's feat . . . the Baʿal Shem confronted R. Yiẓḥaq. "Why has your honor taken from me the power of my amulets—amulets that I dispense to help people?" Said R. Yiẓḥaq, "It is forbidden to make personal use of the Holy Names." "But there are no oaths nor any Names in my amulets," argued the Besht, "save my very own, 'Israel, son of Sarah, Baʿal Shem Tov.'" R. Yiẓḥaq, unwilling to believe this, said that it was not possible for the Baʿal Shem's name alone to possess such awesome powers. Upon opening several amulets that were brought for R. Yiẓḥaqʿs scrutiny, he became convinced of the truth of what he was told. Then he uttered the following: "Lord of the universe, if a man earns his livelihood through the power of his own name, what do You

care? Restore to him the potency of the amulets bearing his name." And so it was.[187]

Thus, the awesome powers of the proper name of the Baᶜal Shem were said to accomplish, alone, deeds commonly attributed to the divine name. It seems highly significant that the proper name of a *Ẓaddiq* was thought to be so powerful. This also seems to be the view underlying the passage from the work of R. Menaḥem Azariah of Fano cited above. Though he was not mentioned in our context, apparently his views were able to influence an eighteenth-century figure such as the Besht. Another legend associated with the Besht may be instructive in this regard. R. Pinḥas of Korecz, an outstanding disciple and companion of the Besht, asserted that "many years after a *ẓaddiq* enters the future world, he is transformed into a divine Name, and he becomes a light for the fear of God." According to another tradition, which is anonymous, he had heard this from R. Ẓevi, the son of the Baᶜal Shem Tov. R. Ẓevi told him that his father had appeared to him in a dream and had told him that "in the next world a *ẓaddiq* is transformed into a divine Name. You should meditate on the Name *ʾAnaʾ Bekoaḥ*, for I am that Name."[189]

As in the legend regarding the confrontation of the Besht with R. Yiẓḥaq of Drohobycz, there is again an affinity between the divine name associated with the prayer *ʾAnaʾ Bekoaḥ*—namely, the name of forty-two letters that emerges from the acrostic of the words of this prayer—and the Besht. In the latter story, the Hasidic master was transformed into this name. It seems therefore that this was the most important divine name used by the Besht. Moreover, according to Menaḥem Azariah of Fano, the personal name of the Besht may have been a transformation of the name of forty-two letters. In any case, the magical use of the Besht's name testifies to a phenomenon described by the Italian Kabbalist. It may well be, then, that just as in the case of the names of the *Ẓaddiqim* mentioned by Menaḥem Azariah of Fano, the letters of the Besht's name caused the descent of the flow from above. Indeed, a power closely related to that described by the Italian Kabbalist was believed to be present in the name of the son of R. Yiẓḥaq of Drohobycz, the famous Hasidic master R. Yeḥiel Mikhal, the Maggid of Zlotchov. He is quoted by R. Jacob Isaac, the Seer of Lublin, as saying that he has seen in books that "in the letters of *refuʾah* (healing) there is the vitality of healing,[189] since that whole Torah is [composed of] the names of God,[190] Blessed be He."[191] As we learn from the sequel to this passage, the letters of the Torah, as divine names, draw downward the vitality that is a synonym for spiritual force (*ruḥaniyyut*).

Toward the middle of the nineteenth century, an important Hasidic figure, R. Yisrael of Ryzhin, explained the magical activity of the Besht in terms that reflect the magical model very accurately. The bad luck of a person is explained by the bad influence of the zodiac, which depends upon the combination of letters that is regnant insofar as that person is concerned. The Besht had the special ability, according to this Hasidic master, to substitute for the bad combination "other letters that will draw down to the person, by their nature, vitality and existence, and this is a very high degree attained by the Besht."[192] Thus, the function of the letters in attracting the supernal spiritual power, in connection with the process of healing or changing the fate of someone, was well known in the entourage of the Besht. According to another passage associated with the Maggid of Zlotchov,[193] in order to help someone in need of healing, the name of the person should be mentioned together with the word *refu ʾah,* for the "light"[194] or vitality that occurs when this word is pronounced dwells on the name of the person and improves his condition. Here, the name of the person is the recipient of the supernal overflow. Perhaps the name of the *ẓaddiq,* the Besht, functioned in the same manner in the amulets: its letters would collect the influx and thereby help to cure the sick person. Or, if the word *refu ʾah* was considered to be endowed with curative power, it seems reasonable that this is one of the possible roles of the letters forming the name of the Besht written in his amulets.

2. Second, we must consider the existence of a magical, "hermetic" understanding of medicine, as revealed in the writings of some Christian figures, since the end of the fifteenth century[195] and later on in the work of R. Abraham Yagel.[196] He, and his possible sources, applied to the theory of medicine the magical principle of using the descending flow, the healing being achieved according to this theory by the power descending from above. This magical understanding of medicine may be found in Yagel's work, *Moshi ʿa Ḥosim,*[197] and could have influenced, directly or indirectly, any eighteenth-century author. Because the magic of the Besht was concerned with healing, and because his mysticism employed the principle of causing the descent of the supernal flow, we may infer that the theory of magical healing of Yagel was known to the Besht. This hypothesis seems to be confirmed by a statement found in a Hasidic work. R. Eliezer, the son of the famous Hasidic master, R. Elimelekh of Lisansk, stated that the *ẓaddiqim,* the religious leaders of the Hasidic communities, "heal maladies and draw downward the influxes on the entire people of Israel."[198]

If this proposal concerning the "Cordoverian" origin of the Hasidic theory of magic is borne out by future studies, then the conclusion we must draw regarding the affinity of Beshtian healing magic and Italian magic is that the latter remained influential in Safedian Kabbalah, especially that of R. Moses Cordovero and his school. In any case, it seems obvious that the later fifteenth-century Spanish conception of demonic magic, and the much older magical practice of creating a *golem,* were quietly rejected by eighteenth-century Hasidism[199] in favor of the Italian type of magic as espoused by Alemanno and Yagel. Again, this is not to say that these authors had a direct influence either in Safed or in Poland, but that their approach to magic, inherited from both

Jewish and Christian sources—drawing upon earlier Hellenistic types of magic—was known to Jewish mystics in these two centers.

Last but not least, though the Italian type of magic seems to be closest to the Beshtian, the latter involves an important characteristic missing in Italian magic. The achievement of the Besht, as well as his self-perception, is directed toward the community and, theoretically, as we learn from some of his rhetorical statements, even to the entire people of Israel. As against the relatively individualistic tendency of authors like Alemanno, eighteenth-century Hasidism focused on the well-being of a people. According to the famous letter of the Besht to his brother-in-law, R. Gershon of Kotov, the Besht believed that the dissemination of his teaching would have eschatological significance. In light of this document, the Besht's magical and mystical teachings may be regarded as having messianic implications, and the Besht himself may be seen as a moderate redemptive figure whose work included magical components. Let us look at the relevant passage of this highly interesting document.

> I [namely the Besht] asked the Messiah: "When will you come?" And he answered: "You will know [the time] as it is when your doctrine will be revealed in public and will be disclosed to the world, and your fountains will well outside [with] what I have taught you and you apprehended, and they also [i.e., the people of Israel] will be able to perform the unifications and the ascents [of the soul] as you do, and then the shells will be abolished and then there will be a time of good will and redemption." And I was surprised by this [answer] and I was deeply sorrowful because of the length of time before which this will be possible; however, from what I have learned there, the three things that are remedies and three divine names are easy to learn and to explain. [Then] my mind was calmed and I thought that it is possible for my contemporaries[200] to attain this degree and aspect by these [practices], as I do, namely to be able to accomplish the ascents of souls[201] and they will be able to study and become like me.[202]

Like R. Aqiva in the *Heikhalot* literature,[203] the Besht brought down the means to ascend on high in order to study the secrets that would pave the way for the advent of the Messiah. As the Besht indicated, this technique of ascent includes divine names, but also certain remedies whose nature is obscure. I have translated the Hebrew term *seggulot* as "remedies" not only because this is the most plausible rendering from the semantic point of view, but also because of a parallel to this Hasidic text found in an early medieval treatise on magic, *Shimmushei Torah*. In the introduction to this text, which explains the magical attainments that can be accomplished by various passages in the Pentateuch, Moses is portrayed as ascending on high in order to receive the Torah and, afterward, contesting with the hostile angels. He prevails, and these angels offer him, together with the Torah, "a remedy [*devar refu'ah*] and the secret of the names that can be derived from each and every pericope and their [magical] uses."[204] Thus, the work of Moses was seen in some sources to be similar to that of R. Aqiva, as well as to that of the Besht, as we have seen above. All three of these major figures in Judaism are portrayed as having brought down divine names—which are at the same time magical names—in addition to other secrets, apparently medical remedies. As such, both the revelation of a mystical technique of ascent and the magical remedies are, in the Hasidic text, part of the future dissemination of the Beshtian doctrine, which opens the way to the Messiah. No less than earlier mystical masters who had engaged in magic as part of a redemptive enterprise, the Besht, the Master of the divine name, saw his work as redemptive.[205] If the remedies are seen as representing the medical aspects of the Besht's activity, in other words a significant aspect of his magic, the divine names may represent his mystical activity, related to the ascent on high apparently through the use of the classical formulas of Jewish mysticism—the divine names. According to this proposal, the Besht received revelations that pertain precisely to the two major aspects of his work: magic and mysticism.

The medical significance of the term *seggulot,* which occurs together with the divine names, is also supported by a historical document describing the Besht as not only a Kabbalist but also as a *Doktor* and *Balsem,* or *Balszam.*[206] These two words are to be found just after the designation of the Besht as a Kabbalist. Indeed, they seem to have been used widely to refer to persons with similar powers. So, for example, we find in the magical writing *Mif ᶜalot ᵓElohim,* attributed to R. Yoᵓel ben Naftali Katz, a famous *magus* described as a Baᶜal Shem, a quote from the "writings of the Kabbalists" that deals with medical astrology, where it is written that astrological details "are necessary both to the master of the name and to the doctor."[207] Therefore, the pair of words in the Besht's revelation is indeed relevant to the practice of the founder of Hasidism.

In this context, the use of the Torah as an instrument by means of which the Besht attained clarivoyant power may be related to the magical understanding of the Hebrew letters and divine names. The companion of the Besht, R. Meir Margoliot mentions, in the context of the Besht's instruction of studying Torah, that by

> cleaving to the holy letters, someone will be able to understand future [events] from the very letters . . . because [the Torah] enlightens the eyes of those who cleave to them [the letters], in holiness and purity, like the *Urim* and *Tummim* . . . because the letters of our holy Torah are all of them holy, and whoever merits to cleave to the letters, when he studies for the sake of heaven, will be able to understand future [things].[208]

Although bibliomancy is by no means a novel magical technique,[209] the way the Besht understood it seems to differ from the more common magical usage, for as he asserted in another context, the primordial light inherent in the Torah is the medium of his clairvoyance. From this we might assume he meant that by cleaving to the letters of the Torah, and bringing within them the divine light, it was possible for him to see both the future and the distant events and objects.[210]

Before leaving the description of the magical model, we should emphasize the elite nature of this type of thought and action. In its medieval versions, it required precise knowledge of the astral order, a very rare type of knowledge. Although astral magic and its Jewish counterparts involve acts that change the course of nature, they also presuppose the existence of laws, in addition to the natural ones, described by philosophical systems of thought. These para-natural laws can interfere with the normal course of nature without altering it in an arbitrary manner. In light of Renaissance discussions of magic, we should designate this form of magic as natural magic, a Jewish version of the Renaissance concept of *magia naturalis*.[211] This practice is far removed from witchcraft, sorcery, miracle-making, or popular medicine, though the latter was indeed practiced by the Besht. Rather, it involved an interaction with the higher powers in accordance with preestablished sympathies. One important characteristic of the Hasidic *Ẓaddiq* is, as I shall attempt to show in detail in chapter 6, his knowledge of how to draw down into this world the supernal spiritual forces for the benefit of the community. Paradoxical as it may appear prima facie, the Hasidic *Ẓaddiq* is the last important reverberation of an ideal type described in fifteenth- and sixteenth-century Italian Renaissance thought. We shall return to this issue in the concluding remarks; here, it should be emphasized again that the use of divine names for medical and other magical purposes, which apparently has nothing to do with hermetic magic, was reinforced by the encounter with a natural explanation of drawing down the influx by means of the divine names. It should be mentioned that the divine names were also used by the Besht, according to some legends, for apotropaic purposes, such as exorcism, but this issue does not concern us here.

4. COMPARISONS BETWEEN THE MODELS

The following is a phenomenological comparison between the above-mentioned three basic models of Jewish mysticism. However, let me start with some broader cultural-historical observations. Both the magical and the ecstatic models were deeply influenced by elements that stem from medieval Muslim culture, though their origin may be much earlier and belong to diverse cultural milieux. Abulafia's Kabbalah is in debt to Maimonides' Neo-Aristotelianism; R. Yiẓḥaq of Acre, and perhaps also Abulafia, were influenced by Muslim Sufism; and in the later stages of ecstatic Kabbalah, Neoplatonic themes are more evident. On the other hand, the theory of magic explicated above is one of three major explanations of magic in the Arab world: in addition to talismatic astro-magic—what may be called hermetic magic—Muslim authors were acquainted with and accepted a Neoplatonic belief in influencing the events in the natural world by cleaving the human soul to the cosmic one; and last but not least is the theory of magic connected to the name of Al-Kindi, which is based upon the assumption that spiritual "rays" are instrumental in the magical influence. We have restricted our analysis only to the first of these three explanations. However, ancient as all those theories may be, it is probable that the main, and perhaps single, channel of information available to Jewish medieval authors was Muslim culture. In the Renaissance, there was a dramatic change, with the large-scale Latin translations of Neoplatonic and hermetic material, which also had a certain influence on Jewish thinkers. However, in general, the magical and mystical models described above owe much to the impact of the vigorous Muslim culture that existed between the tenth and fourteenth centuries. From this point of view, these models, like the Jewish philosophies in the Middle Ages, represent various interactions between Jewish thought and its immediate cultural environment. These models, significantly affected by Muslim culture, were transmitted to Jews in Europe through various channels and were formative in the emergence of Hasidism. Interestingly enough, it is only a certain, relatively small segment of Ashkenazi Jewry, who lived in Eastern Europe, who were receptive to some of the elements of these models and adopted them, elaborating upon them with the result that they become part of a mass movement. On the other hand, the various communities that form Sefardi Jewry, which was crucial in the initial acceptance and transmission of these elements, were less prone to elaborate upon them, and so remained more faithful to the theosophical systems espoused in the *Zohar* and in Luria's writings. Curiously enough, Ashkenazi Jewry, reluctant to adopt the more speculative types of Jewish culture cultivated in the South by Spanish and Italian Jewry, adopted and elaborated upon both the mystical and the magical models, as we shall see below. On the other hand, while the Sefardi authors initially adopted important aspects of these models from their Muslim environment, they did not cultivate them on a large scale. This bizarre situation is less surprising if we compare the above description with the various metamorphoses undergone by the concept of the golem. In Ashkenazi culture, it remained basically a magical notion, while among the Sefardi authors, the magical aspect was eclipsed by more psychological and theosophical interpretations.

Let us now turn to a comparison of the three models. Although historically and phenomenologically different, the mystical and magical models nevertheless share some important traits, which appear to be only rarely the result of historical affinities. There are two main areas of convergence: the locus of the experience and the main technique itself. Both of these models are strongly anthropocentric: man is the center of activity as well as the main beneficiary of the results of these activities. In a more detailed manner, we may also describe man as the place where the encounter with the divine takes place: not a sacred place, a shrine or a temple, but the human person hosts this contact.[212]

Moreover, it is a human activity, the production of language, that is instrumental in such an encounter. However, in sharp distinction to the theosophic-theurgical model, the Hebrew language is only marginally functional on its symbolic level, though this symbolic function was not always negated. In these models, language, namely Hebrew, is conceived as having a cathartic or magical role, sometimes interpreted as the symbolic function. Or, to put it in different words, the two models activate language in order to achieve an experience that is direct and instantaneous, while the theosophical-theurgical model assumes another plane of being paralleled by the mental-linguistic activity, which is impacted by the linguistic activity. The mental aspect of the theosophical-theurgical model assumes a symbolic cargo that transforms language into a universe that reflects and influences another, transcendent universe.

Let us now examine the main differences between the two models: the mystical one is based upon the purification of the human consciousness and its preparation for the encounter with the divine. According to the Aristotelian version, it is the human intellect that is united in an epistemological act with the divine as intellect. According to some Neoplatonic versions, it is the purified human soul that returns to her source on high. The Godhead is not affected by this experience of union, nor is it attracted downward in order to ensure it. The cognitive aspect of the experience is sometimes evident, especially in the Abulafian version of this model, while it is less obvious in the Neoplatonic one.

In the magical model, however, it is not the human spiritual capacities—intellect or soul—that are the main "location" of the encounter with the divine, but the human body and the elements of language that serve as a container of spiritual forces.[213] God is experienced as a descending power, captured or attracted by human activity, but the cognitive aspect of this encounter is marginal. While the Aristotelian version of the ecstatic model assumes the pervasive presence of the Deity as intellect within the cosmos, the Neoplatonic version requires the ascent of the soul to the spiritual by abandoning the material world. In the magical model, the divine energy or spirituality is often brought down into the universe.

Language acts in different ways in these two models: according to the magical model, the precise sequence of the letters in the recited ritual text is vital for the mystico-magical attainment. However, the mystical model emphasizes the cathartic nature of the manipulation of language, the combination of letters,[214] and the importance of each letter in itself,[215] while the magical model focuses upon the inner quality of their precise sequence. Both models exploit the nonsemantic aspects of language, but the magical one is still in debt to the established sequence of the letters in the canonic texts, while Abulafia's technique is based upon combinatory devices stemming from *Sefer Yeẓirah* and its commentaries. To put it differently: by ignoring the semantic dimen-sion of language in the ecstatic state, the ecstatic Kabbalist attempts to reach an experience of fusion with an entity that is absolutely spiritual and undifferentiated. He strives to assimilate himself to it by leaving behind him any personal, idiosyncratic qualities.

Although language is still a significant part of Lurianic mystical performance—being a major component of the ritual and an important factor in the technique of the *Yiḥudim*—it is nevertheless less crucial in Luria's system that in each of the two models.[216] However, the difference between the Lurianic vision of language in mysticism and that of the two models transcends the matter of relative emphases; it has to do more with the differing concepts that inform their attitude to language as part of a mystical system. Lurianism is the inheritor of a long theosophical-theurgical tradition, one that is especially represented by the *Zohar,* and which envisions language from the symbolic point of view. According to this tradition, there is an inner quality in the Hebrew letters and words that relates them to the higher divine manifestations in two different ways: the elements of language are both symbols of the divine processes and organs of theurgical influence on the direction of these processes.[217] Common to these two different functions is the possibility of transcending the normal religious experience by visionary experiences and theurgical operations. In fact, the this-worldly orientation of the linguistic techniques in the two models is contrasted by the otherworldly proclivities of the Lurianic mystical use of this medium.

By deemphasizing the mystical role of the theosophical plurality, the *Sefirot,* on all its levels, a Kabbalist like Abraham Abulafia is able to reach the highest experience. However, the magical model emphasizes the paramount importance of the particular for attaining a certain goal, even one that is mystical. The minutiae of magical ritual and its counterpart in Jewish ritual involves particularity, and implicitly plurality, as part of the system that ensures an encounter with the divine here below. The inner structure of a sacred building, ritual, or language is crucial for this model, and it presupposes a diversified spiritual power on high. This is the reason that the magical model, like the theosophical-theurgical one, is much more nomian, whereas the mystical-ecstatic one is basically anomian, or only rarely nomian. Or, to put it differently: Abulafia was striving to reach an experience of union that can be achieved only by the prior process of self-simplification; he flees, as we shall see below,[218] from lower multiplicity to the utmost divine unity, which was conceived as a never changing reality.

For the theosophical-theurgical Kabbalah, and for the astro-magic of the Middle Ages, the plurality of the spiritual forces was not only a given, but also a situation that could be changed. According to the theosophical Kabbalists, the ultimate aim of this activity is to achieve a harmonious relationship between the divine forces, to unify them without obliterating their particular existence. Complexity, and the ability to manipulate it, is essential to these types of thought. Let me give one example of the positive role of the complex in talismatic magic as understood by the Kabbalists. R. Abraham Azulai, apparently following Cordovero, compares the nature of the letters and their combination into divine names to that of a *mirqaḥat,* a medicine; his assumption is that the more complex the medicine is, due to its different components, the more effective it will be.[219] The combination of letters that attracts a higher spiritual force is powerful precisely because of its complexity. Magical activity, in contrast to the solitary achievement of the individual, is more powerful if performed in a group.[220] It should be emphasized that the analogy with medicine is very suggestive, for it assumes a distinct quality to each of the letters and to the spiritual force that corresponds to it. By combining the different qualities, a much stronger effect is achieved. Although the mentioning of the medicine is apparently only as an analogy to a remedy achieved by drawing down spiritual forces, as we shall see below astral medicine may constitute an interesting parallel to this view.[221]

With Abulafia, however, the highest form of contemplating the canonized text is when is is dissolved into distinct letters.[222] If the combinations of letters or the single letters are intended to propel the ecstatic mystic into another, more spiritual, "simple," level of existence, the talismatic linguistics strives to attract a complex celestial reality here below by means of combining letters and divine names.[223] Moreover, according to Hasidic texts, the commandments are seen as a multiplicity of acts that attract the infinite light into the lower realm.[224]

What are the main differences between the two models described above and the Lurianic one? The most conspicuous divergence between these models is the anthropocentric emphasis in the ecstatic and magical models versus the strong theocentricity and mythocentrism of the Lurianic one. The emphasis upon the transcendence of the theosophical structure, *ʾAdam Qadmon,* which is repaired or restored to its primeval stage by performing the ritual, is crucial in Lurianism. The unifying principle, the supernal *anthropos,* is therefore conceived as shattered, and the whole religious enterprise is geared toward reuniting those particles into a reconstructed transcendental entity. The divine immanence is not excluded from this system, but is the result of a catastrophe in the theogonic process, and the presence of the sparks, the holy *niẓoẓot,* in our world is not an ideal situation. However, this transcendent nature of the supernal *anthropos* is coupled by a very complex divine infrastructure, whose components and dynamics are to be studied in a minute way and understood and manipulated by the performance of the commandments *more cabalistico,* an issue that involves the paramount importance of Kabbalistic theurgy.[225]

On the other hand, the two models under consideration are definitely more open to immanentistic interpretation, which conceives the presence of the divine in a mundane plane not as the inevitable effect of a divine catastrophe, but as a state of being intended by God, or as the individual attainment of the mystic, who is able to see God in all things. To a certain extent, the collection of the sparks of the soul of each *Ẓaddiq* in Hasidism[226] is a micro-anthropic replica of the gigantic Lurianic system, where the supernal anthropos, not the individual soul, is the target of mystical-theurgical religiosity. Using two major examples, let us demonstrate the interactions between the different models. I shall focus first upon the value of *devequt*—which characterizes ecstatic Kabbalah—as it is achieved by drawing down the influx from above. Then I shall present an important concept characteristic of theosophical Kabbalah, the idea of divine contraction, and look at how its interpretation is affected by the mystical model.

5. DEVEQUT

One of the most cherished values of Hasidism is that of cleaving to God. Indeed the term *devequt,* the most recurrent designation for this spiritual value, appears thousands of times in Hasidic literature. In one sense, that is by no means exceptional. As one Hasidic master said, "The quintessence of the worship of God is to comprehend His divinity, blessed be His name, and to cleave to the Infinite, blessed be He."[227] The various sources of the Hasidic notions of *devequt,* its various meanings and its place in the general economy of the Hasidic movement, have been the subject of several studies, and we shall not summarize their findings here.[228] However, when comparing the relative emphasis on *devequt* in the various branches of Jewish thought, there can be no doubt that ecstatic Kabbalah put a greater emphasis on attaining intense mystical experiences, described as union with God, than any other form of Jewish thought except Hasidism.[229] Therefore, at least on this issue, there is a certain phenomenological convergence of spiritual concerns between these two forms of Jewish mysticism.

The ideal of *devequt* has a long history in Judaism, dating to even before the emergence of the historical Kabbalah. Some of the stages of this rich history have already been surveyed in several studies.[230] Of special interest for our discussion here is the intersection between the search for a profound contact between God and man and the magical model.

It should be emphasized that the notion of union, or communion, with God was a well-established ideal in some major Kabbalistic schools in the thirteenth century, especially in ecstatic Kabbalah.[231] We have given a few examples to this effect above.[232] Although this kind of Kabbalah is only one of the many sources for the concept of *devequt,*[233] due to its influence the Safedian Kabbalists also cultivated this value in many of their writings.

Crucial to the special status of this idea is, once again, the position of R. Moshe Cordovero. He quotes the author of *Sefer Ma ͑arakhot ͗Elohim Ḥayyim* as saying that "in order to cleave to Him, by a wondrous cleaving named *͗Aḥdut*[234] it is worthwhile to remember Him in each and every moment of the hour."[235] The unknown Kabbalist quoted by Cordovero assumes that by pronouncing the letters of the divine name in each and every moment, one is clinging to God; the more precise meaning of this cleaving to God is to sustain an uninterrupted awareness of the divine in one's mind.[236] The ideal of oneness with God obliterates the distance between the human and the divine through a continuous act of remembering; both the term *ʾAḥdut* and the practice of uninterrupted awareness of the divine are characteristic of the ecstatic model. In any case, there is no trace of classical Jewish ritual in the notion of union with the divine, and we may consider this quote to reflect an anomian attitude. In fact, the details of the combinations of letters as they appear in Cordovero's statement betray the influence of an Ashkenazi source. These details differ slightly from Abulafia's technique of combining letters and stem from the same types of sources that nourished his thought.[237] However, what is perhaps most notable here is the synthesis between the Ashkenazi linguistic technique and the ideal of total union, a synthesis reminiscent and characteristic of Abulafia's Kabbalah and that of his followers.

In his *Shi ʿur Qomah,* the same Safedian master indicates that *devequt*

> [i]s our *bonum,* that we shall attain this unification, and to illuminate in the light of the Torah, to be integrated light into light up to the level of *Binah* and *ḥokhmah,* since we may only cleave up to there because *devequt* on the higher level is possible only in an intermittent manner . . . all the other *boni* being not [genuine] *boni* at all, but a certain apprehension, *devequt* being the main *bonum,* all the other *boni* being but a preparation to this *one.*[238]

This axiology, which emphasizes the highest status of *devequt,* should be compared to the former passage; there, continuous *devequt* is discussed, while here the more extreme or advanced forms of *devequt* are proposed. In one way or another, these views of *devequt* reflect an approach closer to the ecstatic type of Kabbalah than to any other Jewish mystical system I know.

However, beside this appropriation of the technique and axiology of ecstatic Kabbalah insofar as *devequt* is concerned, in several instances Cordovero also discusses the magical or hermetical understanding of this ideal.[239] So, for example, he indicates that it is "well known that in accordance with the preparations of the lower things, it is the desire of the higher ones to cleave to them."[240] Or, again, in the same context:

> Since the body is similar to the spiritual, it is incumbent[241] upon the latter, despite its spirituality, to cleave to the material out of its great desire for it, because the lower [entities] are the tabernacles[242] of the higher ones. And just as the *causatum* desires to ascend to its *causa,* so it is the desire of the *causa* to have the *causatum* near to itself.[243]

The experience of cleaving takes place here below because of the preparation of the lower, which attracts, or compels, the higher to cleave to it. Of great importance from our vantage point is the use of the term *mishkan* in relation to *devequt*. It should be emphasized that the notion of the attraction of the divine into a building, which is so prominent in hermetic and medieval sources, was adopted by some Jewish thinkers because it was reminiscent of rabbinic sources related to the Tabernacle and the Temple, which were conceived as special buildings where the Divine Presence descended as a result of the performance of ritual.

As is clear from several sources,[244] language was also conceived to be a receptacle and a possible container for the divine. This is also the case of the righteous man, the *Ẓaddiq*, as we shall see later.[245] In the above instance, the ancient Hebrew term for Tabernacle, which refers to a mobile construction to receive or hold the presence of God, was transposed onto the physical structure of man. However, it seems that this hermetical understanding of the *devequt* was given a more philosophical turn here. Cosmic love, which informs the reciprocal attraction of the higher to the lower and vice versa, seems to reflect certain earlier philosophical sources.[246] This seems to be the case also with the term *mishkan,* which was used in some medieval sources in a new way, namely to refer to the concept of substratum.[247] Therefore, the precise structure of the human body, which corresponds according to numerous Kabbalistic sources to the structure of the spiritual world,[248] and also to that of the Temple, is the cause of the attraction of the supernal to the mundane, by virtue of the structural affinity of one for the other. *Devequt* as related to a descent of the divine upon a human being described as a certain type of building is dealt with again in Cordovero's writings. In *Shi ͨur Qomah* we learn that

> wherever the *Ẓaddiqim* are, God is there. The prooftext for this is that while the people of Israel were in the desert, the Temple was with them . . . [H]ence the *Ẓaddiqim* hallow the place, as He cleaves to his *Ẓaddiqim* because of their mental concentration[249] on Him . . . [W]herever the *Ẓaddiqim* are, like the *mishkan* . . . He is there.[250]

Thus, the role of the sacred place as the place of encounter with the divine was attenuated in favor of the righteous, who ensure the descent of the divine and are united with Him. Interestingly enough, this attenuation of the centrality of sacred geography, which will become much more dramatic in Hasidism, was explicated in a book written in Safed.

What is of particular interest in the above discussion is the coexistence of different models that explain the nature and the locus of *devequt*: in some cases, the ecstatic model posits the transcendental realm as the place where the human and the divine meet, while the magical model proposes the mundane realm as the place that the divine will is attracted into in order to meet the human. In fact, these diverging visions of *devequt* are, in my opinion, not a case of peculiar and insignificant incoherence but part and parcel of the Cordoverian vision, which cultivated, concomitantly, diverging approaches to this and other topics. This eclectic attitude of Cordovero's concerning *devequt* is also represented in the writings of some of his students. However, I am not concerned here with a systematic attempt to survey the coexistence of the two models in their writings but simply to make the point that by becoming aware of the different systemic sources of a certain author, we can dispense with the harmonistic approach, which insists on making sense of diverging attitudes; we can easily see the variety of opinions that coexist in the same Kabbalistic systems when we are better acquainted with the different sources of the various models. This view of the cleaving, as the result of the drawing down onto the mystic of divine light, luminosity, vitality, divine presence, holiness, and so on, has also influenced R. Moshe Ḥayyim Luzzatto,[251] and the entire magical model should be considered as a possible source for the Hasidic "hermeneutic" of *devequt*. Let us look at just one example of the Hasidic treatment of this talismatic understanding of *devequt*. R. Ḥayyim of Chernovitz wrote in his *Sha ᶜar ha-Tefillah* about the second kinds of prayer, whose intention is

> the light of spirituality[252] and the divine vitality[253] that flows by [the dint of] each and every blessing, from the light of our God, blessed be His name, in order to cleave to Him and to draw it onto them, to take delight[254] by cleaving to the light of God.[255]

This is a clear example of the mystical interpretation of the magical implications of the hermetic model; it is the mystical aspect of the ritual that dominates the understanding of the role of the prayer. The meaning of the blessing has more to do with bliss than with magical influx. Similar in spirit is a passage of R. Mordekhai of Chernobyl, who emphasizes the attraction of the divine onto man after a long series of stages that constitutes the anabatic move, viewed as preceding the descent of vitality upon man.[257]

6. TWO TYPES OF ẒIMẒUM IN HASIDISM

Some of the most interesting results of the interaction between the various models that influenced Hasidism are the Hasidic interpretations of *ẓimẓum*.[257] This concept is a very rich and influential one, and its history should be given closer analysis.[258] In any case, it appears that two types of Kabbalistic literature had a significant impact upon Hasidic thought with regard to this notion: the Lurianic and the Cordoverian. The first was instrumental in fostering this concept in Hasidism, while its content has much to do with Cordoverian thought and some of its seventeenth-century philosophical interpretations.[259] In fact, the history of *ẓimẓum* since the end of the sixteenth century consists of ongoing interpenetrations between these two versions of this concept.[260] However, several important aspects of the process of *ẓimẓum* seem to be new to the Hasidic masters, possibly the result of the intersection of themes relating the magical and theurgical models.[261]

What are the theological premises that informed the Lurianic concept of *ẓimẓum*? Assuming that the self-withdrawal of the divine essence takes place before any creative process, the Lurianic type of discourse emphasizes the idea of the accommodation of the infinite to the future finiteness, either for the purpose of theogony and cosmogony or for the self-revelation of the infinite divinity. This self-withdrawal permits the emergence of the yet nonexistent finite beings. The main concerns of the Lurianic view of *ẓimẓum,* and to a certain degree of the Cordoverian one as well, are therefore theogonic and cosmogonic. The theogonic concern has to do with the emergence of the world in a relative vacuum originated by and in God's retreat. Indeed, the emanative processes and crises taking place after the withdrawal, especially the breaking of the vessels[262] and the dispersion of the divine sparks, are the inverse blueprint of theurgical activity, whose purpose is to recreate the shattered supernal *anthropos.*[263] The fallen man, who is also responsible for the fall of the sparks, is called upon to restore to their primordial place within the divine *anthropos* the particles of light imprisoned in the realm of the shells, an activity known as *tiqqun.*[264] Man, especially man's soul, benefits only obliquely from this recreative project. Indeed, the individual soul, herself a divine spark, is sometimes depicted as returning to her pristine place by an act of cleaving.[265] The term cleaving, which is rather marginal in Lurianic sources,[266] is related to a relatively lower portion of the divine realm, one of the *Sefirot* or *parẓufim,* but not the *ʾEiyn Sof.* One must bear in mind that the intricacies of the Lurianic theosophical system, which describes the complex processes of withdrawal, emanation, breaking of the vessels, and so on, remained at the periphery of the earliest Hasidic discussions;[267] the shift of emphasis in Hasidism from theosophy to anthroposophy attenuated the concern with the emergence of plurality from the infinite as a process that predates the creation of the lower world.

Other theological matters related to *ẓimẓum,* for example, the epistemological concern may also be discerned in pre-hasidic texts.[268] The divine withdrawal permits an act of cognition that is impossible before creation; in fact, divinity is perceptible precisely because it is limited. However, these two foci, cosmogony and self-revelation, are nevertheless dominant. The epistemological aspect of *ẓimẓum,* which is very important in Hasidism, has been examined by scholars and I will not take up this theme again.[269] Here we are concerned only with two different types of relations between *ẓimẓum* and the mystical and mgaical ideals. One observation should be made regarding the meaning of *ẓimẓum* in these contexts: while in Luria, *ẓimẓum* means the retreat from a certain space, namely its evacuation, in other texts this term refers to concentration of the divine into a certain space.[270] Hasidic thought takes advantage of both meanings. Let us start with the relationship between withdrawal and mystical experience.

In Hasidism, the divine contraction is the only avenue left for God to reveal Himself in an already created world and to bring man toward Him. To a certain extent, by contracting Himself, God comes to encounter man. Either He is seen as contracted from the human, subjective perspective, or He brings man to the experience of union. The main causes for the contraction are not the theosophical vessels, who are ontological beings existing in a supreme plane inaccessible, or hardly accessible, to man, either in space or time, but the mystical experience, on one hand, and human worship on the other, which create the oral and ritual "palaces," "boxes," or vessels that contract the infinite.[271] Thus, the theosophical meaning of *ẓimẓum* changed its logic when it encountered the mystical and the magical models, mainly by shifting its emphasis to the human experience. Let me present a few examples of the new interpretation of *ẓimẓum* as contraction.

A concept of *ẓimẓum* that expresses in Hasidic terms the ideal of union with God assumes that the withdrawal of the divine was intended to prepare the human soul for a gradual disclosure of the divine brightness, *behirut,* and for the cleaving to the ultimate divine substance. R. Qalonimus Qalman Epstein, following earlier formulations, describes the divine "decision" to withdraw Himself several times in order to enable men

> to receive a little bit of the brightness, [in order] to comprehend the divinity, blessed be His name, and the ten *Sefirot* of *ʾAẓilut* were enclothed in ten of *Beriyʾah,* and the latter were enclothed in ten *Sefirot* of Yeẓirah and the latter were enclosed in ten *Sefirot* of *ʿAsiyah* and by those [many] *ẓimẓumim* men can receive, gradually, a little bit of comprehension of His divinity from below to the higher and to remove, gradually, the *ẓimẓumim* and the screens[272] until we shall be able to receive the great brightness [and] cleave ourselves, gradually, to *ʾEiyn Sof,* blessed be He, this being the core of the reward that we receive from the Creator who has created us in this corporeal world, by [means of] several thousands of *ẓimẓumim* and screens that cover His divinity, blessed be His name, and we are able to pierce by our power the screens and the *ẓimẓumim* in order to comprehend His divinity, blessed be His name, and cleave to Him.[273]

An interesting parallel to this view is found in a passage from "the lore of Kabbalah of R. Yiẓḥaq Luria," adduced in R. Yeshaiah Horowitz's *Shaʿar ha-Shamayim.* The details of this discussion are reminiscent of R. Israel Sarug's view of *ẓimẓum,* and we will not go into them here. However, the aim of the divine withdrawal is described as "to do good to His creatures, so that they will acknowledge His grandeur and will have merit to become *Merkavah* on high,[274] and cleave to Him."[275]

It seems very plausible to see this text as the prototype of the Hasidic passage. However, it seems incongruent with the Sarugian, and Lurianic systems to assert that someone can cleave to *ʾEin Sof.* Therefore, a more extreme mystical understanding of the *ẓimẓum* originated in Hasidism, in comparison to what appears to have been the closest Lurianic formulation.

The divine occultations described in the Hasidic text are not retreats that cause a distancing between God and man, that is, a departure into transcendence. On the contrary, all the thousands of screens are invitations to enter, stage after stage, into closer and closer contact with the divine world, and finally to cleave to the Infinite. In fact, the many screens are opportunities to increase the rewards the mystic receives, since otherwise, he would receive nothing for his mystical attainment.[276] Creation was carefully calculated to take into consideration the human ability to overcome corporeality[277] by means of purification and the study of the Torah and the power of the letters.[278] What is evident in this passage, and in at least one other as well,[279] is the view that *devequt* with the Infinite is the highest religious ideal. The mystical attainment, *devequt,* dictates in these instances the meaning of the divine occultation; cosmogony serves mysticism.[280] In other words, a definitively non-immanentist theory, which emphasizes many occultations, can serve a mysti-cal ideal as well as an immanentistic one.[281]

While the mystical ideal leaves the initiative for occultation to God in order to bestow upon man the initiative to pursue the mystical way,[282] the magical model originated a quite different view of *ẓimẓum*. The emergence of limited, or contracted, manifestations of the divine is the result of human acts rather than of sublime processes that have nothing to do with the nature of man. The Great Maggid expressed this view in various ways, a few of which will be discussed here. In *ʾOr ha-ʾEmet,* we find what seems the most magical of the formulations:

> It is as if God has contracted Himself into the Torah. When someone calls a man by his name, he puts all his affairs aside and answers the person who called him, because he is compelled[283] by his name. Likewise it is as if God has contracted Himself into the Torah, and the Torah is His name[284] and when someone calls[285] the Torah, then they draw God, blessed be He, down toward us, because He and His name are one total unity with us.[286]

The text exploits a double meaning of the Hebrew verb *QRʾ*, "to call" and "to read." Reading the Torah is understood as tantamount to calling, or conjuring God by His name, in fact compelling Him to come down upon us, bringing about a mystical experience of union. For our discussion here, it is important to see how the concept of *ẓimẓum* is being used: God's primordial contraction is the starting point of our ability to bring Him down. Elsewhere in the same treatise the Great Maggid emphasizes the need to call, or read, with all one's power, in order to become one with God, because He is "dwelling in the letter . . . and his intellect, which is from the world of the intellect, becomes a limb of the *Shekhinah*."[287]

These are illuminating examples of the transformation of the talismanic magic of language into a mystical technique, in the manner of the descending *devequt,* mentioned above.[288] Again, the Great Maggid is quoted by R. Elimelekh of Lisansk as explaining the meaning of the *ẓimẓum* as follows:

> He contracted Himself within the letters of the Torah, by means of which he has created the world[289] . . . and the *Ẓaddiq,* who studies the Torah for its own sake in holiness draws the Creator downward, blessed be He, within the letters of the Torah[290] as in the moment of the creation . . . and by the pure utterances related to the study of the Torah, he draws down God within the letters.[291]

The affinity between contraction and the divine letters is not new to Hasidism: already the Sarugian view of the theogony depicts the organization of the divine energy immediately after the withdrawal as Hebrew letters.[292] However, unlike the Sarugian theory, in our text the assumption is that the letters did not emerge within the evacuated space that the divine essence left behind Itself, but pre-existed the moment of contraction and served as receptacles for the divine vitality. This conclusion is obvious from the comparison between the *Ẓaddiq* and God: the former brings the divinity into the letters, just as God did during the cosmogonic process. However, even the formulation of the divine activity, "He contracted Himself within the letters," is equivocal; it may stand for the divine self-contraction, but also for a human act that causes it. The magical attraction of the spiritual forces into talismatic entities was translated into cosmogonic terms. At least in one case the Great Maggid even adds the ideas that the contraction of God within the letters and utterances is ensured by the human adherence to the divine; it is that adherence that attracts divinity into this limited world.[293] In another teaching of the same master we learn that

> God contracts himself into and dwells upon this world by means of Torah and commandments, which are here contracted and possess a [certain] size . . . and whoever is worthy . . . sees supernal worlds while he performs the commandments.[294]

The prior contraction of the Torah and the commandments, their peculiar limits and size, dictate the finitude of the divine presence in this world. Although the magical drawing down does not occur explicitly in this passage, nonetheless it shows the priority of the vessels to their divine content, a priority that stems from a process of contraction of the Torah and the commandments. Although the Torah and the commandments are infinite in their source, they receive finite size with their descent.[295] This theory was adopted by R. Eliezer Lippa, the son of R. Elimelekh of Lisansk, and repeated in several instances in his *ʾOrah le-Ẓaddiq*: let me mention just two examples that show the expansion of this theme to other domains of learned activity: the commentary on the Torah and the innovation of halakhic issues are described as drawing the divine infinity into the world and creating thereby an act of *ẓimẓum.*[296]

The question of what type of theology informs these discussions is a crucial one, because the concept of attracting God below will concern us throughout this study. The notion of the Hebrew letters as vessels, which is widespread in Hasidic writing, may be understood in two ways: either the letters are empty receptacles, which can be filled with divine influx by the mystic in prayer or by studying the Torah, or alternatively, the letters are full receptacles whose divine content does not depend on any human activity. Both views are well represented in Hasidic texts and coexist even in the writings of the same Hasidic master. However, they represent different theological approaches, which correspond, sometimes, to different understandings of the ritual. The first view seems to reflect a non-immanentist theology, in which God is not conceived of as present even in the most sacred entities, the letters. Indeed, He, or His presence, is prone to be drawn down, to reveal Himself to the mystic. We may speak about a "spontaneity of the numinous" in response to the human search.[297] The epiphany of the divine is caused by and in human ritual.

The second view, namely the contraction of divinity within the Torah and its letters, or the attraction between the divine and the linguistic elements that encompass it, recurs in some Hasidic sources independently of the concept of drawing the vitality into them.[298] Likewise it should be emphasized that the divine immanence is presented, at least in one crucial passage, in terms related to the talismanic theory of language. In *Toledot Ya^caqov Yosef,* we learn that

> just as there are twenty-two letters of the Torah and prayer, so there are twenty-two letters in all the existent things of matter and body, because the world was created by their means . . . but the letters are clothed in the matter of the things of the world, by several covers and garments and shells. And within the letters, there the spiritual force of the Holy One,[299] blessed be He, is dwelling. Therefore, His Glory, Blessed be He, is filling the entire earth and whatever is within it, and there is no place void of it.[300]

Therefore, the view of *Sefer Yeẓirah* as to the existence of the letters in the various levels of reality was combined with the talismanic view of language, and God's spiritual force was conceived of as present within them. This view is paralleled by a short passage in R. Nathan-Neta^c of Siniewa, who asserts that the letter *Yod,* the first letter of the Tetragrammaton, is found in all the other letters and its presence corresponds to the presence of "the power and the spiritual force[301] from above, in all the things in the world, and His glory fills the world."[302]

Thus, a non-Hasidic master also accepted an immanentist view related to a mystical view of language. Common to these masters is the assumption that the divine immanence is achieved through the linguistic elements of the lower world. God is immanent because the "form" and vitality of any being is the Hebrew name that encaptures, in its letters, the divine influx. Linguistic immanence is a major factor in Hasidic thought that cannot be analyzed here in detail, but to which we will return in the concluding remarks.

7. THE KABBALISTIC MYSTICO-MAGICAL MODEL

Despite very substantial differences between the three models, it is interesting that these divergences were not openly explicated in the Kabbalistic writings or later in Hasidic teachings. They were eventually integrated with each other, creating amalgams that constitute only rarely fully coherent structures. The panoramic landscape described above is, in fact, much more variegated than the different syntheses of the three models, since other forms of thought, Rabbinic thought, for example, were formative in the emergence of Hasidism. However, the exposition of the interactions between the models can solve part of the problem that remained unaddressed by the dominant assumption that, phenomenologically, Hasidism is a kind of interpretation, or coalescence of interpretations, of Lurianism, which in turn can be explained by reference only to the names of Kabbalists, or to generic Kabbalistic systems. More detailed analyses of the sources of certain crucial terms and an investigation of their specific interactions with other terms from different models can help to explain the panoramic viewpoints of various Hasidic masters. In the following, we shall survey various pre-Hasidic syntheses between the mystical model and the magical models.

As seen above, in the description of the ascent of the Besht, the tour of heaven can end with a particular revelation brought down for the benefit of the people of Israel. This pattern is an ancient one, perhaps as ancient as the Psalms. In Psalm 68:19 we read that a certain anonymous figure, identified in the Rabbinic sources as Moses, says, "Thou has ascended on high, thou has made captivity captive." The last phrase was understood, according to traditional interpretations, as referring to the Torah (accompanied according to some versions by divine names and remedies), which was brought down after the confrontation between Moses and the angels. This pattern of ascending and bringing down from the supernal world is thus well known in classical Jewish sources.[303] However, in the following we are concerned not with the ancient versions of this pattern, but solely with medieval and early modern formulations as they recur in mystical texts.

In general, mysticism and magic are not conceived of as coexisting naturally in the same systems. However, examples of such coexistence are not unusual, and some have already been studied. Scholem, for example, has pointed out that the borderline between the mystical and the magical cannot be defined easily.[304] Other discussions of this subject can be found in Tishby's examination of mystical prayer, in Liebes's treatment of the theurgy of the *Zohar*, and in Cohen-Alloro's doctoral thesis.[305] Let me start with the observation that from its very beginning we find in Kabbalah combinations of two mystical ideals: that of cleaving to the divine, *devequt*, together with the subsequent theurgical activity. Though these two ideals are already found separately in Rabbinic literature, they constitute different approaches that apparently remained distinct.[306] A kind of embryonic stage of the mystico-magical model is evident in some texts by the very beginning of the Kabbalah in Europe. For example, in a Geronese text, we learn of an obvious combination between these two models:

> Man comprises all the spiritual entities,[307] and his intellectual soul is superior to all. This is the reason why the Torah and *Miẓwot* come to deter man and warn him that all the ways of man are in his power . . . like the perfectly righteous man who crowns his Creator with crowns,[308] by the means of *devequt* he causes his soul to cleave to its source,[309] and [then] he causes the emanation of the blessing[310] just as someone kindles one candle from another,[311] and he holds and settles and adds.[312] The wicked person is doing the opposite.[313]

The main spiritual concern of this text is the divine infrastructure, which can be affected by a righteous person who has previously caused his soul to return to her source on high. Though the ideal of *devequt* was indeed important for the Geronese Kabbalists, I wonder whether in this context it is considered a value in itself. I am more inclined to see it, in this discussion of the mystical attainment, as instrumental for the second, theurgical ideal. In any case, the return of the soul to the source does not involve, at least in this context, a transformative spiritual annihilation. The theurgical movement is deeply concerned with the drawing down of the influx from the higher to the lower sefirotic realm. In my opinion, the Gestalt-coherence of the model tends to emphasize the centrality of the second constituent to such a degree that insufficient attention has been paid to the first one. This is also the case in another instance, in which Luria, or Vital, regarded the *devequt* as the return of the soul to her primordial state within the structure of *ʾAdam Qadmon*.[314] Here again, a theurgical ideal is combined with a mystical one, but the former is much more dominant in comparison to the latter. In other words, those Kabbalistic systems in which theurgical elements are dominant would only rarely pay equal attention to the mystical-ecstatic ideal. The early Kabbalists, like those who came later, are less interested in reaching the highest level of divine reality, and this is why we may describe the mystical-theurgical model as moderate; moreover, the magical element is less important, the drawing down of the influx beneath the last *Sefirah* being marginal, and this is why the theurgical aspect is so dominant.[315] The Godhead, rather than the soul or the universe, is the center of such a powerful aim of worship, and the other spiritual attainments of the mystic are marginalized, becoming instrumental or peripheral to the general scheme.

However, by the thirteenth century we also find a clear nexus between the cleaving on high and the drawing down of the divine influx beneath the sefirotic realm onto the performer of the ritual. The most distinct example is found in *ʾIggeret ha-Qodesh,* a short and very influential treatise dealing with the mystical significance of sexual intercourse:

> Human thought has the ability to strip itself [of the alien issues] and to ascend to and arrive at the place of its source. Then it will unite with the supernal entity, whence it comes, and it [i.e., the thought] and it [i.e., its source] become one entity. And when one's thought returns downward from above, something similar to a line appears, and with it the supernal light descends, under the influence of the thought that draws it downward, and consequently it draws the *Shekhinah* downward. Then the brilliant light comes and increases upon the place where the owner of the thought stands . . . and since this is the case, our ancient sages had to state that when the husband copulates with his wife, and his thought unites with the supernal entities, that very thought draws the supernal light downward, and it [the light] dwells upon the drop [of semen] upon which he directs his intention and thought . . . [S]ince the thought on it [the drop] is linked to the supernal entities, it draws the brilliant light downward.[316]

In this case, no importance is placed on the theurgical operation but on the drawing down of the brilliant light.[317] Hence, the nexus between the mystical union of human thought with the source, and the operation of drawing down a divine force, is explicit. The major organon of drawing down is identical to that of the mystical union: human thought. However, it should be noted that the drawing down has nothing to do with a ritual: the substratum for the divine light, human semen, is a material factor that has nothing to do with the act of descent, but only with the reception of the light in a certain place. In other words, it is an anomian process that is being described here, both in the anabatic aspect and in the drawing down of the light. One could speculate that the above passage relates to the concept of drawing down the spiritual force, the *ruḥaniyyut,* though this term is not mentioned here. Last but not least: the cleaving to the divine is described here in strong terms, which describe anabasis as a case of *unio mystica*. The text cited above is one of the best-known thirteenth-century texts; it was quoted, printed, and reprinted many times. The mystico-magical model represented by this quote was thus available to any learned Jew in the eighteenth century.

Even better known is the Zoharic version of the mystico-magical model. According to this classic of Kabbalah, by cleaving to God, which means by the intentional performance of his commandments, a supernal spirit is drawn down upon the Jew.[318] It should be emphasized that the *Zohar* envisions the descent of the spirit without assuming a magical function in this attraction. Even the formulations involved in conveying the drawing down, which use the verb *MShKh,*[319] do not always imply an activist attitude; though such an activism is crucial for the performance of the commandments, in many instances in the *Zohar* it seems that there is a certain automatism in the descent of the spirit after their performance. There appears to be a certain downplay of the activist attitude toward the drawing-down activity in Zoharic thought. Moreover, it is implausible to assume that the various forms of the root *DBQ* have clear-cut mystical significance, though they refer to a certain intentional relationship to God. In some instances, the spiritual predisposition of the worshiper is crucial; his awe and the brokenness of his heart contribute toward this purpose.[320]

Though formulated in a totally different mystical milieu, the next passage displays a certain similarity to the earlier one. Written by Abraham Abulafia, it deals with the turning of the spiritual components of man to their highest, unified source. In an epistle to R. Yehudah Salmon of Barcelona, Abulafia writes as follows:

> All the inner forces and the hidden souls in man are differentiated in the[ir] bodies. In fact, when their knots are untied, the essence of each and every force and soul will run to their prime source, which is one without any duality, which comprises all multiplicity *ad infinitum*. This untying reaches up to the highest [degree] such that when someone pronounces there the [divine] name, he ascends and sits on the head of the supernal crown and the thought draws[321] a threefold blessing from there . . . [T]hus the pronouncer of the name is drawing the blessing from above,[322] and he pulls it down.[323]

Of paramount importance for the discussions to follow is the attainment by the mystic of the highest spiritual level by pronouncing the divine Name and the subsequent drawing down of the blessing. If we accept this text on its more literal level, it is obvious that the mystical ascent to the source is coupled with the descent, which is related to the drawing down of the blessing. However, this text may be better understood metaphorically, namely, as describing the arrival of the spiritually united forces at their source in the divine world, thereby obtaining the blessing described as the priestly blessing, namely a mystical-intellectual experience. It should be mentioned that in another text of the same Kabbalist, to be dealt with below,[324] the drawing down of the supernal force is achieved by means of the pronunciation of the letters of the divine name with the vowel *ḥiriq*, and the downward movement of the head. It should be emphasized that the human intellect is united with the highest realm of the divine. Unlike the theurgical discussions, which commonly focus on the union of elements within the revealed Godhead, in ecstatic Kabbalah—that of Abraham Abulafia as well as R. Yiẓḥaq of Acre—God himself is the subject within which one is able to be unified.

A similar approach is found in a passage of R. Yiẓḥaq of Acre, a late thirteenth- and early fourteenth-century Kabbalist, who asserted to the mystic that

> you should live a life of suffering in your house of contemplation,[325] lest your appetitive soul overpower your intellective soul, for by this you will merit to draw down[326] into your intellective soul the influx of the Godhead,[327] and into the Torah, that is to say, in the wisdom of combination and all of its conditions.[328]

Here also the drawing down has nothing to do with ritual; in the case of R. Yiẓḥaq, it is mental concentration and the permutations of letters that are able to endow human intellect or thought with the presence of the divine influx.[329] In another text of R. Yiẓḥaq's, the drawing down of the divine influx is portrayed not only as dwelling in the human soul or intellect but also "on all of reality."[330] Therefore, drawing down was considered by some early Kabbalists a mystical activity that brings the divine into our world. While Abulafia was more concerned with a private mystical experience, which indeed may endow one with magical powers,[331] it seems that in the texts of R. Yiẓḥaq of Acre the more cosmic nature of the mystical act is also prominent. This Kabbalist, who took the drawing down of the blessing more literally in his earlier book, *Me ᵓirat ᶜEynaim,* was one of the first Jewish mystics to propose a synthesis between ecstatic and magical elements.

An interesting passage in a writing of a sixteenth-century ecstatic Kabbalist, R. Yehudah Albotini (especially relevant to discussions that will concern us later) describes the union of the human intellect with the higher entities, the Active Intellect or *Malkhut*. As a result of this experience of *devequt,* the soul becomes part of the higher entity and is consequently able to operate on this world as it chooses.[332] Following this affirmation we learn that the sages were able to do this by "drawing down[333] the supernal force and influx on those whom they wanted to affect, positively or negatively."[334] Mystical transformation is therefore an avenue that opens the way to magical attainments.

Important for the later Hasidic model is also the view of R. Elijah de Vidas; from his widely influential *Reshit Ḥokhmah,* we learn that

> All the worlds are bound together by the soul, spirit, and higher soul of man, and this [bond] causes the illumination of all the worlds by the Emanator, the King of all kings . . . and then the worlds are bound to each other and are comprised in each other and so the soul of man and his spirit and higher soul will illuminate and will be integrated on high and will suck an abundance of influx from the source of all the blessings.[335]

The ascent of the soul, and with it all the worlds, returns the spiritual entity in man to its source and enables the suckling of the influx.

Apparently unrelated to Albotini and de Vidas, though probably influenced by some of their sources, is the model presented by R. Ḥayyim Vital in his *Sha ᶜarei Qedushah.* An attempt to propose a theosophical ontology that expresses the relationship between the individual soul and her root, or roots, within the divine world, Vital's theory does not, however, embrace the mythical ascent of the soul, but prefers the inner contemplation of the supernal sources.[336] However, despite the reluctance to allow a flight on high as part of the mystical experience named prophecy,[337] Vital emphasizes the "practical" effects of spiritual contemplation. Time and again, the Kabbalist uses the verb *MShKh* and its derivatives[338] and the noun *hamshakhah*[339] in order to explain the descent of the influx onto the human soul. With Vital, this descent is related to the cleaving, which occurs here below, and is the quintessence of the prophetic experience.[340] As some explicit quotes from Abraham Abulafia show,[341] the Safedian Kabbalist was influenced by the ecstatic Kabbalah, though he added important elements that stem from the Neoplatonic and theosophical systems. However, his insistence that the prophetic experiences are possible in his generation as well demonstrates that even after the death of R. Yiẓḥaq Luria, the most famous exponent of the later, theosophical Kabbalah emphasizing the theurgical ideal, intensive mystical experiences, coupled with drawing down the influx from above, were explicitly espoused by his most important disciple. Therefore, there is no reason to regard the emergence of the Lurianic theosophical-theurgical model as the final type of kabbalah, or, as in Vital's view, a *dernier cri.* I assume that the different models coexisted in his thought and perhaps also in his practice, just as they did for another Safedian Kabbalist, R. Moshe Cordovero.

These passages indeed contain the crucial elements of the mystico-magical model that will concern us in the following discussions. However, it is important to emphasize the marginality of one important element that will dominate eighteenth-century Hasidism: while the katabatic descent, or the return from the celestial tour, is strongly related in the foregoing to the person who ascended on high, who is the goal of the return, or with an individual affected by the magical power of the master as the passage from Albotini's book shows, the collective or the community is only rarely mentioned in this context.

Nevertheless, I would like to underscore the importance of a discussion found in several works that appeared long before the emergence of Hasidism, and which is of special relevance for Hasidic thought. In Cordovero's *Pardes Rimmonim,*[342] in two books of his follower R. Abraham Azulai, *Ḥesed le-ʾAvraham*[343] and his commentary on *Massekhet ʾAvot,*[344] in the preface by R. Nathan Shapira of Jerusalem to R. Yiẓḥaq Luria's *Peri ʿEẓ Ḥayyim* and in the introduction to Shapira's own book on Lurianic prayer, *Meʾorot Nathan,*[345] these Kabbalists distinguish between the effect of ritual performed by an expert in Kabbalah as opposed to ritual performed by someone who is not a connoisseur of this lore.

> The man whom his Creator has bestowed with the grace of entering the innerness of the occult lore and who knows and understands that by reciting *Barekh ʿAleinu* and *Refaʾenu* the intention is to draw down the blessing and the influx by each and every blessing to a certain *sefirah,* and the blessing of *Refaʾenu* to a certain *sefirah,* as it is known to us, behold, this man is worshiping the Holy One, blessed be He, and his *Shekhinah,* as a son and a servant standing before his master, by means of a perfect worship, out of love, without deriving any benefit or reward because of that worship . . . because the soul of a wise man[346] by the quality of the [mystical] intention[347] he

> intends during his prayer, his soul will be elevated by his [spiritual] arousal from one degree to another, from one entity to another[348] until she arrives and is welcome and comes in the presence of the Creator, and cleaves to her source,[349] to the source of life; and then a great influx will be emanated upon her from there, and he will become a vessel[350] and a place and foundation for [that] influx, and from him it[351] will be distributed[352] to all the world as it is written in the *Zohar,* pericope *Terumah,*[353] until the *Shekhinah* will cleave to him . . . and you will be a seat to Her and [then] the influx will descend onto you . . . because you are in lieu of the great pipe[354] instead of the *Ẓaddiq,* the foundation of the world.[355]

As in some of the other expositions of the mystico-magical model, the cleaving to God means the return to the source of the soul, and thereby to the possibility of receiving the influx. However, what is remarkable in this passage is the coalescence of two important themes: the *perfectus* is described as a *Ẓaddiq,* and, at the same time, he is depicted as a channel. Here we see a view formulated by pre-Hasidic Jewish mystics that is strikingly similar to the Hasidic version of this model. However, apart from the phenomenological affinities, it should be noted that Azulai's text is also found in one of the most influential books on Hasidism, *Ḥesed le-ʾAvraham,* which is in fact mentioned by an important Hasidic author.[356] Indeed, on the basis of this quote, we may assert that the human *Ẓaddiq* is conceived in several influential pre-Hasidic texts not only as an exemplary figure, a magician or a mystic, but also as the lower extremity of the divine continuum. The divine does not only flow upon the righteous man; divinity is extended in order to add him to the divine realm.[357]

To close our survey of the mystico-magical model, let us look at a passage from a magical text influenced by Kabbalistic themes, in which our model reverberates. At the beginning of the collection of magical traditions compiled by R. Abraham Ḥamoi, we read that when

> the perfect man will distance himself from corporeal lust and will separate himself and be alone and cleave to God, blessed be He, then they [!] will emanate upon him the influx of holiness and disclose to him all the issues he wishes to know.[358]

The cathartic path, which culminates with cleaving, is complemented by the conferring of magical powers. Although certainly not a representative text of Jewish magic, this passage testifies to the centrality of the mystico-magical model, which was also adopted by Kabbalistically oriented magicians.

The texts adduced in this paragraph represent the mystico-magical model as expressed in the most important forms of Kabbalah: the Geronese one, the Zoharic, the ecstatic, and the Safedian schools. In fact, the available texts are even more numerous.[359] However, these samples will suffice to show that the occurrence of this mystico-magical model in Hasidism constitutes a profound consonance with already existing mystical ways of thought, though this school of Jewish mysticism added to them one more variation. What seems to me crucial for the Hasidic version of the mystico-magical model is the integration of elements from the magical-talismatic and the mystical-ecstatic models. On the one hand, the frame of the mystico-magical model as described above was fleshed out in Hasidism by additional elements stemming from extreme magical and mystical systems of thought; on the other, this enriched and more extreme mystico-magical model became part of social life. As a social phenomenon, Hasidism represents the encounter between a spiritual model that had already moved in its pre-Hasidic phases toward an emphasis upon its magical aspects, and social circumstances that, though not instrumental in generating the model, contributed to some of its features, once it became active in larger groups. The social life of the model is also one of its forms: the oscillation from the elitist form to one of its possible translations into a social group.

3

The Mystico-Magical Model

1. TWO MODELS IN ḤASIDISM

Hasidic thought can be described as the interaction between various, and sometimes very different, mystical models. However, given the belatedness of this form of Jewish mysticism, we may observe the articulation of links between these models that were either a continuation of affinities discovered between them in earlier phases of Jewish mysticism or were the result of the dynamics of Hasidic thought itself. It would be helpful when looking at Hasidic thought and the experiences of the Hasidic masters to be guided by two main constitutive models, which are themselves the result of the coalescence of elements from different earlier models. I am not acquainted with any scholarly attempt to describe Hasidic thought in terms of the lines of thought and activities represented by these two models. Nor does it appear, from the Hasidic sources, that any such articulated distinction between these different models exists.[1] One of these models may be designated as the katabatic-redemptive model; the other, the anabatic mystico-magical one.

The katabatic model is represented by the concept of the descent of the *Ẓaddiq,* which is better known by the Hebrew phrase, *Yeridah ẓorekh ʿAliyah,* namely, the descent for the sake of ascent, the transgression for the sake of repentance, or the elevation of the sparks. Much attention has been paid to this model because of its essential affinities with the Zoharic and Lurianic Kabbalah[2] and, according to some scholars, with Sabbatean theology.[3] Indeed, there can be no doubt that this model was a very important one in Hasidic thought as well; however, I shall not be concerned here with the details of its constitutive elements or its phenomenological structure.

The model that will concern us here is the anabatic mystico-magical one—its major components, its inner logic, and its interpretation by the Hasidic masters. The general meaning of each of its two components and their influence have already been discussed in the preceding chapter. Here I am concerned only with the nexus established between them in Kabbalah and in several important Hasidic discussions. However, before embarking on a detailed analysis of this model, we will briefly compare it to the katabatic-redemptive one. The latter assumes a very powerful personality who is able to confront evil in its various forms, including its psychological manifestations, in order to change it, or to rescue the divine element that is entrapped within the domain of evil. The holy man who undertakes this task is conceived of as a partial savior, though not a messiah as this concept is commonly understood. He elevates by means of his descent; he improves by his suffering.

The mystico-magical model is anabatic by its very nature.[4] It presupposes the capacity of the *Ẓaddiq* to leave this world by ascending to or by assimilating with the divine. This "ascent" is a deep transformation of the self through its temporal spiritualization, self-effacement, annihilation, and cleaving to the divine. It should be mentioned that the mystical component of the model includes several different versions; the most important one, which will be amply documented in the following pages, emphasizes self-effacement, or abnegation, as the main technique for assimilating into the divine. This may be designated as mystical anabasis, namely the assumption that the contact or union with the supreme instance is established by an inner transformation that causes the encounter within the inner space. From several points of view, this type of anabasis is reminiscent of the Plotinian mystical experience, where the ascent is metaphorical, an experience of light or, as it was called recently, a "luminous area of experience."[5] Despite the centrality of self-effacement and annihilation as part of the mystico-magical model, there are cases where only spiritual anabasis, or the cleaving on high is mentioned, while the concept of annihilation does not appear.[6] The assumption of the Hasidic masters is that a certain ascent of the soul, which penetrates the higher levels of reality, is instrumental in bringing the soul to encounter God. Although such an ascent is not to be understood metaphorically, as I propose to interpret the texts, this spiritual anabasis is substantially different from the ancient Jewish mystical ascent as performed by the "descenders to the *Merkavah*" and some of their medieval followers and, later, by the Besht himself.[7] While the *Heikhalot* literature and its various reverberations include elements of a mythical supernal topography (paradises, divine palaces, etc.) and disclosure of mysteries resulting from conversations with higher beings, the spiritual anabasis consists more in the flight of the soul to her source and her union with it rather than the exploration of a mythical *terra incognita*. These two cases of the flight of the soul or of the mystic approximate the category of ecstasy designated by Laski as "intensity ecstasy."[8] Let me present one example of such a spiritual ascension. In a passage authored by the Great Maggid, we learn that the mystic

> ascends from one world to another and unifies them and he can see actually, by the sense of the eye of the mind, all the supernal lights and it is obvious that such a worshiper merits a great delight, in each and every moment, unceasingly, because the root of his soul is cleaved there on high.[9]

In lieu of the mythical geography of the earlier sources, only the vaguely differentiated lights are mentioned here. It is not so much the pneumatic vision that preoccupies the mystic as the return to the source itself. We can see in Hasidism not only a reticence to emphasize the myth of paradise, with the details of the divine palaces, but also a neglect of the complex structure of Lurianic theosophy. Closer to the Neoplatonic mode of expression, the Great Maggid's style may reflect a more contemplative rather than ecstatic type of experience. This mode would also influence Hasidic masters who were much more influenced by Lurianic thought. Interestingly enough, a later Hasidic master, R. Yiẓḥaq Aiziq Safrin of Komarno, attenuates Vital's description of an inner "flight" in his *Sha^carei Qedushah* in favor of actual anabasis of the soul to her roots within the divine.[10]

In some cases, contact with the divine is described by means of integration images that convey the concept of *devequt*. So, for example, we read in R. Moshe Eliaqum Beri^ɔah, that the union between the *Ẓaddiq* and God is

> actually the entrance into Him, blessed be He, when the cleaving of the *Ẓaddiq* called one within the Holy One, blessed be He, who is also called One, then two times one, which is numerically equivalent to thirteen [i.e., the Hebrew word for one is *ɔeḥad,* whose letters equal thirteen], and are altogether twenty-six, as the value of the Tetragrammaton,[11] blessed be He, and then the perfection of the Tetragrammaton is achieved . . . He enters the Tetragrammaton[12] and cleaves to Him, blessed be He, and this is the reason why he will be able to draw from Him, blessed be He, good influxes.[13]

This entrance into the divine is already referred to in some earlier texts; so, for example, from an interesting text attributed to the Besht by an author at the end of the eighteenth century, we learn:

> The righteous is able to apprehend the innerness, which is the holiness and the *ruḥaniyyut* and Being that maintain everything. In every place that he looks, he sees only the divine and the Being, even etc.[14] And when is he able to apprehend the above? When he sits at the entrance of the tent. Namely in the moment he accomplishes supernal unification[15] up to *ɔEiyn Sof,* that is, at the upper window of all the worlds and of all the heavens and the heavens of the heavens. On them it is said: "He stretched them like a tent" [Isa. 40: 22]. And it is said in the name of the Besht: "Someone should not sit down in the divine[16] but he shall consider himself as if he is entirely stored[17] in the light of the divine. This is the meaning of [Genesis 18:1]: 'He sits at the entrance of the tent.' Namely, the righteous performs a *Yiḥud,* up to *ɔEiyn Sof,* which is at the entrance of all the worlds."[18]

Close contact with the divine constitutes the first stage of the mystico-magical world, whose second phase is the drawing down of the divine influx from the supernal source. Entering the ultimate source allows the mystic not only to cling to it, but also to draw forth from it. In this passage, neither ascent nor annihilation but rather a certain type of immersion into the divine, is the means of establishing the profound relationship between the mystic and God. Only after the performance of the mystical or spiritual anabases is the *Ẓaddiq* able to act on the external, namely on the communal or cosmic levels.

While the *Ẓaddiq* encounters evil, or the holy elements caught within the realm of evil, through katabasis, it is through the anabatic experience that he establishes contact with God. While the katabatic experience produces an encounter with evil in which the divine is imprisoned in order to rescue the sparks, anabasis brings the mystic to a direct encounter with the divine, which is subsequently drawn down onto this lower world. Anabasis is based mainly upon striving to assimilate oneself into the spiritual realm through self-effacement or through entering the spiritual zone; the katabatic model is based upon the assumption that the *Ẓaddiq* is able to maintain his personality intact despite his entering the dangerous situation of dealing with evil. The descending *Ẓaddiq* is concerned more with the individual to be rescued; by virtue of the anabatic movement one operates more on the communal and cosmic levels. Another crucial difference between these models is the question of the dangers involved in these practices. While the former is conceived to be dangerous because the *Ẓaddiq* is prone to be affected by the maleficent powers—and there are numerous warnings concerning these perils—there are only few warnings related to the intensive annihilative experiences. Despite the ancient and medieval preoccupations with the dangerous *Pardes,* the divine orchard envisioned as a mystical experience, Hasidic thought was not haunted by the dangers of the extreme mystical experiences. It should be emphasized that, though there were in Hasidic thought and practices attempts to explain how someone returns from a strong mystical experience, the alternatives envisioned were different from those described in the *Pardes* stories. The mystic may die, that is, he may not be able to return to normal existence, but the assumption is not that he has become a heretic or insane; his death is not a punishment, as in some of the *Pardes* interpretations, but an exalted mystical achievement.

Those profound divergences notwithstanding, the same Hasidic texts cannot be said to adopt either one model or the other. In fact, these models appear, though they are parts of different discourses, in the same Hasidic texts. We may even find them complementing each other. At the beginning of the nineteenth century, R. Mordekhai of Chernobyl writes of the *Ẓaddiq* that he

> has to cause his descent to the lower degrees and elevate by the dint of the "lower arousal." This aspect of the descent of the *Ẓaddiq* himself to the lower degrees is called the "worship of the earth." But this aspect can be attained only by someone who is *ʾAdam,* and this is by dint of the "supernal arousal" . . . [when]he is in the "aspect of Nought,"[19] higher than comprehension, and then he brings all the good influxes and the blessing to the world.[20]

Therefore, at least according to this Hasidic master, the mystico-magical model is a precondition of the katabatic enterprise.

However, despite the vital differences between them, we can see in the anabatic and the katabatic models a basic similarity: the assumption of the indispensability of the *Ẓaddiq's* having a paranormal experience as a prelude to his various transformative activities. In other words, in order to be able to change the other, the *Ẓaddiq* has to change first himself, by entering another realm. However, common to these two models is the assumption that despite the initial importance of transcending this world, the final goal of the mystical activities is the improvement of the mundane realm. The struggle with evil in the katabatic model and the encounter with the divine in the anabatic one are instrumental events, or "means-experiences," which are intended to change the mundane world. This convergence between the aims of the two main models that informed Hasidic thought lends a special note to this mystical movement.

The quintessence of the mystico-magical model can be defined as the sequence of an inner, mystical experience that consists of a cleaving to God, often preceded by a self-induced feeling of "nothingness"—that is, an expansion of consciousness, and the subsequent return to this world and drawing down into it the divine energy by performing the ritual, and then distributing that energy to others. The two main phases of this model are induced actively by the mystic; there is no unexpected mystical union or free retribution through the agency of divine grace in the texts that will be used to exemplify this model. From this point of view, discussions regarding the descent of the influx that results from cleaving to God, or from divine initiative without subsequent human activity, are not the most representative passages of this model as we are attempting to describe it here, given the fact that man is not instrumental in an active manner in the process of the descent of the influx.[21] As we have seen in the previous chapter, different versions of an ascending move combined with a descending magical one had been in existence in Kabbalah since the thirteenth century. However, the idea of self-effacement or annihilation as part of the cleaving to the highest divine aspect did not occur in the above-quoted passages. It seems that the most important pre-Hasidic discussions that approximate an important element of the Hasidic mystico-magical model emerged in the school of R. Moshe Cordovero. But let us start from its beginnings.

2. SOME REMARKS ON IMMANENTISM AND *ʾAyin*

The question of which is the more dominant factor in religion, and especially in mysticism—experience or theology—is not easy to answer. A more open theology, with immanentist leanings, might be considered to open up more easily the way for mystical experiences. However, mystical experiences are reported even within religions that cultivate extreme forms of transcendental theology.[22] Thus, it may be that the spiritual predisposition, the opening of the human to the divine, is more important for the occurrence of mystical encounters than theology. Such an opening would select out of the many available theologies in the speculative reservoir of a particular religion the more immanentist or pantheistic one.[23] As Erich Neumann has said, the "world and its content are numinous, but this is true only because man is by nature a *homo mysticus*."[24] Therefore, the emergence of a certain type of mystical theology should be an indicator of the experiential emphasis of the religious mentality within which this theology appears. Provided that mystical experiences emerge from and are encouraged by both immanentist and transcendental types of theologies, it seems reasonable to conclude that the latter do not impede upon the mystical experiences. Insofar as Hasidism is concerned, its theologies, which include strong immanentist formulations, are apparently not strong determinants of this religiosity, but more the effects of a theological selection determined by the strong openness of the Hasidic masters toward the numinous.[25] This also seems to be true in the case of other Jewish mystical systems, more precisely ecstatic Kabbalah, especially in the forms espoused by R. Yiẓḥaq of Acre and Cordovero.[26] Indeed, a certain correlation between a tendency toward experiential mysticism and immanentism should be presupposed.[27]

That immanentist theology cannot alone explain the emergence of full-fledged mystical experience may be deduced from a comparison between Hasidism and the thought of one of its great opponents. R. Ḥayyim of Volozhin, who used expressions that betray his deep interest in immanentist theology, as M. Pachter has shown.[28] Therefore, the theological assumption that God is immanent in the world is far from being an innovation of Hasidic thought, but is one of the possible theologies that an eighteenth-century mystic could have adopted from a variety of classical Jewish writings. Strong unitive expressions, however, cannot be found in the writings of R. Ḥayyim. It would therefore be more plausible to look for the sources of Hasidic mysticism not in a certain type of theology, or at least not solely in it, but in a special spiritual opening, which drew on classical sources both in order to reach and to express the mystical state. The existence of a long history of mystical techniques, concepts, and systems in medieval Jewish mysticism proves that those texts that revealed them could have informed the Hasidic masters; thus we may assume that the role of immanentist theology in the emergence of Hasidic mysticism may be substantially reduced.

With this observation in mind, let us inspect briefly the history of the concept of "annihilation." This concept is crucial for many of the Hasidic discussions of mystical experience and may be considered one of the most important components of the mystical technique in Hasidism. Indeed, its role as part of the technical aspect of the model is the expansion of consciousness, the breaking of the ego-centered personality, in order to assimilate to the divine and thereby receive the influx from above. It should be emphasized that assimilation by annihilation does not concern divinity in its immanent aspect but, on the contrary, the highest plane in the divine world, the divine Nought. Despite the remoteness of this aspect of the divine, it is possible to encounter the deity by inducing a certain state of mind and/or soul. In these discussions, while we are stressing the importance of experiential starting points over theological ones, the possible impact of the latter should not be ignored. We must assume, however, that the existence of mystical practices is far more important for the actualization of a mystical drive than the theosophical or theological structure within which a particular form of mystical revival takes place. In other words, the emphasis should be placed on the existence of a directive to imitate God by self-effacement as well as on the practices of solitude and mental concentration. Such practices reflect more adequately the emergence of a mystical search that may also adopt a variety of theologies as religious frameworks. Let us therefore examine the availability of a pivotal practice for the nascent Hasidism in earlier mystical traditions.

In a Talmudic discussion, R. Abbahu, a mystically inclined Amora,[29] is quoted to the effect that "the world does not subsist . . . but for the sake of someone who conceives himself as nonexistent."[30] The last phrase is a translation of the Hebrew words *Mesim ᶜaẓmo kemiy she-ʾeino*. This awareness of personal "nothingness" has no direct relationship to a divine way of behavior, though it has, at least implicitly, a certain cosmic connotation: the existence of the worlds is conceived as depending upon this kind of person. The precise nature of such a person is not specified by the Talmudic source, which mentions in this context—though not in this specific case—names of biblical figures. However, in another context, R. Yoḥanan is quoted as saying that the Torah does not subsist except for those who conceive themselves as "nonexistent."[31] In this case, however, a prooftext is given: the famous verse in Job, 28:12, "*Ve-ha-ḥokhmah me-ʾayin timaẓeʾ*." While the original sense of the verse is interrogative ("But where shall wisdom be found?"), in the Talmudic context the sense is that wisdom, namely the words of the Torah, are found in someone who regards himself as nonexistent, the last concept being represented in the verse by the word *ʾAyin*. Interestingly, R. Shelomo Yiẓḥaqi, the most important commentator on the Talmud, uses in the context of the passage the form *ke-ʾAyin,* namely "as nonexistence," or "as nought," instead of *ke-ʾeino*. I cannot embark here on a full description of the implication of such a reading of the biblical verse in the Talmud.[32] However, for our purpose, it is sufficient to point out that according to the above quotes, *ʾAyin* can designate the spiritual state of the few, who play a special role both in sustaining the world and as teachers of the Torah.[33]

A correlation between humility and the concept of *ʾAyin* as the symbol of the highest *Sefirah, Keter,* is already evident in R. Moseh Cordovero's *Tefillah le-Moshe*: "*ʾAyin ʾAniy,* the humble, *ʿAnavim* who are within *ʾAyin,* while the poor ones are within *ʾAniy.*"[34] This statement means that the humble ones can reach the divine Nought, which stands for the first *Sefirah,* while the poor belong to the last *Sefirah, Malkhut.* Even more important for the subsequent evolution of Jewish mysticism is a passage from Cordovero's *Tomer Devorah,* in which he relates the *imitatio dei* to the imitation of the activity of the first *Sefirah*; in the second chapter of this book we read that the

> quintessence of the humility is that man should not find in himself any value but should consider himself as nought [*ʾAyin*] . . . because *Keter* is the first attribute . . . which sees itself as nought in front of its emanator, likewise man should consider himself as nought, indeed, his "non-existence" being better than his existence.[35]

As Bracha Sack has shown,[36] this text has influenced Cordovero's student's important book, *Reshit Ḥokhmah,* and thereby also Hasidism. However, before turning to this work, let us ponder the meaning of the comparison between human behavior and the theosophical processes. The first *Sefirah* recognizes both its nothingness and its dependence when it ascends to receive the power of the Infinite. However, the first *Sefirah* does not disappear, and there is no reason to assume that the concept of self-negation is proposed here even implicitly. The *Sefirot* in Kabbalah can return to their source, but they do not lose their distinctiveness even there. By analogy, humility does not automatically assume a loss of identity, but may signify instead the proper understanding of the nature of reality and the absolute dependence of the individual upon the higher entities.

R. Elijah de Vidas, a major disciple of Cordovero, describes the first *Sefirah* as bowing in front of the emanator; it is called *ʾAyin,*

> since it considers itself as nothing when compared to the Emanator. And it lowers its head in order to watch over and to emanate onto the lower worlds, which all incline to suckle from it.[37] Therefore, it is appropriate for man to think about himself as nought before His Greatness, blessed be He, which has no end or limit.[38]

Although there is no doubt that de Vidas was influenced by Cordovero, it should be mentioned that he also made recourse to the two talmudic texts quoted above.[39] However, there is one element that is hinted at in *Reshit Ḥokhmah* that does not occur in the context of the passage we have quoted above from Cordovero's *Tomer Devorah.* According to de Vidas, the Kabbalist should imitate the first *Sefirah* not only through his humility or "annihilation" but also, he seems to be saying, through his influence on others. It should be emphasized that this is not an explicit statement: the emanation of *Keter* appears in de Vidas, but not explicitly in Cordovero, while the human counterpart of this act is not mentioned. Nevertheless, from the phrase "it is appropriate" we may infer that someone should also attempt to imitate the first *Sefirah* by service to others. Although this is only a possible inference, it is one which, indeed, was drawn by the Hasidic masters. It should be emphasized that the use of the term *ᵓAyin,* in order to express the mystic's attitude of humility in relation to God, does not imply, at least in the above texts, individual disintegration or momentary annihilation. On the contrary, in some instances we may assume that by imitating the divine Naught the mystic is extending his consciousness by removing the boundaries of the self. Just as the divine Sefirotic realm starts with the infinite and moves toward the finite, so it is the case with human consciousness during this experience: by broadening his consciousness one not only transcends his regular, mundane state of awareness, but enhances his spiritual capacity, enabling it subsequently to capture or attract more sublime contents and stronger divine powers. This is the explanation of the ability to imitate the second type of divine act: the emanation or the production of the influx that descends upon the lower entities. This explanation ensures a certain logic of events, a Gestalt-contexture between the two divine acts as imitated by the mystic.

It should be emphasized that in the passages quoted above the Safedian Kabbalists do not mention *devequt,* the union or communion of man and God, but only the imitation of the divine attributes through human action. Consequently, these texts differ from the passages to be adduced below, where the concept of union with the highest levels in the divine world is explicitly mentioned in connection to the drawing down. The Hasidic texts to be analyzed below betray different combinations of terms and different concepts of the models described previously. In addition to the process of expansion of consciousness, union with the divine is part and parcel of the mystical model, combined with the magical one. It would therefore be advisable to understand some of the discussions in which the existents, *Yesh* and *ᵓAyin,* occur together, examples of semantic paradoxes that, nonetheless, do not represent conceptual paradoxes. In other words, though the words *Yesh* and *ᵓAyin* are indeed semantic opposites, in some Hasidic and in several pre-Hasidic texts, they do not represent concepts or states of being that are opposite to each other. This awareness allows a less paradoxical understanding of Hasidism.

3. THE HASIDIC MYSTICO-MAGICAL MODEL

Let us now survey some of the numerous treatments of the Hasidic masters associated with what I have called the mystico-magical model. In my opinion this is a rather widespread topos, which shows that it can be considered a core-model, and not just one of the many themes of which Hasidism was fond; I would say, on the basis of the sources quoted below (and the many others referred to in the footnotes), that this model is ubiquitous in Hasidic literature, a fact that demonstrates the centrality of the mystico-magical model for all the major forms of eighteenth-century Hasidism as well as much of Hasidic thought that followed. In principle, the Hasidic views to be presented below may be understood as variations of the Kabbalistic model presented at the end of the previous chapter. This observation seems crucial for the understanding of those aspects with which we are concerned here, but also for the methodological approach proposed earlier, which attempts to understand Jewish mysticism as consisting of comprehensive underlying patterns.

The mystico-magical model as such has never been discussed in detail in scholarship. Nevertheless, its elements, and sometimes the relations between them, have been treated sporadically by modern scholarship; I am acquainted with few *en passant* references to the combinations between *devequt* and drawing down.[40] A more detailed treatment is found in R. Schatz's discussion of R. Elimelekh of Lisansk; more recently, Rachel Elior has discussed issues related to what I propose to call a model in her interesting study on *ᵓAyin* and *Yesh* and in her treatment of the Hasidic thought of the Seer of Lublin.[41] In these scholarly treatments only a small part of the material has been hinted at, with no formulation of the broader significance of these discussions in the con-text of Jewish magic and mysticism and no analysis of the possible impact of non-Hasidic sources. Neither of these scholars mentions the magical implications, which are I believe crucial for an understanding of the significance of the mysticism-magic nexus in Hasidism. As to the genesis of the model, the only attempt to address this question is that of Rachel Elior; her assumption seems to be that what I have called the mystico-magical model emerged in the late eighteenth or early nineteenth century as the result of socioeconomic changes in central Poland.[42] The restriction of the mystico-magical model to a relatively late phase in early Hasidism, namely the third or fourth generation, seems to me to be implausible. This model, as we have seen above in the examination of pre-Hasidic texts, is part and parcel of the earliest phases of this movement. Given the fact that the emergence of the model was understood as part of a socioeconomic situation in central Poland, it seems that an elaborate analysis of the earlier extant material is necessary. This is one of the reasons for the numerous quotes that will be introduced below—not only to clarify the details of the various versions and interpretations of this model, but also to demonstrate its wide and relatively early dissemination among Hasidic masters. As we will see, the same mystico-magical model is found not only in Podolia, the area of the first Hasidic masters, but also in the Ukraine and central Poland. This wide geographical distribution shows that we must look beyond specific socioeconomic factors (which cannot in any case account for a model in existence several centuries beforehand), to its spread during a certain period. Transcending the differences between these geographical areas is the emphasis upon extreme mystical and strong magical attitudes prevalent in all Hasidic literature.

What seems to be crucial for the understanding of the Hasidic version of the mystico-magical model is the special emphasis on the concept of humility, which occurs widely and which follows the Safedian texts mentioned above. It seems that Hasidism was aware of the arrogance of magic, and attempted to prevent it. The Hasidic masters were afraid, to quote Robert R. Marett, of "the nemesis attendant on all . . . output of vital forces which are not occasionally chastened and purified by means of the pilgrim's progress through the valley of humiliation."[43] The role of "annihilation" and humility in the economy of the mystico-magical model seems to be precisely this chastening of the vital forces.

It is very reasonable to assume that in the Hasidic camp the mystico-magical model was already espoused by the Besht himself. Let me start with a passage from the Besht's important disciple, R. Jacob Joseph of Polonoy: by means of prayer, the last *sefirah, Malkhut* symbolized by the word *ʾAniy,* "I," is connected to the first *Sefirah, Maḥashavah,* namely "Thought," symbolized by *ʾAyin,* "Nought." By this transformation of *ʾAniy* in *ʾAyin* "he draws down the influx from *ʾEiyn Sof* to *Malkhut,* by means of [the *sefirah* named] *Ẓaddiq,* and therefrom onto all the worlds."[44] In fact, this is a classical Kabbalistic exposition, which from the structural point of view partially parallels the early Kabbalistic texts.[45] However, what gives this sentence a special flavor is the mention of the transformation of the *ʾAniy* in *ʾAyin.* The meaning of this change is, in the above text, Sefirotic: the last, namely the lowest, *Sefirah,* by its ascent to the highest, becomes the first one and thereby the divine influx is drawn forth onto the lower worlds. In other words, this is a theosophical discussion that uses symbols of "I," *Ẓaddiq,* and Nought, but it does not speak openly about a psychological transformation. However, these two types of processes, the ascent on high and causing the descent of the influx, are the result of human ritual activity, which can be described as theurgical-magical; the Kabbalist is able to cause the ascent of the lower *Sefirah* and ensure the descent of divine power onto the mundane realm. R. Jacob Joseph mentions, however, that he has already discussed this issue earlier and indeed such a discussion exists, in which the Besht is quoted to the effect that Moses was able to link *Malkhut* to Althought, or *ʾAniy* to *ʾAyin.*[46] Again, in this case no psychological processes are mentioned, but at least the move from I to Nought is identified as the teaching of the Besht.

However, in a relatively later source, we find in his name the following passage, which deals in a psychological manner with one of the symbols mentioned above. In *Doresh Tov,* a collection of teachings of the Besht compiled by R. Shimeon Zeʾev Zelig, the Besht was reported to have said,

> Whoever wishes that the Godhead [*ʾElohut*] should dwell upon him should consider himself to be *ʾAyin,* and the most important thing is to know and

> understand that within him there is [nothing] but Godhead, and this is a preparation for the dwelling of the Godhead on him.[47]

The attaining of the Nought, presented here as the consciousness of human "nothingness," is related, as in the earlier passages, to the descent of divinity into the lower worlds. In fact this passage, attributed to the Besht, apparently constitutes the core of a larger treatment of the subject by the Great Maggid; in one of the collections of his teachings, we learn about the immanence of the divine within all the realms of reality. Accordingly, also in man we find the deity, and whenever someone wishes for the deity to dwell upon him, he must acknowledge that his entire vitality constitutes in the divine Presence that vitalizes him, without which he is nothing. This awareness will ensure the dwelling of the Godhead upon him.[48] According to the first source, the consideration of one's own nothingness is part of the preparation for the dwelling within oneself of the divine. This is explicated in the sentence following the passage quoted, which asserts that one's essence is divine. In the second text, this reading is emphasized and we may conclude that the "annihilation" is not a destruction of the ego, but the discovery of its innermost essence, the divine immanence within man. These passages, as well as another adduced in the Besht's name[49] should suffice in order to reasonably attribute to the Besht an awareness of the mystico-magical model with which we are concerned here.

Let us ponder the significance of the word *nothingness* in the above text. It is not the obliteration of personality, its reduction to nothingness, or the awareness of its nullity; rather it is the dissipation of the ego-centered consciousness and the discovery of the divine within man. In other words, by using the term *nought,* the Hasidic masters refer, at least in some cases, to the disentanglement of the limited, accidental element from the core, the divine spark, which is able to become the locus of the infinite power. Because like is attracted to like, by discovering the divine within man, the mystic draws toward him the divine source.

Furthermore, in one of the teachings of the Besht's grandson, R. Barukh of Miedzyborz we learn that by the effacement of the importance of any existent in the world, the mystic strives to perform only the will of God, and thereby the divine Presence comes to dwell within him. The letters of will, *Raẓon,* are permutated into *Noẓar,* created being. This play, meaning that out of the divine will the divine mercy, *Ḥesed,* is created, is apparently a hint at the influx descending from the divine will. A further permutation of these consonants produces the word *Ẓinor,* the pipe or the channel,[50] meaning the transformation of the mystic into a channel of the influx, which is distributed to the whole world.[51] Thus, as in the Safedian texts mentioned above, the Hasidic sources also assume that man opens himself toward the higher source, an act that enables him to influence the lower levels of existence.

In several of his teachings, the Great Maggid, the other important disciple of the Besht, also espouses the mystico-magical model. In a collection of his doctrines, he succinctly indicates that "the faith[52] of the *Ẓaddiq* is his ascent upward and his causing the descent of the influx like a pipe."[53] This master is also quoted by the Seer of Lublin as asserting the affinity between the mystical attainment and the magical quality of the subsequent action: when describing the meaning of the quality of Nought, *Middat ha-ʾAyin,* a phrase very characteristic of the thought of the Great Maggid, this master indicates that "whoever regards himself as nought, can draw down benefits that are dependent on the *mazzal*[54] that governs 'children, life and sustenance.'"[55] In another similar tradition, quoted again in the name of the Great Maggid, we learn that

> whoever is nought is the *mazzal*[56] that draws down to the people of Israel, and he arouses the supernal World of Unity named Nought, because there is an occultation.[57] Upon this [world] "children, life, and sustenance" are dependent.[58]

The supernal Nought is described here not as a void, a vacuum, but as a fullness that is the source of emanation. Therefore, it would be more adequate to emphasize the "annihilation" as a process of expansion, which allows the mystic to capture more of the divine, in order to be able to transmit more to the lower beings. Assimilation to the higher is a source of emanation onto the lower.

In the spirit of his teacher, the Lubliner Seer, R. Meir ha-Levi of Apta writes in his *ʾOr la-Shamayim*:

> I heard people saying in the name of the Rabbi of Neskhiz[59] . . . that the *Ẓaddiqim* bring themselves[60] to the state,[61] that they are always united with and linked to the higher [world], to the supernal worlds . . . and that King David, blessed be his memory, was always united with and linked to the supernal worlds, and he became a pool and a pipe[62] to draw down the influx from the supernal source to the lower worlds.[63]

Here, and in some of the other texts of this author,[64] the divine influx is attracted by the *Ẓaddiq,* who becomes an intermediary, a channel, to transmit the influx to the lower worlds. Elsewhere R. Meir of Apta emphasizes that the influx should be channeled through those who are humble, openly connecting the prerequisite to "annihilate" before the drawing down with the nature of those people who should enjoy the result of the annihilation.[65] Elsewhere, this Hasidic master describes the combat between the *Ẓaddiq* and the maleficent powers that attempt to obstruct the descent of the divine influx and light.[66] In a rather exceptional statement, R. Meir asserts that the *Ẓaddiq* is able to direct the influx to whomever he wishes. However, he himself is unable to care for his own affairs because of his humility and "annihilation."[67] In this context, it would be pertinent to address the interpretation of humility in some texts of the Great Maggid's school.

As we have attempted to point out above, in some instances the term *ʾAyin* can better be understood as an expansion of the ego rather than asthe annihilation of all its contents. This interpretation is corroborated by instances when humility, or self-debasement, *shiflut,* is understood in terms of broadening the receptive capacity. The Great Maggid mentions the lowering of the intellect as allowing more space for the study of the Torah.[68]

It should be mentioned that the attainment of the annihilation is accompanied not only by the ability to draw down influxes and blessings, but also by the capacity to perform miracles. But this important issue does not concern us here.[69] The Hasidic mystic is, therefore, described as identical to the supernal world in the moment of his "annihilation," and this is the reason for his being able to draw down the influx.[70]

One of the more mystical masters of early Hasidism, R. Menaḥem Mendel of Vitebsk, who opposed the concept of *Ẓaddiq* as leader of a community, nevertheless gave a concise expression of the mystico-magical model when he mentioned the desire of the *Ẓaddiqim* "to cleave to the supernal source and to draw from there and cause the emanation of mercy to all the worlds."[71]

Although only scarcely mentioning the moment of "annihilation" throughout his book, an important student of the Great Maggid, R. Elimelekh of Lisansk, presented a model very similar to that described above: "By the total cleaving of the *Ẓaddiq* he causes the descent of the influx of good to the community of Israel."[72] Elsewhere he distinguished between three degrees: the first being the inner preparation for prayer and the ascent of the soul on high; the second the preparation for causing great influxes on the community of Israel; and the last the minute and intentional observance of the commandments.[73] Although someone may draw from the above passage the conclusion that drawing down the influx and observing the commandments are two different phases or acts, from other contexts it seems that this master is indeed well aware of the nexus between the two.[74]

In a passage penned by one of R. Elimelekh of Lisansk's disciples, we find a very explicit expression of the mystico-magical model; R. Yehudah Leib of Zakilkow indicates that the *Ẓaddiq* has to

> cleave always and be joined to the Life of the Worlds, and he has to strengthen himself and cause his soul to cleave to on High and to the Primordial[75] Will. But, despite the fact that he is united there with the World of Althought,[76] because he is here below in the World of Reality,[77] he has to draw down to himself vitality from the Source of Life and the Root of Roots, within the worlds[78] . . . and he cleaves to the supernal world, to the root of repentance, which is higher than the vitality of the worlds . . . Afterward, from the supernal cleaving, there is a drawing of the influx to sustain the reality of the worlds."[79]

What is especially interesting in this quote is the occurrence of the phrase "*horadat ha-shefa* ᶜ," the drawing down or the descent of the influx; the word *horadah* is reminiscent of the magical term *horadat ha-ruḥaniyyut*.[80]

In fact, the above texts have many important and interesting parallels to a relatively early collection of sermons of the Great Maggid, *Shemu ᶜah Tovah,* where the divestment from materiality brings about the cleaving to the Nought; only then, "after the divestment from materiality is is possible to draw [down] the luminosity, which is the divine influx."[81] This sequence is of paramount importance for the understanding of certain major discussions in the circle of the Great Maggid: the extreme mystical experience opens the way to the more magical one. In our case, the term *behirut,* luminosity, is used but this is only one of the synonyms of the term *ruḥaniyyut*.[82] The two kinds of activity correspond, according to the Great Maggid, to the two parts of the opening verse of the *Shemoneh ᶜEsreh* prayer: "God, open my lips" stands for the divestment from materiality, while the sequence "and my mouth will tell Your praise" stands for the drawing down of the luminosity to the worlds."[83] This last act is related to the recitation of words, an issue that will concern us later.[84] According to a statement of R. Levi Yiẓḥaq,

> there are those who serve God with their human intellect and others whose gaze is fixed as if on Nought, and this is impossible without divine help . . . He who is granted this supreme degree, with divine help, to contemplate the Nought, his intellect is effaced and he is like a dumb man . . . but when he returns from such a contemplation to the essence of [his] intellect, he finds it full of influx.[85]

The return means not only a disengagement from the cleaving to the Nought but also the filling of the mind with divine splendor. "Mind" is conceived here as the vessel for the collection of the divine energy.[86] We may infer that the expansion of the intellect means a certain transcendence of its normal limitations, which brings about its being filled by the divine influx.

The need for elevation to the highest level of reality in order to draw down the influx is also expressed overtly in the writing of another important disciple of the Great Maggid, R. Ḥayyim Ḥayke of Amdura; he affirms that

> when he[87] is elevated[88] to God, blessed be He, he can draw down wisdom for himself.[89] But when the wisdom is emanated from God to man, it emanates by means of heaven and earth, which is the way of *Ẓimẓum*; but when the *Ẓaddiq* links himself[90] to wisdom and he causes an influx, this influx comes to man immediately, without any discernible *Ẓimẓum*.[91]

For our purpose it suffices to point out the recurrence of the anabatic themes of elevation, linking, and elsewhere the joining[92] to the divine *Ḥokhmah,* or the cleaving to God,[93] or coming close to God,[94] as preceding the act of drawing down. What is significant in the preceding two passages is that the human intellect is conceived of as a vessel, a container for the higher wisdom that plays the same role as the influx and the energy or spiritual force that in other Hasidic discussions is collected by language and ritual. In other words, though using the language of the philosophers, the speculative content is understood more in substantial than in epistemological terms. This is only one of the many examples where the ontological language of the magical model shapes the content of terms stemming from other types of thought.[95]

Let us ponder, for a moment, the meaning of the above sequence of concepts: the total divestment, the elevation, and the cleaving to the higher realms are acts that are intended to leave behind corporeality and bring one to the "gate of Nought,"[96] which is the place for change and also the turning point for the return to this world and, at the same time, the place from where luminosity, spirituality, influx, benefit, and so on are drawn forth. The "annihilation" of the self, its spiritualization or elevation, are the technique that precedes the magical act and ensures the descent of the power that strengthens the material, and in some cases also the spiritual, aspects of life here below. To put it differently: the mystical aspect of the mystico-magical model can be conceived as the mystical technique that strives to achieve the ideal, namely the magical drawing down of the influxes. These mystical stages enable the Hasidic mystic to reach the source that provides the influx, and by becoming a vessel the *Ẓaddiq* mediates actively between the fullness of the divine power and the mundane world depending upon it.

However, in a passage that has been aptly described as "most surprising"[97] in R. Levi Yiẓḥaq, an important disciple of the Great Maggid, we may find another meaning of the Nought, which may imply an immersion within the divine that dissolves the worshiper for the period of the experience. This master distinguishes between two types of worshipers, who reach different types of *devequt* with God: those who have attained it outside the land of Israel and without performing the commandments, and those who have done it by means of the commandments. The first type is able to reach the contemplation of the Nought by means of his eye,[98] and represents the highest union of the human spirit[99] with the divine that can be contemplated directly, while the latter worshiper sees God only by means of a reflection. I will not enter here into all the details related to the interesting passage under consideration, as a fine analysis has already been done by Arthur Green.[100] Let us look only at those sentences that are relevant to the present theory of models.

The first type of worship is characterized by the contemplation of the Nought and amounts to a very extreme experience: the mystic himself becomes, as it was expressed by the Great Maggid, nought:

> One who serves through dedication alone, without commandments and deeds, is truly in the Nought,[101] while the one who serves by means of commandments is serving Him through some existing thing. Therefore, the one

who serves in dedication and is wholly within the Nought cannot cause [divine] influx to flow down upon himself: "he" does not exist,[102] but is fully attached to God.[103]

The way of dedication is anomian and extreme: it is the prerogative of those righteous, like Abraham, who lived before the promulgation of the Torah and its commandments. It is extreme because it culminates in a temporal extinction of the individual. From the mystical point of view, this is the most sublime form of experience, and I would classify it as representative of the ecstatic model: indeed, when discussing again the cleaving to the Nought, the same master introduces a view somewhat similar to that of R. Yiẓḥaq of Acre:[104]

When the *Ẓaddiq* cleaves to the Nought, and is [then] annihilated, then he worships the Creator in the aspect of all the *Ẓaddiqim,* since no division of the attributes is discernible there at all. . . . There is a *Ẓaddiq* who cleaves to the Nought and nevertheless returns afterward to himself.[105] But Moses our master, peace be upon him, constantly contemplated the greatness of the Creator, blessed be He, and did not return to himself at all, as is well known, since Moses our Master, peace be upon him, was constantly cleaving to the Nought, and through this aspect was annihilated. . . . When he contemplated the Creator, blessed be He, then there is no sence of self, since he is annihilated . . . he contemplated the Nought and was annihilated . . . Moses was constantly cleaving to the Nought.[106]

As the Hasidic master indicates just before this passage, the Nought transcends all divisions by including them within Itself; hence we can sense the view of God as a prime-matter that can receive all forms.[107] However, in order to confer these forms upon it, one must reach the zone of Nought. It is appro-priate to compare this discussion of R. Levi Yiẓḥaq to the views expressed by R. Azriel of Gerona, who maintained that any change takes place only after the return of the substance to the divine Nought.[108] However, whereas the early Kabbalist was dealing mainly with theosophical and cosmological processes, the eighteenth-century Hasidic master is concerned mainly with the effects of the mystical experience and the role of ritual. He assumes that it is possible to transcend someone's particular way of serving the Nought and become, as Moses did, one who worships God from the aspect of all the other *Ẓaddiqim*.and become, as Moses did, one who worships God from the aspect of all the other *Ẓaddiqim*.

An interesting parallel to some of the ideas in the above quotations is found in the writing of a disciple of R. Levi Yiẓḥaq; R. Aharon of Zhitomir speaks about his master as follows:

There are two kinds of *Ẓaddiqim*: there is the *Ẓaddiq* who receives luminosity from the letters of Torah and prayer; and there is another *Ẓaddiq,* who is greater, who brings the luminosity to the letters from above, despite the fact

> that the letters are in the supernal world. When the great *Ẓaddiq* brings new luminosity[109] to the world, this luminosity cannot come to the world but by its being clothed in the letters . . . and when the luminosity comes down the letters fly upwards[110] whereas the luminosity remains here below. And the [great] rank of this *Ẓaddiq* is connected to recitation of the speeches with all his power and with dedication and with all the two hundred and forty-eight limbs and then to each and every word that he recites, he brings luminosity.[111]

The gradation between the two kinds of *Ẓaddiqim* is obvious; the one who is able to bring down the luminosity is greater than he who merely receives it from the letters. The passivity of the first type of righteous man, though motivated by a stronger mystical experience, is nevertheless conceived to be lower in degree than the activism of the latter. This passive attitude is apparently related to the assumption that the luminosity is present in the letters irrespective of any human action, a view that recurs in Hasidic literature but is not the dominant one.[112]

However, the Nought-experience does not bring about one particular practical attainment, which can be achieved only by means of the second category of worship: bringing down the influx or blessing from above upon the mystic or upon the world. This descent does not assume the mystic's extinction or annihilation, but rather his return to existence, as well as his activist attitude and the performance of the commandments. By causing the presence of God to be upon the mystic, by attracting His contracted manifestation,[113] another kind of mystical experience is achieved, one whose details will be examined immediately—that of God encountering man within the human body. Worship through "existence" involves, therefore, both the body and the ritual acts related to the body. This is the existence that is the alternative to the Nought. Indeed, the practice of the commandments is also intended to bring about the contact between man and the divine without man's losing himself in this experience:

> In fulfilling the Creator's will one intends to reach the Nought, while the selfsame commandment also binds you to existence,[114] since the commandments partake of existence[115] and you draw forth blessing. Thus there are people who sustain themselves through their deeds.[116]

According to the logic of the second type of experience, the greater the material or corporeal involvement and the more comprehensive the deeds, the greater will be the encounter with the divine and the richer will be the descending blessings. Moreover, it is by virtue of the *Yesh,* the existent alone, but not by virtue of the Nought, that the blessings are attained. In the parlance of the text, this achievement is not only a positive one but, by implication, seems superior to worship by the Nought. Let us examine in greater detail the obtaining of blessings here below. The verb used to express the concept of drawing down is *MShKh;* in the *po*ʿ*el* and *hif*ʿ*il* forms, *Moshekh* and *le-Hamshikh.* The latter form of this verb was in use by the beginning of Kabbalah in order to describe the descent of the influx from the higher divine realm upon the lower *Sefirot.* Thus, it is a verb that describes an intradivine process that depends on the mystical intention of the Kabbalist.[117] However, elsewhere this Hasidic master uses this verb to mean the drawing down of the influx upon the mystic himself. This is an anthropocentric act, in comparison to the theocentric activity of the earlier Kabbalists.

Similarly, the fact that the second type of worship appears later in "history" may indicate the more positive attitude of the Hasidic master. In more explicit terms, we can find a preference for the active *Ẓaddiq* over the passive one in R. Levi Yiẓḥaq, as pointed out by R. Aharon of Zhitomir. Also the view of Abraham, as espoused by R. Aharon, shows that the later phase of his life, after his circumcision and the addition of the letter H to his name, is characterized by his drawing down the "graces," *Ḥasadim,* upon the world.[118]

Likewise, a contemporary of R. Levi Yiẓḥaq, R. Abraham Friedman, the Angel, who was the son of the Great Maggid, mentions two forms of worship: that of the *Ẓaddiqim* who perform the commandments in order to induce pleasure in God, and another, described as higher, and performed by the greater *Ẓaddiqim* who intend to bring grace to the entire world.[119] According to this master, the annihilation of the *Ẓaddiq* is the reason for his ability to draw the divine revelation[120] here below.[121] Therefore, we may conclude that Hasidic thought preferred a world-oriented worship to a purely mystical one, without, however, negating or opposing the latter.

Although R. Levi Yiẓḥaq originally spoke about two different types of worship, it seems that it is possible to propose the existence of a sequel to them, reminiscent of the passage quoted above from the Geronese Kabbalah:[122] extreme mysticism is a kind of mystical preparation, becoming *ʾAyin* or "annihilation" and, at the same time, a reconnaissance expedition that culminates in the return from above and the bringing down of the various influxes for all the limbs by performing the commandments:

> It is well known that the *Ẓaddiq* is to be united to *ʾAyin,* and this is the annihilation of his existence, out of his great awe and fear of the Lord,[123] blessed be He, and when the *Ẓaddiq* is united to *ʾAyin,* he brings from there the influxes, goodwill, and blessing[124] to the whole world . . . but he must previously be united to *ʾAyin* . . . [T]he *Ẓaddiq* must be united to the *ʾAyin* and annihilate his existence; and only afterward he is able to bring all the blessings[125] to the world.[126]

While the first move consists in a distancing of the spiritual from the material, so that the spiritual will be able to encounter the Nought, namely *Deus sive modis,* the second stage is concerned with the well-being, the blessing, of the material by bringing the spiritual downward. Although this descent may be understood in purely anthropocentric terms, it may be that there is also a theocentric aspect: the reference to the Nought as the potential power, or as a power prepared to receive all the forms, is surprising. In many of these Jewish texts, God is defined as the actuality, while the lower entities are defined as the potentialities[128] here, however, the forms related to human activities are conceived as actualizing the divine potentiality.[129] By his ritual activity, man causes the descent of the divine upon himself, that is, he brings about the actualization of the divine.

This analysis may serve as a clue for the understanding of the relations between Nought-service and the existent-service: the first is an encounter with the all-comprehensive potentiality, the supernal Nought, while the latter points to the actualization of this potentiality. Extreme mysticism is indeed highly anthropocentric, while the more moderate approach is much more magical and theocentric. I wonder if we can draw a conclusion from the possible implications of the above discussion: if the ritual is the activity that brings down the divine as existence, and if man by his dedication cleaves to the Nought and becomes nought, perhaps the absence of the ritual is instrumental in the annihilation of the revealed divinity and the reduction of the *Deus revelatus* to the Nought. This conclusion is not obvious in the Hasidic text but is explicit in several Kabbalistic texts since the thirteenth century.[130] Thus R. Levi Yiẓḥaq's dedication-service is an absorptive experience that allows the individual to annihilate his personality by a total, spiritual experience, in which he encounters God as Nought, namely the deity beyond all attributes. God, however, can be encountered also as "existent" by means of the Jewish ritual, which not only enwraps man with a divine aura but also displays the divine in this world. The sequence of the extreme form of *devequt* (a fine example of *unio mystica*) and the magical drawing down may be compared to a similar pattern that has recurred since early Kabbalah, in which we also find the unitive experience preceding theurgical activity.[131]

The second ideal, though not absent in the work of this master, is, as we shall see below, attenuated in Hasidism and here the magical experience was preferred. Thus, the structure of two models, where the first is a *devequt*-type and the second a performative model, is still evident here, despite the shift from theurgy to magic.[132] However, we should also be aware that in the Hasidic structure the first model apparently implies a much more extreme and intense mystical experience. Is this sequence a matter of Gestalt? In other words, is the functional significance of one constituent of the structure linked to the nature of the second one?

Levi Yiẓḥaq, following the Besht and his own mentor, the Great Maggid, was aware of the existence of two types of worship, which we have attempted to distinguish above. Indeed, the Hasidic master is close enough to the phenomenology of religion proposed by Friedrich Heiler, who also distinguishes between mystical and prophetic religiosity. The mystical model seems to have nourished the Nought-service and experience, while the existent-service corresponds to the magical model. This distinction was expressed in the two different stages of the religious life of the biblical Abraham—his worship outside the Land of Israel corresponding to the Nought-service, and his worship in the Land, by means of the commandments, corresponding to existent-service.[133] Nevertheless, I assume that the inspiration for this classification was not an exegetical approach to the biblical episodes but the two models called upon by the Hasidic master. The Nought-service is focused on the human experience, which takes place by means of the mystic entering the divine zone; the existent-service involves the presence of the divine in a realm where it was absent previously and the well-being of man as a whole. While the above views of the Berditchever Rebbe are concerned basically with the experience of the mystic, another emphasis is evident in the writings of one of his colleagues, the Seer of Lublin, another disciple of the Great Maggid.[134]

However, it seems that the most sophisticated and elaborate treatment of the mystico-magical model is to be found in the most influential Hasidic sect to emerge from the circle of the Great Maggid's entourage: the Ḥabad movement. Its founder, R. Shneor Zalman of Liady, and his various followers have paid special attention to the relationship between ecstatic experience and the role and nature of the performance of the commandments, in a manner that seems based in the model presented above. The details of the two forms of worship, by means of self-annihilation and by means of reading the Torah and performing the commandments, have been admirably analyzed by several scholars,[135] especially by Rachel Elior[136] it remains to explicate some passages in order to show that, despite the highly complex formulations of the masters of this school, the principle they espoused is very similar to the mystico-magical; in a manner reminiscent of R. Levi Yiẓḥaq, his acquaintance R. Shneor Zalman of Liady distinguished between two kinds of worship:

> There are two aspects in the worship of God: one, intense love, with burning fire, to leave the body. . . . This is the aspect of "great love," which the vessel of the heart cannot contain, for the heart cannot contain such tremendous ecstasy.[137] Thus, it cannot stand in the vessel of its body and wishes to leave the sheath, the matter of the body. The second is that of ecstasy that dwells in the heart, and whose concern is to draw down the divinity from above to below, intentionally, into the various vessels, by means of Torah and commandments. And this is the issue of *Razo*ʾ *va-shov*.[138] [139]

It is possible to emphasize the dialectical nature of this passage, as Elior indicated the "paradox and the dialectic of contradiction" as one of its fundamental elements.[140] I would like to stress that though I have my own, nondialectical explanation of the precise relationship between the two eyes of worship, this does not mean that in general Elior's dialectical analysis of Ḥabad thought is not correct. On the contrary, I am convinced by the texts she uses in order to show that Ḥabad's thought is dialectical. However, in the light of numerous parallels adduced above from R. Shneor Zalman's contemporaries, I would propose a less dialectic understanding, not one of "mutually contradictory" values, but rather of complementary ones. The first type of worship, the uninhibited ecstatic one, the intensive love, brings the worshiper to leave the body. The second type is not just another form of worship but, in my opinion, that which succeeds the first, a lower type of mystical striving, which intends to draw God down by means of performing the ritual.[141] At least twice in his writings this sequence is clearly stated: in *Liqqutei Torah,* R. Shneor Zalman indicates that only after the sowing, namely the breaking of the heart or the annihilation of the soul, *biṭṭul ha-nefesh,* is the growing of the redemption possible, the last phrase meaning the drawing down of the divine power; while in another discussion, in *Torah ʾOr,* he summarizes the relationship between the major concepts involved in our discussion as follows: "It is precisely the effacement of the existence into the Nought that causes the drawing down of the Nought to Existence."[142] The sequel between the two types of worship is indicated also in a text of R. Aharon ha-Levi Horowitz, a faithful disciple of R. Shneor Zalman. He affirms that:

> the worship of the Jew[143] is to self-annihilate so that the soul will vanish to her source and root . . . and afterward he should draw the revelation of His Godhead, blessed be He. . . . [B]ecause this is the intention[144] of the worship, to be in the aspect of revelation.[145]

"Afterward" stands between the processes of extinction and drawing down. Consequently, the disciple supplies a clue for the proper understanding of the relation between the two manners of worship, which is fully consistent with the views of the other Hasidic masters. I would say that in the line of the axiology of R. Levi Yiẓḥaq, the second type of worship is not only second in time but also higher; in Ḥabad thought, the *Kelim,* the vessels that are repeatedly related to the commandments,[146] are regarded as stemming from a very high source within the divinity, and thus the worship by Torah and commandments seems to be also higher.[147]

The phenomenology of the ritual service as understood by the Great Maggid, R. Levi Yiẓḥaq, R. Elimelekh of Lisansk, R. Shneor Zalman of Liady, the Seer of Lublin, and their various followers, is deserving of a more elaborate analysis: while the Nought-service is able to bring the mystic to a much higher, direct mystical experience, it was not preferred by the Hasidic masters to the other service. The role of ritual in R. Levi Yiẓḥaq's view, or the spiritual-mate-rial synthesis in the writings of the Seer, consist both of the actualization of extreme mysticism by annihilation and of an encounter, though moderate, with a manifestation of God on the human plane. However, there can be no doubt as to their origin in the thought of their common teacher, the Great Maggid, or even earlier. Although each of his disciples has elaborated on the synthesis between annihilation and the subsequent drawing down of influx in his own way, the difference between them is more an issue of emphasis than innovation.[148]

Indeed, a perusal of the literary corpus of the Seer of Lublin confirms his particular concentration on the question of drawing down not influx and blessing in general but benefits that are more specific and that are oriented to others, not just to the mystic himself. Thus, the picture of this mystic as portrayed by Elior is adequate, although I am reluctant, given the significance of the earlier Hasidic texts mentioned above, to agree to the view that this unique material-communal preoccupation is indeed an innovation. Perhaps we may resolve this quandary by assuming that already existing ideas came to the fore in certain geographical areas under certain socioeconomic circumstances. In my opinion, the resort to socioeconomic explanations cannot and should not solve questions related to the origin of a certain spiritual model, but should rather give a post factum explanation for its attractiveness and success. I would prefer to analyze the structure of the model itself in an attempt to understand its inner logic and its relationship to the religious background of the group that cultivates it. In any case, it seems that the combination of the mystico-magical model, on the one hand, and the ascent in importance of the *Ẓaddiq* as the ideal according to this model, on the other, is crucial for the structure of Hasidism both as a mode of mysticism and as a social organization.

In a highly significant text whose milieu cannot, unfortunately, be located precisely, we learn explicitly that this model cannot be cultivated by everyone, but by those few whose souls stem from the divine world, *ᶜOlam ha-ʾAẓilut.* In a collection of Hasidic traditions named *Darkhei Ẓedeq,* compiled by R. Zekhariah Mendel of Yaroslav, and author from the circle of R. Elimelekh of Lisansk, we find the following statement:

> A man cannot draw down the influx but from the place of the root of his soul.[149] This is the reason why nowadays, when there are not many souls from *ʾAẓilut,* and he cannot draw from *ʾAẓilut,* the substitute[150] is to link and unite his soul to the soul of the *Ẓaddiqim,* who are known to him, according to the degree of their soul in the [world of] *ʾAẓilut.* And this is a very important principle concerning Torah, good deeds, rescue [of prisoners], and all the commandments.[151]

The basic premise is that the drawing down can be accomplished only by someone who is able to reach the highest of the spiritual worlds, and thereby reach the source of the soul, which is also the source of the influx that is drawn down. Thus, anabasis and talismatic magic are closely related here. In principle, the drawing down may be achieved by everyone whose soul stems from the world of *ʾAẓilut.* However, in the epoch of Hasidism, such persons are few, and so the drawing down cannot be achieved except by adhering to the *Ẓaddiqim,* the recognized elite, whose souls stem from the highest spiritual level. It is very significant that the mystical aspect, the cleaving to the source or, in lieu of it, to the *Ẓaddiqim,* seems to be regarded as somewhat instrumental—important because it makes possible the attainment of an even more important goal and experience: the drawing down. If the centrality of this magical ideal for Hasidic thought, along with that of *devequt,* is indeed compelling, then the mediating function of the *Ẓaddiq* in the general economy of Hasidism will appear in a somewhat different light. The righteous alone, according to this text, can draw down the influx and distribute it to the others,[152] and it is precisely this role, more than that of achieving the extreme union with God, by him or others, that is crucial for his special status.[153]

This emphasis on the magical function of the righteous also seems to come to the fore in another nineteenth-century text, penned by R. Yiẓḥaq Shapira of Neskhiz, which affirms that the self-annihilating *Ẓaddiq* becomes similar to God, as he is able to perform the miracles of reviving the dead and curing barrenness. In a dramatic hermeneutical move, he interprets the biblical verse "There is no one like Thee, God" *ʾEiyn kamokha ba-El[oh]im* [Psalm 86:8], as follows: *ʾEiyn* means *ʾAyin,* which is conceived as a symbol for a *Ẓaddiq* who is *kamokha,* similar to God.[154] When becoming *ʾAyin,* the *Ẓaddiq* is able to draw down the thirteen divine attributes of mercy, and by means of them he is able to do "deeds like those of God, blessed be He, by the dint of His Will."[155] In fact, the act of drawing the divine attributes hints at the identification of the *Ẓaddiq* with the highest *sefirah, Keter,* which is related to the concept of the thirteen attributes.[156] God and the *Ẓaddiq* are portrayed as almost identical in the context of the mystico-magical model; R. Moshe Eliaqum Beriʾah describes the righteous as alive, *Ḥayyim,* which is numerically equivalent to the divine names *ʾEheyeh, YHWH, ʾEheyeh,* because of their cleaving to their "supernal source." Afterward, he mentions that because of the act of cleaving between them, there is no difference between God and the righteous. Although there is a great difference between the infinite, which is limitless, while man is composed of matter and form, in the moment of their cleaving there is no "change," *shinnui,* between them. This is why the righteous one decrees and God fulfills, and he can operate and emanate all the goods.[157] By an interesting pun, this Hasidic master describes the model under discussion as follows: "By their cleaving to the Life of Lives, they draw down all kinds of vitality."[158]

As late as the end of the nineteenth century the total cleaving to God was connected to drawing down vitality and influxes to the worlds.[159] From a tradition related to R. David of Tolna, we learn about two interpretations of one word, which represent, each in its own way, the two major components of the mystico-magical model. Reflecting on a talmudic passage that compares the rabbi with an angel,[160] he offers two interpretations to the designation of the angel as *Pelʾiy,*[161] one meaning "separation," *Opgescheid* in Yiddish, the other meaning "wonder," *Wunder.* Like the rabbi, the angel separates himself from this world, and like the angel, the rabbi is able to perform wonders.[162]

Let me turn now to a more general analysis of the structure of the mystico-magical model. It combines intense mystical experiences, attained in many cases using anomian practices, with the subsequent praxis of the commandments, conceived now as fraught with a mystico-magical cargo. The commandments are the vessels that attract and contain the divine in this world, just as the *sefirot* do in the supernal world. Are these two parts of the model artificially linked elements, a forced effort to combine the *frui* with the *uti,* as Saint Augustine described these two kinds of religiosity? Is the extreme spiritualization characteristic of self-annihilation able to interact logically with the later, magical component of this model? Is the mystical facet of the magical model, the drawing down of spirituality upon the mystic, a logical sequel to the earlier, ascending experience? In other words is there a Gestalt-coherence discernible in the above model? And is such a coherence explicable in psychological terms alone? Or may there also be a more systemic coherence, involving the theological elements that enter the interaction between the two models, fusing them into the mystico-magical one? And last, but not least, is there a discernible social significance for this model? These questions have nothing to do with the history of ideas, namely with the attempt to find out the affiliations among ideas and terms in different historical periods and literary *corpora* and to determine the changes they underwent, as well as the directions of these changes; we have already attempted above to answer questions related to the history of ideas. It is important to also pay due attention to the phenomenological aspects of the model, as well as to the comparative potential involved in this magic-encrusted pattern.[163]

4. ENTRY VERSUS EXIT RITES

The ascent to the divine and the contact with or immersion within it creates the situation that the mystic must ponder: how to return to regular life. This return may be problematic either because of the desire to remain immersed in the divine, or because of the need for a technique to retreat from it in a proper manner, in order to ensure a smooth return. This was indeed a question dealt with by Kabbalists and Hasidic masters. The Besht himself was aware of the natural aspiration of the human vitality to return to God, and he indicates that his striving is balanced by "issues of this world," which may keep the righteous man in the world and not allow his annihilation.[164] In several instances, some of which are mentioned above[165] and others that will be discussed shortly, the mystico-magical model itself refers to the aspect of the return of the mystic from his extreme mystical experience: it constitutes the method of retreat from the annihilation-experience or from the Nought-experience to the state of existence, to use the terminology of the Berdichever Rebbe. So, for example, we read above that the *Ẓaddiq,* after attaining the experience of *ʾAyin,* returns to his essence, or to the realm of existence. R. Levi Yiẓḥaq writes that

> by the performance of the commandments and good deeds, he cleaves to the existence, because the commandments are existence and by their performance he is drawing upon himself influx from God.[166]

We should perhaps pay attention to the fact that both the mystical experience—annihilation and full cleaving—and the magical one, are portrayed in strong terms: whoever is able to become Nought is subsequently able to obtain everything, sometimes even for the whole community. This return to "existence" from the state of annihilation by means of religious deeds can also be described as an "exit rite," namely a procedure to escape the inchoate state, sublime as it may be, in order to produce "material" effects. If the "entry rites," what we called the mystical techniques, are in the mystico-magical model, anomian as they are, they are intended to produce extreme experiences. The commandments help the mystic to descend from this state and attain a more moderate unitive experience, one that is also fraught with magical effects. I would like to emphasize the nexus among commandments, existence, and personality or "essence": the commandments invert the effects of the anoniam techniques. While the divestment of corporeality brings someone to the state of nought, which is, at least in *Qedushat Levi,* a trans-intellectual state, the commandments bring one back to the "intellect."[167] In other words, the descent of the divine influx is concomitant with the return of a worshiper to his regular senses. The nexus between returning from a strong mystical experience and the commandments is evident in a passage in the name of the "Rabbi of Pinsk," namely R. Levi Yiẓḥaq, quoted by the Seer of Lublin:

> One who wishes to live should disregard the concerns of his body and let his thought cleave to God, blessed be He. He will mortify himself and will depart from himself but he is nevertheless alive, as he cleaves to the Life of [all] Lives.[168] . . . [W]hoever is impoverished by his cleaving to God, blessed be He, is certainly considered . . . as if dead, as freed from [actual] death, but [nevertheless] lives by them [i.e., the commandments].[169]

Poverty,[170] death, and cleaving are mystical states that are overcome by the practice of the commandments. Although there is nothing here that deals with the idea of drawing down, the passage overtly relates the return to life to the commandments. It should be mentioned that this Hasidic master states that when someone understands the "inner essence of each commandment, how much influx he causes in all the worlds by the commandment he fulfills, he will perform it with greater enthusiasm."[171] However, the most powerful description of the superiority of the drawing-down *Ẓaddiq,* in comparison to the extinctive one, who remains absorbed in his fascination with the divine, is expressed in a description of the "perfect prayer." According to the Berditchever Rebbe, only prayer that brings down an influx is perfect, while that of the extremely righteous, which does not return, is not conceived as perfect. The latter worshipers are devoid of the title "performing" righteous, *Ẓaddiqim po ͨalim,* while the nonperformative righteous one's prayer, for whom mystical experience is an end in itself, is called "incomplete," as the influx is not attracted.[172] Extreme mysticism, which preaches a complete immersion in the divine and loses sight of responsibility toward the world, is not openly condemned here, but, at the same time, it is not exalted as the highest form of mystical attainment.

An extremely interesting example of the relation between the commandments and the return from the intense cleaving to God is found in a passage of R. Ḥayyim of Chernovitz. After describing the love and devotion of man to God in very strong terms (a fine example of mystical union), this Hasidic master writes of someone immersed in the unitive experience:

> Then, even fulfillment of the Torah is irrelevant because the passion of attachment is so great. This is like the case of a father and his much-loved only son who have not seen one another for many years. When they see one another face to face they embrace and kiss with a love that is as strong as death, their souls going out to one another. All their senses cease to exist, just as in the moment of death. This is the love that the children of Israel should have for their Creator, blessed be He and His name, a love of such great passion and desire, since they are a part of Him. But if they were constantly in this state there would be no Torah. One who has left the bounds of humanity can fulfill no *miẓwah* and can study no Torah because he has left the human condition. This is why God put it into our nature that we be cut off and fall back from too much love. Then it is possible for one to fulfill the Torah . . . because he falls back from the aspect of *Ḥokhmah*, . . . which is the annihilation of [his] existence.[173]

This remarkable text assumes that though it is possible to attain an anaesthetic experience, which obliterates all the senses and thus also ritualistic acts, it is also natural to return to regular religious life. The need for the Torah and its performance regulate human nature; although, in leaving the human condition, *Ki yaẓa᾽ mi-geder ha-᾽adam,* he becomes united with God, being human consists in returning to the Torah and the commandments. As we learn from the context of this passage, by nature the soul strives to return to her source, but once there, it has to retreat in favor of the religious life.

It may well be, though I do not presently find definitively convincing proof for this speculation, that in Ḥabad Hasidism, also, the return, *shov,* is related to the second type of worship, which draws down the Godhead and constitutes a return type of experience.[174] The question is whether the view of the Berdichever Rebbe is idiosyncratic, or whether his opinion reflects a broader approach to the role of the commandments. In my opinion, this master was not an exception; neither was he the first to express such a view. Let me first inspect some sources written in the circle of the Great Maggid.

It should be noticed that this psychological dimension of return by means of the commandments is absent from the writings of students of the Great Maggid like R. Elimelekh of Lisansk, who almost completely avoids terms referring to the state of annihilation and is very reluctant to use the term *ᵓAyin.*[175] It seems that, in lieu of the theme of annihilation, the dominant emphasis is on the will of the righteous, who is able to change the will of God.[176] Nevertheless, we learn from one of his discussions that "the *Ẓaddiq* is allowed to stop his cleaving from Him, blessed be He, in order to go and perform the commandments."[177] Likewise, R. Elimelekh emphasizes that it is desirable to "leave" God in order to keep His commandments.[178] At least in this case, for this master, *devequt* is only a means-experience rather than an end-experience, to use Abraham Maslow's terms.

An interesting version of the mystico-magical model is found in an important mid-nineteenth century Hasidic master, R. Yiẓḥaq Aiziq Yehudah Yeḥiel Safrin of Komarno; he explicitly mentions that when someone hallows himself by effacement and annihilation, so that his soul goes out, he undergoes an ecstatic experience, and "he is able to elevate *Malkhut* to *ᵓEiyn Sof* and cancel all the bad decrees, and draw down all the good things, remedy, blessing and life on the entire people of Israel, food, blessing, life and sustenance."[179] Moses is described as being able to draw down the "vitality of the divinity because of his likeness to an angel of the Lord of Hosts, out of his divestment of corporeality, and his cleaving to the Life of Lives."[180] Elsewhere, he maintains that it is the unique capacity of the children of Israel to become

> just like the Nought . . . and they stir all the worlds to return to the aspects of the Nought, and then the unification is attained, since all the aspects of unification and intercourse[181] are an ascent to the aspect of *ᵓEiyn Sof.* And the world would be annihilated and would completely return to the Nought, to the aspect of *ᵓEiyn Sof.* There, however, in this annihilation, is comprised also Israel, the holy nation, which necessarily has a body[182] and a vessel and being and an ego[183] which are necessary for the worship. This is the reason why they [Israel] draw all the worlds, so they will not be completely annihilated.[184]

The necessity of worship, that is, the performance of the commandments, as well as social and communal responsibility, represents a barrier that prevents the total absorption into the Nought. However, this Hasidic master, who was also an accomplished Kabbalist, as the use of the terms "unifications" and "intercourses" demonstrates, is concerned not only with the experience of the individual, but also with the maintenance of the universe. The role of the commandments is therefore to force the mystic to return not only to his normal state of consciousness, but also to religious life with all its responsibilities.

The psychological aspects of the combination of the two models are obvious: precisely because the ecstatic experiences were so extreme and intense, it was necessary to find a way to return to a normal state of consciousness. The danger of remaining in a state of self-effacement is that someone will not be able to return to normal consciousness.[185] Indeed, the danger of death haunts extreme forms of mysticism, as we learn from discussions in various ecstatic texts, such as those of Abraham Abulafia,[186] R. Yiẓḥaq of Acre,[187] and the author of an ecstatic handbook written at the beginning of the sixteenth century, R. Yehudah Albotini. Albotini wrote in his *Sullam ha-ʿAliyah* that those who do not want their souls to separate during the mystical experience should, while conscious, that is, before they pass from the human to the divine realm,

> adjure their souls by a terrible oath or by the Great and Terrible Name, that during the appearance and the vision, when the soul is not in its own realm, she should not separate and go to cleave to her source, but should return to her sheath and her body, as [she was] at the beginning.[188]

Compare this quote to a similar description of the early Hasidic masters, found in R. Moshe Eliaqum Beriʾah, the son of the Maggid of Kuznitz. In his *Beʾer Moshe,* he says of the *Ẓaddiq that he* is not satisfied except when he is

> actually annihilated out of the strength of the union with God, blessed be He, by his dedication to God . . . as I have seen some of my teachers and masters, . . . especially my teacher, the holy Rabbi, the man of God . . . R. Meshullam Zusha,[189] who totally divested himself from this world when he ascended in order to cleave to God, to such an extent that he was actually close to annihilating his existence.[190] Thus it was necessary that he should take a vow and give alms that his soul will remain in him.[191]

It is not my claim that the last two texts are historically related; although one scholar has proposed that Albotini's book was a source of a certain Hasidic concept,[192] I would be more cautious in this respect. The phenomenological affinity, it seems to me, is much more important: the masters of R. Moshe Eliaqum Beriʾah were aware of the danger of extinction during the mystical experience and used a certain device in order to survive, just as Albotini had done centuries beforehand. Given the anomian nature of ecstatic Kabbalah, the commandments did not play a role in its mystical system and could not serve as exit-rites. Indeed, it seems, in other passages, that this Hasidic master assumes that though the extreme mystical experience can culminate in death, this does not happen because God returns the soul to the body and supplies vitality to it.[193] It is divine grace, not a drawing down performed by the mystic after his annihilating experience has vanished, that supplies human needs by emanating the vitality; or, as we learn from another passage, "for the *Ẓaddiq,* it is an easy thing to ascend on high."[194] Much more difficult is, according to this master, to come down in peace.[195] Again, it is divine grace that enables the *Ẓaddiq* to descend, with all the influxes He grants him. Overtly, this is an attempt to attenuate the magical aspects of the model we are examining.[196] However, in another work by this master the return from ecstasy is expressly motivated by the necessity to provide the needs of his generation.[197]

Discussions about returning from a deep experience of *devequt* occur in the Nadvorna dynasty; R. Berish of Nadvorna is described as "descending" from a state of union because of the need to go to the synagogue. Even then, according to his son, he was still in a high mystical state.[198]

This emphasis on the return, which in the Hasidic texts has magical, ritual, and psychological components, seems to be a constant in Jewish mysticism. The encounter with the divine Nought is not an uroboric absorption, a return to the maternal womb, but, to again use Neumann's categories, a "world-transforming" type of experience.[199] The Nought is a "creative void" or "creative nothingness"[200] that engenders an even stronger activism than was possible before embarking on the experience. Indeed, the Hasidic emphasis on the need to efface the ego in order to reach the supernal Nought is reminiscent of Neumann's definition of "mystical" as "a fundamental category of human experience which, psychologically speaking, manifests itself wherever consciousness is not yet, or is no longer, effectively centered around the ego."[201] The distancing from the ego in Hasidic thought is double: the mystic first has to negate the ego in order to be able to identify himself with the Nought (in psychoanalytical terms the "self"), while by returning to the world he becomes helpful to the community. The divine Nought, can, therefore, not only be described as a theological intuition or an ontological statement about the ineffable nature of the divine; it can serve at the same time as an expression of the transformative experience of the Hasidic mystic, who has selected from the store of Kabbalistic symbolism that symbol that best serves his own experience. From this point of view, the mystico-magical model overcomes the dichotomy between the prophetic and the mystical as proposed by Heiler. The momentary, or more constant obliteration of the ego, its simplification, serves as a powerful tool for the quasi-prophetic mission of the Hasidic *Ẓaddiq*. He is able to escape time, in his ascent to total atemporal perfection, but he is also able to return in order to act in time. This concept of the *Ẓaddiq,* therefore, implies that he is not only a mystic who acquires magical powers, but also an ecstatic who is able to control his experience by coming back to function as a communal leader. He is able to encounter the *Deus absconditus,* yet leave Him in order to experience *Deus revelatus*.

A very important question related to the status of the above model in Hasidism is its *Sitz im Leben*. Do all the numerous passages quoted above, those referred to in the footnotes, and some others not introduced here reflect only the existence of a topos, a recurring idea about the role of the mystic, or do they reflect a much more social function? Are these discussions an idea, like the Great Chain of Being, or an abstract model, or did they actually shape the mystical life of certain Hasidic masters? Or, to formulate it differently, though the mystico-magical model was indubitably a well-known topic, has it also been a source of inspiration for the Hasidic elite? In the case of Kabbalistic discussions, the more magical aspects were less obvious and the responsibility of the mystic for the emergence of concrete events was, by and large, very vague. Theosophical-theurgical activity was not intended to have an immediate effect on one's surroundings, and though inspiring the spiritual life of many of the Kabbalists, the question of its efficacy was not of pressing concern. The Hasidic master, however, who was less focused on the theurgical aspects of Jewish mysticism, preferred the magical aspect as part of his role as spiritual leader of a community whose expectations, both as a group and as individuals, were fairly concrete. Although the mystical aspect of the model created the relationship between the *Ẓaddiq* and God, the magical aspect represented the responsibility of the leader for the well-being of his followers. Given the fact that this aspect of spiritual life was considered to be attainable by means of the commandments, which attract the spiritual forces, and given the fact that the commandments were performed by the *Ẓaddiq*, there is little room for doubt as to the formative role of this model in the actual religious life of the Hasidic elite. The mystico-magical model in Hasidism reflects a moment in the history of the model when the magical aspect was not only emphasized much more than it had been earlier, both by more explicit formulations and by dint of its recurrence, but also when it became part of the unwritten "communal contract." More than the katabatic model, the anabatic one regulates the relationship between the leader and the group. Thus, it may be concluded that the mystico-magical model indeed informed the self-awareness of the Hasidic elite, and became part of the function of the *Ẓaddiq* in real life. The descriptions above do not take any position as to the efficacy of the righteous as elite magicians; we are asserting only that the new kinds of mystical communities were informed by the dual ability of the righteous to realize the maximum mystical attainment and to help their adherents in ways that were considered effective.

5. EROTIC INTERPRETATIONS OF THE MYSTICO-MAGICAL MODEL

Another important aspect of the Hasidic mystico-magical model is its erotic implications. Like many other forms of mysticism, Jewish mysticism has developed a rich series of erotic images and symbols in order to describe mystical theology and experience. However, though the Kabbalistic contributions to this area of expression were relatively well explored by scholars, the Hasidic erotic imagination has been less elaborated by modern scholarship.[202] There can be no doubt that when compared to the luxuriant Kabbalistic contribution, Hasidic literature is relatively poor as far as this type of religious imagery is concerned. Here we cannot embark on a discussion of Hasidic eroticism, and the following remarks are intended solely to explore the erotic implications of the mystico-magical model. For this purpose I shall present here several passages, and then turn to some other aspects of this issue.[203]

The Besht is quoted by R. Jacob Joseph of Polonoy as proposing that the biblical verse on the female discharge may be interpreted as providing a criterion for determining the gender of the child.[204] However, in the various versions of his interpretation, the Besht has apparently not linked his view to that of the mystico-magical model. Such a nexus is found in a passage of R. Jacob Joseph of Polonoy, who speaks about the sequel of *Mayyim nuqbbin,* the human initiative, which is followed by the *mayyim dukhrim,* the divine influx descending from above.[205] It is in the book of R. Moshe Ḥayyim Ephraim of Sudylkov, the Besht's grandson, *Degel Maḥaneh ʾEfrayim,* that such a nexus becomes evident:

> In comparison to God, blessed be He, all the worlds are as a female versus a male, receiving their vitality from God, and He is like a male in comparison to the worlds, because He emanates the vitality and grace that is called male. Thus, when man wishes to cleave to God, he is elevating the aspect of the "female waters," and on high the aspect of "male waters" are aroused, and the influx and the vitality were born to him and to all the worlds . . . when the higher soul is in man then he wishes to [return to] her source, to God. This is hinted at in the verse [Lev. 12:2] "If the woman discharges," i.e., the soul that is the aspect of a woman and female in relation to the Holy One, blessed be He, discharges" that is, she desires the Holy One, blessed be He, and thereby she discharges the aspect of the "female waters" through the lower arousal from below to above, then [it is written] "then she shall bear a male child," as it is written above that it arouses the grace and life and influx from above downwards, as the aspect of the "male waters."[206]

The mystical impulses of the *Ẓaddiq* are described in classical Kabbalistic terms, such as "female waters" and "lower arousal." However, in most of its theurgical-theosophical sources "female waters" refers to the arousal of the last *sefirah, Malkhut,* when she is sometimes excited by lower energies, stemming from the human sphere, and she then excites the male divine powers, and it is part of the description of the intradivine world. In the Hasidic text it stands for the relationship between the mystic's soul and the divinity, and its ultimate aim is union with God. This is a clear instance of a psychological reading of theosophical terminology. However, in the case of the second phrase, "the lower arousal," the situation is much more complex: in its Zoharic sources and in Lurianic Kabbalah it stands for the lower, human, activity that is impacting the higher activity. Nevertheless, the Hasidic master uses the phrase in a slightly different way than a classical Kabbalist would. While the latter would describe the influence of the lower arousal as the generation of an intradivine dynamic that reflects the human dynamic, the former emphasizes the emergence of a new type of relationship between the divine and the human.[207] In at least one instance, however, again in a discussion of R. Abraham Azulai, the lower arousal, described as "feminine waters," induces the descent of the influx after the attainment of the higher, theosophical union between the divine powers.[208] In other words, while the weight of the term in the Kabbalistic nomenclature is to establish the sexual relationship between the divine powers, in the Hasidic passage it creates an erotic arousal of the divine toward the human. It should, nevertheless, be noticed that the Kabbalistic meaning of the terms did not disappear in Hasidic literature, but the weight of their meaning shifted toward anthropocentrism. Vacillations between the theocentric and anthropocentric poles can be easily detected in some Hasidic discussions.[209]

What seems to be original in the Hasidic interpretation of *devequt* is its presentation as an act of arousal that will be answered by descending acts: influx, grace, and so forth. In fact, these descending entities could be understood as sexual emissions that emerge as the response to the arousal coming from below. In other words, the ascending ecstatic or unitive element is conceived as determining the erotic reaction of the divine, which is represented by the influx. This erotic interpretation is afterward reinterpreted in terms closer to what we have found in the abovementioned masters. The soul recognizes its humble nature and thereby becomes prepared to receive the dwelling of the *Shekhinah* upon the mystic.[210]

There can be no doubt that this manner of exposing the dynamic between the two entities or between the two types of processes is less magical than in the other cases. However, the fact that the biblical verse is used in order to serve as a prooftext for the entire situation implies an organic event that is less erotic than sexual. Less sentimental than classical erotic description in other mystical *corpora,* where longing plays a greater role, the descriptions of the Hasidic master describe a programmed event. God is responding almost automatically to the human arousal. However, by being able to stir the divinity to "ejaculate," the mystic is able to bring down the influx, and is identified with this process; that is, he is conceived as a male: "She shall bear a male child: namely she merits to reach the degree of becoming a male, because by her mediation influxes and life descend upon all the worlds."[211]

Two interesting erotic descriptions of the mystico-magical model occur in the writings of R. Abraham Yehoshuʿa Heschel of Apta and R. Moshe Eliaqum Beriʾah of Kuznitz. It seems that both are independent of the above discussion, and consequently, all three masters reflect earlier traditions. I shall address here only the view of the Rabbi of Apta. In his well known *ʾOhev Yisrael,* this master affirms, in a fashion reminiscent of Jung's anima-animus theory, that

> everything in the world necessarily possesses aspects of male and female. This is especially true in the case of the worshiper of God, who has to possess the aspect of male and that of female . . . namely that of emanator and recipient.[212] The aspect of male means, for example, that which is always emanating; by dint of his holiness and great cleaving and the purity of thought, he emanates a spiritual delight into the supernal lights, worlds and attributes. And he has also a female aspect, namely that which is the recipient and draws down to the lower worlds the influx from the supernal worlds and [draws down] to all [the members of] the community of Israel whatever they need and all kinds of good graces, like "sons, life, and sustenance,"[213] healing, etc.

> The aspect of male causes influx on high and this influx becomes semen[214] and becomes an aspect of male to the female . . . and the female aspect of the *Ẓaddiq* is his faculty of receiving the supernal influx and to draw from above to below all kinds of good things and material issues.[215]

The sexual aspect of the model is here even more explicit than that described earlier; the divine descending power is His semen,[216] which results from the stimulation provoked by the cleaving of the *Ẓaddiq qua* female. The mystical experience is envisioned in these texts not only as a highly individualistic attainment, a spiritual achievement that concerns only the mystic, but a technique to induce a fertile reaction to the lower arousal in the Godhead. In fact, the transformation of the mystic from a female-like to a male-like entity,[217] when he passes from the ascendant to the descendent role, implies a very activist approach; longing for the divine, self-effacement, and annihilation are means of achieving the magical, energetic accomplishments.

The dual nature of the *Ẓaddiq* is important because it may reflect the double nature of the Godhead, which may function both as male and female in relation to the *Ẓaddiq*. So, for example, we learn from certain traditions of the school of the Great Maggid, who was R. Israel of Kuznitz's teacher, that the *Ẓaddiq* induces the emergence of a feminine aspect in the divine. R. Levi Yiẓḥaq adduces in the name of his master, the Great Maggid, the following passage:

> As it is well known, the word *Zʾot* refers to the feminine facet . . . and as we have already mentioned above[218] the quintessence of the worship of God is to cause delight to the Creator, blessed be He, [and] then the Creator has been called as if he is Recipient[219] this being the meaning of the verse: "This came from God" [Psalms 118:23], namely that the Holy One, blessed be He, implies the facet of the female, the facet of *Zʾot,* which is a wondrous thing in our eyes.[220]

The ritual is understood as creating a delight for God, who is now perceived in the aspect of a recipient, namely a feminine entity affected by a masculine one. This inversion of the traditional roles is reminiscent of theurgical activity in the mainstream of Kabbalah, where the divine is deeply affected by human activity.[211] Here, it is not man who enjoys the effect of the worship but the divine *qua* feminine. Indeed in a parallel discussion, God as Creator is described as "if He is the female of the righteous."[222] It should be mentioned that the erotic relation between the righteous man and an aspect of the Godhead is not unknown in Hasidism, where the swaying of the person at prayer were understood in terms of sexual movment.[223] Both the magical and the theurgical models, which assume that after the experience of self-annihilation the mystic enters an other-oriented way of activity, represent patterns of thought and experience that differ conspicuously from the quietist attitude that is indeed expressed, as shown by Schatz-Uffenheimer, in a few cases.[224]

In an interesting passage, R. Aharon of Zhitomir[225] distinguishes between two kinds of *Ẓaddiqim*: the first draws down the influx from above upon himself and all the children of Israel, and may be described by the mystico-magical model; the other, higher kind of *Ẓaddiq* worships God only for the sake of the delight he is able to produce.[226] It is this nonmagical worship that may reflect a conspicuous turn toward an erotic theurgy. In one case, it is obvious that delight is produced by the act of cleaving to God.[227] Because of this delight, God desires to emanate onto the lower world.[228] The sequel of *devequt,* delight, and emanation may be understood, against the background of the above texts, as fraught with erotic overtones.[229]

As seen above, the Hasidic masters were eager to distinguish, in different ways, between two forms of worship: one that starts with human initiative, the lower arousal, and the other that is initiated by God, and is less positive—the supernal arousal.[230] Bearing those distinctions in mind, let us examine an interpretation of a teaching of R. Shneur Zalman of Liady, found in his *Liqqutei Torah*:

> There are two types of worship, from the low to the high consisting of the aspects of run and return[231]. The aspect of *raẓo* is called the protruding seal, that of *shov,* the receding seal. The former aspect is love and "sparks of fire"[232] and desire, the revelation of the hidden love from the low to the high, from Yisrael to the Infinite, blessed be He. . . . [T]his is the lower arousal, the aspect of the *raẓo,* that is, the aspect of the protruding seal, which is the aspect of the existent.[233] However, whoever loves in such a manner draws down the supernal arousal from above in its aspect of the receding seal, namely that the revelation[234] and the lights within the vessels are drawn down . . . The second type of worship, from below to the high, is the aspect of *shov,* namely the total annihilation of the will, the soul becoming as dust, the awe, the shame;[235] this is the aspect of the receding seal from below, and thereby the supernal arousal is drawn down in the aspect of the protruding seal, namely the revelation of the light of the Infinite, without any garment at all. . . . By means of love and performance of the positive commandments, it is impossible to draw from above, from the chain [of being][236] because love is also an aspect of existence and vessel. This is why the revelation and the lights are drawn from above within the vessels.[237]

The erotic expressions related to the two types of seals, love and desire, deal with the ascending type of service, which is done out of love but cannot draw down the influx from the realm of the divine attributes, the chain of the *sefirot,* because the *sefirot* are existent just as human love is. The effect of this service is the entering of the light of the Infinite within the existent. The second type of service, done but of self-effacement, is stronger, as it annihilates the existent and draws down the influx in its purity, without any garment or vessel. Different as these types of worship and their results indeed are, there is a conspicuous common denominator: the human religious attitude, love or annihilation, initiates a divine response, the descent of the "revelation" and "light" with or without the mediation of the vessels. Thus, our model is well represented by both types of worship. The first assumes an activist attitude. The divine is approached with a strong feeling, and the response is a veiled revelation; or, alternatively, the annihilating self is able to induce a total revelation. It seems reasonable to describe the first type of worship as that of a human male toward the divine female, while in the second case, the mystic assumes the role of the female in relation to the divine male. This comparison is invited by the context of the whole discussion, which is part of an interpretation of the verse "Put me on thy heart as a seal" from the Song of Songs. Moreover, it is also explicitly related to a Talmudic passage that asserts that if the woman discharges seed first, then she will bear a male child."[238]

Let me compare the above to the main patterns of erotic imagery in the two major Kabbalistic schools: the theosophical-theurgical and the ecstatic. In the former, the Kabbalist, or the *Ẓaddiqim,* and Moses, played the role of the male in comparison to the divine feminine manifestation, the *Shekhinah,*[239] and it was by means of the performance of the commandments that the impact of the lower on the higher was achieved.[240] In the ecstatic Kabbalah, however, there are many discussions where the Kabbalist, or more precisely his soul or intellect, were conceived as feminine in relation to the higher entities, the Agent Intellect, or God Himself. Elsewhere I have had the opportunity to discuss in detail the erotic language of this kind of Kabbalah:[241] here I would like to present just one example, in order to compare it to the Hasidic treatment of a similar theme, as shown above. In his *ʾImrei Shefer,* Abraham Abulafia distinguishes between

> two kinds of impregnation,[242] that is, two forms which alternate with little difficult and are similar in most respects and in their common use, and which differ in their offspring, to bear fruit similar to themselves. And if the upper one passes on the seed prior to the lower one, which is impregnated, the offspring will be similar to the lower one, possessing the opening, which is called female [*neqevah*] or woman [*ʾishah*]; and she is Eve [*Ḥawah*], because she desired mystical experience, and obliged herself to be material to the upper one, [who] conquers and inscribes himself in his place below, and is rooted and becomes a model to what comes after him, and it sealed in his form and image to protrude out. And when the lower matter comes to him and is connected with him, and embraces and kisses him and is attached and united with him . . . and they become connected to one another, then the latter becomes a concave seal, and her opening is opened. And this is the secret [meaning of] "when this is opened that is shut, and when that is open this is shut. . . ." and if the action is reversed between the two who are giving seed, and the lower matter conquers the upper, then the names formed are four: *ʾAdam* (Adam), *Zakar* (Male), *ʾIsh* (Man), *Ḥayah* (Living Creature); "and no man remembered that unfortunate man." [Ecclesiastes 9:15] And as is the

offspring between the two of them, so is the offspring of [mystical] "prophecy" in the two substances: the lower and upper matter.[243]

This passage is a fine example of the cryptic style of Abraham Abulafia, which is in stark opposition to the far more exoteric expressions of the Hasidic masters. Nor are the details of the thirteenth-century Kabbalist echoed in the Hasidic texts quoted above, despite the fact that they attempt to offer mystical interpretations of the same biblical verse. Although the above text might have influenced a discussion of R. Shneor Zalman of Liady, as has been recently suggested by Bezalel Naor,[244] here I would like to address the phenomenological affinities between the ecstatic Kabbalist and the Hasidic masters, rather than the possible historical links.[245] In both cases the mystic is identified with the female; the unnatural identification may indeed reflect mystical experiences that induced in the mystic the feeling that he has become passive or receptive in relation to God during the experience, or at least during part of it. This type of experience seems to be stronger in both Abulafia and the Hasidic master; it allows a direct encounter with the divine. While for Abulafia the active role of the soul renders the result of the encounter a negative one, in the Hasidic text the effect is less sublime, but in no case is it negative. In other words, the two types of worship discussed above are understood as positive. In fact, the ecstatic emphasis on the soul as feminine, and the theurgical approach to the mystic as male, were integrated as two positive and complementary avenues in Hasidism. Just as the ascending phase is mystical and the descending one is magical, so also the ascending one reflects the ecstatic understanding of the status of the mystic, whereas the descending one represents the magical phase and envisions the *Ẓaddiq* as male.

One final remark is necessary in order to understand the centrality of the erotic implications of Hasidism. One of the most common terms in Hasidic literature is *Taʿanug,* "delight." It recurs thousands of times in a large variety of sources, and any understanding of Hasidic thought must take this ubiquity into consideration. At least in some cases, the divine delight has some erotic overtones, as seen above. However, I would like to note a certain role this term fulfills in comparison to the earlier stages of Jewish mystical literature. In ecstatic Kabbalah, especially as it was formulated by Abraham Abulafia, God does not react, enjoy, or respond to the human worship of mystical attainments. However, in the Rabbinic and theosophical-theurgical literature, there occurs the assumption that by human worship, or performance of the divine will, God's power can be increased. This is one of the crucial moments in certain Rabbinic attempts to explain the meaning of ritual, and this line was amplified in the theosophical-theurgical school of Kabbalah. In Hasidism, *Taʿanug,* the delight of God in the deeds of men, occupies a similar position to that of the idea of power occupied in the previous phases of Jewish thought. Namely, instead of providing the divine dynamis with additional energy, as many of the Kabbalists understood their mystical and theurgical task, the Hasidim assume that their role is to cause delight or pleasure. The Great Maggid asserts that

> when [the sons of] Israel perform the will of the Place [i.e. God], they are adding delight on the high. . . . [W]hen Israel are repenting and cause the return of everything to its source, they add delight on high.[246]

In lieu of the relatively mechanical concept of the Deity on the part of the theosophical Kabbalists, which provoked the negative reactions even of accomplished Kabbalists like Sabbatai Ẓevi, Hasidic thought preferred a much more personal concept, as the kinds of erotic imagery discussed above amply demonstrate. By emphasizing the idea of the drawing down of the divine influx, and the possibility of distributing it to the community, the descriptions of the more passive experience of the Hasidic masters are highly complicated. While the theosophical-theurgical Kabbalist emphasizes his contribution of power to the divine infrastructure and the induction of a higher harmony as the vital quality of his mystical religiosity, the mystico-magical model emphasizes the reception of power in lieu of its channeling upward. Less a contributor, the Hasidic mystic is a recipient of power. While the theosophical-theurgical model turns its focus on the intradivine processes and ecstatic Kabbalah gravitates about the mystical experience, that is, on the divine psyche, the Hasidic mystico-magical model turns its attention to what happens a) in the divine—the induction of delight; b) in the psyche—the various forms of mystical communion and union with God; and c) on the communal and cosmic levels.

6. PHILOSOPHICAL INTERPRETATIONS

As mentioned above, one of the standard Hasidic designations for God is "Nought." Although not new to the eighteenth-century masters, the use of this term to refer to God is nevertheless characteristic of Hasidic parlance, apparently because it became a decisive term in matters of inner human processes, in particular the process of "annihilation." Man has to obliterate his illusion of separate existence, which is the experience of his normal state of consciousness, and recognize his total dependence upon the Nought. Only after such an experience of nullification does the *Ẓaddiq* return to the realm of existence enriched by the divine energies that he will draw down. This process was portrayed in several discussions from the circle of the Great Maggid in terms that are reminiscent of Aristotelian physics and metaphysics. Indeed, they constitute a separate type of understanding of the mystico-magical model, distinct from the erotic and entrance-exit readings of the model.

With respect to the concept of Ḥabad, analyzed above, where the active mystic is able to leave his imprint (the protruding seal) on the Infinite (the receding seal), R. Levi Yiẓḥaq of Berdichev also assumes the possibility of shaping the infinite potentiality by imprinting a certain form on it. He follows the Great Maggid's fascination with the metaphysical Nought, a notion that is influenced, as R. Levi Yiẓḥaq indicated, by the *Commentary on Sefer Yeẓirah* attributed to Rabad.[247] The view of God as both the Nought and as potentiality is rather interesting from the theological point of view: man is conceived here as the shaper of God, which means that he is able to draw the influxes where he needs them. What is the precise meaning of this drawing, in relation to the service by "Nought"? The answer is supplied by R. Levi Yiẓḥaq himself:

> The Nought is the most general category of all the wisdoms,[248] because it is a potential power that may receive [every] form.[249] And when man wants to cause the descent of wisdom from there, as well as anything else, it depends only upon the will of man, because if he wants to worship God he can draw down [Him] upon himself.[250]

Commandments,[251] like words and letters, are tools that ensure the descent of the influx upon the worshiper; they cause the influx to descend.[252] Since the commandments correspond to all the limbs of man, the performance of the maximum number of commandments corresponds to the attraction of the divine influx upon each and every limb. In fact, the Hasidic rabbi indicates that the *ḥiyyut,* namely the vitality or the life-force of each and every limb depends upon the commandment related to it. The attachment to the Nought is, therefore, the encounter with the unshaped prime-energy, the pure potentiality, while worship by means of the commandments signifies the actualization of the divine potential by drawing the divine into the mundane world, upon the human body. It should be emphasized that the potentiality related to the Nought may reflect the lower status of this type of experience, in contrast to conferring forms or actualizing some energy or luminosity by the performance of the commandments. Elsewhere, R. Levi Yiẓḥaq speaks about the possibility of transcending the "concentrated influx," and the cleaving to the unshaped power is mentioned. Perhaps it can be said that the dedication that enables someone to cleave to the Nought is actually a dissolving of the individual in an attempt to transcend the stage of creation by concentration of the influx in limited structures. According to this passage, Abraham loses his name while clinging to the influx.[253]

Another version of the theme *ʾAyin-Hyle* is found in R. Abraham the Angel's view of the righteous person. With this author, the *Ẓaddiq* himself becomes "nought" and *hyle* because he serves as the medium of the divine revelation and of miracles to the entire people of Israel.[254] This use of the *hyle* image may point to an understanding of the Nought as expansion, as we have seen in some of the texts analyzed above. The *hyle* is, after all, matter that does not possess a form, a limiting definition; it is the potentiality open to all forms. It is the extension of all the possibilities, rather than their annihilation. However, the passivity implied in this hylic view of the divine is obvious and differs from the view of R. Levi Yiẓḥaq, with regard to the divine *hyle* that is shaped by man's act. In comparison to the activist version discussed above, a quietist attitude is reflected in this way of thought.

Although these two ways of speaking about the *Ẓaddiq's* contact with the Nought differ, they may still reflect a larger scheme that includes both of them, one that fits the mystico-magical model we are describing here. If R. Abraham the Angel's "annihilation" of the *Ẓaddiq* represents an initial stage, or the mystical part of the model, the shaping of the divine Naught and bringing down the influx may represent the magical aspect of the model. In any case, the annihilation and the encounter with the unshaped divine forces are the two poles of experience that constitute the model under consideration here. Indeed, such a representation of the whole mystico-magical model, emphasizing the issue of psychic annihilation and the divine as the supernal Nought, is found in a succinct discussion by the founder of the Ḥabad movement. He describes the worshiper as

> changing his nature, which means the annihilation of existence, and changing the existence into Nought, and by means of this [change] he draws down from the aspect of "Out of Nought it [namely the existence] will emerge."[255]

Last but not least, the influx drawn down by the *Ẓaddiq* is described in one instance as "hylic," namely as an undifferentiated flow of "spiritual force" received by the *Ẓaddiq* during his prayer. This flow is not particularized and induces, according to R. Barukh of Kossov, a feeling of delight. Only after the end of the worship does this hylic flow receive the form of the preoccupation of the mystic: it may become instrumental in his winning some money or attaining spiritual insights; it may even become physical force, if strength is needed.[256] In any case, the assumption is that the supreme unified energy takes the precise form of the recipient's preoccupation.

7. ON SPIRITUALITY AND POWER

It is of paramount importance to be aware of a fascination in Hasidism with the concept of power as an integral part of the mystico-magical model. Even the most spiritually powerful of the Hasidic masters were aware of their nothingness, which, they recognized, was precisely what allowed them to fulfill their powerful role. R. Yisrael of Ryzhin answered those who asked him the meaning of his being a "*gutter yud*"[257] by saying, "I am not a *gutter yud*, but I myself am nothing [*ʾAyin*] . . . And whoever speaks about me just as he speaks about God,[258] he will be punished[259] in this world and in the next one."[260]

Thus, the power with which a master was invested by his flock, and even his special status, did not distract from the self-awareness of nothingness.[261] A similar feeling is expressed in a story related to another classical thaumaturge among the Hasidic *Ẓaddiqim*, the Seer of Lublin.[262] Indeed, the move toward a concern with power is obvious and crucial for Hasidism in general, and it becomes more conspicuous with the strengthening of the institution of the *Ẓaddiq*. However, seen within the more general framework of the magical-mystical model, it may be understood as more than a mere lust for power. In any case, crucial for the proper understanding of Hasidism is the awareness that though the mystico-magical model was almost uniformly related to the person, and later onto the institution, of the *Ẓaddiq,* that is, with an elite, the magical model—namely the view that it is possible to draw down the divine influx and in some cases even the divinity by means of ritual language without always resorting to extreme mystical attainments, is quite widespread in Hasidic sources, as we shall see in the next two chapters. Therefore, we must look at the relationship of various social strata to different aspects of the model. The simpler Hasidim were taught that, in principle, the divine influx could be attracted and captured with and within linguistic and ritualistic acts, although one assumes that this attainment had more of a personal than a communal impact. In other words, the *Ẓaddiq* was considered to be a specialist more because of his mystical capacity to attain a deep adherence, or extreme union, with God than because of his ability to capture the divine power. Indeed, I assume that as a specialist, the *Ẓaddiq* was also conceived as able to channel that power more than the average person. We primarily analyzed here documents stemming from the higher Hasidic elite, and there is no doubt that there is an emphasis in them on the importance of the role of the *Ẓaddiq*.

However, less extreme forms of the mystico-magical model, which do not refer to the *Ẓaddiq* at all, may also be detected relatively early in the history of Hasidism. An interesting example in this direction is R. Aharon Shemuel ha-Kohen's *Ve-Ẓiva ha-Kohen,* a book written by someone well acquainted with both the Great Maggid and R. Pinḥas of Koretz.[263] Himself a member of the elite—he served as a rabbi in several significant communities in Poland and wrote halakhic books—and apparently also immersed in Kabbalistic studies, R. Aharon Shemuel ha-Kohen mentions the mystico-magical model several times without emphasizing the concept of the *Ẓaddiq*. So, for example, he writes:

> The goal of man's coming to this lower world is to adapt himself to[264] Torah and commandment[s], which are a ladder that stands on earth and the top of which reaches to Heaven,[265] in order to draw down, by his performing the Torah and commandment[s], influx upon all the worlds, and to give power to the supernal retinue.[266]

Theurgy, mentioned in the final clause, is combined here with the attraction of the influx into the extra-deical world by means of the ritual and study of the Torah. However, the mystical part of the mystico-magical model appears to be represented by the concept of the ladder, which symbolizes the notion that the student reaches heaven by his religious behavior. Indeed, immediately after the above passage, the author mentions the cleaving of the scholar on high as part of the drawing down of "the vitality and influx."[267] From our vantage point, it is crucial to point out that these discussions are related to the goal of man and not of the *Ẓaddiq*. Therefore, it is a quite democratic model.

A comparison of the evolution of concepts related to sanctity in Christianity and Judaism is quite illuminating. The starting point in Christianity was an identity between the sanctity and power of kings, princes, and leaders; as it was formulated in the eleventh century, "sanctity was power and power was holy."[268] Only later on did "Christ-like humility" come to the fore and become dominant.[269] In Judaism it seems that the concept of power connected to sanctity in late antiquity, namely that found in Rabbinic literature, was somewhat attenuated by the more intellectual approach of the Middle Ages, though it never disappeared. It has resurged in a powerful manner in the mystico-magical model adopted by the Hasidic masters. The split between lay power and sanctity in Christianity, though not total, remained crucial; in Judaism, where the leadership consisted very often of the spiritual leaders, such a split could rarely take place. The synthesis between them has, in fact, been buttressed by those elements of the magical model that were integrated into Jewish mysticism.

The learned and more popular traditions about the magical powers of the founders of various trends of Jewish mysticism are well known. R. Abu Aharon of Bagdhad, who is conceived of as the person who brought mystical treatises from the East to Europe, the attribution of magical concerns, and even writings, to no other than the paragon of Jewish philosophy, Maimonides, the legends about R. Eleazar of Worms and Naḥmanides, the occult powers attributed to R. Yiẓḥaq Luria in so many legends, demonstrate that the holy man in Judaism was oftenly enwrapped in a magical cloak. From this point of view, there is some truth in the cultural image that R. Qalonimus Qalman Epstein expresses, in the text which will be analysed in Appendix C, that the transmission of power is a long tradition in Judaism. Indeed, S. Sharot has already correctly emphasized in the importance of the magic aspect in the Hasidic leadership and viewed it as one of the main reasons of its success.[270] I would, however, put the accent on the recurrence of the magical motifs throughout the history of Jewish history, Hasidism being the most outstanding example of the floruit of this type of attitude on a larger scale than earlier. It would suffice to explore some of the developments in more recent forms of devotion in Judaism in order to see that this observation is not a matter of the past.

The above analyses assume that a systemic approach to developments in Jewish mysticism, which can explain later developments in Hasidism, is better served by a more experiential starting point than it is by theoretical-theological premises. Magic and ecstasy, the material and the spiritual attainments, encompass, in their various aspects, phenomena of intense religious life, and the focus on the manner in which they interact seems to me to provide a better, though not exclusive, explanation of one major aspect of Hasidic religiosity than the theological premises do. Therefore, let ua analyze two major types of Jewish practice as understood by the Hasidic masters: prayer and study of the Torah.

Part II
Drawing Down

The general view of the relationship between magic and religions has been that the latter is the outcome of the former. Although this view, whose most famous exponent was none other than James G. Frazer, is to some extend simplistic, we may allow a certain importance to the axial changes that stress the importance of the individual and spiritual over the collective and material. In terms of verbal worship, this change can be described, as Marett has done, as a move from "spell" to prayer. Examining the various versions of Jewish mysticism, we can add an additional stage. Vocal prayer has been regarded as fraught with deeper meaning by various medieval Jewish mystical theories. A certain interiorization took place: the mystical intention, the inner dimension of prayer, became a vehicle of the influx rather than the verbal aspect, which was envisioned as a vehicle of the spiritual. From this perspective, the impact of prayer is achieved more through the intense channeling of human powers than the powerful performance of the liturgy. This is the main contribution of medieval Jewish mysticism as far as prayer is concerned. In order to explain the path of this influx the medieval mystics used a very complex theosophical structure that functioned as a map for the correlations between the text of prayer and the supernal powers that should be addressed and affected by the one who prays.

The Hasidic way of prayer emerged after the proliferation of an extraordinarily complex theology and a tenuous type of practice, especially as represented by the Lurianic system. The main movement in the Hasidic theory of prayer is a turning from mental, interiorized performance to a much simpler and vocally oriented version of prayer. Although preserving the more spiritual requirements for the ideal prayer, as a divestment of corporeality, the Hasidic masters also emphasized the oral aspect of prayer as a major creative component, one that minimalizes the mental quality of prayer and restores the glory of the prayer as production of sounds. In a sense, Hasidism is a return from prayer to spells. Implicitly, this meant a weakening of Lurianic theory and practice, and some evidence in this direction is pertinent to understanding the return of a model of prayer that was already in existence in several circles of Jewish mystics. In other words, the mystico-magical model may be regarded, when related to prayer, as a combination of two religious modalities—those described by Friedrich Heiler as the mystical and the prophetic. The more depersonalized attitude of mystical religiosity is paralleled by the mystical part of the model, while the descending facet, which means the return to society in order to impart the influx and abundance, would correspond to prophetic religiosity.

Closely related to this transformation of prayer is the study of the Torah. An eminently intellectual undertaking, Torah study also gave rise, through the ages, to deeper emotional and even ecstatic moments. In Hasidism there was a deepending of this emotional element, and in many cases the study of the very complex texts was conceived as a mystical path, and as a way, like prayer, to draw down the influx from above. In practice, this meant, again as in the case of prayer, an atomization of the studied text and a magical belief in the canonical text as a sacrosanct talisman.

Last but not least, one of the ideals of Jewish religion, the scholar, who studies the Torah and prays in a perfect way, was fused with the ideal of the mystical and magical *Ẓaddiq*. Like prayer and study, the *Ẓaddiq,* too, was conceived as efficacious when he was able to ensure the descent of the supernal influx. In other words, it is the concept of power, which means in this context the capacity to bring down the divine energy, that moves to the center of the mystical preoccupation in Hasidism.

These three transformations—which affected major issues in Judaism—are characteristic of and congenial to Hasidism, but they did not emerge with it. In all three cases important antecedents will be presented and analyzed, attempting to put these metamorphoses into a large perspective, namely, the broader history of Jewish mysticism; we are especially interested in the repercussions of the magical model through either the mediation of Cordoverian writings or other channels. In the following discussion an emphasis on the magical will become evident, especially in the chapter on prayer. This does not mean that the phenomenon of the *Ẓaddiq,* or the study of the Torah did not involve more mystical elements. This will become evident in Chapter five, as well as in the two appendices. However, I will not take up the issue of mystical prayer in Hasidism here, since it is an issue upon which those scholars who have studied it separately agree.

4

Mystical and Magical Prayer in Hasidism

1. EIGHTEENTH-CENTURY ATTITUDES TO LURIANIC *KAVVANOT*

One of the most interesting features of the Hasidic modus vivendi is its way of praying. This is also the case in Lurianic Kabbalah, which had its special version of mystical intentions. However, despite the importance of prayer in Jewish ritual in general and in Jewish mysticism in particular, there is hardly any attempt by the Hasidic masters to encourage mystical prayer as described in Lurianic sources. In fact, from its very beginnings, Hasidism minimalized the importance of the Lurianic theurgic technique of *kavvanot* in favor of a more devotional form of prayer.[1] This abrogation of the Lurianic way of prayer had a clear antecedent: Sabbatai Ẓevi never used Luria's *kavvanot,* and Nathan of Gaza viewed it as an unsuitable religious practice in the Messianic era. Scholars who have dealt with the similarity between these two abrogations have differed on the possibility of an historical affinity between them. Joseph Weiss maintained that there is "no historical connection[2] between the two parallel phenomena," a view also affirmed by Schatz-Uffenheimer.[3] Yehuda Liebes' research indicates that the affinity between the Sabbatean and Hasidic rejection of *kavvanot* is greater than previously thought. In both cases the reason for this rejection was the ineffectiveness of Lurianic *kavvanot* in clearing the praying man's consciousness of alien thoughts.[4] It would therefore be instructive to analyze other negative attitudes toward Lurianic prayer,[5] in order to enrich our discussion with regard to Hasidic discontent with Luria's *kavvanot.* As we shall see, the comparison of the Hasidic abrogation of *kavvanot* to Sabbateanism in the second half of the eighteenth century is only one of several significant comparisons that can be proposed.

A very curious attitude toward *kavvanot,* apparently in the Lurianic vein, is found in R. Elijah ha-Kohen of Smyrna. In his *Midrash Talpiyot*[6] he stresses the fact that Satan tries to disturb the prayer of those who use *kavvanot,* and thus, since alien thoughts are prone to be attracted and to intervene, it is necessary to renounce this way of praying. The prayers therefore concentrate either on earthly things, in which Satan was not interested, or on subjects related to the study of Torah, thereby deterring the possibility of being attacked by alien thoughts; however, one had to pray without *kavvanot*. The Kabbalistic way of prayer, though it was considered superior to the conventional one, had therefore to be postponed because of these demonic attacks, which were directed primarily at the elite.[7] R. Elijah's view differs from Nathan of Gaza's rejection of Lurianic *kavvanot*;[8] the former conceived the present period as imperfect, since Satan has the power to disturb even the prayers of the perfect; the latter, however, considered his period close to perfection, making the performance of Lurianic *kavvanot* no longer necessary. Emden, a fierce enemy of Sabbateanism and an adversary of Hasidism, firmly rejected the use of Lurianic *kavvanot*.[9]

> I did not read the book *Mishnat Ḥasidim* at all, since, in my view, the author collected it from the writings of the Ari. However, I say and command to my sons and my descendants, my lovers and friends, and whomever is obeying my orders: I decree and prohibit praying according to *Mishnat Ḥasidim*, or [to use] a manuscript named "Prayer according to Luria's writings," by R. M[eir] Poppers, since it has not been compiled either by Luria or R. Ḥayyim Vital, his student. Even the book *Kavvanot* by the Ari was not composed for the purpose of using the *kavvanot* de facto, but only to study them. And even if Luria, and likewise his students, could use the *kavvanot* during prayer, in the way he taught them, in any case nowadays the understanding of people is limited, and whoever will use the *kavvanot*, his understanding will doubtless be confused and he will certainly lose more than he intended to profit. Therefore I warn and admonish the people who are listening to my voice not to attempt to achieve grand and marvelous things, surpassing them; would that they be able to use the more general *kavvanot*, which I have arranged in a clear fashion in my prayer book. Do not think that I defame Luria's works, God forbid; our generation is not worthy of that [i.e. the *kavvanot*], until the [Divine] Spirit will descend from above; now, because of our sins, we are not worthy, and therefore let no one say, "I shall multiply the use of *kavvanot* and will not turn aside," since he will deceive himself, because all of the works of Luria were falsified, and all copies contain a multitude of errors and scribal mistakes. I have seen with my [own] eyes, a prayer of Luria in the hands of a quasi-Hasid, and it is full of serious and not small errors, but he does not sense it. Therefore, intelligent men, hear me and do not desire to ascend and fly to heaven without wings,[10] since you will surely fall . . . and it is better [to have] a bit of fear of God, [since] He[11] prefers the intention of the heart. Let Him be your hope.

Emden, like some of the Sabbateans, abrogated the Lurianic *kavvanot*, but for diametrically different reasons. Nathan of Gaza rejected Luria's *kavvanot* because he considered his epoch to be the age of the messiah, whereas Emden viewed his days as unworthy of Luria's way of prayer; he implicitly indicates that this way may be suitable in the Messianic period. Furthermore, in Emden's eyes the versions of Luria's writings are so corrupt that any use of them is dangerous, and simple prayer, with good intentions, is preferable to Lurianic *kavvanot*. Emden's testimony, as well as his recommendation, is corroborated by a passage in R. Shemuel ben Eliezer of Kalvaria's *Darkhei No*ᶜ*am,* a work written around 1760. Describing the prayer of unspecified Kabbalists, he asserts that their

> prayer books are manuscripts and they were copied from one copy to another, and the *Kabbalah* or the [Divine] Names written above a word change their place from one word to the another, and those of one word are transposed upon another and vice versa, and God's glory is despised. And they [the prayerbooks] are full of mistakes, almost at each word, and their owners are not able to correct their faults, since they are ignorance and cannot distinguish between good and bad which they prepared [namely the prayerbooks], and it would be better for them not to pray at all, like the gentiles around them, than to pray from the prayerbooks before their eyes.[12]

This criticism is directed at those who prepared for themselves prayerbooks with Lurianic *kavvanot* without a solid Kabbalistic education.[13] According to the evidence of Emden and R. Shemuel, the infiltration of the Lurianic way of praying at the end of the first half of the eighteenth century constituted a theological problem,[14] and both of them viewed the erroneous practice of Lurianic *kavvanot* as worse than not praying at all, or praying with simple prayer. The tacit assumption is that using a corrupt text may have a pernicious influence on the supernal divine powers. Interestingly, it was the view that the peculiar arrangement of the words of prayer was intended by the men of the Great Assembly to influence the *Sefirot,* whereas the rationale of the Lurianic *kavvanot* was used in order to diminish the practical importance of the men of the Assembly by putting them on a pedestal. R. Ḥayyim of Volozhin was a connoisseur of the Lurianic system and a fervent devotee of the theurgic *kavvanot*.[15] In the manner of Luria's Kabbalah, he asserts that the elders and prophets who formed the Great Assembly comprehended the structure of the supernal worlds through their prophetic faculty by means of the Divine Spirit and instituted the blessings and prayers in such a fashion that their words could modify the configurations of the supernal worlds. R. Ḥayyim implies that the power to change these worlds is inherent in the exact arrangement of the words. He did not mention in this context that the *kavvanot* are necessary for the attainment of the theurgic operations. Moreover, he approvingly quotes a highly significant passage from R. Joseph Qaro's *Maggid Meisharim*:

> As the *Maggid* said to the author of *Beit Yosef,* in the second warning, . . . be careful not to think any thought during prayer, even [thoughts] connected to Torah and *Miẓwot*; [concentrate] solely on the words of prayer. See that his words are not mentioned [so as] to intend the meaning of the words, since indeed the deep inner sense of the meaning of prayer is unknown to us. Even if some of the meanings of prayer were revealed to us by our ancient rabbis,

> blessed by their memory, until the last [of them] . . . the Ari, blessed be his memory, who exceeded [everyone] in his creation of wonderful *kavvanot,* [these meanings] are no more than a drop in comparison with the sea with respect to the deep inner meaning of the members of the Great Assembly, who instituted prayer.[16]

Therefore the inner structure of prayer includes a multitude of esoteric significances and theurgic values, of which only a small part have been transmitted to us, even by Luria himself; this perspective explains why we may ignore the Lurianic *kavvanot,* or *kavvanot* in general, and why the authority of a Maggid is invoked in order to strengthen this view. The main contribution to the words he pronounces of the person who prays is his spiritual preparation and his intention to achieve union with God by means of the words of prayer.[17] Lurianic *kavvanot* are conceived as valuable and influential, but their contribution, nevertheless, is viewed as negligible.

2. HASIDIC VIEWS OF *KAVVANOT*

A similar appreciation of the Lurianic *kavvanot* to that of R. Ḥayyim, a great opponent of the Hasidim, is perceptible in the Great Maggid of Miedzyrec, who writes in one passage:

> He who uses in prayer all the *kavvanot* knows that he can do no more than use the *kavvanot* that are known to him. But when he says each word with great attachment,[18] all the *kavvanot* are by that very fact included, since each and every pronounced letter[19] is an entire world. When he utters the word with great attachment, surely those upper worlds are awakened, and thus he thereby accomplishes great actions. Therefore, a man should see to it that he prays with great attachment and enthusiasm. Then he will certainly accomplish great actions in the upper worlds, for each pronounced letter awakens [things that are] above.[20]

The Great Maggid recognized, as did R. Ḥayyim of Volozhin a few decades later, that the theurgic nature of words of prayer does not depend upon the awareness of the details of the *kavvanot* inherent in them;[21] moreover, both agree that we are conscious of only a part of these *kavvanot.* However, the views of the two masters differ in other ways. Here we shall focus on an issue that seems crucial. R. Ḥayyim speaks about words of prayer as the primary element of prayer; the Great Maggid considers the sound of these words, which are all-inclusive entities, as the most significant element. It seems that we are confronted here with a monadic perception of sounds that changes them into a microcosm worthy of a particular act of contemplation and attachment. The statement "each and every pronounced letter is an entire world" deserves a more detailed explanation.

The Besht recommends that

during your prayer and your study [of the Torah] you shall comprehend and unify each and every speech and utterance of your lips, since in each and every [pronounced] letter, there are worlds and souls and divinity and they ascend and combine and unify with each other and with the Godhead and afterward they [the sounds] combine and unify in a perfect union with the Godhead, and the soul [i.e. your soul] will be integrated [into the Godhead] with them.[22]

Thus, it is evident that the Great Maggid adopted a view already at least partially present in the teachings of his master. In these passages, the monadic nature of the pronounced letters is explicit: each has to be contemplated and continues, independently, its way upward; only later do they combine into a word. It is worthwhile comparing this perception of the founders of Hasidism with that of one of their contemporaries, R. Nathan-Neta^{c} of Sieniawa,[23] the author of the commentary on the prayerbook *^{c}Olat Tamid*.[24]

Sometimes, when a person recites the verses of the Psalms, a voice is stirred up for him, [namely] a voice to him, and this is from his [own] soul, for out of his joy a great voice enters him, to urge the love of lovers. This happens sometimes even when the person does not known the intention [*kavvanah*—of the words]; his soul knows and is enjoying a spiritual delight. In the *Qeri $^{\supset}$at Shema ^{c}*, as well, a person brings upon himself, with each and every [pronounced] letter, light to the soul [and to] the 248 limbs.[25] And it is incumbent [upon the worshiper] to pray with intention [as concerns] each and every [pronounced] letter, since [he] hints to the supernal worlds, by each letter [pronounced] in holiness.

The affinities of this passage to Hasidic thought are numerous.[26] Here, I would like only to point out the similarity between the emphasis upon the utterance of each letter and the lights resting upon man.[27] The letters are, according to this author, "lights and supernal worlds." Again, it seems that the process of treating the words as monads is essential for a proper mystical prayer that intends to invest the person with spiritual forces. The view of R. Nathan-Neta^{c} about the aim of prayer is similar to that of the Hasidic masters—to cause the descent of higher entities:

By means of prayer we cause the holiness to descend from above; hence, everyone has to intend, by his prayer, to cause the holiness to descend from above to overflow into his soul.[28]

These similarities notwithstanding, the passages quoted from *^{c}Olat Tamid* omit the main characteristic of the texts we shall discuss below, where the utterance of the letters of prayer creates palaces or vessels into which the supernal influx is attracted downward. Again, according to the Great Maggid, who probably follows a Beshtian tradition,[29]

> when he [man] speaks with knowledge, then "and by knowledge shall the chambers[30] be filled" [Prov. 24: 4], since he causes the presence of the Godhead,[31] may He be blessed, into the [pronounced] letters, and when he brings the Godhead into them, everything is in them.

The monadic view is a result of two different actions: the separation of the utterance into discrete sounds, and the incorporation into them of the Godhead. Let us begin with an analysis of the sources and views of two great masters of Hasidism. The unearthing of the sources will yield a better understanding of the real meaning of Hasidic prayer and the way it emerged. It will show the emphasis in Hasidic mysticism on the vocal aspect of prayer, that is, on the pronounced letters rather than on contemplation of the written letters. This emphasis on the oral nature of prayer, which is in complete accordance with *halakhic* regulations, has been rather neglected by the modern study of Hasidism. Its significance is that it constitutes the response the Hasidic masters proposed to the Lurianic *kavvanot* in prayer. It is probable that there was no total and overt rejection of the Lurianic way of prayer; it was still considered by the Great Maggid as "applicable to all,"[32] though R. Eleazar ben R. Elimelekh of Lisansk, the son of one of his most important disciples, distinguished—in a manner reminiscent of R. Meshullam Phoebus of Zbarazh's perception of Lurianic Kabbalah[33]—between the Lurianic *kavvanot* intended solely for *Ẓaddiqim* and the use of the ancient Ashkenazi prayerbook by the masses.[34]

3. PRE-HASIDIC MONADIC VIEWS

It is, therefore, only natural to look for the sources of Hasidic references to prayer in the Cordoverian treatises, especially those dealing with the meaning of *kavvanah*.[35] Such research convincingly demonstrates that key concepts that were considered to be Hasidic stem from Cordovero, who served as an intermediary between earlier, magical sources and Hasidism. The proper understanding of the Hasidic way of prayer is closely connected to the unearthing of the evolution of certain concepts and the formulation they received means of Cordovero's writings.[36] We shall focus our attention in the remainder of this chapter on the sources of some Hasidic notions related to prayer. The contribution of these sources, however, goes beyond the question of Hasidic prayer, for they were also extremely important in the elucidation of Hasidic motifs concerning *Talmud Torah*, the *Ẓaddiq*, and so forth. These subjects will be taken up in subsequent chapters.

Let us turn to a brief description of the view of letters as worlds, and then to their delineation as vessels or palaces. In the monadic perception of the Hebrew letters, which is apparently an ancient view, the letters are often personified, each of them being attributed by God with a particular character.[37] An ancient text of the Heikhalot literature, *Heikhalot Zutarti*, maintains that "the twenty-two letters are twenty-two [divine] names formed out of one letter of the Torah."[38] According to the *Pesiqta Rabbati*,[39] "Every letter of the Tetragrammaton forms a plurality [*ẓava*ʾ] that corresponds to the whole name." Each of the letters of the Tetragrammaton is similarly viewed as a divine Name in an anonymous commentary on the *Havdalah de-Rabbi* ʿ*Aqiva*:[40] "The Tetragrammaton is mentioned at the beginning of the periscope, and the letters of this name, each and every one of them, is a [divine] name when it is written separately . . . since each and every letter is a [divine] name in itself."

An interesting parallel is found in one of R. Abraham Abulafia's works; in his commentary to his own *Sefer ha-Meliẓ* he asserts:[41]

> Raziel intended to announce to us His Name, may He be blessed, according to the occult way, in order to bring us near to Him, may His Name be blessed, . . . and he divided the words and sometimes set one letter aside, as if it were a whole word in order to announce that according to the Kabbalah each and every letter is a separate world. And he ordered those who see[42] this divine and marvelous power to acknowledge His Name, may He be blessed.

The letters referred to here are those of the Tetragrammaton, but Abulafia did not limit this atomization into single letters of the Tetragrammaton; he considered this technique to be a comprehensive way of mystically understanding the texts—the climax of seven ways of interpretation. The description of the last of these seven includes the sentence:[43] "each and every letter [of the biblical verse] by itself, stands separate." This way of dividing the verses culminates in a state of cleaving to the All in which man receives power to perform miracles.[44] Furthermore, the atomistic approach to the written letters has a significant parallel with regard to their utterance;[45] in a magical fragment that is very close to Abulafia's *Ḥayyei ha-* ʿ*Olam ha-Ba*ʾ, the author writes:[46]

> It is necessary to know how it [the Divine Name] is read during its pronunciation, since each and every letter has to be pronounced during one single breath, as if the spirit is going out of the person [who pronounces it] with a high voice. The result of this practice is "to receive the influx of wisdom and [the power] of creation."[47]

The magical nature of the loud pronunciation of a single sound in a very discrete way is obvious and it may be relevant for a better understanding of Abulafia's view in the commentary to his *Sefer ha-Meliẓ* and elsewhere, as well as for the evaluation of the period when magical practices infiltrated the Kabbalah. In his mystical handbook, ʾ*Or ha-Sekhel,* the same author describes the process of pronunciation of the letters of the Divine Name: "Then play the *ḥiriq* that extends downward and [it] draws downward the supernal force in order to cause it to cleave to you."[48] Abulafia thus explicitly indicates that his technique is intended to collect or attract spiritual power to the person who permutates the letters. The exact nature of this supernal force is not clear; it may be connected to astral bodies, though this is not a necessary interpretation.

The context of this quotation mentions the enwrapping of the mystic with a *talit* and putting on the *tephillin,* so that the ritual of pronunciation of letters has the external features of the morning prayer.[49] Indeed, in a commentary on prayer composed in Abulafia's period, and presumably by one of his disciples,[50] we learn about a combination of the concepts of prayer and permutation of letters; the purpose of this combinations reminds one of Abulafia's *ʾOr ha-Sekhel.* The anonymous Kabbalist recommends:[51]

> The person who prays has to transfer his *kavvanah* onto the two lower alphabets in order to draw downward the blessing from the fountain of the source of life to the other *Sefirot,* onto each and every letter[52] from the letters of the [two] alphabets, . . . and the person who blesses has to move his head[53] in order to show the drawing down of the blessing from above.

The anonymous author, hints, like Abulafia, at the descent of the influx, which is allegorized by the movement of the head. Unlike Abulafia, however, he explicitly introduces the term *kavvanah* in order to describe the synthesis between the liturgical ritual and a mystical technique very similar to that of Abulafia.

4. LETTERS, PRAYER, AND SPIRITUAL FORCE IN PRE-HASIDIC SOURCES

In a Kabbalistic text that was probably composed in the fourteenth century, we learn of the combinations of letters in explicit connection with astral magic:[54]

> If the Creator will decree, He will decree to cause the influence of the force of the success of this combination, [and] the zodiac and the planets will reveal to you their forces and their nature and [you] operate through them.

Let us turn our attention now to a term that is missing in Abulafia's own works, but occurs several times in books written by Kabbalists who were influenced by him: the term *ruḥaniyyut*—"spiritual force" or "spirituality." The sources of this term are Sabian Arabic texts, which use *ruḥaniyyut* in order to designate the supernal forces or lights. Because of the centrality of this concept for the following discussion, as well as for the understanding of the Hebrew terminology used later in Kabbalah and Hasidism, let me quote at length Shelomo Pines' description of this concept as it appears in al-Shahrastani's *Kitab al-Milal wa ʾl-Niḥal*:

> Intermediaries between God and the other created beings and the planets, called the supernal temples (*al-hayakil al-ʾulwiyya*), are in relation to them as it were, bodies and individual persons. These supernal beings receive an influx from the *ruḥaniyyut* that set them in motion with a view to order and to the good; they in turn are the causes of everything that happens (in the sub-lunar world). Men honor each of these "temples" with various kinds of observance and worship, such as magical and astrological operations, fumigations,

> and prayers. For addressing oneself to the *ruḥaniy* to which it pertains, and, beyond that, to the Lords of Lords.[55]

In other texts, mainly Arabic magical texts, the aim of the magicians is to draw downward this *ruḥaniy*; this concept is also widespread in Jewish texts of a magical vein.[56] As a magical term, *ruḥaniyyut* entered some fourteenth-century Jewish texts, some belonging to Abulafia's Kabbalistic school. R. Yiẓḥaq of Acre, whose affinity to Abulafia's school is indisputable,[57] describes the process of permutating letters in the "chamber of seclusion" as intended to draw upon us the divine intellect.[58] However, when dealing with the separation of the mystic from this union, he uses the term *divine supernal force*.[59] We may conclude that this *ruḥaniyyut* is tantamount to the divine intellect that is caused to descend by the permutation of letters and their pronunciation.[60]

It is important to emphasize the similarity between R. Yiẓḥaq's view and that of Abulafia: both maintain that through the combinations of letters and their pronunciation a supernal force descends upon the mystic and cleaves to him. According to the *Epistle on Secrets,* spuriously attributed to Maimonides, which stems from Abulafia's school,[61] there is a close relation between "the spiritual force of the angels and the twenty-two letters of the Hebrew alphabet. After quoting from *Sefer Yeẓirah* the anonymous Kabbalist writes:

> . . . and these are the twenty-two simple letters. He intends by these that everything He created out of the spiritual force of the angels for the external souls will be engraved in these twenty-two words, and man will have knowledge concerning the world.[62]

Whoever reads the text of this pseudepigraphic epistle cannot miss its astrological and magical character; recitations of magical names are openly connected to the seven planets and their angels,[63] and it seems that the incorporation of spiritual force into the letters is part of the method of drawing down the influx of the astral bodies.[64] As far as I know, this is the first Jewish or Hebrew text that overtly states that the Hebrew letters are pregnant with "spiritual force." in the late fourteenth-century the term *ruḥaniyyut* as a designation for spiritual forces superior to the astral bodies became widespread. At the end of the fifteenth century the term occurs several times in the work of R. Yoḥanan Alemanno, who was influenced by both Abulafia and magical texts.[65] For our purpose, the perception of the words of prayer found in Alemanno's *Collectanaea* is of utmost importance. As part of a threefold classification of prayers as drawing down einfuxes, he mentions that there are

> a) prayers performed by persons who know nothing about the things of which they are speaking, and who do not pray out of choice and free will, but because of the custom of their ancestors. [These prayers] receive the influxes that descend onto them because of the existence of human voices, which are arranged in such a fashion that they are worthy of receiving the influxes, which are ready to descend onto them, even if the performers [of the prayers]

do not prepare them with [proper] intention, or [pray] out of choice and free will, but as a blind man errs in darkness . . .[66]

Even this brief passage suffices to show that the proper arrangement of the words of prayer enables the worshiper to cause the descent of spiritual influxes even when the persons praying are totally ignorant of the virtues inherent in the sounds they are uttering. A fortiori, says Alemanno in the continuation of the text, there are persons who acknowledge the significance of the text of prayer, the times it is to be performed, and the necessary intention that has to accompany the utterance of the words.[67] What is more important, however, is that Alemanno uses two terms that will occur in Cordovero's late Kabbalistic jargon: in his *Shir ha-Ma ᶜalot,* the introduction to his commentary on the Song of Songs, the phrase "the spiritual force of the letters" is attributed to R. Isaac ibn Latif.[68] Alemanno uses this phrase in a context dealing with the magical impact of the oral prayer. Moreover, in his *Collectanaea* he asserts:[69]

This is the secret of the world of letters; they are forms and seals [made in order to] collect the supernal and spiritual emanation as the seals collect the emanations of the stars.

As the magical seals serve to attract the astral influx, so are the letters capable of attracting the spiritual force of the *Sefirot*:[70]

How shall we know to make any image for the spiritual force of the *Sefirot*? He has shown to him[71] the movements of the letters that are moved by the other letters. . . .[72]

Therefore, at the end of the fifteenth or very beginning of the sixteenth century, a clear conception of letters as talismanic objects, which can be traced to works that deal with permutations of letters from Abulafia's school, was in existence; in some of these texts an allusion or direct mention of prayer is notable.

Highly interesting discussions on related subjects are found at the beginning of the fifteenth century in Spain. R. Shem Tov ben Shem Tov, the famous Kabbalist, asserts in his *Sefer ha-ᵓEmunot* that through Moses' cleaving to the supernal world, he comprehended the forms under the *Shekhinah,* probably the supernal *heikhalot,* and that[73]

from the force of these forms [his] speech was formed, and the voice of that speech is in these letters like a body to the inner, spiritual, and holy intellects,[74] the names of God, which are like drawing deep waters by means of a vessel; so was [Moses] drawing to his form, by means of that voice, the innerness of the intellects . . . the building of the letters, which are vessels of the inner intellects.

It is highly significant that the vessel for the collection of the supernal influx is the voice that articulates letters. However, even the written text of the Torah has magical qualities, and since they are related to the single letters, they had to be written separately.[75] It is interesting to remark that although R. Shem Tov refers several times to talismanic magic, which in his opinion is completely idolatrous,[76] he never draws a comparison between it and the technique based on the Hebrew letters, as Alemanno has done.[77] Apparently R. Shem Tov was acquainted with Arabic texts or translations that were known to some of the Jewish-Spanish theologians since the middle of the fourteenth century, wherein astrological magic dealing with *ruḥaniyyut* occurs more than once.[78] A decisive development in the perception of letters as talismans is evident in the writings of R. Shelomo ha-Levi Alqabetz. He was acquainted with R. Shem Tov's book and even quotes from it a passage dealing with the idolatrous practice whose aim is to cause the spiritual force to descend, and with the letters as vessels.[79] However, whereas in his *Pirqei he-Ḥakham,* Alqabetz does not add anything to R. Shem Tov's view, in the presumably later *Collectanaea of Introductory Theses to Kabbalah* he not only reviews the material on letters as found in R. Shem Tov, but apparently adds some new metaphors. We will present here only one pertinent passage. According to Alqabetz:

> All the letters of our holy Torah . . . are by themselves an extreme holiness, since they are like bodies and palaces to the spiritual forces that are in them, coming from above, and this is the reason the scribe who copies the Torah [scroll] or *tephilin,* says: "I write for the sake of holiness etc.," since by this intention he infuses spiritual force into the bodies of the letters from above.[80]

Therefore the letters, as well as the divine names,[81] are designated as palaces that are capable, like the Sabian temples, of collecting spiritual power. However, with Alqabetz—as with Alemanno before him—the origin of the supernal force is no longer the astral body, whose spiritual force can be collected by seals or temples, but the *Sefirot.* The pagan temples become letters, written or pronounced, and the astral force is changed by Sefirotic influx.

Alqabetz's view appears to be an important channel for the incorporation of this semi-magical perception of the letters into the main trend of Kabbalistic literature, and he could have influenced, as scholars already pointed out,[82] Cordovero's *Pardes Rimmonim.* However, Alqabetz was not the only source for Cordovero regarding letters as talismanic objects. He knew and quoted Abulafia's text from *ᵓOr ha-Sekhel* cited above, as well as an unknown Abulafian text.[83] Cordovero was the first Kabbalist to endow the talismanic perception of letters and their permutations with the highest status in the hierarchy of Kabbalistic studies. In his *Pardes Rimmonim*[84] he classifies the students of Torah into four groups: (a) those who deal solely with plain meaning; (b) those who study the Halakhic and Midrashic aspects of Torah; (c) those who study the secrets included in the *Zohar*; and (d) those who study the spiritual forces inherent in the letters and their combination. Those who understand this science can "create worlds." This science, being so sublime, is very rare.

Although Cordovero mentions only *Berit Menuḥah* as belonging to this brand of Kabbalah, he also hints that issues like combinations of letters or pronunciation of Divine Names are part of this science. Therefore Abulafia's Kabbalah is an important formative element of the highest part of Kabbalistic lore, together with other texts dealing with the nature of letters and divine Names. In this branch of Kabbalah, the ultimate element of contemplation is the separate letter or sound. Time and again we find discussions concentrating on the nature of a single letter or combination of letters.[85] We shall deal with some passages of Cordovero wherein the nature of letters or sounds and one's *kavvanah* are related. It should be emphasized that the following discussions gravitate around one view of the *kavvanah,* the talismanic one. This is indeed a relatively simple understanding of this issue, but we should be aware that in many other places Cordovero exposes very complex theurgical views of *kavannah.* However, these treatments will not concern us here.

In the last gate of *Pardes Rimmonim,* Cordovero defines the essence of *kavvanah*:

> A worshiper using *kavvanah* has to draw the spiritual force from the supernal levels downward onto the letters he is pronouncing so as to be able to elevate those letters up to that supernal level, in order to hasten his request.[86]

The concept of material sounds that can be filled with spiritual influx or supernal light is central to Cordovero's thought, and he repeats this view dozens of times, mainly in *Pardes Rimmonim.* The above-mentioned passage was copied by Abraham Azulai in his compendium *Ḥesed le-ʾAvraham*[87] and it was quoted from there by R. Jacob Joseph of Polonoy in his introduction to *Toledot Yaʿaqov Yosef.*[88] An evaluation of the context of this passage clearly indicates that it includes several peculiar Cordoverian views, which are presented here as R. Jacob Joseph of Polonoy's own concepts. A single example will be sufficient:[89]

> The human body[90] is not considered to be only the flesh; rather the soul within it is the [real] man, and so also with all the commandments, even those dependent on speech, as the commandment of prayer, the commandment to study Torah, and the [saying of] Blessings of Enjoyments.[91] The pronounced letters are only a vessel and garment. It is incumbent to draw downward into the interior part of the letters when he is pronouncing them the spiritual forces of the *Sefirot,* together with the light of *ʾEiyn Sof,* who vivifies them.

5. LETTERS AND PRAYER AS VESSELS

The Cordoverian vein of this and other passages concerning letters and or sounds is evident and demonstrates that the Lurianic definition of *kavvanah* was replaced by Cordovero's; both include magical overtones, but the latter's is simpler and more "literary." Moreover, Cordovero's view of religious activity in the terms referred to above enables the encounter and cleaving to the godhead's manifestation even in the sounds pronounced by men, and therefore turns the most widespread commandments into opportunities for *devequt*.[92] I would like to emphasize that the talismatic understanding of *kavvanah* is not the sole definition found in Cordovero's writings. On the contrary, in many other cases the more theosophical-theurgical attitude is dominant. This is but one more example of how different models are active within the same corpus. What is more important for the history of Jewish mysticism, however, is that the Hasidic masters were attracted by precisely this aspect of Cordovero's thought, or by this specific model, despite the fact that the theosophical-theurgical model, in its different versions, was shared by both Cordovero and Luria. The hermeneutical *grille*, active in Hasidism with an emphasis on the magical aspects of a body of writing, is very conspicuous in this case.

It is worth dwelling for a moment upon the use of the term "vessels" for sounds. Its origin is obviously Cordoverian; however, this view of the Safedian Kabbalist was apparently used not only among the students of the Besht but also by one of his contemporaries, R. Naḥman of Kossov. In a context very similar to that adduced above from the *Toledot Ya^caqov Yosef*, its author quotes R. Naḥman as saying that "the speech [of the prayer] becomes vessels into which the influx of influx is infused."[93] This view is incorporated in R. Jacob Joseph's formulation of the same attitude, immediately following this passage.[94] According to Cordovero, as cited by his student R. Elijah de Vidas:[95]

> Out of His love for man God has fixed these letters in the mouth of man, in order to enable him to cleave to his Creator; by the very pronunciation of the sounds here below, when he studies Torah or prays, he shakes and stirs up the roots above. The meaning of the verb "fixed" is similar to sticking the end of a chain[96] in one place, and the other end in another place; the distance between the places notwithstanding, when a man shakes the end of the chain, which is in his hand, he shakes the whole chain . . . and so we can understand the virtue of our ancestors whose prayers were answered immediately, since they were careful not to defile the twenty-two letters that are [pronounced by] the five places in the mouth.

This passage is very significant for at least two reasons: (a) it explicitly clarifies that the phrase "study of Torah and prayer" refers to oral activity, not contemplation of written forms; (b) we learn that the pronunciation of letters is a way of cleaving to God because of the emanational continuum that connects sounds and their supernal roots. De Vidas' text was paraphrased by R. Menaḥem Naḥum of Chernobyl, who added, however, some important motifs totally absent in *Reshit Ḥokhmah*:[97] (a) the five inner places of the mouth are named "the inner speech," *dibbur penimi*; (b) the lights of the letters are also located there; these "lights" are an emanation from God, which invests the five places with thought and divine vitality. Therefore the very emission of the Hebrew letters is an activation of the light of *ʾEyin Sof* dwelling in the five places, thereby creating the opportunity to cleave to the inwardness of the sounds.

With these two conclusions in mind, let us explore in a more detailed fashion some important Hasidic texts. The aforecited passage of the Great Maggid explicitly refers to oral activity: "he says each word," "he utters"; therefore, the actual utterance, and not only mystical contemplation, is the modus operandi of prayer.[98] The same assertion is also true regarding the passage from *Toledot Yaʿaqov Yosef.* It is worthwhile elaborating on this magical feature of Hasidic prayer. According to Cordovero's *Pardes Rimmonim,* the letters or the pronounced letters are palaces or temples where the spiritual forces dwell.[99] This perception is closely related to and influenced by medieval and Renaissance discussions about astral magic; structures, like palaces, were considered to be a means to attract the spiritual powers dwelling in the planets or stars. This magical conception, as we have pointed out above, was already combined in a Kabbalistic source known to Cordovero and Abulafian Kabbalah:[100]

> By the combination and permutation of the Name of [seventy-two letters] or other [divine] names, after a great concentration[101] [of mind], the righteous . . . will receive a revelation of an aspect of the *Bat qol* [the divine voice] . . . until a great influx will descend upon him, with the condition that he who deals with this will be a well-prepared vessel to collect the spiritual force.

This passage, whose source escapes me for the time being, is apparently the prototype of Cordovero's own view:

> The prophets comprehended the spiritual force that enters the letters through the letters themselves, by great concentration and the merit of the pure soul.[102]

Let us return to Hasidic texts. R. Dov Baer of Miedzyrec, in the name of the Besht, makes the following comment:

> Concerning that which is written in the *Zohar,* that man is judged in each [supernal] palace, this is to be [viewed as dealing with] speeches and pronounced letters of prayer, which are called palaces, wherein a man is judged, whether he is worthy of entering the pronounced letters or the prayer; if he is unworthy, he is cast out, i.e. an alien thought is sent to him, and he is pushed away.[103]

We can easily see how the supernal palaces of the *Zohar* were transformed into the pronounced letters that man pronounces during prayer. This anthropological shift changes the magical significance of the sound qua palace into a mystical spiritualization of prayer. In the Cordoverian magical view, man is requested to draw downward supernal forces in his own "sounds"; in the

Hasidic interpretation, he himself has to enter the articulated letters, apparently referring to penetration of the intention of the words of prayer, or to cleave to the spiritual force found in the sounds. If he is unable to do this he will be attacked by alien thoughts. Again, according to the tradition attributed to the Besht:

> the main purpose of the study of Torah and of prayer is to cleave himself to the inwardness of the spiritual force of the light of *ʾEiyn Sof* that is within the pronounced letters of Torah and prayer.[104]

One has to enter the palace—i.e., the material aspect of sounds or letters—in order to cleave to the divine Presence represented by the term "spiritual force." Although the magical terminology remained, this passage reflects only the mystical facet of the encounter. The nature of this cleaving is clarified in another teaching ascribed to the Besht,[105] where this process is identified with the entering into the palaces referred to in the ancient Jewish mythical literature; he overtly mentions in that context the entering into the *Pardes* of the four famous Tannaitic scholars. This penetration is tantamount to the understanding of the inner sense of Torah, i.e., Kabbalah. Furthermore, cleaving to the Torah is interpreted in erotic terms:[106]

> And when he [Jacob] lay down and cleaved himself with attachment and desire to the pronounced letters of the Torah, he divested[107] himself of materiality.

The Besht evidently hints at the erotic encounter between the Kabbalist and Kabbalah, personified by a maiden in the famous parable of the *Zohar*.[108] The magical element is here totally conquered by the mystical experience. Although this passage deals with sounds or letters of Torah, its basic principle is valid for prayer as well. The Great Maggid comments in the same vein that when the "utterances of the prayer" are spoken, the worshiper in a state of *qatenut* is in the position of "back to back;" however, when the one who prays becomes aware that he stands before God,[109]

> and is aware of the nature of the utterances and combinations [of utterances] and names and the lights that are in them, and cleaves to them in an extremely marvelous manner, then he turns to the state of "face by face," with the utterances . . . in the secret of the divestment[110] of materiality.

Here, the verbal nature of the activity that may end in an erotic union is here explicit. The "lights" referred to are but another term for "spiritual forces." According to the Great Maggid, they are infused in the utterances by the process of praying:

> By the prayers of Israel the new influx and vitality are drawn downward onto the pronounced letters, combinations, and utterances.[111]

The vocal prayer is therefore the best way to draw the spiritual force—in Hebrew *ruḥaniyyut* is of female gender—onto the sounds in order to enable the cleaving. However, a superior method of attaining it is the nonverbal act of thought, *maḥashavah:*

> Indeed, any worthy person who prays cleaves by his thought to Him, may He be blessed, and the drawing down of the influx is not necessary, as it is possible that this [kind of] prayer is better [when performed only] in thought . . . since this prayer does not need a vessel in order to draw the influx downward.[112]

However, this supreme form of prayer is exceptional, and it is discussed in the context of Moses' prayer before his death. The last stage of the triad, *ma ͨaseh, dibbur,* and *maḥashavah,* is thus an ideal that cannot be recommended; hence *dibbur* remains the highest form of worship by prayer.[113] This being the nature of the pronounced words, it is quite understandable that Hasidic prayer took so long to perform; it resulted in an erotic union that the worshiper was eager to prolong:

> The cleaving occurs when someone says a word and he prolongs that word for a long time, since on account of his cleaving he is unwilling to separate himself from the word, and this is why he prolongs the [utterance of the] word.[114]

In this context it is pertinent to mention the superiority of prayer with closed eyes over prayer performed while gazing at the written letters in the prayerbook:

> When man is on a lower level, it is better to pray from a prayerbook, since the very sight of the letters causes him to pray with *kavvanah.* However, when he cleaves more to the supernal world, it is better for him to close his eyes, so that the sight of letters will not suspend his cleaving to the supernal world.[115]

Closing one's eyes during prayer is well known from Kabbalistic as well as non-Kabbalistic recommendations regarding prayer;[116] nevertheless, none of the sources known to me refer to the elimination of vocal prayer, even when the eyes are closed. The oral activity is supposed to continue; the Besht himself reportedly indicates this in the context of discussing the nature of prayer:

> When I cleave my thought to the Creator, I let my mouth say whatever it wants, since I thereby bind the words to [their] supernal root, to the Creator, blessed be He.[117]

The Besht declares that the cleaving to God is closely connected with joy, and the latter is to be cultivated especially at the time of "the speech."[118] Passages quoted in his name often deal with "crying" in a whisper without any corporeal movements; there, however, do not include the cessation of speech.[119] According to an important passage:[120]

> Sometimes man can say the prayer with love and fear, and with great enthusiasm, without any movement [i.e., sway] and he may appear to another man as if he says these things [i.e., his prayer] without any attachment. This a man can do when he is cleaving greatly to God, [and] then man can worship Him solely with his soul, out of great love. This worship is better and faster and [helps us] cleave to God, [much] more than the prayer that is seen outside, on his limbs, and the *qelippah* has no hold on this prayer [of man], which is in its entirety in the inwardness [of man].

In this context the "saying" of prayer is explicitly mentioned; therefore, the movements of the body can refer only to the swaying of the body, not including the expression of the words by the lips. The problem dealt with in this text is very similar to that found in a text of R. Elijah ha-Kohen of Ismir; who claims that prayer without swaying is a result of the fear that Satan may attack the worshipers:

> Satan only spends his time causing important persons to fall; . . . hence the perfect [men], knowing this way of Satan . . . did not show themselves as preparing for the *kavannah* of their prayer, lest Satan see them and come to disturb their *kavvanah*. Therefore, they prepare themselves solely in their hearts, since the thought does not reveal the things [i.e., *kavvanah*] to Satan. When they stood to pray, they did not show themselves [performing] the movements of the *mekhavvenim*.[121]

The swaying of the *mekhavvenim* is liable to stir Satan, and so also the movements of the limbs that may be seizures of the *qelippah* in the Hasidic text. None of the texts, however, exclude oral prayer, and the "intention" is now an inner movement.

Let us elaborate upon the other way of reaching God, namely, through the ascent of the sounds to God rather than penetration and cleaving to their inner spirituality. According to Cordovero's definition of *kavvanah* cited above, prayer culminates in the elevation of sound to the highest level. How is this achievement possible? According to Cordovero,

> When someone pronounces and causes one of the letters [or sounds] to move, [then] the spiritual force of that [letter] will necessarily be stirred, and the vapor[s] of [his] mouth, out of which holy forms are formed, will ascend and be bound with their root, for they are (!) the root of the emanation [i.e., the revealed God].[122]

And again in the same chapter:

> From it [i.e., the pronunciation of a word], the vapor of his mouth, appears a spiritual force and entity, which is as an angel that will ascend and will be bound with its source and will hasten to perform its operation in a speedy and

rapid way, and this is the secret of the pronunciation of [Divine] Names and the *kavvanah* of prayer.[123]

Oral pronunciation, therefore, is the substantial source of the formation of a spiritual force; this is apparently to be achieved, through the emission of "spirit," *ruaḥ,* by the very act of pronunciation, and the collection of a supernal element on this substratum. This view, which underlies some Hasidic discussions, is explicitly adopted by R. Meshullam Phoebus of Zbarazh from *Pardes Rimmonim* through a passage in the introduction to *Sha ᶜar ha-Shamayim*:[124]

When a person pronounces the letters he moves the supernal vitality, and when he cleaves by his thought to God in a complete manner, he returns the vitality that is emanated from the supernal thought, until it reaches the speech and is [finally] placed in the mouth of man; and he longs[125] through the words of the prayer for God, by his causing the sounds to fly upward to their source . . . if he succeeds in drawing downward the spiritual force from above onto his words, in order to cause the pronounced letters to fly upward, as it is written in *Pardes Rimmonim.*

The cleaving of one's thought to God is a necessary precondition for correct prayer, which culminates with the return of human vitality to its source. R. Meshullam tends to see human vitality as an emanation from the human soul, which is presumably divine, and therefore the returning speech is the restitution of that vitality to its origin. Similarly, according to the Great Maggid, human "utterances and prayers" are described as substrata that attract and collect the divine vitality:

Man is full of vitality and vapor, which is in his innerness *in extenso.* However, when he wants to speak, he limits the vapor through the throat to the five places of the mouth [where the voice appears], to whatever place he wants and thereby his speech is heard and his voice and his wisdom, since his vitality, his wisdom, and his voice are limited in this speech. Therefore, the *Ẓaddiq,* when he prepares to pray before his Creator, may His name be blessed, certainly cleaves and binds his thought and his vitality to the *ʾEyin Sof,* may he be blessed, which is the Simple Unity, without any image. And when he begins to speak, he draws the vitality of the Creator, may He be blessed, [downward] into his speech and the words that he emits from his mouth, which are closely joined to his vitality and vapor, which are limited by the utterance of these sounds that he speaks. It seems as if by his vapor and his vitality bound to *ʾEiyn Sof,* may He be blessed, he utters and limits by his utterance of these sounds.[126]

The mystical universe implicit in this passage deserves detailed treatment. It is not an immanentist theology that is represented here. God does not dwell on the letters or on the utterances because of His essence, which penetrates all, as we find in several Hasidic sources, but because the bond between man and God that is created by the cleaving of man ensures the descent of the divine within the linguistic material. Talismatic as the concept of language may be, it does not work automatically. The mystical act of cleaving, which is preliminary to prayer is crucial for the drawing down of the divine. Here then is one more source that demonstrates that Hasidic thought was not invariably immanentist, and that the mystical and magical models of activity are necessary in order to establish the ascending and descending act or cleaving.

Some final remarks about the loudness of the utterances are pertinent here. Commenting upon the names of *Pu ᶜah* and *Shifrah,* R. Dov Baer of Miedzyrec writes:

> *Pu ᶜah* signifies speech, since the *shofar* causes all the prayers to ascend upward, and all the prayers ascend by means of the voice of the *shofar* . . . and we pray [on *Rosh ha-Shanah*] the *shaḥarit* prayer, and afterward we send you, the blower [*Ba ᶜal Toqe ᶜa*], for the purpose of arousing our ancestors, and they will cause our prayer to ascend before Him . . . and all our prayers will ascend by means of this *Teqi ᶜah* of yours, and they will be clothed by this voice [of the *shofar*].[127]

The prominent role of the voice of the *shofar* in elevating the speech or pronounced letters of prayers is evident. However, this high appreciation has nothing to do with a depreciation of the regular oral prayer itself. Against this background let us consider another text of the Great Maggid dealing with similar elements; in a parable regarding the children of the king who went astray in a wood, the Hasidic master tells:

> And they were crying so that perhaps their father would hear them, but they were not answered. And they pondered: Perhaps we have forgotten the language of our father. Therefore, he does not hear our cry; hence, let us cry with a [loud] voice, without [discreet sounds of] speech. And they decided to send one of them to cry, and they warned him, "See and comprehend that all of us depend upon you." The meaning of this parable is: God has sent us to elevate the holy sparks, and we went astray from our father. And it may be that since we have forgotten the speech of our father, we cannot pray by means of speech. [Therefore] we send you, *Ba ᶜal Toqe ᶜa,* in order to arouse the compassion upon us by means of the voice without speech; see and be careful: all of us depend upon you.[128]

The articulated speech of prayer is the ancient and efficient technique of communicating with God; children speaking to their father need not cry in order to be understood. However, the obstacle of the dispersion in the diaspora constitutes a hinderance that the regular worshiper cannot overcome; in order to succeed one needs stronger means—the loud, though inarticulate, voice of the *shofar,* which can elevate the sounds of our common prayer. Under the inspiration of the Great Maggid, a text included in *Shemu ᶜah Tovah* maintains that:

> in speech there are no voices and letters [or sounds], and during speech both voice and speech are heard together. But voice is the inwardness and is above

> the letters [or sounds]. However, when the speaker thinks about speaking some novel things that he wants to innovate [through] speech, then his thought is [focused] solely upon the letters [or sounds] of the speech and not upon the voice. And he separates the speech from the voice, and the voice is dormant. Hence we blow the *shofar* which is the voice without speech, and we arouse the supernal voice, so that God will ponder again the [supernal] voice. And this is the meaning of the [*shofar-*] blowing: that [we shall cause] God to enter His thought into the [supernal] voice.[129]

The voice is the primal element that can influence supernal processes—here involving the divine Althought that exerts its influence on the Supernal Voice. In the previous passage the blowing of the *shofar* is supposed to arouse divine compassion. Mental prayer is thus not the most powerful means for Israel, but rather the blowing of the *shofar,* which is viewed as superior to speech and pregnant with theurgical qualities. The Besht himself is reported to have prayed "with a great cry" that was unbearable for the Great Maggid, who thus had to leave the room.[130] According to R. Alexander of Shklov, the *Mitnaggedim*

> claim that we must pray as they do, and pray hurriedly and without any bodily movements or raising of the voice just like those angels . . . But this is only said of the highest rank of angels known as Seraphim, and it does not apply to the other ranks, as it is said, "And the Ophanim and the Holy Beasts with a great noise of great rushing." Even of the Seraphim it is written, "A noise of tumult like the noise of a host [Ezek. 1:24]."[131]

Criticism of the loud shouting prayer can be found even in Hasidic writings,[132] testifying that this phenomenon attained extreme forms. Let us examine, at the end of this analysis of Hasidic mystical prayer, one more passage that exemplifies many of the themes dealt with earlier while illustrating the mystico-magical model insofar as prayer is concerned. In the school of the Great Maggid we learn that

> when he has to request something from the Creator, blessed be He, he should think that his soul is a limb of the *Shekhinah*[133] as if he is a drop of the sea.[134] And he should make that request as if it is the need of the *Shekhinah.* He should believe that he certainly operates above, onto the *Shekhinah.* [But] only if he is united to the *Shekhinah* in an appropriate manner will the influx be drawn down on him . . . and he should imagine that he is a vessel, and the thought of his speech is worlds that are spreading, namely the world of speech, which is the *Shekhinah,* that is asking from the world of thought for the sake of these speeches. When the light of the Creator, blessed be He, is enclothed within his thought and speech, he should ask that the influx should spread from the world of thought upon the *speeches.* And thus our Creator is found in our requests . . . Israel makes the words of their mouths into vessels in order to clothe the *Shekhinah* within."[135]

Again, the assumption is that only our cleaving to God is able to bring down the divine force within the words of prayer. Actually, the mystical identification with the *Shekhinah* alone ensures the dwelling of the influx within the letters as vessels. Through this identification, the descent of the influx from the world of thought to that of speech becomes an inner divine affair. By emotional or intellectual identification, the distance between the *Shekhinah* and man is obliterated, and she comes to dwell upon man and is clothed by his words. A magical element is thus still identifiable, as the speeches as vessels demonstrates; nevertheless, the mystical element is by far stronger. Not only does the soul become a limb of the *Shekhinah*; the latter is also embraced by the words of man. The image of the drop is therefore to be understood against the intertwined situation of man's soul entering the *Shekhinah* and the *Shekhinah* entering the human words. Strong as this union may be, it still has another goal: receiving the influx. Therefore, the mystical union in this case is a means-experience, unlike other Hasidic discussions where *devequt* is an end-experience. In other texts, however, we find a much more explicit expression of the magic element in the mystico-magical mode. R. Eliezer Lippa of Lisansk writes very explicitly that

> we are operating, by means of our prayer, remedies on the sick, or similarly, all the needs of people, by our drawing down His Divinity, blessed be He, by means of our prayer, on the supernal world that is pertinent to this need. Then the good influx comes in any case to this world, either for the many or for the individual.[136]

This is only one example of the use of the more general theory of drawing down for facilitating a specific outcome, even in the case of the individual. Beyond the preoccupation with the community, the possibility of channeling the influx for the benefit of an individual expresses the return to the fore of the magical element in Hasidism, once the theory of drawing down in Kabbalah was understood as emphasizing more theurgical concerns. This fascination with the drawing down can be exemplified in the interpretation offered by R. Elimelekh of Lisansk, who interprets the term *maggid,* normally meaning preacher, in terms of drawing down. Commenting on the verse, "the deeds of His hands are declared by the firmament" [Psalms 19:2] this master states that the righteous ones are the deeds of God's hands, who draws down, *maggid,* the subtle things, symbolized by the firmament.[137] Buber's attempt to differentiate between Kabbalah and Hasidism on the basis of the latter being free of magic while the former is imbued with magical thought presents an idealized categorization, one that does not reflect the evidence presented here.[138]

To summarize the findings of our previous discussion, Lurianic *kavvanot* lost their complete supremacy among Kabbalists in the eighteenth century. However, no particular mystical alternative was proposed outside the Hasidic camp; only there was the talismanic concept of prayer adopted and disseminated. The magical overtones of Cordovero's view are still evident in the writings of the first Hasidic masters, but already a transformation of magic into mysticism is perceivable in their discussions; this tendency apparently became a dominant line in the further development of Hasidic prayer in later periods. Hasidism adopted and adapted mystical and magical models different from the theurgical one dominant in the various versions of Lurianism; the mystical and magical models of Kabbalah, which have been neglected in modern scholarship, contributed substantially to the emergence of Hasidism.

We have elaborated in some detail upon the nature of the Hasidic view of the mystical intention and its sources not only because it can tell us about the metamorphoses of earlier themes into latter concepts of prayer; the above filiation is emblematic of a long series of related religious acts, especially those performed by oral activity. After the acceptance of the magical model, the oral mode was considered preeminently creative, more than contemplative or theurgical activity.[139] We shall turn our attention now to another crucial activity, which follows in many ways the magical understanding we have explored above regarding prayer, namely the study of the Torah.

5

Mystical and Magical Study in Hasidism

Mystical hermeneutics is ordinarily a strong form of exegesis; the fact that intense experiences may inform the approach of the mystic to the canonic texts can explain the audaciousness that characterizes the readings of the mystics. In the case of Hasidism, it seems that the two models discussed above, the mystical and the magical, have contributed, separately, to the emergence of similar trends among the eighteenth-century Jewish mystics. The mystical model has influenced the Hasidic assumption that the spiritual predisposition is crucial for disclosing the secrets of the text, or for encountering it experientially, while the magical model prefers to regard the canonic text, especially the Bible, as a talismatic entity. There are obvious differences—and frictions—between these two approaches. While mysticism emphasizes the emotional and intentional attitude and is less concerned with a precise performance of the text, the talistmatic approach is less interested in the inner attitude and more in the exact production of the linguistic talisman. We shall not attempt to harmonize these two tendencies, but rather strive to describe them succinctly.

1. PSYCHOLOGICAL-EXPERIENTIAL READINGS IN HASIDISM

It would be helpful to distinguish between two different, though partially and intermittently overlapping, readings of classical canonic texts and the theosophical-theurgical material that recurs in the writings of the Hasidic masters: the experiential and the psychological. The former assumes that religious texts, including the classical mystical ones, are to be read with a certain emotional arousal, which transforms the study into a mystical experience or a mythical event. The psychological approach argues that complex and sublime theosophical systems are also to be understood as reflected in the human personality, especially its spiritual aspect. The experiential reading or interpretation is less interested in penetrating the content of the interpreted texts and emphasizes the intensity of the approach, while the psychological approach is first and foremost a special form of hermeneutics, whose details may be easily described. Despite these distinctions, it seems that the transposition of the meaning of a canonic text to the spiritual life of the individual, a characteristic of the psychological approach, sometimes contributes to the experiential aspect of Hasidism.[1]

Let me adduce some examples for the experiential turn of the Hasidic axiology. One of the most famous stories of *In Praise of the Baal Shem Tov* is a description by the Great Maggid, his most important disciple, of the encounter with the founder of Hasidism:

> He asked me whether I had studied Kabbalah. I answered that I had. A book was lying in front of him on the table and he instructed me to read aloud from the book. The book was written in short paragraphs, each of which began, "Rabbi Ishmael said, 'Metatron,[2] the Prince of Presence, told me.'" I recited a page or half a page to him. The Besht said to me: "It is not correct. I will read it to you." He began and read, and while he read he trembled. He rose and said: "We are dealing with *Ma^caseh Merkavah* and I am sitting down." He stood up and continued to read. As he was talking he lay me down in the shape of a circle on the bed. I was not able to see him any more. I only heard voices and saw frightening flashes and torches.[3]

According to this version of the legend, it is not a Kabbalistic text that has engaged the attention of the two Hasidic masters but one of the earliest texts of Jewish mysticism.[4] However, what is important here is not the content of the text or its precise identity but the mode of its performance: its vocal recitation. The difference between the Besht and the Great Maggid was, it seems, not a matter of knowledge of the topics dealt with—the Maggid had already acknowledged that he studied Kabbalah—or their ability to read the text, but the special way it had to be recited; a text should be studied not only for the sake of its content but for the experience it is able to induce. According to this story what concerned the Besht was the revelation that he experienced by performing the text rather than the gnosis inherent in it.

What is characteristically Hasidic in this story? Someone can argue that the mystical experience, accompanied by fire, lights, and angelic revelations, contains nothing new, for indeed these phenomena are also mentioned in the ancient *Heikhalot* and *Merkavah* literature. It seems, however, that in the older forms of mysticism it is the precise details of the topic that are crucial for the experience, not a certain written formulation of *Ma^caseh Merkavah*. The discussions about the topic, or the absorption of its content, not its recitation—or to put it differently, the intellectual, gnostic-like nature of the discourse and not the text's performance—is vital for the occurrence of the experience. This seems also to be the case in those ancient Jewish texts where study of the various parts of the Bible is described as inducing a revelatory situation. Again, the ability to find out the hidden links between the different layers, an exegetical enterprise par excellence, is involved in the induction of the paranormal experience.[5] The two media relevant to the ancient texts were the written and the mental, even in cases when oral discussions were mentioned. It seems also that the recitation of the *Mishnah* in Safed, which become a famous mystical device, reflects much more a technical type of phenomenon, which combines expertise with induction of revelations.[6] Apparently, it is the study, the preoccupation with the text from a more mental point of view, that creates the revelation mediated by the hypostatized status of the personified text. The *Mishnah,* embodied as a *Maggid,* reveals to R. Joseph Qaro issues that have nothing to do with the content of the *Mishnah,* nor does a situation described in the *Mishnah* materialize in a visionary form.[7]

However, in the Hasidic story, it is precisely the recitation, the oral performance, and even orality itself, that play a central role in creating the experience. However, we may assume that this oral performance involves a far more emotional orientation; moreover, it seems that the direct nexus between the content and the occurrence, namely the recitation of an account of the relationship between a mystic and an angel on the one hand, and the immediate revelations that took place on the other, should be understood as reflecting a nonsymbolic attitude to the text. When recited in a proper manner, the ancient text becomes an invocation, or conjuration, that brings about the experience mentioned in it. The text is not ancient history, not a metaphor or symbol for something else, but the appropriate performance; the text, when performed enthusiastically, incudes the experience itself.

According to another version of the encounter between the founder of Hasidism and the Great Maggid, the book involved in this situation was not an ancient mystical text but Luria's *ᶜEẓ Ḥayyim*; here, instead of the contest of recitations, as in the previous passage, the Great Maggid, as the representative of the learned elite, is asked to explain a certain passage in Luria's book. Although the Besht acknowledges that this explanation is valid, he describes the study of the Maggid as "lacking a soul," *beli neshamah.*[8] In the Beshtian manner of study, the same text becomes a continuum of names of angels,[9] who also appeared to the eyes of the two masters.[10] To a certain extent, the *Maggid* may be regarded as the classical representative of speculative Kabbalah, and the Besht that of practical or experiential Kabbalah. Their attitudes are exemplified by their respective approaches to the same texts; it is the general attitude that counts more than the nature of the text and its precise understanding.[11]

While the above example reflects a more experimental, or practical, aspect of the oral performance, with the emphasis on the "objective" efficacy of studying the text, the following examples reflect the spiritual efficacy, the effort to focus on the inner experience. The Great Maggid affirms that there are different degrees of divestment of materiality, which reflect the ascent of the human spirit on high, which means, at the same time, the perception of the more sublime dimensions of the Torah and the commandments.[12] One of the early Hasidic masters defined the meaning of "hidden" in relation to Kabbalah in these words:

> *Nistar* is the name given to a matter that one cannot transmit to another person; just as the taste of [a particular] food cannot be described to a person who has never tasted this taste[13] so it is impossible to explain in words how it is and what it is; such a thing is called *seter*. Thus is the love and fear of God, blessed be He—it is impossible to explain to another person the love [of God] in one's heart; [therefore] it is called *nistar*. But the attribution of the term *nistar* to the lore of Kabbalah is bizarre, because for one who wishes to study [Kabbalah] the book is available to him, and if he does not understand he is an ignoramus, as [indeed] for such a person, the *Gemara* and *Tosafot* are also *nistar*. But the concealed matters in the *Zohar* and the writings of R. Yiẓḥaq Luria are those based upon the cleaving to God, for those who are worthy to cleave and to see the supernal *Merkavah*,[14] like Yiẓḥaq Luria, to whom the paths of the firmaments were clear and who walked on them [seeing his way] with his mental eyes, like the four sages who entered *Pardes*.[15]

This passage from R. Menaḥem Mendel of Premislany, like that of the story about the Besht and the Great Maggid, betrays the dilemma that Hasidism as mysticism had to face: it had to choose between complicated forms of Kabbalah—the Lurianic and Zoharic literary corpora, which have to be studied in a very intense manner in order to penetrate their theosophic gnosis—and a more experiential type of mysticism, revolving around the idea of *devequt*, the mystical communion and union with God. The result was not a selection of one of these two alternatives but the assumption that one could discover within the studied texts the taste of the experience, an experience that was known to the authors of those texts, who were predisposed to mystical experiences. Likewise the study of the Halahkic corpus was not rejected or underestimated, but approached from another angle.[16] The ideal of *devequt* was projected onto the earlier Kabbalistic texts, where it did not play the crucial role the late Hasidic rabbi imagined it had played. The perspectives provided by a more experiential lore had drastically transformed the perception of the mystical theosophy. This shift is paradigmatic for a whole realm of similar phenomena; the ideal of *devequt* is not an addition to an already existing, stable, and accepted Lurianic system. The increase in the importance of *devequt* deeply affected the manner in which this system was understood.

What connects the last passage to the stories about the Besht is the assumption that the spiritual riches one brings to the text are of tantamount importance, even more important than the technical knowledge of the "plain" sense of the text. From this point of view, Hasidic mysticism presupposes the mystical maturity of the reader or interpreter more than it does any accumulation of knowledge of the secrets stored in an esoteric Kabbalistic book. In fact, the legend about the Besht's mode of study can be understood as an example of studying *bi-devequt*, namely with intensive mystical devotion, while the passage of R. Menaḥem Mendel of Premislany requires the experience of *devequt* in a sense that is closer to Kabbalah. While the need for an extraordinary state of mind for the understanding and commenting upon a canonic text is not new in Jewish mysticism in which from time to time we see the concept of a pneumatic reader,[17] in Hasidism the Kabbalistic primacy of the revelation of secrets is marginalized.

By strongly emphasizing the attitude of the student, the nature of the text becomes less important: at least in the case of R. Meshullam Phoebus of Zbarazh, who approvingly quotes another teacher of his, R. Yeḥiel Mikhal, the Maggid of Zloczov, as saying that he never distinguished between what is written in the texts he studies, be it Gemara or *Kabbalah,* since he sees in all of them only one thing: how to worship God.[18] This is considered to be a very elitist kind of reading, that of a *Ẓaddiq* who was the sone of a *Ẓaddiq*. Similar is the view of R. Barukh of Medzibush, the grandson of the Besht, who said that the Hasidic interpretations "touch and [at the same time] do not touch" the text, because of the implicit assumption that it is the effect of the divine spirit that informs the interpreter.[19] His brother, the author of *Degel Maḥaneh ᵓEfrayim* speaks about the revelation of the secrets of the Torah by means of the divine spirit.[20] Their acquaintance, R. Levi Yiẓḥaq of Berdichev, indicates that the *Ẓaddiqim,* "now have the power to interpret the Torah in the way they like," even if in heaven this interpretation is not accepted.[21]

In many other discussions, with which the work of R. Zeᵓev Wolf of Zhitomir, *ᵓOr ha-Meᵓir,* is replete, the inner spiritual status of the reader drastically affects the "combinations" of letters that occur to him while reading the Bible. For the righteous, these combinations will be positive, for the wicked—negative. The dialectical nature of the Torah, already espoused by rabbinic sources, is exploited here by emphasizing the "response" of the Torah to the human, psychological starting point of the reader.[22] To an ancient ontology of the text, then, the Hasidic masters added a psychology of the reader. This attitude is exemplified by a story about R. Aharon Aryeh of Premislany, who explained to one of the younger disciples that, while praying in Hebrew, he nevertheless thinks in Yiddish. When asked whether the Yiddish thought does not detract from the holiness of the prayer, he answered that when he recites *Barukh,* he thinks of God, when he recites *ᵓAtah,* he thinks of God, when he recites "the Lord," he certainly thinks of God. Indeed, this is a more popular version of the Great Maggid's teaching that the "Kabbalistic prayer" transforms the words of the prayer into divine names. Therefore, the text of the prayer uniformly refers to God, irrespective of the specific meaning of the recited words. This is indeed a very interesting version of the Kabbalistic notion that the whole Torah is composed of divine names, an idea that was also cherished by the Hasidic masters.[23] The spiritual predisposition toward approaching a sacred text seems crucial to the Hasidic attitude, not only in matters of hermeneutics, but also for the Hasidic way of life in general. Without assuming such a strongly enthusiastic approach to mystical life, it is hard to understand many Hasidic attitudes.

2. SOME VIEWS ON TORAH LI-SHEMAH

One of the main goals of studying the Torah, according to the Besht, is the attainment of cleaving with God through the letters or sounds of the Torah. One of the most representative passages attributed to the Besht, which shows the direction that would later be followed by many of the Hasidic masters, is found in the writing of one of the Besht's acquaintances and companions, R. Meir Margoliot:

> Whoever prepares himself to study for its own sake, without any alien intention, as I was warned by my great teachers in matters of Torah and Hasidism, included [among them] my friend, the Hasid and the Rabbi, who is the paragon of the generation, our teachers, Rabbi Yisrael the Besht, blessed be his memory, let his desirable intention concerning study for its own sake be to cleave himself in holiness and purity to the letters, *in potentia* and *in actu,* in speech and in thought, [so that he will] link part of [his] *nefesh, ruaḥ, neshamah, ḥayah,* and *yeḥidah* to the holiness of the candle of the commandment and Torah, [to] the enlightening letters, which cause the emanation of the influx of lights and vitality, that are true and eternal.[24]

It should be mentioned that although this passage comes down to us in the name of the Besht, as Weiss has already emphasized, the Besht was not the only master who taught this view to R. Meir Margoliot, but only one of his teachers. The Besht was giving expression to an idea that was already known, at least to a small group of masters. The idea of the Hasidic study of Torah is expressed here by the particular interpretation of the phrase *Torah li-shemah*—namely, that someone should study Torah for its own sake, which means for the sake of "the letter" or "the sound."[25] Two main themes are present in this passage: the idea of cleaving to the letters and that of the descent of the lights and vitality by means of letters. Although the sequence of these two events is not specified, at least on the basis of the order of their presentation one may assume that cleaving precedes the descent of the influx. If this is the case, then it is probable that we have in this passage another example of the mystico-magical model, one attributed to the Besht himself.

Another important passage cited in the name of the Besht partially parallels that of R. Meir Margoliot and is worthy of detailed analysis. In a collection of Hasidic excerpts from the beginning of the nineteenth century, we learn about a tradition that stems from the spiritual mentor of the Besht, Aḥijah the Shilonite, who revealed it to the Besht, who in turn transmitted it to the Great Maggid. It was then passed to R. Levi Yiẓḥaq of Berdichev, who apparently handed it down to his student, R. Aharon of Zhitomir.

> The way of the truth is as follows: In the moment of prayer one ought to divest himself of [his] corporeality [of belonging to] this world, so that he will conceive himself as if he were no [more] in this world at all. [Then] he should pronounce the letters by voice and simple speech, and cleave and link his thought to the holy letters and understand the sense of the holy words. Then, by itself, suddenly, the fire of the flame of the blaze of the burning of the supernal awe and love will flame up and become incandescent, in a very strong manner. This is the path that the light is dwelling in sofar as the holy and inner worship is concerned.[26]

Let me admit from the very beginning that there is no special reason to assume that this passage deals with the study of the Torah. It is much more reasonable to assume that the Besht has in mind the right way of prayer, by means of cleaving to the Hebrew letters, although I would not insist too much on this distinction. As we have seen in previous chapters, both prayer and the study of the Torah are viewed as identical, and this is also the case in many other texts not dealt with here. What is nevertheless relevant for our discussion is the fact that it diverges with the Besht's views as adduced by R. Meir Margoliot and allows a better and more general understanding of the oral activity (in my opinion, activities), as stages of the authentic *via mystica*. Let us examine these stages as they are found in the last passage: a) divestment of corporeality; b) the extreme feeling that results from this divestment, which is that someone does not feel himself as being in this world; c) the pronouncement of the letters; d) the cleaving to these letters; e) the understanding of the meaning of the words; f) the arousal of awe and love. There is no magical dimension to this path; while according to R. Meir Margoliot the letters bring down the influx, here the extreme feelings of love and awe are aroused. Here worship is the organon that enables someone to reach the emotional acme, while in the previous passage it is the means of receiving the divine influx. In the latter passage worship propels someone to the heights of experience, in the former it attracts the divinity downward. What is the reason for these divergences?

When we compare the two passages it becomes obvious that the peak is achieved as part of an inner path that includes divestment of corporeality and a feeling of elation, followed by cleaving to the pronounced letters. In the case of the drawing down of the influx, the stage of divestment of corporeality is not mentioned. Cleaving alone to the letters suffices to initiate the descent of the influx. Thus, we may regard these two passages as expressions of two forms of worship that apparently reflect different sources and models; the mystical model, as present in the quote of the *Tur,* informs the passage of R. Aharon of Zhitomir, while the magical form stems from the magical model. Here we shall focus on this second aspect of understanding the study of the Torah, as a mystico-magical event.

Although the nature of the mystical concept of studying the Torah has been discussed by several scholars,[27] one important aspect of this topic has nevertheless been ignored: how exactly did the Hasidim conceive of "the cleaving" when studying Torah? The answer accepted by these scholars is appropriate only for a limited series of Hasidic texts; namely, the perception of the Hasidim as contemplating the letters of the Torah and then cleaving to the lights included therein.[28] There is, however, another possible explanation, one that is consistent with the notion that R. Meir Margoliot's words in the name of the Besht served as an impetus for a long series of Hasidic texts.

In order to comprehend properly the Hasidic stand on this subject, we will first survey some pre-Hasidic antecedents, dealing with the nature of the study of the Torah. Luria's model assumes that the last letter of the *li-shemah,* the letter H, is a symbol for the *Shekhinah,* and devoted study is directed to the *Shekhinah* in order to unify Her with the divine masculine attribute.[29] According to a view attributed to Luria, the meaning of this dictum is to link and cleave the soul to her source by means of prayer and study of the Torah, in order to complete the structure of the supernal *anthropos* and to restore him.[30] However, though the mystical goal is explicit, the linguistic mechanism involved in cleaving was not explained. However, according to Cordovero,

> when someone pronounces and causes one of the letters [or sounds] to move, then the spiritual force of that [letter] will necessarily be stirred . . . so also regarding their [i.e., the letters'] existence, namely even in their written form spiritual force dwells upon those letters. And this is the reason behind the holiness of the scroll of the Torah.[31]

Cordovero hints at the superiority of the uttered sounds in comparison with the written letters; this superiority is referred to in the expression "even in their written form," and it corroborates his more explicit expression of this idea in the same context. However, in the text discussed here the issue is not letters in general but the letters of the Torah, which are considered to be inferior to their form. Hence, in Cordovero's view, it is incumbent upon man to raise the status of the written letters of the Torah by reading them aloud. The conclusion Cordovero draws from this assumption is rather surprising:

> Even if someone has no knowledge except that of the oral reading of the Torah, namely only the [biblical] verse, by necessity he will receive a reward for that oral reading, and his reward will be great.[32]

Immediately afterward, Cordovero identifies the concept of the oral reading of the written Torah with the Oral Law; the latter is the real explanation of the Written Torah, and whoever really reads the Torah has to intend its inner meaning[33] or "the spiritual force," and by the act of oral reading he uncovers the spiritual force. Therefore, the very utterance of the letters[34] of the Torah has a revelatory role with respect to the reader, and also elevates the letters to a higher level. Cordovero conceives the reading as transformations taking place concomitantly in man as well as in the letters. As seen in our discussion above on oral prayer, the utterance of sounds is necessary since it prepares the substratum for the collection of the spiritual forces; in one text adduced above, indeed, prayer and the study of Torah were mentioned together, and there are several other passages that can be cited, all of them pertaining to Cordovero's disciple, de Vidas.[35] Therefore the oral activity either uncovers the hidden spiritual immanent in the letters or draws it down. At least according to de Vidas, the sounds were fixed in the mouth in order to enable man, by utterance of sounds, to cleave to the Creator.[36] Since in this context de Vidas mentions both the Torah and prayer, we may conclude that the uncovering of the spiritual force, or alternatively its drawing down, is tantamount to cleaving to God.

Another Cordoverian thinker, R. Abraham Azulai, regards the study of the spiritual Torah as attracting the influx upon the student and causing its distribution to the entire world.[37] As we have already seen, this descent of the influx is tantamount to an experience of *devequt*.[38] Again, under the impact of Cordovero's synthesis between ecstatic Kabbalah and talismatic linguistics, Azulai distinguishes between those who study the Torah in accordance with its plain sense, and those who engage in its study on the level of its esoteric sense. Azulai assumes that the kinds of *ruḥaniyyut* received by such students are different, but he nevertheless assumes that even the study of the plain sense attracts a spiritual force.[39] Both Kabbalists envisioned this descent of the spiritual force by means of combinations of letters as fraught with radical magical potentialities, thought they were reluctant to declare those possibilities in their own time. This Cordoverian conception is certainly not an innovation of the Safedian Kabbalist; it continues a tradition of magical perceptions of the Torah, which was interpreted by some Jewish thinkers in terms of Hermetical magic. The most important of these thinkers is R. Yoḥanan Alemanno, who discussed the magical nature of the Written and Oral Torah in the sense that Cordovero espoused it in the texts cited above,[40] stemming from fourteenth- and fifteenth-century Jewish literature.[41]

Let us turn now to some Hasidic texts: Cordovero's view on the study of the Torah is shared by the two most important students of the Besht. In *Liqqutei Yeqarim,* from the school of the Great Maggid, the Besht is quoted as saying that[42]

> a person who [orally] reads the Torah, and sees[43] the lights of the letters [or sounds] that are in the Torah, even if he does not properly know the cantillation [of the biblical text], because he reads with great love and with enthusiasm, God does not deal with him strictly even if he does not properly pronounce them [i.e. the cantillations].

It seems that an enthusiastic reading according to the cantillation of the letters, accompanied by the seeing of the lights that dwell—according to our interpretation—in the utterances, is a meritorious religious activity. Here the emphasis is on the reading, while the contemplative aspect is marginal and may itself be connected to the sounds as vessels and not necessarily with the letters. The Cordoverian origin of this view of reading the Torah is obvious.[44]

The strong impact of Cordovero on our topic is evident in a passage from R. Jacob Joseph of Polonoy, who adopts the magical terminology found in Cordovero;[45] the occurrence of the terms *keli* and *ruḥaniyyut ha-Sefirot* constitutes irrefutable evidence for the source of the above view of the role of study and prayer in an oral activity that is magical both in its essence and source.

Again, according to a teaching of the Great Maggid:

> He [i.e., God], may He be blessed, concentrated Himself into the Torah; therefore, when someone speaks on issues of Torah or prayer, let him do it with all his power, since by it [i.e., the utterance] he unites himself with Him,[46] may He be blessed, since all his power is in the pronounced letter, and He, may He be blessed, dwells in the pronounced letter.[47]

Here, the utmost importance of the utterance is evident: the union with God is a function of the power invested in the pronunciation of the sound. The louder the sound is, the stronger will be man's union with Him. However, it seems that one more aspect of the study of one Torah has to be elaborated; like the sounds of the prayer, the sounds of the Torah attract God to them. According to R. Moshe Ḥayyim Ephraim of Sudylkov, the Besht's grandson, who was, apparently, under the latter's influence:

> Since the Torah, God and Israel—all of them are one unity,[48] only when they [namely Israel] study the Torah for its own sake [or name] is there in her [i.e., the Torah] the power of God and she becomes the secret of emanation, to vivify and heal.[49]

Also, in this case, study is an oral activity whose final aim is to achieve cleaving with God, for

> by study and involvement with the Torah for its own sake [or name], he can vivify his soul and amend his 248 limbs and 365 sinews, [and] cleave himself to their root, and to the root of their root, which is the Torah and the Tetragrammaton, blessed be He, . . . all of this is [achieved] by the study of Torah for its own sake [or name] and for the sake of asking from the letters themselves, and I heard the interpretation of the Besht . . . from "the secret of God" that is in them, which [i.e., "the secret of God"] will help them [i.e., the students of Torah] to speak the letters with a firm interpretation "for its own sake."[50]

The "speaking," that is, the utterance of the letters, is obvious evidence of the way the Torah was studied; the sounds produced by the study of the Torah[51] are the means to cleave with the inner divine force inherent in them, probably—as expressed in the passage—as a result of human activity that invests sounds with spiritual forces.[52]

The drawing downward of the spiritual forces by the sounds of the Torah is, according to some texts, completed by their ascension back to God, as we have already remarked in the case of the sounds of prayer.[53] Finally, the relation of the students to the Torah is expressed, as in the case of prayer,[54] in erotic imagery.[55] According to R. Jacob Joseph of Polonoy, the study of Torah has two aims: to embellish it by the study of its plain sense, which is the garments of the Torah; afterward, as the bride already possesses ornaments and garments, it is the time of

> union and copulation and then he strips his garments and he cleaves unto his wife and they shall be one flesh [Gen. 2:24]. So also in the [various] ways to study Torah: after it is dressed and embellished comes the union with and the cleaving unto the innerness of Torah in which is indeed His name.[56]

Actually, it is a Zoharic parable that is the prototype of this passage;[57] however, the Hasidic interpretation stressed the "cleaving," *devequt*, as a superior way to study Torah, and it is achieved by the entrance of the student into the inner part of the sounds, since the union is with the twenty-two letters.[58] The study of the Torah with a loud voice seems to be connected with a certain kind of revelation, as the Great Maggid indicates:

> When he speaks, [being] in [a state of] cleaving to the supernal world, and having no alien thoughts . . . [then] a thought reaches him, as in the state of prophecy. It is certainly so. And this thought comes [to him] because of the celestial herald on that thing. And sometimes he will hear as if a voice were speaking, because of the cleaving of the supernal voice[59] to his prayer and the voice of his [study of] Torah, [and] he will hear a voice foretelling the future.[60]

The sounds of prayer and the study of Torah are, therefore, the substrata whereupon the supernal voices cleave and announce future things,[61] which also reach man by hearing. It seems as if, were a student or a worshiper to concentrate strongly upon the sounds he pronounced, not only would he cleave to them, but he would also eventually receive messages from above.

It is interesting to notice a different treatment of the issue of study and attraction of divine power. R. Mordekhai of Chernobyl, following some earlier traditions, offered a view of letters as palaces that differs from the view analyzed in a previous chapter. He describes the letters of Torah and prayer in a manner reminiscent of the mystico-magical model; the letters are conceived as monads,

> palaces for the revelation of the light of *ʾEiyn Sof,* blessed be He and blessed His Name, that is clothed within them.[62] When someone studies the Torah and prays, then they [!] take them out of the secret places and their light is revealed here below. . . . By the cleaving of man to the letters of the Torah

> and of the prayer, he draws down onto himself the revelation of the light of *ʾEiyn Sof.*[63]

In contrast to the conspicuously magical view of the drawing of the influx within the letters, the letters were also conceived as palaces full of divine light from the very beginning, and study as the way to extract that light and reach an experience of union with the divine. Thus, in lieu of the talismatic view of the sound in the great majority of Hasidic texts, that is, the power to bring down the higher forces by uttering the letters, in some of the texts of R. Mordekhai of Chernobyl these forces are seen as simply passing to the performer from their hidden status within the canonic texts.[64]

We have described above the kabbalistic sources for the study of the Torah for its own sake, which means cleaving to the divine force inherent in, or drawn into, the letters. Let us look at another aspect of the Hasidic understanding of *torah li-shemah,* study for the sake of the Divine Name, in which the influence of the mystical model will be proposed. First, we shall discuss the earliest evidence dealing with the drawing of the divine Presence onto the student by contemplating the Divine Name. R. Moshe Ḥayyim Ephraim of Sudylkov, in the name of his grandfather, the Besht, reveals the following tradition, which includes elements of the mystico-magical model—though the magical element is obliterated, becoming another form of cleaving, the descending one:

> How is it possible to take the Holy One, may He be blessed, as if He will dwell upon man; it is by the means of the Torah, which is indeed the names of God,[65] since He and His name are one unity,[66] and when someone studies the Torah for the sake of God and in order to keep His commandments and abstains from what is prohibited, and he pronounces the letters of the Torah, which are the names of God,[67] by these [activities] he takes God indeed, and it is as if the Divine Presence dwells upon him, as it is written [Exodus 20:21]: "in all places where I pronounce the name of God," which is the holy Torah, which is in its entirety His names, then "I will come unto thee and I will bless thee" [ibid.].

By his studying the Torah for its name, "it is as if he thereby takes the name, and he draws onto himself the dwelling of the Divine Holy Presence."[68] This passage implies also that each and every letter of the Torah is a Divine Name, and by its pronunciation can cause the Divine Presence to dwell upon the pronouncer because of the identifications with one other of the letter, the names of God, the Torah, the Name of God, and God. Therefore, to study Torah "for the sake of the letter" is a very representative Beshtian tradition and is tantamount to studying it for the sake of God's name.[69]

The assumption that links these two interpretations is that a letter of Torah is a Divine Name; from Abulafia, in a passage already partially quoted above, we learn that the seventh and highest way to interpret Torah consists of separating letters from their original word, so that

> each and every letter of it [i.e. the verse] by itself stands separate . . . and according to the [the seven] ways and others similar to them . . . you will understand the whole Torah, which is the name of God.[70]

Thus, Abulafia, like the Besht, maintans that there is a way of approaching the text whereby the letters become separate entities that altogether form the Torah, which is considered to be a continuum of Divine Names.[71] Interesting enough, the same seventh method for interpreting the Torah is referred to in a text that presumably was written by Abulafia himself, or at least by someone in his circle, as

> the study of Torah for its own sake, and the secret of [the word] *li-shemah,* which was mentioned by our masters in every place, is always the Divine Name that is in it [i.e. the Torah].[72]

Transformation of words into letters, letters into Divine Names, their pronunciation, and viewing the *Torah li-shemah* as Torah for the Divine Name—these resemblances between the Hasidic and the Kabbalistic texts must be taken seriously when dealing with probable sources of the Besht's view. Whatever the conclusion of such an exploration may be, the phenomenological affinity between this description of the Hasidic scholar studying the Torah and Abulafia's seventh way to interpret it is, in my opinion, startling. In both cases the final purpose was a pneumatic experience, attained by means of the letters of Torah *qua* Divine Names.[73]

Let us analyze now a clear-cut expression of the oral interpretation of *Torah li-shemah.* R. Menaḥem Naḥum of Chernobyl writes:

> *Li-shemah* [*leshem he* ʾ*]*, for the sake of the letter *H,* i.e. the five places, which is Primordial Speech.[74] . . . Man has to pronounce the letters while being in a state of cleaving to the "Primordial Speech," and thereby it is possible to draw downward the "Primordial Speech"—which is an aspect of God—to Israel in a general way. Since this is the quintessence of the revelation of the Torah, which is an aspect of God, and is in His Name, part of God is drawn and infused into the Children of Israel by means of speech that emanates from the Primordial Speech.[75]

Here, speech is conceived not only as containing a spiritual force that can draw downward other spiritual forces by the intention—*kavvanah*—of the worshiper or the student;[76] R. Menaḥem Naḥum assumes that the very act of speech is a divine emanation, if it is performed in a pure way.[77] In his revision of the Cordoverian conception, "speech," *dibbur,* rather than the letters or "sounds" are the palaces of the Divine Light.[78] In this version of Beshtian Hasidism, the magic of drawing supernal forces downward is obviously attenuated and "the mystical speaker" comes to the fore in lieu of the magical and mystical contemplations of letters and sounds.[79] The mystico-magical model is obviously represented here; in order to draw down, the worshiper must be in a state of cleaving.

In an interesting passage from R. Yiẓḥaq Shapira of Neskhiz we learn also that the initial and final letters of the Written and Oral Torah point to the fact that one should study the Torah for its own sake in order to attain the *Yiḥudim* and

> draw down blessings and salvations[80] on Israel, and draw down holiness on himself, and he merits to be called a holy man.[81]

According to this text, it is the magical achievement of drawing down that confers upon the student the title of Holy man. Accordingly, this passage assumes that the magic operation can be undertaken not only by the elite, but also by someone who reaches the higher status as the result of the magical success. R. Yiẓḥaq Shapira mentions also the *Yiḥudim,* which means in this context the unification between two divine names that symbolize the two kinds of Torah.[82] Thus, a theurgical attainment is perceived as preceding the drawing down of the spiritual force. Although this passage does not mention the mystical component of the model, this seems to be presupposed, as we see from another text of this Hasidic master; in the name of the Besht, he states that

> it is incumbent that by [or during] the study, illumination and vitality will [come] from the cleaving to Him,[83] Blessed by He. And because of it, the study will last.[84]

Both the study and performance of the commandments constitute a means to attract the supernal light, according to another Hasidic master:

> According to the greatness of the commandment he performs out of awe and love, he draws down the light of the Torah upon the performance of the commandments, in accordance with the arousal that he arouses in the letters of the Torah that constitute that commandment.[85]

The assumption that the very reading of the Torah attracts the supernal influx into the letters raises the question of the status of the recitation of other Hebrew texts, those that were not considered to be divine or were not so carefully composed by the ancient Jewish authorities as was the text of prayers. In principle the answer is positive: as Alemanno has already stated it in a text cited above,[86] it is a matter of efficiency, namely of finding the propitious correspondences between the sequence of uttered letters, the timing of their pronunciation, and the goal to be achieved by these pronounced letters. However, the strong astrological view of this Renaissance Jewish thinker is not found in the vast majority of Hasidic texts.[87] In lieu of the higher constellations, another celestial principle was established: the canonical texts have a certain ontological status on high, and their specific content represents a special type of event that may be reproduced by the recitation of the appropriate text. Some of the sources of this metaphysics of the canonic texts may be found in earlier mystical literature,[88] but we shall be concerned here only with its Hasidic version.

3. STORYTELLING

Hasidism, in most of its major forms, has cultivated storytelling as a major vehicle for spiritual teaching. Its creativity in this field is well known and need not concern us here. However, the more abstract explanations offered by the Hasidism as to the religious aims of this activity are pertinent to our discussion. According to some masters, the stories were told as a diversion from the mystical study of the Torah or, as we shall see below, in order to come back from an intense mystical experience. The *Ẓaddiqim* also used this medium in order to attract the masses and elevate them to a higher spiritual status. However, it seems that an additional reason, one that was expressed in some instances by the Hasidim themselves, appears to have been overlooked in the scholarship dealing with this issue. This rationale is strongly reminiscent of the talismatic understanding of studying the Torah, and it merits a more detailed examination.

R. Yeḥiel Mikhal, the Maggid of Zlotchov, is quoted several times to the effect that the telling of a story about miracles influences the "root of the miracles"[89] and causes the repetition of the miracle mentioned in the biblical story.[90] This view does not in itself explicate the precise mechanism of the repetition of the miracle. We may surmise that an Avicennian version of magic has been adopted here, and the mentioning of the root of the miracles points in this direction.[91] However, in all the various versions of this tradition, causality is explained in terms of talismatic linguistics: the Hasidic masters are asserting in this context the view that the letters of a certain word are the container of the "vitality" of that word.[92] Therefore, the repetition of a certain sacred text may cause the reiteration of the primordial event in the present by virtue of the inherent powers of the letters that constitute the story.[93] In the important collection of Hasidic directives named *Darkhei Ẓedeq*,[94] the remedy is acquired by the study of stories on medical miracles in the Talmud; similarly, R. Ḥayyim of Chernovitz recommends reciting the wonders performed by God according to the Bible whenever someone needs a miracle.[95] This principle, which is explained by the talismanic principle, may be the key for understanding the following Hasidic story:

> Our holy master[96] told us a story of the Baʿal Shem Tov, blessed be his memory. Once there was a stringent necessity to save an only son, who was a very good person, etc.[97] He[98] ordered that a candle of wax be made, and he traveled to a forest where he attached this waxen candle to a tree,[99] and [did] some other things and performed some *yiḥudim*, etc., and he succeeded in saving [the son], with the help of God. Afterward, there was such an incident involv-

> ing my grandfather, the Holy [Great] Maggid, and he did likewise, as mentioned above, and he said: "The *yiḥudim* and the *kavvanot* performed by the Besht are not known to me,[100] but I shall do this on the basis of the *kavvanah* that the Besht intended"; and his [prayer] was also answered. Afterward, a similar thing happened to the holy R. Moshe Leib of Sassov, blessed be his memory, and he said: "We do not even have the power to do that, but I shall only tell the story to God,[101] so as He will help." And so it happened, with God's help.[102]

The magical act of the Besht—the preparation of the candle—was accompanied by theurgical acts: *kavvanot* and *yiḥudim*. The next stage is represented only by the prayer, which takes in account the theurgical operation, despite the fact that the details of its theurgical aspect was forgotten. By the time of R. Moshe Leib of Sassov, both the external deed and the theurgical prayer were forgotten. In lieu of the magico-theurgical behavior characteristic of its founder, the later Hasid emphasizes the more personal approach. It should be emphasized that in this version, the effects of the magico-theurgical acts of the Besht, of the prayer of the Great Maggid, and of R. Moshe Leib of Sassov's telling of the story, are identical: all of them achieved their purpose.[103] If there was a decline, it was in the knowledge of magic, that is, of the deed, of theurgy, namely the *yiḥudim* and *kavvanot*; but these losses were complemented by a direct, verbal address to God. The loss of sympathetic magic and theurgy, still present in the practice of the Besht, is compensated by the discovery of forms of personal mysticism. However, the very performance of the story is effective because of the act of repetition of the accomplishments of the earlier Hasidic masters.

In any case, a tale found in another source mentions that the Besht was able to "unify *yiḥudim* and repair the broken supernal pipes by telling stories."[104] Thus, we may assume that from the very beginning, storytelling was, according to the Hasidim, laden with extraordinary powers. Indeed, in lieu of regarding the story as a symptom of the decline of the generations, we may consider it a display of the tools at the disposition of the *Ẓaddiqim*. If the Besht used storytelling from the very beginning as a theurgical instrument, then not too much of the original intent was lost or changed. Indeed, a passage found in R. Qalonimus Qalman Epstein's book seems to indicate that the above story represents a gamut of possibilities for mystico-magical activities. He enumerates the techniques of the *Ẓaddiqim* as follows:

> There are *Ẓaddiqim* who operate miracles and wonders by means of their speech; and there are those who operate by means of a certain deed, [*ma ᶜaseh*], and there are those who do it by means of prayer.[105]

Thus, different techniques can achieve the same results, but they are used by different righteous men. The speech in this text corresponds to the storytelling of R. Moshe Leib of Sassov, while the deed is reminiscent of the Besht and the prayer reflects the technique of the Great Maggid. In the passage immediately following the one above, the Hasidic master explains whom the letters of the speech influence on "the high" by presenting a mystico-magical theory of language. Accordingly, the category of deeds is shared by sorcerers, while speech is characteristic of the children of Israel and obviously superior to any external deed. Perhaps we should read each of the above modes of activity as precisely parallel to the above story; however, the preference for speech may indicate the uniqueness of the Hasidic perception of oral activity.

The concept of sacramental repetition may also explain the special value of telling stories about the Hasidic masters. The holiness of the *Ẓaddiq,* his being the chariot (*Merkavah*) of God, as well as his being an imitation of God, endow the repetition of his deeds with a special aura. By telling stories someone is counted as if he is studying the secrets of the *Merkavah.*[106] G. Scholem has shown a remarkable parallel to this view in the Sabbatean literature.[107] Pending research to determine if similar claims exist in sources before Sabbatai Ẓevi,[108] Scholem's observation must be taken at its face value. However, even if, historically speaking, Scholem is correct, it is likely that the Hasidic authors' understanding of this saying may be related to the talismatic linguistic. The *Ẓaddiqim* were conceived, from the very beginning of Hasidism—apparently under the influence of a long tradition starting with Rashi, Abraham Azulai, and the *Shelah,* to mention only the most important examples—as the limbs and the chariot of the *Shekhinah,*[109] and as a result events related to their life apparently became related to the divine chariot, the *Merkavah.* Indeed, some parallels to Besht's statement to this effect have been offered by Piekarz and Gries from late eighteenth- and nineteenth-century Hasidic authors.[110] In one of them it is possible to detect an interpretation that confirms this connection between storytelling and talismatics: The telling of "the good qualities of the *Ẓaddiqim,*" asserts R. Zekhariah Mendel of Yaroslav, "draws good things to the world."[111] According to a Hasidic story, the term *Maᶜaseh Merkavah* means that mundane stories are necessary in order to ensure the return of the soul from intense states of ecstasy, so that the *Ẓaddiqim* will become the chariot of the *Shekhinah* here below. This is a very audacious interpretation, which diminishes the significance of the personal and individual aspects of the lives of the righteous; it is the distraction of the soul from its sublime experience, by anomian topics, that is instrumental in bringing the *Ẓaddiq* down to normal life and with him also the *Shekhinah.*[112] Thus we witness two interpretations: one related to the magical implication of the storytelling, the other related to the ecstatic life of the *Ẓaddiq.* Therefore, even if the ultimate source of the Hasidic statement is Sabbatean, it was interpreted in Hasidic literature according to the other models, and the messianic element was obliterated.

Last but not least, the recitation of the canonic text was not the only technique for drawing down the influx. In an interesting passage, we learn that even the act of committing to writing someone's innovations on the Torah affects the supernal vitality; the writer is drawing upon his soul vitality from the Life of lives[113] by every move of his pen.[114] This text seems, again, to reflect a talismanic view of studying the Torah, as presented, for example, in Azulai's *Ḥesed le-ʾAvraham,* where the innovations in matters of Torah are described as been drawn down from above.[115]

6

Ẓaddiq as "Vessel" and "Channel" in Ḥasidism

1. SOURCES OF HASIDIC VIEWS OF THE *ẒADDIQ*

The Hasidic views of the *Ẓaddiq* have been explored in several studies;[1] this is understandable as the numerous concepts of *Ẓaddiq* are undoubtedly a crucial topic in Hasidic thought and experience. It is both a mystical and magical ideal, playing a formative role both in the abstract formulations of the Hasidic teachings and in the practical life of Hasidic communities. As pointed out several times in this book, I do not propose to attempt a strong and systematic reading of the various Hasidic sources in general, but rather to present a more panoramic perspective that will encompass different nuances and even diverging strands, not only in the Hasidic literature in general, but even within the writings of a given Hasidic group.[2]

In the specific case of concepts about the righteous, the variety of sources that nourished the Hasidic version of the *Ẓaddiq* was duly recognized by modern scholars. G. Scholem has enumerated three major types of literary sources that informed the Hasidic masters: the older Rabbinic[3] and Kabbalistic concepts; the moralistic preachers known as *Maggid* and *Mokhiaḥ*, represented by a whole range of homiletical literature;[4] and last but not least, in the view of Scholem, the Sabbatean concepts.[5] Although the first two types of sources are openly referred to by the Hasidic masters, the impact of the third is much more difficult to demonstrate. The Hasidic masters do not refer, at least not openly, to the pertinent Sabbatean concepts, and Scholem's hypothesis still requires additional evidence. Such an attempt was made by Tishby's detailed analyses of the impact of the views of R. Moshe Ḥayyim Luzzatto on the Hasidic understanding of the *Ẓaddiq*.[6]

There can be no doubt that Scholem and Tishby have presented some interesting and specific correspondences between Sabbatean and Hasidic concepts of the *Ẓaddiq*; however, not all of these affinities have withstood the subsequent examination of scholars.[7] For example, Piekarz has strongly argued in favor of a different explanation for the affinities between the two forms of the mystical concept of the *Ẓaddiq* than the one Scholem and Tishby have advanced: according to Piekarz, both Sabbateanism and Hasidism were informed by the same sources, the ethical mystical literature that predated these two strata of Jewish mysticism.[8] Using a very impressive series of texts to corroborate his thesis, Piekarz is in my opinion very convincing. However, the ultimate significance of his thesis for our discussion is that greater emphasis should be placed on the second, rather than the third, type of source in Scholem's list.[9] In my opinion, we should add other types of sources, which were vital to some Hasidic views on this subject: those dealing with the *Ẓaddiq* as a "Neoplatonic" and as a talismanic magician. Although most of the immediate texts that informed the Hasidim belong to the first two strata mentioned by Scholem, Kabbalistic and ethical Kabbalistic writings, these sources were not, as seen in several cases above, the primary sources of the concepts; rather they served as channels for the transmission of views that emerged in medieval magic. Thus, though basing much of the discussion below on books that were known to modern scholars, the concepts and nomenclature on which we shall focus in the following pages have been marginalized in recent scholarship. It is important to mention that the proposal being put forth here is based not upon a conceptual comparison alone, but also on terminological comparisons, which help to uncover, in many cases, both the textual sources and the specific model that informed the Hasidic masters. I would like to emphasize that neglecting the analysis of the specifically magical aspect of the role of the *Ẓaddiq* produced not only a less comprehensive image of the *Ẓaddiq,* but also a rather limited understanding of his special role in the Hasidic communities. Before embarking on the talismanic view of the *Ẓaddiq,* which is consonant with the views on prayer and the study of the Torah analyzed before, it should be emphasized that in addition to the Hermetic type of magic, the Hasidic masters were also acquainted with the more Neoplatonic form of magic. Indeed, R. Moshe Eliaqum Beriʾah describes two aspects of the performance of the commandments:

> One is the performance of the commandment here in this world, *in corpore*; the second is the performance of the commandment in its supernal root.[10] Each and every commandment has a root above in the supernal worlds. There, the commandments shine in their supernal root, in an infinite manner and fashion. The perfect *Ẓaddiqim* perform the commandments in accordance with the two aspects: they perform them here *in corpore,* but the essence of their thought is united with them in their supernal root above, that is, [with] the supernal secret of each commandment. And the inner aspect and core of the commandment in the supernal root is the essence and the root of all the worlds. And when the *Ẓaddiq* wants to perform some good deed for the sake of Israel, such as a remedy or similar action, he is elevated up to the supernal essence and root of the thing and he operates there and automati-

cally it is done also below, as it is known to the perfectly righteous. Especially, I have seen this in the case of my honorable holy father, blessed be his memory.[11]

The turn to the supernal source in order to change something below is reminiscent of the Neoplatonic type of magic. According to the author, this explanation is not his own, but is a well-known conception, ascertained by his father, the Maggid of Kuznitz, who was well-known as a thaumaturge.[12] The commandment is conceived according to the Neoplatonic chain of being, which starts on high and reverberates alongside an ontological continuum here in the lower world.[13] This notion of the double existence of the commandments is not new to the nineteenth-century Hasidic master; it had already appeared in the first half of the thirteenth century.[14] However, the magical effects of this theory seem to be explicated only much later in our text. The lower performance is the starting point for a process of ascent. However, unlike the talismanic system, the magical operation does take place here below by the performance of an act, but in the source of the world, within the supernal lights.[15] It should be emphasized that this is an exceptional passage, in which are explained the magical acts of a Hasidic master by his own son in a manner that differs from the talismanic concepts. However, in line with the energetic understanding of the commandments as attracting the supernal power onto the lower world, there is also in this Neoplatonic discussion the commandment that serves as the starting point for the magical operation. Last but not least, the regular talismanic view of magic, part of the mystico-magical model, is found both in the writings of the Maggid of Kuznitz and in those of his son.[16] Therefore, more than one system of explaining magic was acceptable in the same type of Hasidic writing.

2. THE *ZADDIQ* AS A VESSEL

The *Zaddiq* is the person who performs the Hasidic way of prayer and studies Torah for its own sake. Since these two acts sometimes have magical overtones—drawing spiritual forces downward onto the letters and sounds—the *Zaddiq* in many Hasidic texts is understood as a type of archmagician[17] who is able to cleave to God in mystical union and afterward to bring down spiritual force.[18] As we have already mentioned, Cordovero inherited a Kabbalistic tradition that conjoined Abulafian elements with a talismanic perception of letters and sounds.[19] When referring to the possibility of receiving an influx from above, Cordovero quotes a passage that ends with the sentence, "the righteous [*Zaddiq*] . . . with the condition that he who deals with this will be a prepared vessel to collect the spiritual force."[20] Therefore, long before Cordovero—who refers in this context to the "ancients"—the *Zaddiq* was viewed as a well-prepared vessel.[21] On the basis of this quote alone, we may conclude that a synthesis between talismanic magic and ecstatic Kabbalah took place sometime at the end of the thirteenth century and early in the fourteenth century, and the literary remnants of this blend were still in the hands of Safedian Kabbalists.

In the following pages we shall inspect the metamorphoses of two images of the *Ẓaddiq*, as a vessel and as a pipe. It should be noted that the Hebrew terms *kelim* and *ẓinorot* are very important in the theosophy of R. Moshe Cordovero.[22] By using these terms, the Safedian Kabbalist, and implicitly those who followed him, conceived the righteous human being as a corporeal replica of the spiritual *anthropos*, both the vessel and the pipe of the divine influx and the main tool of divine action in this world. The *Ẓaddiq* imitates the revealed divinity by becoming instrumental in the transmission of the divine influx from the Sefirotic realm to the mundane one, just as the *Sefirot* are transmitting the influx from the Infinite to the lower levels of reality. This phenomenological view of the *Ẓaddiq* as a replica of the revealed divinity does not seem to be corroborated by an explicit statement in the Hasidic writings; the closest discussion known to me that implies this comparison is found in an interesting passage of R. Ḥayyim of Chernovitz, who elaborates upon the nature of the first sefirah, *Ḥokhmah*, which receives from the Infinite and transmits the force to the lower divine powers, as a paradigm for man.[23]

The concept of the Kabbalist being a vessel is also espoused by an author who was deeply in debt to Cordovero's thought, R. Abraham Azulai. In a passage already referred to,[24] the soul of the praying Kabbalist ascends on high and cleaves to God and a great influx descends upon her. However, what is of particular importance to our present discussion is a certain change that occurs in the text: while the feminine gender, related to the soul, *neshamah*, is mentioned in the first part of the discussion, immediately afterward Azulai, following Cordovero, shifts to the masculine: "and *he* will become a vessel[25] and a place." Consequently, it is the soul that ascends and first receives the influx; spiritual anabasis is the first step. But it is the whole person, apparently including the body, that becomes the vessel and the place for the descending influx. Indeed, in his *Ben Porat Yosef*, the Hasidic master Jacob Joseph of Polonoy elaborates upon the Cordoverian view and stresses the correspondence between the letters, viewed as a vessel, and the body within which the spiritual force is drawn forth.[26] This change from the ascending spiritual capacity to the descent of the spirituality within the body reflects, in an interesting manner, the two aspects of the mystico-magical model: while the soul performs the mystical act, it is the body that seems to be the locus for the descent of the influx. In other words, the psychosomatic structure informs the two aspects of the mystico-magical model. This conclusion is of special importance if we remember that the role of the commandments, as acts performed by the body, is crucial for the magical drawing of the influx.[27] It is this text, in the version of *Ḥesed le-ʾAvraham*, that was read by R. Jacob Joseph of Polonoy, who describes the righteous as a vessel of the *Shekhinah*, who is, at the same time, also drawing down the divine sparks; he thereafter mentions Azulai's book.[28]

However, apart from the influence of Cordovero via Azulai, the text of R. Jacob Joseph is highly interesting for another reason: the Hasidic master presents the book of the *Zohar* as a prooftext for the magical concept of the *Ẓaddiq* as a vessel.

> The *Ẓaddiq* is called a vessel of the *Shekhinah,* as it is written in the *Zohar,* that "they are his broken vessels" etc.[29]

There can be no doubt that the nature of the righteous person is understood in relation to the magical concept of the container of the supernal power. We shall return later to some aspects of this passage. What is crucial here is the attempt of the Hasidic master to use the classic text of theosophical-theurgical Kabbalah in order to substantiate his view. However, even in the short phrase quoted from this book, it is clear that it is scarcely plausible to consider a broken vessel as a container. Indeed, in the *Zohar*[30] what is important is the spiritual breaking of the heart, not the corporeal aspect of the perfect religious person. Therefore, this strong Hasidic interpretation of the *Zohar,* in effect a misinterpretation, is the result of a magical model that is even stronger than the ethos of the most important classic of Kabbalah.

Before embarking on the other pertinent Hasidic discussions, it should be mentioned that the righteous are described by means of the term *keli,* already found in Midrashic literature,[31] but with the meaning of "instrument"; that is, the *Ẓaddiqim* are the tools of the divine action, but not His vessels. Therefore, by describing the righteous as a vessel in the context of the Zoharic text, the Hasidic master actually misinterprets this classic of Kabbalah in favor of the talismanic view, which insists upon the vessel as a perfect receptacle, not a broken vessel. This is an interesting case of the hermeneutical *grille* of Hasidism, which imposes one model of understanding the *Ẓaddiq* as a *keli* upon another. This move can also be understood against the background of the reinterpretation of the higher world in terms of the lower, mundane plane. Just as the *keli* as a magical tool is intended to become a receptacle of the divine, and just as the supernal divine manifestations, the *Sefirot,* are the vessels of the divine essence, so also the lower *Ẓaddiq* imitates the higher one, who, as we shall see below, receives from above in order to transmit the influx onto the lower worlds. Indeed, this correspondence constitutes an anthropological interpretation, in comparison to the Lurianic Kabbalah, and the dynamics seem to be different from those agreed upon by modern scholars. In lieu of an application of the higher structures and processes on the lower, it is possible to speak about the adoption of already existing concepts of human acts in order to create such a correspondence. The active role of the vessel in magic, namely the view that it both attracts and contains the supernal spiritual force, is not paralleled by the theosophical view of the *Sefirot* as vessels; there, only the container-role is evident. Therefore, to conceive of the *Ẓaddiq* as a vessel reflects a problematic of the inner-divine structure as a receptacle, but also, and more markedly in my opinion, it implies the magical notion of an "attractive" factor.

According to the Great Maggid, "God does not dwell except in someone who belittles himself.[32] Hence, the *Ẓaddiq* is called by all the terms that are related to the vessel."[33] Only a person who is ready to recognize his limitations and his nothingness will become a vessel of the Divine Presence. The very term "vessel" reminds us of the perception of the letters or sounds as vessels containing divine light or spiritual force. Therefore, the *Ẓaddiq* may well be associated with the sounds or letters. Likewise, in the writings of Jacob Joseph of Polonoy, we find clear-cut expressions regarding the affinity between the *Ẓaddiq* and the letters. Let us start with his description of *Ẓaddiq* as a palace or a temple:

> and I shall dwell amidst them[34] since the *Ẓaddiq* is named the temple of God and the Sanctuary of God, wherein *YH* dwells as it is known and [is] widespread in the words of the ancients. And when someone cleaves to a scholar [of the Torah],[35] upon whom the Divine Presence dwells,[36] he automatically cleaves with Him indeed.[37]

It is of paramount importance to emphasize that this early Hasidic master was aware that this formulation is not an innovation of Hasidism but, on the contrary, is both ancient and widespread, a statement that perfectly fits our conclusions from the analysis of the texts. Little doubt remains that R. Jacob Joseph had seen some of the texts he alludes to, and considered them as ancient. The comparison of the *Ẓaddiq* to "a temple," "a sanctuary," or "a vessel," turns in a very significant way, into a comparison to "letters"; later in the same work, the Hasidic master comments:

> "And I shall dwell amidst them"[38] . . . upon the scholars who are the temple of God, neither on trees nor on the stones of the Tabernacle[39] . . . [but] upon the scholars who are worthy of that [dwelling], as it is written, "It is a sign[40] between me and you" [Exodus, 31:13], thereby, the Divine Presence will dwell in Israel.[41]

The Hebrew term for "sign," *ʾot,* is the very term for "letter"; as seen above, the Divine Presence dwells in letters, and the scholars are represented here both as "signs" for the connection between God and Israel and as "letters." Let us turn to another passage in the same treatise, which states that when He causes the spiritual force to descent upon the *Ẓaddiq,* through his prayer and his Torah study, there is no delight greater than this.[42] Hence, because of the attraction of spiritual force onto letters or sounds produced by the *Ẓaddiq,* he himself will also be invested with that force. We learn about the same phenomenon from another classic Hasidic text: "There is a faculty in the letters that enables them to comprise[43] the supernal degrees, and draws them downward onto them, and by the means of these sounds, they [i.e. the supernal degrees] dwell upon the person who utters them."[44] The sounds, therefore, are intended not solely to perform a particular commandment, prayer or study, but also to draw downward the supernal forces upon man.

In order to appreciate better the Hasidic transformation of magical traditions stemming from medieval texts into a mystico-magical technique, let us compare the Hasidic conceptions described above with two similar contemporary perspectives: that of the *miẓwah* in the circle of the Gaon of Vilna and the purely magical view in Salomon Maimon's earlier work, *Ḥesheq Shelomo.*

In R. Naftali Hertz ha-Levi's commentary to the *Siddur ha-Gera,* he states that

> at the time we perform commandments, it is as if we are vessels [or tools] of God and it is as if this Will dwells on its vessles, and we are in His hands as they are in the hands of the stonecutter[45] . . . since this Will dwells onto us and we are its [or His] vessels.[46]

Here the commentator plays with the polysemy of the term *kelim*: it may signify "vessel," "tools," or "instruments." The meaning of "vessel" is readily apparent; man's acting in accordance with God's commandments becomes the vessel of the divine will or, according to another passage of R. Naftali Hertz ha-Levi, of the Divine lights: "at the time when man performs God's commandments, then the divine will dwells on him and they [perhaps the Will] are called Lights of *ʾAẓilut* . . . "[47] These formulations are confirmed by several similar passages occurring in R. Ḥayyim of Volozhin's *Nefesh ha-Ḥayyim.* According to one of his discussions,[48] the words of the Talmudic innovations are "kissed" by God, and are described as building "a new world by itself"; compare this to the above-mentioned views on "sounds," that is, discrete elements, which are considered worlds in themselves. However, in his view, the vitality or light inherent in the commandments is inferior to that existing in "the letters of the Torah that spell the issue of that [particular] *Miẓwah.*"[49] This interesting view notwithstanding, only the actual performance of the commandments can ensure the influence of the supernal light dwelling in the letters.[50] The terms "lights' and "vessels," or letters, seemingly reached the circle of the Gaon of Vilna not only through Cordoverean sources, but also by means of Lurianic texts; however, they function here in the sense we have already discussed, namely that our actions have the capacity to attract the divine into the frames prepared by us. Nevertheless, the difference between the Hasidic application of Cordoverian Kabbalah and the way it is applied here is very significant; as we have seen above, the Hasidim were interested, under the direct and indirect influence of Cordovero, in monadizing the words of the prayer or text they were studying, for even in its atomic state, the atomic component, mainly the sound, is capable of becoming a vessel for the divine presence. In the view of R. Ḥayyim of Volozhin and R. Naftali Hertz ha-Levi, ritual is necessary in order to induce divine will or lights onto our actions. In the latter's theology, only a sequence of actions performed simultaneously may capture the divine lights. The difference between the emphasis on oral elements—sounds—occurring in Hasidism as vessels, and the written letters and the commandments in general, shows the evident divergence between these two perceptions. Moreover, the Hasidic act is focused upon the presence of God Himself in the sounds created by man; in the view of R. Ḥayyim of Volozhin and R. Naftali Hertz ha-Levi, the divine will is attracted to actions that strictly follow the will of God. The magical overtone of causing the presence of God to come into human actions has evaporated.

Furthermore, the immanence of God in the performance of the commandments has striking affinities to the general Hasidic perception of God's acting through man. The passage of R. Naftali Hertz ha-Levi is especially reminiscent of a passage of R. Shneor Zalman of Lyady's *Sefer ha-Tanya,* describing the contemplative mood that has to precede the performance of commandments. He writes that

> before the study of Torah or the [performance of] a *miẓwah,* as well as before the wrapping the *Talit* and *Tefillin,* and also he has to contemplate how the light of the *ʾEin Sof,* blessed be He, encompasses all the worlds and fills all the worlds. It [the light] is the supernal will which is clothed by letters and the wisdom of the *Torah* or the *ẓiẓit* and *Tefillim,* and by its(!) [oral] reading or its wrapping he causes the light of God, blessed be He, to descend upon himself, namely upon the "part of God from above" that is in his body in order to integrate[51] himself and vanish into the light of God, Blessed be He.[52]

The terminological affinities—the mentioning of the supernal light *qua* Will and the discussion of the inherence of supernal light or will onto the commandments as well letters—are remarkable. Thus, we can say that the technique of drawing downward the divine light onto man through the performance of the commandments recurred in a large spectrum of Hasidic schools and even in the circle of the Gaon of Vilna.

Let us now turn to the most striking description of the magical-astral technique, according to Shelomo Maimon, one of the contemporaries of the Hasidic masters. The text translated below will serve as unequivocal evidence for the fact that medieval astral magic was well known in eighteenth-century Poland and could be employed for the building of an intellectual *Weltanschauung* in the manner it was used earlier by R. Yoḥanan Alemanno or R. Moses Cordovero. After a short examination of the differences between the views of Maimonides and R. Abraham ibn Ezra on the rationales of the commandments, Maimon states that

> according to the view of the Kabbalists, the entire Torah and all the commandments are befitting preparations [made] in order to receive the requested effluxes, in a perfect way,[53] without the mixture of any deficiency, and this is the focus upon which the commandments concentrate, those con-

> nected with a certain time or a certain place or with a certain operation, and all of them [namely the commandments] are intended for their own sake, in a very minute fashion, so that if a certain issue will miss the requested operation it will not be accomplished . . . and this is the building of the Temple,[54] the courtyard, and the Sanctuary, and the Adytum and its instruments: the table, the *Menorah,* and the altars, the basin and its basis, and all the kinds of priestly garments and all sorts of sacrifices, all of them based upon what we have mentioned.[55]

According to Maimon and his sources in medieval and Renaissance Jewish authors, the Jewish religion, in its kabbalistic version, intends to attract supernal influences upon places and persons; here it is the priests who are being evidently hinted at. In other words, all the aspects of ancient Jewish ritual are arranged so as to enable the Jews to collect the divine influx. However, Maimon does not mention the "oral" ritual or activities—like prayer or study of Torah—as vessels that may attract the spiritual forces unto them. Nevertheless, a person—the priest—may become a vessel, as we learned from the Hasidic texts. The magical Kabbalah, or magical mysticism, is not only a continuation of fifteenth- and sixteenth-century Kabbalah; apparently, it also serves as the starting point of Maimon's later perception of Kabbalah, which was mentioned above: Kabbalah in its authentic and ancient form "can contain nothing but the secrets of nature."[56] Indeed, Maimon viewed actual magic as containing natural subjects. Dealing with the dissemination of magic in Egypt and Babylon, as well as the idol worship of King Solomon, Maimon asserts that

> all of them were not ignoramuses, but great wise men, whose little finger was larger than the philosophers' loins;[57] the former knew and comprehended the ways of nature—as well as the ways of the preparations to receive the operations of nature according to the will of man who requests.[58]

In Maimon's view, Kabbalah is even higher than the magician's wisdom, using the licit ways of the Torah, but nevertheless able, like the magic of the magicians, to receive "the operations of nature."[59] We may well assume that the Kabbalist, like the magician, attracts upon himself the supernal forces. This understanding of Maimon's view proves that the Hasidic perception of the *Ẓaddiq* as an ideal person who becomes a vessel for the supernal force has an interesting parallel in a contemporary, non-Hasidic Polish Jewish book.[60] Moreover, some of the *Ẓaddiqim* were conceived of as being able to perform miracles, thereby bringing them closer to Maimon's ideal Kabbalist.[61] Let us briefly exemplify how Cordoverean magical Kabbalah was accepted by Maimon and probably applied by R. Dov Baer of Miedzyrec. According to Cordovero, as quoted by Maimon,

> when someone needs to draw downward the influx from *Ḥesed,* let him imagine before him [i.e., his eyes] the name of the *sefirah* in a perfectly white

> color . . . [T]he [high] priests have drawn down the influx from Ḥesed and hence their garments were white garments and this is the reason that the High priest in the *Yom Kippur* service changed the golden garments into white garments . . . and likewise they said of the operations of amulets that when a person prepares an amulet for the operation of *Ḥesed* let him design that name with white . . .[62]

The magical overtone of the color of the garment is obvious; like the magus, the Kabbalist also has to conform the details of his behavior to the peculiar features of the supernal forces he desires to draw downward. When describing the entrance of the Great Maggid to a Sabbath meal, Maimon wrote that

> . . . the great man appeared in his awe-aspiring form, clothed in white satin.[63] Even his shoes and snuffbox were white, this being among the Kabbalists the color of grace (*Gnade*).[64]

As background to the view in this earlier *Ḥesheq Shelomo,* and to the explicit reference to the Kabbalistic link between whiteness and *Ḥesed,* Maimon's emphasis upon the details of the Great Maggid's garments seems to imply that this peculiar way of dressing has theurgic significance. Furthermore, Maimon describes R. Dov Baer's way of concentration: He "held his hand for some time upon his brow and then began to call out."[65] However, shortly beforehand, when Maimon relates the preparation of an unidentified Hasid for a sermon, probably a disciple of the Great Maggid, he writes: "He clapped his hand on his brow as if he were waiting for inspiration from the Holy Ghost."[66] Therefore, according to Maimon, the Great Maggid also must have induced the Divine Spirit by holding his hand upon his brow. Moreover, the anonymous Hasid deals in his sermon with the passivity of man, who holds himself

> like an instrument in a purely passive state. The meaning of the passage is therefore this: When the minstrel becomes like his instrument, then the spirit of God comes upon him.[67]

Although the background of this passage is clear enough, in dealing with a quietist approach to mysticism, at least in Maimon's perception, this text may also imply magical overtones:[68] the Maggid clothed in white garments, concentrating in order to receive inspiration from above, may well be a mystical master who is interested in the same ideal as the kabbalistic magician: the attraction upon himself, by a particular way of behavior, of the Divine Spirit.

3. ẒADDIQ AS A PIPE

The image of the vessel, which apparently attempts to describe the body as the receptacle of the supernal influx, is only part of a larger scheme: the descent of the divine influx not only upon the mystical magician himself but also its distribution throughout the whole world by means of him. Another image, which is coherently related to the "vessel," recurs in Kabbalistic and Hasidic writings, that of the ideal righteous man as a pipe, *ẓinor,* or a channel for the divine power. Again, most of the crucial texts for the pre-Hasidic history of this concept are related to the school of R. Moshe Cordovero, though I have no doubt that he has elaborated upon some pre-existing elements.[69] B. Sack has already pointed out the affinity between several Cordoverian texts that describe the soul of the *Ẓaddiq,* or the souls of the people of Israel, as a pipe and the corresponding Hasidic views.[70] Here I am presenting other sorts of evidence in order to clarify the significance of this image for the magical aspects of Hasidism, namely discussions of the whole person of the *Ẓaddiq* as a channel, and not only his soul.

In an innovative article, Azriel Shoḥat has pointed out the possible contribution of a passage from one of R. Yehudah Albotini's books for the history of the concept of *Ẓaddiq* in Hasidism.[71] Although it is difficult to point out a possible historical filiation between these early sixteenth-century ecstatic treatises and eighteenth-century Hasidism,[72] from both the phenomenological and historical point of view it is worthwhile to analyze this passage again. Because it predates Cordovero's writings by at least one generation, Albotini's text serves as an indicator that the vision of the *Ẓaddiq* as a channel of divine energy preexisted the emergence of Safedian Kabbalah. Therefore, here again Cordovero and his students are important as transmitters of Kabbalistic motifs that were less central before the sixteenth century, to later generations of Jewish mystics.

In his *Yesod Mishneh Torah,* a Halakhic writing that contains several substantial Kabbalistic passages, Albotini describes man as the shadow of the supernal original found in the world of *ᵓAẓilut*[73] but at the same time the descent of the influx from that world to the lower ones depends upon the deeds of man. In this context he mentions the great power of the *Ẓaddiqim,* who are able to cause the descent of the *Shekhinah* below. With the existence of the divine Presence below, the influx, the blessing, the splendor, and the light[74] descend

> from the heights of the high through the pipes of all the worlds[75] to this lower world, where the *Ẓaddiq* dwells. Therefore all the creatures of the worlds are nourished[76] from that influx, splendor, and majesty coming from Him, blessed be He, from above. Thus, the *Ẓaddiq* who is in this world causes the blessings of both the supernal and mundane entities, [which benefit] because of him . . . and he himself gains the merit and causes the benefit of the many, and the merit of the many are depending upon him.[77]

It should be emphasized that the term *ẓinorot* does not reflect here the status of the *Ẓaddiq per se*; the pipes are only activated by him. On the other hand, this term does not stand for an intradivine mechanism, but rather for the channels that transmit energy from God to this world. The righteous are conceived as acting upon the dynamics of this intermediary realm rather than on the divine itself. Moreover, it is the *Ẓaddiq* sitting in this world gaining merit for himself that may constitute the place where the *Shekhinah* dwells and upon whom all the good things descend. In other words, though the *Ẓaddiq* is not the "pipe," he may nevertheless be the lower extremity of a channel that starts with God. It would perhaps be wise, therefore, not to envision this Kabbalist as a source of Hasidism, as Shoḥat assumes, but to see his text as a stage in the development of the Jewish concept of the *Ẓaddiq*. In any case, it is pertinent to mention that at least in one case, which is apparently unrelated to Albotini's passage, the term *ẓinor,* used to mean an extradivine entity that transmits energy from God to the world, is mentioned in a magical context in the late fifteenth century by R. Yoḥanan Alemanno.[78]

The "channel" concept of the human righteous occurs, without using this very term, in an anonymous Kabbalistic passage preserved in a North African manuscript that seems to be independent of the Cordoverian or Hasidic traditions.[79] In addition to some other more common descriptions of the role of the *Ẓaddiq,* we learn that just as the influx comes down to the lower worlds by means of the *Shekhinah,* so it reaches us by means of the *Ẓaddiqim.* This special status is achieved by the cleaning of the material of their body,[80] so that they become transparent, "a clear glass," *zekhukhit levanah,*[81] and are able to cleave to their source. The light of *Shekhinah,* therefore, shines through these bodies. Thus the lower *Ẓaddiq* has to prepare himself so that the "influx will be emanated by his mediation from the supernal *Ẓaddiq*."[82] Important for our analysis here is the emphasis on the role of the body; the *Ẓaddiq* does not draw down the influx: its transmission is automatic, due to the cleaving of the *Ẓaddiq,* whose body was purified by the source of the light and the influx, which necessarily means that a translucent body will be a trident of the light to the lower entities. Therefore, without using the magical language that is characteristic of the hermetical sources, this anonymous text envisions the righteous person as the appropriate channel for the supernal influx. However, the initiation of the process is in their hands: they must prepare their body, and they must cleave to the *Shekhinah.*

A more explicit position is expressed in a passage occurring in Cordovero, Azulai, and Nathan Shapira of Jerusalem, where the Kabbalist is described as standing in lieu of the "great pipe." What is important in the texts of these Kabbalists is the assessment that a righteous man can stand in place of the divine manifestation that is designated as "the great pipe." However, in one case, following the quote we have analyzed above, Cordovero states that

> he[83] will be the foundation for the *Shekhinah.* And since the influx comes by his mediation, the *Ẓaddiq* is in lieu of[84] the great pipe, the foundation of the world, and this is the reason why he is worthy that the *Shekhinah* will cleave

to him . . . Happy is he and happy his lot, because he himself gained the merit and caused the others [to receive] merits, and the whole world is judged as meritorious.[85]

Again, the *Ẓaddiq* is not defined as a pipe but functions as one. In other words, the righteous person fulfills the same function here below as the ninth *sefirah, Yesod,* fulfills on "high." There seems to be an erotic element here, which assumes, following Zoharic erotic mysticism, that the righteous human being can cleave, sexually, to the *Shekhinah.*[86] If so, the image of the "great pipe" has an obvious sexual implication. It should be noted that the expression "in lieu of the great pipe" found in Cordovero and in Azulai's commentary to *Massekhet ᵓAvot* in his *Ḥesed le-ᵓAvraham,* is slightly different in the passage from R. Nathan Shapira of Jerusalem: in Hebrew, he writes *Meqom ha-ẓinor ha-gadol,* which means that the *Ẓaddiq* is the very place where the great pipe arrives. Thus the reader of these versions can understand Cordovero's text as suggesting that the *Ẓaddiq* is the lower extremity of the supernal *membrum virile.* However, an important step toward the Hasidic vision of the *Ẓaddiq* is found immediately following the last passage. Cordovero writes that

when a *Ẓaddiq* and a *Ḥasid* are present in this world, the entire world is nourished, as it is written[87] "the entire world is sustained for the sake of R. Ḥanina, My son."[88]

It is very difficult to fathom the precise implications of this text. The Hebrew term *bi-shevil* is translated as "for the sake of." We can therefore decode the text as referring solely to the great role played by the *Ẓaddiq* in this world, which is created for his sake, just as Jewish authors from a much earlier time affirmed that the world was created for the sake of Israel.[89] However, the Hebrew word can also be construed to mean "by the path." Such a reading is not explicit but is fostered by the occurrence of the term "*pipe.*"[90] In both cases, there is the notion that the world is nourished by a transmitted divine energy that reaches us through a certain mechanism. According to such a reading, "Hanina" stands for a path, just as the *Ẓaddiq* is a pipe or a tube. It seems very plausible that, following the Kabbalistic symbolism of the *sefirah* of *Yesod* as both *the Ẓaddiq* and the divine phallus,[91] the earthly *Ẓaddiq* was conceived in similar terms, as being the locus that both receives the influx and distributes it. Indeed, this is the very basis of the Besht's vision of the *Ẓaddiq,* which was perhaps influenced by an interesting discussion found in *Sefer ha-Shelah*[92] that, in its turn, represents the views of the Cordoverian tradition. Thus, Shoḥat's view that the peculiar interpretation of the dictum of R. Ḥanina was an innovation of the Besht, an application of the idea of the pipe to the Talmud,[93] or Piekarz's view that the *Shelah* is the source of the Hasidic interpretation,[94] have to be qualified in favor of emphasizing the central role in the Hasidic version of this concept of Cordovero, who was himself influenced by other sources. Another important source of the Hasidic view of the *Ẓaddiq* as pipe is found elsewhere in Azulai's *Ḥesed le-ʾAvraham,* where the righteous are described as

> a path and a channel and a pipe, for the sake of causing the descent of the waters of the influx,[95] in order to enhance the fruits of our material and spiritual successes, because causing the descent of the influx of the waters of the supernal pool cannot be done but by the large and strong channels . . . since it is incumbent that by the large and strong channels the waters will be drawn in order to irrigate the vineyard and its plantations.[96]

The corporeal images refer, apparently, not only to the souls of the righteous, but to their bodies as well. This view of transmission is so explicit that a precise parallel is hard to find in any of the later Hasidic discussions on the *Ẓaddiq* as a pipe. Before embarking on some Hasidic reverberations of the above motif, it is interesting to note that the vision of the *Ẓaddiq* as a pipe was also adopted by Lurianic sources, though it does not play an important role in Luria's system. So, for example, Cordovero's text was anonymously copied almost *verbatim* in R. Nathan Shapira's preface to Luria's *Peri ʿEẓ Ḥayyim,*[97] while R. Moshe ben Menaḥem Graff refers to Luria as the "great, holy, and pure pipe."[98]

There can be no doubt that Hasidic masters were acquainted with the version of the Cordoverian text presented in Abraham Azulai's *Ḥesed le-ʾAvraham*; the famous definition of prayer, dealt with above, and which also stems from *Pardes Rimmonim* and is quoted by various Hasidic masters,[99] occurs immediately after the text on the *Ẓaddiq*. This issue, among others, was expounded by the Besht and was traced to *Ḥesed le-ʾAvraham* by Scholem.[100] Thus, the combined influence of *Pardes Rimmonim,* the *Shelah* and *Ḥesed le-ʾAvraham,* and other similar texts, provides solid ground in order to describe crucial Hasidic theories of the *Ẓaddiq* as elaborations on Cordoverian material in this elemental sense.

There is one important issue that should be addressed in order to understand better the deep Hasidic concern for the *Ẓaddiq* as a vessel and pipe. The first image corroborates a long range of discussions connected to the "vessel"-nature of language in general and prayer and study of the Torah in particular. However, the last topics do not involve the image of the pipe. It seems that language and ritual were conceived, at least in many of the texts inspected by this writer, as capturing spiritual forces by their very nature. Thus, they are at least partially efficacious, even when performed by an ignorant person.[101] These practices achieve their greatest efficacy, however, only when performed by the ideal righteous, who are not only able to attract the divine here below but, as seen in the Cordoverian passage analyzed above, are also able to distribute the divine influx to the entire world. Without this critical stage, the *Ẓaddiq* cannot be influential in the community or in the cosmos. The magical origin of the "vessel"—concept of man, which limits the *Ẓaddiq*"s influence to very particular instances, was enhanced to the degree that it transformed the *Ẓaddiq* into a cosmic magician; but Hasidic thought was much more interested in the faculty of transmitting the divine influx to others. So, for example, we read in a collection of the Great Maggid's teachings that the

> *Ẓaddiq* is the foundation of the world. Now it is known that *Yesod* has the power to ascend and draw abundance from above, because it includes everything. The same is true of the earthly *Ẓaddiq*: he is the channel who allows the abundance to flow down for his entire generation. Thus the rabbis said: "The whole world is sustained for the sake of Ḥanina, My son." This means that Ḥanina brought the divine flow forth for all of them, like a pathway through which all can pass; R. Ḥanina himself became the channel for that overflow.[102]

Insisting upon the transformation of the *Ẓaddiq* into a channel or pipe is related in this text to the idea of "the *all*,"[103] because *all* is a Kabbalistic symbol of the *Sefirah* that corresponds to the earthly *Ẓaddiq* and because the whole abundance is intended for the entire generation. Indeed, according to R. Jacob Joseph of Polonoy, if the *Ẓaddiq* does not distribute the influx he has received to others, he restricts his own reception of it.[104] Elsewhere, in the continuation of a sentence quoted above about the righteousness as a vessel, the same master indicates that

> the *Ẓaddiqim* are the chariot of the *Shekhinah*,[105] as it is written regarding Abraham: "and God ascended from him" [Genesis 17:22] namely that they are pipes, so that the sparks of the *Shekhinah* are emanated within them in order to emanate the entire world.[106]

The *Ẓaddiq* is portrayed not only as the channel for the influx, but also as transmitting the sparks from the divine to the mundane plane. The occurrence of the term *spark* is rather unusual. In the classical Lurianic texts it stands for the scattering of the divine particles as the result of the traumatic breaking of the vessels. Consequently, it is a negative event whose repercussions are disastrous. In our text, it is the positive mission of the righteous. Is this connected to the notion, to be discussed immediately below, of the sparks that belong to the soul of the *Ẓaddiq*?

4. COMMUNAL CONCERNS

This nexus between the *Ẓaddiq*'s role as "vessel" and "pipe" is an interesting example of what Aron Gurwitsch has called the Gestalt-contexture. The deep interest in the communal function of the righteous contributed to the emphasis upon his "pipe-role," which also contributed to enhancing his function as a vessel: a *Ẓaddiq* who intends to be a "classical" magician—cultivating a clientele but not a "church,"[107] or restricting the influx to himself alone—is regarded as self-contradictory. A vessel cannot be a perfect vessel unless it becomes a pipe. The concept of the Hasidic *Ẓaddiq* is not that of an individualistic images who alone enjoys the divine influx he receives; in Hasidism, the Ẓaddiq must share it with the community or, sometimes, even with the entire world. It is the "channel" role that become statistically and conceptually dominant in the Hasidic sources, while the "vessel" role was conceived to be either characteristic of the performance of everyman, or of minor importance in the definition of the nature of the *Ẓaddiq*. What may be central for the nature of the Hasidic righteous man is, therefore, not only his "annihilation," the expansion of his consciousness, but his capacity to bring down and distribute divine power, or influx, to the community he serves as spiritual mentor,[108] and also, in many instances, to perform miracles. Thus we should conceive of the mystico-magical model of the *Ẓaddiq* as including three decisive moments: the opening toward the divine and the cleaving to God; the attracting of the divine influx by means of religious activities; and last but not least, its distribution to the community.

Indeed, there are important instances when Hasidic authors explicitly emphasize the altruistic nature of these activities. So, for example, R. Naftali Ẓevi of Ropshitz affirms that it is impossible to draw down the holy influx if the *Ẓaddiq* does not previously cleave to the whole community of Israel out of concern for their material needs.[109] R. Meir ha-Levi of Apta, a student of the Seer of Lublin, describes, in an hermeneutically impressive passage, both the channel-role and the imposed nature of the thaumaturgical role of the righteous:

> "You shall not do after all the things that we do here this day [Deut, 12:8]." The word *here* [*Poh*] seems to be superfluous. But the verse should be interpreted as follows: Behold that the genuine *Ẓaddiq* performs *miracula* and *mirabilia* in the world because the supernal light is emanated into his heart,[110] and the influxes go by his mediation, by the way of the five places of his mouth[111] because the mouth is the end of the head.[112] But another person is not allowed to do as the *Ẓaddiq* does in this case. And even the *Ẓaddiq* himself should not, God forfend, desire it. But from heaven, help and remedy are emanated onto him for the needs of Israel. And "you should not do all the things that we do here this day," namely that you should draw down from the supernal light called "this day" into the mouth, as mentioned above, because whoever does not possess this aspect, God forfend that he might imitate the *Ẓaddiq* in his deeds.[113]

The *Ẓaddiq* is portrayed here in a way similar to that found in the text of Cordovero/Azulai/Nathan Shapira: not as an active agent in the descent-phase of the model, but as chosen by heaven after his mystical attainment.[114] The activistic aspect of the magical achievement is here obliterated. Envisioning the needs of Israel as the primary aim of the descent of the influx, the *Ẓaddiq* himself is conceived as merely a channel; his mouth is simply an organon of transmission.[115] This is the solution for the quandary of the occurrence of the word "here," *Poh*: the consonants stand for another term, *Peh,* namely mouth.[116] The Hasidic master does not comment upon the possibility that mouth is related to wonders, the *mirabilia* performed by oral techniques—incantations of divine names, but this nexus to mouth seems very plausible. The unique status of the *Ẓaddiq* as an effective vessel and tube is emphasized in order to restrict the magical implictions, which could be misinterpreted by larger circles.

The emphasis on the mouth is symptomatic of the bodily nature of the attraction of the divine influx in Hasidism. It is not only the soul that is able to come in contact with the divine; the body, too, as seen above, becomes the container of the divine revelation. However, the stress on the mouth and on oral activity should be seen also as part of the social structure of Hasidism as a mass movement; gravitating around the vocal activities of its masters, Hasidism, much more than Kabbalah, relies upon direct communication rather than written dissemination of its teachings.

This preoccupation with the body should be compared to the way a contemporary of the first Hasidic masters espoused a view very similar to those presented above. In his commentary on the prayerbook, R. Nathan-Netaᶜ of Siniewa describes the people of Israel as bringing down by their prayers

> the Holiness[117] within their palace, which is the synagogue[118] the palace of God, the *Ẓaddiq* himself, whose soul is the bride of God, which is the soul of Israel, which is called *Knesset Yisrael,* bride.[119]

The description of the *Ẓaddiq* as a palace is immediately qualified as applying to his soul, which becomes a bride. Therefore, the holiness descends on the spiritual, rather than the corporeal aspect of the *Ẓaddiq*. Alternatively,[120] the souls of Israel are the locus for the descent, but their bodies are not mentioned. Elsewhere, when the holiness is mentioned as descending upon the brain, the author insists that it is so because it is the place of the soul.[121] In another instance, however,[122] the reception of the influx by the limbs is described, but in this case also they are supposed to become subdued to the soul. The soul is described as a cosmic ladder in terms reminiscent of medieval traditions.[123] Therefore, though presenting a scheme similar to that of the early Hasidim, this contemporary author does not adopt the concern with the magical aspect of the drawing down but is content mainly with its spiritual aspects. The activism or "masculinity" that occurs in most of the cases of Hasidic reception of the influx is less prominent, giving way to a more passive and "feminine" attitude.[124]

The strong emphasis upon the body of the *Ẓaddiq* as transmitter is a fascinating parallel to the well-known concept of *axis mundi*. As Arthur Green has duly analyzed this aspect of the Hasidic *Ẓaddiq,*[125] I shall not dwell here on this topic. However, it should be stressed that some descriptions of the *Ẓaddiq* are reminiscent of ancient rabbinic concepts of the land of Israel. Using a geo-omphalic notion, some Talmudic texts viewed the land of Israel as the sacred center that not only receives the divine power but also distributes it to all the world.[126] This special relationship between divinity and a particular piece of land was absorbed and spiritualized in Hasidism, but the sacred space was transformed into a holy man who, unlike the land, actively ensures the descent of the divine influx.

The above discussions are intended to illuminate the concept of *Ẓaddiq* as informed by the mystico-magical model. As mentioned above,[127] Hasidism as a religious system consists of an interplay between different models. (The katabatic model, which was not discussed here, contributed important elements to the Hasidic concept of the *Ẓaddiq*.) However, beyond the various types of concepts, it should be emphasized that in analyzing the abstract statements, we must bear in mind that they served only as a framework for daily life, where the *Ẓaddiq* had to function, practically, in a given society. The *minutiae* of the acts of the *Ẓaddiqim*, namely the various translations of the theories into praxis, are, in my opinion, as important for the understanding of Hasidism as the more general, and necessarily abstract, descriptions. The fervor of the intensive religious life, the profound sense of responsibility for the flock,[128] are crucial elements that shaped the religious life, just as much as theoretical presuppositions. As important as it is necessary, this emotional aspect remains, however, beyond the scope of our analysis.[129]

Nevertheless, one crucial theoretical question concerning the *Ẓaddiq* and his community should be addressed. As several scholars have already pointed out, the social structure of the Hasidic groups, namely the special relationship that is assumed between the *Ẓaddiq* and his followers, is reflected upon the ideational level by the assumption that their souls belong to the "family" of the soul of the *Ẓaddiq*.[130] This concept, which emerged with particular force during the last third of the eighteenth century, was understood as the theoretical underpinning of the social reality. It is not my intention here to argue against this assumption; however, the contribution of the *Ẓaddiq*, or the distribution of the sustenance or influx that he draws down, was not explicitly related in the sources mentioned above, or in other sources I am aware of, to the belonging of the Hasidim to the same spiritual genealogy. This spiritual organization into soul-families in paradise is related in most of the sources I have inspected to the Lurianic model, since the role of the righteous is to rescue the sparks of his own soul and to redeem or repair the souls that are akin to his. This is, to a great degree, part of the katabatic model.[131] Moreover, it is part of the self-redemption of the *Ẓaddiq* that those souls should be redeemed. On the other hand, the magical model reflects a much more altruistic approach; less concerned with the souls of the others, it emphasizes helping them in more "practical" matters. It is the body, his own and that of the disciple, in addition to the soul, that concerns the activity of the *Ẓaddiq* qua magus.

Last but not least, as we learn from some early descriptions of the relationship between the *Ẓaddiq*[132] and his adherents, we must allow room for an additional type of magic, designated by Walker as "transitive magic"[133] and by Couliano as "intersubjective magic,"[134] namely the quasi-hypnotic interaction between the magician and his audience, especially as understood by Giordano Bruno. Not part of the mystico-magical model, and not mentioned by Hasidic sources, this type of influence does not concern us here; but we should be aware of another interesting category of magic, influential in the Renaissance, that can help us understand the emergence of Hasidism.

We have attempted to illustrate the magical sources and the magical nature of the Hasidic concept of *Ẓaddiq*. Although these discussions cover important aspects of this concept, they do not exhaust its variegated nature; nevertheless, at least methodologically, it is clear that one must check all the pertinent material before a typology of the sources of Hasidism can be presented. Sabbateanism, conceived of as a major source, only very rarely offers precise and crucial parallels to major Hasidic concepts, as the ecstatic and magic literature do. If modern scholarship wishes to transcend the repetition of earlier hypotheses regarding the emergence of Hasidism without independent research in new bodies of literature, one still virgin domain is Jewish magic.

Concluding Remarks

1. WHAT IS NEW IN HASIDISM?

What are the implications of the previous discussions for a more general understanding of Hasidism? We have attempted to show that a variety of mystical and magical elements, concepts, and practices have been adopted, and somehow also transformed, by Hasidic masters. In many cases this has happened only after strong adaptations, which brought the magical concepts and practices even closer to mysticism than the mystical formulations in the magical sources that informed the Kabbalistic texts. On the other hand, the fact that extreme mystical experiences were often coupled with ritual acts performed for the sake of the community shows that Hasidic mysticism should not be categorically identified with "extreme mysticism," since only in some cases were the ecstatic or mystical experiences also "end-experiences."[1] The above analysis of the various versions of the mystico-magical model has shown that Hasidic thought and experience are characterized by sustained effort to keep together the two extremes, the spiritual and the material, as part of both a religious and social system. This type of cultural *coincidentia oppositorum* is reminiscent of the cult of the saints in Christian Europe; those persons who cultivated a life of spirituality and developed a special sense for it became, *post mortem,* the object of cults intended to obtain very material goals.[2] Indeed, in eighteenth- and nineteenth-century Hasidism, as in contemporary North-African Judaism,[3] Islam[4] and Christianity, the religious perfecti, the masters of spirituality, become the source of blessings for material nature. However, while the blessing of the saints was pursued for a particular problem—health for example—the religious theory that underlay the healing was not incorporated into a mystical system and, outside of accidental meetings, could not attract the constant devotion of followers.

On the one hand, Hasidism had no reason not to encourage the extreme experience of the individual, in keeping with the spirit of ecstatic Kabbalah. It is sometimes the way of the lonely mystic to achieve his highest spiritual experience by mental concentration and isolation from society.[5] However, while the ecstatic Kabbalist would consider his own achievement as religiously paramount and meaningful in itself, though it may also have social implications, Hasidic masters would in most cases consider the mystical experience as a stage on the way toward another goal, namely the return of the enriched mystic who becomes even more powerful and active in and for the group for which he is responsible.[6] The notion of redeeming a small elite group, rather than the whole Jewish "nation,"[7] seems to be alien to ecstatic Kabbalah.[8] On the other hand, the theosophical-theurgical Kabbalah has always regarded the common mystical enterprise as superior to that of the isolated individual. As Yehuda Liebes has shown, the *Zohar* and Lurianic Kabbalah have emerged out of the interaction of mystically inclined individuals who cooperated in groups in a common mystical enterprise.[9] This is also the case insofar as some Jewish magicians are concerned.[10] Although such small groups operated around a leader, it is the joint effort that marks the critical difference between the "regular mysticism" of individual perfection and their theurgical aims that fascinated the members of those groups. Hasidism represents another model: the group is a much more expanded one, but it is of such a nature that, as far as we know, it cannot help the mystic in the moments of extreme experience. From this point of view, the group is not functioning mystically, though it will become the final aim of the mystical experience. However, while ecstatic and theosophical-theurgical Kabbalah focus their efforts on transcending mundane conditions and needs in favor of trans-natural aims—total spiritualization in the case of ecstatic Kabbalah and repairing the inner structures of divinity in the theurgical-theosophical Kabbalah—both ideals have become directly instrumental in Hasidism in the improvement of the life of the group. This shift of the focus of religious interest from the theocentric and anthropocentric toward an anthropocentric type of experience that serves, in many cases, a more altruistic way of life, is crucial for the understanding of this distinct type of religious mentality.

The eschatological implications of these forms of Kabbalistic spirituality were attenuated in the mystico-magical model. Even those who emphasized the spiritual redemption of the individual, which would seem to belong to models constituting what can be generically designated as "Jewish Messianism"[11] and are not a form of its neutralization, still sought to experience this perfect state in this world. By centering the weight of the consequences of the mystical experience not upon a subject who is in the realm of the human or the divine spiritual, but on the welfare of the community or the group, the Hasidic model as described above narrowed the scope of its final achievement, which became much more palpable. Magic is as imponderable for the outsider as mysticism, and probably as palpable for the insider as a mystical experience can be. The question of the efficacy of the magical element is therefore easier to deal with. While the theosophical structure is very difficult to contemplate and establish, the precise effect of the theurgical operation is much more subjective. Instances of the financial success of a Hasidic disciple, of the birth of a child by a previously barren woman, recovery from what seemed to be a fatal illness, and so forth, are more concrete than the reestablishment of the relations between two divine *Sefirot, Tiferet* and *Malkhut*.

Neither the escapism of ecstatic Kabbalah nor the bias toward material gain and the resolution of private problems characteristic of the popular magicians are the gist of the Hasidic ethos. Indeed, in some instances we find explicit warnings that magic and miracle-making are detrimental to the true religious life. So, for example, a Hasidic Legend attributes to R. Barukh of Medziebuz the following reaction to the rumors that R. Elimelekh of Lisansk performed miracles:

> How utterly useless they are! When Elija performed miracles, we are told that the people exclaimed, "The Lord is God" (Kings 1, 18:19). But nowadays the people grow enthusiastic over the reputed miracle-worker, and forget entirely to say The Lord is God."[12]

We also learn that the Seer of Lublin, one of the most famous thaumaturges in the history of Hasidism, told his disciple, R. Alexander of Komarno, "I do not pray for anything unless I see in advance whether it is the divine will to pray for it."[13] Even prayer, the most common means of trying to influence the divine, is conditioned by a certain type of revelation of the divine will.

It may be appropriate to offer at this point a more complex description of Hasidism as a spiritual phenomenon. Although operating with concepts and models found in various Kabbalistic schools, Hasidism differs from them because of its syntheses between the extreme mystical and the extreme magical claims of the *Ẓaddiqim*. By offering a synthesis between the magical and the mystical, the Hasidic masters were not being innovative; both of these ideals were in existence long before the eighteenth century. Even various syntheses between them were in existence; apparently, however, the two extremes of the mystico-magical model were never before emphasized and at the same time implemented. Understood in such a manner, Hasidism is not merely a popularization of Kabbalah, a psychological interpretation of Lurianism, or the generic name for social groups rotating around charismatic figures. Rather, it has a unique spiritual countenance, one that is both a continuation of and a significant divergence from earlier types of thought.[14] It is a diversified movement, and this diversity does not mean merely a series of Hasidic groups that differed in a number of details. Even within the writings of a particular author, there may be found more than one view on the same issue. Yet, this inconsistency does not diminish the mystical nature of Hasidism; it reflects a dynamic shared even by the systems of most of the speculative Kabbalists like Cordovero.[15] What seems to me crucial to the mystical aspect of this movement is therefore not the theology embraced by the Hasidic masters, or that there are many answers to the same problem, but the presence of mystical practices and techniques, mystical and magical interpretations of the role of the commandments, and testimony as to the mystical experiences and magical achievements themselves.

Last but not least, in Hasidism as a movement we witness an intensification of mystical phenomena in comparison to all the other phases of Jewish mysticism. With respect to the Hasidic masters alone, we can easily see that a dramatic change occurred in the number of persons who dedicated themselves to the mystical life in an intensive manner. By all these criteria, one could say, Hasidism is indeed a mystical movement, despite Piekarz's recent attempt to argue against such a characterization.[16] By assuming, in order to negate the distinctive nature of Hasidism, that Hasidism mainly adopted earlier views on *devequt,* Piekarz is only partially right. Although he was able to trace some of the sources of the Hasidic masters, this alone is not sufficient for characterizing the thought of the Hasidim. What is necessary is not only an understanding of the views of the Hasidic masters, but the conceptual model that informed these passages. In other words, for an appropriate history of these ideas, it is important to detect the direction of the changes, especially when integrated into a larger model.[17] *Devequt,* therefore, may mean something different, and may play a different role, in a purely mystical model than it does in the mystico-magical model. We should especially emphasize the drawing down of the divine influx as fraught not only with magical overtones but also, as the speech of the *Shekhinah* from the throat of the mystic is understood in some Hasidic texts, with mystical ones. It is hoped that when a more detailed analysis of the katabatic model in Kabbalah and Hasidism is available, a more comprehensive discussion of the interactions between the anabatic and the katabatic models will make possible a more accurate understanding of Hasidism. The fragmentation of Hasidic discourse into small passages in order to offer a history of a certain concept, the ignoring of the interaction between ideas, and the cultivation of a simplistic history of ideas must be transcended by a more complex, panoramic picture of the Hasidic spiritual landscape. Of the possible ways of doing this, one is to adopt a theory of models. Indeed, the syntax of the Hasidic metalanguage, in particular the affinities that were established between the various concepts and the interactions between the models (in the above discussions between the mystical and the magical, and in future studies between the anabatic and katabatic models), are a better means for creating this portrait than enumerating the various nuances of a certain concept outside this context. If the history of ideas can be compared to morphology, namely the analysis of the separate components, their life within the large discourse can be approached by means of the theory of models that functions as the syntax.

2. SOME THEORIES OF MAGIC AND THE HASIDIC NOTION OF *ẒADDIQ*

The Hasidic attempt to synthesize the two extremes casts serious doubt on Martin Buber's characterizations of this form of Jewish mysticism. One of the finest phenomenologists of religion, Buber emphasized in several of his works that one feature of Hasidic religiosity was the retreat from magic. So, for example, he declared that the manipulation of letters and divine names was indeed adopted by Hasidism, "but this magic ingredient never touched the center of Hasidic teaching."[18] This characterization, which is quantitative, appears to be very subjective. Indeed, in the legendary literary corpus of Hasidism Buber's interest in the magical-talismatic theory of language is less apparent. However, in the more theoretical literary corpus, I see no support for Buber's statement. On the contrary, the linguistic theories of Hasidism betray not a marginalization of talismatic magic but, on the contrary, a certain movement of it to the center, combined with the mystical experience. What seems to have limited Buber, when he attempted to juxtapose the Hasidic *yiḥud* practices to linguistic magic, is the possibility of an "either/or" approach. Hasidism is, according to Buber, either devotional, through its investment of energy in the sacramental act, which brings the greater union of the powers above, or magical, meaning circular, since it starts with man and ends in his magical achievement.[19] However, by inspecting not separate statements, but larger passages as we have done above, it is possible to see that Hasidic texts combined more than one ideal. The mystical ideal envisions the union of man with the divine much more strongly than the unification of divine powers that was emphasized by Buber. Inclined to present Hasidism more as a devotional rather than a unitive type of mysticism, Buber at the same time attenuated the more practical-magical "ingredients."

The rich descriptions of the mystico-magical model in chapters two and three may not only contribute to the understanding of Hasidism but to the academic view of magic in general. Let us compare the Hasidic views with the way Marcel Mauss, one of the most influential theoreticians of magic in the last generation, has described magic in comparison to religion. In the tradition of Durkheim,[20] Mauss emphasizes the distinction, even the stark divergences, between these two religious phenomena.

> Magical and religious rites often have different agents; in other words, they are not performed by one and the same person.[21]

In Hasidism, the various entry and exit rites are not only performed by the same person but they are also part of the same sequence of acts or model. Therefore, though they are different in their nature and effect, the mystical and magical acts of the Hasidic *Ẓaddiq* are part of one coherent model, a fact that invalidates the radical distinction drawn between them by the modern anthropologist. Moreover, Mauss proposes to characterize the magical rites as secret, "shrouded in mystery," in comparison to the more exoteric nature of the religious rites.[22] However, this claim also does not hold in the case of Hasidism: the magical rites, the commandments, are precisely that of the "religion" in Mauss's nomenclature, and there is no sign of esotericism in their performance, even when they are understood magically. On the contrary, the magical effect is achieved by those who have a deeply religious orientation, directing their deeds to creating delight in God. R. Asher Ẓevi of Ostraha gave a fine description of this phenomenon:

> He who directs all his deeds in order to create delight in his Creator, he draws down the ʾ*Alef,* the symbol of the Ruler of the World, in all his deeds.[23] But if he takes the delight[24] for himself [alone], not in order to create a delight in his Creator, he is separating the ʾ*Alef,* the Ruler of the world.[25]

Therefore, the drawing down is part of inducing the delight into the higher world (apparently envisioned as male) but not for the sake of the worshiper alone. We can discern here an attempt to minimize the magical aspect of drawing down. Also the "irreligiosity" or even "anti-religiosity," attributed by Mauss to the magical rites,[26] its "abnormality" and liminality, up to becoming a "prohibited rite," do not fit the Hasidic model as presented above. Not only do the magical rites of Mauss not reflect the Hasidic phenomena, but the nature of the magician, as portrayed in Mauss's intellectual circle, is not reflected in the Hasidic concept of *Ẓaddiq.*

A fascinating version of a mystical magician, the *Ẓaddiq,* should be understood from various points of view: unlike the magician described by Durkheim, who has clientele rather than a church,[27] the Hasidic *Ẓaddiq* has (and sometimes even creates himself) not merely a clientele but a full-fledged religious community. By becoming the embodiment of the ideals of the community, he is also able to fulfill, according to the ideology of Hasidism and the expectations of its followers, with a broad range of its needs. Not only is he the spiritual guide of the community and the psychological adviser of its individuals, but he is also expected to be helpful in meeting the material needs of both private persons and the collective. To a certain degree, the *Ẓaddiq,* as described above, functions in a way that is reminiscent of the shaman: "[T]he society becomes the shaman's collective patient. . . . [T]he shaman mediates with the sacred; he heals and is the ritual mediator in his dual sacred and social role."[28] Magic, as it appears in the mystico-magical model, is therefore a religious-natural phenomenon that, far from introducing tension within the religious group, serves as a cohesive factor. On the other hand, the status of the more miraculous forms of magic, which may or may not be connected with the mystical phase, may attract some forms of criticism, as we have already seen above. It should be noted that, if the emphasis placed here on the theory of magic as an important explanatory tool for the understanding of Hasidism is correct, we can see a move from what Frazer would call religion toward what he would call magic, a direction that counteracts the well-known theory of this anthropologist. The theory of alternating fluctuations of the relative roles of the magical, mystical, and theosophical-theurgical is, one could argue, a better description of the "history" of Jewish mysticism than any linear or Hegelian vision of the development of this mystical lore, in the spirit of Frazer's "great transition."

Much more pertinent than modern, sociologically oriented theories of magic is the comparison between the Hasidic theory of the *Ẓaddiq* and Renaissance views of the *magus*. The affinity between these two phenomena, which flourished in different geographical areas and in different centuries, may not seem apparent. However, if we put aside for the moment simplistic historical considerations in order to look at these two visions of the *magus* from a more conceptual point of view, the similarities are remarkable. We shall focus our comparison around a problem that has already been touched on in various ways, but never systematically: magical-talismatic conceptions of language.

3. IMMANENTIST CONCEPTS OF LANGUAGE

As we have mentioned, Hasidism has adopted immanentist kinds of expressions, which are, it seems, closely related to its openness to paranormal experiences.[29] Expressed in terms of "vitality," "spiritual forces," sparks[30], "parts" of the whole that are inherent in this world, or branches and roots,[31] the immanentist approach in Hasidic texts owes a lot to Cordoverian views. This is also the case with another major type of terminology, one that reflects the presence of the divine in the world: the "mystical linguistic."[32] This ontological vision of language was well known in Jewish mysticism long before the Safedian Kabbalah.[33] Indeed, it is the more magical aspects of language that attracted the attention of the Ashkenazi figures in the twelfth and thirteenth centuries, whereas the Sefardi mystics, though deeply immersed in an ontological-theosophical attitude to the Hebrew language and its components, were less inclined to emphasize the practical aspects of their mythical linguistic. From this point of view it is interesting that the ontology of language, which was articulated and elaborated in the Sefardi Kabbalah, and especially in that of Cordovero, was in many ways adopted and elaborated by the Ashkenazi masters. It is their fascination with language, more than that of the Sefardi, that explains the Ashkenazi recourse to Sefardi theories about linguistic immanence and the expansion of those theories in numerous discussions, a few of which will be presented below. While the theosophical Kabbalists used language in general and its components and process as part of their attempts to understand and explain to others the theosophical system, the attenuation of the importance of this system in Hasidic thought left language with a greater role in the general economy of Hasidic mystical thought.

In his *ʾElimah Rabbati,* Moshe Cordovero offers, in a way unparalleled by any prior Kabbalist, a very complex mystical and mythical interpretation of the organs of speech.[34] Expanding upon Zoharic, anthropomorphic views, he regards the five place of the mouth where the speech is generated as the sources of the *Sefirot* and "the secret of the chain of emanation" of all reality;[35] the letters are conceived of as the tools or instruments or vessels of the "divine will," as well as the "secret of the supernal spiritual force," because the latter is emanated, drawn forth, by their means. The very source of emanation is therefore a process understood in terms of pronouncing sounds, and the whole process of emanation is explained in linguistic terms,[36] as we see in Cordovero's commentary on the *Zohar*:

> There is no doubt that the letters that compose each and every periscope of the periscopes of the Torah, and every *Gemara ᵓ* and chapter [*Pereq*] someone is studying, which concern a certain *Miẓwah,* have a spiritual reality that ascends and clings to the branches of this *Sefirah,* namely that [peculiar] *Sefirah* that alludes to that *Miẓwah,* and when the person studies the [corresponding] *Miẓwah* or the chapter or the periscope or the verse, those letters will move and stir on "the high," on this reality [*Meẓiy ᵓut*], by the means of a "voice" and a "speech," which are *Tiferet* and *Malkhut* and *Maḥashavah* and *Re ᶜuta ᵓ de-Libba ᵓ*[37] . . . since *Maḥashavah* and *Re ᶜuta ᵓ de-Libba ᵓ* are like a soul to the "speech" and to the "voice," which are the [lower] soul [*Nefesh*] and the spirit [*Ruaḥ*]. And behold, the voices and the realities of the letters [produced by] the twist of the lips bestow on them a certain act and movement [like that] of a body. And the reality of the letters ascends and is found everywhere on the way of their ascent from one aspect to another, following the way of the [descending] emanation from one stage to another.[38]

This view had deep repercussions in his circle. R. Elijah de Vidas, in a passage quoted above,[39] affected pre-Hasidic[40] and Hasidic views of language. Let us look at some of the immanentist expressions that serve as the framework for both the mystical and the magical concepts of language. R. Shneor Zalman of Liady, for example, writes in his *Sha ᶜar ha-Yiḥud va-ha-ᵓEmunah,* in the name of the Besht,[41] that letters and words that were creative of a certain entity in the particular case discussed there, the firmament,

> stand upright forever within the firmament of the heaven and are clothed within all the firmaments forever, in order to enliven them, . . . because should the letters disappear for a second, God forfend, and return to their source [then] all the heavens would become nought and nil indeed and become as if they never existed at all. . . . And this is also [the case for] all the creatures that are in all the worlds, higher and lower, even this corporeal earth, and even the aspect of mineral. Would the letters of the ten *logoi*[42] disappear from it [the earth] for a second, God forfend, by means of which the earth was created . . . it would return to nought and nil indeed, . . . and the combination of letters that form the name *ᵓEven* [stone] is the vitality of the stone, and this is the case of all the creatures in the world, [that] their names in the Holy language are the letters of the speech that are emanated from one gradation to another from the ten *logoi* in the Torah, by their substitutions and permutations of letters according to the 231 gates, until they arrive and are enclothed within that creature.[43]

This widely read text is important because it shows that the immanentist linguistic was attributed to the very founder of Hasidism. It assumes that everything created by the ten creative *logoi,* and mentioned in the first chapter of Genesis, is maintained by the letters of the words that were pronounced in *illud tempus*. Other entities not mentioned there, like the stone, can subsist only by various derivations from the letters that constitute the ten *logoi*. R. Levi Yiẓḥaq of Berdichev likewise claims that

> the existence of all the different existing entities are the letters of the name of each and every entity, because the letters are emanated from the aspect of the supernal Speech.[44]

Just as in medieval Aristotelianism the forms are said to emanate from the supernal Agent Intellect and constitute, together with matter, substance, so also the name, formed out of letters, descends upon the lower material and sustains the created entities.[45] Like Abraham Abulafia, who interpreted the continuum between the Agent Intellect and the human intellect in terms of language,[46] so also the Hasidic master uses the phrase "Supernal Speech" as the source of letters that will enter the mundane world and constitute its spiritual aspects. Linguistic terms have been projected upon the higher entities, and the emanational scheme was also described in linguistic terms. However, whereas in Abulafia, because of his emphasis upon the superiority of the intellect over all forms of material reality, the material nature of linguistic processes sometimes created an ambiguous attitude, for the Hasidic masters there is no embarrassment concerning this material aspect of language.

In the middle of the nineteenth century, R. Yiẓḥaq Aiziq of Komarno declared that "everything depends upon the letters by means of which all the worlds are unified, becoming one."[47] They were conceived as including the

> inner spiritual force and the vitality of the world. And each of these letters has a spiritual form, a sublime light descending from the very essence of the *Sefirot,* coming down degree after degree until that light will be clothed within the letter [i.e., the sound] on his lips, and they have within them the supernal light.[48]

It is language, among those few other phenomena, such as the divine spark of the human soul, that ensures an unbroken link between the lower and the higher worlds. As we have already seen, it is the talismatic view that confers the more magical aspect of the linguistic activity. However, the immanentist view offers an opportunity to reach back to the divine source by liturgical and other linguistic forms of activity.[49] Despite the obvious impact of the talismatic view of language upon the Hasidic texts, it should be noted that the immanentist approach, as important as the talismatic, is based upon positions that cannot be found, at least for the time being, in magical sources. From one perspective the linguistic continuum does not imply the talismatic assumption. If the talismatic aspect ensures the attraction of the higher within the lower, the immanentist nature of language ensures the return of man to his source.

When compared to the classical models of understanding the nature of language, the Hasidic texts quoted above reflect a strong "natural theory": the correspondence between the word and the thing, or between the *signifiant* and its *signifié,* is not a matter of convention or agreement between men. The created entity is an exteriorization of a linguistic core, the materiality whose essence is informed by the letters that dwell within it. The continuum from God to matter that occurs in the concept of form in certain philosophical arguments in the Middle Ages, which links God and any object here below, was sometimes replaced by the supreme divine speech, which generates the principle of any essence. A deep affinity between name and object pervades Hasidic thought. This fascination with the linguistic continuum is paralleled in Hasidism by the spiritual, or vitalistic type of *continua,* by the possibility of man becoming a Nought, and by the ability of the righteous to draw down divinity.[50] Like many Kabbalists before them, the Hasidic masters would fiercely combat the Aristotelian theory of language as conventional.[51]

4. RENAISSANCE PARALLELS

Any variegated human phenomenon can be approached from numerous perspective, much more so the subject of our study here: Hasidism, a mass movement with strong mystical and magical aspects, which spread over several countries, and whose history dates back more than two and a half centuries, can be considered not only as a chapter in Jewish mysticism and a phase in Jewish history, but also as a form of mysticism that is Jewish, a form of magic that is Jewish, and as a sectarian development that can contribute to a better understanding of the dynamics of sectarianism. Similarly, there is no reason not to compare some of the paranormal aspects of Hasidism with reports of the extraordinary attainments of the shamans. Some attempts to do this may be found in the notes.

Prima facie, a less obvious approach would be to include Hasidism in the European history of Hermeticism. A rather evasive term, Hermeticism was considered by some scholars in the last generation, particularly D. P. Walker and Dame Frances A. Yates, as a central factor in the occultic *amalgam* of the Renaissance and its offspring. Indeed, a comparison of the particular type of magic that informed Renaissance intellectuals shows that they are greatly indebted to Hermetic texts that had been recently translated into Latin.[52] However, while focusing their analyses upon the corpus of Ficino's translations, these scholars paid less attention to other channels for the transmission of Hermetic texts to the West. In more recent studies, the role of the Hermetic texts was somewhat reduced[53] and, at the same time, alternative channels were highlighted.[54] While the general trend of Hermeticism in Christian Western Europe was described as declining somewhat,[55] it is in the Galillean city of Safed, and in Eastern Europe, that Jewish mysticism became the most prominent conduit of moderate talismatic-magical traditions, which flourished, as we have seen above, in an unprecedented manner. We cannot embark here on a comprehensive discussion of this process of Hermetization of significant aspects of Jewish mysticism; nevertheless, one crucial issue shared by some forms of Renaissance thought and Hasidism invites a comparative approach: the way they understood the magical role of language.

The magical theory of language in Jewish mysticism is reminiscent of views expressed by such Renaissance thinkers as Marsilio Ficino, Lodovico Lazarelli, Cornelius Aggripa, and Paracelsus. In a series of modern studies on these authors, scholars have emphasized their common assumption than an identity exists between the word and the thing it signifies.[56] This presupposition is a basic premise of their magical vision of the universe. In other words, in addition to the Neoplatonic theory of magic, which substantially informed the Renaissance view of the magus, the Kabbalistic one—gravitating around the mystical theory of language—also contributed to the emergence during the same era of the magical universe. Hasidism brought to an extreme Kabbalistic assumptions concerning language as the spiritual underpinning of reality. This emphasis was consonant with the emergence of its magical universe and with the paramount role of liturgical texts and the study of the Torah as producing talismatic entities. While for Renaissance thinkers mythical language was only one factor in their magical picture of the universe, which was prominently Neoplatonic, for Hasidism mythical language was pivotal; the Neoplatonic aspects were relatively marginal to its magical configuration.

However, Renaissance thinkers were individualists par excellence, since their emphasis on their particular problems motivates their concerns for astral magic.[57] Cosmology rather than society, or a group, forms the center of their intellectual preoccupations. Magic was not integrated into a social framework, but remained the prerogative of the elite; although they were ready to share their knowledge with the public, the fate of this public remained beyond the scope of their concerns. Operating with the same models of magic, the Italian Renaissance intellectuals and their European followers did not create groups that lived according to their magical assumptions. There are several reasons for the absence of popular religious organizations around the magical ideal in the Christian milieux.[58] The first has already been mentioned: the strong, individualistic proclivities of the Italian thinkers. Flourishing at the courts of magnates, kings, and emperors, Christian intellectuals directed their efforts toward the higher rather than the lower classes. The courts of Cosimo and Lorenzo de Medici, and that of Rudolf the second, attracted intellectuals who were involved in occultism because of the spiritual orientation of those rulers and neglected the multitudes. The other reasons are not less consequential: the strong criticism of the Church had intimidated propagandistic activities in favor of magical world views. Moreover, soon after the articulations of the magic of language, adopted by Christian Kabbalists mainly from the Jewish

Kabbalah, some "scientific" forms of critique were addressed to the mythical linguistic.[59] The abstract language of science had been attributed by some thinkers to the confusion between image and source, *signifiant* and *signifié,* word and thing.[60] The views that sixteenth- and seventeenth-century thinkers criticized constituted, in fact, a theory that was alien to Christian thought in general, which has never substantially cultivated a mythical vision of language.[61] Moreover, this split between Ficino and Pico's private beliefs in astral magic and their adoption of classical Christian rites may reflect a certain distance from the magic as they themselves espoused it. It is possible, as Trinkaus has said of some aspects of Renaissance philosophy, that these were more part of a "poetic vision"[62] than a *regimen vitae* that was performed daily for its own sake. This seems to be the case insofar as one critical aspect of the Renaissance philosophy of man is concerned: from a sociological standpoint, the view of the magus as an intermediate entity between heaven and earth, able to unite them by magic, expressed by Pico under the influence of Ficino,[63] has remained without any practical consequences. They were not only written by an elite, but also intended for an even higher elite, their patrons. On the other hand, the Hasidic *Ẓaddiq,* operating under the impact of similar types of thought, made more concrete efforts to function in a manner that had consequences for the public, social scene.

Hasidic discussions on linguistic immanence were, on the other hand, fully consonant with what the Hasidic masters, as well as other Jewish thinkers, considered to be classical views found not only in Cordovero, but also in many of his Kabbalistic, and sometimes even non-Kabbalistic predecessors. This is also true in many cases of non-Hasidic Jewish authors. Even the fiercest opponents of the Hasidic religious mentality would not protest against the belief in the power of language, as this is indeed not the prerogative of this form of Jewish mysticism. In fact, the magical-talismatic interpretations of Jewish ritual and liturgy, which were formulated long before Hasidism,[64] opened the way to the gradual acceptance of magical world views, whereas in Christianity the magical cosmology was kept separate from the tenets of Christian faith—the Florentine intellectuals being unable to advance a more comprehensive synthesis between the newly arrived Neoplatonism *cum* Kabbalah and the details of the Christian worship. Such an attempt would have imperiled them even more than their hidden allegiance to the pagan philosophy and magic.

There can be no doubt that the development of Western culture has produced an world view that is dramatically different from the occult *Weltanschauung* of some Renaissance thinking and its reverberations. Its final result is modern science. Kabbalah, which has informed some of the occult currents in the West, has had its own resurgence both in Italy, in the writings of R. Yoḥanan Alemanno and some of his followers, and in Safed. It is the repercussions of the Safedian school of Cordovero, a type of mystical lore that has incorporated talismatic magic and ecstatic Kabbalah, that affected the emergence of Hasidism. The enchanted world of Kabbalah was elaborated by the eighteenth- and nineteenth-century Hasidic masters far beyond what is found in Kabbalistic literature. Both the emanative scheme and linguistic immanentism have created a world view replete with divine Presence.

The "warm" cosmology of Hasidism, which emphasized not only theological immanentism but also care for the community and the attempt to improve its well-being by means of the talismatic-magical concept of the whole range of Jewish ritual, was confronted with one of the reverberations of the "cold" scientific approach, placed in the service of a nationalistic mythology: Nazism. The results are well-known. They raise the problem of what is finally the more dangerous, magical lore that cares and is responsible, though the object of this care is a small community, or of a scientific-technological approach that is apparently more powerful but, at the same time, radically hostile to other human beings. When comparing the two worldviews, scholars must take the historical repercussions into consideration.[65]

5. RETREAT?

As mentioned above, the talismatic-magical elements were absorbed over a long period of time in Jewish culture, from the early twelfth to the middle sixteenth century. However, crucial to the acceptance of these elements were the syntheses created between them and the Jewish rites. By proposing that the commandments are the main avenue for returning from the extreme experience of annihilation,[66] the strain between the spiritual and enthusiastic aspirations on one hand and the Jewish conservative way of life on the other was to a great extent solved.[67] Moreover, as we have already emphasized beforehand, on the social level the Hasidic master was portrayed as the leader of the community not only because of his spiritual attainment but also because of his ability to return from his mystical journey and provide sustenance for his flock. The magical model, which is based upon nomian practices, complements the strong spiritual drive of the ecstatic model and ensures the emergence of a much more comprehensive and, from the social point of view, more balanced model, which takes into consideration on one hand the mystical attainment of the individual and his corporeal well-being, and on the other the needs of the masses. In the above discussions we have dealt with the activist solution, namely with instances where there is no reason to assume a "passive performance," namely a quietist submission to God's will while keeping the commandments.

By pointing out the compensating part of the mystico-magical model in the "exit" understanding of the rite in the school of the Great Maggid,[68] we may reformulate a question that has concerned modern scholarship on Hasidism: the retreat of the later generation of Hasidic masters from extreme forms of mystical experience. So, for example, Schatz-Uffemheimer maintained that there was a retreat from quietistic formulations,[69] while Green has pointed out a turn among the later masters toward more moderate expressions of mystical union.[70] In this regard, we should pay due attention to two issues: already at the beginning of Hasidism there was a more balanced relationship between mystical union, ecstasy, and quietism on one hand, and activism on the other. The magical model was accepted in many cases as complementing the extreme mystical one, and I assume that this was already the case in the world view of the Besht himself. Moreover, the assumption that some masters were afraid of the extremity of the stand of their predecessors is based upon two other implicit assumptions: one, that mystical union and quietist elements were novel in the eighteenth century and, at the same time, that they were regarded as somewhat problematic in Jewish mysticism; and that in nineteenth century Hasidism there was a retreat from these formulations. However, an inspection of earlier Kabbalistic sources, as well as the writings of later Hasidic masters like R. Moshe Ḥayyim Ephraim of Sudylkov,[71] R. Dov Baer, the middle Rebbe of Ḥabad, R. Aharon ha-Levi of Staroselye, and later on those of R. Yiẓḥaq Aiziq Yehudah Safrin of Komarno,[72] may lead to a different conclusion.

The first Hasidic masters indeed constitute a group inclined to extreme formulations, which were nevertheless less audacious and less problematic to the Jews, including their elite, than modern scholars would assume. A more mystical understanding of certain spiritual phenomena, already in existence centuries before Hasidism—in ecstatic Kabbalah for example, or in Safedian spirituality[73]—may help to give a more nuanced picture of the whole range of Jewish mysticism. Instead of regarding the extreme mystics as marginal exceptions within the economy of the history of Hasidism, some of the students of the Great Maggid may be seen as inspiring later generations with Hasidic versions of mystical experiences, which were, apparently, experienced and recapitulated time and again.[74] Indeed, the later masters did not contribute novel formulations, but in itself this fact does not constitute decisive proof of the retreat; rather it implies the routinization of a certain mystical phenomenon, which gives rise not to new formulations but to their widespread implementation in practice. In other words, the "cooling" of Hasidic enthusiasm in the nineteenth century is not a clear-cut process; it occurred in many cases, but there was also a continuation of mystical fervor among many of the Hasidic masters. Up to the end of the third quarter of the nineteenth century, with the death of R. Yiẓḥaq Aiziq Safrin of Komarno, a rather vital mystical, sometimes ecstatic, uninterrupted line is apparent. It should be mentioned that around the middle of that century, an important line of Hasidic spirituality, represented by the Kotzk, Izbica, and Radzin schools, preferred a less enthusiastic form of spirituality, but nevertheless proposed new lines of Hasidic religious modalities. From these points of view, it seems that some of the formulations of anthropologists or sociologists of religion regarding the routinization of the initial charisma in revivalist movements—like Knox's generalization, formulated in the context of Christian revivalist movements, that "always the first fervours evaporate; prophecy dies out, and the charismatic is merged in the institutional"[75]—are not so pertinent as far as Hasidism is concerned.[76] Today it is sufficient to observe, even superficially, the followers of the various nineteenth-century trends of Hasidism to see that the terrible encounter between their ancestors, in their strongholds in Poland and Russia, and the bearers of scientific-mythological Nazism, was unable to extirpate their vital religiosity. The "magic" of language is sometimes able to prevail over the efficiency of technology.

6. HASIDISM AS MYSTICISM

The luxuriant Hasidic literature should not be identified too easily, and certainly not in toto, as a full-fledged mystical literature. Replete with hermeneutical, homiletical, ethical, theosophical, magical, and other kinds of topics, it may nevertheless be understood to reflect, in many cases, intense mystical experience. Some, as discussed above, are means-experiences, which, intense as they might have been, were understood as part of the broader picture of the communal role of the *Ẓaddiq*. However, it must be emphasized that there are many instances in Hasidic mysticism where extreme experiences, which can be designated as *unio mystica* experiences, may also be found as end-experiences. We have dealt elsewhere with expressions of this type.[77] However, I would like to address, at the end of this study, some connections to mysticism in Hasidism, based upon our analyses above.

Mystical experiences, though sometimes attained only after a much longer period of practice, were said to be achieved in a rather easy manner.[78] Many of the ascetic practices found in Kabbalistic literature were abrogated by the Hasidic masters.[79] However, what characterizes Hasidic mysticism, especially because of its intensity, as expressed by the desire for annihilation and self-effacement, is the absence of negative post-experience feelings, known in other forms of mysticism as the desert-experience of the feeling of barrenness, or the dark night of the soul. R. Naḥman of Braslav aside, the retreat from the experience of union with God was not conceived as a return to a state of mind, or soul, in which one experienced an abyss between oneself and God, a state that implied a fall of the soul. The Hasidic formulations concerning the energetic plenitude of the mystic who returns to normal life leave little room for the assumption that a dark night of the soul was haunting his consciousness. The end of the experience was conceived of not as a long period of divorce but as a short break. In many cases it is obvious that the "fall" or state of *qatenut* is but an occasion for attaining a higher type of experience. Given the assumption that Jewish ritual time served as a clock for returning to the mystical experience, contact with the divine was considered a daily occurrence. Moreover, strong union with the divine was followed by what can be conceived to be a weaker form of union with the descending divinity or vitality or spiritual force.

The separation is to be understood as a gradual process, not as an abrupt and forced distancing of the soul from the divine. Images of the righteous as a vessel or channel reflect this dissipation of the contact with the divine, which passes through the soul and body of the mystic to others.

The Hasidic assumption as to the case of achieving the mystical experience,[80] a rather exceptional view in the phenomenology of mysticism, is also found in Abraham Abulafia's Kabbalah. In many cases he too mentions this "easiness,"[81] which should be understood against the background of the presence of strong and detailed mystical techniques in ecstatic Kabbalah. If the first phase of the mystico-magical model includes activist components like mental concentration and divestment of corporeality, in the magical phase there is room for more active and passive attitudes. The passive attitudes were analyzed by Schatz-Uffenheimer; as she has explicitly noticed, they do not represent Hasidic mysticism as a whole.[82] According to her analyses, quietist experiences represent the most important innovation that Hasidism has invented as a mystical phenomenon in Judaism.[83] In the descriptions above we have attempted to stress the active side, which ensures the magical nature of the drawing down of the influx. This activist attitude is not merely one of many characteristics of Hasidic mysticism, but is indeed central, far more dominant than the passive, quietist characteristics analyzed in the studies of Weiss and Schatz-Uffenheimer. If our analysis is correct, the awareness of the magical component in Hasidism can contribute to a fresh look at the nature of this form of mysticism.

The basic Hasidic approach to the encounter with the divine is much closer to the mysticism of love, whereas ecstatic Kabbalah is more inclined to the mysticism of knowledge and understanding. To be sure, we find in Hasidism many cases where philosophical terms are used, including several important instances where the term intellect, *sekhel,* or *maskil,* was used to point out the higher entities.[84] In Abraham Abulafia's Kabbalah, as in Maimonides, the language of love portrays the longing of the soul or the intellect for God, or as in the case of the ecstatic mystic, the unitive contact with divinity.[85] Nevertheless, we can differentiate between these two forms of Jewish mysticism as representing two distinct mystical modalities. The move toward a much more emotional or affective form of mysticism[86] was mediated both by the Safedian Kabbalistic-ethical literature, written by mystics who were well-acquainted with Abulafia's philosophical mysticism, and by the mystical thought of the Maharal. It seems that despite the acquaintance of the Safedian Kabbalists with ecstatic Kabbalah, they decided, apparently following the Zoharic approach,[87] to opt for a less elitist form of mysticism, as the emergence of the literary genre of ethical literature demonstrates. The ideal of *devequt,* discussions of *hitbodedut,* recommendations of *hishtawwut,* and the practice of combinations of letters, all occurring in the Cordoverian literature, occupy a relatively smaller place than they do in ecstatic Kabbalah as presented in the writings of Abraham Abulafia, Yiẓḥaq of Acre, or Yehudah Albotini. The extreme mysticism of the ecstatics was domesticated in the ethical literature. On the other hand, Spanish Kabbalah as a whole, with the Zohar as its main representative, was less interested in strong ecstatic experience and devoid of mystical techniques to attain *unio mystica* experiences, absorbed, in Cordovero's school, deeper mystical dimensions because of the encounter with ecstatic Kabbalah. The Safedian Kabbalists, however, did not give up the theosophical system as a major focus; it became a paradigm to be imitated. The Safedian Kabbalists assumed that through *imitatio Dei* they would attain a profound mystical experience. The discursive emphasis of the Cordoverian school, and even more of the Lurianic one, easily balanced the importance of the ecstatic elements.

However, because of the attenuation of the role of theosophical components in the mystical systems of Hasidism, some elements of ecstatic technique, and the importance of the mystical ideals, came to the fore more easily, together with the magical aspects. Hasidic forms of mysticism, certainly those belonging to the mystico-magical model, should be understood as part of fluctuations taking place within the basic motifs, themes, and models of Jewish mysticism as a whole. Without a more comprehensive understanding of all the mystical possibilities inherent in the literary corpora that constitute Jewish mysticism, the explanations concerning Hasidism as mysticism will be more inclined to reductions to the seemingly similar of the immediately preceding historical periods. Thus a panoramic approach to Jewish mysticism, and especially to Hasidism, is required for a more accurate understanding of the processes related to the various encounters between models and historical circumstances. However, while emphasizing the vital contribution of the earlier stages of Jewish mysticism to the spiritual physiognomy of Hasidism, we must not remain solely within the perimeter of Jewish mysticism and history; rather, efforts must be made to compare Hasidic mysticism and magic to pertinent phenomena in European occultism, with its intellectualist propensities and general religious categories, such as Shamanism, with its more concrete elements. To paraphrase a recent definition of the Sufi philosophy of illumination, Hasidism is a unique synthesis of primordial themes and concepts, traditions as old and primal as those of the paleolithic age and as late and refined as those of Renaissance and early modern religiosity.[88] It seems to me that without paying due attention to the primal, magical aspect of this spiritual phenomenon, and by contemplating Hasidism only from the refined—that is, the mystical—perspective, modern scholarship offers a unilateral and somewhat distorted picture of the latest phase of Jewish mysticism. Hasidism is a religious modality that combined both preaxial and axial traits,[89] and the awareness of this synthesis is decisive for the understanding of its dissemination among the masses and its attractiveness to the elite.

Appendix A: Psychologization of Theosophy in Kabbalah and Hasidism

One of the main scholarly explanations for the shift from Lurianic Kabbalah to Hasidism is the psychological interpretation of Lurianic theosophy offered by the Hasidic masters.[1] Indeed, there are numerous examples of such a psychological orientation in the writings of most of the eighteenth-century Hasidic figures.[2] However, though this is an indisputable fact, a deeper understanding of this phenomenon would take consideration more than one factor. In other words, in addition to the inner drive of the Hasidic masters to interpret their sources in a particular manner, we must also take into account extant Kabbalistic trends, which may have contributed to the Hasidic emphasis on the reflection of the divine attributes within man, thus reducing to a certain extent the novelty of Hasidism.

First, it is a fact, pointed out recently, that at least in one case, that of *qatenut* and *gadelut,* a psychological interpretation is inherent in the Lurianic sources.[3] Second, psychological interpretations of theosophical-hypostatic entities are found since the thirteenth century in two different Kabbalistic schools, a fact that requires a substantial qualification of the sharp distinction between the psychological understanding of the theosophical system of Hasidism and that of the early Kabbalah. In other words, just as magic and ecstasy, which were already in existence in Kabbalistic thought, were given a much more prominent role in Hasidism, so also the psychological understanding of Kabbalah was already present in certain earlier sources without coming to the fore. In the absence of an appropriate recognition of these facts, it will be difficult to understand one major aspect of Hasidic hermeneutics.

The psychological understanding of the whole range of Jewish canonic texts as allegories of the inner life of the mystic and his spiritual achievements is much more common than the experiential reading described above.[4] This fact was indeed prominent in the eyes of the opponents of Hasidism among the Kabbalists, who protested against this transformation of divine attributes into human ones.[5] Although this accusation might be considered an indication that the Hasidic move constitutes an innovation, this argument is part of an assault that does not pay attention to historical truth; it is similar to what occurred when Hasidic thought was accused of pantheism, a view already found in Cordovero, as the Hasidim themselves pointed out in their response.[6]

However, there is a certain point in the critique that is worthy of deeper investigation: the claim that the Hasidic spiritualization of the divine attributes is reminiscent of the philosophical allegory of the late thirteenth century.[7] Indeed, there are many precedents to the allegorizations of eighteenth-century Hasidism; first and foremost were the philosophical allegories, both Neoplatonic and Aristotelian, which were applied to both Biblical and Talmudic texts. This represents just one of several forms of allegory cultivated by the Jewish philosophers.[8] The main tendency was represented by physical exegesis, which can be characterized as the "objective" approach, namely the decoding of the ancient and early medieval sources, which are assumed to point to the experiences of the ancient heroes and protagonists, or to psychological processes in general, without expressing, at least not in explicit terms, the spiritual experiences of the interpreter. It is also exceptional to find in the medieval sources overt indications of the religious significance of imitating those figures on their psychological journey, though this may be implicit in some cases.

A major exception to the "objective approach" in hermeneutics is found in the ecstatic Kabbalah. Although deeply influenced by Maimonidean exegesis, Abraham Abulafia interpreted the biblical texts as pointing first and foremost to spiritual attainments whose meanings are found, in most cases, beyond time and place. We may assume that, at least in some instances, the psychological interpretations also reflect the impact of the mystical experiences of Abulafia himself, and this is one of the reasons it seems appropriate to designate this form of experiential, psychological exegesis as spiritual interpretation.[9]

Another form of exegesis found in the writings of Abulafia is also relevant to the later development of Jewish mysticism: the psychological transformation of the Kabbalistic-theosophical hypostases. The *Sefirot,* constituting one of the features of theosophical Kabbalah, were conceived either as divine manifestations, when they were described as forming the essence of the divine,[10] or, in other kinds of theosophies, as its tools or vessels.[11] Although there was widespread use of anthropomorphic imagery in portraying a homologous realm within the divine, the analogies between the various parts of the human body and its spiritual constitution did not contribute to an articulated psychological exegesis that could interpret the scriptures on the psychological as well as the symbolic-theosophic level. However, in the case of two thirteenth-century Kabbalists, we may detect an attempt to understand the Sefirotic ontology as a homologue of the human personality, in body and spirit. This psychological tendency to interpret the theosophical *anthropos* psychologically can be explained in two different ways: First, these Sefirotic hypostases represent projections of psychological experiences or spiritual states, as R. J. Z. Werblowsky has suggested.[12] In this case, theosophical Kabbalah constitutes yet another example in the history of religion of scholars tending to prefer an experiential over a theological basis for the supernal ontological structures. So, for example, some scholars have described Gnostic theosophy as projection[13] while others have interpreted the Plotinian hierarchy as representing inner faculties and experiences.[14] However, though such a view seems reasonable in the case of the sources of the theosophical system, the fact is that the explicit spiritual interpretations of the Sefirotic hypostases that concern us here appear only one century after the emergence of the full-fledged theosophical system. Thus, at least in the case of Abraham Abulafia, I am inclined to see his interpretation not so much as retracing the psychological roots of the theosophical system, but as part of an intellectual competition between two different and competing forms of Kabbalah: his ecstatic one versus the theosophical one.[15] This is, then, a strong hermeneutical move on the part of the founder of the ecstatic Kabbalah, who apparently attempted to integrate the main points of his adversary into his own system by transforming them drastically. This shift is best represented in one of Abulafia's epistles, where he envisions the *Sefirot* as entities reflecting human spiritual activities:

> The masters of the *Sefirot* call them by names[16] and say that the name of the first *Sefirot* is "Althought," and they add another name in order to explain its meaning, which they call *Keter ᶜEliyon,* since the Crown is something lying on the heads of Kings . . . and the [master of *Sefirot*] will add another name and will call it "Primeval Air" . . . and so will he do to each and every *Sefirah* of the ten *Sefirot Belimah.* But the master of the [Divine] Names have [quite] another intention, completely superior to that;[17] this path of Names is of such a profundity that in the profundities of human thought there is no one thing more profound and more excellent than it, and it alone unites human thought with the Divine [Thought],[18] to the extent of human capability, and according to human nature. And it is known that human thought is the cause of his wisdom, and his wisdom is the cause of his understanding, and his understanding is the cause of his mercy, and his mercy is the cause of his reverence to his Creator; and his fear is the cause of his beauty, and his beauty is the cause of his victory,[19] and his victory is the reason of his splendor, and his splendor is the cause of his essence,[20] which is named Bridegroom,[21] and his essence is the cause of his Kingship, named his Bride.[22]

Abulafia therefore reinterprets the theosophical hierarchy, which is basically hypostatical, to refer to a hierarchy of human actions, partly psychological, partly corporeal. It should be emphasized that this scheme is proposed as being a superior understanding of the *Sefirot,* the aim of which Abulafia sees as mystical union rather than theurgical operation or even theosophical gnosis. In Abulafia's text it is depicted as a translation of divine thought, which has come into contact with human thought, into physical and external activity into which the recondite human thought "descends," through wisdom and understanding, onto a rather external quality—mercy, and gradually to more corporeal aspects of man. The last two *Sefirot,* which have obvious sexual valences, are to be understood, not on the theosophical level, in which they point to infradivine relations, but as alluding to the relationship between man and God, or between Bride and Bridegroom.[23] In his *Mafteaḥ ha-Sefirot,* Abulafia's Commentary on Deuteronomy, the entire Sefirotic realm is described as referring, again, to human activities:

> The influx expanding from the "one who counts the numbers"[24] is comprised in and passes through ʾA[lef] to Y[od], from the first *Sefirah* to the tenth, that is, from "Althought" to "Justice," and [only] through them will human thought be right.[25] That is, Wisdom will emerge from Althought, and understanding will emerge from the wise Althought; and from the thought of wisdom and understanding Greatness, which is the attribute of Ḥesed, [will emerge], and those who think on them will become great; and out of all of them *Gevurah* [will emerge], and the power of the thinker will increase, since he thinks that he is the counter of the *Sefirot.* And from them Truth will emerge, and immediately Beauty forcefully reveals itself and causes the person attaining it to be proud of it and of prophecy, according to truth. However, prophecy [comprises] degrees of comprehension, and thus, whoever comprehends the truth is similar to Jacob, our ancestor, as it is written: [Micah 7:20] "Thou wilt show truth to Jacob, . . . " And the nature of Victory necessarily emerges from "Truth" and whoever knows the Truth, can subdue even the structure of planets and stars,[26] and then he will be blessed through the name *ʾEl Shaddai,* and Victory will produce from itself Splendor, as in the verse [Num. 27:20]: "And thou shalt put some of thy splendour upon him. . . . " And the ninth *Sefirah* . . . is called by the name *kol neshamah Yesod be-Yah* . . . and it is the source of influx and blessing . . . and the tenth *Sefirah,* which is the *Shekhinah,* whose name is Justice . . . and from this issue hinted in the *Sefirot*—according to [someone's] comprehension of them, and according to the force someone received from them, which depends upon the knowledge of the true names,[27] the power of one prophet will surpass and become greater than the power of another prophet.[28]

In another epistle, he asserts that:

> man can cleave to each and every *Sefirah* by the essence[29] of the influx expanding from its emanation on his *Sefirot,*[30] which are his attributes . . . [31] And it is necessary to mentally concentrate[32] [in order to attain] an apprehension, until the expert Kabbalist will attain from them an influx of which he is aware.[33] This is so given the fact that the written letters are like bodies, and the pronounced letters are spiritual [by nature] and the mental [letters] are intellectual[34] and the emanated [letters] are divine[35] . . . and out of [his] concentration[36]—to prepare the power of the bride to receive the influx from the power of the bridegroom, the divine [letters] will move the intellectual ones, and because of the sustained concentration and its greatness and power, and the great desire [of the Kabbalist] and his forcible longing and his mighty infatuation to attain the *devequt* and the Kiss,[37] the power of the bride[38] and

> her name and her essence[39] will be positively known[40] and preserved for eternity, since they were found to be righteous, and the separated [entities] were united[41] and the united ones were separated[42] and the reality is transformed,[43] and as a consequence, every branch will return to its root and will be united with it[44] and every spiritual [entity] [will return] to its essence[45] and will be linked to it [Exod. 26:6], "and the Tabernacle will become one" [Zech. 14:9], "and the Tetragrammaton[46] will be the King of the entire world, and in that day, the Tetragrammaton will be one and His Name one," and if he will do so to the order of the *Sefirot* and the structure of twenty-two letters [Ezek, 37:17], "and join them one to the other to make one stick, and they shall become one in they hand.[47]

For Abulafia, mystical union is to be attained by means of the ten *Sefirot,* or attributes intrinsic in human nature, by means of which one is able to collect or to capture the emanation flowing from the supernal *Sefirot.* What is critical for the understanding of Abraham Abulafia's view is that the cleaving is not attained by establishing a direct contact with the supernal *Sefirot,* but only by means of their emanation, a view that is repeated in other instances. Interestingly enough, Abulafia does not elaborate on the nature of these higher *Sefirot,* but only on the means or technique by which the Kabbalists, using combinations, pronunciations, and meditations on the letters, can capture the emanations or divine letters. The above passage is an illuminating example of the Hermetic conception, whereby union is attained by causing the spiritual forces to descend upon the mystic, rather than via his ascent to the divine. This approach is evident in another book of the ecstatic Kabbalah:

> The receiver of the names of the *Sefirot* should make an effort to receive the divine influx from themselves [i.e. the names], in accordance with his attributes. And he should cleave to each and every *sefirah* separately and he should integrate his cleaving with all the *Sefirot* together, and will not separate[48] [between] the branches.[49]

The focus of Kabbalistic activity is not the ten *Sefirot* but their names, which enable the Kabbalist to attain *devequt.* Moreover, as in the epistle, the human attributes are mentioned in terms of receiving the divine emanations. Especially important for our discussion of the Hasidic understanding of the *Sefirot* is the fact that this text was copied, anonymously, in *Sefer ha-Peliy ᵓah,* with few variations[50] and could, therefore, have come to the attention of the Hasidic masters.

Elaborations upon the affinities between human attributes and the *Sefirot* are found in the school of ecstatic Kabbalah. So, for example, we read in the anonymous treatise *Ner ᵓElohim* that

> there is a war within the heart of man, which is generated by the first *Sefirah,* which is, in man, the good and the bad thought, and by the root, the branch and the leaves, the fruits will be borne and so likewise will happen to its ema-

nation,[51] for good and for bad, namely the thinker will become wise, to act by means of wisdom [in] whatever he will do, good or bad, and likewise [in the case of] the understanding and knowledge of good and bad, that he may understand good and bad and discern between them . . . and the *Sefirot* emanate the influx onto the heart, and this influx is differentiated according to different sorts, some of them natural, others accidental, others necessary, some of them voluntary . . . and God wishes the heart,[52] which means that the Merciful wishes the merciful heart, which pursues His attributes, as it is said that "just as He is merciful, so also shall you be merciful" and so also all the other attributes.[53]

What is pertinent in this passage for our discussions later on is the assumption that the divine attributes are conceived in terms of *imitatio Dei*. If the divine influx is taking the shape of, or the nature of, the *Sefirot* in the heart of man, he is called to apply the divine attributes in his actions. Before leaving Abulafia's reinterpretation of the theosophical scheme, it should be remarked that Abulafia's statement that man ought to cleave to each and every *Sefirah* is echoed by a rather obscure Kabbalist, R. Joseph ben Ḥayyim, who is reported to have maintained that:

All that the Creator, blessed be His Name, commanded to us is to cleave to Him . . . Therefore, I shall explain the [meaning of] the ten *Sefirot*, the universal and divine ones, according to the Kabbalah, in order that [you] will cleave to them . . . and by his cleaving to them, the divine and Holy spirit will enter him, and into his senses and movements.[54]

Even more significant, however, are the views found in another school of Kabbalah, that of R. Joseph ben Shalom Ashkenazi, which understood the *Sefirot* not only as theosophical realities but also as corresponding to powers and limbs within the physical structure of the human being. In an anonymous commentary on *Shir ha-Yiḥud,* written no later than the middle of the fourteenth-century,[55] an unknown Ashkenazi Kabbalist envisions the *Sefirot* as existing not only in the *Causa causarum,* and also outside it as the *Sefirot* of the unit, *Sefirot ha-Yiḥud,* but likewise in the human soul and body. This psychological understanding of the *Sefirot,* which is rare in theosophical Kabbalah, has theurgical implications in our commentary. The author mentions the contemplation of "the Binah in my soul": *Ba-binah etbonen she-be-nafshi.*[56] This phrase is interpreted as pointing, esoterically, to the meaning of the divine image, *Ẓelem Elohim,* which is to be understood as *koaḥ nafshekha*. However, the details of this view are, unfortunately, described as part of a topic to be transmitted orally: *Ka ʾasher tishma ʿ mi-peh el peh.*

During prayer the Kabbalist is supposed to ascend to, or into, "the tree of myself," *ʾIlan shel ʾAẓni,* a conspicuous reference to a personal tree of *Sefirot.* After arriving at Keter, apparently the inner, individual, *Keter,* the Kabbalist is supposed to draw the influx from the *Ketarim,* apparently *Ḥesed* and *Gev-*

urah. This drawing is conceived in terms of the filling of the personal tree: *Nitmala*ʾ *ha-*ʾ*Ilan sheli min ha-shefa*ʿ. The author mentions the pipes, or the channels, *ha-Ẓinorot,* stemming from the "head of my Keter" to the channels of "my throat," *Ẓinorei geroni,* and later on "my diadem," ʿ*Atarah sheli.* Therefore we may assume that, according to this Kabbalist there is a complete Sefirotic system, starting with the highest *Sefirah, Keter,* down to the last one, ʿ*Atarah,* which constitutes the personal, spiritual, Sefirotic tree, which is filled by dint of the theurgical-magical activity of the Kabbalist.[57]

This understanding of the tree of the *Sefirot* is, as mentioned above, quite exceptional: nevertheless, it seems implicit in the Kabbalah of R. Joseph Ashkenazi. He indicates that "the soul of the tree of [*nishmat* ʾ*ilano*] each of the sons of Israel is planted in Paradise."[58] We can understand the phrase *nishmat* ʾ*ilano* as pointing to the supernal soul that provides power to the personal tree of *Sefirot.* At least in one case, it seems that this Kabbalist speaks about the "channels," *Ẓinorot,* that emanate onto "the spirit of God that is in him [namely in man]."[59]

It is plausible that under the combined influence of the two different psychological interpretations of the *Sefirot,* Cordovero may have moved in this direction. This Kabbalist was certainly acquainted with several of Abulafia's books,[60] including those passages of the ecstatic Kabbalist copied in *Sefer ha-Peliy*ʾ*ah.* He emphasizes the fact that the soul is composed of ten *Sefirot,* as mentioned above,[61] and elsewhere he elaborates upon the necessity for human imitation of the activities of the *Sefirot.*[62] In any case, the magical model that Cordovero absorbed in his writings allows for more of an emphasis upon the significance of inner processes than the purely theosophical-theurgical model. The combined influences of ecstatic Kabbalah, of the school of R. Joseph ben Shalom Ashkenazi, and of talismatic magic opened the way to creating another focus of mystical activity, one that strives to valorize the reflection of the theosophical structure onto the human psyche and body.

Another independent, but similarly significant development is the philosophization of Kabbalah, including Lurianic Kabbalah, in the writing of certain authors from the end of the fifteenth century until the first part of the seventeenth century. In the writing of R. Abraham Kohen Herrera and R. Joseph Rofe' del Medigo, known also as Yashar of Kandia, the impact of medieval and Renaissance philosophy contributed to the understanding of theosophical and mythical events in philosophical, mostly Neoplatonic, terms.[63] Hasidism was acquainted with the two different interpretations of theosophy: one that uses the more "human" nomenclature, and deals with inner processes, and another, employing philosophical terms (including sometimes even psychological ones) in order to offer a less mytho-theosophical explanation of the sacrosanct lore. Therefore, tendencies that emerged, and to a certain extent even crystallized, before the emergence of Lurianism could later on serve a less theosophical understanding of Kabbalah. However, just as the impact of Lurianism and Sabbateanism marginalized, to a certain extent, earlier cultural and intellectual trends, such as rationalistic Jewish attitudes, it also contributed to change in the direction of mystical thought. Hasidism, at least insofar as the psychologically and philosophically oriented visions of the Kabbalah are concerned, does not innovate ex nihilo, but rather reorganized the structure of mystical themes and tendencies that were peripheral to the immediately preceding generations. Thus, it would seem that instead of attempting to find out what the innovations of the Hasidic masters were, as Buber and Elior have done, or by denying any novelty at all, as Scholem and some of his followers did,[64] it would be more advisable to look for a change in emphasis, movement from the center to the periphery (and vice versa) of already existing notions. The pulse of Hasidism may be better understood by inspecting the direction of such changes than by speculating about the degree of innovation, or overemphasizing Hasidic conservatism. The impulses that characterized Hasidism must be analyzed in the domain of the ascent of certain hermeneutical devices, in our case psychologization, or the interaction of tendencies, as seen above.

In the name of the Besht we learn, from a passage in one of R. Jacob Joseph of Polonoy's books, that

> there are ten *Sefirot* in man, who is called *microcosmos,* since the thought is named *ʾAbbaʾ*, and after the *Ẓimẓum* it was called *ʾImmaʾ* and so on, down to faith, which is called "two loins of truth"; and delight[66] in worship of God is called *Yesod, Ẓaddiq,* and sign of the Covenant.[66]

Indeed, the Besht is interpreting here not the simple theory of ten *Sefirot* that confronted Abulafia, but the complex Lurianic system, where *Sefirot* and anthropomorphic configurations created a theosophical web uncommon even in Gnosticism. From the point of view of the interpreted material, at least, there is no way to compare Abulafia's interpretation to that of the Besht. Indeed, from a strictly historical perspective, Hasidism differs considerably from ecstatic Kabbalah by virtue of its encounter with a different theosophy. However, even if there is truth to such an argument, the crucial elements shared by Hasidism and ecstatic Kabbalah are significant enough to compare these two phenomena both historically and phenomenologically. Theosophy, despite its amazing development between the thirteenth and sixteenth centuries, is still a phenomenon whose appearances in various historical periods share crucial elements. If we disregard academic rhetoric, which too often engages in generic distinctions that do not do justice to the nuances of phenomena, Lurianism and Zoharic Kabbalah are much closer than we expect; classical scholarly studies tend to overemphasize the "new Kabbalah" of Luria. The fascination with a complex theology haunted by syzygies, sexual couplings, emanations, and questions of good and evil, is common to the two forms of Jewish theosophy. They are two forms or versions, of one basic structure.

Historically, the concept of *ta ᶜanug* may bear more than just a phenomenological resemblance to the ninth *Sefirah.* But, from the conceptual point of view, Hasidism focuses its attention on the inner human constitution after a long period in which Jewish mysticism was fascinated more with the inner structure and processes of the divine. This reorganization is accompanied, as in ecstatic Kabbalah, by an emphasis on *devequt.* Moving from the external to the internal, Hasidism focuses on topics related to the soul and the body of man, including his immediate environment, in lieu of the more grandiose ideal of theosophical Kabbalah of repairing the cosmic rift and the divine disharmony. With human experience at the center of their concerns, the Hasidic masters shifted the vision of theosophical Kabbalah from *visio rerum omnium in Deo,* to a *visio Dei attributi in hominem.*

> Once the Rabbi admonished someone because he was discussing Kabbalah in public. That person answered him: "Why do you discuss Kabbalah in public too?" He [the Great Maggid] answered him: "I teach the world to understand that everything written in *Sefer ᶜEẓ Ḥayyim* also exists in this world and in man. However, I do not explain the spiritual matters of *Sefer ᶜEẓ Ḥayyim;* but you discuss everything that is written in *ᶜEẓ Ḥayyim* literally, and thus you transform the spiritual into corporeal;[67] but the sublime, spiritual world is [indeed] ineffable."[68]

The argument of ineffability, rare in Kabbalistic writings, is more widespread in Hasidism, with its emphasis on the experiential over the cognitive.[69] The Great Maggid follows the path opened by the Besht, who had already applied the Lurianic symbols to human entities, as seen above. However, what is apparent from this passage is the attempt to disseminate a psychological, which is also felt to be the more correct, form of Kabbalistic theosophy. This tendency, also expressed by a close disciple of the Great Maggid[70], may betray a much deeper affinity between the psychologization and (in some other cases) the philosophization[71] and magical interpretation[72] of Kabbalah, on one hand, and exotericism on the other. In any case, Abraham Abulafia and Moshe Cordovero, who are to be considered among those who attempted to disseminate Kabbalah, are also involved in psychological, magical, and philosophical interpretations of theosophical Kabbalah. On the other hand, it is R. Yiẓḥaq Luria, the great theosophical Kabbalist, who restored the importance of esotericism to its former status.[73] From this perspective, the breaking of esotericism is, to a certain degree, a deviation from Lurianism and a return to a politics of esotericism and to mystical rhetoric. Indeed, the esoteric is connected to the psychological. One of the Hasidic masters describes the path of the founders of Hasidism as follows:

> The path of the Besht and of the "Great] Maggid was that they have drawn down the aspect of revelation of the light of the Infinite into the plurality of the modi of epiphany, as in the aspect of [Job, 19:26], "Out of my flesh I shall

> contemplate God,"[74] namely that this is the vitality of the soul in the body, that arrives and is drawn forth by the path of the hidden and the revealed. This, however, is not the way of the Kabbalists, who spoke about the aspect of the light and the luminary etc.[75]

Moving away from the Kabbalistic discussion of the intricacies regarding the supernal lights as symbols and manifestations of a complex theosophical system, the Besht and his followers shifted the mystical discourse to the manifestation of the divine attributes within the human constitution. The *ḥiyyut,* the divine within man, becomes the focus rather than the source of their speculations. Following Kabbalistic speculations connected to the verse in Job, the Hasidic master hints at the possibility of contemplating God by starting with the contemplation of human nature. However, while for the Kabbalists, the main topic of their discussion was the human body, which reflected the supernal *anthropos* and thus could serve as the starting point of the contemplative path, in the Hasidic interpretation of the verse, it is the inner vitality that serves as the bridge between the *Deus absconditus* and the mystic. It is not the multiplicity of the Sefirotic system that is fathomed by means of the human anatomy, but the vitality of the divine reality that is traced by introspection. This understanding may elicit a much more precise interpretation of the text cited in *ʾOr ha-ʾEmet.* The Kabbalistic discussions, because they are immersed in anthropomorphical symbolism, gravitate around topics that may be misunderstood as corporeal. The Great Maggid is actually indicating that by addressing the supernal world, one is already prone to cause a misunderstanding. However, through a more modest approach of focusing on issues that are part of our world, it is possible to ascend from the material to the spiritual, apparently by inspection of the spiritual aspects of man. The corporeal element in man is significant only as the garment of the divine power that activates it.

It should be mentioned that the term used by the Hasidic master to describe the emergence of the Hasidic path is also of some importance for our thesis. Again, the verb *MShKh* occurs, alluding to the disclosure of a realm of religious life that was not invented, but brought down from on High, by the founders of Hasidism. One must assume that it was their ecstatic and enthusiastic capacities that facilitated this bringing down, just as the holiness of Luria was instrumental in the revelations that produced the evolution of the Kabbalah from Zoharic concepts. Just as the great founders of religion brought down the divine revelations that changed the course of the spiritual life of their peoples, so also the two founders of Hasidism brought down their own revelations.

To disclose traces of the divine within this world and in man, to reveal the divinity that underlies corporeal manifestations, is tantamount to disclosing the Kabbalah to the masses. In Hebrew the same verb is used to point to this discovery and disclosure: *GLH*. Thus, the Besht believed that he revealed only what was necessary for mystical worship, while the secrets that depict the supernal worlds were kept from the ordinary person. Indeed, in a rather interesting tradition found in a manuscript of R. Yiẓḥaq Aiziq of Komarno, R. Yiẓḥaq states that his father-in-law told him that the Besht had argued with Luria about why he spoke so openly of the secrets instead of dealing with "the path of worship." Luria answered that should he live two years more, he would redress this problem.[76] Thus, according to this tradition, the center of the Besht's way is worship, while Luria is seen as dealing with Kabbalistic secrets. This view is also expressed elsewhere, when students of the Besht are presented as employing Kabbalah in order to explain "issues of worship."[77]

Let us return to the concept of *ḥiyyut,* which occurs in the passage from R. Hillel ha-Levi of Paritch's *Pelaḥ ha-Rimmon.* This is a crucial concept in Hasidism, and it has recurred in many of our discussions above.[78] It has played a role in the mystico-magical theory of Northern European mysticism since the late twelfth century, and it was adopted and cultivated by Cordovero and some of his followers.[79] *Ḥiyyut* stands, as we have seen above, for the divine Presence in the world. As such, it represents the dynamic image of God in man. However, in certain cases this term underwent a certain semantic shift, in which it came to denote not only divine vitality but also an act performed in a vital, powerful manner.[80] This change is reminiscent of that undergone by the term *devequt,* which means in Hasidism not only the act of cleaving to God, but also the performance of a pious deed with devotion and enthusiasm. Thus, the change in emphasis by the Hasidic masters from the supernal lights to the vitality of the human soul means not only a shift from theosophy to anthroposophy, but also a shift toward performing religious acts in a less mental and more vital and enthusiastic manner. This also seems to be the case in the way the verse from Job is understood in a passage of R. Menaḥem Mendel of Kossov, where it is used to illustrate the total dedication required in the performance of a religious act.[81] In other words, another change introduced by Hasidism was deep emotional investment in the religious performance. According to at least one text, *hitlahavut,* enthusiastic devotion, is by itself able to draw down the influx.[82]

This shift from *ḥiyyut,* from pointing to the immanence of the divine in man, to the manner in which one acts, also represents the shift from a given theology, the immanentist one, to what may be called, following André Breton, *un êtat d'ésprit,* a state of the spirit. If the understanding of divine immanence is the matter of a mental state, a discovery of mystical theology, the act of discovery requires an intense mystical effort. Man is able to activate the divine within himself in order to discover Him within the nature of reality. This seems to me to be the meaning of the Great Maggid's statement about the revelation of divinity in the world and in man. If the noun *ḥiyyut* is part of a worldview, *be-ḥiyyut* stands for the ethos.[83] From this perspective, Hasidism, as Buber has already mentioned, transformed the Kabbalistic worldview into a mystical way of life; but in doing so it did not innovate, but expanded a possibility already exploited by earlier Kabbalists. This transformation must be properly understood: the interiorization of the divine attributes and their perception as a modus vivendi did not obliterate their existence, just as the *ḥiyyut* remains active even when someone acts enthusiastically. Thus, transformation was there, or perhaps one could say there was the extension of the divine attributes to man; but this shift still left both the supernal and the immanentist divine as powerful and as active as they were in Kabbalah. It is the dynamism of devotion and the enthusiasm that penetrated the worship that is characteristic of Hasidism, together with the unmediated encounter with the divine on high, and with the pervasive presence below. This was achieved by the exploitation of potentialities inherent in the various forms of Kabbalah.

Appendix B: Rabbi Yisrael of Ryzhin Who Cries

In a letter written by the famous student of the Gaon of Vilna, addressed to the much less known R. Yehudah Leib de Butin, he accuses some unidentified Hasidim, *inter alia,* of speaking vain things and conceiving them to be the "words of the Torah."[1] This is, apparently, not his own formulation; from the context it appears that his addressee, who had some leanings toward Hasidism, had informed him of it in a previous, and no longer extant, letter. In fact, it is a characteristically Hasidic practice to refer to the sermon delivered by the Hasidic Rabbi at the end of Shabbat,[2] as *Torah.* It is, indeed, a quite remarkable claim, to argue that the mystical sermons delivered each and every Shabbat in many communities are part of, or in some way identical to, the sacrosanct *Torah.* In any case, it seems that this assumption was instrumental in bringing about the printing of the greater part of Hasidic literature, which consists of sermons. The question may be raised, how serious is this claim? Were these sermons, delivered in Yiddish,[3] indeed considered by the homilist or his audience as *Torah,* in the usual sense of the word? Although they were explanations of the pericopes of the *Torah,* they were no more and no less than interpretations. We may therefore ask whether this phenomenon represents a statement, reminiscent of modern debates in the fields of literature and hermeneutics, about the relationship between text and commentary. Without offering an answer for the whole range of Hasidic literature, one can say without any doubt that in some schools the teachings of the Hasidic leader immediately became canonical. This is obviously the case with teachings of the great-grandson of the Besht, R. Naḥman of Braslav, each of them having been designated as a *Torah.* According to his closest student, R. Naḥman repeatedly recommended that his disciples will transform his Torot into prayers.[4] Thus, R. Naḥman himself openly regarded his teachings as *Torah.* His student, however, went a little bit further; he describes the teachings of his master as "containing, each and every one of them, the entire *torah,* the whole people of Israel, and all the things in the worlds."[5] Indeed the whole introduction is a lengthy description of the way to transform the teachings into prayers.

However, this is just one extreme phenomenon, because of the highly original nature of R. Naḥman's mystical thought and, perhaps, also becaues of a theory he elaborated according to which

> When one finally is integrated in *ʾEiyn Sof,* his *Torah* is the *Torah* of God Himself, and his prayer is the Prayer of God Himself . . . there exists a *Torah* of God and a Prayer of God. When a person merits to be integrated in *ʾEiyn Sof,* his *Torah* and prayer are those of God Himself.[6]

Mystical union, the integration of one's soul within the Infinite, will change the status of the human verbal activities so that they will become attributed to God.[7] This view is in line with the assumption, mentioned several times above, as to the *Shekhinah* which speaks from the mouth of the mystic.[8] Mystical experiences are, therefore one of the reasons for the claim of the divine status of the Hasidic creativity.

However, it seems that long before the beginning of the nineteenth century, when the two texts dealt with above were composed, the special status of the Hasidic teaching was already formulated in a tradition in the name of the Great Maggid, adduced by his great-grandson, R. Yisrael of Ryzhin. In a highly interesting passage, according to a certain story, or tradition, there was a

> great debate between the disciples of the Great Maggid concerning the *Torah* said by the Maggid, blessed be his memory. One argued that he said so, another otherwise. And the [Great] Maggid told them that both versions are the words of the living God, because the words I said include all of these [interpretations]. End of the words of the Maggid. And he [the Great Maggid], blessed be his memory, said that there are seventy facets to the *Torah,* and indeed it [the *Torah*] emerges from the place of true unity. Though in its source the *Torah* is one, only by its descent upon these worlds it became seventy facets. This is the reason why in the *Torah* of R. Meir it is written *kutonet ʾor*; spelled with *ʾAleph* because R. Meir took over the *Torah* from its source, and this is why it was written with *ʾAleph,* while with us it is written with *ʿAyin.*[9]

The comparison between the *Torah* of the Maggid and the divine *Torah* is brought out by the assumption that the teaching of the Great Maggid bear seventy interpretations just as the *Torah.* This assumption in itself is similar to some, indeed few, parallels found in Middle Age Jewish mysticism, the most prominent of them being Abraham Abulafia. Also in their case interpretations were offered, by themselves or by angels, to their "own" writings.[10] In the case of the Great Maggid the argument is less extreme, since no full-fledged commentaries were composed on his teachings. The debates between the students of the Great Maggid are therefore justifiable, because his teachings possess, implicitly, the depths of the divine *Torah.* However, what seems to be intriguing is the second part of the discussion; what is the *raison d'être* of putting these two parts together? Let me attempt to explain the meaning of the second part. In our text of the Bible, the garment of Adam is described as made of skin, *ʿOr,* while, according to a Midrashic tradition, the original spelling was *ʾOr,* spelled out with *ʾAleph* [light] and, accordingly, Adam was conceived as possessing a garment of light.[11] This variation is understood in the Midrash as pointing to two different phases in the life of Adam; the "lighty" one, before the sin, the "skinny" one, after the fall. The common version of the *Torah* reflects, therefore, the present fallen situation.

However, this is not the way the Great Maggid explained the story. The two spellings of the *Torah* coexist; a saintly figure like R. Meir whose name, symbolically enough, means "the shining one," was able to capture the primordial *Torah,* while the other mortals are able to perceive only the lower, revealed *Torah.* While the letter *ʾAleph* points to the one, or the unified *Torah,* the letter *ʿAyin,* whose numerical value is seventy, points to the multiple meanings, that emerge out of the descent of the *Torah* in the lower worlds. The seventy facets represent the lower, both ontologically and hermeneutically, status of the *Torah,* while the unified one seems to be higher than all its interpretations. With these remarks in mind, let us return to the first part of the quote; if the different interpretations of the students stand for the seventy facets, a fact that seems to be obvious, then the original teaching of the Great Maggid stands for the unrevealed *Torah.* If the arguments of the students are called *Divrei ʾElohim Ḥayyim,* much more so would be the teachings of their teacher.

The status of the Great Maggid in this passage is, indeed, paralleled by his achievement in history. Not only was he admired and surrounded by many disciples, but most of the Hasidic literature is, indeed, attempts to interpret the views of the Great Maggid, incomparably more than those of the other students of the Besht. The splendor of his ancestor is reflected, however, in a much stronger light in another passage related to his great-grandson, which cannot be properly understood except against the above-mentioned passage. In his *ʿIrin Qaddishin Tanyyanaʾ* there is a story about the Rabbi of Ryzhin, as follows:

> Once, in the eve of the feast of *Shavuʿot,* he was sitting at the table and did not say any *Torah,* neither did he speak one word; but he was crying very much. The second night he did the same. After the grace after the meal he said: When the [Great] Maggid was saying *Torah* at the table, the students were repeating it afterwards among themselves, going back to their houses; one saying he heard it in such a way, another saying he heard it in another way, because each of them had heard it in a different way. I say that this is not a novelty, since there are seventy facets to the *Torah* and each of them heard the *Torah* of the Maggid according to the facet he had [heard] in the *Torah.*[12] And he said, "When I look attentively to the faces,[13] there is no need to say *Torah,* because the 'show of their faces[14] witnessed against them' [Jes. 3:9]. And this suffices for someone who understands."[15]

The tragic situation of being silent in the night when, according to the Jewish tradition, the *Torah* was revealed and the time when the study of *Torah* is a legal requirement,[16] of crying instead of being joyful, stems form the comparison between the glory of the great-grandfather and that of his descendant.

However, the comparison has nothing to do with external, material success. The Ryzhin dynasty is one of the most successful Hasidic schools; R. Yisrael was, perhaps, the most powerful and richest of all the Hasidic masters.[17] Neither was he regretful over his personal insufficiency as a master, for it seems that in this realm, too, he was successful enough, due to his unusual charisma. The one problem that seems to haunt him is the nature of his students. Their faces did not, assumingly, correspond to any facets in the *Torah,*[18] or to put it even more blatantly, they had no part in the riches of the *Torah* he could deliver to them. This alienation between the aristocratic leader and his apparently common followers seems to have been the existential basis for his crying. To deliver a sermon, or a Torah, meant—at least according to the implicit message of this passage—to open the gates for multiple interpretations, to offer to everyone in the audience something that belonged uniquely to him.[19] Torah without the capacity to arouse the imagination of its listeners is worthless, and it would be better for the *Ẓaddiq* not to deliver a sermon that lacks this quality. Without producing the spiritual debate, or interpretations, the text may be insignificant. The sense of destiny of this *Ẓaddiq* as the descendant of the Great Maggid, named after the founder of Hasidism, Yisrael, certainly contributed not only to the messianic expectations of his followers[20] but also to his own feeling of being in exile, which, golden as it was, kept him far from the great centers of Jewish learning.[21]

Let us investigate further some of the more obvious aspects of the last passage. It seems to me that, in comparison to Kabbalistic literary creativity, it represents the spirit of Hasidism. The Hasidic sermon is preeminently an oral event taking place between the leader and his disciples, and it is the main tool of creating and communicating his ideas. This is why the vernacular is crucial. The Hebrew versions of the sermons are important for modern scholarship, but they reflect the events in the field to a smaller degree.[22] Communication[23] to the sympathetically predisposed audience therefore invites creativity in a new medium. In modern terms, we can say that the reader is present at the act of creating the text and that the oral text is conceived of as meaningless unless the reader interprets it immediately. There is no barrier between the author and his text, or between him and its consumer.[24] The preacher, therefore, is not only attempting to influence and shape the audience, but also—at least indirectly—to be shaped by its response.

This situation is both reminiscent of and fundamentally different from, most of the situations related to the Kabbalists. We know about different groups of Kabbalists who were spending time together; this seems to have been the case by the beginning of Kabbalah in Gerona and Castile,[25] and later on in sixteenth-century Safed and eighteenth-century Italy. However, the sermon was hardly their most important literary genre. We may assume that these were conclaves of experts who may have had a recognized leader but operated more on the level of producing secrets, or explaining them in a very technical manner. There was no popularization among these groups. Whenever a step toward popularizing the secrets was taken, it was done by producing books—the ethical-kabbalistic literature. However, even then the message was very general, intended to speak to the whole "nation," irrespective of country or circumstances. Hasidism seems to differ on this crucial issue: having been produced in the presence of the "consumer," it attempted to answer his questions, even his unasked ones. The feedback of the audience was undoubtedly crucial for the leader. The weeping of the rabbi, together with his silence, is therefore an act of communication about the lack of communication. Unlike the Kabbalists, who were writing to an unknown and therefore silent audience, the Hasidic master had to create his small audience by his act of literary creativity, and to be able to absorb its reaction. The weeping Hasidic rabbi must also be seen against the background of the mystico-magical model discussed above. Ironically, the *Ẓaddiq,* who is said to be able to affect the will of God, is unable to create an appropriate audience. This situation is reminiscent of a story attributed to the Rabbi of Kotzk, who reacted to the rumor that someone who came to his town was able to produce miracles by asking whether he would also create a Hasid.[26] The real miracle is in the spirit, and this seems to transcend even the [quasi]-omnipotence of the *Ẓaddiqim.*

Historically, the above tradition seems to reflect the period of the residence of the Ryzhiner Rabbi in Sadigura, after he had to flee from Russia to Bukovina, the periphery of the Hapsburg empire. Away from the centers of Hasidism and learning in Podolia and Galicia, he had to rebuild his hyparchy in a relatively forgotten territory, and it seems that the human entourage with which he was thrown together did not meet his expectations. Again, from the perspective of history, he was right: neither he nor any of his followers and descendants have contributed substantially to the development of Hasidism as a mystical movement. Feeling of intellectual inferiority, which stems according to the second text not from his own inability to teach but from the absence of a learned audience, is probably the reason for the image of R. Yisrael, cultivated in some Hasidic and non-Hasidic circles, as ignorant.[27]

This historical observation brings us again to the problem of whether or not Hasidism is cooling down, like other mass movements that grew out of enthusiasm and ecstasy. The answer is basically no, for the reasons already presented; but let us look at this question from the perspective of the passages above. There can be no doubt that there is an immense gap between the students of the Great Maggid and the disciples of the Ryzhiner Rabbi. But this gap was present not only at the end of the forties of the nineteenth century, before the death of the *Ẓaddiq* in Sadigura, but also in the middle of the eighteenth century. The students of the Great Maggid were part of an elite whose spiritual drive brought each of them to the inspired preacher, and many of them become *Ẓaddiqim* themselves. By comparing the students of the Great Maggid to the Hasidism of Sadigura, we are thus, in a sense, following R. Yisrael, comparing advanced students to freshmen; we compare the incomparables. What should be compared is the elite of mid-nineteenth-century Hasidism, figures like the rabbis of Komarno, of Gur, of Kotzk, and of Izbica, to those of the eighteenth century. We should compare *Ẓaddiqim* to other *Ẓaddiqim* and not the founding fathers of Hasidism to regular *Hasidim*. With these as the terms of comparison, the question of "retreat" from deep spiritual life becomes less easy to answer. R. Yisrael felt that he was not going to produce a spiritual effervescence among his followers that was comparable to that produced by the Great Maggid, and in this feeling he was quite right. However, the message of the Besht and the Great Maggid did not produce an ongoing revolution. Its very success meant its dissemination and appropriation by sociological and spiritual strata different from those that produced it. Even by creating an effervescence among the masses, Hasidism could not bring them to the level of its spiritual leaders, some of whom were extreme mystics. While the Besht appears to have been content with any spiritual improvement he was able to produce, this was not the case for later phases of Hasidism; in the nineteenth century complaints about the impossibility of inducing deep spiritual change in the community began to multiply. It is the feeling of the enormous gap between the *Ẓaddiq* and his community, which sometimes coexists with the total dedication of the leader to it, that haunts, on the social level, the greatest achievement of Jewish mysticism. The direct and regular contact of the mystic leader with the people who became his followers seems to have produced not only his feeling of responsibility towards them, as represented by the magical preoccupations of the *Ẓaddiq*, for example, but also at times a negative reaction toward their inability to reach his spiritual level.

Appendix C: On Intentional Transmission of Power

R. Qalonimus Qalman ha-Levi Epstein of Crakow, a late eighteenth- and early nineteenth-century Hasidic master, authored *Maʾor va-Shemesh,* one of the most widely read Hasidic books of the time. For the general thesis of this book regarding the importance of the nexus between mysticism and talismatic magic, we shall examine in some detail a passage that represents a significant illuustration of the mystico-magical model. We will show that this master accorded an important role to this model and thus support our methodological assumption that the awareness of the importance and preexistence of one of the models (the mystico-magical one, as proposed in the present study) is shared also by a Hasidic text. Commenting upon the verse, "Behold I set before you this day a blessing and a curse,"[1] R. Qalonimus Qalman wrote:

> This issue is very famous, as [it is known] from the mouths of books and from the mouths of writers[2] that the *Ẓaddiqim,* who follow the path of the prophets,[3] are able to draw down blessings from the supernal worlds[4] to whomever they like. Likewise they are able to draw curses onto the foes of Israel, as we found in the case of the *Tannaim* and *Amoraim,* especially the companions, who were the sages of the *Zohar,* the disciples of Rabbi Shimeon bar Yoḥai. There are *Ẓaddiqim,* generation after generation, who are wonder-makers,[5] and who possess the power, [*zeh ha-koaḥ*], as it is known and famous in our generation. And the *Ẓaddiq* is likewise able to transmit it to his disciple and also to a man who directs his attention, every minute and moment,[6] so that divinity will be dwelling in him[7]. He [the *Ẓaddiq*] transmits this power [*zeh ha-koaḥ*] so that he [the recipient] will be able to draw the blessings to whom-ever he likes and vice versa. This is the meaning of the issue of *Semikhah,*[8] when Moses our master, may he rest in peace, put his hands upon Joshuʿa, the son of Nun, and so also generation after generation. However it is impor-tant to declare that notwithstanding the fact that the *Ẓaddiq* is able to bless [every man], it is paramount that he do so [only] to an Israelite whom he knows wishes to worship God.[9]

The transmission of the magical power is conditional, according to this author, on one's being either the disciple of a righteous man or being aware of the divine dwelling within oneself. One must assume that this awareness is also required in the case of the disciple. Thus, mystical consciousness is a prerequisite for the magical drawing down of supernal power, which may be activated either for good or bad purposes. Initiation in matters of magical power presupposes a prior mystical attainment. The formulation of this prerequisite is important: The mystical moment is a phase that may be complemented by a magical one; however, the two are not conceived here to be exclusive of each other, or to contradict each other. In fact, the mystical stage, in which the divine is said to be present within the body or soul of the mystic, is supplemented by a manipulation of the energy that is drawn so that it will be effective outside his body.

This view is presented here as a widely known fact, which is found not only in written texts and oral tradititions, but is also part and parcel of the Jewish tradition from biblical times, and was continued by Halakhic and mystical masters. In other words, according to R. Qalonimus Qalman, this view was an essential part of Jewish tradition and was alive during his lifetime. In fact, in lieu of the Kabbalistic genealogy chain of the transmission of secrets, this Hasidic master argues for a genealogy that stems from deep antiquity up to his contemporaries. The author might have been influenced by genealogies of transmission of the divine Name or names found in some Kabbalistic sources.[10] Like the Kabbalists, especially R. Joseph Gikatilla and Moses Cordovero, the recipients of the magical tradition are elitist figures, as he takes pain to mention later on; thus, though the more mystical aspect of Hasidism is conceived as open to a larger audience, the magical aspect, including sometimes a theurgical phase, is conceived of as more restricted, or even esoteric.[11] Unfortunately, this master does not elaborate on the precise manner by which the power is transmitted. Is it part of a more detailed technique, like the use of divine names, or is it a capacity that can be learned, or a potential spiritual trait that can be developed? In any case, the nexus between the blessing and the drawing down is indeed well represented in many Kabbalistic and Hasidic texts, as we have already seen above.[12]

The alleged ubiquity of the tradition described in the passage under discussion, as claimed by the author, is rather intriguing, as I am unable to find, prior to R. Qalonimus Qalman, a similar formulation of this theory.[13] Thus, we may assume that he had in mind not a precise quotation that he was reproducing but a more general theory, apparently similar to Gikatilla's or Cordovero's views, which one may consider to be identical to the mystico-magical model.

It should be mentioned that the transmission of power by blessing is not to be practiced indiscriminately, but only for those who intend to worship God. The magical power thus put in the service of religious ideals; the blessing is to be distributed only to those who share the same religious beliefs and practices as the thaumaturge. The powerful blessing is therefore understood as part of an effort to form, or ensure, the continuation of a religious community, not as the act of a person found on the margin of society.[14]

Last but not least, this passage was formulated in a rather articulated phase of Hasidism; the succession of *Ẓaddiqim,* which was somehow related to the inheritance of power, is not presented here as a matter of family-relation but is exclusively conditional on mystical attainment. It is possible that the absence of a father-son succession may point to the fact, explicitly claimed by the author, that he is indeed preserving an earlier view. It should be mentioned that, although he was at the beginning a disciple of R. Elimelekh of Lisansk, at the end of his life Epstein became a follower of the Seer of Lublin, and his emphasis on the transmission of the thaumaturgic powers may be related to the practices of this latter figure.[15] In any case, the claim found in the above passage regarding the transmission of power, though formulated in a way that seems unparalleled beforehand, is not a total innovation of the Hasidic author, but may be traced to earlier Kabbalistic discussions about transmission of the capacity of blessing. The occurrence of the term *power, koaḥ,* twice in the above passage may be seen as part of the general restructuring of theosophical Kabbalah, which emphasized more the act of transmitting power to the divine realm, but was less inclined to elaborate upon the precise distribution of the descending power. Nevertheless, these two forms of Jewish mysticism are concerned with manipulating power, a fact that demonstrates its concerns with the idea of energy or power.

To extrapolate from this example, I propose to see in Hasidism not so much a speculative innovation, but different emphases on some elements in a model that was already in existence in various writings, though it has been now applied in a social context.

Abbreviations

AJS Review—*Association of Jewish Studies Review*
HUCA—*Hebrew Union College Annual*
JJS—*Journal of Jewish Studies*
JQR—*Jewish Quarterly Review*
JSJT—*Jerusalem Studies in Jewish Thought*
MGWJ—*Monatschrift fur Geschichte und Wissenschaft des Judentums*
PAAJR—*Proceedings of the Academic Academy of Jewish Research*
QS—*Qiriat Sefer*
REJ—*Revue des Études Juives*

Notes

NOTES TO INTRODUCTION

1. On the reception of Buber's rendering of Hasidic tales in Europe see the introduction of Paul Mendes-Flohr and Ze᾿ev Gries to the reprinting of Buber's *The Tales of Rabbi Naḥman,* trans. M. Friedman (Atlantic Highlands, N.J., 1988), pp. ix–xxviii.

2. Martin Buber, "Interpreting Hasidism," *Commentary* 36, 3 (September, 1963): 218–25; Gershom Scholem, "Martin Buber's Interpretation of Hasidism" in his *The Messianic Idea* pp. 228–50. This is the expanded version of the article originally printed in *Commentary* 32 (1961): 305–16. On this controversy, see Rivka Schatz-Uffenheimer, "Man's Relationship to God and World in Buber's Rendering of Hasidic Teachings," in *The Philosophy of Martin Buber,* ed. Paul Schilpp and Maurice Friedman (La Salle, Ill., 1967), pp. 403–35 and her introduction to *Quietistic Elements* (Jerusalem, 1974) pp. 10–18 (Hebrew); as well as the studies of Michael Oppenheim, "The Meaning of Hasidut: Martin Buber and Gershom Scholem," in *Journal of the American Academy of Religion* 49, 3 (1981): 409–21; Steven D. Kepnes "A Hermeneutic Approach to the Buber-Scholem Controversy," *Journal of Jewish Studies* 38 (1987): 81–98, the introduction by Samuel H. Dresner to Abraham J. Heschel, *The Circle of the Ba*ʿ*al Shem Tov: Studies in Hasidism,* ed. S. H. Dresner (Chicago, London, 1985), pp. xvi–xix and David Biale (note 33 below).

Buber's view of Hasidism, including the description of the criticism of Scholem, has been discussed extensively in Grete Schaeder, *The Hebrew Humanism of Martin Buber,* trans. N.J. Jacobs (Wayne State University Press: Detroit, 1973), pp. 287–338; Rahel Shihor, "Buber's Method in his Research of Hasidism" *Da᾿at* 2/3 (1978–79): 241–46 (Hebrew). On Scholem and Hasidism, see Louis Jacobs "Aspects of Scholem's Study of Hasidism," *Modern Judaism* 5 (1985), reprinted in Harold Bloom, ed., *Gershom Scholem* (New York, New Haven, Philadelphia, 1987), pp. 179–88, and Rivka Schatz-Uffenheimer, "Gershom Scholem's Interpretation of Hasidism" in *Gershom Scholem, The Man and His Activity* (Jerusalem, 1983), pp. 48–62 (Hebrew); Jon D. Levenson "The Hermeneutical Defense of Buber's Hasidism: A Critique and Counterstatement," *Modern Judaism* 11 (1991): 297–320. See also Tishby's stand in relation to Buber and Scholem's views of the neutralization of messianism in Hasidism, in *Messianic Idea,* pp. 1–45.

3. See e.g., Ze᾿ev Gries, "Hasidism: The Present State of Research and Some Desirable Priorities," *Numen* 34 (1987): 97–108, 180–213; Mendel Piekarz, *The Beginning of Hasidism: Ideological Trends in Derush and Musar Literature* (Jerusalem, 1978), pp. 299–302 (Hebrew).

4. A main exception is Schatz-Uffenheimer's *Quietistic Elements.* See also Scholem's essays on the *Ẓaddiq* and *devequt.*

5. See the studies of Ben Ẓion Dinburg and Shemuel Ettinger, printed in Rubinstein, *Studies in Hasidism,* pp. 53–121, 227, 240, and even Weiss in some instances, ibid., pp. 123, 125–27. More prominent in this vein is Raphael Mahlerʾs, *Hasidism and the Jewish Enlightenment: Their Confrontation in Galicia and Poland in the First Half of the Nineteenth Century,* trans. E. Orenstein (Philadelphia, 1985).

6. See e.g., Arthur Green, *Tormented Master: A Life of Rabbi Naḥman of Bratslav* (Alabama, 1979); Siegmund Hurwitz, "Archtypische Motive in der Chassidischen Mystik," in *Zeitlose Dokumente des Seele* (Zurich, 1952), pp. 123–212; Mordekhai Rotenberg, "Hasidic Contraction: A Model for Interhemispheric Dialogue" *Zygon* 21 (1986): 201–17; and his *Dialogue with Deviance: The Hasidic Ethic and the Theory of Social Contraction* (Philadelphia, 1983); Shelomo G. Shoham, *The Myth of Tantalus* (Queensland, 1979), pp. 73–93; idem, *The Bridge to Nothingness* (Tel Aviv, 1991), pp. 112–40, 212–27 (Hebrew); Micha Ankori, *The Heart and the Spring, A Comparative Study in Hasidism and Depth Psychology* (Tel Aviv, 1991) (Hebrew). A much greater effort to apply Jungian psychoanalysis to Judaism, and especially to Jewish mysticism, was undertaken many years ago by Erich Neumann, who unfortunately did not publish the monograph he prepared. See nevertheless, his "Mystical Man," in *The Mystic Vision: Papers from the Eranos Yearbooks,* 375–415, ed. Joseph Campbell, trans. R. Manhein (Princeton University Press: Princeton, N.J. 1982), where he refers several times to Hasidism. See also the Ph.D. thesis of Jonathan Shatil, "The Conception of Mental Energy in Psychological Theories and in the Cabalistic-Hasidic View" (Hebrew University: Jerusalem, 1986) (Hebrew), now printed as *A Psychologist in a Braslav Yeshiva, Jewish Mysticism in Actual Practice* (Tel Aviv, 1993) (Hebrew).

7. See his *The Origin and Meaning of Hasidism,* ed. and trans. Maurice Freedman (Atlantic Highlands, N.J., 1988) p. 239, where he describes Hasidism as the encounter between two lines of religiosity that do not meet regularly: the line of inner illumination and the line of revelation.

8. See Martin Buber, *Tales of Rabbi Nachman* (note 1, above), p. 10, *Origin and Meaning,* p. 252; Scholem, *Major Trends in Jewish Mysticism,* p. 342 and Zeʾev Gries, "From Myth to Ethos: Lines to the Personality of R. Abraham of Kalisk" in Shmuel Ettinger, ed., *Nation and History, Studies in the History of Jewish People* (Jerusalem, 1984), vol. 2, pp. 117–18 (Hebrew); on Gnosticism in this context, see below, notes 33 and 39. In a more general context, Buber regards Judaism as a struggle against magic, conceived of as being of Egyptian origin, and Gnosticism, which stems, according to him, from Mesopotamia. See Martin Buber, *Teʿudah vi-Yiʿud* (Jerusalem, 1963) vol. 1, p. 188 (Hebrew).

9. *Major Trends,* pp. 327–29; see pp. 338–39. This approach was accepted by the school of Scholem, and it is reflected in many expositions of the emergence of Hasidism. See e.g. the title of Yoram Jacobson's *From Lurianic Kabbalah to the Psychological Theosophy of Hasidism* (Tel Aviv, 1986) (Hebrew).

10. Isaiah Tishby, "Les traces de Rabbi Moise Haim Luzzato dans l'enseignement du Hasidism," in *Hommage à Georges Vajda, Études d'histoire et de pensée juives,* ed. G. Nahon and Ch. Touati (Leuivain, 1980), pp. 421–62; Hebrew version, *Ẓion* 43 (1978): 201–34. See also his great efforts to show that a certain dictum that recurs in

Hasidic texts as quoted from the *Zohar* actually stems from R. Moshe Ḥayyim Luzzatto's book: see his "*Qudsha᾽ Berikh Hu᾽*." Interestingly enough, precisely this same conclusion was reached five years before Tishby, in an article by Abraham J. Heschel, "God, Torah, and Israel," in *Theology and Church in Times of Change: Essays in Honor of John C. Bennett*, ed. E. LeRoy and A. Hundry (Westminster, 1970), pp. 81 and 89, note 60. However, while Tishby is concerned with the "Sabbatean" aspects, namely with an historical approach, and spends page after page in order to make the point, it was made by Heschel in one footnote. Meanwhile, more material that included the triple identification surfaced. See Bracha Sack, "More on the Metamorphosis of the Dictum: *Qudsha᾽ Berikh Hu᾽*, *ᶜOrayyta᾽*, and *Yisrael* are One" *QS* 57 (1982): 179–84 (Hebrew), who pointed out several discussions, including Cordoverian evidence; and Moshe Idel, "Two Remarks on R. Yair ben Sabbatai's *Sefer Ḥerev Piffiyot*"*QS* 53 (1979): 213–14 (Hebrew).

11. See note 15 below.

12. On this issue see immediately below. My criticism of proxism is not an opposition to contextualism. In my opinion, the panoramic view expands the context from the preceding phrase, assuming the importance of other literary corpora as relevant contexts, even if they were remote in history.

13. In his otherwise very valuable *Beginning of Hasidism*, I did not find an attempt to differentiate between the types of thought that underlie these two Kabbalistic systems and the ethical-mystical literature written under their influence.

14. See, especially, his article mentioned in the next footnote.

15. Buber, "Interpreting Hasidism," pp. 218, 221. In his *Origin and Meaning*, pp. 29–38, Buber explicitly relates Hasidism to Sabbateanism, as he does also several times later on throughout this book; however, even when Buber points out the historical relationship between Sabbateanism and Hasidism, he does not assume that Sabbateans were among the founding fathers of Hasidism, as it is possible to infer from some of Scholem's discussions and more manifestly from Tishby's essay, "Between Sabbateanism and Hasidism: The Sabbateanism of the Kabbalist R. Yaᶜaqov Kopel Lifshitz of Miedzyrec," in his collection of studies, *Paths of Faith and Heresy*, pp. 204–26, especially pp. 225–26.

16. This is the general nature of Buber's *Origin and Meaning*.

17. See his *Major Trends*, pp. 327–31. See also the presentation of Joseph Dan, "The Historical Perceptions of the Late Professor Gershom Scholem," *Ẓion* 47 (1982): 170–71 (Hebrew).

18. See Paul Mendes-Flohr, "*Fin-de-Siécle* Orientalism, the *Ostjuden* and the Aesthetics of Jewish Affirmation," in *Studies in Contemporary Jewry* (Bloomington, 1984), pp. 96–139.

19. See note 9, above.

20. See Scholem, *Messianic Idea*, pp. 223–27.

21. The *Erlebnis*-phase is well represented by the composition of the *Ecstatic Confessions* in 1909. See Paul Mendes-Flohr, ed. (Harper and Row: San Francisco, 1985).

22. Buber, "Interpreting Hasidism," p. 218.

23. See note 26, below.

24. See note 26, below.

25. Hasidism was defined as the place where Buber found the "primal Jewish reality," and it embodies the "inner truth" of Judaism. See Buber, *Hasidism and Modern Man,* p. 59: Mendes-Flohr, "*Fin-de-Siécle*" (note 18 above), pp. 115–16; on the nature of Gnosticism and Apocalypticism, see Buber, ibid., p. 27.

26. Scholem, *Messianic Idea,* p. 231; Compare Buber, *Origin and Meaning,* pp. 133–34, 179–80; "Interpreting Hasidism," p. 225. See also ibid., p. 218, Oppenheim, "Meaning of Hasidut," p. 409, and below, Concluding Remarks, par. 2.

27. On Heschel's views on Hasidism see Dresner's introduction to Heschel, *Circle of the Baal Shem Tov,* pp. 20–39.

28. I shall not discuss here those peculiar points of agreement that were already referred to by Scholem himself; see his *Messianic Idea,* pp. 236–37. See also Buber "Interpreting Hasidism" pp. 221–22. Another formulation of what I call proximism is found in Schatz-Uffenheimer, *Quietistic Elements,* p. 13: "These questions [related to the mystical aspects of Hasidism] cannot be understood but from the acquaintance with the Lurianic Kabbalistic worldview." Any other types of Jewish spirituality were not mentioned in this context; see now her *Hasidism as Mysticism,* p. 42.

29. See notes 9 and 17, above.

30. See notes 15 and 28, above.

31. See e.g. *Origin and Meaning,* p. 30, where Hasidism is described as a "countermovement."

32. See Buber, ibid., pp. 174–78 and Scholem, *Messianic Idea,* p. 232.

33. The importance of Gnosticism in Scholem's explanation of the nature of Kabbalah was discussed in David Biale's *Gershom Scholem, Kabbalah, and Counter-History* (Cambridge, Mass. 1982), pp. 51–64, 65–67, 71–72, and especially 89–91, where he discusses the controversy between Scholem and Buber on the place of Gnosticism in the frame of Hasidic thought. On Scholem and Gnosticism, see Harold Bloom in *Gershom Scholem,* pp. 207–20. For a criticism of Scholem's emphasis of the role of Gnosticism in the constitution of Kabbalah, see for the time being, Idel, *Kabbalah: New Perspectives,* pp. 30–32; idem, "The Problem of the Sources of the Bahir" in *The Beginnings of Jewish Mysticism in Medieval Europe,* ed. J. Dan (Jerusalem, 1987), pp. 55–72 (Hebrew); idem, "Subversive Catalysts: Gnosticism and Messianism in Gershom Scholem's View of Jewish Mysticism" (forthcoming); Ithamar Gruenwald, *From Apocalypticism to Gnosticism* (Peter Lang: Frankfurt am Main, 1988), pp. 65–124, 191–232.

34. *Der Jude und sein Judentum* (Koeln, 1963), pp. 194–97.

35. See the very beginning of Scholem's seventh unhistorical statement: "The doctrine of the emanation is to be considered as the special misfortune of Kabbalah," in *ᶜOd Davar* (Jerusalem, 1989) p. 36.

36. See Idel, "Subversive Catalysts" (note 33 above).

37. Although Buber was well aware of both the variety of Hasidic teachings and legends, as is apparent from his collections of Hasidic tales and his introductions, when dealing with Hasidism as a religious phenomenon he never elaborates upon the possible implications of this diversity and approaches the whole religious core of Hasidism as one unified doctrine.

38. Buber, *Origin and Meaning,* pp. 119–21, 176–77; "Interpreting Hasidism," p. 219.

39. Scholem opposed Buber's assumption that Hasidism neutralized the Gnostic elements existent in Kabbalah; see *Messianic Idea,* p. 241. He agreed that only the messianic elements were neutralized.

40. "Interpreting Hasidism," pp. 219–20.

41. Scholem, *Messianic Idea,* pp. 233–34.

42. See Green, *Tormented Master,* pp. 337–71 especially pp. 368–69, note 4.

43. As for example Cordovero's *Pardes Rimmonim* and R. Abraham Azulai's *Ḥesed le-ʾAvraham.* For the influence of those treatises on Hasidism see more below, chap. 4 note 87 and Scholem, *Messianic Idea,* p. 241.

44. The assumption that several mystical paradigms were in existence in Jewish sources since the Tannaiticc period cannot be dealt with here. It is sufficient to mention that the Talmudic literature includes what was called a "normal mysticism," to use Kadushin's terminology, the *Heikhalot* literature differs substantially from the theories of *Sefer Yeẓirah,* and to these three trends we may add esoteric trends that generated the medieval Kabbalah, which in itself is a multifaceted form of mysticism. Even in the frame of the *Heikhalot* literature, there are different views, as it appears from recent papers of Joseph Dan; see e.g. "Anafiel, Metatron and *Yozer Bereshit*" *Tarbiẓ* 52 (1983): 456–58 (Hebrew). See also Idel, *Kabbalah: New Perspectives,* pp. 74–111.

45. This issue will be dealt with in a further study of the emergence of Kabbalah in Europe. It is indisputable that the views of the book *Bahir* differ substantially from those of the Provençal Kabbalists.

46. See par. 39, printed together with *Liqqutim Yeqarim,* fol. 132b (Appendix 1). See also the testimony of R. Shneur Kalman of Liady, who mentions four Kabbalistic books that are studied: Giqatilla's *Sha ᶜarei ʾOrah,* R. Moshe Cordovero's *Pardes Rimmonim,* R. Shabbatai Sheftel Horowitz's *Shefa ᶜ Tai* (See also chap. 1, note 64), and Luria's *ᶜEẓ Ḥayyim.* See Mondshein, *Kerem CḤABAD,* vol. 1, p. 50 (Appendix 2). Thus, the panorama of this important Hasidic master includes one earlier Kabbalistic book, two Cordoverian ones, and only one Lurianic text. See also chap. 1, note 71.

Another writing composed by a follower of Cordovero and replete with quotations from the writings of his master is *Qinat Setarim* of R. Abraham Galanti, which was also widely printed.

47. See below, especially chaps. 2 and 4, as well as note 43 above.

48. Byron Sherwin, *The Mystical Theology and Social Dissent: The Life and Works of Judah Loew of Prague*, pp. 53–55, 130–33, 138–40; Bezalel Safran, "Maharal and Early Hasidism," in *Hasidism: Continuity or Innovation?* pp. 47–144. See also *Major Trends*, p. 339. Quotations from Maharal appear by the second generation of Hasidic masters. See R. Moshe of Dolina, *Divrei Moshe*, fol. 39c.

49. See Idel, "The Magical and Neoplatonic Interpretations," pp. 186–242; idem., "The Magical and Theurgical Interpretation," pp. 33–62. See also below, Concluding Remarks, par. 4.

50. See Idel, "Jewish Magic," p. 91.

51. See, for the time being, Idel, "The Magical and Theurgical Interpretation" pp. 57–60, idem, "Jewish Magic," pp. 105–6, and below, chap. 1, par. 3 and chap. 6 par. 2.

52. See the Seer of Lublin, *Zikkaron Zot*, fol. 10b, and *Benei Yisaskhar* II, fols. 42ab, 108d quoting *Sefer ha-Roqeaḥ*, a book printed under the aegis of R. Levi Yiẓḥaq of Berdichev or R. Qalonimus Qalman Epstein, *Ma᾽or va-Shemesh* IV, fol. 15c, and R. Barukh of Kosov *ʿAmud ha-ʿAvodah* fol. 172a quoting *Sefer Ḥasidim* etc. It should be mentioned that Ashkenazi material of 12th and 13th centuries could have come to the attention of the Hasidic masters of the 19th century through the mediation of the writings of R. Ḥayyim Joseph David Azulai, who was quoted by masters like R. Ẓevi Elimelekh of Dinov. See e.g., *Benei Yisaskhar* II, fol. 108c. For quotations from *Paʿaneaḥ Raza᾽*, see *Ben Porat Yosef*, fols. 51a, 53b.

53. Their writings were printed long before the emergence of Hasidism and were quoted by early Hasidic masters. On their Kabbalah, see Scholem, *Sabbatai Ṣevi, the Mystical Messiah* (Princeton, 1973), pp. 79–86; Yehuda Liebes, "Mysticism and Reality: Towards a Portrait of the Martyr and Kabbalist, R. Samson Ostropoler," in *Jewish Thought in the Seventeenth Century*, ed. I. Twersky and B. Septimus (Cambridge, Mass., 1987), pp. 221–25; idem, "Yonah ben Amitai ke-Mashiaḥ ben Yosef," *Studies in Jewish Mysticism, Philosophy, and Ethical Literature Presented to Isaiah Tishby*, eds. J. Dan and J. Hacker (Jerusalem, 1986), pp. 273–311 (Hebrew) and his "On a Secret Judaeo-Christian Sect Stemming from Sabbateanism," *Tarbiẓ* 57 (1988): 381–83 (Hebrew). R. Nathan Shapira and Shimshon of Ostropoler were quoted several times in the writings of the early Hasidic masters. See, e.g., *Ben Porat Yosef* (Pietrkov, 1884), foo. 54a; R. Barukh of Kossov, *Yesod Torah* (Chernovitz, 1864), fol. 23a; R. Menaḥem Mendel of Kossov, *᾽Ahavat Shalom* (Jerusalem, 1984), p. 1; R. Yehudah Leib ha-Kohen of Hanipoly, *᾽Or ha-Ganuz* (Zolkiew, 1899), introduction, fol. 8b, and fols. 3c and 8d; *Benei Yisaskhar* I, fol. 20b and II, fols. 94d, 95d.

54. See R. Barukh of Kossov, *ʿAmud ha-ʿAvodah*, passim and below chap. 3, note 247.

55. See Idel, *Studies*, pp. 126–34.

56. See, for the time being, Idel, "Universalisation and Integration," pp. 31–33 and 53–55, and the very important remark of Amos Goldreich in his edition of R. Yiẓḥaq of Acre's *Me ͗irat ͑Einayim,* pp. 399–400, to the effect that R. Yiẓḥaq combined in his work some of the features of Hasidism, such as using divine names, his proclivity for storytelling, his concern with the ideal of *devequt,* and the merging of conservatism and radicalism.

57. Idel, *Kabbalah: New Perspectives,* pp. 88–96, and below, chap. 5, in our discussion of *Ma ͑aseh Merkavah.*

58. This point, obvious as it seems to be from an inspection of the sources, was not sufficiently taken into consideration in the context of the modern description of the emergence of Hasidic mystical thought. See, e.g., the very important study of Piekarz, *The Beginning of Hasidism,* which seems to miss this cardinal point, which separates the Musar literature—profoundly influenced by Cordovero's Kabbalah—from the Lurianic literature. The fact is that without a theory of models that can organize the great variety of themes, ideas, and motifs in a meaningful manner, beyond merely quoting the sources, modern philological-historical approach may even induce someone to negate the nature of Hasidism as a distinct mystical movement; see his "The Devekuth as Reflecting the Socio-Religious Character of the Hasidic Movement," *Daat* 24 (1990): 47 and *Ideological Trends of Hasidism in Poland During the Interwar Period and the Holocaust* (Jerusalem, 1990), p. 47. More on this issue see below, in the Concluding Remarks, par. 6.

59. See below, chap. 2, par. 1.

60. Idel, *Studies,* p. 132, where the single discussion on *hitbodedut,* quoted in the name of Luria, is analyzed.

61. See below, chap. 2, note 326.

62. See Ze͗ev Gries, *The Book in Early Hasidism* (Hakkibutz Hameuchad: 1992), pp. 59–60 (Hebrew); Arieh Tauber, "Defusei Koretz," *QS* 1 (1924/25): 303–6; vol. 2 (1925/26): 64–69, 215–28, 274–77 (Hebrew); Ḥayyim Lieberman, "Defusei Koretz" *Sinai* vol. 67 (1970): 63 and vol. 68 (1971): 182–89 (Hebrew). An inspection of the detailed list of the books printed at Koretz shows that more non-Lurianic Kabbalistic books (twenty-five) were printed there than Lurianic ones (twenty-two), not including the Hasidic books, of which there were twelve. If we add the books of the Hasidic masters to the non-Lurianic mystical books, it becomes obvious that Lurianism was a major area of interest, but in any case, more non-Lurianic books were printed. This finding concurs with the more general picture of the period I am trying to present throughout this study: the modern scholarly emphasis upon the singular centrality of Lurianism should be moderated, allowing more room for other forms of Kabbalah and for the various interactions among them.

63. *Liqqutim me-Ray Hai Gaon* (Warsaw, 1798). This collection of early Kabbalistic texts was commented on by the Maggid of Kuznitz, see below, note 64.

64. See *Rimzei Yisrael* (Warsaw, 1899); *Ner Yisrael,* printed in *Liqqutei R. Hai Gaon* (Lvov, 1800); *Nezer Yisrael* (Lvov, 1864). It should be remarked that the Maggid

of Kuznitz's literary activity in glossing the important Jewish texts is reminiscent of that of R. Elijah, the Gaon of Vilna, the great opponent of Hasidism.

65. See *Beginning of Hasidism.* However, see Bracha Sack, "The Influence of R. Moshe Cordovero on Hasidism," *Eshel Be ͗er Sheva ͑* 3 (1986): 229–46 (Hebrew). By emphasizing this fact an important step was taken in overcoming the simplistic resort to the notion that Lurianic Kabbalah was the only significant type of Kabbalistic thought relevant to the nature of Hasidic mysticism. However, the awareness of the paramount importance of Cordoverian thought is not sufficient, and we should be more conscious of the eclectic nature of his thought and look for the various models that were incorporated in his writings. See below, chap. 2, pars. 1–4.

66. See R. Dov Baer of Lubavitch, the Maggid of Kuznitz, R. Ẓevi Hirsch of Zhidachov, R. Yiẓḥaq Aiziq Safrin of Komarno, and his son, R. Eliezer.

67. See the decision included in the ban of Brody prohibiting the study of Lurianic Kabbalah before the age of forty, whereas the Cordoverian Kabbalah could be studied after the age of thirty; see Isaiah Tishby, "The Messianic Idea and Messianic Trends in the Growth of Hasidism," *Ẓion* 32 (1967): 4–5 (Hebrew); Moshe Idel, "On the History of the Interdiction to Study Kabbalah before the Age of Forty," *AJS Review* 5 (1980): 14–15 (Hebrew), and the introduction of R. Shelomo of Lutzk to *Maggid Devarav le-Ya ͑aqar,* pp. 1–2. See also the answer of R. Shneur Zalman of Liady to the secret committee regarding the beginning of the study of Kabbalah at the age of twenty, which is based upon Cordovero's *͗Or ha-Ne ͑erav.* Cf. Mondshein, *Kerem CḤABAD,* vol. 1, p. 81 and note 3. See also Scholem, "Two Testimonies," p. 230.

68. See Buber, *Origin and Meaning,* pp. 107–12; Scholem, *Messianic Idea,* 178–202. Scholem's article is a response to Tishby's "The Messianic Idea," and cf. Scholem's more extreme stand in Rivkah Schatz-Uffenheimer, "Self-Redemption in Hasidic Althought," in *Types of Redemption,* ed. R. J. Zwi Werblowsky and J. Bleeker (Leiden, 1970), pp. 207–12.

69. Scholem, *Messianic Idea,* 180–202; pp. see also Schatz-Uffenheimer, *Quietistic Elements,* p. 173 and *Hasidism as Mysticism,* p. 333.

70. I am inclined to accept Scholem's stand on this point, because the material adduced by Tishby in "The Messianic Idea" in order to demonstrate the importance of the messianic trend in Hasidism is relatively scanty in comparison to the huge Hasidic literature. Although Tishby's evidence is convincing with regard to the fact that Kabbalists contemporaneous with the early phase of Hasidism did indulge in various forms of Lurianic eschatology, much more so than Scholem would admit, the paucity of the Hasidic material he presented is surprising when compared with the rich documentation Tishby adduced from the Kabbalistic sources. I am interested here not in the debate between Scholem and Tishby concerning whether there was an acute messianism in Hasidism, but in the source of the type of personal redemption which Scholem, and many others following him, have correctly attributed to Hasidism. See also R. J. Z. Werblowsky, "Mysticism and Messianism: The Case of Hasidism," in *Man and His Salvation: Essays in Memory of S. G. F. Brandon,* (Manchester, 1973), pp. 305–13. On the question of messianism, influenced by Lurianic sources, in early Hasidism see Lie-

bes, "The Messiah of the Zohar," p. 114 and note 116 and Elliot Wolfson, "Walking as a Sacred Duty: Theological Transformation of a Social Reality in Early Hasidism," pars. 2–3, notes 10, 63 (forthcoming).

71. See Moshe Idel, "'One from a Town, Two from a Clan.' The Diffusion of Lurianic Kabbalah and Sabbateanism: A Reexamination" *Pe ᶜamim* 44 (1990): 6–8 (Hebrew), now in English, *Jewish History* 7 (1993): 82–85.

72. This point was duly recognized also by Scholem, *Messianic Idea,* p. 200, who attributed it to Kabbalistic preachers, apparently writing in the 16th and 17th centuries. However, he does not explain what precisely is novel with the Hasidic spiritualization of these terms and why messianism was spiritualized in reaction to heretical messianism if such a trend was already in existence. See Idel, *Studies,* pp. 100–1; idem., "The Land of Israel in Medieval Kabbalah," in *The Land of Israel: Jewish Perspectives,* Lawrence A. Hoffman, ed. (University of Notre Dame Press, Indiana, 1986), pp. 178–80; on the spiritualization of the Sefirotic ontology of the theosophical Kabbalah, which is already evident in 13th-century ecstatic Kabbalah, and its early Hasidic manifestations, see Idel, *Kabbalah: New Perspectives* pp. 146–153, and below, Appendix A.

73. See Idel, "Some Conceptions of the Land of Israel in Medieval Jewish Thought," in *A Straight Path: Studies in Medieval Philosophy and Culture: Essays in Honor of Arthur Hyman,* ed. Ruth Link-Salinger (Catholic University Press of America, Washington, 1988), pp. 137–41.

74. Idel, "Types of Redemptive Activity in the Middle Ages," pp. 254–58.

75. Scholem, *Major Trends,* pp. 140–41; Idel, ibid., 259–63.

76. Scholem, ibid., pp. 127–28; Idel, *Studies,* pp. 45–61. Compare also to Werblowsky's view that the concepts related to historical and collective messianism coexisted in Hasidic writings with the spiritual interpretation of messianism; cf. "Mysticism and Messianism," pp. 311–13 and Idel, *Messianism and Mysticism,* pp. 84–85.

77. See Idel, *Studies,* pp. 6–18.

78. See Scholem, *Messianic Idea,* pp. 223–25, *Kabbalah* (Jerusalem, 1974), pp. 144–52, Schatz-Uffenheimer, *Quietistic Elements,* 28, 104, 125, 128; Yoram Jacobson, *La Pensée Hassidique,* trans. C. Chalier (Paris, 1989) pp. 15–27.

79. Elior "The Affinity." See also Scholem, ibid., and Tishby-Dan, "Hasidism" p. 770. Elior assumes that the meaningful type of Kabbalah to be taken into account when dealing with the peculiar nature of Hasidism is the Lurianic one; see especially her formulations ibid., pp. 108–9. On the theory that regards immanentism as the revolutionary background of Hasidic mysticism, see Schatz-Uffenheimer, *Quietistic Elements,* pp. 104, 128.

80. Scholem, *Messianic Idea,* p. 223. See also Pachter, "The Concept of Devekut," p. 205 and below, chap. 1, note 71.

81. For more on immanentism in Judaism, see Moshe Idel, "An Epistle of R. Yiẓḥaq of Pissa (?) in Its Three Versions," *Qovertz ʿal Yad* 10 (OS, vol. 20) (1982): 191–92, note 187; ibid., *Kabbalah: New Perspectives,* pp. 144–46, 153–4; Dov Schwarz, "The Immanentistic Concept of the Divinity in Middle Ages Jewish Philosophy" (Hebrew) (forthcoming). On this issue in the 18th century, see also Norman Lamm, *Torah Lishmah, Torah for the Torah's Sake in the Works of Rabbi Ḥayyim of Volozhin and His Contemporaries* (New York, New Jersey, 1989), pp. 19, 66, and 81, and below, chap. 3, par. 2.

82. *ʾElohut ve-Ḥiyyut shelo.*

83. This Zoharic formula is the slogan of immanentism in Hasidic writings; of many discussions, see e.g., Weiss, in *Studies in Hasidism,* ed. Avraham Rubenstein (Jerusalem, 1977), pp. 173–74 (Hebrew); *Meʾor ʿEinayim,* p. 105 and Lamm, *Torah Lishmah,* p. 19.

84. Quoted in *Siddur Beit ʾAharon ve-Yisrael,* by R. Aharon of Karlin (Brooklyn, 1952), no pagination, in the discussion of *Sukkot* (Appendix 3). See also Menaḥem Mendel Viznitzer, *Sefer Mishnat Hasidim* (Benei Beraq, 1981), p. 319. A very close formulation to that adduced by the Maggid of Bar occurs in R. Menaḥem Naḥum of Chernobyl, *Meʾor ʿEinayyim,* p. 96, where he describes the Shekhinah as "the vitality of God, blessed be He, that dwells in every thing." Similar phrases recur in this work, even later on the same page and on p. 105. See also chap. 2, notes 221, 254. See Cordovero's view of the existence of *ḥiyyut* and *ruḥaniyyut* in every entity; *Pardes Rimmonim,* vol. XXIV, chap. 10; II, fol. 50b; Ben Shelomo, *The Mystical Theology,* pp. 288–29 and Idel, *Golem,* p. 197. See also Abraham Azulai's *ʾOr ha-Ḥamah* vol. I, fol. 63d, and the way the teaching of the Great Maggid was described in R. Yisrael ben Yiẓḥaq Simḥah, *ʿEser ʾOrot,* fol. 12a. See also below, Appendix A note 78.

The thought of R. Menaḥem Mendel of Bar did not attract the attention of scholars; the only longer piece of writing apparently written by him was printed, under the name of the Besht, by Rivka Schatz as "The Besht's Commentary." Scholem has sometimes expressed doubts as to whether the text was indeed authored by the Maggid of Bar. See, e.g., *Messianic Idea* p. 189; see also Weiss, Rubinstein, ed., *Studies in Hasidism,* pp. 141–42, and Viznitzer's collection of teachings by R. Menaḥem of Bar in his *Beʾer Menaḥem,* mentioned at the beginning of this note.

85. Compare to Cordovero's *Tefillah le-Moshe,* fol. 244b, where the divine emanation or extension within the world consists of the existence there of souls, Torah, and divinity (*ʾElohut*)." Compare this use of *ʾElohut* in order to point out an immanentistic view to that of R. Menaḥem Mendel of Bar. Compare also to another triad that become ubiquitous in Hasidism, that of worlds, souls, and divinity, which are present in each and every letter, according to the Besht. Cf. chap. 4, note 22. On *ḥiyyut* as the divine immanence in Cordovero and the *Shelah,* see Sack, "The Influence of Cordovero in the Seventeenth-Century," p. 369. See also the quote from Cordovero in Horwitz's *Shaʿar ha-Shamayim,* p. 182. See also below, chap. 2, note 176.

86. On this issue see below, chap. 2, par. 2

87. Idel, *Kabbalah: New Perspectives,* p. 154.

88. See Scholem, *Messianic Idea,* pp. 223–24.

89. An examination of the writings of Martin Buber, Joseph Weiss, Rivkah Schatz, and others an early Hasidism demonstrates that the question of the Kabbalistic sources of Hasidism was considered a minor issue, given the preconception that, in principle, Hasidism is either a continuation of Lurianism or an interpretation or a reaction to Sabbateanism. The need for an examination of Kabbalistic literature was put forth, at least theoretically, by Schatz-Uffenheimer, *Quietistic Elements* p. 11 and *Hasidism as Mysticism,* p. 39. It is only recently, in the studies of I. Tishby, M. Pachter, B. Sack, and G. Nigal that the issue of the Kabbalistic sources, especially the Safedian and those influenced by those Kabbalists, has been dealt with in a more elaborate manner. However, even in these studies, there is no systematic assertion of the need for a panoramic view, since they deal with Kabbalistic material and its relationship to Hasidism in a sporadic manner, without addressing the need to survey the whole range of Jewish thought as potentially relevant, or else they assume that some other models informed both the Kabbalistic texts and those of the Hasidic masters.

90. See a recent criticism of the opinion that Hasidism was a popular movement that came to solve the problem of a crisis in Emanuel Etkes, "Hasidism as a Movement: The First Stage," in *Hasidism: Continuity or Innovation?* ed., B. Safran. (Cambridge, Mass., 1988), especially p. 23.

91. The view that Jewish mysticism produces spiritual solutions for historical crises is characteristic of the explanation of Scholem and his disciples (see Dan, "The Historical Perceptions" [note 17 above], pp., 170–71, which stresses the importance of the crisis) for the emergence of the Lurianic Kabbalah as a response to the expulsion from Spain; I disagree with this view of Scholem; see Moshe Idel, "Particularism and Universalism in Kabbalah: 1480–1650," in David B. Ruderman, ed., *Essential Papers on Jewish Culture in Renaissance and Baroque Italy* (New York, 1992), pp. 335–37, and *Kabbalah: New Perspectives,* pp. 264–66. See also Ivan Marcus, "Beyond the Sefardic Mystique," *Orim* 1 (1985): 40–47.

92. *Present Past, Past Present: A Personal Memoir,* trans. Helen R. Lane (Grove Press: New York, 1972), p. 140.

93. Andrew Samuels, *Jung and the Post-Jungians* (Routledge and Kegan Paul: London, 1985), p. 74. See also Walter A. Shelburne, *Mythos and Logos in the Thought of Carl Jung* (State University of New York Press: Albany, 1988), pp. 66–68. It should be mentioned that at the beginning of the century, a psychologist, William M'Dougall, in *An Introduction to Social Psychology* (London, 1908), formulated a theory about what he called the "central part" of an emotional religious event or experience, in a way reminiscent of Rudolf Otto's *numen.* See R. Marett, *The Threshold of Religion* (London, 1914), p. 187. His views, which were accepted by Marett, emphasized the priority of the emotional over the rational aspects of religion, in a way that seems to me to be very interesting, ibid., p. X. Although I would not like to generalize to religion as such, at least in the case of Hasidism it seems that the emphasis in modern scholarship on the theological is reminiscent of Frazer's theory, which was criticized by Marett, stressing the emotional, religious impulses as formative. Therefore, even without relying on the more speculative aspects of religion, which could provide

abstract systems which may be more constant, it is possible, at least on the basis of M'Dougall and Marett's views, to speak about rather stable forms of experience, which have a recurring core.

94. *Peregrinations: Law, Form, Event* (New York: Columbia University Press, 1988), p. 8. In one way or another, the above quotations are reminiscent of the famous theory of Empedocles concerning the notion of recurrence.

95. See, e.g., some of the more recent discussions collected in Dominick La Capra, *Soundings in Critical Theory* (Ithaca and London, 1989); the collection of studies edited by Daniel Guerriere, *Phenomenology of the Truth Proper to Religion* (Albany, 1990); John E. Toews' review article, "Intellectual History after the Linguistic Turn: The Autonomy of Meaning and the Irreducibility of Experience," in *The American Historical Review* 92 (1987): 879–907; Carlo Ginzburg, *Ecstasies: Deciphering the Witches' Sabbath* (New York, 1991); Jean-Francois Lyotard, *Phenomenology,* trans. Brian Beakley, (State University of New York Press: Albany, 1991), pp. 73–92; Lawrence E. Sullivan, *Icanchu's Drum. An Orientation to Meaning in South American Religions* (New York, London, 1988), pp. 3–4, 866, note 4; idem, "Seeking an End to the Primary Text," or "Putting an End to the Text as Primary," F. E. Reynolds and S.L. Burkhalter, eds., *Beyond the Classics?* (Scholars Press: 1990), pp. 41–59.

96. Cf. Isadore Twersky, "Joseph ibn Kaspi: Portrait d'un intellectuel juive," *Cahiers de Fanjeaux* (*Juifs et Judaisme de Lanquedoc*) 12 (1977): 189–90.

97. See also the view expressed by Yehuda Liebes in "New Directions in the Study of Kabbalah," *Peʿamim* 50 (1992): 154–56 (Hebrew).

98. Hans Jonas, "Myth and Mysticism," *Journal of Religion* 49 (1969): 328–29.

99. Liebes, "New Writings," pp. 205, 231, 241–42, 289–90, 302–4, 327–28, 338–39, and the pertinent footnotes, as well as his "R. Naḥman of Bratslav's *HaTikkun HaKelali* and his Attitude towards Sabbateanism," *Ẓion* 45 (1980): 201–45 (Hebrew). See also above, note 15, and chap. 3, note 2 and chap. 4, note 5. See also Weiss, in Rubenstein, ed., *Studies in Hasidism,* p. 132.

100. Tishby, "Les traces."

101. See *The Beginning of Hasidism,* pp. 299–302, 331–37.

102. In this context, Azriel Shoḥat's study of "joy" in Hasidism was paradigmatic, as it chartered the history of one important Hasidic theme from Cordovero to the ethical-kabbalistic literature and then to Hasidism. See "On Joy in Hasidism," *Ẓion* 16 (1951): pp. 30–43 (Hebrew).

103. See his *The Conduct Literature.*

104. I propose this term in order to cover a concept that was expressed by the term "macrocosmic approach" in *Saints and Society: Two Worlds of Western Christendom, 1000–1700,* by Donald Weinstein and Rudolph M. Bell (Chicago and London, 1986), pp. 2–3. Micro-analyses would therefore stand for attempts to deal with the history of an idea within the Hasidic literature or with the thought of a certain Hasidic master. It

goes without saying that both avenues are important and complementary, and the use of the terms micro and macro does not represent any evaluation with regard to their primacy.

105. It should be emphasized that there is no reason to adopt an exclusive approach; even if, for example, the Hasidic concepts of *devequt* or *ʿavbdah be-gashmiyut* were influenced by R. Moshe Ḥayyim Luzzato, as Tishby has shown (see his "Les Traces," pp. 428–60), there is no reason to restrict the Hasidic sources of inspiration solely to one type of text. Cumulative influences are as good an explanation as maintaining that one particular source can solve the question of the emergence of a certain type of thought.

106. See below, chap. 2.

107. Let me mention here a more specific example of the poverty of the proximist approach. Dealing with the identity of R. Adam, the Master of the Name, Scholem proposed to identify this legendary figure with a Sabbatean author. See Scholem, *Major Trends* pp. 332–34; ibid., *Researches in Sabbateanism,* pp. 591–97; and Liebes' notes pp. 597–59. Nothing in the legends connected to this figure necessitated such an identification; the fact that Scholem resorted to such an explanation was, undoubtedly, part of his preconception of the paramount importance of Sabbatean figures for the understanding of the genesis of Hasidism. However, as Chone Shmeruk has convincingly shown, it is possible to trace the prehistory of the R. Adam legends long before the emergence of Hasidism, and of Sabbateanism, in the early 17th century. See his *Yiddish Literature in Poland* (Jerusalem, 1981) (Hebrew), pp. 119–39. See also Abraham Rubenstein, "On the Mentor of the Besht and the Writings He Studied," *Tarbiẓ* 48 (1978–79): 156–58 (Hebrew). This is but one characteristic example of the need to allow richer possibilities for the understanding of Hasidism than both Scholem and Buber were interested in doing.

108. The first chapter of the present study is devoted to this last question.

109. See below the many references to the writings of R. Moshe Eliaqum Beriʾah, the son of the Maggid of Kuznitz; those from R. Aharon of Zhitomir's *Toledot ʾAharon,* the disciple of R. Levi Yiẓḥaq of Berdichev; R. Reuven Horowitz's *Dudaʾim ba-Sadeh*; R. Yisrael of Ryzhin's books; R. Qalonimus Qalman Epstein's *Maʾor va-Shemesh*; and R. Yiẓḥaq Aiziq Safrin of Komarno, among other 19th-century Hasidic authors. I have perused some collections of Hasidic legends, and some references to Hasidic stories that concur with my understanding of the teachings were mentioned in the footnotes.

110. Since Buber's and Weiss's comparative and phenomenological observations, and Schatz-Uffenheimer's *Quietistic Elements,* only a few remarks have been devoted to this issue. See e.g., Joel Orent, "The Transcendental Person," *Judaism* 9, 3 (1960): 235–52; Joseph A. Schultz, *Judaism and the Gentile Faith* (Toronto, 1981), pp. 91–97, and Arthur Green, "The Ẓaddiq as Axis Mundi in Later Judaism," *Journal of the American Academy of Religion* 45, 3 (1977): 327–47.

111. See Gries, *The Book,* pp. 85–92.

112. See "ḤABAD: The Contemplative Ascent to God," *The Theory of Divinity; The Paradoxical Asent.*

113. Green, *Tormented Master.*

114. "Hasidism as a Movement"; idem., "The Study of Hasidism: Trends and Directions," *Jewish Studies* 31 (1991): 5–21 (Hebrew); "R. Shneur Zalman of Liady's Ascent to Leadership," *Tarbiẓ* 54 (1985): 429–39 (Hebrew); "The Way of R. Shneur Zalman of Liady as a Leader of Hasidism," *Ẓion* 50 (1985): 321–54 (Hebrew).

115. See especially her "The Hasidic Movement." It should be mentioned that some significant distinctions between earlier and later Hasidic generations are also implicit in Piekarz's recent study, "Devekuth," but he draws the conclusion that after all, Hasidism as mysticism is not a distinct form of thought, but mainly a socio-religious movement.

116. *The Lord's Jews* (Cambridge, Mass., 1991), p. 211 and his study mentioned below, chap. 2, note 207.

117. For more on this issue, see below, Concluding Remarks, par. 6.

118. See above, note 114.

119. Cf. "Spiritual Renaissance," p. 34.

120. See Valerie I. J. Flint, *The Rise of Magic in Early Medieval Europe* (Princeton, New Jersey, 1991) p. 3.

121. See Idel, *Kabbalah: New Perspectives,* p. 157.

122. Compare Joachim Wach, *The Comparative Study of Religions,* ed. Joseph M. Kitagawa (New York, London, 1958), pp. 52–53; Marett, *Threshold of Religion,* p. 72; Michel Meslin, *L'experience humaine du divine* (Paris, 1988), pp. 82–83 and see also below, Concluding Remarks, par. 2.

NOTES TO CHAPTER 1

1. See Jacob Katz, "On the Question of the Connection between Shabbateanism and the Enlightenment and the Reform," in *Studies in Jewish Religious and Intellectual History Presented to Alexander Altmann,* eds. S. Stein and R. Loewe (Alabama, 1979), p. 95 (Hebrew section).

2. Some important reports of criticism against the widespread study of Kabbalah in the eighteenth century were collected and discussed by Piekarz, *The Beginning of Hasidism*: 320–38. In the following discussion we shall be concerned with other sources than those quoted by Piekarz. The main interest will be the criticism regarding the very nature of Kabbalah.

3. See Tishby, *The Wisdom of the Zohar* I: 52–56.

4. See Scholem, *Major Trends*: 181–89.

5. According to a widespread medieval dictum, occurring inter alia in Yehudah

Halevi, *Sefer ha-Kuzari* II, 72, we must study from the mouth of teachers, rather than from written texts: *mi-pi soferim we-lo᾿ mi-pi sefarim.* Cf. n. 13, and Shalom Rosenberg, "Joseph ibn Caspi, *Sefer ha-Hata᾿ah* (Sophistical Refutations)," *ʿIyyun* 32 (1983), 280, n. 17 [Hebrew]. A similar stand to that of Emden can be found in R. Shemuel ben Eliezer of Kalwaria's work *Darkhei Noʿam* (Koenigsburg, 1764) fol. 981; Tishby "The Messianic Idea," pp. 20–21. This Lurianic Kabbalist, who apparently was close to R. Eliahu, the Gaon of Vilna, bitterly attacks the Hasidic tendency to study Kabbalah without authoritative mentors.

6. Cf. *Ḥagigah,* fol. 14b.

7. On Lurianic works contaminated by incorrect versions and spurious attribution of Sabbatean inventions see Emden, *Mitpaḥat Sefarim*: 78, 112.

8. Seemingly the Ottoman Empire, since immediately afterwards Emden mentions inter alia Poland and Hungary as influenced by Sabbatean customs.

9. R. Jacob Emden, *Mitpaḥat Sefarim* p. 77 (see Appendix 1).

10. Compare also to R. Joseph del Medigo's critique in *Maẓref le-Ḥokhmah,* chap. 17 (see Appendix 2). On the whole subject see Jacob Katz "Halakhah and Kabbalah as Competing Subjects of Study," *Daʿat* 7 (1981), 37–68 [Hebrew].

11. Emden, *Mitpaḥat Sefarim,* p. 78.

12. The passage is quoted in Emden's name in R. Pinḥas Eliyahu Hurwitz, *Sefer ha-Berit,* p. 292. At present I am not able to locate it in any of Emden's works. (See Appendix 3) Compare also ibid., p. 299.

13. On the superiority of oral transmission to written documents, see Abraham Abulafia's view discussed in Idel, *Language, Torah and Hermeneutics*: 46–55. On the paramount importance of the oral transmission of Kabbalah, see Alexander Altmann, "Lurianic Kabbalah in a Platonic Key: Abraham Cohen Herrera's Puerta del Cielo," *HUCA* vol. 53 (1982), 321–24. See also Isadore Twersky, "The Contribution of Italian Sages to Rabbinic Literature" *Italia Judaica, Atti del l Convegno Internaẓionale*—Barri, 18–22 maggio, 1981 (Rome, 1983): 386–87. Compare also to the view of R. Menaḥem Mendel of Premislany, mentioned in n. 24 below.

14. *Leshem Shevo᾿ ve-᾿Aḥlemah* (Jerusalem, 1948) fol. 2a (see Appendix 4).

15. *᾿Aspaqlariah ha-Me᾿irah* (Firth 1776), fol. 1b (see Appendix 5).

16. See M. A. Perlmuter, *Rabbi Jonathan Eibeschuetz and his Attitude Towards Sabbatianism* (Jerusalem, Tel-Aviv, 1947) [Hebrew]; Liebes, "New Writings."

17. *Ḥesed le-᾿Avraham,* fol. 3a (see Appendix 6). This argument recurs in the Ḥabad Hasidism; see Monshein, *Migdal ʿOz*: 363, 372 and n. 28 where a tradition in the name of the Besht is quoted from R. Menaḥem Mendel of Lubavitch, *Derekh Miẓwoteika,* fol. 115b, to the effect that the Besht himself has disapproved the study of Kabbalistic books, because of their anthropomorphic understanding by some Kabbalists. In this context, Luria's books are mentioned. Compare also the whole discussion ibid., fol. 115ab and in the "Additions" to *Keter Shem Tov,* from the circle of Ḥabad,

fols. 76b–77a. This attitude to Lurianic Kabbalah is corroborated to a stand attributed by R. David of Makov to R. Ḥayyim Ḥaike of Amdura, to the effect that the latter derided those who study Lurianic books and pray according to this form of Kabbalah; see *Shever Poshe ʿim* in Wilensky, *Hasidim and Mitnaggedim* II, p. 165. See also ibid., II, p. 107, 244. However, despite these statements, adduced here in order to point out the fact that Lurianism poses some problems to its students. I do not imply that the Besht, or others, did not study Lurianic sources and even practiced Lurianic mystical practices. See also below Appendix A beside n. 67.

18. See the first introduction to R. Shelomo of Lutzk, *Dibrat Shelomo* fol. 1c and *Maggid Devarav le-Ya ʿaqov,* p. 3 (see Appendix 7).

19. Shelomo of Lutzk, *Dibrat Shelomo,* fol. 1c and *Maggid Devarav le-Ya ʿaqov,* p. 2 (see Appendix 8). Compare below our discussion on the relation between philosophy and Kabbalah in Solomon Maimon's works, especially, n. 35 below.

20. Shelomo of Lutzk, *Dibrat Shelomo,* fol. 1c and *Maggid Devarav le-Ya ʿaqov,* p. 2. See also below Appendix A n. 70.

21. See Immanuel Schochet, *The Great Maggid,* (New York, 1978) vol. 1: 70–71. See also the *haskamah* of R. Moshe of Sambur to R. Barukh of Kossov's *ʿAmud ha-ʿAvodah,* fol. 1b-2a, where he regards the study of Cordoverian writings and that of *Sha ʿarei ʾOraḥ* as helpful in avoiding an anthropomorphic understanding of Luria's writings. Implicitly, this is the content of the haskamah of R. Menaḥem ben Eliezer of Premislany, ibid., fol. 1b.

22. See *ʿOmer Man,* (Vilna, 1883) p. 10; R. Meshullam Phoebus, *Yosher Divrei ʾEmet,* fol. 138a (see Appendix 9). Also see n. 23 below.

23. R. Meshullam Phoebus of Zbarazh, *Yosher Divrei ʾEmet,* fol. 138a (see Appendix 10). See also Idel, *Kabbalah: New Perspectives,* p. 58.

24. R. Meshullam Phoebus, *Yosher Divrei ʾEmet,* fol. 122a (see Appendix 11). See below, chap. 5 par. 1 and *Maggid Devarav le-Ya ʿaqov*: 234–35.

25. See R. Shneor Zalman's letter printed by David Hilman, *Letters of the Author of the book Tanya and his Contemporaries* (Jerusalem, 1963), p. 97 (Hebrew); Wilensky, *Hasidim and Mitnaggedim* I: 201-2 (see Appendix 12); see Ross, "Two Interpretations," pp. 153-54 n. 4.

26. See also Lamm, *Torah Lishmah*: 19-23, 311. R. Elijah's reported assertion regarding human wisdom as the real source of Luria's Kabbalistic teachings contradicts one of the most central conceptions of Lurianic Kabbalah which perceived itself as superior to other kinds of Kabbalah exactly because of its divine source. See Moshe Idel, "Inquiries into the Doctrine of *Sefer ha-Meshiv*", *Sefunot* (NS), vol. 2 (17), edited by Y. Hacker (Jerusalem, 1983): 240-43 [Hebrew]. Compare to R. Pinḥas Hurwitz's statement in *Sefer ha-Berit,* p. 291 on Luria's Kabbalah (see Appendix 13).

27. Compare, however, R. Ḥayyim of Volozhin's statement in the introduction of R. Elijah's *Commentary on Sifra di-Ẓeni ʿuta*: "he [R. Elijah] brought them [i.e. the Lurianic works] out of darkness, caused by scribal errors."

28. On this subject, common to Emden and Hasidism, see our discussion below.

29. Shimeon Ginzburg (ed.), *R. Moses Ḥayyim Luzzato and his Contemporaries—A Collection of Letters and Documents* (Tel Aviv, 1937): 284–85 [Hebrew].

30. Meir Balban, *The History of Frankist Movement* (Tel Aviv, 1934), p. 126; compare also Tishby, "The Messianic Idea," p. 17.

31. See Moshe Idel "On the History of the Interdiction against the Study of Kabbalah before the Age of Forty," *AJS Review* vol. 5 (1980): 1–9 (Hebrew section).

32. See Ginzburg, *R. Moses Ḥayyim Luzzato,* (n. 29 above), pp. 286–87.

33. Maimon, *An Autobiography*: 94–95.

34. The view of hieroglyphs as pregnant with hidden lore, which is in our specific text the Kabbalah, was widespread since the late 15th century. See Don Cameron Allen, *Mysteriously Meant* (Baltimore, 1970): 107–33; F. A. Yates, *Giordano Bruno and the Hermetic Tradition* (Chicago, 1979): 163–64, 416–18, 428. Athanasius Kircher, the great theosophist of the 17th century, named one of the chapters of his *Oedipus Aegyptanus* "De Allegorica Hebraicorum veterum Scientia, Cabalae Aegyptiaca et hieroglyphicae parallela." Interestingly enough, R. Pinḥas Eliahu Hurwitz refers several times to hieroglyphs in his *Sefer ha-Berit,* (pp. 292, 294, 297), asserting that they were a mode of ciphering among ancient Jewish masters, without, however, combining hieroglyphs with Kabbalah. Compare, however, the view of Thomas Vaughan, in his work *Magia Adamica,* who asserts that the true Kabbalah uses letters as an artifice with which it observes and hides God's physical secrets as the Egyptians used the hieroglyphics; cf. Liselotte Diekmann, *Hieroglyphics—The History of a Literary Symbol* (Seattle, 1970), p. 78.

35. It is instructive to compare Maimon's view on the peculiar way the Kabbalah reached us with that of R. Aharon ha-Levi of Starosielce, one of the most important theologians of the Ḥabad movement. See Appendix 14 for the doctrines of the *Zohar* and Luria according to the latter. According to R. Aharon, the role of the Hasidic tradition he inherited from R. Shneor Zalman of Liady was to disclose the real meaning of Kabbalistic texts. According to Tishby, "The Messianic Idea," pp. 39–41, the text of R. Aharon ha-Levi has eschatological overtones, since in this context it is said, inter alia, "through his merit the Messiah shall come." Tishby's eschatological interpretation has been questioned by Elior, *The Theory of Divinity*: 374–75, n. 9, who concludes that R. Aharon merely used commonplace formulae. However, an interesting parallel to the aforecited text, which also includes messianic phraseology, is found in R. Pinḥas Hurwitz's *Sefer ha-Berit,* p. 291 (see Appendix 15). Compare also Hurwitz's statement in *Ta ʿam ʿEẓo* (commentary on *Mishnat Hasidim*) on his explanation of Lurianic Kabbalah (see Appendix 16) and *Sefer ha-Berit*: 290–91. On this author in general, as on his peculiar Kabbalistic background, see Manferd Harris, "The *Book of the Covenant*: An Eighteenth Century Quest for the Holy Spirit," *The Solomon Goldman Lectures,* vol. 6 ed. Nathaniel Stampfer (Chicago, 1982): 39–53.

36. Compare also to Maimon, *An Autobiography,* p. 97: "The modern Kabbalists prefer the latter (i.e. the Lurianic Kabbalah) because they hold that only to be genuine Kabbalah, in which there is no rational meaning."

37. Ibid., p. 103. See also below, chap. 6 par. 2.

38. Ibid., p. 97; Vital's booklet and its wide propagation and profound influence in the second part of the eighteenth century will be discussed elsewhere.

39. *Ḥagigah,* fol. 15b.

40. Ms. Berlin, fol. 142 (see Appendix 17). Compare also fol. 130 passim where Maimon attacks the gross misinterpretation of the Kabbalah by Kabbalists who did not study Maimonides. On the whole problem see also Moshe Idel, "Divine Attributes and *Sefirot* in Jewish Theology" in *Studies in Jewish Thought,* eds. S. O. Heller Wilensky and M. Idel (Jerusalem, 1989), pp. 89–111, esp. pp. 107–10 [Hebrew].

41. Compare also to the similar view of Jacob Emden, *Mitpaḥat Sefarim*: 110–11.

42. The whole problem was dealt with at length by Sara Klein-Braslavy, "Verité prophetique et verité philosophique chez Nissim de Gerone," *REJ* 134 (1975), 75–99.

43. See e.g. Meir ibn Gabbai, *ᶜAvodat ha-Qodesh* IV, chaps. 1–2; fols. 113c–115c, and Idel, "Differing Conceptions," pp. 153–54. Sharp criticism of philosophical interpretations of *Maᶜaseh Merkavah* are found even among contemporaries of Maimon who were indeed Kabbalists, but nevertheless relatively close to the general culture, not to say to the Jewish Enlightenment, like R. Jacob Emden, *Mitpaḥat Sefarim*: 65–66 or R. Pinḥas Eliahu Hurwitz, *Sefer ha-Berit*: 222–23. See Idel, "Maᶜaseh Merkavah."

44. *Ḥesheq Shelomo,* Ms. Berlin, p. 129 (see Appendix 18). See also n. 50 below. On *Ḥesheq Shelomo* see Abraham Geiger, "Zu Salomon Maimon's Entwickelungsgeschichte," *Juedische Zeitschrift* vol. 4 (1866): 189–99. I quote from photocopies made by the late Prof. G. Scholem, which can be found in the National and University Library, Jerusalem. I hope to edit substantial parts of this manuscript in the near future.

45. I excluded a long series of Lurianic issues, mainly dealing with anthropomorphic configurations. It is obvious that Maimon has chosen this type of subject in order to deride its understanding in a simplistic way.

46. Maimon, *An Autobiography,* p. 105. On this passage see Harry W. Wolfson, *The Philosophy of Spinoza* (New York, 1969), vol. 1, p. 395; Alexander Altmann, "Lessing und Jacobi; Das Gesprich ueber den Spinozismus" *Lessing Yearbook,* vol. 3 (1971): 29–34.

47. On Spinoza and Kabbalah see Maimon's *Giveᶜat ha-Moreh,* eds. S. H. Bergman and N. Rotenstreich (Jerusalem, 1965) p. 161 [Hebrew], where the Kabbalistic notion of "withdrawal" *(ẓimẓum)* is compared to Spinozistic pantheism, and the discussions referred to in the previous note. This topic will be discussed in detail elsewhere.

48. See immediately afterwards (*An Autobiography,* p. 105) where the *Sefirot* are depicted as the ten Aristotelian categories which Maimon learned from *The Guide of the Perplexed.*

49. The understanding of Kabbalah as a superior type of talismanic system will be dealt with in chap. 4, par. 4.

50. Maimon, *An Autobiography,* p. 106. Compare to *Ḥesheq Shelomo,* Ms. Berlin, p. 18 (see Appendix 19). See also n. 44 above.

51. See Herrmann Meyer, *Moses Mendelssohn, Bibliographie* (Berlin, 1965), p. 113; Altmann, *Moses Mendelssohn,* p. 866, n. 8.

52. This term *oriental philosophers* for Kabbalists reminds one of the Latin version of the subtitle of the Kabbalistic work *ʾImrei Binah*: "Metaphisica cabbalistica, sive Philosophia orientalis antique." This work was seemingly written by Isaac Satanov, or at least published by him; Satanov was part of Mendelssohn's entourage; see Altmann, *Moses Mendelssohn,* index, s.v. Satanov.

53. Compare Scholem, *Messianic Idea*: 216–17. Scholem's assertion that the Hasidim were the first who substituted *tiqqun* for *devequt* will be discussed at length elsewhere. See meanwhile Idel, *Messianism and Mysticism* pp. 84–89.

54. *Sefer ha-Berit*: 2, 338, 340, 352, 354, 358–59.

55. Ibid.: 45–46.

56. See Maimon, *An Autobiography,* p. 97, quoted above n. 38.

57. (a. The versions of R. Yisrael Sarug's Kabbalah which were known to the eighteenth-century Kabbalists in their authentic forms as compared by Sarug, in the Neoplatonic interpretations of R. Abraham Kohen Herrera and R. Joseph Shelomo del Medigo, and even the latter's atomistic interpretation; (b) the version of R. Ḥayyim Vital.

58. The interpretation of R. Emanuel Ḥayy Rikki which stressed the plain meaning of the Lurianic texts versus that of R. Joseph Ergas and R. Moshe Ḥayyim Luzzatto, who tended to a more allegorical understanding of the Lurianic thought. On the attribution of an allegorical sense to Lurianism by R. Yiẓḥaq Ḥaver, one of the greatest exponents of Luria's Kabbalah in the nineteenth century, among the followers of Elijah, the Gaon of Vilna, see Ross, "Two Interpretations" p. 154 n. 7.

59. See Liebes, "Sefer Ẓaddiq Yesod ʿOlam."

60. On the "struggle" between Lurianic and Cordoverian types of Kabbalah in the early 17th century, see Tishby's two articles in his *Studies in Kabbalah,* pp. 177–267.

61. *Pardes Rimmonim* was printed, inter alia, in Cracow in 1590; *Tomer Devorah,* Cracow, 1592; *ʾOr Neʿerav* Cracow, 1647, Fiorda, 1701.

62. See Mordekhai Pachter, "*Sefer Reshit Ḥokkmah* by R. Eliyahu de Vidas and Its Abbreviations," *QS* vol. 47 (1972): 686–710 [Hebrew].

63. Cf. R. J. Zwi Werblowsky "O Felix Culpa Version" in *Studies in Jewish Religious and Intellectual History Presented to Alexander Altmann,* edited by S. Stein and R. Loewe (Alabama, 1978): 355–62. Compare, however, Joseph Dan, *Hebrew Ethical and Homiletical Literature* (Jerusalem, 1975), 223 [Hebrew] who believes that this

is a Lurianic-ethical book! See E. R. Wolfson, "The Influence of Luria on the Shelah," *JSJT* 10 (1992): 423–48. On the influence of the *Shelah* on Hasidism see Piekarz, *Hasidism in Poland*: 38–40 and also the next footnote.

64. On the importance of the "mussar" literature for the study of Hasidism, see Piekarz, *The Beginning of Hasidism,* Index, s.v. *Reshit Ḥokhmah, ha-Shelah, Ḥesed le-ʾAvraham.* This fact was also emphasized by other scholars, like Dan, ibid., p. 205, without, however, distinguishing between the Cordoverian dominance and the marginality of Luria's thought. It should also be emphasized that at least in the writings of R. Barukh of Kossov, there is a deep influence of R. Menaḥem Azariah of Fano's compendium of Cordovero's *Pardex Rimmonim* as well as a profound impact of R. Sabbatai Sheftel Horowitz's *Shefa ͑ Tal.* (On this book see also Introduction, n. 46.) Therefore, in the writings of one major contemporary of the Besht and the Great Maggid, there was an impressive range of Cordoverian writings that were available and influential. The pervasive impact of Cordoverian writings, and especially quotations concerning the attraction of the spiritual powers, show that even a Kabbalist immersed in Lurianic writings, proposed Cordoverian readings inspired by the magical model.

65. See above, n. 29–30. See also below chap. 2 n. 347, where an important text of Cordovero, quoted anonymously, has been chosen in order to open Lurianic treatments of mystical prayer.

66. Maimon, *An Autobiography,* p. 96.

67. Cf. ibid., p. 99, when speaking about Lurianic anthropomorphic subjects: "With all my efforts I could not find in these representations any rational meaning."

68. It is highly significant that the first edition of *͑Eẓ Ḥayyim* was initiated and accomplished by a *maskil,* Yiẓḥaq Satanov; see Altmann, *Moses Mendelssohn,* p. 353.

69. The controversy on the interpretation of the significance of *ẓimẓum* (contraction), which is referred to in Maimon's *An Autobiography*: 103–4, 106, and hinted at in *Ḥesheq Shelomo,* is an edifying testimony that any endeavor to understand Luria in an unorthodox way was dangerous. I will return to this point at length elsewhere. See meanwhile, Idel, "The Concept of *Ẓimẓum,*" pp. 106–10 and below chap. 2 par. 6. It should be mentioned that as late as the middle of the nineteenth century Cordoverian Kabbalah was considered as an alternative to the Lurianic one; see the story related to R. Simhah Bunim of Perzisha, where the Cordoverian Kabbalah is conceived to have a very high pedigree but not being beautiful, while the Lurianic one is very beautiful but has no pedigree. When asked what to prefer, the *Ẓaddiq* answered that "*was shein is shein*" namely he preferred the Lurianic one, but Cordoverian Kabbalah was nevertheless an alternative. See *ʾOr Simḥah,* printed by R. Yisrael ben R. Yiẓḥaq Simḥah in *Simḥat Yisrael* (Pieterkov, 1910) fols. 7b–8a.

70. R. Shelomo of Lutzk, *Dibrat Shelomo,* preface, and n. 18–21 above.

71. See Schochet, *The Great Maggid* (n. 21 above), pp. 70–71, n. 7. Nevertheless, Cordovero has not been included by some modern scholars among the main sources of Hasidism: see, e.g. Tishby-Dan, "Hasidism," p. 770 or Schatz-Uffenheimer, *Quietistic Elements,* index. See, however, the discussion of Elior on the influence of Cordovero

on later Ḥabad theology, *The Theory of Divinity,* index, s.v. Moshe Cordovero. See also above, Introduction, n. 46.

72. See chap. 4 par. 1.

73. See Buber, *Tales of the Hasidim, Early Masters*: 75–76; see also the text brought by Mondshein, *Migdal ʿOz,* p. 364, and Wilensky, *Hasidim and Mitnageddim,* vol. 2, p. 170 and n. 302. Compare also to the tradition adduced in R. Ḥayyim Liebersohn, *Ẓeror ha-Ḥayyim,* fol. 4c, on the confrontation between the Besht on one hand, and Luria and R. Shimeon bar Yohai on the other, over the plain sense of the *Zohar,* which ends with the victory of the Besht. In Kaidaner's *Sippurim Noraʾim* pp. 36–37 another version of a confrontation between the Besht and Luria, reminiscent of that adduced by Buber, is found.

See also the accusation of R. Abraham of Kalisk, that his friend, R. Shneor Zalman of Liady, has garbed the teachings of the Besht in the terminology of Luria; cf. Green, *Tormented Master*: 97–98. However, even the Ḥabad attitude to Lurianic Kabbalah was considered as too metaphorical by R. Ẓevi Hirsch of Zhidachov, one of the most radical followers of Luria in the Hasidic camp; see Loewenthal, *Communicating the Infinite*: 172–73 and Dov Schwartz, "R. Ẓevi Hirsch of Zhidachov: Between Kabbalah and Hasidism," *Sinai,* vol. 102 (1988), pp. 241–51 (Hebrew).

NOTES TO CHAPTER 2

1. On the peculiar meaning of this term, which differs from the classical Kabbalistic use of it, see below, chap. 4, n. 75; chap. 6 par. 2.

2. Introduction, par. 3.

3. Scholem, *Major Trends,* pp. 328–30; *Messianic Idea* pp. 180, 184–85.

4. See Scholem, *Devarim be-Go,* pp. 357–58 and below, Appendix A.

5. See above, Introduction, n. 8.

6. Compare, Elior, *Paradoxical Ascent,* pp. 5–6. See however, the more detailed discussion of Tishby, "Les traces," pp. 452–53 and below, Appendix A.

7. Scholem, *Messianic Idea,* pp. 185–86.

8. See Etkes, "Hasidism as a Movement"; Rappoport-Albert, "The Hasidic Movement."

9. See above, Introduction, par. 4.

10. See Idel, *Kabbalah: New Perspectives,* pp. 146–53. See now M. Pachter, "Katnut ("Smallness") and Gadlut ("Greatness") in Lurianic Kabbalah," *JSJT* 10 (1992): 171–210 (Hebrew).

11. *Major Trends,* p. 250.

12. See Nissim Yosha, note 261 below.

13. Introduction, pars. 1, 2.

14. See, e.g., the innovative study of Katz, "Models," and his contribution to Steven T. Katz, ed., *Mysticism and Religious Traditions* (Oxford, New York, 1983), pp. 43–51. Katz, as well as some other scholars, like John J. Collins and George W. E. Nickelesberg (*Ideal Figures in Ancient Judaism: Profiles and Paradigms* [Scholars Press, 1980]), are more interested in the paradigmatic concept of ancient or primoridial figures, while my approach has to do much more with the organization of knowledge, with relations, and processes. Compare also to the interesting essay of Frederick Ferré, "Mapping the Logic of Models in Science and Theology," in *New Essays in Religious Language,* ed. D. M. High (Oxford University Press, New York, 1969), pp. 54–96.

15. See his "Phenomenology of Perception: Perceptual Implications," *An Invitation to Phenomenology,* ed. James M. Edie (Quadrangle Books, Chicago, 1965), p. 21. See also Katz, "Models," pp. 251ff., which also deals with various forms of coherence, a little bit differently from the way it was presented by Gurwitsch. Interesting from our point of view is also the concept of "magical coherence" found in Gustav Mensching, *Structures and Patterns of Religion,* tr. H. F. Klimkeit and V. Srinivasa Sarna (Delhi, Varanasi, Patna, 1976), pp. 8–10, where he assumes that the magical view of existence is characteristic of primitive religiosity. However, as we shall try to show, not only is the Hasidism of the eighteenth century replete with crucial magical elements, which indeed may be regarded as constituting a coherent magical attitude to reality, but this attitude was also quite widespread in certain European circles from the late fifteenth-century Renaissance in Italy. See below, Concluding Remarks, pars. 2, 4.

16. Tishby, *Paths of Faith and Heresy,* pp. 26–27, Ben Shelomo, *The Mystical Theology.* See, more recently, Yehuda Liebes, who proposed a much more mythical, rather than theoretical, understanding of Cordovero's Kabbalah. Cf. his study, "Towards a Study of the Author of *Emek Ha-Melekh*: His Personality, Writings, and Kabbalah," *JSJH* 11 (1993): 101–38 (Hebrew) and now Bracha Sack, "The Attitude of R. Moses Cordovero to the Literature of the *Zohar* and to R. Simeon bar Yohai and His Circle," in *The Frank Talmage Memorial Volume,* ed. Barry Walfish (Haifa University Press: Haifa, 1993) vol 1, pp. 63–75 (Hebrew).

17. See, for example, below, par. 5, our discussion on *devequt.*

18. See his *Mystical Theology.*

19. *Torat ha-Ra ᶜ ve-ha-Qelippah be-Qabbalat ha-ʾAri,* (Jerusalem, 1952).

20. See Liebes, "New Directions," pp. 150–54, Idel, *Kabbalah: New Perspectives,* pp. 27–29, where the overemphasis upon a systematic approach was criticized. See also, Introduction, n. 93.

21. On this issue see below, chap. 3, par. 2.

22. From my point of view, it is not important whether the technique of achieving the *devequt* is nomian or anomian. In Hasidism, following the Kabbalistic traditions, this ideal can be attained in both ways.

23. See e.g., Scholem, *Major Trends,* pp. 244–86.

24. On this pivotal concept in Lurianism see Scholem, ibid., pp. 256, 267. On its source see Moshe Idel, "The Image of Man above the *Sephirot*: R. David ben Yehudah he-Hasid's Doctrine of the Supernal *Sephirot* [ẒAḤẒAḤOT] and its Evolution" (forthcoming).

25. See n. 5 above.

26. See Lewis, *Ecstatic Religion*; Lasky, *Ecstasy*; Ioan P. Couliano, *Experiences de l'extase* (Payot, Paris, 1984), Sullivan, *Ichancu's Drum*, Carlo Ginzburg *Ecstasies* (introduction, n. 95), *Religious Ecstasy*, ed. Nils G. Holm (Stockholm, 1981), Heiler, *Prayer*, pp. 137–42. See also below, n. 164 and n. 186.

27. See Werblowsky, *Joseph Karo*, pp. 78–81, 256–86; Idel, "Jewish Magic," pp. 106–7; idem, *Kabbalah: New Perspectives*, p. 311, n. 1.

28. Werblowsky, ibid., pp. 140–42.

29. Gedalyah Nigal, "*Dibbuk*" *Tales in Jewish Literature* (Jerusalem, 1983) (Hebrew); ibid., *Magic, Mysticism and Hasidism*, pp. 71–77.

30. See Idel, "Jewish Magic," pp. 106–8.

31. See below, chap. 5, par. 1. See also the Hasidic descriptions of the Sabbatean attempts to reach revelatory experiences adduced by Gershom Scholem, *Studies and Texts Concerning the History of Sabbateanism* (Jerusalem, 1976), p. 39, note 27.

32. An oneiric technique, namely a device to obtain a revelation in the dream state, is attributed to the Besht; see Scholem, "Two Testimonies," p. 240, n. 40 and Dubnow, *The History of Hasidism*, p. 485; and see also n. 34 below. On his ascent of the soul, a practice widespread in some Hasidic circles, see below, par. 3.

33. See below, chap. 5, par. 2 beside n. 60 and the interesting quote of R. Qalonimus Qalman Epstein analyzed in Schatz-Uffenheimer, *Quietistic Elements*, pp. 118–19 and translated into English in Jacobs, *Jewish Mystical Testimonies*, pp. 217–18. On the great importance of "prophets" in the lifetime of the Besht, see Scholem, "Two Testimonies," p. 239. See also below, n. 74. Another interesting comparison of the ecstatic experience of the *Ẓaddiqim* to prophets is found in the circle of R. Naḥman of Braslav; see Gries, *The Conduct Literature*, p. 240. See also R. Barukh of Kossov, *ᶜAmud ha-ᶜAvodah*, fol. 132a, where a passage from Luria's praises on the subject of revelations from above was interpreted in terms of Hermetic magic. An interesting earlier parallel to the ecstatic state of consciousness, where the mystic is possessed by the *Shekhinah* that speaks from his mouth, is found in ecstatic Kabbalah and in Jewish mystical sources that might have been influenced by it. See e.g., R. Nathan Netaᶜ of Helm, *Netaᶜ Shaᶜashuᶜim*, fol. 19c, and Idel, *The Mystical Experience*, pp. 84–88. See also the interesting material collected by Tishby, "The Messianic Idea," p. 40 on the various revelations that started in the Hasidic camp with the Besht and Heschel, *The Circle of the Baal Shem Tov*, p. 20, as well as the numerous references to prophetic phenomena in the critique of the opponents to Hasidism, cf. Wilensky, *Hasidim and Mitnaggedim*, vol. 2, pp. 105, 166, 249.

34. *Degel Maḥameh ʾEfrayim,* pp. 284–85. His contemporary, R. Yisrael, the Maggid of Kuznitz, reports on an encounter with the Besht in a dream, *ʿAvodat Yisrael,* fol. 38a. See also R. Yiẓḥaq of Radvil, *ʾOr Yiẓḥaq,* p. 197, which mentions a wondrous secret Yiẓḥaq was taught in the supernal paradise a night beforehand. It seems that this master received answers to questions he asked, and it is quite probable that this was part of an oneiric practice. See also R. Aharon Shemuel ha-Kohen, *Ve-Ẓivah ha-Kohen,* p. 136 and R. Ẓadoq ha-Kohen of Lublin, *Quntres Divrei Ḥalomot,* printed together with *Resisei Laylah* (Lublin, 1903), and see also Idel, *Golem,* pp. 220–24.

35. See below, chap. 3, par. 4.

36. *Beʾer Moshe,* fol. 182c (Appendix 1).

37. See below, n. 253 and chap. 3, n. 9.

38. *Zohar Ḥai* II, fol. 449c (Appendix 2). See also *Netiv Miẓwoteikha,* pp. 56–58. In his son's commentary on *ʾAvot,* R. Eleazar Ẓevi of Komarno's *Zeqan Beiti* (Jerusalem, 1973), pp. 83–84 offers a typology that diverges from that of his father's. According to him, R. Shimeon bar Yoḥai, Luria, and the Besht had the extraordinary power to see the higher worlds, while the disciples of the Besht were only to hear supernal voices. See the text referenced by n. 36 above.

39. As I shall elaborate in chap. 3, in my opinion Hasidism incorporates more than one formative model already in existence in Kabbalah.

40. See Idel, *Studies,* pp. 103–34.

41. Ibid., pp. 107, 112–13, 122–24, 132, 146–48, 151, and 157, n. 90.

42. Idem, *Mystical Experience,* pp. 22–24; *Studies,* pp. 64–67. On the power of the divine Name, see Urbach, *The Sages,* pp. 124–34. This magical view of the divine Name is shared also by the influential twelfth-century Jewish thinker, R. Abraham ibn Ezra; see e.g., his commentary on Exodus 3:15. The divine names are conceived to be both the instrument for reaching an experience of union of man and God as well as a powerful means to perform miracles. Whether these two perceptions of the divine names were combined into a more coherent paradigm, similar to the mystical magical model to be analyzed in the following discussions, is a question that requires special investigation. See especially Reuchlin's *De Verbo Mirifico* as analyzed by Charles Zika in "Reuchlin's *De Verbo Mirifico* and the Magic Debate of the Late Fifteenth Century," *Journal of the Warburg and Courtault Institutes* 39 (1976): 106–7, 111, 113, and 115.

43. See Idel, *Studies,* p. 147, n. 36.

44. This is part of a study in progress on the influence of ecstatic Kabbalah in different periods.

45. Compare the very sensitive remark of R. Ḥayyim Joseph David Azulai, *Midbar Qedemot* (Jerusalem, 1962), fol. 21c, that he did not see in Luria anything related to the "lore of combination of letters," a term characteristic of the ecstatic Kabbalah. Compare this to his *Shem Gedolim* I, fol. 54ab.

46. *Mayyim Rabbim,* fol. 21b (Appendix 3). Compare this to the discussion in Weiss, *Studies,* pp. 129–35.

47. Apparently, the *Zohar* refers to the Talmudic view that Bezalel knew how to combine the letters. See *Berakhot,* fol. 55a. See the discussion of the Zoharic text in Wolfson, "Letter Symbolism," pp. 219–20. On the mystical and magical significance of the combinations of letters, see Idel, *Golem,* p. 316 index s.v. Combinations of letters; *Mystical Experience,* pp. 21–24; Ithamar Gruenwald, "Uses and Abuses of *Gimatria,*" in *Rabbi Mordechai Breuer Festschrift,* ed. Moshe bar Asher (Jerusalem, 1992), vol. 2, pp. 823–32 (Hebrew), as well as his "Jewish Mysticism's Transition from *Sefer Yeṣira* to the *Bahir,*" *JSJT* vol. 6 (1987), pp. 28–29 (Hebrew), and the magical text printed recently by Lawrence H. Schiffman and Michael D. Swartz, *Hebrew and Aramaic Incantation Texts from the Cairo Genizah* (Sheffield, 1992), pp. 71, 74, 78.

48. *Zohar* III, fol. 2a.

49. *Sefer ha-Peliy'ah* I, fol. 17b.

50. Ibid., fol. 17a. Compare to *Sanhedrin,* fol. 22a.

51. See Idel, *Language, Torah, and Hermeneutics,* pp. 53–54, 176, n. 123.

52. Ibid., p. 53.

53. See e.g., the view expressed in the name of the Besht in *Keter Shem Tov* I, fol. 12c; R. Abraham the Angel, *Ḥesed le-'Avraham,* fol. 26b; *Degel Maḥaneh 'Efrayim,* p. 135; *'Or ha-Me'ir,* fols. 190a–d, 191a etc.; *Darkhei Ẓedeq,* fols. 4ab, 5a; R. Moshe Eliaqum Beri'ah, *Be'er Moshe* I, fol. 45ab. See also below, chap. 5. The recombination of letters of a certain word in order to amend its meaning and impact is called by the Great Maggid *tiqqun*; see Weiss, *Studies,* pp. 129–36. Indeed, this may be an interesting case of interpreting a term that was important for Lurianic Kabbalah, though not congenial to it, in terms closer to ecstatic Kabbalah. For the possible source of this reinterpretation in an important text quoted below by Cordovero, see text referenced by n. 137, below, and Idel, *Studies,* p. 162, n. 123. This also seems to have been the case in another instance, when the great *Yiḥudim* were caused by the combinations of letters. Again, a Lurianic term, *Yiḥudim,* is connected to a practice from ecstatic Kabbalah. See R. Yiẓḥaq of Radvil, *'Or Yiẓḥaq,* p. 114; R. Qalonimus Qalman Epstein, *Ma'or va-Shemesh* II, fol. 31a. On *Yiḥudim* and permutations of letters, see R. Yiẓḥaq of Acre, Idel, *Studies,* p. 114. See also R. Moshe Eliaqum Beri'ah, *Qehilat Moshe,* fol. 8a. I consider Abulafia's technique of combining letters in order to achieve an ecstatic experience a practice that is definitively different from the Lurianic technique of *Yiḥudim,* and I doubt very much Scholem's statement as to Abulafia's influence on Luria. See *Major Trends,* p. 277, *Kabbalah,* p. 180. Also Scholem's view, ibid., p. 181 as to the affinity between Abulafia's technique and the goal and that of the Geronese Kabbalists seems to me more than doubtful; Scholem probably has in mind *Sha'ar ha-Kavvanah li-mequbbalim ha-rishonim,* an anonymous text authored, according to Scholem, by R. Azriel, while its composition seems to me to belong to the end of the thirteenth century. See also below, n. 317. For the origin of the Lurianic practice of *Yiḥudim* see Marc Verman, "The Development of Yiḥudim in Spanish Kabbalah," in *The Age of the Zohar,* ed. Joseph Dan (Jerusalem, 1989), pp. 25–42. Although Abulafia was acquainted with

the technique of the conjugation of two divine names, and sporadically also used it, this should not be confused with permutations of the letters of the divine names. I hope to return to this issue in a separate study.

54. *Peri ha-ʾAreẓ,* fol. 81 (Appendix 4). See also a similar discussion, ibid., fol. 8ab. Compare also to *Degel Maḥaneh ʾEfrayim,* p. 238.

55. *Ḥesed le-ʾAvraham,* fol. 12c (Appendix 5). More on prayer and *zerufei ʾotiot,* see below, chap. 4, n. 89 and 123. See also *Keter Shem Tov* II, fol. 56ab, where the Besht is described as assuming that prayer is related to the practice of moving from one letter to another while contemplating how they are combined with one other. For an analysis of this text, see Daniel Merkur, "The Induction of Mystical Union: Two Hasidic Teachings," *Studia Mystica* 14 (4) (1991): 71–73. I fear that Merkur's assumption—that the Beshtian approach inspired him to a better understanding of Abulafia's concept of the combination of letters (ibid., p. 70)—is problematic not only historically and phenomenologically (Abulafia speaks about an anomian technique, the Besht about a nomian one), but also philologically, since it is not the one who prays that combines the letters, as in the techniques of ecstatic Kabbalists; the letters are combined with one other by themselves. Unfortunately Merkur's claim as to the improvement in understanding the ecstatic Kabbalah by resorting to Hasidism remained unfulfilled in his article, inasmuch as he does not come back to Abulafia's views in order to explicate his proposed improvement. He implicitly assumes that the fourfold theosophical scheme of Luria, which was combined with the technique of combining letters, can be helpful for better understanding Abulafia's thought. Although I assume that, indeed, Abulafia's concept of combining letters was known to the Besht, I assume that there were also other crucial elements that were combined with the views of ecstatic Kabbalah. See below, chap. 4 par. 3; on the divergences between Abulafia's Kabbalah and Hasidism, see here below, par. 4 and Concluding Remarks, par. 6.

56. Ibid., fols. 23cd, 26a. This master has an entire ontology of the concept of *Ẓerufim,* which cannot be analyzed here. Compare also to the view of the contemporary of this master, R. Aharon Kohen of Apta, *Ner Miẓwah,* fols. 15a and 31a, where revelations are obtained by means of combinations of divine names. See also the passage from his *ʾOr ha-Ganuz,* fol. 46ab in n. 74, below.

57. Sefer *Mafteaḥ ha-Ḥokhmot,* Ms. Parma 141, fol. 91a. For more on this type of interpretation, see Idel, *Language, Torah and Hermeneutics,* pp. 101–9.

58. *ʾOẓar ʿEden Ganuz,* ms. Oxford, 1580, fol. 171a.

59. See below, chap. 4, par. 3.

60. *ʾOr ha-Meʾir,* fol. 190b. See also ibid., fol. 247d. Compare to a view found in a tract belonging to ecstatic Kabbalah, where the assumption is that the "hidden light," *ha-ʾor ha-ganuz,* is found in the letters of the Tetragrammaton; cf. the anonymous *Sefer ha Mardeʿah,* ms. Oxford 1649, fol. 200b. This text was copied in middle Europe, around 1475. The idea that the "hidden light" is found in the letters of the Torah recurs in many Hasidic texts. See also below, note 185.

61. *Degel Maḥaneh ʾEfrayim,* p. 13.

62. I, p. 44, n. 17. Interestingly enough, as the compilator has correctly remarked in this footnote, the same view was also accepted in *Collectanaea* of R. Eliahu of Vilna's *Commentary on Sefer Yeẓirah,* without mentioning the original source.

63. See *Pardes Rimmonim,* XXI, chap. 1; I, fol. 97ab; *Shelah* I, fol. 105a. also below chap. 4, n. 48 and 123 and Idel, *Mystical Experience,* pp. 22–23.

64. Fol. 3c.

65. A lengthy quote from one of Abulafia's manuscripts in a work by the student of R. Eliahu of Vilna, and its implications, will be discussed separately. See also below, chap. 3, n. 244.

66. See *Ḥayyei ha-Nefesh,* ms. München 408, fol. 67b and especially *Ḥayyei ha-ᶜOlam ha-Ba᾿,* ms. Oxford 1582, fol. 11b. This work of Abulafia's is quoted by a Hasidic author of the eighteenth century; see R. Jacob Ẓevi Yalish, *Sefer Qehilat Ya ᶜaqov* (Lemberg, 1880) III, fol. 19b. Another topic that occurs in this manuscript and recurs in a Hasidic text deals with the acronym of the word *Ẓ᾿on* which stands for *Ẓeruf, ᾿Otiot, Nequdot.* See ms. Oxford 1582, fol. 45b and R. Joseph Moshe of Zalovich, *Berit ᾿Abram* (Brod, 1875, rpr. Jerusalem, 1972), fol. 114b. For more on this acronym see Idel, *Studies,* pp. 137–38. Last but not least, it is precisely this work of Abulafia's whose publication was announced by R. Yehudah Leibush Rappoport, an inhabitant of Brod, in 1855. See R. Ḥayyim Vital, *Sefer Sha ᶜar ha-Yiḥudim* (Lvov, 1855) the verso of the first, unnumbered page. The plan of printing was done under the aegis of the Rabbi Yisrael of Sadigura, namely Ryzhin. See Assaf, *Rabbi Israel of Ruzhin,* pp. 210–11. It should be mentioned that a long passage from this book was copied anonymously in the introduction to R. Yiẓḥaq Shani, *Me᾿ah Sheᶜarim,* a book that was reprinted twice at the end of the eighteenth century in Poland, at Koretz in 1786 and at Zolkiev in 1797.

67. See e.g., *Ktoneth Passim,* p. 302; R. Yehudah Leib of Hanipoly, *ᶜOr ha-Ganuz,* fol. 29c; *Degel Maḥaneh ᾿Efrayim,* p. 275; *Be᾿er Moshe,* fols. 49c, 92ab. In some texts *sof tokh rosh* is presented as representative of the status of the three letters *ᶜEmet.* See R. Dov Baer of Lubavitch, *Be᾿urei ha-Zohar,* fol. 62d. Abulafia's acronym occurs already in Cordovero's *Sefer ha-Gerushin,* pp. 128–29, this book being also a plausible source of its influence on Hasidic masters.

68. It is also possible to see Cordovero's use of these terms, again under the influence of Abulafia, in *Pardes Rimmonim* XXX, chap. 5; II, fol. 69c was a channel for the Hasidic uses, but there are details that are common to the Hasidic texts and those of Abulafia that are not quoted in Cordovero's *summa.* See also in R. Yiẓḥaq of Acre the recurrence of this triad of terms, e.g., in his *Commentary on Sefer Yeẓirah,* printed by Gershom Scholem, *QS* 31 (1956): 383.

69. See below chap. 4, par. 3 and chap. 5, par. 2.

70. See also below, Concluding Remarks, par. 3 and Idel, "Reification of Language," pp. 52–58, 64, 66–69.

71. Chap. 4, par. 5.

72. *The Messianic Idea,* p. 213. See also p. 211. For a further discussion of this issue see below, chap. 5, par. 2.

73. See Idel, *Language, Torah and Hermeneutics,* p. 109. *Sha'ar ha-Niqqud,* printed in *'Arzei Levanon* (Venice, 1601), fol. 38a (Appendix, 6.) This collection of early Kabbalistic material was reprinted in 1748 in Cracow and later in Koretz, and Hasidic masters quoted it; see Idel, "The Magical and Theurgic Interpretation of Music," p. 61, note 164. Compare also to some texts of Abulafia and his school, discussed in Idel, *Language, Torah, and Hermeneutics,* pp. 18–19 and Giqatilla's *Sha'arei 'Oraḥ* I, pp. 48, 206, passim. See especially the Hasidic version of Giqatilla's view in *'Or Torah,* p. 115. See also the view of R. Elijah de Vidas dealt with below, chap. 4, par. 5 and chap. 5 n. 36, where cleaving to God is also related to linguistic elements. Compare also to Scholem's remark that the formula used by Hasidic masters in order to convey the idea of cleaving to God, *devequt ha-Shem,* may be related to views of Giqatilla found in (the unfortunately unmentioned) manuscripts of this Kabbalist. See "Two Testimonies," p. 236 and the different opinion of Tishby, *The Wisdom of the Zohar* II, p. 302, n. 151. Last but not least, the cleaving to the divine Name is described in a magical text as the longing for ultimate union: "let my soul cleave to you a cleaving without any separation." Cf. R. Abraham Ḥamoi, *Lidrosh 'Elohim* (Livorno, 1879) fol. 22b. I assume that this text, like another one in this collection of earlier magical and magical-mystical traditions, is somehow related to Abulafia's school. See below chap. 4, n. 62. The cleaving to the Name in Ḥamoi's text is connected also to the dwelling of the divine spirit.

74. *'Or ha-Ganuz,* fol. 46ab (Appendix 7). On this work see Ḥayyim Lieberman, *'Ohel RaHel* (New York, 1980), pp. 8–11 (Hebrew), Gries, *The Conduct Literature,* p. 125 and n. 84, Tishby, "*Qudsha' Berikh Hu',*" p. 484 n. 22. On this author's better-known collection of Beshtian material, *Keter Shem Tov,* see Nigal (chap. 4, n. 132). Another partial version of this passage is found in this author's *Keter Nehora'* (unpaginated introduction, *haqdamah sheriyah,* par. 7 [Appendix 8]). Interestingly enough, the topic of prophecy recurs in *'Or ha-Ganuz* several times; see fols. 17b, 18a, where the rank of prophecy is described as the divestment of corporeality, apparently under the impact of the passage from the Tur that is discussed later in this passage. See also the emphasis on the divine spirit as a level that can be reached in our own time that is found in the introduction to and other passages of *Keter Nehora'*. It is significant that the influence of R. Ḥayyim Vital's *Sha'arei Qedushah* on the introduction is conspicuous. Compare also the description of the mystical experience as being encompassed by the divine light, as in some phenomena known in ecstatic Kabbalah, found in this book and discussed below, chap. 3, par. 1 as well as his passage bout reaching the level of prophecy in *Ner Miẓwah,* fol. 19a. See also the mystical-cathartic way that culminates with prophecy, to the sequel of requirements presented in R. Moshe of Dolina's *Divrei Moshe,* fol. 38c as necessary in order to attain *devequt.* The mystical way is able to induce, according to passages preceding and immediately following this text, in the hearing of the divine speech. See fols. 38d–39a and especially fol. 14b. It should be mentioned that at least one of Abulafia's relatively lengthy discussions on prophecy, his "Secret of Prophecy" from *Sefer Ḥayyei ha-Nefesh,* has been copied, with some interpolations, in *Sefer ha-Peliy'ah.* See below n. 79 and chap. 35 n. 246. The transmis-

sion of the divine names, as part of the technique of achieving prophecy, is reminiscent of the technique of achieving an elevation of the soul, according to the famous letter the Besht wrote to R. Gershon of Kotov, which mentions "the incantation for the ascent of the soul known to you." See Mondshein, *Migdal ᶜOz*, p. 122. Although the Hebrew phrase translated here, *hashbaᶜat ᶜaliyat ha-Neshamah* does not occur in any of the earlier manuscripts, its absence is perhaps the result of an attempt to deemphasize the magical, that is incantatory, aspect of the event. In any case, the Besht states that a certain technique, which could contain divine names, as we shall see below, par. 3, was known to R. Gershon of Kotov. Was it part of an esoteric tradition? See also beside n. 189 below, in the text, and n. 202. On the phrase "the way of prophecy," see Idel, *Studies*, p. 144, n. 22. See also above, n. 56.

75. Cf. R. Ḥayyim Joseph David Azulai, *Shem ha-Gedolim* I, fol. 54a; Idel, *Studies*, p. 114.

76. See Gottlieb, *Studies*, pp. 234–38; Idel, *Kabbalah: New Perspectives*, pp. 67, 70–71.

77. *Sod ha-Hishtawwut*. This is a very peculiar use of the term sod, which, though it means "secret," stands here for a certain state on the mystical path.

78. In this context this term means mental concentration.

79. *Meʾirat ᶜEinaym*, p. 218. This text may be counted also among those that betray a variant of the mystico-magical model, because the end of the experience is telling the future. Compare to the important passage of R. Yiẓḥaq of Acre's *ʾOẓar Ḥayyim*, ms. Moscow-Gunzburg 775, fol. 183ab, where the reception of the spirit of prophecy is preceded by *hitbodedut*, and divestment of the soul (*hifshit nafsho*) from material things. See also below (at the end of this paragraph) the text from the Tur, where the sequel *hitbodedut, hitpashshetut*, and prophecy occurs. Compare to the text of R. Nathan Netaᶜ of Helm, referred in chap. 35, n. 145, and that of R. Abraham of Pohrebusht, the brother of R. Yisrael of Ryzhin, *ᶜIrin Qaddishin*, fols. 44d–45a, where the reception of prophecy is conditioned by becoming thought.

80. To R. Yiẓḥaq of Acre.

81. *Mitbodedim*. See n. 78 above.

82. *Hishtawwut*. Compare n. 77 above. This term is precisely that used by the Hasidic masters in order to express the idea of equanimity. It should be mentioned that in addition to the deep influence of the Sufi concept on Hasidism, also by the mediation of Yiẓḥaq of Acre, some similar nuances reached Hasidism from the writings of the Maharal; see Safran, "Maharal and Early Hasidism," p. 119, n. 111. On Hasidism and Sufism see below, n. 221, 257, 281, 326 and Idel, *Kabbalah: New Perspectives*, p. 305 n. 55.

83. p. 218. See also Gottlieb, *Studies*, pp. 236–39.

84. For the centrality of these terms in both ecstatic Kabbalah and Hasidism, see Idel, *Studies*, pp. 133, 148, n. 41, and n. 326 below; Elior, "Spiritual Renaissance," p. 38, enumerates several mystical concepts crucial in Hasidic mysticism, some of them

mentioned in R. Yiẓḥaq of Acre, but does not point out that the Hasidic masters adopted major components of their mystical path from Kabbalistic sources.

85. *Studies,* pp. 134–40.

86. See Gries, *The Conduct Literature,* pp. 170–71, n. 84; see also pp. 210–12, where the important passages on equanimity at the beginning of Hasidism were quoted. See also Pachter, "The Concept of Devekut," pp. 226–27.

87. Namely in the cemetery.

88. *Hitbodeduto.* See above, n. 78.

89. *Reshit Ḥokhmah, Sha ʿar ha- ʾAhavah,* chap. 4; I, p. 426. See also above, n. 79. This text also should be seen as reflecting the mystico-magical model.

90. Idel, *Studies,* pp. 115–18.

91. Symposium, 211–12.

92. Cf. Fenton, *Deux traites,* p. 104, n. 218, which draws some more parallels to R Yiẓḥaq of Acre's text on loving women. It is important to bear in mind that the possibility of finding the spiritual within the material was a technique recognized by Cordovero; see the text translated and analyzed in Idel, *Studies,* pp. 129–30. Therefore, the immanentist views of the Hasidic masters, who discovered God in the world, should not surprise anyone acquainted with Safedian Kabbalist thought. It is of special importance to note that Cordovero's recommendation is related in that text, as in Hasidism, to the notion of *devequt*; compare, however, Elior, "Spiritual Renaissance," p. 36.

93. See Idel, *Studies,* pp. 117–18.

94. Ibid., p. 91–101.

95. *Reshit Ḥokhmah, Sha ʿar ha- ʾAhavah,* chap. 4; I, p. 426; Pachter, "The Concept of Devekut" p. 220.

96. Idel, *Studies,* p. 117.

97. *The Beginning of Hasidism,* pp. 208–9, 234. It should be noted that the trace of the above passage is apparent also in an additional early Hasidic text, quoted in R. Jacob Joseph of Polonoy, *Ẓafnat Pa ʿaneaḥ,* fol. 49a. See Piekarz, ibid., p. 261.

98. "The Traces of the Influence," pp. 576–77.

99. *The Conduct Literature,* pp. 206–7. See also Goldreich's more guarded observation in his edition of *Me ʾirat ʿEinayim,* pp. 399–400.

100. *Toledot Ya ʿaqov Yosef,* fol. 45b. See also his *Ẓafnat Pa ʿaneaḥ,* fols. 49a, 83ab, 116b, *Ben Porat Yosef,* fol. 21ab. This explicit awareness of the founders of Hasidism as to the Kabbalistic source of the immanentist view should have been taken into consideration in "Spiritual Renaissance," where Elior claims (pp. 35–39) that Hasidism has introduced a far-reaching transformation of Kabbalistic concepts, and presents as her major example the concept of the disclosing of the divine within this world. Likewise, Tishby, in "The Messianic Idea," p. 27, n. 122, mentions the theme of

tracing the beauty of a beautiful woman to its supernal source of R. Barukh of Kossov, *Yesod ha-ʾEmunah* (Chernovitz, 1864), fol. 100a, as the view of the Great Maggid, without being aware either of the discussions of R. Jacob Joseph of Polonoy or of R. Yiẓḥaq of Acre. For the direct influence of the story of R. Yiẓḥaq on a mid-nineteenth-century Hasidic master, see R. Yiẓḥaq Aiziq Safrin of Komarno, *Noẓer Ḥesed,* p. 22.

101. The term is *Havayah,* which may stand for the Tetragrammaton, and it seems that there is an influence of the same term as it recurs in Giqatilla's *Ginnat ʾEgoz.*

102. *ʾOr ha-Ganuz,* fol. 9b (Appendix 9). Compare to the view of R. Menaḥem Mendel of Bar, quoted above, Introduction, par. 5. Especially interesting is the passage of R. Zeʾev Wolf of Zhitomir, *ʾOr ha-Meir,* fol. 16ab, where two different reactions to the beauty of women are expressed. One, from an incident in the life of the Great Maggid, is the rather conservative repulsion to beauty, activated by an intellectual retracing of the origin of that beauty to low corporeal elements. The other, in accord with the view of R. Yiẓḥaq of Acre, traces the source of beauty in the *Shekhinah,* called, "the most beautiful of all the women, the image of all the images [demut le-kol ha-dimiynot] that are reflected in Her." On this definition of the *Shekhinah,* see *Zohar* I, fols. 88b, 91a. (See Elliot Wolfson, "The Hermeneutics of Visionary Experience: Revelation and Interpretation in the Zohar," *Religion* 18 [1988]: 314–15.) See also Louis Jacobs, "The Relevance and Irrelevance of Hasidism," *The Solomon Goldman Lectures,* ed. Nathaniel Stampfer (Chicago, 1979), vol. 2, p. 23.

103. See above, Introduction, par. 5.

104. Compare also to discussions in R. Menaḥem Naḥum of Chernobyl, *Meʾor ʿEinayyim,* pp. 6, 94 and *ʾOr Torah,* pp. 26, 87, 105, and Krassen, "*'devequt' and Faith,*" pp. 179–80.

105. *ʾOr ha-Ganuz,* fol. 10b (Appendix 10). See also the text that appears just before that, quoted and analyzed below, chap. 3, par. 1. Compare to the accusation addressed to a practice of Hasidim that they are looking for women in the marketplace and elevate the thought to God. Cf. R. David of Makow, in Wilensky, *Hasidim and Mitnaggedim* II, p. 235.

106. The immanentist view of this Kabbalistic master requires a special discussion that cannot be gone into here.

107. See *Toledot Yaʿaqov Yosef,* fol. 45b.

108. On another topic, which is shared by R. Yiẓḥaq of Acre and Hasidism through the mediation of R. Moshe Cordovero, namely the mystical translation of "Enoch the Shoemaker," I hope to elaborate elsewhere. See meanwhile, *Meʾirat ʿEinayyim,* p. 398, n. 19, of Goldreich; Scholem, *On the Kabbalah,* p. 132; Buber, *Origin and Meaning,* pp. 87, 126–27; Wolfson, "Walking as a Religious Duty" par. 3. The transformation of Enoch into Metatron is already found in traditions attributed to the Besht; see *Keter Shem Tov* I, fol. 12d.

109. *Tur, ʾOraḥ Ḥayyim,* par. 98. The passage was quoted also in R. Joseph Qaro's 16th version of this codex known as *Shulhan ʿArukh,* ad locum. See Aryeh Kaplan, *Meditation and Kabbalah* (York Beach, 1985), pp. 283–84, which points out some

sources and influences of this passage, and Idel, *Studies,* pp. 163–64 n. 136; and see *Keter Shem Tov* I, fol. 31a and n. 79 above, and below, n. 110 and chap. 5, par. 2. See also Scholem, *On the Mystical Shape,* p. 291, note 91.

110. Although Abulafia's ecstatic Kabbalah, which he designated as prophetic, came under attack by an important Halakhic authority, R. Shelomo ibm Adret, the passage in the *Tur* was quoted hundreds of time with the result that mystical terms were disseminated. I hope to do a special study of the different uses of this text in both Kabbalistic and Hasidic literature. For the time being, see the occurrence of the *hitbodedut* as a prerequisite before prayer, in *No ᶜam ᵓElimelekh,* fols. 39a, 40b. Just as mental concentration in Geronese Kabbalah preceded prophecy, or, in ecstatic Kabbalah, it preceded the ecstatic experience, so also in some versions of Kabbalah and Hasidism ecstatic prayer was envisioned as a stage that requires the prior practice of concentration.

111. On the magical elements in Jewish mysticism, see Alexander Altmann's essay of 1934, printed in his *The Meaning of Jewish Existence, Theological Essays 1930–1939,* ed. Alfred Ivry (Hanover and London, 1992), pp. 58–60; Scholem, *Kabbalah,* p. 477, the numerous references mentioned under the item *Magic*; Werblowsky, *Joseph Karo,* pp. 38–83. More recently, the importance of magic for the *Heikhalot* literature was emphasized in some studies; see Schaefer, *Hekhalot-Studien,* pp. 84–95, 118–53, 277–95. On magic in mystical Judaism, see e.g., Michael Fishbane, "Aspects of Jewish Magic in the Ancient Rabbinic Period," in *The Solomon Goldman Lectures* (n. 102 above), pp. 28–38; Cohen-Alloro, "Magic and Sorcery"; Idel, "The Concept of the Torah," "Jewish Magic," "Magical and Neoplatonic Interpretations," "Magical and Theurgical Interpretation," "On R. Yiẓḥaq Sagi-Nahor's Mystical Intention," and "Magic and Kabbalah in the Book of the Responding Entity," in *The Solomon Goldman Lecture Series,* ed., Mayer Gruber, vol. 6 (1993), pp. 125–38 as well as Ithamar Gruenwald's forthcoming article in the *Memorial Volume* dedicated to Prof. Ephraim Gottlieb and his *Apocalyptic and Merkavah Mysticism* (Brill, Leiden, 1980), pp. 106–110, 225–231, and Zafrani (below chap. 6 n. 3.)

112. See Aviezer Ravitsky, "The Anthropological Theory of Miracles in Medieval Jewish Philosophy," in Isadore Twersky, ed., *Studies in Medieval Jewish History and Literature,* vol. 2 (Cambridge, Mass., 1984), pp. 231–72. On Avicenna see pp. 231–33; Howard Kreisel, "Miracles in Medieval Jewish Philosophy," *JQR* vol. 75 (1984): 94–133; Idel, "Universalization and Integration," pp. 28–30. In print there were R. Shemuel ibn Ẓarẓa, *Meqor Ḥayyim* (Mantua, 1559) and Shemuel ibn Motot, *Megillat Setarim* (Venice, 1564); we also find awareness of astro-magic in manuscripts originating in seventeenth-century Poland. See e.g., ms. Oxford 1309.

113. See notes 37, 253.

114. Fol. 15cd (Appendix 11). See also below, n. 228.

115. See below, chap. 6 pars. 2,3 and n. 103, and chap. 6, n. 37.

116. Cf. n. 118 below. See also Idel, "The Magical and Neoplatonic Interpretations," p. 233, n. 68. On magic in the Hermetic sources see the important study of Grese, "Magic in Hellenistic Hermeticism."

117. See Pines, "On the Term *Ruḥaniyyut* and Its Sources" pp. 523–24.

118. Pines, pp. 523–30; ibid., "Shiʾite Terms and Conceptions," pp. 165–219; see also Elliot Wolfson, "Merkavah Traditions in Philosophical Garb: Judah Halevi Reconsidered," *PAAJR* 57 (1991): 190–92; Idel, "Universalization and Integration," pp. 28–30.

119. See Idel, "The Magical and Neoplatonic Interpretation," pp. 204–10, and see now the detailed analyses of Schwartz, "Forms of Magic," pp. 21–26 and below chap. 6, n. 56.

120. Mostly in the writings of R. Shem Tov ben Shem Tov and R. Yoḥanan Alemanno; see below, n. 125 and Concluding Remarks, par. 3.

121. See below n. 123, 124.

122. This issue still awaits a more detailed analysis. See meanwhile the interesting study by Ronald C. Keiner, "Astrology in Jewish Mysticism from the *Sefer Yeẓirah* to the *Zohar*," in *The Beginnings of Jewish Mysticism in Medieval Europe*, ed. Joseph Dan (Jerusalem, 1987), pp. 1–42, especially pp. 28–291; Jacques Halbronn, *Le Monde Juif et l'Astrologie* (Arche, Milano, 1985), pp. 291–326.

123. *Shaʿar ha-Ḥesheq*, fol. 34a.

124. See e.g., Cordovero's commentary on the *Zohar* printed in Azulai's *ʾOr ha-Ḥamah* III, fol. 85d; *Tefillah le-Moshe*, fol. 75a.

125. See chap. 4, beside n. 66.

126. See below, chap. 4, par. 4.

127. See chap. 4, n. 84, as well as Idel, "The Magical and Neoplatonic Interpretation," pp. 194–215; "Jewish Magic," pp. 84–90.

128. X, chap. 1; I, fol. 59b (Appendix 12). See my *Kabbalah, New Perspectives*, pp. 110–11; Nicholas Sed, "La 'kavvanah' selon le XXXIIe chapitre du 'Pardes Rimmonim' de R. Moise Cordovero," in *Priére, Mystique et Judaïsme*, pp. 187–207. A typology of illicit magic, based upon the drawing-down influx from the stars, sometimes using talismans, is offered by R. Moshe Cordovero in his commentary on the *Zohar*, printed in Abraham Azulai's *ʾOr ha-Ḥamah* I, fol. 106c. See also below, chap. 6, n. 62.

129. *Pardes Rimmonim* X, chap. 1; I, fol. 59bc.

130. In Kabbalah, gold is a symbol of the attribute of stern judgment.

131. Ibid., X, chap. 1; I, fol. 59b (Appendix 13). On the magical effects of the garments in Hasidism see below chap. 6, n. 63.

132. See Abulafia's own views, based also on the combinations of the letters of the divine Name of seventy-two in his *Ḥayyei ha-ʿOlam ha-Baʾ*, translated and discussed in Idel, *Golem*, p. 99.

133. In Hebrew, *hitbodedut*. For the significance of this term, see Idel, *Studies*, pp. 128–29.

134. *Maskil.*

135. *Bat Qol.*

136. See Idel, *Studies*, p. 162 n. 124. On the dangers involved in the technique of combining letters, see also the description of this lore in R. Ḥayyim Joseph David Azulai, *Shem ha-Gedolim* I, fol. 54a.

137. Ibid., XXX, chap. 3; II, fol. 69b (Appendix 14). The combination of letters has something to do with enhancing the influx that is drawn down. See below, par. 4. In principle, the above passage deals with the righteous one who permutates the letters. However, even wicked persons can do this in order to attain their goal. Compare *Zohar* III, fol. 2a, as interpreted by R. Dov Baer of Lubavitch, *Be*ʾ*urei ha-Zohar*, fol. 62ab. See also above, n. 53. On combinations of letters and the body as the instrument of the divine spirit, see Idel, *Mystical Experience*, pp. 55–57 and the footnotes that refer to the Hasidic discussions of inducing a passive experience; see also Matt, "*Ayin*," p. 142. On combinations of letters and the reception of the divine blessing, see the anonymous treatise from the school of Abraham Abulafia, *Ner* ʾ*Elohim*, ms. München 10, fols. 129b–130a and see also below Appendix A.

138. See also Cordovero's commentary on the Zohar, printed in Azulai, ʾ*Or ha-Ḥamah* II, fol. 190a.

139. *Pardes Rimmonim*, XXVII, chap. 1; II, fol. 59c. See my *Studies* pp. 138–39; Azulai, *Ḥesed le-*ʾ*Avraham*, fol. 10a.

140. For the most elaborated discussions of the mystical nature of the forms of the written letters both in classical Hasidism and in contemporary writers, see R. Levi Yiẓḥaq of Berdichev, *Qedushat Levi*, fols. 117a–118b; see also R. Barukh of Kossov, ʿ*Amud ha-*ʿ*Avodah*, e.g., fol. 112cd, Menaḥem Mendal of Vitebsk, *Peri ha-*ʾ*Areẓ*, fol. 9ab; R. Naḥman of Braslav, *Liqqutei Moharan*, fol. 4b; R. Dov Baer of Lubavitch, *Be*ʾ*uri ha-Zohar*, fol. 107ab.

141. *Meshu*ʿ*abbadim*. See also ibid., pp. 75, 77.

142. *Derishot*, p. 76 (Appendix 15). See also *Pardes Rimmonim*, XXIV, chaps. 10–11; II, fols. 50d–51b; XXX, chap. 3; II fol. 69b.

143. This issue will be dealt with in detail in chap. 6. See also here below, par. 7.

144. *Derishot*, p. 76.

145. ʾ*Or ha-*ʾ*aẓilut*.

146. Ibid., p. 75.

147. On Cordovero's magical view of the *Ẓaddiq* see also below, chap. 6, par. 2.

148. See below, n. 196.

149. *Derishot,* pp. 77–80. See Ben-Shelomo, *The Mystical Theology,* pp. 29–31; Moshe Idel, "R. Shelomo Molkho as a Magician," *Sefunot* (NS) 18 (1985): 199–202 (Hebrew).

150. Cf. *Derishot,* pp. 86–87.

151. *Keli u-deli*; compare to R. Moshe Eliaqum Beri᾿ah, *Qehilat Moshe,* fol. 90d, where the *Ẓaddiq* is conceived to be a bucket and a channel for the divine power. See also *Ḥesed le-᾿Avraham,* fol. 10d, which hints at the concept of the bucket.

152. On this phrase, see also below chap. 6, n. 95, in the quotation from Abraham Azulai. See also his *Ḥesed le-᾿Avraham,* fol. 10c, where the assumption is that there is a multiplicity of spiritual powers that came from the depths of the Torah. This is one of the few statements where the plural of the term *ruḥaniyyut* is quite evident.

153. *Tefillah le-Moshe,* fol. 4a (Appendix 16). It should be emphasized that Cordovero expresses very complex types of theurgical understandings about drawing forth the influx, which involves complicated intradivine processes. See e.g., ibid., fols. 344a–346b. Compare to the explicit nexus between *berakhah* and *hamshakhah* in the Great Maggid's *Maggid Devarav le-Ya῾aqov,* p. 205, and R. Yisrael of Ryzhin, *῾Irin Qaddishin Tanyyana᾿,* fol. 10c. Interestingly enough, according to a Lurianic source, R. Ḥayyim Vital's *Liqqutei Torah,* fol. 122a, it is the highest spiritual faculty in man, the *Ẓelem* that surrounds his head, that draws vitality, *ḥiyyut,* or life, *ḥayyim,* to man. This drawing is not the direct effect of one's own *kavvanah* or the performing of a commandment, but the act of an occult faculty in man. On drawing life by the soul each night, see *Genesis Rabba* 14:9: 133–34.

154. Compare to our discussion immediately below of texts from Provencal and Geronese Kabbalah.

155. See Idel, *Studies,* p. 150 n. 53, Abraham Nuriel, *The Philosophy of Abraham Bibago* (Ph.D. thesis, Hebrew University, Jerusalem, 1975), pp. 94–98 (Hebrew). The source of some of the medieval Jewish philosophical sources is the influential book of Abu Bakher ibn Tufail, *Ḥayy ibn Yoqtan.* There is good reason to assume that R. Moshe Cordovero was acquainted with this type of philosophical terminology. See also Maurice R. Hayoun, *La Philosophie et la theologie de Moise de Narbonne* (Mohr, Tubingen, 1989), pp. 210–213.

156. Idel, "On the Mystical Intention"; Vajda, *Le commentaire,* p. 464, index, s.v. *hamshaka.*

157. Namely the third *sefirah, Binah,* which is designated in Sagi-Nahor's system as Repentance.

158. Namely the sixth *sefirah, Tiferet.* See R. Shem Tov ibn Gaon's *Keter Shem Tov,* printed in *Ma᾿or va-Shemesh,* ed. Yehudah Qoriat (Livorno, 1839) fol. 36a. (See a similar sequel in Hasidism, in R. Menaḥem Naḥum of Chernobyl's *Me᾿or ῾Einayim,* p. 197.) This text is to be understood as part of the Provencal-Geronese Kabbalah and read together with the text adduced below, par. 7 and n. 314.

159. *Ma᾿or va-Shemesh,* ibid., fol. 35b. See Idel, "On the Mystical Intention," n. 89. This sequel of theurgical and magical understanding of the drawing remained stable enough in Kabbalistic texts, which tended to stress the theurgical element. See, as late as the sixteenth century, R. Yiẓḥaq Luria, *Sefer ha-Kavvanot,* fol. 38a. Interestingly enough, the mystical experience is not mentioned as a prerequisite for the performance of the theurgical-magical *kavvanah.* Elsewhere, fols. 11a, 22b, there is another theory regarding the consequence of prayer: it permits a link between the different worlds by the descent of holiness upon the man who conceives himself to be the seat of the *Shehkinah.* This descent of the "supernal holiness" induces a deep transformation in the Kabbalist, who is described as attaining a state in which he can know whatever he wants and becomes like an angel from above. On a Renaissance version of this view see below, Concluding Remarks, n. 63. It should be mentioned that becoming an angel is already implicit in the descriptions in the *Heikhalot* literature of Enoch, who was transformed into the archangel Metatron, and see also an ancient Jewish magical text, discussed by Morton Smith, *Jesus the Magician* (San Francisco, 1981), pp. 133, 206, as well as in medieval texts. See Idel, "Universalization and Integration," p. 31, idem, "Enoch is Metatron," *Immanuel* 24/25 (1990): 223–228; 231–237.

160. See the important remarks of Shlomo Blickstein, *Between Philosophy and Mysticism; A Study of the Philosophical-Qabbalistic Writings of Joseph Giqatila (1248–c. 1322)* (Ph.D. thesis, The Jewish Theological Seminary of America, 1983), pp. 63–79, 83, 134–36.

161. Cf. Boaz Huss, "Theurgic Trends in the Kabbalistic Teaching of R. Simeon Lavi," *Daat,* 28 (1992), p. 312 (Hebrew).

162. See e.g., *Tefillah le-Moshe,* fol. 248b. This view is also expressed in R. Meir ibn Gabbai's *ʿAvodat ha-Qodesh* II, chap. 10, fol. 30c.

163. See Clifford Geertz, *Islam Observed: Religious Development in Morroco and Indonesia* (New Haven: Yale University Press, 1968), p. 44; Felicitas D. Goodman, *Ecstasy, Ritual, and Alternate Reality* (Indiana University Press: Bloomington, 1992), pp. 150–51. Compare also to the way Georges Vajda described the blessing in early Kabbalah: "Benediction, flux vivifiant l'universe," *Le commentaire,* p. 196. Compare this view of the blessing to the principle of dynamis in theurgical Neoplatonism, where it is conceived in terms reminiscent of mana; see Georg Luck, "Theurgy and Forms of Worship in Neoplatonism," in Neusner and alia, eds., *Science, and Magic,* pp. 189–90.

164. *Shemu᾿ah Tovah,* fol. 55b.

165. See Ruderman, *Kabbalah, Magic, and Science,* p. 117.

166. Ms. Berlin, pp. 130–32 (Appendix 17).

167. In Hebrew, *kokhavim,* but Maimon refers afterward only to planets. See also Maimon's *Giveʿat ha-Moreh,* p. 96, and Maimonides' *Guide of the Perplexed* I, 63, III, 29.

168. *Genesis Rabba* X, 6, p. 79. See also ibid., ms. Berlin, p. 33, where this dictum is interpreted again in a mystical vein. See also the description of the thought of the

Great Maggid in R. Yisrael ben Yiẓḥaq Simḥah, *ᶜEser ᵓOrot,* fol. 12a, where this dictum was interpreted in a Hasidic manner. See also immediately below for other Hasidic interpretations.

169. See Idel, "Magical and Neoplatonic Interpretations," p. 213; ibid., "Hermeticism and Judaism" p. 66.

170. On the magical perception of the *Teraphim* see Idel, "Jewish Magic," pp. 84, 112 n. 12; ibid., "An Astral-magical Pneumatic Anthropoid," *Incognita* 3 (1991): 19–23; Schwartz, "Forms of Magic," pp. 24–25.

171. See Idel, "Magical and Neoplatonic Interpretations," p. 204.

172. Cp. the pseudo-Ibn Ezra's *Sefer ha-ᶜAẓamim,* ed. M. Grossberg (London, 1901), pp. 17–18 (Hebrew). This book is a highly influential magical treatise, based on a talismatic approach.

173. The passage following this quote, dealing with the nature of Kabbalah, will be cited in chap. 6, par. 2.

174. See above, Cordovero's text referred by n. 129.

175. R. Yehudah Leib ha-Kohen of Hanipoly, *ᵓOr ha-Ganuz,* fol. 23a. Another astrological interpretation of this passage is found in R. Qalonimus Qalman Epstein, *Maᵓor va-Shemesh* II, fol. 6b. A less astrological formulation, apparently an attenuation of the quoted interpretation to the Midrash, is found in *ᵓOr ha-ᵓEmet,* fol. 52ab. It should be mentioned that already in quotations in the name of the Besht the nexus between *ruḥaniyyut* and *ḥiyyut* as descending entities, was apparent; see *Toledot Yaᶜaqov Yosef,* fol. 171c, *Ẓafnat Paᶜaneḥ,* fol. 2c, *Keter Shem Tov* I, fol. 59b. On *ḥiyyut,* see Weiss, *Studies,* p. 46, where he proposes to see in the Neoplatonic theory of emanation and its Kabbalistic reverberations the source of the Hasidic concept of *ḥiyyut.* However, given the occurrence of this term in connection to *ruḥaniyyut,* I am inclined to see in a more plausible source the magical model. Indeed in his *Teshuᵓot Ḥen* (Brooklyn, 1982) p. 98, R. Gedalyah of Linitz mentioned *ḥiyyut* in a conspicuously astrological context: he speaks about drawing down the *ḥiyyut* onto the respective zodiacal planet. It should be noticed that though *ḥiyyut* recurs in Cordoverian sources, it is also found in Lurianic ones, though its occurrence there is relatively rare, and the use of it reflects a Cordoverian influence. See e.g., Vital's *Taᶜamei Miẓwot,* printed in his *Liqqutei Torah,* fol. 74a, as well as *Liqqutei Torah,* fol. 96ab. See also Introduction, n. 85 and R. Menaḥem Azariah of Fano's *Pelaḥ Rimmon,* xxvii, 1, fol. 65a.

176. *ᵓOraḥ le-Ẓaddiq,* p. 126.

177. Chap. 4 par. 4, the text of R. Shem Tov ibn Shem Tov.

178. Ms. Munchen 214, fol. 51a. On the importance of this treatise for the understanding of the theory of the *ruḥaniyyat,* see Pines, "On the Term Ruḥaniyyat and Its Sources," pp. 518–20; Idel, "The Magical and Neoplatonic Interpretations," pp. 192–93, 199. See also chap. 3 n. 96. On the use of the divine Name in Hermetic magic, see Grese, "Magic in Hellenistic Hermeticism," pp. 49–50, the details of this practice being similar to some formulas for creating the *Golem* and attaining ecstatic experiences in

Abraham Abulafia; see Idel, *Mystical Experience,* pp. 22–23, 45, n. 36. On this issue I hope to elaborate elsewhere. On Aristotle as a magician in the Middle Ages, see the spurious *Secretum Secretorum.*

179. *ʿAsarah Maʾamarot* II, fol. 41b (Appendix 18). Compare also the quotation from Menaḥem Azariah of Fano's compendium of Cordovero's *Pardes Rimmonim, Pelaḥ ha-Rimmon,* cited in R. Barukh of Kossov, *ʿAmud ha-ʿAvodah,* fol. 113c. On this Italian Kabbalist, see Alexander Altmann, "Notes on the Development of Rabbi Menaḥem Azariah Fano's Kabbalistic Doctrine," in J. Dan and J. Hacker, eds., *Studies in Jewish Mysticism, Philosophy, and Ethical Literature Presented to Isaiah Tishby* (Jerusalem, 1986), pp. 241–68 (Hebrew); Robert Bonfil, "Halakhah, Kabbalah, and Society: Some Insights into Rabbi Menaḥem Azariah de Fano's Inner World," *Jewish Thought in the Seventeenth Century,* eds. I Twersky and B. Septimus (Cambridge, Mass., 1987), pp. 39–61; Joseph Avivi, "R. Menaḥem Azariah of Fano's Writings in Matter of Kabbalah," *Sefunot* 4 (XIX) (1989), pp. 347–76 (Hebrew). On the various discussions on the affinities between the vitality and the proper name of a certain person, see also the sources collected in Menaḥem Mendel Viznitzer, *Sefer Milei de-ʾAvot* (Benei Beraq, 1981), pp. 166–70. See also the view of R. Jacob Kopel of Miedzyrec as to the existence of two names for every righteous man, one here below and another on high, cf. *Qol Yaʿaqov,* fol. 1a. This view is reminiscent of the Neoplatonic notion of the soul of man that exists both in the upper and the lower worlds. See also R. Menaḥem Mendel of Kossov, *ʾAhavat Shalom,* p. 88.

180. See his *Tiferet ʾAdam* (Lvov, ND), fol. 2b. See also R. Elimelekh of Lisansk, *Noʿam ʾElimelekh,* fols. 68c, 69a which assumes that someone may become a *Ẓaddiq* just because he was called by the name of *Ẓaddiq,* which causes a lighting of the light of the *Ẓaddiq* in the upper world.

181. *Ben Porat Yosef,* fol. 21a. This description, derived from Cordovero's thought via Azulai's *Ḥesed le-ʾAvraham,* recurs in a series of Hasidic texts. See below, chap. 4, par. 3.

182. See below, par. 5.

183. *An Autobiography,* pp. 158–59. The mention of the healing reflects a relatively positive attitude toward the founder of Hasidism, who is nevertheless described by Maimon as using divine names. It seems that Maimon was sympathetic to linguistic magic. See below, chap. 6, n. 56. For the Jewish Enlightenment's attitude to medicine, which was opposed to astrology, Hasidic practices, and various superstitions, see Maimon's contemporary Moshe Markuse, as described by Shmeruk, *Yiddish Literature,* pp. 199–201. On the term *Baʿal Shem Tov,* see the historical survey of Nigal, *Magic, Mysticism and Hasidism,* pp. 13–32, and Shmeruk, ibid., pp. 201–2. In other cases, his magical activities were described as that of a *qosem,* namely someone who performs wonders by producing illusions; this is the way, according to the report of R. David of Makow, that the Gaon of Vilna described the Besht's influence on the Great Maggid. See Wilensky, *Hasidim and Mitnaggedim,* vol. 2, p. 236. Compare also to p. 209. I would like to emphasize that the present study focuses upon the more theoretical premises of Hasidic magic, while the interesting questions as to the relationship between praxis and theory, between magical praxis and social circumstances, and even between

this form of magic and what is called "practical Kabbalah," still await special study. From the many manuscripts and some printed material, including information about details of the practice of magic known in Hasidic circles, it is quite difficult to draw a line between the general theory and the practices that were in existence for centuries in various Jewish circles. In any case, fascinating material about magic known to Hasidic masters is found in manuscripts in the possession of Mr. Joseph Goldman of New York, who has kindly allowed me access to them.

184. See *Shiveḥei,* ed. Rubinstein, pp. 84–85 and n. 20, Ben Amos-Mintz, *In the Praise of Baal Shem Tov,* pp. 49, 89. See also Weiss, "Talmud-Torah," pp. 155–56. See also the quotations in the name of the Besht in R. Naḥman of Braslav's *Liqqutei Moharan* I, fol. 102c and R. Shemuel Shemariah of Ostrowce, *Sefer Zikhron Shemuel* (Ostrowce, 1925) I, fol. 38bc. See also above, note 60.

185. On similar phenomena in Shamanism see Mircea Eliade, *Shamanism: Archaic Techniques of Ecstasy* (Princeton, 1974), pp. 60–61, Sullivan, *Icanchu's Drum,* pp. 422–24.

186. See chap. 4, par. 4.

187. Heschel, *The Circle of the Baal Shem Tov,* pp. 167–70; Nigal, *Magic, Mysticism and Hasidism,* p. 32. To the sources mentioned by Heschel, ibid., p. 170, n. 65, and Nigal, also R. Shimeon Zeʾev Zelig of Miedzevo, *Doresh Tov,* fol. 54cd, should be added. See, however, the attempt to deny the Besht's use of divine names in the Ḥabad school, cf., the addition in *Keter Shem Tov,* fol. 133ab and Kaidaner, *Sippurim Noraʾim,* pp. 37–8. An interesting parallel to the above story is told in connection to R. Abraham of Ulianov, the son of a better-known figure, R. Yiẓḥaq Ḥarif of Sambur, who is reported to have distributed amulets, which, instead of divine names, contained acronyms of Tannaitic figures whose teaching he studied during the day on which he wrote the amulets. See R. Yisrael ben R. Yiẓḥaq Simhah, *ʿEser ʿAtaret,* fol. 10ab. There, a contest between the Rabbi of Ulianov and other, unmentioned *Ẓaddiqim,* is reported in a way reminiscent of the story regarding the Besht. Therefore, it is clear that during the nineteenth century some Hasidic *Ẓaddiqqim* did distribute amulets, while other *Ẓaddiqqim* opposed this practice. See the very interesting preface of R. Yehudah Leibush Rapoport in this edition of *Shaʿar ha-Yiḥudim* (Lvov, 1855), in which he enumerates the *Ẓaddiqim* who were concerned with amulets; this was the reason for this plan, which apparently was not realized, to print a collection of amulets. On the basis of these and other texts, I see no reason to accept Buber's interpretation of Hasidism as a retreat from magic; see also Scholem, *Devarim be-Go,* pp. 296, 297–98, 312; see especially Buber's treatment of the topic in *Tales of the Hasidim: The Early Masters,* pp. 12–13. See also note 220, below.

188. Heschel, ibid., p. 15. Compare to *Shiveḥei,* ed. Rubinstein, p. 312, where the divine Name given by the Besht to his son is not mentioned. For the magical use of the name of the Besht in another context see Ben Amos-Mintz, *In Praise of the Baal Shem Tov,* p. 181: "Since the name Yisrael, son of Eliezer, is a name, it means that he is a *Ẓaddiq.*" This passage was kindly drawn to my attention by Prof. E. Etkes. Thus, a contemporary of the founder of Hasidism, who apparently was not a Hasid at that time, was convinced of the Besht's extraordinary powers and cognizant of the particular power

that the name of a *Ẓaddiq* possesses, just as R. Menaḥem Azariah of Fano indicates. On the basis of the preceding, it is understandable that Joseph Perl, in his sarcastic criticism of Hasidism, would hint that the name of the Besht, transcribed according to a cryptic alphabet, was a magical name that could open all locks: see Ch. Shmeruk and Sh. Werses, eds., Joseph Perl, *Hasidic Tales and Letters* (Jerusalem, 1969), pp. 116, 229. In this context is is highly significant that in the circle of the great-grandson of the Besht, R. Naḥman of Braslav, a treatise enumerating all the names of all the Righteous, beginning with Adam, was composed, the recitation of which was said to have overt magical influence. This work, *Shemot ha-Ẓaddiqim,* went through several editions, some of them together with R. Naḥman's *Sefer ha-Middot.* Thanks are due to Mr. Mikhah Oddenheim, for bringing this work to my attention.

189. *Ḥiyyut.*

190. On this magical view, see my "The Concept of the Torah," pp. 52–58.

191. See *Mayyim Rabbim* fol. 42b, quoting from the Seer's *Zikkaron Zot,* fol. 15c. See also ibid., fol. 31c and R. Moshe of Dolina, *Divrei Moshe,* fol. 14a, 15a, and R. Asher Ẓevi of Ostrog, *Ma ͑ayan ha-Ḥokhmah,* fol. 84c. See also below, chap. 5, n. 90.

192. *Ba ͑al Shem Tov* I; 17–18 (Appendix 19). A very similar view is expressed by R. Qalonimus Qalman Epstein, *Ma ͗or va-Shemesh* IV, fol. 22a. See also R. Hillel ha-Levi of Paritch, *Pelaḥ ha-Rimmon* (Brooklyn, 1957), vol. 2, p. 77, where the assumption is that the name is the aspect of the letters within the soul that attract the manifestation of the soul within the body.

193. *Mayyim Rabbim,* fol. 23a.

194. *͑Or.* According to a Hasidic tradition, which cannot now be located, told to me by my wife, Shoshannah Idel, the word *refu ͗ah* consists of two roots, *͗or* and *poh,* namely, "light" and "here," these words containing the consonants of *Refu ͗ah.* On drawing down the remedy, *refu ͗ah* see also R. Meir ha-Levi of Apta, *͗Or la-Shamayim,* fol. 14d.

195. See Couliano, *Eros and Magic*: 107–43; Eugene F. Rice, "The *De Magia Naturalis* of Jacques Lefevre d'Etaples," in *Philosophy and Humanism: Essays in Honor of P. O. Kirsteller,* E. P. Mahoney, ed. (Leiden, 1976), pp. 24–25, and Paola Zambelli, "Le Problème de la magic naturelle à la Renaissance," *Magia, Astrologia e Religione nel Rinascimento* (Wrotslav, etc., 1974): 65–66; Ruderman, *Kabbalah, Magic, and Science* pp. 110–11. For medieval studies on astrological medicine, see Marcelino V. Amasuno, *Un Texto Medico-Astrologico del siglo XIII—"Eclipse del sol" del licenciado Diego de Torres* (Salamanca, 1972); Joseph Shatzmiller, "In Search of the 'Book of Figures': Medicine and Astrology in Montpellier at the Turn of the Fourteenth Century," *AJS Review* 7–8 (1982–83): 403; Dov Schwartz, "The Neoplatonic Movement in Fourteenth Century Jewish Literature and Its Relationship to Theoretical and Practical Medicine," *Koroth* 9 (1989): 272–84 (Hebrew). English summary pp. 708–10. On magical healing in Judaism, see the remarks of Hyman C. Enelow, *Selected Works* (Kingsport, Tenn., 1935), 4, pp. 487–89, and note 220 below.

196. See Ruderman, *Kabbalah, Magic, and Science* pp. 27, 30, 40–41.

197. [Venice, 1587] fols. 3b, 16ab, 17ab, 27a–28a. Compare the slightly different version of this treatise in ms. Oxford, Catalogue Neubauer 2310, fol.s 4b, 15a, 24ab. On this treatise in general see Ruderman, ibid., pp. 32–34.

198. See R. Eleazar (the son of R. Elimelekh) of Lisansk's *ᵓIggeret ha-Qodesh* and the criticism of this issue in Joseph Perl; see Abraham Rubenstein, ed., *Ueber das Wesen der Sekte Chasidim* (Jerusalem, 1977), p. 101.

199. See Idel, *Golem,* pp. 247–50.

200. *ᵓAnshei giliy.* This term is understood in a restrictive sense as the members of the circle of the Besht by Etkes, "Hasidism as a Movement," p. 17. This understanding can be reinforced by a similar situation related to the Besht. In the Yiddish version of the *Praises of the Besht,* he asks his *hechste leit,* that is, the highest among his people, to keep his special mystical practice a secret as long as he is alive. See Yaᵓari, "Two Editions," p. 552. The Yiddish version uses a Hebrew term for mystical practice, *hanhagah.* Thus, one can assume that knowledge of a secret mythical path, known by the Besht and his companions, was kept from the masses. Moreover, in the epistle, the techniques of the Besht were related to the ascent of the soul. In the Yiddish version of the legend, the context is the utter concentration of the thought of the Besht, to such an extent that he is described as out of this world. In these two cases, ecstatic or trance-like experiences were related on one hand to a certain way of life, *hitbodedut* and *hanhagah,* and on the other to a certain type of *yiḥudim.* The *hanhagah,* namely the regimen vitae, of the Besht is mentioned as if it was a quite structured issue in R. Meir Margoliot, *Sod Yakhim u-Vo ᶜaz,* p. 41; and in the additions to *Keter Shem Tov,* fols. 113a–114b. An interesting passage, printed in the name of R. Aharon of Zhitomir, in *Ge ᵓulat Yisrael,* fol. 17c, deals with some of the elements mentioned above as part of an allegedly secret tradition stemming from Ahijah the Shilonite and transmitted to the Besht, the Great Maggid, and R. Levi Yiẓḥaq of Berdichev. See below, chap. 5, par. 2 and n. 26.

In the manuscript printed by Mondshein, *Migdal ᶜOz,* the phrase *ᵓAnshei giliy* does not appear; instead the phrase *ᵓAnshei seggulah,* namely eminent people, or closest disciples, occurs. See Mondshein, ibid., p. 124, n. 10.

201. For a bibliography on the ascent of the soul, see below, chap. 3, n. 4. This mystical technique was also used by the Besht, according to some Hasidic sources, in other instances (see e.g., Kaidaner, *Sippurim Noraᵓim,* pp. 36–37, as well as by R. Yeḥiel Mikhal, the Maggid of Zlotchov. See *Mayyim Rabim,* p. 140. This technique was known and reportedly practiced, though not very highly appreciated, by R. Eliahu, the Gaon of Vilna. See R. Ḥayyim of Volozhin's introduction to his master's *Commentary of Sifraᵓ de-Ẓeniutaᵓ* (Vilna, 1891).

202. See Mondshein, *Migdal ᶜOz,* p. 124; see also Ben Amos-Mintz, *In Praise of the Baal Shem Tov,* p. 57, and Tishby, "The Messianic Idea," pp. 29–32; Scholem, *Messianic Idea,* pp. 182–84; Piekarz, *Studies in Braslav Hasidism*, p. 66; Liebes, "The Messiah of the Zohar," pp. 113–14; Etkes, "Hasidism as a Movement," pp. 16–17; Katz, "Models" p. 259, Abraham Rubinstein, "The Mentor of the Besht and the Writings from which He Studied," *Tarbiẓ* 48 (1978–79): 146–58 (Hebrew), Nigal, *Magic,*

Mysticism and Hasidism, p. 30. The analysis below shows that at least those details that describe the activity of the Besht concur with the way medical magicians were regarded in his lifetime. Our analysis below adds some modest contribution to the concept of the *Shiveḥei ha-Besht* as close to the *realia;* see, more recently, Rosman (n. 207 below) and Jacob Barnai, "Some Clarifications on the Land of Israel's Stories of 'In Praise of the Baal Shem Tov,'" *REJ* vol. 166 (1987): 367–80.

On the Besht as someone who is able to cause the ascent of his soul very easily, see also the manuscript text of R. Yiẓḥaq Aiziq Safrin of Komarno, printed in *Ba ͑al Shen Tov* I, pp. 17–18.

203. See *Heikhalot Zutarti,* Rachel Elior, ed. (Jerusalem, 1982), p. 22; Peter Schaefer, ed., *Synopse zur Hekhalot-Literatur* (Tuebingen, 1981), pp. 143–44.

204. See *ʾOẓar Midrashim,* J. D. Eisenstein, ed. (New York, 1915), p. 307. Cf. Idel, "The Concept of the Torah," pp. 27–29, Halperin, *Faces of the Chariot,* pp. 289–319. In this context, it is perhaps pertinent to mention that the text related to the magical interpretation of the Pentateuch, *Shimmushei Tehilim,* which decodes the magical names found in the Psalms, was printed in 1724 in Hamburg under the title *Kawwanath thillim,* by Eliaqim Getz of Premislany. Thus, the term *Kavvanah* was understood as having a magical meaning. On *kavvanah* as the magical significance of prayer, see below, chap. 4.

205. This is also the case with other magical figures, like R. Joseph della Reina and R. Shelomo Molkho.

206. Moshe Rosman, "Medziebuz and R. Israel Baʾal Shem Tov," *Ẓion* 52 (1987): 185 (Hebrew). On the Besht as a practical magician, see Wertheim, *Law and Custom,* pp. 235–36. There is plenty of magical material attributed to the Besht, in print and in manuscripts, which consists of classical remedies, *seggulot,* and apotropaic amulets. No attempt has been made to study them; I have perused many of them in writing this book, but it is very difficult to discern a unified theory of magic. See, nevertheless, immediately below.

207. (Zolkiew, 1865) No pagination, under the rubric *Kokhavim* (Appendix 20). As Thomas has aptly remarked, "all the evidence of the sixteenth and seventeenth centuries suggests that the common people never formulated a distinction between magic and science, certainly not between magic and medicine." *Religion and the Decline of Magic,* p. 668.

208. *Sod Yakhim u-Vo ͑az,* pp. 41–42 (Appendix 21). Compare also the descriptions of the Besht's way of studying the texts, dealt with below, chap. 5, pars. 1, 2.

209. See Joshua Trachtenberg, *Jewish Magic and Superstition* (New York, 1934), p. 216.

210. On the presence of the divine within letters see below, chap. 4, par. 5. As to the relation between cleaving to the letters of the Torah and lights, see below, chap. 5, par. 2, the quotation attributed to the Besht in R. Meir Margoliot, *Sod Yakhin u-Vo ͑az* p. 41. The concept of *Urim* and *Tummim* is also related to the idea of the light and

enlightenment, which already appears in Rabbinic and Kabbilistic sources. See Idel, *Mystical Experience,* pp. 105–8, and the pertinent footnoes, pp. 158–60.

211. See Idel, *Golem,* pp. 174–75, 179–82.

212. For more on this issue, see below, ch. 6.

213. See below, par. 7, the quote from *ʾIggeret ha-Qodesh.*

214. See Idel, *Mystical Experience,* pp. 37–41.

215. Idem, *Language, Torah, and Hermeneutics,* pp. 101–9.

216. However, see Sarug's version of Lurianism, where the letters play a greater role; see below, note 293.

217. See Idel, "Reification of Language," pp. 49–52, 59–62. An interesting attempt to classify the Lurianic theurgy is found in a quote in the name of R. Moshe of Fes, a student of Luria, found in Vital's *Ta ʿamei Miẓwot,* printed in his *Liqqutei Torah,* fol. 15cd, where Luria is said to distinguish between a) the reparation on high of the deleterious repercussions of sins by means of performing the commandments; b) by the induction of the unification between *ʾAbba ʾ* and *ʾimma ʾ*, namely two high, divine configurations; and c) induction of the conjugation between the male and female lower attributes.

218. par. 7. On simplification as part of the mystical model, see Heiler, *Prayer,* pp. 145–46.

219. *Ḥesed le-ʾAvraham,* fol. 10a; compare Cordovero, *Pardes Rimmonim,* XXVII, chap. 2; II, fols. 59d–60a, where, however, the analogy to medicine does not occur. This text was reproduced by one of his famous descendants, the famous R. Ḥayyim Joseph David Azulai, *Shem Gedolim* I, fol. 54b. In fact, after quoting almost verbatim two passages from *Ḥesed le-ʾAvraham,* this author offers another passage, which reiterates the analogy between combinations of letters and medicine in a very interesting manner. I have not yet found the source of the last passage. See also *Ḥesed le-ʾAvraham* fol. 10d, in a text obviously influenced by the above mentioned passage from *Pardes Rimmonim,* where the mixtures of the letters and words of the Torah reflect the supernal spiritual force, *ruḥaniyyut.* See also his passage in another book, *Devash le-Fi,* discussed by Scholem, *On the Kabbalah,* p. 76. It should be mentioned that R. Yehudah ha-Levi, one of the earliest and most important exponents of the astro-talismatic theory in Judaism, uses the metaphor of medicine several times in order to point out the necessity of worshiping God in a precise manner. See e.g. *Kuzari* I, par. 97, Pines, "On the Term *Ruḥaniyyut* and Its Sources," pp. 527–28, 529; H. J. Zimmels, *Magicians, Theologians, and Doctors* (Feldheim: New York, 1952), pp. 137–39, 250, notes 153–54; see also Karl-Erich Grözinger, "Baʿal Shem oder Baʿal Ḥazon: Wunder-doctor oder charismatiker, zur Fruhen Legenden bildung um den Stifter des Hasidis-mus," *Frankfurter Judaistische Beitrage* vol. 6 (1978): 71–90.

220. Apparently under Azulai's influence we find the same idea in R. Barukh of Kossov, *ʿAmud ha-ʿAvodah,* fol. 137c. See also ibid., fol. 113d, where this author, a contemporary of the Great Maggid, differentiates between the spiritual force of the

Shekhinah and that of God. This is a rather rare example of assuming a multiple type of ruḥaniyyut in the extant Jewish literature. On the concept of the *ruḥaniyyat* of God see the text of R. Abraham he-Ḥasid, an early thirteenth-century Sufi-oriented master in Egypt, as interpreted by Pines, "On the Term Ruḥaniyyut and Its Sources," p. 512 and below, n. 300. See also R. Yiẓḥaq Aiziq Safrin of Komarno's *Noẓer Ḥesed,* p. 111, where both God and the *Shekhinah* are found within the letters. This issue requires a more detailed analysis that seems to point, according to R. Jacob Joseph of Polonoy, to the direction of a more complex divine structure that is to be attracted into the letters See below, chap. 4 par. 4, and n. 88, 89.

221. In one case, we learn that by emphasizing a certain letter in a word of prayer someone causes this letter to attract a certain type of spiritual force. Qalonimus Qalman Epstein, *Ma᾿or va-Shemesh* I, fol. 21b.

222. See Idel, *Language, Torah, and Hermeneutics,* pp. 101–9, and also below, chap. 4, par. 3.

223. See par. 3 above the quotation of Cordovero from unidentified ancient sources, and Idel, *Kabbalah: New Perspectives,* p. 308, n. 96.

224. See R. Shneur Zalman of Liady, *Liqqutei Torah* III, fol. 38d.

225. The Lurianic theurgy, like its theosophy, is a very complex topic that was not studied in a detailed manner. The most important studies on this issue are those of Lawrence Fine; see e.g., his "The Contemplative Practice of *Yiḥudim* in Lurianic Kabbalah," in Green, *Jewish Spirituality,* vol. 2, pp. 64–97.

226. See below, chap. 6, par. 4.

227. R. Qalonimus Qalman Epstein, *Ma᾿or va-Shemesh* I, fol. 3b; see also ibid., fol. 11b, IV, fol. 3d; v, fol. 46c and below, beside n. 280; R. Jacob Joseph of Polonoy, *Toledot Ya᾿aqov Yosef,* fol. 167d, *Ben Porat Yosef,* fols. 32d, 33c, 55d. R. Elizer Ze᾿ev of Krechinev, *Raza᾿ de-᾿Uvda᾿,* part 2, fol. 20b. On the occurrence of both the comprehension of God and cleaving to Him as the acme of Hasidic worship, see R. Meir Margoliot, *Sod Yakhin u-Vo᾿az,* p. 41, where the context may allow the assumption that this passage was influenced by the Besht himself. See also the Besht's grandson's similar view, in R. Barukh of Miedzybort's *Boẓina᾿ di-Nehora᾿,* p. 113, where the aims of the Torah are said to be comprehension and cleaving, as well as R. Meshullam Phoebus of Zbarazh, *Yosher Divrei ᾿Emet,* fol. 144b, and R. Qalonimus Qalman Epstein, *Ma᾿or va-Shemesh* III, fol. 16a. See also the fascinating passage of R. Yisrael of Ryzhin, *ʿIrin Qaddishin,* fols. 30d–31ab, where the quintessence of the religious life is described as the entering of the light of the Infinite in the body of the purified mystic. Compare the view of Cordovero on this issue printed in Bracha Sack, "A Fragment from R. Moshe Cordovero's Commentary on Raʿya Mehemna᾿" *Qoveẓ ʿAl Yad* [NS] vol. 20 (1982), p. 264: "The purpose of the worship is to cleave to the simple Divinity." See also ibid., p. 269. This view was reiterated verbatim by R. Abraham Azulai, *Ḥesed le-᾿Avraham,* fol. 10c and thereby came to the attention of the Hasidic masters. R. Jacob Joseph of Polonoy is actually referring to another passage from this book found on the same page of *Ḥesed la-᾿Avraham*; see below, Appendix A, n. 48. See also another note from this book discussed above, at the beginning of par. 3.

228. See Weiss, in Rubinstein, ed., *Studies in Hasidism,* pp. 136–41; Gedalyah Nigal, "Sources of 'Devekut' in Early Hasidic Literature," *QS* 66 (1970–71): pp. 343–48 (Hebrew), and the studies mentioned below in n. 230–31, 234.

229. See also Sherwin, *The Mystical Theology,* pp. 124–41.

230. See Scholem, *Messianic Idea,* pp. 203–26; Tishby, *The Wisdom of the Zohar* II, pp. 304–5; Pachter, "The Concept of Devekut," Idel, *Kabbalah: New Perspectives,* pp. 35–58.

231. Idel, *Mystical Experience,* pp. 124–34.

232. See above, par. 2.

233. See Pachter, "The Concept of *devequt,*" p. 227, n. 267.

234. This term is a rather exceptional way to describe cleaving; nevertheless it occurs in many Hasidic texts as a way of pointing to a mystical experience. On the drawing down of the "power of *ʾAḥdut*" by means of prayer, see Cordovero's text quoted in Azulai's *ʾOr ha-Ḥamah* II, fol. 232b. Compare also the view of Alemanno, *Shaʿar ha-Ḥesheq,* fols. 42b–43a. See also here below, chap. 5 n. 46, the quotations from the traditions of the Great Maggid, and also chap. 5, n. 11.

235. *Pardes Rimmonim* XXI, 1; I, fol. 97b (Appendix 22). Compare to the text of another Safedian mystic, R. Elazar Azikri, discussed in Idel, *Studies,* pp. 132–33.

236. *Pardes Rimmonim,* ibid., fol. 97c. See also de Vidas, *Reshit Ḥokhmah,* Gate of Holiness, chap. 6; II p. 87, the *Shelah* I, fol. 105a.

237. Idel, *Mystical Experience,* pp. 22–23.

238. Fol. 10d (Appendix 23). For more on this quotation see Idel, "Universalization and Integration," p. 38. On *devequt* as *bonum* see also in R. Joseph Ẓarfati's *Yad Yosef,* put forth and discussed by Piekarz, "Devekuth," p. 134.

239. On the sources of this view see Idel, *Kabbalah: New Perspectives,* pp. 40–41.

240. *Pardes Rimmonim* XXXI, chap. 8; II fol. 75c.

241. *Lakhen hukhraḥ.*

242. *Mishkan.* See also the text quotation by Sack (note 16 above, p. 74. On similar issues see the discussion below, chap. 6, par. 2. Cordovero's view of the tabernacle as attracting the *ruḥaniyyut* was repeated several times in R. Qalonimus Qalman Epstein, *Maʾor va-Shemesh* II, fols. 30ab, 33d, 36a; R. Moshe Eliaqum Beriʾah, *Qehilat Moshe,* fol. 8a. See also R. Aharon Kohen of Apta, *Keter Nehoraʾ,* fols. 19a, 33a, 80b and his *Ner Miẓwah,* fol. 31a. On the attraction of the *Shekhinah* into the Tabernacle and the temple as a concept in Rabbinic sources similar to the Hermetic magic, see Idel, "Hermeticism and Judaism," pp. 61–62, *Kabbalah: New Perspectives,* pp. 166–70. See also below, chap. 3 n. 42. On the human body as a building, see Byron L. Sherwin, "The Human Body: A House of God," in *Three Scores and Ten, Essays in Honor of Seymour J. Cohen,* ed. A. Karp, L. Jacobs, and H. Z. Dimitrovsky (New Jersey,

1991), pp. 99–107, and another version of it in Byron Sherwin, *Toward a Jewish Theology* (Lewiston, Queenston, Lampeter, 1991), pp. 149–58.

243. *Pardes Rimmonim,* ibid., fol. 75d (Appendix 24). For the Arabic and Jewish sources of this view, well known in the Renaissance, see Moshe Idel, "The Sources of the Circle Images in R. Yehudah Abravanel's *Dialoghi d'Amore*" *ʿIyuun* 28 (1978): 166 n. 40 (Hebrew) and Pachter, "The Concept of *devequt,*" p. 213, *Reshit Ḥokhmah,* Shaʿar ha-ʾAhavah, chap. 2; I, 368–69. Compare also to the quotation given by *Qedushat Levi* in the name of the Besht, fol. 121c; *Maʾor va-Shemesh* I, fol. 3c, and R. Ẓevi Elimelekh of Dinov, *Benei Yisaskhar* II, fol. 65d. See also below, chap. 4, n. 125.

244. See above, par. 3 and below, chaps. 4, 5, and Concluding Remarks, par. 3.

245. See below, chap. 6.

246. Cf. n. 244 above.

247. See Jacob Klatzkin, *Thesaurus Philosophicus Linguae Hebraicae* (Lipsiae, 1928), vol. 2, p. 294. This meaning of the term recurs several times in other discussions of Cordovero: see e.g. *Derishot,* pp. 63, 76.

248. See Alexander Altmann, *Von der mittelalterlichen zur modernen Aufklaerung* (Tuebingen, 1987), pp. 12–23. See also below, Appendix A.

249. *Mi-ẓad hitbodedam bo.* On *hitbodedut* as mental concentration in Cordovero, see Idel, *Studies,* pp. 127–31.

250. Fol. 36c (Appendix 25). For more on this "masonic" understanding of the *Ẓaddiq,* see Scholem, *On the Mystical Shape,* pp. 135–36. See also the important passage of the Vidas, *Reshit Ḥokhmah,* "Gate of Holiness," chap. 6; II, p. 87, to the effect that the pure soul becomes "a seat for the supernal spiritual force [ruḥaniyyut]." See also ibid., p. 110 and the text from *Pardes Rimmonim,* XXXII, chap. 1; II, fol. 78bc, to be quoted and analyzed below in chap. 7. See also Green, "The *Ẓaddiq* as *Axis Mundi.*"

251. See the text quoted by Tishby, "Les traces," pp. 451–52. Since Luzzatto's Kabbalah was not studied in the context of talismatic concepts it is very difficult to assess its general impact, but at least this passage quoted by Tishby should be considered as reflecting talismatic views. I hope to return to this question in a more detailed study elsewhere.

252. Elsewhere, fol. 105b, the author uses the term spiritual lights, *ʾOrot ruhaniyyim.* See also Idel, *Studies,* p. 165, n. 149; *Mystical Experience,* pp. 77–81, 183–84. On *ruḥaniyyut* as lights, see Pines, "On the Term *Ruḥaniyyut* and Its Sources," pp. 514, 522 and below, chaps. 3, par. 1 and 4, par. 4. See also the description of the Besht seeing supernal lights in R. David of Makov's *Zemer ʿAriẓim,* printed in Wilensky, *Hasidim and Mitnaggedim* II, p. 200, *Noʿam ʾElimelekh,* fol. 69a. See also Jacobs, *Jewish Mystical Testimonies,* pp. 7–8, *Maʾor va-Shemesh* IV, fol. 22c.

253. *Ḥiyyut ha-qodesh*; in many other cases this author uses the term *ruḥaniyyut ha-qodesh.* See ibid., fol. 112d. This last phrase is interesting as it constitutes an example of the complete integration of the astral-magical term into a religious scheme. See

already Cordovero's *Pardes Rimmonim* XVIII, chap. 6; I, fol. 86c. See also above, Introduction, n. 84. The term *ḥiyyut ha-qodesh* recurs in R. Menaḥem Mendel of Kossov, *ʾAhavat Shalom*. See e.g., p. 88.

254. On fol. 105ab, this delight is described as the supernal one.

255. Fol. 112c (Appendix 26). A similar view is also found in ibid., fols. 105a, 110cd. For the experience of cleaving to the divine light, see also Vital, *Shaʿarei Qedushah,* pp. 112–13; Azulai's *Ḥesed le-ʾAvraham,* fol. 15c (to be quoted immediately below); R. Abraham Yehoshuʿa Heschel of Apta, *ʾOhev Yisraʾel,* fol. 63b; R. Moshe Eliaqum Beriʾah, *Daʿat Moshe,* fol. 101b, and the medieval antecedents, some of them influenced by Sufism, cited in Idel, *Studies,* pp. 81–82, 111, 120–21, 129.

256. *Liqqutei Torah,* fol. 8ab. See also R Yiẓḥaq Aiziq Safrin of Komarno, *Noẓer Ḥesed,* p. 110.

257. See also our discussion of the Hasidic interpretation of the *Ẓaddiq* as vessel in the *Zohar,* chap. 6, par. 2.

258. See meanwhile Idel, "The Concept of *Ẓimẓum*" pp. 59–112 where the relevant bibliography is cited; Christoph Schulte, "*Ẓimẓum* in the Works of Schelling" *ʿIyuun* 41 (1992): 21–40, Ross, "Two Interpretations."

259. On *Ẓimẓum* in Cordovero see Bracha Sack, "R. Moshe Cordovero's Doctrine of *Ẓimẓum*" *Tarbiẓ* 58 (1989): pp. 207–37 (Hebrew).

260. See Nissim Yosha, *Abraham Cohen Herrera's Philosophical Interpretation of Lurianic Kabbalah* (Ph.D. Thesis, Jerusalem, 1991), pp. 134–59, 249–51, 254–64 (Hebrew).

261. On *Ẓimẓum* in Hasidism see Schatz-Uffenheimer, *Quietistic Elements,* pp. 122–27; Jacobs, *Hasidic Prayer,* pp. 89–91; idem, *Seeker of Unity* (Valentine, Mitchel: London, 1966), pp. 49–63; Amos Funkenstein, "*Imitation Dei* and the Concept of *Ẓimẓum* in the Doctrine of Ḥabad," in *Raphael Mahler Jubilee Volume* (Merhaviah, 1974), pp. 83–88 (Hebrew); Tishby-Dan, "Hasidism" pp. 772–73; Green, "Discovery and Retreat" pp. 114–17. For a very interesting treatment of the concepts of *Ẓimẓum* and *hitpashshetut* as informing Hasidic mysticism see Joel Orent, "The Transcendent Person," *Judaism* 9 (1960): 235–52; Schatz-Uffenheimer, *Quietistic Elements,* p. 125; Elior, "'Yesh' and 'ʾAyim,' and *Paradoxical Ascent,*" pp. 79–91; David Novak, "Self-Contraction of the Godhead in Kabbalistic Theology," in Goodman, ed., *Neoplatonism and Jewish Thought,* pp. 299–318.

262. On this issue, see Isaiah Tishby, "Gnostic Doctrines in Sixteenth-Century Jewish Mysticism," *JJS* 6 (1955): 147–52; idem, *The Doctrine of Evil and the "Kellipah" in Lurianic Kabbalah* (Jerusalem, 1984), pp. 21–61 (Hebrew).

263. On this conception of the relationship between Lurianic theosophy and theurgy against the background of several ancient myths, I hope to elaborate elsewhere. Compare to the illuminating, but quite ignored observation of Buber, *Origin and Meaning,* p. 121 and to the myths described by Bruce Lincoln in *Myth, Cosmos, and Society* (Cambridge, Mass., 1986).

264. See Louis Jacobs, "The Uplifting of Sparks in Later Jewish Mysticism," in Green, *Jewish Spirituality* vol. 2, pp. 99–126.

265. See Idel, *Kabbalah: New Perspectives,* p. 57.

266. Vital's *Sha ͨarei Qedushah* does not, in my opinion, belong to the literary genre of Lurianic writings despite the fact that it was composed after the death of Luria.

267. Nevertheless, there are several instances where Hasidic authors espoused rather simplified versions of Lurianic and Sarugian views on *ẓimẓum.* See, e.g., R. Qalonimus Qalman Epstein, *Ma ͗or va-Shemesh* I, fol. 2c.

268. See Idel, "On the Concept of *Ẓimẓum,*" pp. 105–110; idem, *Kabbalah: New Perspectives,* p. 304, note 44.

269. See above n. 242.

270. This is the way the classical Midrash understands the act of the descent of the divine Presence into the Holy of the Holies.

271. On palaces and boxes see more below, chap. 4.

272. *Masakhim.* See also the Seer of Lublin's discussion of the necessity of the screen for creation; cf. *Zot Zikkaron,* fol. 9bc where the scenes are related to a famous parable of the Besht's concerning seven walls. On this parable, see *Keter Shem Tov* I, fol. 8a, Weiss, in *Studies in Hasidism,* ed. Rubenstein, pp. 174–76; Green, "Discovery and Retreat" p. 107; Joshua Finkel, "A Link between Hasidism and Hellenistic and Patristic Literature" *PAAJR* 26 (2957): 1–24 and 27 (1958): 19–41; R. Jacob Joseph of Polonoy, *Ẓafnat Pa ͨaneaḥ,* fol. 126d, *Ben Porat Yosef,* fol. 111ab; R. Yiẓḥaq Aiziq Safrin of Komarno, *Noẓer Ḥesed,* p. 93. For more on *ẓimẓumim* and screens see *Ma ͗or va-Shemesh* V, fol. 10a. The notion of screens in connection with the divine withdrawal occurs already in R. Abraham Kohen Herrera, *Sha ͨar ha-Shamayim* (Warsaw, 1884) fol. 36b in a context that is related to another, epistemological view of *Ẓimẓum* that was influential in Hasidism. See also *Sefer ha-Tanya,* chap. 51; Loewenthal, *Communicating the Infinite,* p. 156; Idel, "The Concept of *Ẓimẓum*" p. 106 n. 6–7.

273. *Ma ͗or va-Shemesh* I, fol. 11b (Appendix 27). See also ibid., V. fol. 13b. On the divine occultation see also below, chap. 3, n. 57. For another example of using Lurianic terminology in order to point to unitive experience, see ibid., I, fol. 19d, where the cleaving to the five Lurianic configurations, *parẓufim,* is described as being achieved by means of cleaving to the letters of the divine Name. For an earlier formulation, see *Maggid Devarav le-Ya ͨaqov,* pp. 38–39; see also Krassen, "*Devequt*" and Faith, p. 340.

274. See below, chap. 5, n. 109.

275. *Sha ͨar ha-Shamayim,* p. 110.

276. *Ma ͗or va-Shemesh* V, fol. 9c.

277. Ibid., I, fol. 11c.

278. Ibid., fol. 11d.

279. See above, n. 228.

280. Compare to the Sufi views described in Eva de Vitry-Meyerovitch, *Mystique et poesie en Islam* (Descless de Brouwer, 1972), pp. 204ff; Chittick, *The Sufi Path of Knowledge*, s.v. veil. The idea that veils hide the divine was adopted by a late 14th- and early 15th-century descendant of Maimonides, R. David ben Yehoshuᶜa; see his *Guide for Detachment*, in Fenton, *Deux traites*, p. 299 and n. 160. There, too, the overcoming the veils is complemented by a cleaving to God. The nexus between contraction and garments that veil the divine is evident in R. Menaḥem Naḥum of Chernobyl, *Me'or ᶜEinayim*, p. 207 and R. Yisrael of Ryzhin, *ᶜIrin Qaddishin Tanyyana'*, fol. 6c.

281. On this issue see below, chap. 3, par. 2.

282. This situation probably reflects the more feminine view of the mystic, versus the male nature of the transcendent God. See below, chap. 3, par. 5.

283. *She-hu' 'asur bi-shemo.*

284. See Scholem, *On the Kabbalah*, pp. 39–41; Idel, "The Concept of the Torah," pp. 49–52.

285. The verb *Qore'* means both to read and to call. See also R. Jacob Kopel of Miedzyrec, *Qol Yaᶜaqov*, fol. 169b. A very similar passage occurs also in R. Aharon Kọhen of Apta, *'Or ha-Ganuz*, fol. 30ab. From a preliminary comparison between the versions of some Hasidic ideas as found in this book, versus their presentation in other sources, my impression is that this author, or compiler, was inclined to more extreme mystical expressions.

286. Fol. 14c (Appendix 28). See also the text from the same collection quoted below, chap. 5 par. 2, as well as the view of R. Menaḥem Naḥum of Chernobyl discussed there. Compare also the text of R. Menaḥem Mendel of Vitebsk, translated and analyzed in Idel, "Reification of Language" pp. 62–63. See also below, note 292.

287. Ibid., fol. 15a. See also ibid., fol. 39c, quoted below, chap. 4 n. 133.

288. See par. 5.

289. See a similar view in R. Aharon of Zhitomir, *Toledot 'Aharon* II, fols. 1a, 36b.

290. Compare also ibid., fol. 7d, where the *Ẓaddiq* draws the Creator within the worlds.

291. *Noᶜam 'Elimelekh*, fol. 8a (Appendix 29). See also *Maggid Devarav le-Yaᶜaqov*, p. 324, quoted below, chap. 4, par. 5. See the very interesting passage of R. Shelomo Lutzker, *Dibrat Shelomo*, fol. 6a, dealt with by Schatz-Uffenheimer in *Quietistic Elements*, pp. 132–33. The drawing down of the Godhead into the worlds is a leitmotif of R. Eliezer Lippa, the son of R. Elimelekh, in his *'Oraḥ le-Ẓaddiq*; see also *Maggid Devarav le-Yaᶜaqov*, p. 227. See also note 287 above and recently, Elliot Wolfson, "Beautiful Maiden Without Eyes," in Michael Fishbane, ed., *The Midrashic Imagination* (SUNY, Albany, 1993), pp. 189–90.

292. See Idel, "Differing Conceptions of Kabbalah," pp. 179–88; ibid., "The Relationship of the Jerusalem Kabbalists and R. Israel Sarug," *Shalem* 6 (1992): 165–74 (Hebrew). At least in one case, the possible relation between the Sarugian *Malbush* and the contraction into letters is implicit in R. Aharon of Zhitomir's *Toledot ᵓAharon* II, fol. 45b. However, even in this case the letters are those created by man, and they ascend in order to form the divine garment. Compare also to *ᵓOr Torah,* p. 85, on letters as divine garment in a context dealing with *ẓimẓum.*

293. See *Maggid Devarav le-Yaᶜaqov,* p. 324, analyzed below, chap. 4, par. 5.

294. *Maggid Devarav le-Yaᶜaqov,* p. 235; see also *Shemuᶜah Tovah* fol. 55b, discussed above beside n. 165.

295. See below, n. 299.

296. pp. 32–33 and ibid., pp. 1, 105. See also R. Aharon of Zhitomir's *Toledot ᵓAharon* II, fol. 47d.

297. Cf. Neumann, "Mystical Man" p. 382.

298. See R. Menaḥem Naḥum of Chernobyl, *Meᵓor ᶜEinayim,* pp. 40, 284. See also below, chap. 5, n. 63.

299. *Ruḥaniyyut ha-Q[adosh] B[arukh] H[uᵓ].* A similar expression recurs later on on the same page. See also, n. 221 above.

300. Fol. 7a (Appendix 30). See also the observation of R. Shimeon Menaḥem Mendel, *Baᶜal Shem Tov* I, pp. 39–40, n. 10.

301. *Ruhani.*

302. *ᶜOlat ha-Tamid,* fol. 11a. See also above, Introduction, par. 5 and below, chap. 3, par. 2.

303. On the entire question, see Peter Schaefer, *Rivalitaet zwischen Engeln und Menschen* (Berlin, New York, 1975) and Idel, "The Concept of the Torah," pp. 25–29. It should be clear that the idea of the founding figure of a new religious concept is ordinarily seen as ascending on high, or having a deep contact with the divine, and then coming back with a message, be it a book, the tables, or some form of religious wisdom. See G. Widengren, *Muhammad, The Apostle of God and his Ascension* (Uppsala-Wiesbaden, 1955). Compare also the combination of *via contemplaiva* and *via activia* in Christian Mysticism: cf., Roger Bastide, *The Mystical Life,* New York, 1935), pp. 136–50; Raymond Bailey, *Thomas Merton on Mysticism* (New York, 1975), pp. 117–118.

304. *Devarim be-Go,* p. 233.

305. See, respectively, *The Wisdom of the Zohar* II, pp. 253–55; "The Messiah of the Zohar," pp. 180–81; *Magic and Sorcery,* pp. 18, 274 n. 60.

306. See Idel, *Kabbalah: New Perspectives,* pp. 38–39; 156–66.

307. *Ha-devarim ha-ruḥaniyyim.* This phrase points in early Kabbalistic texts to the ten *Sefirot*; see Idel, ibid., pp. 43, 290–91, n. 29–30.

308. On the earlier sources of this concept, see Idel, ibid., pp. 191–97.

309. *Meqom moẓa ʾah.* This phrase occurs in several Geronese sources. See Scholem, *Origins of the Kabbalah,* pp. 303–4; Idel, ibid., pp. 52, 293 n. 64.

310. Berakhah. On the ontological concepts of blessing in Geronese Kabbalah, see Vajda, *Le commentaire,* pp. 196–209. See also below, n. 323.

311. The term translated as candle is *NER*. The assumption is that the descending emanation does not create a diminution of energy in the divine source. See also below, chap. 5, n. 99.

312. *Mosif.* This verb occurs in the Rabbinic literature in the context of adding power on the high. See Idel, ibid., pp. 157–66.

313. Ms. Oxford 1947, fol. 26b; ms. Vatican 202, fol. 54a–54b (Appendix 31). For more on this text, see Idel, "Some Remarks on Ritual" pp. 14–15; other texts from early Kabbalah pertinent to our issue were discussed by Tishby in *The Wisdom of the Zohar,* vol 2, pp. 253–55. See also above, n. 59. Compare also to R. Meir ibn Gabbai, *ʿAvodat ha-Qodesh* II, chap. 10, fol. 30c.

314. See Idel, *Kabbalah: New Perspectives,* p. 57. See also below, chap. 5 n. 30.

315. See, nevertheless, R. Asher ben David and R. Ezra of Gerona, cf. Vajda, *Le commentaire,* pp. 197–98.

316. Printed in Ch. D Chavel, ed. *Kitvei ha-Ramban,* vol. 2 (Jerusalem, 1964), p. 333. For more on this text see Idel, "Sexual Metaphors," pp. 204–5. See also another formulation of the mystico-magical model in *Sod vi-Yisod ha-Qadmoni,* ms. Jerusalem 8° 1959, fol. 200a, translated in Idel, "Enoch is Metatron," p. 235 and R. David ben Yehudad he-Ḥasid's formulation in ms. Cambridge, Add. 505.5 Ḥ fol. 8a, where the imaginative ascent, caused by the visualization of the letters of the Tetragrammatom in different colors during the prayer reaches the divine *Sefirot,* and then the influx is brought down from the heights of the infinite divinity unto the lower worlds by means of the imaginative faculty. Here, as in the earlier quotations, the theurgical and the magical moments are combined. See Idel, *Kabbalah: New Perspectives,* p. 104, and below, Appendix A, the texts from the anonymous Ashkenazi Kabbalist. See also the mystico-magical technique espoused by an anonymous short text, entitled in some manuscripts *Shaʿar ha-Kavvanah li-mequbbalim ha-rishonim,* printed and analyzed by Gershom Scholem, "The Concept of Kavvanah in the Early Kabbalah," *Studies in Jewish Thought,* ed. Alfred Josep (Detroit, 1981), pp. 169–74. Under the influence of these views we find the mystico-magical model in R. Shimeon Lavi's *Ketem Paz* (Djerba, rpr. Jerusalem, 1981), vol. 1 fol. 182c. The school of R. David ben Yehudah he-Ḥasid, and especially R. Joseph ben Shalom Ashkenazi, was more interested in the concept of causing the divine influx to descend beneath the Sefirotic realm, which I have proposed to call the vertical axis, while other contemporary schools were focusing more, though not exclusively, on reestablishing harmony within the divine world, a view that can be designated as the horizontal axis. See Moshe Idel, "The Meaning of *ʾTaʿamei HaʿOfot Ha-Temeʾimʾ* of Rabbi David ben Yehudah he-Ḥasid," in Hallamish, *ʿAlei Shefer,* pp. 24–25 (Hebrew).

317. For more on the non-theurgical though mystical views of thirteenth-century Kabbalists, see Idel, "Some Remarks on Ritual."

318. An elaborate discussion of this issue in the *Zohar* is found in Cohen-Alloro, *Magic and Sorcery,* pp. 100–4, 274 n. 60. The Zohar was acquainted with the Neoplatonic link between cleaving and magic; see Idel, *Kabbalah: New Perspectives,* p. 53.

319. See Cohen-Alloro, ibid., p. 185.

320. *Zohar* II, fol. 69a; Cohen-Alloro, *Magic and Sorcery,* p. 104; see also *Zohar* I fol. 43a which is much closer to the mystico-magical model that preoccupies us here. See Idel, *Kabbalah: New Perspectives,* p. 53.

321. *Sho'ev.* Compare to the Midrashic concept that the soul is ascending each night on high in order to draw forth *sho'evet,* life to the body. See *Genesis Rabba'* XIV, 9, pp. 133–34, *Ta'anit,* fol. 11b, *Zohar* I, fol. 92b. This concept occurs also below; see n. 337. It should be mentioned that this verb also means in many texts the drawing down of the influx from above by non-human beings; see e.g. Tishby, *Paths of Faith and Heresy,* pp. 209, 334 n. 40. On the other hand, this verb denotes also the magnetic attraction of the lower entities, especially the soul, by the higher entities. This view is found in both early Kabbalah and Hasidei Ashkenaz writings. See Idel, "*Be-'Or ha-Ḥayyim.*"

322. See also immediately below, the idea of drawing the comprehensive blessing from the supernal one. On the concept of blessing as the divine influx, see also the anonymous treatise stemming from Abulafia's school, *Sefer Ner 'Elohim,* ms. Munchen 10, fol. 132a. Here the divine influx is described as causing health, money and sons for many years, as well as exerting an influence on the souls. The first three effects remind one of the Talmudic triad *Ḥayyei, Banei, Mezonei,* which will be discussed in the next chapter, par. 3.

323. Ms. New York, JTS 1887, fols. 99b–100a; *Ve-Zot li-Yihudah,* pp. 20–21 (Appendix 32); Scholem, *Major Trends,* p. 131; Idel, *Mystical Experience,* p. 132; idem, "Universalization and Integration," p. 37, Stace, *Mysticism and Philosophy,* p. 116. See also below, Appendix A.

324. See chap. 4 par. 3 and n. 51.

325. *Beit hitbodedutkha.* This term, apparently of Sufi extraction, which is found also in other Kabbalistic texts, like the *Commentary on Sefer Yeẓirah* of R. Joseph Ashkenazi, fol. 52c—and under his influence in *Sefer ha-Peliy'ah* I fol. 57d; R. Yoḥanan Alemanno, ms. Paris BN 849, fol. 74a; and R. Eliahu of Smirna, *Midrash Talpiyot,* fol. 163b—had influenced the similar expression and practice of Hasidism. See e.g., Ben Amos-Mintz, *In Praise of the Baal Shem Tov,* index s.v., "Seclusion, house of"; Assaf, *Rabbi Israel of Ruzhin,* p. 217 n. 43. To this issue I hope to devote a larger study. See meanwhile Idel, *Mystical Experience,* pp. 39–39, ibid., *Studies,* p. 142 n. 11, 150 n. 52.

326. *Lehamshikh.*

327. *Shefa ᶜ ha-ʾElohut.* Bringing down the divine plenitude into both the mystic and the Torah is reminiscent of the Hasidic practices to be discussed below in chaps. 4 and 5.

328. *ʾOẓar Ḥayyim,* ms. Moscow-Ginzburg 775, fol. 170b (Appendix 33), discussed also in Idel, *Studies,* p. 115. On the phrase "the wisdom of combination," see above, par. 2.

329. See ibid., pp. 114–15.

330. *Kol ha-Meẓiyʾut. ʾOẓar Ḥayyim,* ms. Moscow-Gunzburg 775, fol. 40a. See ibid., fol. 35a and also the very important text of this Kabbalist translated in Idel, *Studies,* pp. 118–19.

331. See Idel, *Language, Torah and Hermeneutics,* pp. 106–9.

332. *Sullam ha-ᶜAliyah,* p. 75. See also pp. 73, 76.

333. *Mamshikhim.*

334. Ibid., p. 75.

335. Gate of Love, chap. 3; I, p. 400 (Appendix 34); Idel, "Universalization and Integration," pp. 38–39. On the image of the suckling see chap. 3, n. 37 and also above, n. 322. Two other important instances of the mystico-magical model occur again in *Reshit Ḥokhmah,* Gate of Holiness, chap. 6; II, p. 81; Gate of Love, chap. 3; I, p. 400. See also the passage quoted in the name of the Besht quoted in chap. 5, par. 2 and the discussion in R. Qalonimus Qalman Epstein, *Maʾor va-Shemesh* V, fol. 13a,b. Compare also Cordovero's views discussed chap. 3, n. 35 and in his commentary on *Raᶜyaʾ Meheimnaʾ* (n. 228 above), pp. 270–71, where the ascent on high of the sounds of study causes the cleaving of man to God, and then the emergence of apprehensions that could not be attained beforehand.

336. Wee Werblowsky, *Joseph Karo,* pp. 65–72; Idel, *Kabbalah: New Perspectives,* pp. 93–94, 110.

337. *Shaᶜarei Qedushah,* p. 97.

338. Idem, pp. 95, 96, 98, 102–3, 104, 106, 112.

339. Ibid., pp. 97, 98. See also below, chap. 4, n. 53.

340. Ibid., pp. 93, 97, 103–4, 105. For a translation and discussion of the pertinent text on p. 115 see Idel, *Studies,* p. 135.

341. See ibid., pp. 131–32. See also Pachter, "The Concept of Devekut," pp. 227–28.

342. XXXII, chap. 1; II, fol. 78bc. This passage was included almost verbatim in R. Shemuel Gallico's compendium of *Pardes Rimmonim, ᶜAsis Rimmonim.* See also above, n. 251.

343. Fol. 14a. For more on Cordovero's influence on Azulai in general see Sack, "The Influence of Cordovero on the Seventeenth-Century," pp. 372–78 and ibid., "On

the Sources of R. Abraham Azulai's book *Ḥesed le-ʾAvraham,*" *QS* vol. 56 (1981), pp. 164–75 (Hebrew).

344. Fol. 3a.

345. Respectively fol. 1b and, for *Meʾorot Nathan* (Jerusalem, ND), pp. 4–5. Neither Abraham Azulai nor Nathan Shapira mentioned their common source in Cordovero's book. An inspection of R. Nathan Shapira's version shows that he copied the text from Azulai and not from Cordovero. R. Jacob Joseph of Polonoy alludes to this passage in his *Ben Porat Yosef,* fol. 21a, and he supplies an inconvertible link between Cordovero and the theory of *Ẓaddiq* of early Hasidism. It is important to mention that still in the middle of the seventeenth century, such classical Lurianic writings, as *Peri ʿEẓ Ḥayyim* and *Meʾorot Nathan* served as tradents of Cordoverian Kabbalistic traditions. For more on Cordovero's influence on Nathan Shapira, see Sack, "The Influence of Cordovero on Seventeenth Century Jewish Thought," pp. 372–79.

346. *He-Ḥakham.* From the context it is obvious that the intention is to the Kabbalist.

347. *Tuv kavvanato.*

348. The Hebrew term translated as "entity" is *sibbah.* Cordovero mentions here also the ascent from one *ʿIllah* to another. The expression of ascending from one degree or gradation to another became a topos in Hasidism. See the sources collected by Wolfson in "Walking as a Sacred Duty," notes 5 and 6.

349. On the cleaving of the soul to the source in a similar context see chap. 3, par. 1, the quotation from the Great Maggid. This is a clear neoplatonic theme known since the very beginning of Kabbalah; cf. Idel, *Kabbalah: New Perspectives,* pp. 42–46 and idem, "Universalization and Integration," pp. 28–33.

350. *Keli.* This term is absent in Cordovero and Nathan Shapira, though it occurs elsewhere in Cordovero's writings. See e.g., the texts quoted and analyzed in chap. 4, par. 5.

351. The influx.

352. *Yitḥalleq.* Another pertinent translation is "will be divided."

353. *Zohar* II, fol. 169a. The pertinent text is quoted in Cordovero, but I do not deal with it here because in my opinion this *Zoharic* text is not the actual source of this view. See, however, *Zohar* I, fol. 43a and Idel, *Kabbalah: New Perspectives,* p. 53.

354. *Bi-meqom ha-ẓinor ha-gadol.* On this expression see below, chap. 6, par. 3.

355. Azulai, *Massekhet ʾAvot* (rpr. Jerusalem, 1986), fol. 3a (Appendix 35). I prefer to analyze this version, because it has some formulations that synthesize the views of Cordovero. For more on this quotation see chap. 6, par. 3, below.

356. See chap. 4, n. 87.

357. Compare Green, *Upright Practices,* pp. 252–253.

358. *Lidrosh ʾElohim* (n. 73 above) fol. 1a (Appendix 36).

359. See above, n. 79, 89, 317, 332, 334, 337.

NOTES TO CHAPTER 3

1. The closest discussion I could find occurs in R. Eliezer Lippa of Lisansk's *ʾOraḥ le-Ẓaddiq,* p. 99, in which a distinction is drawn between the *Ẓaddiqim* who perform operations on the supernal worlds by means of *Yiḥudim,* and those who are closer to the ideal of the learned person, and act by means of the Torah and thereby the elevation of the sparks.

2. See Scholem, *On the Mystical Shape,* pp. 125–29; Schatz, "The Besht's Commentary"; Weiss, in ed. Rubinstein, *Studies in Hasidism,* pp. 145–79; Piekarz, *The Beginning of Hasidism,* pp. 280–91; Tishby-Dan, "Hasidism," pp. 783–91, 797–98; Elior, *The Theory of Divinity,* pp. 262–67; Dresner, *The Zaddik,* pp. 173–90; Green, *Tormented Master,* p. 295; Jacobs, *Hasidic Prayer,* pp. 104–20; Liebes, "The Messiah of the *Zohar,*" p. 179, note 215. I hope to elaborate on the history of aspects of this model in my monograph on the mystical interpretations of the Pardes story. In general, I would like to emphasize that our survey of these models is an attempt that requires a more elaborated articulation.

3. *Messianic Idea,* pp. 221–22.

4. On the concept of ascension of the soul in ancient religions, see Mircea Eliade, *Myths, Dreams, and Mysteries* (Harper Torchbooks: New York, 1975), pp. 99–122; for this phenomenon in ancient Christianity, see Pierre Benoit, "Lʾascension," *Révue Biblique* 56 (1940): 161–203; see also Charles H. Talbet, "The Myth of a Descending-Ascending Redeemer in Mediterranean Antiquity," *New Testament Studies* 22 (1976): 418–39. On the ascent of soul in Judaism, see Martha Himmelfarb, "Heavenly Ascent and the Relationship of the Apocalypses and the Hekhalot Literature," *HUCA* 59 (1988): 73–100; Schaefer, *Hekhalot-Studien,* pp. 234–49, 285–89; Annelies Kuyt, *Heavenly Journeys in Hakhalot Literature* (Ph.D. thesis, University of Amsterdam, 1991); Idel, *Kabbalah: New Perspectives,* pp. 88–96, ibid., *Golem,* pp. 285–86. The scholarly literature on the entrance, or ascent to Pardes, which is particularly pertinent to our issue, is too vast to be included here. See, e.g., Schaefer, ibid., p. 239, n. 35, and Halperin, *Faces of the Chariot,* pp. 5–7, 63–113, 289–376, 414–26, and ibid., "Ascension or Invasion: Implications of the Heavenly Journey in Ancient Judaism," *Religion* 18 (1988): 47–67. See also Elior, *Paradoxical Ascent.*

5. See Loewenthal, *Communicating the Infinite,* p. 30. This category is reminiscent of Laski's category of "withdrawal ecstasy"; see her *Ecstasy,* pp. 57–66.

6. See e.g., R. Naftali Ẓevi of Ropshitz, *ʾImrei Shefer,* fols. 2d, 3c, and below, n. 267. Especially important is one of the earliest discussions, found in R. Barukh of Kossov, *ʿAmud ha-ʿAvodah,* fol. 117c, where the intensive cleaving of the thought and oral expression of someone's will induces the descent of the influx of the divine attribute that someone intends to attract. See also ibid., fol. 118a. The Cordoverian

source of this formulation of the mystico-magical model in the formative years of Hasidism is apparent, as the term *ruḥaniyyut* recurs in the context of these discussions.

7. See Idel, *Kabbalah: New Perspectives,* pp. 88–96.

8. *Ecstasy,* pp. 47–66, 67–76.

9. *ʿOr Torah,* p. 179 (Appendix 1). On the ascent from one gradation to another, see above, chap. 2 par. 7, the text of Cordovero/Azulai/Shapira. This text, as some other in Hasidic literature (see e.g. the next note), expresses the mystical experience in terms of an ascent, which assumes a hierarchy. See also *ʾOr ha-ʾEmet,* fol. 76d. The hierarchical use of the Lurianic four worlds is implicit in the theory of prayer in some Hasidic schools, and is perhaps already found in the name of the Besht, who describes the ascent of the mystic during his prayer from one world to another, though it is possible to read this ascent as an inner process. See e.g. *Keter Shem Tov* II, fol. 56ab, and some of its parallels mentioned below, chap. 4 n. 103. Therefore, the assumption that an immanentist theology that rejects hierarchies, divine or human, informs Hasidic mysticism (Elior, "Spiritual Renaissance," pp. 37, 39) should be at least somewhat modified. The text of the Great Maggid quoted above is just one strong example for divine hierarchy; the existence of a human hierarchy in a mystical system where the *Ẓaddiq* is one of the pivotal factors needs no examples. The emphasis upon seeing the supernal lights, an issue that recurs in Hasidic mysticism (see above, chap. 2, n. 37, 253) also requires a qualification of Elior's overemphasis on the role of immanentism in Hasidism.

10. See *Zohar Ḥai* II, fols. 267a–269a. I hope to deal with this transformation elsewhere.

11. See also *Toledot Yaʿaqov Yosef,* fol. 168b. A very similar computation in order to exemplify the mystical union is found in Abraham Abulafia's *ʾOr ha-Sekhel,* as analyzed in Idel, *Studies,* pp. 7–8.

12. The *Ẓaddiq* is conceived of as the letter *D,* which enters the Tetragrammaton and all the letters form the name *Yehudah.* Compare to a similar passage in the same author's *Qehilat Moshe,* fol. 101b. On entering God see also *ʾOr Torah,* p. 107 as well as the text in *ʾOr ha-Ganuz,* quoted here below, n. 18. See also Idel, "Universalization and Integration," pp. 33–50.

13. *Binat Moshe,* fol. 8b (Appendix 2). See also R. Yiẓhaq Aiziq Safrin of Komarno, *Zohar Ḥai,* vol. II, fol. 267d. Compare also R. Qalonimus Qalman Epstein, *Maʾor va-Shemesh* I, fols. 3c, 7a, 11d, 35c; II, fol. 5c; III, fol. 15cd; for more on the mystico-magical model in this book, see below, Appendix C.

14. My assumption is that this is a hint at the need to discover divinity even by contemplating a woman. See above, chap. 2 par. 2.

15. *Yiḥud ʿElyon.* See also below, n. 140.

16. *Lehityashshev ʾet ʿaẓmo ba-ʾElohut.*

17. *Ganuz.* This is indubitably a pun upon the Rabbinic phrase *ha-ʾor ha-ganuz,* the hidden, or stored light, that is also the title of the book. See also the view of the Besht quoted by R. Menaḥem Naḥum of Chernobyl, *Meʾor ʿEinayim,* p. 161. The phenomenon of being encompassed by light as part of a mystical experience is widespread. See, insofar as Kabbalah (and its sources) is concerned, Idel, "*Be-ʾOr ha-Ḥayyim,*" pp. 193–95, 197, 208–9; idem, *Mystical Experience,* pp. 77–83. For a remarkable passage that betrays the influence of ecstatic Kabbalah, see above, chap. 2, par. 2. On the shaman's immersion in pure light, see Sullivan, *Icanchu's Drum,* p. 655. On the immersion in light during a mystical experience see Mircea Eliade, *The Two and the One,* tr. J. M. Cohen (Harper Torchbooks: New York, 1969), pp. 19–77.

18. R. Aharon Kohen of Apta, *ʾOr ha-Ganuz,* fol. 9c (Appendix 3). On the feeling of being stored within the light of Godhead, see ibid., fols. 6b, 8b, 11a and his *Keter Shem Tov* I, fol. 21d and *Ner Miẓwah,* fols. 30b, 31a. See also Idel, "Universalization and Integration," pp. 36, 199 n. 32 and n. 12 above. See also the view expressed by the same author in his commentary upon prayerbook, *Keter Nehoraʾ* (unpaginated) in his interpretation of the morning service, on the Psalm 91. Compare also to the legend on the light that, according to R. David of Mikhelaiev, enwrapped the Besht when he was asleep, presented in Menaḥem Mendal Viznitzer, *Mishnat Ḥasidim* (Benei Beraq, 1981) p. 330. See also below, chap. 2, end of par. 2. Tishby, "*Qudshaʾ Berikh Huʾ,*" p. 484 n. 22, warns that R. Aharon of Apta was an uncareful compiler, who attributed to the Besht passages he did not write. Whatever the case may be, the fact that some of the most important Hasidic masters were ready to approve the publication of the book shows that the views found in it did not meet any opposition in Hasidic circles.

19. This phrase, which will also recur in many passages to be quoted below, is characteristic of the Hasidic parlance. On *ʾAyin* in Hasidism in general see Matt, "*Ayin,*" pp. 139–43 and the numerous examples adduced by Elior in "*Yesh ve-ʾAyin*" and *Paradoxical Ascent,* pp. 73–77.

20. *Liqqutei Torah,* fol. 43d (Appendix 4). See also the view of R. Yisrael of Ryzhin, who was a relative to R. Mordekhai, in *ʿIrin Qaddishin Tanyyanaʾ,* fol. 2b.

21. See e.g., R. Israel Shapira of Gradzisk, *Binat Israel* (Warsaw, 1939), fol. 12c.

22. See Idel, *Kabbalah: New Perspectives,* pp. 60–61.

23. Compare to the emphasis on the theology of immanence in several modern studies, e.g., Schatz-Uffenheimer, *Quietistic Elements,* pp. 110–21, Elior, "*Yesh ve-ʾAyin*", *Paradoxical Ascent,* pp. 93–95.

24. "Mystical Man," p. 385. Compare also to Laski, *Ecstasy,* pp. 257–58, where she describes a certain type of feeling, occurring both among ecstatics and certain manic-depressives, that seems to hallow existence, so that it is perceived in its adamic state, in which distaste does not exist. Therefore, even without a certain theological predisposition, the feeling of a sanctified reality can emerge. Compare also to William James' description of the feelings of the saints in *The Varieties of Religious Experience* (London, 1902), pp. 278–79. See also the interesting discussions found in Rudolf Otto, *Mysticism East and West,* tr. B. L. Bracey and R. C. Payne (New York, 1970), pp. 158–60, whose approach is relatively close to that proposed here. See R. Yisrael of Ryzhin,

ʿIrin Qaddishin Tanyyanaʾ, fol. 4d–5a, where *devequt,* faith, and the belief in divine immanence are presented as three mystical stages. The mystical search will, according to this master, bring someone to faith and belief in immanence. See however, ibid., fol. 14d, where the discovery of the divine within everything is envisioned as cleaving to God.

25. The emphasis on the mystical, or pneumatic, starting point of Hasidism, within groups of mystics that evolved into a mystical movement, is one of the recurrent points in recent scholarship; see e.g. Scholem, *Major Trends,* pp. 337–38; Weiss, *Studies,* pp. 27–47; Etkes, "Hasidism as a Movement," pp. 11–12; Elior, "Spiritual Renaissance," pp. 30–33. There can be no doubt that the existence of such a dynamic group of ecstatics was crucial for the emergence of Hasidism. The question is, however: What were the sources for these ecstatic, and mystico-magical, leanings? More has to be done in order to find out the sources in the Jewish mystical literature. See also above, chap. 2 par. 2.

26. See Ben-Shelomo, *The Mystical Theology,* pp. 281–86, 290–91, 300–1; Scholem, *Messianic Idea,* p. 223; and Karl-Erich Grözinger, "Neuplatonisches Denken in Hasidismus und Kabbala," *Frankfurter Judaistische Beitrage* 11 (1983): 71–73.

27. See Idel, *Kabbalah: New Perspectives,* p. 154; see also the view of *Sefer ha-Peliyʾah* quoted below, Appendix I, n. 49. Krassen, "*Devequt*" and Faith, pp. 101–3, 186.

28. See Mordecai Pachter, "Between Acosmism and Theism: R. Ḥayyim of Volozhin's Concept of God," eds. S. O. Heller Willensky, M. Idel, *Studies of Jewish Thought* (Jerusalem, 1989), pp. 143–44 and n. 16 (Hebrew).

29. On R. Abbahu see Lee I. Levine, "Rabbi Abbahu of Caesarea," in *Christianity, Judaism and Other Greco-Roman Cults: Studies for Morton Smith at Sixty,* ed. Jacob Neusner (Leiden, 1975), vol. 4, pp. 75–78, Halperin, *Faces of the Chariot,* pp. 160–61. See also Joshua Finkel, "The Guides and Vicissitudes of a Universal Folk-Belief in Jewish and Greek Tradition," in *Harry Austryn Wolfson Jubilee Volume* (Jerusalem, 1965) vol. 1, pp. 238–54.

30. *Ḥulin,* fol. 89a. See also the cosmological discussion of the transformation of the nonexistent into the existent, according to some versions of *Sefer Yeẓirah*; see Ithamar Gruenwald, "Some Critical Notes on the First Part of *Sefer Yezira,*" *REJ* 132 (1973): 505. God has, according to this treatise, made the *ʾEino,* the non-existent, into *Yeshno,* the existent. See Matt, "Ayin" p. 125. While God is conceived as transforming the Nought into existence, the Talmudic sage argues that the world will be maintained by someone who obliterates himself, and becomes nought. These two opposite moves were related to each other in Hasidism, where the greatness of the *Ẓaddiq* has been often described precisely by his capacity to do something that is contrasting the divine activity. See e.g., the Great Maggid's influential formulation in *Maggid Devarav le-Yaʿaqov,* p. 24, R. Shneor Zalman of Liady, *Torah ʾOr,* fol. 22c. This Hasidic issue is dealt with in detail by Matt, "*Ayin*" p. 143 and Elior, "*Yesh* and *ʾAyin,*" Schatz-Uffenheimer, *Hasidism as Mysticism,* pp. 67–79 (*Quietistic Elements,* pp. 22–31.)

31. *Sotah,* fol. 21b. See also Matt, "*Ayin,*" p. 156, n. 102, Elior, "Between *Yesh* and *ʾAyin*" p. 450 n. 68.

32. I hope to do this in my study of Kabbalistic symbolism.

33. Indeed, in some Hasidic texts, the term *ʾAyin* alone suffices in order to point out to a person of high spiritual degree, the *Ẓaddiq*: see e.g. R. Yiẓḥaq Shapira of Neskhiz, *Toledot Yiẓḥaq,* fols. 10c, 14a. For an elaborate analysis of the concept of nought in Jewish mysticism, see Matt, "*Ayin.*"

34. Fol. 219b. For the Kabbalistic sources of this symbolism, without including, however, the psychological elements, see Matt, "*Ayin,*" p. 156, n. 97–98, 102.

35. See also Charles Mopsik, *Le Palmier de Debora,* ed. and tr. Rabbi Moise Cordovero (Lagrasse, 1985), p. 78. See also his notes p. 145, notes 175–76. Cordovero's book was mentioned in the context of the theory of *devequt* in R. Qalonimus Qalman Epstein, *Maʾor va-Shemesh* I, fol. 6d, together with another Cordoverian book, Azulai's *Ḥesed le-ʾAvraham.* For our discussions below, it is important to remark that earlier, in chap. 1 p. 70, Cordovero mentions the effect of human behavior as opening the supernal sources to emanate upon him. One formulation is especially relevant for the present analysis: "Just as he behaves, so does he cause the emanation from above." In the way I am reading this phrase, human behavior induces a corresponding reverberation on high. However, the final result of this behavior is not the infradivine structure, but the world "he causes to that, that attribute will illuminate the world." Ibid.

36. "The Influence of *Reshit Ḥokhmah,*" and see also Idel, *Kabbalah: New Perspectives,* p. 351 n. 357.

37. The image of a suckling from the higher world already appears at the beginning of Kabbalah; see Scholem, *Origins of the Kabbalah,* pp. 279–83, Tishby, *The Wisdom of the Zohar,* vol. 2, p. 254, n. 45; Idel, *Kabbalah: New Perspectives,* p. 182, and *Reshit Ḥokhmah,* Gate of Love, chap. 3; I. p. 400 and in the text analyzed above, chap. 2 par. 7; see also R. Shelomo Rocca, *Kavvanat Shelomo,* fol. 104a, where the higher entities are described as striving to elevate themselves to their source in order to suck from there and draw down the influx in order to distribute it to the lower entities. This image is crucial for an interesting formulation of the mystico-magical model, as found in R. Abraham of Kalisk, *Ḥesed le-ʾAvraham,* fol. 7ab, where the mystic that annihilated himself and reached the realm of *Ḥokhmah,* is sucking from there. See also Qedushat Levi, fol. 48a. This view of the highest *Sefirah* as a supernal mother is interesting, and should be added to the views of the divinity as feminine, to be discussed immediately below, par. 5. Another description of the mystico-magical model occurs in ibid., fol. 8c. See also R. Uzziel Meisels, *Tiferet ʿUzziel* (Warsaw, 1963) fol. 28c.

38. *Reshit Ḥokhmah,* The Gate of Humility, chap. 1 par. 15, p. 582 (Appendix 5). See also R. Yehudah Leib ben Simeon of Frankfurt's commentary on R. Menaḥem Azariah of Fano's *ʿAsarah Maʾamarot* II fol. 5b, where he argues that *ʾAyin* is the zodiac that rules over the *Ẓaddiqim,* while *Yesh* corresponds to the repentants. For this Kabbalist, *ʾAyin* stands for the three highest *Sefirot,* while *Yesh* represents the lower seven. Compare above Cordovero's text where *ʾAyin* corresponds to the humble ones.

39. See ibid., p. 618, I would like to emphasize that the imitation of the first *Sefirah* does not imply a total self-effacement, and thus the pre-Hasidic and the Hasidic discussions of union with God in the context of annihilation should be carefully inspected in order to differentiate between the *unio mystica* form of expression and that in which the annihilation is instrumental. See this distinction in the case of Hasidic discussions in Weiss, *Studies*, pp. 84–90.

40. See Scholem, *On the Mystical Shape*, p. 130; Buber, *Origin and Meaning*, pp. 133–34; Weiss, *Studies*, pp. 87, 192–93; Jacobson, *La pensée hassidique*, pp. 176–77; Loewenthal, *Communicating the Infinite*, pp. 31–32.

41. "*Le-Mahuto*," pp. 373–75; Elior, "Better *Yesh* and *ʾAyin*," pp. 401, 402, 407, 408, 414–15, 426–27. See also her "*Yesh ve-ʾAyin*" and *Paradoxical Ascent*, passim. In this richly documented paper, the recurrent discussions on Existent and Nonexistent, or nought, are exposed, with a special emphasis on the "double nature of reality" and on the two faces of the existence and nonexistence, though also more ethical and mystical aspects are dealt with. This rather theological approach, which emphasizes the dialectics of being and its paradoxes, differs from the present theory of models, which is interested in ways of operations more than modes of cognitions, which are, in my opinion, the focus of Hasidism, and they can be described in less paradoxical terms, as I shall attempt to show below.

42. See Elior, "Between *Yesh* and *Ayin*," pp. 394, 401–2, 406, 427–28, 440–41. See also her "*Yesh ve-ʾAyin*," n. 73, where she describes the view that the *Ẓaddiq* is the tabernacle of the *Shekhinah* and is able to perform miracles as extraordinary things. In fact, the quotation from the Seer of Lublin is just one of the numerous examples of the mystico-magical model that started long before this Hasidic master, and the many examples Elior presents in footnote 74 from the works of the Seer demonstrate that there was nothing extraordinary in this linkage between the divine Presence and magic. Moreover, see above, chap. 2, n. 243. On the descent of the divine light and spiritual forces upon the mystic, who is described as a tabernacle, see *Keter Shem Tov* II, fol. 63d. This whole discussion is overtly influenced by R. Eleazar Azikri, a student of Cordovero.

43. Marett, *The Threshold of Religion*, p. 201, quoted and discussed also in Joachim Wach, *The Comparative Study of Religions*, ed. Joseph M. Kitagawa (New York, London, 1958) p. 53.

44. *Ktoneth Passim*, p. 299. Compare also the passage brought in the name of the Besht in *Ẓafnat Paʿaneaḥ*, fol. 105c, where a quite plausible interpretation would be that the perfect man, who is the palace of God (see chap. 6 n. 37) transforms his *ʾAniy* into *ʾAyin*. Compare also to his *Ben Porat Yosef*, fol. 121d. See also another quotation in the name of the Besht cited in *Kaftor va-Peraḥ*, in the part named *Luḥot ʾErez* (Jerusalem, 1937–8), fol. 67a, from *Ẓafnat Paʿaneaḥ*, about the transformation of *ʾaniy* to *ʾayin*. On the mystical union with the divine Naught, see Daniel Merkur, "Unitive Experiences and the State of Trance," in Idel-McGinn, *Mystical Union*, pp. 141–43.

45. On the ascent of the last *sefirah* to the highest one, in order to receive the influx from the highest instance, see Idel, *Kabbalah: New Perspectives*, pp. 182, 196.

46. *Ktoneth Passim,* p. 297. See also the quotation in the name of the Besht in R. Ḥayyim Liebersohn, *Ẓeror ha-Ḥayyim* fol. 4c: "The paragon of the generation has to amend himself turning the matter into form [namely spirit] by the transformation of the attribute of *ʾAniy* into the attribute of *ʾAiyn.*" See especially Aharon Kohen of Apta, *ʾOr ha-Ganuz,* fol. 49ab (Appendix 6), where the Besht is quoted to the effect that the annihilation is the only way to bear the infinite. Since there is no vessel capable of containing this infinite, man should annihilate himself for this purpose. Compare, however, Scholem, *Messianic Idea,* p. 214. See also the tradition from the circle of Ḥabad, where the view that the ascent is by means of the divine Name *ʾElohim,* while the drawing down, *ha-hamshakhah,* is by means of the Tetragrammaton. Cf., additions to *Keter Shem Tov,* fol. 83a. See also the strong emphasis on extreme humility and modesty as a prerequisite for attaining truth, in a quoted adduced in the name of the Besht in R. Yehoshuʿa Abraham ben Yisrael, *Geʾulat Yisrael,* fol. 1b.

47. Fol. 32c, quoting *ʾOr ha-Ganuz,* apparently the passage referred to in the previous note. Compare also to R. Ezeqiel of Kazimir, *Sefer Neḥmad mi-Zahav* (Pieterkov, 1909) fols. 31c, 31c–32a. An issue that cannot be explored here in detail is the connection between the mystico-magical model and some expressions related to the drawing down of the *ʾAlef* into the corporeal man, represented by *dam,* blood, and the formation of *ʾAdam.* This widespread discussion is sometimes formulated in terms identical to the model we analyze here; for example R. Menaḥem Mendel of Kossov writes in his *ʾAhavat Shalom* fol. 299b (and see also ibid., fols. 299a, and 68a) as follows: "Whoever merits to cleave to God, blessed be He, and draw down on himself the "Leader of the World" (*ʾAlufo shel ʿOlam*), he attains that the two shall be together." R. Jacob Joseph of Polonoy adduces, in the name of the "Hasid R. Dov Baer Torchiner" who is apparently no other than the Great Maggid, a version of this issue very similar to that of R. Menaḥem Mendel of Kossov. See *Ben Porat Yosef,* fol. 110c. Compare this explanation of drawing down the *ʾAleph,* to that found in the Great Maggid, as to cleaving by ascending to the *ʾAleph* in order to form the perfect Adam. Cf. Idel, *Kabbalah: New Perspectives,* p. 304 n. 41, 47. These two kinds of contact with the divinity, by attracting the *ʾAleph* or by ascending to him, reflect two types of *devequt* we have discussed in the previous chapter. Compare also to the discussion of R. Menaḥem Naḥum of Chernobyl, in Green, *Upright Practices,* p. 154 and R. Naḥman of Braslav, *Liqqutei Moharan,* fol. 5a, where the drawing down of an *ʾAleph* is described as part of the mystico-magical model. See also below, Concluding Remarks, n. 23.

48. *ʾOr ha-ʾEmet,* fol. 51d. See also ibid., fol. 76d. Other important themes also support the notion of seeing in annihilation a positive expansion of consciousness. See above, n. 37, the image of suckling, which presupposes an active entity that draws the influx from the source. See, also, the parable of the sown seed, Weiss, *Studies,* p. 154, and the material discussed by Gries, *The Conduct Literature,* p. 176, *ʿOr ha-ʾEmet,* fols. 53c–54a, *Maggid Devarav le-Yaʿaqov,* pp. 134, 205–6 etc., or R. Abraham of Pohorobisecz's passage, printed in his brother's book, R. Yisrael of Ryzhin *ʿIrin Qaddishin,* fol. 44d. See also Krassen *"Devequt" and Faith,* pp. 332–39, n. 106 below.

49. See below, chap. 5, par. 2, the quotation in the name of the Besht cited by R. Meir Margoliot, *Sod Yakhin u-Voʿaz,* p. 41; chap. 5 n. 84, the quotation of R. Yiẓḥaq Shapira of Neskhiz. See also *Degel Maḥaneh ʾEfrayim,* p. 5, where the Besht is quoted

as assuming that because of the cleaving of someone to God and becoming the chariot of the *Shekhinah,* God will send him speeches, *dibburim,* which will help him to repair the world. See also ibid., p. 201. Of paramount importance is the quotation in the name of the Besht preserved in R. Moshe of Dolina, *Divrei Moshe,* fol. 9c, where trivial conversations were concluded while someone cleaved his thought to God, thereby ensuring the drawing down of the holiness upon his words and his negotiations. Thus, early in Hasidism, the mystical cleaving was said to ensure material success. See also ibid., fols. 13a, 31c, and 39d. On fol. 47c, R. Moshe describes the drawing down of the *Moḥin,* the inner influx, by means of the prayer during the festivals. See also fol. 46d. On the *Ẓaddiq* as the chariot of the *Shekhinah* see chap. 5, n. 109. On speeches, see also chap. 5 par. 3 and n. 109.

50. On this image see below, chap. 6, par. 3. The link between *Raẓon* and *Ẓinor* occurs already in R. Menaḥem Azariah of Fano, *ᶜAsarah Ma'amarot* I, fols. 55a, 110b, II, fol. 32a. See also R. Jacob Kopel of Miedzyrec, *Qol Yaᶜaqov,* fol. 1a, and see also *Toledot Yaᶜaqov Yosef,* fol. 168b and R. Shemuel Shmelke of Nikolsburg, *Divrei Shemuel,* p. 1, 96.

51. *Boẓina' di-Nehora',* pp. 115–16; although in this context strong unitive expressions are not mentioned, this Hasidic master speaks elsewhere about a total union with the divine; see ibid., p. 111 and R. Yisrael of Ryzhin, *ᶜIrin Qaddishin,* fol. 4b.

52. *'Emunato.* On faith as related explicitly to the drawing down of the influx, see R. Yiẓḥaq of Radvil's quotation in the name of his father, R. Yeḥiel Mikhal of Zlotchov, in *'Or Yiẓḥaq,* p. 104; see also R. Dov Baer of Miedzyrec, *Maggid Devarav le-Yaᶜaqov,* pp. 244–46, R. Menaḥem Naḥum of Chernobyl, *Me'or ᶜEinayim,* p. 198. Compare also to R. Shemuel Shmelke of Nikolsburg, *Divrei Shemuel,* p. 96, on awe as maintaining the pipe, which safeguards the drawing down of the influx. According to this master, ibid., p. 97, the awe is tantamount to faith. On faith in some forms of Jewish mysticism see R. J. Z. Werblowsky, "Faith, Hope and Trust: A Study in the Concept of *Bittaḥon,*" *Papers of the Institute of Jewish Studies,* vol. 1 (Jerusalem, 1965), pp. 95–139. See also below, Appendix A, n. 82.

53. *'Or Torah,* p. 28. More on the idea of the pipe, see ibid., p. 179 and below, chap. 6, par. 4. It should be emphasized that in this collection of teachings, the verb *horid,* namely "causes to descend," which is reminiscent of the magical terminology, recurs.

54. This term means, in the parlance of the Great Maggid and the Seer of Lublin, the divine flow. See *'Or ha-'Emet* fol. 49b.

55. *Zikkaron Zot,* p. 9. See again, a similar quotation in the name of the Great Maggid, ibid., p. 13; *Zot Zikkaron,* p. 62, and also on p. 22 (to be discussed below); on ibid., p. 32 a similar view is brought as a tradition he heard, without mentioning the Great Maggid. A similar view is presented in the name of the Great Maggid in a manuscript printed and discussed by Schatz-Uffenheimer, *Hasidism as Mysticism,* pp. 76–77 (*Quietistic Elements,* p. 29.) See also the statement quoted by R. Yiẓḥaq Shapira of Neskhiz, in his *Toledot Yiẓḥaq,* fol. 14c, in the name of R. Levi Yiẓḥaq, where the same

Talmudic dictum is interpreted in the manner the Great Maggid was quoted by the Seer of Lublin. See, however, the extensive discussion of Elior, "Between *Yesh* and *Ayin,*" especially p. 428, who apparently was not sure whether the attribution of this quotation by the Seer of Lublin to the Great Maggid is reliable. The existence of additional quotations, referred to above, as well as the following discussions, point to the genuineness of this quote, and implies a different interpretation of the evolution of the role of the *Ẓaddiq,* as emerging out of particular historical circumstances, as proposed by Elior; for more on this issue see immediately below.

56. See n. 54, above.

57. *Ha˒alamah.* See also above, chap. 2, par. 6 on the screens and contractions of the divine.

58. *Zot Zikkaron* II, fol. 11c. (Appendix 7). For another instance of this model see the Seer's text quoted by his disciple, R. Meir ha-Levi of Apta, and adduced below (chap. 6 n. 114) as well as his own view ibid., fols. 15bc, 52cd, 89d (to be quoted immediately below), and the Seer's quotation cited in Elior, "Between *Yesh* and *Ayin,*" p. 429. The mystico-magical model occurs again in the directives of the Great Maggid printed at the end of *Ḥayyim ve-Ḥesed,* the writing of the Great Maggid's student R. Ḥayyim Ḥaike of Amdura, fols. 35c, 79bc. See also below, n. 151. Therefore there can be no reason to deny the firm expressions of this model in the teachings of the Great Maggid.

59. According to another version this text is attributed to the Great Maggid.

60. This is a literal translation of *˓osim le-˓aẓmam,* which means that they bring themselves to the state of. See also the following note.

61. *Le-middat.* This is a rather elliptical version, and I assume that the intention is not different from the expression "the attribute of Nought." See ibid., fols. 52cd, 99b.

62. On this issue, see below, chap. 6.

63. Fol. 89d (Appendix 8).

64. See chap. 6 par. 4 and n. 115.

65. Ibid., fol. 52d. See also ibid., fols. 54d, 65d, 84d, where, again, he insists that the *Ẓaddiq* should draw the influx only onto the children of Israel.

66. Ibid., fol. 54c.

67. Ibid., respectively fols. 84d and 65d.

68. *˒Or ha-˒Emet,* fol. 49c.

69. See e.g., R. Ḥayyim of Chernovitz, *Sidduro shel Shabbat,* fol. 29bc; the quotation in name of the Great Maggid, in R. Yisrael ben Yiẓḥaq Simḥah, *˓Eser ˒Orot,* fol. 16b, no. 51; R. Abraham Yehoshu˓a Heschel of Apta, *˒Ohev Yisrael,* fols. 71c, 72d, 73a; R. Qalonimus Qalman of Epstein, *Ma˒or va-Shemesh* I, fol. 34b and R. Abraham of Radomsk, *Ḥesed le-˒Avraham,* fol. 13b. See also below, beside n. 254.

70. A special turn to this mystical model is found in R. David of Mikhelaiev, who explains the drawing down of goods from the Godhead as the result of the contribution of the mystic to God by his cleaving: see the very important passage printed in R. Abraham ha-Malakh, *Ḥesed le-ʾAvraham,* fol. 37cd. Compare also *ʾOr ha-ʾEmet,* fol. 51b and R. Moshe Eliaqum Beriʾah, *Daʿat Moshe,* fol. 71d. On the view that by mystical union someone is adding to the divine, see R. Shneor Zalman of Liady's text dealt with in Idel, "Universalization and Integration," p. 44.

71. *Peri ha-ʾAreẓ,* fol. 31a.

72. *Noʿam ʾElimelekh,* fol. 1b. See also fol. 109d. See also below, the view that in order to perform the commandments, the *Ẓaddiq* is allowed to leave the state of cleaving. See also above, the passage of R. Moshe Eliaqum Beriʾah on cleaving and drawing down.

73. Ibid., fol. 38b. This view stems from Cordoverian sources. See *Tefillah le-Moshe,* fol. 344b and, as Dr. Bracha Sack has kindly drawn my attention, the view that commandments are prone to draw down the influx is expressed also in Cordovero's *Sefer ha-Gerushin,* p. 21, "The light of the commandment generates a channel for the influx." The concept of the "light of the commandments," implicit already in the Bible, Proverbs 6, 23, has developed since the beginning of Kabbalah, in the context of the efficacy of the performance of the commandments even without a Kabbalistic intention. See Idel, "*Be-ʾOr ha-Ḥayyim,*" pp. 193–203.

74. See ibid., fols. 8a, 107a, 108a.

75. In the printed text it is written *Qodem,* but I assume that the correct version is *Qadum.*

76. *ʿOlam ha-Maḥashavah*; on this concept see Schatz-Uffenheimer, *Quietistic Elements,* pp. 121–28.

77. *ʿOlam ha-Meziʾut.*

78. On the drawing of the influx into the world, see chaps. 2 and 6. "The Root of Roots," or sometimes simply "Root" stands for the Infinite. See the interesting story about R. Moshe Leib of Sassov, adduced in R. Yiẓḥaq of Radvil, *ʾOr Yiẓḥaq,* p. 131, where he is presented as expecting joyfully his return to God, designated as "my root."

79. *Liqqutei Maharil,* fol. 3b (Appendix 9). See also ibid., fol. 3a, 9ab.

80. See also ibid., fol. 12b where the author explicitly mentions the drawing down of the *ruḥaniyyut.* Compare already in R. Moshe of Dolina, *Divrei Moshe,* fol. 16cd, where the verbs derived from *horadah* and *hamshakhah* are semantically indentical.

81. Fol. 80a. On drawing down the luminosity see also *Qedushat Levi* fols. 4a, 48c and in R. Aharon of Zhitomir's *Toledot ʾAharon,* passim; some examples can be found immediately below in quotations from this author. See also R. Reuven Horowitz's *Dubaʾim ba-Sadeh,* fol. 35a, where the drawing down of the "Holiness" after the experience of cleaving is mentioned. On another occasion, ibid., fol. 70ab, the whole model is explicitly described: "when man is humble he is united to God, blessed be He, . . .

and he can draw down the blessings from the source of all blessings." See also R. Moshe Eliaqum Beri'ah, *Binat Moshe,* fol. 16a. Compare to his *Da'at Moshe,* fol. 176b; ibid., *Be'er Moshe,* fol. 93d; idem, *Qehilat Moshe,* fol. 102b. The term *Qedushah* signifies the descending divine influx in Cordovero's commentary on the Zohar, printed in Azulai's *'Or ha-Ḥamah* II, fol. 231c; in R. Nathan-Neta''s *'Olat Tamid,* passim, and in R. Aharon of Zhitomir, ibid., II fol. 36b; R. Asher Ẓevi of Ostraha, *Ma'ayan ha-Ḥokhmah,* fol. 39b. It should be mentioned that at least since Cordovero, the verb used in order to describe the drawing down of the Holiness is also *morid,* as in the magical sources, and not only *mamshikh,* which is dominant in the theosophical-theurgical texts. Compare also to R. Shemuel Shmelke of Nikelsburg, *Divrei Shemuel,* p. 143, and R. Ḥayyim of Chernovitz, *Be'er Mayyim Ḥayyim* I, fols. 8c, 9b, and R. Naḥman of Braslav, *Liqqutei Moharan* I, fol. 95b. See also below, chap. 4 n. 28.

82. The source of this term seems to be in the circle of Cordovero; see his commentary on the *Zohar,* printed in Abraham Azulai's *'Or ha-Ḥamah* I, fol. 39a; III, fol. 10a. See also the Beshtian text quoted in *Keter Shem Tov* I, fol. 59c where *ruḥaniyyut, behirut and ḥiyyut* are used in an almost interchangeable way.

83. Cf. *Shemu'ah Tovah,* fol. 70b. On the interpretation of the verb *NGD,* here represented by the form *yaggid,* as drawing down, see below, chap. 4, n. 137.

84. See chaps. 4 and 5.

85. *Qedushat Levi,* fol. 60a (Appendix 10); for another translation see Scholem, *Major Trends,* p. 5; see also Stace, *Mysticism and Philosophy,* pp. 106–7. Compare also to *Qedushat Levi,* fol. 65b, where the contemplation of the divine luminosity causes the same loss of the sense of identity and reality as the contemplation of the Nought.

86. See also *Shemu'ah Tovah,* fol. 63a. Compare above, the examples from the thirteenth century Kabbalah where the intellect is also connected to the cleaving and the drawing down the of influx.

87. The *Ẓaddiq.*

88. *Higbiah 'et 'aẓmo*; this phrase occurs again in a similar context on the same page. See also ibid., fols. 52d–53a. For the use of this verb in a somewhat similar context, see *Toledot Ya'aqov Yosef,* fol. 6c and below, n. 267. These cases are to be understood as inner flights, or metaphorical expressions, to be distinguished from the elevation of the soul in other cases in Hasidism. See the discussion in Laski, *Ecstasy,* p. 496, on "up-words and phrases."

89. In fact, God stands here for the Nought in the writings of other early Hasidic masters, as the mention of the wisdom implies.

90. *Meqashsher 'et 'aẓmo.* See also ibid., fol. 74b.

91. *Ḥayyim va-Ḥesed,* fol. 43cd (Appendix 11). See also ibid., fol. 35c.

92. Ibid., *lehitḥabber.*

93. Ibid., fol. 70d.

94. *Lehitqarev*. Ibid., fol. 72c.

95. See also chap. 2, par. 6, our discussion of *Ẓimẓum*.

96. *Shemu ᶜah Tovah* fol. 70b. It should be mentioned that a certain resemblance between the feeling of nothingness and mystical and magical-theurgical attainments, is already found in Iamblichus' *Mysteries of Egypt* I, 15; cf. Iamblicus of Chalcis, *On the Mysteries*, ed. S. Ronan, trans. Th. Taylor and A. Wilder (Chtonios Books, 1989), p. 41. See also Gregory Shaw, "The Geometry of Grace: A Pythagorean Approach to Theurgy," *Incognita* 2 (1991): 48–49. On Iamblicus and the concept of *pneumata*, the Greek source of the Arabic *ruḥaniyyat*, see Pines, "On the Term *Ruḥaniyyat* and Its Sources," pp. 521–22. This thaumaturge has developed a view of magic that involves mystical experiences, like enthusiastic states produced by the descent of the *pneumata* onto the magician. See *The Mysteries of Egypt*, vol. III, 7, and Pines ibid., p. 522.

97. See Green, "Discovery and Retreat," p. 128.

98. *Be-ʾAyin*. I have no doubt that the contemplation of the Nought by the eye is a paradoxical concept, because it is not the result of a consistent type of speculation but of a pun related to the actual identity of the pronunciation of the terms *ʾAyin*, Nought and *ᶜAyin*, eye. This impression is corroborated by the recurrence of the phrase *lehistakkel be-ʾAyin*, namely "to look at the Nought," whose pronunciation can be easily understood as "to watch by means of the eye." See ibid., fol. 55d, where the two phrases occur in the same passage.

99. I use this term because according to another discussion this Hasidic master asserts that the human intellect cannot contemplate God.

100. See *Devotion and Commandment*, pp. 20–24, ibid., "Discovery and Retreat" pp. 126–28; Sack, "The Influence" pp. 234–35; see also Moshe Idel, "On the Land of Israel in Jewish Mystical Thought," in *The Land of Israel in Medieval Jewish Thought*, ed. M. Ḥallamish and A. Ravitzky (Jerusalem, 1991), pp. 206–7 (Hebrew).

101. *Be-ʾAyin mamash*; this phrase, very characteristic of this Hasidic master, can be also translated as "within the true Nought." The disciple of the author, R. Aharon of Zhitomir, mentions several times the ascent of the *Ẓaddiq* as transcending the contracted levels. See *Toledot ʾAharon* II, fol. 36bd. See also above, chap. 2 par. 6, the texts of R. Qalonimus Qalman Epstein.

102. Compare also to the view of R. Levi Yiẓḥaq, ibid., fols. 55c, 65b.

103. *Qedushat Levi*, fols. 5d–6a (Appendix 12); Green, *Devotion and Commandment*, p. 20; ibid., "Discovery and Retreat" p. 126.

104. See Idel, *Kabbalah: New Perspectives*, pp. 70–72.

105. *ᶜAẓmuto*. See also above, the quotation on the return to the intellect after contemplating the Nought.

106. *Qedushat Levi*, fol. 102b (Appendix 13). See also Idel, *Kabbalah: New Perspectives*, p. 72. This text has been used by R. Elimelekh ben Ḥayyim of Kuznitz, *ʾImrei ʾElimelekh* (Warsaw, 1876), fol. 63, and *ᶜEser ʾOrot*, fol. 42a, in a very interesting

context. The author brings, in the name of his father, the R. Ḥayyim Meir Yeḥiel of Magalinitza, a tradition concerning their ancestor, the Maggid of Kuznitz, who presented himself as "a servant that is standing before God ready to be sent," *mukhan kemo na ʿar meshulaḥ*. The Rabbi of Magalinitza interprets this statement as follows: The Maggid of Kuznitz was in a state of annihilation, beyond any quality, just like the state described in *Qedushat Levi*. Is this state of being, described by the Maggid and his descendant, indeed a realization of the more abstract description in *Qedushat Levi*, as argued by the Hasidic masters? The Maggid of Kuznitz was, as we know, a disciple of the Berdichever Rebbe. This state of annihilation means, according to R. Ḥayyim Meir Yeḥiel, that the person can receive more than the "aspect of his vessels," *mi-beḥinat ha-kelim shelo*. According to this interpretation, that is consistent with the view of R. Levi Yiẓḥaq, namely, that by annihilation one expands his capacity to receive the influx even more than before he "annihilates himself." See also the Maggid of Kuznitz's formulation in *ʿAvodat Yisrael*, fol. 24d, mentioned in *ʾImrei ʾElimelekh*, on the need to be ready and prepared, *mukhan u-mezuman*, to receive divine influxes. Is it possible that beyond the "objective" description in the book we have a rather autobiographical confession? See also n. 48, above.

107. This view stems from the thought of the Great Maggid; see e.g., *Maggid Devarav le-Ya-ʿaqov*, pp. 134, 227. See more on this issue in another quotation to be analyzed below, par. 6.

108. See Scholem, *Origins of the Kabbalah*, pp. 420–26; Schatz-Uffenheimer, *Quietistic Elements*, pp. 24, 45, 100; Safran, "Maharal and Early Hasidism" pp. 55, 80–91, Matt, "*Ayin*" pp. 127, 133–36.

109. The term *Behirut ḥadashah versus Behirut yeshanah* recurs in this book: see e.g., part I, fol. 32b, and it is reminiscent of the pair of terms *Neshamot ḥadashot* and *Neshamot Yeshanot* in early Kabbalah; and of the renewal of the Mohin, *hitḥaddeshut ha-moḥim* in Lurianic Kabbalah; cf. ibid., fol. 37d.

110. See the view of Cordovero on *kavvanah* discussed below, chap. 4, par. 4.

111. *Toledot ʾAharon* I, fol. 6b (Appendix 14), quoted also in *ʿEser ʾOrot*, fol. 31b. See also another similar quotation in the name of R. Levi Yiẓḥaq, ibid., fol. 40a. Compare also to R. Shemuel Shmelke of Nikolsburg, *Divrei Shemuel*, p. 127. The activist mode that is connected to the concept of drawing down the divine energy is evident also in R. Yisrael of Ryzhin, *ʾIrin Qaddishin Tanyyanaʾ*, fol. 2cd, where the assumption is that the ritual acts performed *in corpore*, are performed by the divine power and vitality drawn down by the mystic after his own vitality was effaced.

On fol. 31c of *Toledot ʾAharon* I, this author offers another typology, which situates the magical activity as lower in comparison to the theurgical one. On this issue see also below, beside notes 131 and 266. See also below, chap. 4, n. 25. The most explicit preference for the total union of the *Ẓaddiq* with the Infinite, for worship for the sake of bringing down the *Shekhinah* upon themselves here below (an approximation of the drawing down model) is found quite late, in R. Yisrael Shalom Joseph of Buhush's *Peʾer Yisrael*, fol. 9b. See also ibid., fol. 12a, where another distinction is proposed between the *Ẓaddiqim* who worship in solitude and those who attempt to improve other people. It should be mentioned that attempts to distinguish between two forms of worship of the *Ẓaddiqim* is a topos in Hasidic literature, which varies from one author to another. See e.g. *Liqqutim Yeqarim,* fol. 90b, no. 273, a distinction that is quoted and expanded later on in the name of the Besht in R. Menaḥem Mendel of Kossov, *ʾAhavat Shalom,* fols. 32b–33a; see also ibid., fol. 99a; R. Jacob Joseph of Polonoy, e.g., *Ben Porat Yosef,* fol. 87c, R. Yisrael of Kuznitz, *ʿAvodat Yisrael,* fol. 25a, R. Ẓevi Elimelekh of Dinov, *Benei Yisaskhar* I, fol. 18b. R. Menaḥem Mendel of Viznitz, *Sefer Ẓemaḥ Ẓaddiq* (Haifa, 1988) p. 347. See also Elior, "Between *Yesh* and *Ayin*" p. 437, and for another distinction in R. Naḥman of Braslav's writings, Gries, *The Conduct Literature,* p. 262.

112. See below, chap. 5.

113. See above, chap. 2 par. 6.

114. *Yesh.*

115. On the connection between worship and return from the Nought in R. Levi Yiẓḥaq, see Idel, *Kabbalah: New Perspectives* p. 69, and for a later parallel see the view of R. Yiẓḥaq Aiziq Yehudah Safrin of Komarno as described in Idel, "Universalization and Integration" p. 48.

116. *Qedushat Levi,* fol. 5d (Appendix 15); Green, *Devotion and Commandment,* pp. 20–22; ibid., "Discovery and Retreat" p. 127.

117. See Moshe Idel, "On R. Isaac Sagi Nahor's Mystical Intention of *Shemoneh Esreh,*" *Massuʾot: Studies in Kabbalistic Literature and Jewish Philosophy in Memory of Prof. E. Gottlieb,* eds. M. Oron and A. Goldreich (Jerusalem, Tel Aviv, 1994), pp. 25–52 (Hebrew).

118. *Toledot ʾAharon* I, fols. 7d–8a. See also R. Abraham of Kalisk, *Ḥesed le-ʾAvraham,* fol. 7b, where Abraham is described as cleaving to God and thus performing all the commandments.

119. *Ḥesed le-ʾAvraham* fol. 7bc.

120. *Hitgallut ʾElohuty.* Compare also below, the quotation from *Liqqutei Torah.*

121. *Ḥesed le-ʾAvraham,* fol. 12c.

122. Chap. 2, par. 7 n. 314.

123. Compare the same sequel of words in the quotation from *Liqqutei Torah,* adduced below.

124. Compare *Qedushat Levi,* fol. 102b, where the reception of the luminosity, *behirut,* is mentioned in a similar context. The term *behirut* occurs already in Cordovero's system as a synonym to influx. See his *Sefer ha-Gerushin,* p. 60.

125. *Berakhot.*

126. There is an indisputable affinity between this last formulation and that of the master of R. Levi Yiẓḥaq, the Great Maggid, which was mentioned above. Thus, there is no good reason to doubt the attribution of the above view to the Great Maggid. Like-

wise, the affinity between this text and another one, from the Ḥabad school, which will be dealt with below, may strengthen the probability that they represent an earlier phase in Hasidic thought.

127. *Qedushat Levi,* fol. 5b (Appendix 16). See also ibid., fol. 140ab, where another description of the mystico-magical model occurs.

128. This view occurs in the writings of R. Moshe ben Shimeon of Burgos, R. Joseph ben Shalom Ashkenazi, R. David ben Yehudah he-Ḥasid, as well as in writings influenced by them. I hope to analyze this view in a separate study.

129. The use of the term *ʾAyin* for an hypostatical potentiality represents indeed a change in the Kabbalistic terminology which, paradoxically enough, emphasized the fullness of being; see Matt, "*Ayin,*" pp. 128–38.

130. See Idel, *Kabbalah: New Perspectives,* pp. 181–91.

131. See ibid., pp. 53–57.

132. See also Sack, "The Influence," p. 234.

133. See a similar distinction between the view of R. Ezra of Gerona, who invokes the dedication which culminates with the acceptance of martyrdom, in lieu of coming to the Land of Israel and that of Naḥmanides, Idel, "On the Land of Israel" (note 100 above), pp. 204–7.

134. See Elior, "Between *Yesh* and *Ayin*" pp. 429–31.

135. Especially Green, *Devotion and Commandments,* pp. 62–72.

136. "ḤABAD: The Contemplative Ascent to God" pp. 178–81; *Paradoxical Ascent,* pp. 127–38.

137. *Ha-hitpaʿalut ha-ʿaẓumah.* Interestingly enough, one of the first uses of the verb *hitpaʾel* in order to express a state of ecstasy I am acquainted with is found in one of the writings of Abraham Abulafia: see, e.g., the text brought by Scholem, *Major Trends,* pp. 140, 382 n. 75.

138. On this expression, which means ascent and descent, literally run and return, see Elior, *Paradoxical Ascent,* pp. 29–31. See also below, the analysis of the quotation from *Liqqutei Torah.*

139. *Torah ʾOr,* Va-Yishlaḥ, fol. 25b (Appendix 17), analyzed by Elior, "*ḤaBaD*: The Contemplative Ascent to God," p. 181. (On the authorship of this tract, see Elior, *The Theory of Divinity,* p. 123, n. 12.) Here a slightly different translation is brought. Compare also the important passage ibid., fol. 3b, and our discussion here below on the text from *Liqqutei Torah.*

140. Ibid., p. 181. See also ibid., p. 159, her discussion of the relationship between *Yiḥud ʿeliyon* and *Yiḥud taḥton.* See also above, n. 15.

141. See Elior, ibid., pp. 199–203. See also R. Shneor Zalman, *Commentary on the Liturgy,* fols. 16d–17a; ibid., *Liqqutei Torah,* part III, fol. 75cd.

142. *Liqqutei Torah,* part III, fol. 75d (this issue recurs twice on this page) and *Torah ʾOr* fol. 111a.

143. Literally, "a person of Israel."

144. *Kelal.*

145. *ʿAvodat ha-Levi, haftarat Piqqudei* (Lemberg, 1842), fol. 55b (Appendix 18). This text was adduced and discussed by Elior in the Hebrew version of her article on ḤABAD, p. 176, but not dealt with in the English version, p. 201. See also her *The Theory of Divinity,* pp. 194–95. Also apparently relevant for our discussion is the treatment by R. Dov Baer, the son of R. Shneor Zalman, of two types of ecstatic dances: the chaotic, equivalent to the annihilation-state, and the rhythmical, which is connected to drawing the Beyond-reason into Reason. Cf. Loewenthal, "'Reason' and 'Beyond Reason,'" p. 121. In the above quotation revelation stands for both the act of emanation, and the mystical epiphany of that emanation. However, in an interesting text by R. Nathan Netaʿ of Helm, *Netaʿ Shaʿashuʿim,* fol. 19c, it is said that the *Ẓaddiq* can answer a question dealing with the future only after he is divested from his corporeality and cleaves to God. Only then does the *Shehkinah* speak from his throat. Again, a magical revelation is preceded by the mystical preparation and experience. This view should be compared to a similar passage of R. Yiẓḥaq of Acre; see chap. 2 n. 79. The ḤABAD approach to the mystico-magical model is somewhat closer to the later formulations found in the Gur school. See e.g. *Sefat ʾEmet* III, fol. 85ab.

146. See *Liqqutei Torah* III, fol. 75c.

147. See Loewenthal, "'Reason' and 'Beyond Reason,'" pp. 116–17; Elior, "ḤABAD: The Contemplative Ascent to God" pp. 198–203.

148. Compare however, Schatz-Uffenheimer, *Hasidism as Mysticism,* p. 155 (*Quietistic Elements,* p. 87), where it is said that the more pragmatic attitude toward prayer, though recurring in the school of the Great Maggid, was never attributed to the Great Maggid himself; see also her "*Le-Mahuto,*" pp. 371, 373. Also Elior's stand, though more cautious (see n. 42 above), is still very strongly inclined to see in the social and economic background of late eighteenth- and early nineteenth-century Poland one of the main reasons of the innovation of the orientation of the Seer of Lublin toward the material well being of his flock and the active involvement of the *Ẓaddiq* in this issue: see especially "Between *Yesh* and *Ayin,*" pp. 432–34, 436–37.

149. Compare the somehow similar view in the Geronese Kabbalah, cf. Idel, *Kabbalah: New Perspectives,* p. 52.

150. In Hebrew *Taqanato* can be interpreted also as the repair of the plight.

151. Fol. 15b (Appendix 19). On this book see Gries, *The Conduct Literature,* pp. 112–14, 116–21, 314–53. See also R. Qalonimus Qalman Epstein, *Maʾor va-Shemesh* III, fol. 16b and ibid., fol. 16c where the mystico-magical model is quoted in the name of the Great Maggid. See also ibid., IV, fol. 15c; V, fols. 6b, 49c. See also the texts translated by Jacobs, *Jewish Mystical Testimonies,* pp. 217–22.

152. More on this issue see below, at the end of this chapter and chap. 6 passim.

153. Compare Weiss, *Studies in Braslav Hasidism,* pp. 153–54 n. 3; Rapoport-Albert, "God and the Zaddik," p. 313. I would like to mention that though Rapoport-Albert is certainly right to draw the attention to the mediation-role of the *Ẓaddiq* in Hasidism, the feeling of the presence of the light of the Infinite within all souls can be also attained directly, without any intermediary. See e.g., R. Menaḥem Naḥum of Chernobyl, quoting R. Meshullam Zushia of Hanipoli, *Me᾽or ʿEinayim,* p. 207 and R. Mordekhai of Chernobyl, *Liqqutei Torah,* fol. 44d. Moreover, according to the Seer of Lublin, the *Ẓaddiq* brings down the divine influx and enables the cleaving of the people to God. See *Zikkaron Zot,* fol. 10a. His follower, R. Qaloniums Qalman Epstein, in *Ma᾽or va-Shemesh* IV, fol. 26a, speaks about the *Ẓaddiq* who attains the state of divestment of corporeality and union with God, to behave in such a way that his followers will see him and he will become an example. In other words, the *Ẓaddiq* is an elitist mystic who is also able to ensure the mystical achievement of the masses, whose mystical attainments had remained, in earlier forms of Jewish mysticism, beyond the scope of the mystics' concern. See also the discussion of R. Yisrael of Ryzhin, where he asserts that the Hasid should pray directly to God in order to obtain the influx by the mediation of the *Ẓaddiq*. *ʿIrin Qaddishin Tanniyyana᾽,* fol. 13b and below, n. 258. On the other hand, it is possible to adduce an important example for the Rapoport-Albert thesis from R. Menaḥem Mendel of Kossov, *᾽Ahavat Shalom,* fol. 68a, where the *Ẓaddiqim* are called the "faces of the Divine Presence," and as such, by being in their presence, someone may lose his senses, or become effaced, but the *Ẓaddiq* then gives him a new power to return to himself. In fact, the experience of the *Ẓaddiq* is portrayed in terms that are identical to those used to describe the encounter between the mystic and the Divinity. Elsewhere, ibid., fol. 13b, this experience of annihilation in the presence of a *Ẓaddiq* is atrributed to the lower types of *Ẓaddiqim.*

154. *Toledot Yiẓḥaq,* fol. 10cd. A similar interpretation is found also in the Maggid of Kuznitz, *ʿAvodat Yisrael,* fol. 25b and in R. Moshe Eliaqum Beri᾽ah, his son, *Daʿat Moshe,* fols. 176b, 54d; in R. Yehudah Leib of Zakilkov, *Liqqutei Maharil,* fol. 5ab, and in another version, in *Sefer Zikhron Shemuel,* written by a disciple of the Maggid of Kuznitz, R. Shemuel Shemariah of Ostrowce (Ostrowce, 1925) I, fol. 61a, as a quotation from the Maggid Yisakhar Ber. See also Rapoport-Albert, "God and the Zaddik" pp. 321–23; Jacobs, *Hasidic Prayer,* p. 131; Elior, "Between *Yesh* and *Ayin,*" pp. 424–25. See also the passage from R. Yiẓḥaq of Radvil, *᾽Or Yiẓḥaq,* translated by Samuel H. Dresner, "The Holiness of Man," *Judaism* 37 (1988): 157–59. On deification as the result of the theurgical process see Georg Luck, "Theurgy and Forms of Worship in Neoplatonism," in eds. Neusner and alia, *Religion, Science, and Magic,* p. 189.

155. *Toledot Yiẓḥaq,* ibid., this last phrase recurs several times in this passage. See also R. Reuven Horowitz's *Duda᾽yim ba-Sadeh,* fol. 52b, where he quotes in the name of Rebbe of Neskhiz, an interesting passage on the difference between the deeds of the *Ẓaddiq* and those of God. Compare also to R. Moshe Eliaqum Beri᾽ah, *Be᾽er Moshe* I, fol. 26d.

156. Compare to the view expressed by R. Joseph Giqatilla in his *Shaʿarei ᾽Oraḥ* II, p. 107 and 90–91, where the topic of the magical achievements of the ascending prayer is dealt with explicitly.

157. *Da*ᶜ*at Moshe,* fol. 176ab; see also ibid., fol. 99b; ibid., *Qehilat Moshe,* fol. 65c.

158. *Da*ᶜ*at Moshe,* fol. 176a. The pun is *Ḥayyei ha-Ḥayyim,* an epitheton for God, and ḥiyyut. Compare also R. David of Mikhelaiev, a student of the Besht, printed in *Liqqutei* ᵓ*Amarim,* fol. 4a and in R. Abraham the Angel's *Ḥesed le-*ᵓ*Avraham,* fols. 36d, 37c, and R. Menaḥem Naḥum of Chernobyl, *Me*ᵓ*or* ᶜ*Einayim,* p. 135. On p. 143 this master describes even the ability of the *Ẓaddiq* to "create worlds" if he is united with the Creator. On this issue see additional sources discussed by Idel in *Golem,* pp. 106–8. See also below, chap. 5, n. 113.

159. See *Liqqutim Ḥadashim,* fol. 5d and *Pe*ᵓ*er Yisrael,* fol. 151a.

160. *Mo*ᵓ*ed Qatan,* fol. 17a.

161. Cf. Judges, 13:18.

162. Quoted in a collection of Hasidic teachings preserved by R. Jacob Shemuel ha-Levi Horowitz, and printed in "Yalqut Shemuel," ed. Y. L. ha-Kohen Maimon, *Sefer ha-Besht* (Jerusalem, 1960), p. 304 (Hebrew). See also R. Moshe Eliaqum Beriᵓah, *Be*ᵓ*er Moshe,* fol. 26cd.

163. For more on this issue, see also below in the Concluding Remarks, pars. 2, 4, 6.

164. See R. Jacob Joseph of Polnoy, *Ẓafnat Pa*ᶜ*aneaḥ,* fol. 33a; *Ben Porat Yosef,* fol. 121cd and compare also to the story of R. Moshe Ẓevi of Savaran, adduced by Piekarz, *Studies in Braslav Hasidism,* p. 110 n. 62. The Besht himself was reported to be unable to come out of his mystical state of concentration, or union, *devequt,* and speak with men in a normal way. He was taught by his mystical mentor, Ahiyah the Shilonite, a technique for this purpose. See Yaᶜari, "Two Editions," p. 552, where the Yiddish version is more complete. See also, Ben Amoz-Mintz, *In Praise of the Baal Shem Tov,* p. 129, Weiss, in *Studies in Hasidism,* ed. Rubinstein, p. 140. The device, the recitation of Psalms, is a nomian type of activity. See also the tradition that stems from the Besht and the Great Maggid passed to R. Shneor Zalman of Liady, concerning the recitation of the Psalms every day. Cf. *Keter Shem Tov,* Additions, fol. 113b.

165. See the quotations referred to in notes 127 and 145 above.

166. *Qedushat Levi,* fol. 5d (Appendix 20). On this issue see also Cordovero's view adduced above, chap. 2, par. 3. In Hasidism the correlation between performing the commandments and the attraction of the influx from above is a topos. See above, beside n. 73 and 103 and R. Moshe Eliaqum Beriᵓah, *Be*ᵓ*er Moshe* I, fols. 26c, 27a, 94a.

167. Cf. *Qedushat Levi,* fol. 60a. See also above beside n. 103 and 127.

168. There is a certain stroke of irony that by cleaving to the "Life of Lives" someone reaches an experience of metaphorical death.

169. *Zikkaron Zot,* fol. 29c (Appendix 21). See also Idel, *Kabbalah: New Perspectives,* pp. 69–70, where I have analyzed some sources and details of this quote; there I

was inclined to see it as being closer to the quietist attitude that I assume the passage actually suggests.

170. On the mystical dimension of poverty see Louis Dupré, *The Deeper Life* (Crossroad Press, New York, 1981), pp. 39–46, Tishby, *The Wisdom of the Zohar,* vol. 2, pp. 692–98.

171. *Shemu ʿah Tovah,* fol. 94a. See also ibid., fol. 63a.

172. See *Qedushat Levi,* fol. 65bc. See also a passage of R. Nathan of Nemirov, discussed in Green, *Devotion and Commandments,* pp. 61, 90, n. 126, on the need to return from the negation and attract the light into measures and vessels. See also R. Pinḥas Menaḥem Eleazar of Piltz (formerly in Gur), *Siftei Ẓaddiq* (Jerusalem, 1956), fol. 71a.

173. *Sidduro shel Shabbat,* fol. 81ab (Appendix 22); I have used Green's translation, with some slight changes; cf. *Devotion and Commandment,* p. 87 n. 103. See also R. Jacob Joseph of Polnoy, *Ẓafnat Pa ʿaneaḥ,* fol. 115d, where the *Ẓaddiq* is described as someone who has left the human condition; *Nitroqen me-ʾAdam.* Compare also to the tradition found in *Keter Shem Tov* I, fol. 21d, translated by Jacobs, *Hasidic Prayer,* pp. 93–94. See also above beside n. 69 and below, n. 184.

174. See especially Elior, "ḤaBaD: The Contemplative Ascent to God," p. 201.

175. See nevertheless, *No ʿam ʾElimelekh,* fol. 48a.

176. See, however, the tradition adduced by R. Alexander Safrin of Komarno, according to which the Seer of Lublin has told him that he never prayed in order to receive something, before he sees that it is the will of God that he will pray for it. Cf. *Zikhron Devarim,* pp. 148–49.

177. *No ʿam ʾElimelekh,* fol. 98c.

178. Ibid.

179. *Netiv Miẓoteikha,* p. 103. Compare also to his *Heikhal ha-Berakhah* IV, fol. 12bc.

180. *Heikhal ha-Berakhah* IV, fol. 12cd.

181. *Yiḥudim we-ziwwugim.*

182. The importance of the body in this context will be dealt with below, chap. 6, pars. 3, 4.

183. *ʿAniy.*

184. *Netiv Miẓwoteikha,* p. 19 (Appendix 23). See also ibid., pp. 17–18, 100, ibid., *Heikhal ha-Berakhah* V, fols. 35c, 172a; and Idel, "Universalization and Integration," p. 48. The assumption that the descent of the influx by the power of the *Ẓaddiq* is related to the unification of all the worlds to the highest divine instance occurs long beforehand, in R. Ḥayyim of Chernovitz's *Sidduro shel Shabbat,* fol. 52bc. For other

interesting discussions of the mystico-magical model see this author's *Be᾿er Mayyim Ḥayyim* I, fols. 8a, 88cd, 93a.

185. See also the opinion of R. Jacob ben Sheshet, a thirteenth century Kabbalist of Gerona, who envisioned divine interdictions as necessary for preparing the body in order to receive the soul that returns from the *devequt* experience. Cf. Idel, "Some Remarks on Ritual," pp. 125–127.

186. See Idel, *Mystical Experience,* pp. 180, 208 n. 18. See also by Albotini, *Sullam ha-ʿAliyah,* p. 69 and also the passage on p. 74, adduced immediately below.

187. Ibid., *Studies,* p. 94.

188. *Sullam ha-ʿAliyah,* p. 74 (Appendix 24).

189. On the ecstatic proclivities of R. Meshullam Zushia of Hanipoli as well as some stories about him; e.g. Buber, *Tales of Hasidim: The Early Masters,* pp. 236, 243, 249, 252, and below, chap. 5, n. 11.

190. *Qarov lehitbattel bi-meẓiy᾿ut.* This phrase occurs also *Be᾿er Moshe* fols. 9b, 85c. See also *Ma᾿or va-Shemesh* IV, fols. 25d–26a.

191. Ibid., fol. 8c (Appendix 25). This story recurs also in *Sefer Boẓina᾿ Qaddisha᾿* of R. Nathan Netaʿ ha-Kohen of Kalbiel (Brooklyn, 1984), fol. 12b. Compare also the description of the ecstatic state of R. Moshe Eliaqum's father, the Maggid of Kuznitz, in *Daʿat Moshe,* fol. 73a, to be discussed immediately. See also the interesting passage of R. Yisrael of Ryzhin, *ʿIrin Qaddishin,* fol. 34ab, and *Razin de-᾿Oraita᾿* (no pagination), where he describes R. Abraham Yehoshu᾿a of Apta's ability to predict the future by means of his feeling in his limbs. From the context of this story we may extrapolate that R. Yisrael himself would claim this ability for himself. Compare to ibid., fol. 53a.

192. See Shoḥat, "*ha-Ẓaddiq,*" pp. 302–3. See also below, chap. 6.

193. See *Be᾿er Moshe,* fols. 9b, 85c. See also more recently R. David Yiẓḥaq Aiziq Rabinowitz, *Ẓemaḥ David* (Brooklyn, 1941), fol. 65cd.

194. *Be᾿er Moshe,* fol. 127c.

195. Ibid. See also his *Daʿat Moshe,* fol. 73a.

196. It should be mentioned that in other passages in this book the more common version of the mystico-magic model is also represented. See *Be᾿er Moshe,* fols. 49c, 56a.

197. *Daʿat Moshe,* fol. 73a. See also the description of the state of ecstasy that is connected with *devequt,* in R. Yisrael of Kuznitz, *ʿAvodat Yisrael,* fol. 69ab.

198. R. Eleazar Ze᾿ev of Kretchinev, *Raza᾿ de-ʿUvda᾿, Shaʿar ha-᾿Otiyot,* fol. 20a.

199. "Mystical Man," pp. 404–5, 412, 414.

200. Ibid., pp. 383, 388, 403.

201. Ibid., p. 378. I wonder whether the two stages in the life of the Besht, and in the biography of Hasidic masters, the hidden, *hester*, and the manifest, *gillui*, do reflect, respectively the mystical and the magical—the latter being related to the open activity as a leader of the community. See Weiss, Studies, pp. 256–57.

202. On erotic imagery in Jewish mysticism in general, and on Hasidism in particular, see Georg Langer, *Die Erotik der Kabbala* (Prague, 1923), especially pp. 59–73; Idel, *Mystical Experience*, pp. 179–205; Charles Mopsik, *La lettre sur la sainteté* (Lagrasse, 1986); E. R. Wolfson, "Female Imagery of Torah: From Literary Metaphor to Religous Symbol," in *From Ancient Israel to Modern Judaism: Intellect in Quest of Understanding: Essays in Honor or Marvin Fox*, ed. J. Neusner, E. S. Frerichs, and N. M. Sarna (Atlanta, 1989), vol. 2, pp. 302–5; idem; "Walking as a Sacred Duty," David Biale, *Eros and the Jews* (Basic Books, New York, 1992), pp. 121–48. See also below, note 223.

203. See also Abraham Y. Heschel, *Kotzk, The Struggle for Integrity* (Tel Aviv, 1973) vol. 1, pp. 235–43 (Yiddish) and S. H. Dresner's English exposition of Heschel's view in *Shefa* II 2 (1981): 23–25 and below, chap. 4 n. 108–9.

204. *Toledot Ya ʿaqov Yosef*, fol. 92a; *Ktoneth Passim*, p. 120; *Ben Porat Yosef*, fol. 115c. See also Dresner, *Zaddik*, pp. 230, 307 n. 42, a fragmentary English translation of *Ben Porat Yosef.*

205. *Ben Porat Yosef*, fol. 115d. On the concept of "female waters" see Liebes, "The Messiah of the *Zohar*," p. 179, n. 314 and the forthcoming article of Elliot Wolfson, "On Becoming Female: Crossing Gender Boundaries in Kabbalistic Ritual and Myth." See also Idel, *Kabbalah: New Perspectives*, p. 57.

206. Page 168 (Appendix 26). Compare also to the view that the righteous contribute vitality and luminosity to God, precisely those terms that occur in connection to the drawing down processes. Cf. R. Moshe Eliaqum Beriʾah, *Beʾer Moshe*, fol. 93c and R. Qalonimus Qalman Epstein, *Maʾor va-Shemesh* II, fol. 7ab. See also below, n. 246.

207. See e.g., R. Naftali Ẓevi of Ropshitz, *ʾImrei Shefer* fol. 4a where the lower arousal is the preparation of the soul for the study of Torah and prayer, for their own sake, while the supernal arousal will emerge, namely that we shall receive an illumination from above. This situation is reminiscent of that described in Azulai's passage mentioned in n. 208 below. See also R. Naftali's *ʾAyalah Sheluḥah*, fol. 18b.

208. Commentary on *Massekhet ʾAvot*, fol. 2b. More on this passage see below, chap. 6, par. 3.

209. See R. Yiẓḥaq Shapira of Neskhiz, *Toledot Yiẓḥaq*, fol. 10c.

210. Ibid. See also in *Darkhei Ẓedeq*, fols. 4b–5a, where the person at prayer is told to visualize that the *Shekhinah* is enclothed in him during a prayer performed in deep devotion, *bi-devequt*. Is this directive part of the "feminine" feeling of the mystic, who identifies himself with the divine feminine in order to pray to the divine male? Compare also to *ʾOr ha-ʾEmet*, fols. 15a and especially 17c; see also Gries, *The Conduct Literature*, p. 330 and footnote 10.

211. *Toledot Yiẓḥaq,* fol. 10c on the cosmic implications of the drawing down see below, chap. 6, pars. 3–4.

212. Compare the text of R. Menaḥem Mendel of Vitebsk, analyzed in Idel, "Universalization and Integration," p. 40.

213. This phrase occurs also in the passage from the Great Maggid cited above, and it became a leitmotif of R. Elimelekh of Lisansk and even more of the Seer of Lublin: see also the similar discussion of R. Yisrael's son in his *Be᾽er Moshe,* fol. 92b.

214. *Zera᾽.* In a passage that occurs in the context of this quote, the Maggid of Kuznitz proposes a very interesting pun on the term *Zera᾿,* whose letters, when permuted, form the word *᾿Ezer,* namely helper or counterpart, an obvious allusion to Eve, namely the feminine aspect of man.

215. *᾽Ohev Israel,* fol. 81cd; compare also to R. Moshe Eliaqum Beri᾽ah's *Be᾽er Moshe,* fols. 91d–93a, ibid., *Binat Moshe,* fols. 14a, 16b; R. Reuven Horowitz, *Duda᾽im ba-Sadeh,* fols. 59ab, 79ab; R. Shimeon Ashkenazi of Yaroslav, *Naḥlat Shimeon,* fol. 20a and especially to R. Qalonimus Qalman Epstein, *Ma᾽or va-Shemesh* II, fol. 6ab, who interprets the Rabbinic description of man as *du-parzufin* in the light of the concepts discussed above. On the issue of healing by the *Ẓaddiq* see also R. Menaḥem Naḥum of Chernobyl, in Green, *Upright Practices,* pp. 156–57. The sexual designations of the two stages of the model is reminiscent of the way Heiler describes the mystical path as feminine and the prophetic one as masculine. See his *Prayer,* p. 146.

216. See Ronit Meroz, *Redemption in the Lurianic Teaching* (Ph.D. thesis, Jerusalem, 1988), pp. 97–98, 102, 104, 107 (Hebrew). Compare to R. Ze᾽ev Wolf of Zhitomir, *᾽Or ha-Me᾽ir,* fol. 213b.

217. This issue itself is hinted at by the Behst; see *Ben Porat Yosef,* fol. 115d.

218. See below, n. 246.

219. *Beḥi[nat] meqabbel.*

220. *Qedushat Levi,* fol. 66c (Appendix 28); see also ibid., fol. 65c. This tradition was cited and discussed by R. Moshe Eliaqum Beri᾽ah, *Da᾿at Moshe,* fol. 75a, and see also his relative, R. Elimelekh ben Ḥayyim of Kuznitz, a later descendant of the Kuznitzer Rebbe, in his *᾽Imrei ᾽Elimelekh* (Warsaw, 1876), fols. 6d, 136d. Compare also to a similar interpretation in a collection of the views of the Great Maggid, *Shemu᾿ah Tovah,* fols. 51a, 55b, 94ab and *᾽Or ha᾽Emet,* fol. 6d, R. Ze᾽ev Wolf of Zhitomir, *᾽Or ha-Meir,* fol. 16c, where an important quotation on our issue, in the name of the Great Maggid, occurs; R. Asher Ẓevi of Ostraha, *Ma᾿ayan ha-Ḥokhmah,* fols. 39b, 86ab and his text quoted below in Concluding Remarks, par. 2 and in R. Meir ha-Levi of Apta's *᾽Or la-Shamayim,* fol. 98d. See also below, n. 246.

221. See Idel, *Kabbalah: New Perspectives,* pp. 156–99.

222. See *᾽Or ha-᾽Emet,* fol. 6d: "*Hu᾽ Itbarakh kiveyakhol nuq[ba] le-ha-Ẓaddiqim.*" However, it should be mentioned that according to the same text, nowadays, after

the creation of the world, when someone performs the commandments he receives the "mind," *sekhel*, from God, and the relationship between the worshiper and God is, respectively, that of female and male. When someone performs a commandment he is conceived as a female, who gives birth to it. See also ibid., fols. 51b, 53ab.

223. See Yehuda Liebes, "A Treatise on Zoharic Language," by R. Wolf, son of R. Yonathan Eibeschuetz, on His Company and on the Secret of Salvation," *Qiryat Sefer* (1982): 177–78 (Hebrew). See also D. Biale, *Eros and the Jews*, pp. 121–48. See also below, chap. 4, n. 106 and note 202 above.

224. *Quietistic Elements*, pp. 75–76.

225. *Toledot ʾAharon* I, fol. 31c.

226. See also ibid., fols. 39c and 40a.

227. Ibid., fol. 39c.

228. Ibid., fol. 39d.

229. See especially ibid., II, fol. 4a–d; see also the very interesting discussion of R. Yiẓḥaq Aiziq Isaac Safrin of Komarno, *Heikhal ha-Berakhah* IV, fol. 12ab.

230. See par. 3 above the texts of R. Levi Yiẓḥaq of Berdichev and R. Abraham the Angel.

231. *Raẓo va-shov*.

232. This type of description occurs several times in this book; see e.g,. III, fol. 38b.

233. *Beḥinat ha-Yesh*.

234. On the revelation of the infinite God within His attributes in a context that is very similar to our discussion here, see R. Abraham the Angel, *Ḥesed la-ʾAvraham*, fols. 23d–24a.

235. Compare above, the quotation from *Qedushat Levi*, fol. 5b. See also R. Shneor Zalman's formulation in the same book, III, fol. 75d, where the brokenness of the heart is presented as the cause of the drawing down of remedies and blessings. See also the view that self-abnegation is the reason for drawing down from above in an anonymous Ḥabadic text, printed by Mondshein, *Migdal ʿOz*, p. 290, and ibid., p. 129.

236. *Me-ha-hishtalshelut*.

237. *Liqqutei Torah on the Song of Songs* IV, fol. 46ab (Appendix 29). The interpreted text is found in ibid., fol. 45ac. See also *Torah ʾOr*, fol. 99c. See also Elior, *The Theory of Divinity*, pp. 186–89, 358–59.

238. *Niddah*, fol. 31b. See *Liqqutei Torah*, fol. 46b and compare to the above quotations from the Hasidic sources.

239. See Tishby, *The Wisdom of the Zohar*, vol. 1, pp. 298–99. Interestingly enough, the single master that was described as the husband of the *Shekhinah*, in addi-

tion to the mythical figure of Moses, is R. Pinḥas of Koretz; see R. Yiẓḥaq Isaac Safrin of Komarno, *Netiv Miẓwoteikha,* p. 92, where R. Jacob Shimshon, a student of R. Pinḥas, describes his vision of the master.

240. See Liebes, "The Messiah of the *Zohar,*" pp. 205–7. As Elliot R. Wolfson has pointed out, in the theosophical Kabbalah it is possible to find also the myth of gender change as the male becomes female. On the description of the Ẓaddiq as female vis à vis God, who is portrayed as male, see his "Circumcision, Vision of God, and Textual Interpretation: From Midrashic Trope to Religous Symbol," *History of Religions* 27 (1987): 204–5 and Daniel Boyarin, "This We Know to Be the Carnal Israel: Circumcision and the Erotic Life of God and Israel," *Critical Inquiry* 18 (1992), p. 493–97.

241. Idel, *Mystical Experience,* pp. 179–227.

242. *ᶜibbur.*

243. Ms. Paris BN 777, pp. 46–47; ms. Muenchen 40, fol. 247ab. See Idel, *Mystical Experience,* pp. 193–94.

244. See his "The Song of Songs, Abulafia and the Alter Rebbe," *Jewish Review,* April–May, 1990: 10–11; ibid., "*Ḥotam Bolet Ḥotam Shoqeᶜa,* in the Teaching of Abraham Abulafia and the Doctrine of Ḥabad," Sinai 107 (1991): 54–57 (Hebrew).

245. On this issue I shall elaborate elsewhere; see meanwhile the parallel discussion of R. Yisrael of Kuznitz, *ᶜAvodat Yisrael* fol. 7b.

246. *ʾOr ha-ʾEmet,* fol. 51b (Appendix 30). On the question of theurgy and power see Idel, *Kabbalah: New Perspectives,* pp. 157–66. The same phenomenon of substituting a rabbinic theurgical term by *Taᶜanug* occurs also in the case of the view that Israel is providing sustenance to God, which becomes in Hasidism "Israel provides delight to God"; see *ʾOr ha-ʾEmet,* fol. 53c. According to the Besht, the intermittent coming close to God and the retreat, *raẓo va-shov,* are intended to continuously recreate the feeling of delight, that is "the quintessence of the worship to God," cf. *Toledot Yaᶜaqov Yosef,* fols. 92b, 139c; *Keter Shem Tov* I, fol. 16b. See also above the quotation of R. Levi Yiẓḥaq, in the name of the Great Maggid, beside n. 220 and *Toledot Yaᶜaqov Yosef,* fols. 86a (quoted below, Appendix A) and 170a, where the Besht is quoted as defining the *Ẓaddiq* as "someone who delights in the worship of God." See also Idel, *Kabbalah: New Perspectives,* pp. 150–51, p. 352 n. 366. See also above, n. 206 and Tishby-Dan, "Hasidism," p. 796; Schatz-Uffenheimer, *Quietistic Elements,* pp. 86–87, 92, 102. See also below, chap. 6 n. 42. Compare also to R. Aharon of Zhitomir, *Toledot ʾAharon* II, fol. 20c.

It should be mentioned that one of the texts of Abulafia dealing with the "delight" as part of the mystical experience, which was analyzed in my aforecited book, was preserved not only in the manuscripts of this work, but also in *Midrash Talpiyot,* fol. 22c, which quotes it from *Sefer ha-Peliyʾah* I, fol. 59a. This is a verbatim quotation from Abulafia's *Sefer Ḥayyei ha-Nefesh,* ms. Munchen 408, fol. 65a. This book of Abulafia indeed influenced *Sefer ha-Peliyʾah.* Therefore, the Hasidic masters had access, at least to *Sefer ha-Peliyʾah* and to *Midrash Talpiyyot,* where the passage on the delight, *taᶜanug,* involved in the mystical experiences was copied. On the whole issue of Abulafia's Kabbalah, see Idel, *Mystical Experience* pp. 186–87.

247. *Qedushat Levi,* fols. 118d, 119a; Matt, "*Ayin*" p. 145 and his important accompanying footnotes. The general impact of this important Kabbalistic book for Hasidism, and even for the Lurianic Kabbalah, still awaits a detailed analysis. Here I would like to note the extensive influence of this book on R. Yisrael, the son of R. Levi Yiẓḥaq of Berdichev. See his *Liqqutei Maharin* (Jerusalem, 1960), which is replete with quotations from this book. See also R. Jacob Joseph of Polonoy, *Ben Porat Yosef,* fol. 112cd, where he points out the source of one of the most important phases of the metaphysics of Hasidism, *koaḥ ha-poʿel be-nifʿal,* in this Commentary on *Sefer Yeẓirah.* For the importance of the theory of ʿAyin for the Great Maggid's theory of magic, see Weiss, *Studies,* p. 150.

248. *Ḥokhmot.*

249. *Koaḥ mukhan leqabbel ẓurot.* The phrase *koaḥ mukhan* as a description of the *hyle* is found in R. Shem Tov ben Shem Tov (the philosopher) in his commentary on the *Guide of the Perplexed* I, chap. 28. His view was copied by R. Barukh of Kossov, *ʿAmud ha-ʿAvodah,* fol. 25a. I wonder whether this phrase and its parallels do not reflect the Neoplatonic concept of intelligible matter; see John M. Dillon, "Solomon Ibn Gabirol's Doctrine of Intelligible Matter," in Goodman, *Neoplatonism in Jewish Thought,* pp. 61–76. See also the quotation of R. Menaḥem Naḥum, from anonymous books, to the effect that the *steresis* must precede existence, *havayah, Meʾor ʿEinayim,* p. 196. See also Weiss, *Studies,* pp. 150–51, where he explains the magical view of R. Ḥayyim Ḥaike of Amdura as related to changing the will of God, namely by drawing forth from the divine will a possibility that is actualized.

250. *Qedushat Levi,* fol. 6a–6b (Appendix 31). Compare also to R. Dov Baer of Miedzyrec, *Maggid Devarav le-ʾYaʿaqov,* pp. 68–69 where the "annihilation" ensures the descent of vitality.

251. See *Qedushat Levi,* fol. 72b.

252. In some instances, not only the ritual acts draw down the influx but also the human limbs that correspond to these religious deeds. This theme occurs in several treatments; see e.g., R. Abraham of Kalisk, *Ḥesed le-ʾAvraham,* fol. 8c. For more on this issue, see below, chaps. 4 par. 4; 5, par. 2.

253. *Qedushat Levi,* fol. 9b.

254. *Ḥesed le-ʾAvraham,* fol. 28a; see also fols. 17b, 21a.

255. *Liqqutei Torah* III, fol. 22c (Appendix 32).

256. *ʿAmud ha-ʿAvodah* fol. 44a. See also ibid., fols. 30d and 108bc. On fol. 30d, R. Barukh compares the *hiyuli* to the supernal light, which can receive all forms. See also the view that the *golem,* which means in some texts prime matter, stands for the highest hypostasis in R. Yiẓḥaq Aiziq of Komarno, *Noẓer Ḥesed,* pp. 90–91. See also Idel, *Golem,* pp. 145–47. It should be mentioned that this materialistic view of using the influx, as well as others (see e.g. R. Shemuel Shmelke of Nikolsburg, *Divrei Shemuel,* pp. 97–98, in a sermon delivered in 1777), demonstrate that the materialistic view of our model seems to predate, or at least to be independent of the writings and social conditions of R. Elimelekh of Lisansk. Especially important in our context is R.

Jacob Joseph of Polonoy's text, *Ben Porat Yosef,* fol. 53b, where the attraction of the "influx and money" *shefa ͑ u-mamon* is safeguarded by the creation of the speech and voice of the prayer. Therefore, in the other branch of Beshtian tradition, that of R. Jacob Joseph, the magical or materialistic views are also explicit. See also R. Ḥayyim of Chemovitz, *Be ͗er Mayyim Ḥayyim* I, fol. 8a and the very illuminating passage of R. Ze ͗ev Wolf of Zhitomir, *͗Or ha-Me ͗ir,* fol. 251d, where this student of the Great Maggid conditions the amount of the influx by the "greatness" of the pronounced letters. He mentions explicitly the letters of the word *Parnasah,* namely living which attracts the material influx. Compare to ibid., fols. 14c, 247b, 248a.

257. On this expression, see also *Pe ͗er la-Yesharim* (Jerusalem, 1921), fol. 12b and Gershom Scholem's remark in "The Controversy against Hasidism and Its Leaders in *Sefer Nezed ha-Dema ͑,*" *Ẓion* 20 (1955): 75, n. 10 (Hebrew).

258. See above, n. 153.

259. In the original, in Yiddish, *Er vet far schwarzt verin.*

260. *͑Irin Qaddishin,* fol. 53a. See also fol. 53d, where he asserts that the *Ẓaddiq* receives only in order to give to others, the distribution of the abundance being his delight. (See also his *Pe ͗er la-Yesharim,* fol. 55b.) From our point of view more interesting is the quotation in the name of his father, R. Shalom Shakhna, who is reported to have said that the *Ẓaddiq* who uses the chariot here below will become a chariot to God in the next world. Moreover, he continues, the *Ẓaddiq* uses the chariot in this world in order to be able to draw from the supernal worlds, which are, as I propose to understand the text, also a chariot. See ibid., fol. 54ab. Is the chariot understood as a talisman! In any case, we know that R. Yisrael used very luxurious chariots. Quoted in the name of the father, this concept seems to amount to a mystico-magical interpretation of the lifestyle of the son. See especially, his formulation of the nexus between the affluence of the *Ẓaddiq* and his drawing down the influx onto the world. *Knesset Yisrael,* fol. 18ab and Assaf, Rabbi Israel of Ruzhin, p. 179.

261. See however, Scholem, *Major Trends,* p. 337, "Israel of Rishin . . . is to put it bluntly, nothing but another Jacob Frank . . . but the secret of his power is the mystery of the magnetic and dominant personality and not that of the fascinating teacher." Some lines beforehand Scholem wrote about the "lust for power." See also Weiss, *Studies,* p. 261. More recently, Mendel Piekarz has formulated a very critical attitude to the "double standard ethic" of the Hasidic institution of the *Ẓaddiq* from its very beginning; see *Hasidism in Poland,* p. 168. It is not my task here to become involved in these kinds of considerations, but I assume that a better understanding of the manner the *Ẓaddiqim* understood their role may be connected to a better understanding of the mystico-magical model. See also Assaf, *Rabbi Israel of Ruzhin,* pp. 178–79.

262. See the story adduced by Samuel H. Dresner, *Levi Yizhak of Berditchev, Portrait of a Hasidic Master* (New York, 1974), pp. 132–33. See also the insistence of the Maggid of Kuznitz that only total effacement and consciousness of one's nothingness transforms him into a source of blessing for others; cf. *͑Avodat Yisrael,* fol. 25ab. On the Seer of Lublin's discussions on nothingness see also Elior, "Between *Yesh* and *Ayin,*" p. 411. See also Assaf, *Rabbi Israel of Ruzhin,* pp. 136–37.

263. On this figure, see Gedalyah Nigal, "On R. Aharon Shemuel ha-Kohen—One of the Studies of the Maggid of Miedzyrec," *Sinai* 78 (1976): 255–62 (Hebrew).

264. *Lesaggel.*

265. Using the image of Jacob's vision of the ladder in Genesis the author hints at the ascent of religious activity on high, and the descent of the influx afterward. This is quite an exceptional understanding of the ladder of ascent. Compare to Altmann, "The Ladder of Ascension" (chap. 6 n. 123) and R. Jacob Joseph of Polonoy, *Ben Porah Yosef,* fol. 53d.

266. *Ve᾽Ẓivah ha-Kohen,* p. 45 (Appendix 33). See also ibid., pp. 45, 52 where religious activity causes the ascent of the worlds to the Infinite and the reception of the vitality and influx. Interestingly enough, this view is presented as found in "books." The synthesis between the theurgical and the magical models is more apparent in ibid., pp. 109, 146, 150 where the theurgical activity precedes the magical one. See also above, n. 111.

267. p. 45. See also pp. 45–46, where the author maintains that the soul of man has to elevate herself (*lehagbiah*) from this world in order to come closer to holiness and vitality. Compare above, n. 88. See also two other important discussions on p. 46, where the ascent on high and the cleaving there are followed by the descent of the holiness upon the mystic. See also p. 47, where the assumption is that by performing the commandments someone brings down the influx and sustains thereby the world. The idea of becoming a pipe, or channel, for the descent of the vitality, which appears explicitly on this page, is not related to the idea of the *Ẓaddiq*. Even in the entourage of the figure that is considered to be the founder of the "material *Ẓaddiqism,*" R. Elimelekh of Lisansk, the assumption was that the influx from above can be reached by everyone who participates in the communal religious service; see R. Qalonimus Qalman Epstein, *Ma᾽or va-Shemesh* II, fol. 16a. See below, chap. 6, n. 4 and 102.

268. Weinstein and Bell, *Saints and Society,* p. 246.

269. Ibid., p. 265.

270. See his *Messianism, Mysticism, and Magic* [Chapel Hill, 1982] pp. 158–164.

NOTES TO CHAPTER 4

1. On Lurianic *kavvanot* versus Hasidic prayer, see Weiss, Studies, pp. 95–96; Schatz-Uffenheimer, *Quietistic Elements,* pp. 128–47, *Hasidism as Mysticism,* pp. 215–241. The Lurianic view of mystical prayer, which constitutes a very important factor in this system, has not been studied in great detail. See, for the time being, Roland Goetschel, "Le probleme de la *kawwanah* dans le *Yosher Lebab* d᾽Emmaneul Hay Ricchi (1937)" in Goetschel, ed. *Priére, Mystique, Judaisme,* pp. 207–24, Joseph Avivi, "Derushei Kavvanot le-Rabbi Yosef ibn Tabul," *Studies in Memory of the Rishon Le-Ẓion R. Yizhak Nissim,* ed. Meir Benayahu (Jerusalem, 1985), vol. 4, pp. 75–103 (Hebrew). On Hasidic prayer in general see Wertheimer, *Law and Custom,* pp. 83–109.

2. Weiss, *Studies,* p. 99. On Nathan of Gazza's abrogation of Lurianic *Kavvanot*

see also Scholem, *Sabbatai Ṣevi,* pp. 272, 277–78; ibid., *Messianic Idea,* pp. 102–3; Tishby, *Paths of Faith and Heresy,* pp. 224–25; Green, *Devotion and Commandment,* pp. 81–82, n. 43; Rapoport-Albert, "God and the Zaddik," pp. 315–25.

3. *Quietistic Elements,* p. 143, n. 57; *Hasidism as Mysticism,* p. 235, note 56. According to this scholar, ibid., p. 139, the reason for the rejection of the Lurianic mystical intentions is the quietist proclivity of the Hasidic masters.

4. Yehuda Liebes, "Shabbetai Ẓevi's Attitude towards His Own Conversion," *Sefunot* (N.S.) vol. 2 (17), ed. Y. Hacker (Jerusalem, 1983), p. 289, n. 148 (Hebrew); see also idem, "A Treatise Written in Zoharic Language by R. Wolf, the son of R. Yonathan Eibeschuetz, on his Group and the Secret of Redemption," *QS* 57 (1982): 377 (Hebrew).

5. See Piekarz, *The Beginning of Hasidism,* pp. 125–27, 335–36, where he deals with other types of critiques, mainly regarding the length of prayer when the *kavvanot* were performed, and Jacobs, *Hasidic Prayer,* pp. 83–84. For additional instances of rejecting Lurianic *kavvanot,* see Moshe Ḥallamish, "Luria's Status as an Halakhic Authority," eds. R. Elior-Y. Liebes, *Lurianic Kabbalah,* (Jerusalem, 1992), pp. 282–85 (Hebrew).

6. R. Elijah ha-Kohen, *Midrash Talpiyot,* fol. 162c–d. This work was already printed in 1736. See also the discussion below, n. 1221 and Heschel, *The Circle of the Baal Shem Tov,* p. 174, n. 82.

7. Compare R. Moshe Cordovero's view in *ʾOr Neʿerav* (Israel, 1965), p. 4 where he maintains that idle thoughts attack solely those who pray without *kavvanot.*

8. On the connection between R. Elijah and Sabbateanism, see Gershom Scholem, "R. Elijah ha-Kohen ha-Itamari and Sabbateanism," *Alexander Marx Festschrift* (New York, 1950), pp. 451–70 (Hebrew section).

9. Emden, *Mitpaḥat Sefarim,* p. 112 (see Appendix 1). See also Elozor Flekels, *Olas Zibbur* (Prague, 1787), fols. 29b–30a.

10. *ʾAVR.* It seems that Emden is alluding as well to the "limb," and it may be connected with his criticism of the Hasidic movements during prayer; compare to *Mitpaḥat Sefarim,* p. 78 (see Appendix 2). Compare also R. Moshe Cordovero's *Pardes Rimmonim* 32, chap. 1; 2, fol. 78c. See below, our discussion of the Hasidic conception, influenced by Cordovero, of the ascension of the spiritual forces of the sounds of prayer.

11. Compare R. Pinḥas Eliahu Hurwitz's assertion in *Sefer ha-Berit,* p. 284 (see Appendix 3). R. Pinḥas warmly recommends the Lurianic system of *Yiḥudim,* but has no detailed or elaborate description of it, and has to limit himself to the general knowledge of the Sefirotic world and the trance the soul has to pass through during its ecstatic ascent and descent. Like Emden, he concludes that "God desires (one's) heart." Interestingly enough, in his book *Taʿam ʿEẓo,* R. Pinḥas commented on the first part of Emanuel Ḥayy-Riqqi's *Mishnat Ḥasidim,* whereas the parts concerning prayer remained without his commentary.

12. R. Shemuel ben Eliezer of Kalvarija, *Darkhei No ʿam* (Koenigsberg, 1764), fol. 98a (see Appendix 4). On this author see Tishby, "The Messianic Idea," pp. 16–24; Piekarz, *The Beginning of Hasidism,* pp. 89–90, 153–64, 326–28. Cordoverian and Lurianic *kavvanot* were hinted at by the Sefirotic values written above the words of the prayers. The origin of this technique to allude to the Kabbalistic meaning of prayer is to be found in R. David Ben Yehudah he-Ḥasid's commentary on prayer *ʾOr Zaru ʿa*; see Idel, *Kabbalah: New Perspectives,* pp. 104–11.

13. Ibid. (see Appendix 5).

14. Complaints similar to those of R. Shemuel can be found also among the Hasidim, as R. Ẓevi Wolf of Zhitomir, one of the Great Maggid's disciples, attests (see Appendix 6); see *ʾOr ha-Meʾir,* fol. 132c. Compare below, the complaint of another Hasid, R. Eleazar, the son of R. Elimelekh of Lisansk; see n. 88, 90.

15. For an analysis of R. Ḥayyim's view of prayer see Emmanuel Etkes, "R. Ḥayyim of Volozhin's Doctrine and Activity as a Reaction of the Mitnagdic Society towards Hasidism" *PAAJR* 39–39 (1972): 40–42 (Hebrew); Lamm, *Torah Lishmah,* pp. 76–79; Benjamin Gross, "La priére dans le Nefesh Ha-Ḥayyimʾ de R. Ḥayyim de Volozhin" in Goetschel, ed. *Priére, Mystique et Judaïsme,* pp. 225–44.

16. R. Ḥayyim of Volozhin, *Nefesh ha-Ḥayyim,* fol. 25b (see Appendix 7). Another interesting passage, that concurs with the above, is found in R. Yiẓḥaq ben Eliezer, *Sefer ha-Gan ve-Derekh Moshe* (Duehrenfurt, 1818) col. 7, fol. 3a and quoted in *Liqqutei ʾAmarim,* fol. 15c, where a short prayer to be recited before the regular prayer is adduced, to the effect that "because of the greatness of the deficiency of our knowledge, there is no way for us to direct our thought to the plain meaning of the words, *a fortiori* to direct it to the secret of the *Sefirot,* and the *kavvanah* etc." This prayer is, reportedly printed also in *Liqqutei Ẓevi* and in some prayerbooks. The assumption is that despite the fact that the prayer does not know the mystical *kavvanot,* by this short acknowledgement all the *kavvanot* introduced by the men of the Great Assembly will be performed during his prayer, since the words act in the way a medicine does, namely also without the knowledge of their inner potentialities.

17. Ibid., fol. 25d (see Appendix 8), fol. 26b (Appendix 9). Cf. also fols. 26c, 27a. A very similar stand was that of R. Ezekiel Landau in his polemic against Hasidic prayer; see Jacobs, *Hasidic Prayer,* pp. 146–48.

18. *Hitqashsherut,* attachment, apparently has two possible meanings: (a) cleaving to articulate words (this problem will be clarified below); (b) spiritual concentration on the pronounced words. See also below, Appendix A. On this matter, it seems that there is no divergence between the views of the Besht and the Great Maggid and that of R. Pinḥas of Koretz; compare, however, to Heschel, *The Circle of the Baal Shem Tov,* p. 20–21. In general, the approach to Hasidism in the teachings of these masters differ substantially: see Green, *Tormented Master,* pp. 97–98.

19. For Weiss's letter, I substitute "pronounced letter" for reasons that will be elucidated in the following discussions; see especially n. 45 below.

20. R. Dov Baer of Miedzyrec, *ᵓOr ha-ᵓEmet,* fol. 77b; idem., *Liqqutei Yeqarim,* fol. 67a (see Appendix 10); R. Aharon of Apta, *Ner Miẓwah,* fol. 6a, Buber, *Origin and Meaning,* pp. 136–37; Green, "Discovery and Retreat" pp. 110–11. See also the similar view of R. Abraham the Angel, the son of the Great Maggid, printed by Mondshein, *Migdal ᶜOz,* pp. 196–97. Cf. the translation by Weiss (slightly modified by this author), *Studies,* pp. 106–7; see Schatz-Uffenheimer, *Quietistic Elements,* p. 131; compare also to *Maggid Devarav le-Yaᶜaqov,* p. 324 (Appendix 11). See also our discussion below, and the Besht's view quoted in R. Menaḥem Naḥum of Chernobyl's *Meᵓor ᶜEynayim,* p. 104 (see Appendix 12) and R. Jacob Joseph of Polonoy, *Ben Porat Yosef,* fol. 9a. See also the view quoted by R. Qalonimus Qalman Epstein, in the name of R. Elimelekh of Lisansk, that attachment during prayer causes "the *kavvanot* and unifications to be effected automatically." *See Maᵓor va-Shemesh* 5, fol. 31b (translated by Jacobs, *Hasidic Prayer,* p. 80), and ibid., 5, fol. 13a. See also Buber, *Origin and Meaning,* pp. 136–37.

An incisive critique of the use of the Lurianic *Siddur,* followed by the quotation of Cordovero's definition of the *kavvanah* and the view of the Great Maggid, which will be described below, is found in R. Aharon of Zhitomir, *Toledot ᵓAharon* II, fol. 36b. Another interesting comment regarding the Lurianic *kavvanot* is transmitted by R. Moshe Eliaqum Beriᵓah, in the name of his father the Maggid of Kuznitz; the latter asserted that the extant kavvanot of Luria represent just one set that are pertinent for one day, and they are supposed to change each and every day. In order to become a true Lurianic Kabbalist one has to receive a new revelation every day. Thus, though revering Luria, his *kavvanot* were put on a pedestal of inaccessibility. See *Beᵓer Moshe,* fol. 182bc. Compare also to the view of R. Dov Baer of Lubavitch, translated in Jacobs, *Hasidic Prayer,* pp. 91–92 and compare to Elior, *The Theory of Divinity,* pp. 318–19. See also Idel, *Kabbalah: New Perspectives,* pp. 247–48.

21. On the theurgic forces of the words of prayer see *Nefesh ha-Ḥayyim,* fol. 25c (see Appendix 13).

22. *Epistle on the Ascent of the Soul, Shivhei ha-Besht,* ed. Mondshein, pp. 235–36 (see Appendix 14). See also R. Israel of Kuznitz, *ᶜAvodat Israel,* fol. 97a. Compare Jacobs, *The Hasidic Prayer,* pp. 75–77, 97; R. Menaḥem Naḥum of Chernobyl, *Meᵓor ᶜEynayim* p. 161; R. Abraham of Kalisk in *Peri ha-ᵓAreẓ, Epistles,* p. 81 (see Appendix 15); R. Qalonimus Qalman Epstein, *Maᵓor va-Shemesh,* 1, fol. 21ab; R. Asher Ẓevi of Ostraha, *Maᶜayan Ḥokhmah,* fol. 84c, Yehudah Arieh Leib of Gur, *Sefat ᵓEmet,* 4. fol. 33d (see Appendix 16) and fol. 33bc; R. Yiẓḥaq Aiziq Safrin of Komarno, *Heikhal ha-Berakhah,* 3, fol. 25c. Compare to Cordovero's view cited in n. 95 below and Introduction, n. 85. On the infinities related to single letters, see Idel, "Infinities of Torah," pp. 148–49 and the pertinent footnotes. See also below, Appendix B, n. 5. It seems that we have a Kabbalistic perception akin to the atomistic and, later on, Neoplatonic concept of 'all in all'; see Idel, "Differing Conceptions," p. 189, n. 255. On sounds and Renaissance magic see Walker, *Spiritual and Demonic Magic,* pp. 8–10. On the integration of the soul see Idel, "Universalization and Integration," p. 200, n. 49.

23. On this author see Piekarz, *The Beginning of Hasidism,* pp. 85–86.

24. R. Nathan-Neta of Sieniawa, *ʿOlat Tamid* I, fol. 33b (see Appendix 17); cf. also ibid., fols. 47b–48a.

25. On the parallelism between the 248 limbs and 248 letters of *Qeriʾat Shemaʿ* see Israel Ta-Shema, "'*El Melekh Neʾeman*: The Metamorphosis of a Minhag," *Tarbiẓ* 39 (1970): 184–94; ibid., 40 (1981): 105–6 (Hebrew); Elliot Wolfson, "Anthropomorphic Imagery and Letter Symbolixm in the *Zohar*," *JSJT* 8 (1989): 161–63 (Hebrew). See also above chap. 3 n. 111.

26. For example, the connection between the emergence of the voice out of the soul and love has interesting parallels in *Shemuʿah Tovah*; and I shall elaborate elsewhere on the significance of this link.

27. R. Nathan-Netaʿ, *ʿOlat Tamid* I fol. 52b (see Appendix 18); cf. also with fol. 68b (Appendix 19).

28. Ibid., I fol. 57a–b (see Appendix 20). The occurrence of the term *qedushah* may be the result of the influence of Lurianic Kabbalah, probably via R. Emanuel Ḥayy-Rikki's *Mishnat Hasidim, Masekhet Tefillat ha-ʿAsiyah,* chap. 1. See above chap. 3, note 81.

29. *Maggid Devarav le-Yaʿaqov,* p. 71 (see Appendix 21). Compare to the statement adduced in the name of the Besht in R. Aharon of Apta, *ʾOr ha-Ganuz,* fol. 18a that "the letters of the Torah are vessels and chambers of God, and by means of the *kavvanah,* man draws down within them the emanation of the supernal light" and ibid., *Ner Miẓwah,* fol. 6a. See also in the book of a student of the Besht, R. Moshe of Dolina's *Divrei Moshe,* fol. 46d, where a similar interpretation of the word *chamber* is offered. Cf. R. Menaḥem Naḥum of Chernobyl in *Meʾor ʿEynayim,* p. 121 (Appendix 22). On God's immanence in the letters of Torah, see ibid., *Meʾor ʿEynayim,* pp. 112, 122, and R. Zeʾev Wolf of Zhitomir, *ʾOr ha-Meir,* fol. 14cd, where the Hebrew letters are conceived as houses and boxes. Compare to the view of R. Joseph of Hamadan, a late thirteenth-century Kabbalist (see Appendix 23). See Idel, "The Concept of the Torah," p. 67 where the sources and general conceptual context of this passage are discussed. See also R. Menaḥem Mendel of Vitebsk, *Peri ha-ʾAreẓ,* fol. 10b and below, Concluding Remarks, par. 3.

30. On the specific meanings of the "chambers" see the discussion below on pronounced letters as "palaces."

31. "Godhead" stands here for the term *ruḥaniyyut ha-Sefirot* discussed later on. See also R. Asher Ẓevi of Ostraha, *Maʿayan ha-Ḥokhmah,* fol. 39b, where he speaks about the drawing down of *ʾElohit,* apparently a form of *ʾElohut,* into letters. It is interesting to remark that the Great Maggid consciously refrains from using the expression, "spiritual force of Sefirot" or "of sounds," notwithstanding their occurrence in both the sayings of the Besht and R. Jacob Joseph of Polonoy; see *Toledot Yaʿaqov Yosef,* fols. 3a, 6a, 169a. He mainly speaks of "spiritual force" without any further qualification. We can, however, conclude that the latter master not only quotes texts important for the unearthing of the sources of Hasidism but also tends to preserve the authentic terminology, which had already been obliterated in the homiletic discussion of the Great Maggid.

32. See Jacobs, *The Hasidic Prayer,* p. 42.

33. See n. 34, 86 below.

34. Jacobs, ibid., pp. 41–42 and n. 14 above. See also Loewenthal, *Communicating the Infinite,* pp. 158–59, Krassen, "*Devequt and Faith,*" pp. 88, 136–47. Interestingly enough, a disciple of R. Elimelekh, R. Qalonimus Qalman Epstein of Cracow, reports that his master did not pray using the Lurianic *kavvanot,* though he used the prayer book of Luria, since it was typographically better as regards the letters of the Divine Name. See *Ma᾽or va-Shemesh* 5, fols. 13a, 31b, Weiss, *Studies,* pp. 116–17. For another explanation for the use of the Lurianic *nusaḥ* of prayer, which disregards theurgical prayer, see R. Ẓadoq ha-Kohen, *Quntres Divrei Ḥalomot,* printed together with his *Resisei Lailah* (Benei Beraq, 1967), p. 185. Nevertheless, the printing of various prayer books with Lurianic *Kavvanot* in the eighteenth century is an issue that has to be examined in detail as it has been neglected by modern studies of Hasidic prayer. See also the attitude of the Rabbi of Zanz, R. Ḥayyim, who declared that through the recitation of the first verse of the Eighteen Benedictions he could achieve whatever was been achieved by the Kabbalists who used the *Kavvanot* for three hours; cf. R. Eliezer Ze᾽ev of Kretchinev, *Raza᾽ de-ᶜUvda᾽, Shaᶜar ha-᾽otiot,* p. 47. Even more extreme is the critique, attributed by an opponent to Hasidism, R. Ḥayyim Ḥaike of Amdura, addressed to those who pray with Lurianic kavvanot; they were reportedly described as *narin, shwentz* and *epicurus,* namely "stupid, bigots, and heretical." See R. David of Makov, *Shever Posheᶜim,* in Wilensky, *Hasidism and Mitnaggedim,* II, p. 165.

35. For example, Cordovero's commentary on liturgy *Tefillah le-Moshe* and R. Isaiah Horowitz's *Shaᶜar ha-Shamayim* or R. Nathan Netaᶜs *ᶜOlat Tamid.* It is strange that these, as well as other commentaries on Jewish liturgy, in existence long before Hasidism, were not taken into consideration by modern research on the Hasidic way of prayer. It is an important desideratum of the proper study of Hasidism to peruse these commentaries as possible sources of inspiration for the Hasidic masters; see Moshe Idel, "Kabbalistic Prayer and Colors," *Approaches to Judaism in Medieval Times,* ed. David R. Blumenthal, (Atlanta, Georgia, 1988), vol. 3, pp. 17–19.

36. See e.g. Sack, "The Influence of Cordovero on Seventeenth-Century Jewish Thought," pp. 365–79; ibid., "Prayer," pp. 5–12, and Krassen, "*Devequt*" *and Faith,* pp. 149, 162–87.

37. See the commentaries on the alphabet found in *BT. Shabbat,* fol. 104a–b, *᾽Otiyot de-Rabbi ᾽Aqiva* in its various versions, as well as the voluminous Kabbalistic literature on this subject which deserves a comprehensive monograph. See for the time being Elias Lipiner's pioneering study, *Ideologia del Alfabeto Hebreo* (Buenos Aires, 1967) (Yiddish) [and see now the expanded Hebrew translation *Ḥazon ha-᾽Otiyot* (Jerusalem, 1989)]. Cf. Elliot R. Wolfson, "Anthropomorphic Imagery and Letter Symbolism in the *Zohar,*" *JSJT* 8 (1989): 147–81 (Hebrew); ibid., "Letter Symbolism and Merkavah Imagery in the *Zohar, ᶜAlei Shefer: Studies in the Literature of Jewish Thought Presented to Rabbi Dr. Alexandre Safran* (Bar-Ilan, 1990), 195–236 (English section). On the monadic perception of letters in *Heikhalot* literature see also Karl Erich Groezinger, "The Names of God and the Celestial Powers: Their Function and Meaning in the Hekhalot Literature," *JSJT* 6 (1987): 53–69 (English section).

38. See Rachel Elior (ed.), *Heikhalot Zutarti, JSJT* suppl. 1 (1982), 28 (Appendix 24). The same phrase occurs in *Havdalah de-Rabbi ʿAqiva*; see the edition of Gershom Scholem in *Tarbiẓ* 50 (1980–81): 255, as well as the parallel sentence on p. 256. On the link between writing Arabic letters as separate characters and magic, see E. Doutté, *Magie et Religion dans l'Afrique du Nord* (Algier, 1908), p. 174. On concentration on a single letter of a prayer as a mystical practice see the text of *Heikhalot* literature printed in Elior, ibid., p. 36 (Appendix 25). R. Ishmael was the recipient of this practice. Interestingly enough, R. Aqiva, his contemporary, is reported to have also dealt with meditation upon separate letters; see *ʾAvot de-R. Nathan,* chap. 6.

39. *Pesiqta Rabbati,* edited by M. Freidmann (Jerusalem, 1963), fol. 104a (see Appendix 26). See Scholem, "The Name of God," pp. 169–70, n. 44.

40. Ms. Vatican 228, fol. 99b (see Appendix 27). See also Scholem (n. 38 above), p. 254, n. 14 and the text printed by G. Scholem, *Kitvei Yad be-Qabbalah* (Jerusalem, 1930), p. 217. On monadic views in early Kabbalah see Idel, "Reification of Language" p. 59.

41. Ms. Roma-Angelica, 38, fol. 6a; ms. München, 285, fol. 10a (see Appendix 28) and Idel, *Language, Torah and Hermeneutics,* pp. 106–7. Weiss, *Studies,* p. 104, remarks, *en passant,* that the Besht's method "is not far from the medieval technique of Abraham Abulafia," without any further elaboration. Another illuminating term was proposed by Shalom Rosenberg in his paper "Prayer and Jewish Thought—Trends and Problems," in *Prayer in Judaism: Continuity and Change,* edited by G. H. Cohen (Ramat Gan, 1978), p. 97: "The mystical prayer sometimes caused the disintegration of the text" (Hebrew). On the atomistic view of letters see R. Cadiou, "Atomes et elements graphiques," *Bulletin de l'association Guillaume Budé* (October, 1958), pp. 54–65. Compare also to R. Nathan Shapira of Cracow, *Megalleh ʿAmuqot,* ed. Shalom Weiss (Benei Beraq, 1982) 2, pp. 35–36 where the assumption is that each of the twenty-two letters of the alphabet consists of the divine Name. Immediately beforehand and afterward, pp. 35–36, this Kabbalist mentions that there are pipes that come from each letter, obviously influenced by Cordovero. A similar view occurs also in the other version of this book (Jerusalem, 1981) fols. 12d–13a. These two books are additional channels for the possible influence of Cordovero's view of language on Hasidic sources. This whole concept was accepted by R. Shelomo Rocca from *Megalleh ʿAmuqot,* in his *Kavvanat Shelomo,* fol. 78c. Although this is a book deeply influenced by Luria's theory of *kavvanot,* Cordovero's influence is nevertheless conspicuous in several instances. See also below, ch. 6, note 85. See also the very interesting discussion of R. Ḥayyim of Chernovitz, *Beʾer Mayyim Ḥayyim* I, fol. 8d.

42. The meaning of the "vision" of the "force" is vague, and seems to suggest that the division of words into letters is connected with a certain kind of contemplation, and probably with letters and not sounds. This may be compared to the Hasidic contemplation that attends the perception of the spiritual force inherent in the letters.

43. Abraham Abulafia, *ʾOẓar ʿEden Ganuz,* ms. Oxford-Bodleiana 1580, fol. 172b (Appendix 29). For the context of this sentence see Idel, *Language, Torah and Hermeneutics,* pp. 106–7. Compare also to *Shaʿarei Ẓedeq,* written by an anonymous

Kabbalist in Abulafia's circle (see Appendix 30) (ms. British Library Or. 10809, Gaster 954, fol. 19b; now in print, pp. 28–30.) See also above, chap. 2, par. 2.

44. Cf. Idel, ibid., pp. 107–9.

45. In Hebrew, as well as in Arabic, the term *ʾot* stands for both the written and vocal forms of the letters; see Georges Vajda, "Les Lettres et les sons de la langue arabe dʾaprés Abu-Hatim al-Razi," *Arabica* 8 (1961): 114–15, n. 3. Given the magical characteristics of some of the texts discussed below, it is obvious that the pronunciation of the letters is strictly necessary in order to achieve the aim of prayer. For the magical features of the articulate form see the interesting passage on the peculiar power of the Egyptian language when spoken; William Scott (ed.), *Hermetica* (Oxford, 1924), vol 1, pp. 264–65. For more on *ʾot,* see below, chap. 6 par. 3 beside n. 40.

46. See Idel, *Mystical Experience,* p. 26 (see Appendix 31). Two close parallels are quoted, see pp. 24–26, and see also in *Ner ʿElohim,* a treatise from Abulafia's school, ms. Munchen, 10, fol. 164b (see Appendix 32). Compare, especially to the interesting passage from Abulafia's *Gan Naʿul,* ms. Munchen 58, fol. 335b, where he discusses the way of achieving prophecy, or according to another version, the prophetic comprehension, by means of letters (*ʾOtiyot*) the attributes of numbers (*Middot ha-Sefirot*) and seals (*Ḥotamot*), in order to draw down by their means the supernal, divine forces and cause them to dwell here below on earth. This text was copied in *Sefer ha-Peliyʾah* I, fol. 80a. Compare also to the passage from Abulafia's *Mafteaḥ ha-Sefirot,* cited below, Appendix A. See also Scholem, "The Name of God," pp. 185–86.

47. See ms. Vatican 528, fol. 71b and Idel, *Mystical Experience,* p. 26 (Appendix 33). The creation referred to here is that of the *Golem.* On this issue see Scholem, *On the Kabbalah,* pp. 169–204 and Idel, *Golem,* pp. 96–118. Compare the quotation from Abulafia's *ʾOr ha-Sekhel,* cited below, n. 48, where the drawing downwards of supernal force by pronunciation of letters is obvious. See also the previous footnote, the text from Abulafia's *Gan Naʿul.* On magic combined with prophecy, i.e., the highest mystical state, which is reached according to Abulafia by permutation of the letters, see Idel, "The Study Program," pp. 320–21.

48. Abulafia *ʾOr ha-Sekhel,* ms. Vatican 233, fol. 110b (see Appendix 34). On the significance of this text, see Idel, *Mystical Experience,* pp. 62–63, and n. 124 below, as well as Appendix A, n. 27. On the soul as receiving the supernal force, see R. Abraham ibn Ezra's Long Commentary on Exodus 3, 15 and 4. Bahya ben Asher's introduction to his *Commentary on Torah,* edited by Ch. D. Chavel (Jerusalem, 1981) vol. 1, p. 3. Abulafia's passage was quoted verbatim by Cordovero in *Pardes Rimmonim* XXI, chap. 1; 1, fol. 97ab; see below, n. 123. See also *Shelah* III, fols. 183b–184a (*Torah shebi-khetav,* par. Reʾeh). Cf. our discussion above, chap. 2, par. 2. See also Cordovero's *Derishot,* p. 80, who combines Abulafia's letter-magic as expounded in *ʾOr ha-Sekhel* with talismanic issues and amulets. Another important passage of Abulafia's, where the drawing down of the influx is discussed, is found in his *Sefer Shomer Miẓwah,* Ms. Paris BN 853, fol. 48b.

49. See Idel, *Mystical Experience,* pp. 37–40 and n. 194 below.

50. See Idel, *Abraham Abulafia,* pp. 77–78. I hope to analyze this important treatise in a separate study; see meanwhile Moshe Idel, "Ramon Lull and Ecstatic Kabbalah," *Journal of the Warburg and the Courtauld Institutes* 51 (1988): 170–74. This work should be compared with the views of R. Yehudah ben Nissim ibn Malka, where the process of divination by astral *hayakil* is mentioned as well as talismanic practices; see Georges Vajda, "La doctrine astrologique de Juda ben Nissim ibn Malka," *Homenaje a Millas Vallicrosa* (Madrid-Barcelona, 1956), vol. 2, pp. 483–500. The same author describes permutations of letters in a context dealing with the worship of *hayakil*; see Nicolas Sed, "Le *Sefer ha-Razim* et al methode de 'Combinations de Lettres'," *REJ* 130 (1971): 295–304. Since this thinker wrote in the middle of the thirteenth century, he may well be one of the first Kabbalists who offered a synthesis between the theory of combination of letters and astro-magic theories. See Moshe Idel, "The Beginning of Kabbalah in North Africa? A Forgotten Document by R. Yehuda ben Nissim ibn Malka," *Pe ᶜamim* 43 (1990): 4–15 (Hebrew).

51. Ms. Paris BN 848, fol. 23b (see Appendix 35). Compare also n. 86, 96 below and above, chap. 2 par. 7, on the texts regarding the mystico-magical model in ecstatic Kabbalah.

52. The monadic view of letters is also obvious in this work; see e.g., ms. Paris BN 848, fol. 32b (Appendix 36).

53. Compare to Abulafia, *ᵓOr ha-Sekhel,* ms. Vatican 233, fol. 110b. Concerning the movements of the head in accordance with the places of the Hebrew vowels, see the passage by Abulafia in Appendix 37. See Idel, *Mystical Experience,* pp. 28–29. It is worth noting the similar usage of the verb *mashakh* in order to convey the operation of drawing downward the supernal influx onto the mystic. Compare also the earlier texts belonging to the school of Kabbalists in Gerona; see R. Ezra of Gerona's Commentary on the Talmudic Aggadot in *Liqqutei Shikheḥah u-Feah* (Ferrara, 1556), fol. 7b; R. Azriel's *Commentary on the Talmudic Aggadot,* ed. I. Tishby (Jerusalem, 1945), p. 40, where the descent of prophecy is described as *hamshakhah.* See also R. Jacob ben Sheshet's *Sefer ha-ᵓEmunah ve-ha-Bittaḥon,* ed. Ch. D. Chavel, *Kitvei ha-Ramban* (Jerusalem, 1978), vol 2, p. 370 and n. 58 below. On the usage of *hamshakhah,* see also Idel, *Studies,* p. 150, n. 53 and also n. 19 above and the texts referred to in notes 51, 129, 158, 161, 165, 182, 185, and 196 below. It is worth remarking that the term *hamshakhah* occurs several times in *Sha ᶜarei Ẓedeq,* an anonymous treatise from Abulafia's school; see ms. Jerusalem Heb. 8° 148, fols. 33a, 55b, 60a–b, 63a, 65a, and especially fol. 59b (now in print p. 22) where the phrase *hamshakhat ha-maḥashavah* is found. See n. 58 below. This phrase apparently influenced by R. Ḥayyim Vital's *Sha ᶜarei Qedushah* III, 6, p. 106 where Vital describes the descent of the (supernal) thought as the result of the use of *Yiḥudim* and *kavvanot;* see Werblowsky, *Joseph Karo,* pp. 74–76. This phrase recurs in the Hasidic terminology.

54. Ms. New York, JTS (Adler col.) 1653, no pagination (see Appendix 38). Compare also R. Abraham Yagel's view at the end of his treatise *Bat Sheva ᶜ,* ms. Oxford-Bodleiana 1306, fol. 85b (see Appendix 39). Therefore, the natural magic is the preparation of the matter by pronunciation of Divine Names and permutations of letters in

order to receive the supernal influence. See Ruderman, *Kabbalah, Magic and Science,* p. 32, 110–11.

55. Pines, "Shi^{c}ite Terms and Conceptions" pp. 196–97. On the magical meaning of the terms *ruḥaniy* and *ruḥaniyyut* in Jewish sources, see Idel, "The Study Program," pp. 310–11, n. 69; 319–20.

56. On drawing the spiritual force downward, see Idel, "The Magical and Neoplatonic Interpretations," pp. 201–4; Shlomo Pines, "Le *Sefer ha-Tamar* et les *Maggidim*" in *Hommage Georges Vajda,* edited by G. Nahon and Ch. Touati (Louvain, 1980), pp. 336–37, 353–57. See also chap. 2, n. 119. It is interesting to point out that "spiritual force"—*ruḥaniyyut*—is tantamount, in Cordoverian as well as Hasidic texts, to "light." See the view of the *ruhani* as light in Sabbean texts; Yves Marquet, "Sabéens et Iḥwan al-Safa," *Studia Islamica* 24 (1964): 64 and cf. Cordovero, *Pardes Rimmonim* XI, chap. 2; 1, fol. 62a. See also Pines, "On the Term Ruḥaniyy*ut* and Its Sources," pp. 514. Interestingly enough, R. Levi Yiẓḥaq of Berdichev uses several times the phrase *ᵓOr ve-ḥiyyut* as pointing to immanence; see his *Qedushat Levi,* e.g., fols. 63c–64b.

57. Idel, *Studies,* pp. 91–101, 112–19.

58. R. Yiẓḥaq of Acre, *ᵓOẓar Ḥayyim* ms. Moscow-Guenzburg 775, fol. 1a (Appendix 40). See above chap. 2, par. 2. See also n. 53 above, and see R. Yiẓḥaq's view in his comments on R. Yehudah ben Nissim ibn Malka's *Commentary on Pirqei de-R. ᵓEliezer* (Appendix 41). Cf. Georges Vajda, "Les Observations critiques dᵓIsaac dᵓAcco (?) sur les ouvrages de Juda ben Nissim Ibn Malka," *REJ* 115 (1956), 66. Interestingly enough, here the very fact that someone contemplates the divine issues enables him to attract a supernal influx by means of his thought. See also Vajda, "Les Observations," p. 67 (Appendix 42). See also R. Yiẓḥaq of Acre's *ᵓOẓar Ḥayyim,* ms. Moscow-Guenzburg 775, fols. 40a, 44b, 67b, and in particular fol. 7a, where the author describes the state when the soul is enclothed by "the spiritual force of the intellect" (Appendix 43).

59. Ibid., fol. 2a (Appendix 44).

60. The term *ruḥaniyyut* and its derivatives occur several times in R. Yiẓḥaq of Acre's texts: see Idel, *Studies,* p. 150, n. 56 and *ᵓOẓar Ḥayyim* (n. 58 above), fol. 46b (Appendix 45) and ibid., fol. 35b. See also n. 58 above and R. Yiẓḥaq of Acre's *Meᵓirat ᵓEynayim,* pp. 222–23.

61. See Gershom Scholem, "From Philosopher to Kabbalist—The Kabbalistic Legend on Maimonides," *Tarbiẓ* 6 (1935): 338–39 (Hebrew).

62. *Ḥemdah Genuzah,* ed. Z. Edelmann (Koenigsburg, 1856), vol. 1, p. 43 (Appendix 46). This text was also printed in a famous collection of magical traditions compiled by R. Abraham Hamoi, *Liderosh ᵓElohim* (Livorno, 1879) fols. 19b–20a. Other passages in this compilation may reflect also traces of the influence of ecstatic Kabbalah; see above, chap. 2, n. 73, 360.

63. This epistle is closely connected, as Edelmann has already recognized, to the pseudo-ibn Ezra *Sefer ha-ᶜAẓamim,* one of the most important Jewish texts dealing with astral magic, which several times uses the term *ruḥaniyyut* and also mentions the divine

names. On the influence of this work, see Idel, "The Magical and Neoplatonic Interpretations" p. 210. This epistle is probably one of the earliest testimonies to the substantial interaction between the concept of permutation of letters from the circle of Abraham Abulafia and astral magic.

64. See the texts referred to in the studies mentioned in n. 56 above, and our discussion on R. Shem Tov ibn Shem Tov's *Sefer ha-ʾEmunot* below.

65. Idel, "The Study Program," pp. 310–12, 319–29.

66. The original Hebrew text is printed in Idel, "The Magical and Theurgical Interpretation," p. 41. See also p. 39.

67. See also Idel, "The Magical and Neoplatonic Interpretations," pp. 207–8; see also pp. 209–10, where texts dealing with the Hebrew language in astrological contexts are adduced.

68. See Alemanno, *Shaʿar ha-Ḥesheq,* fol. 38b (Appendix 47). I could not locate the occurrence of any such phrase in ibn Latif's extant works. Alemanno, nevertheless, was well acquainted with the former's works: see Idel "The Study Program," p. 309, n. 64.

69. Yoḥanan Alemanno, ms. Oxford 2234, fol. 95b (Appendix 48). This is a note added by Alemanno on the margin of an astrological quotation; its context is examined at length in Idel, "Hermeticism and Judaism," pp. 69–70.

70. Ms. Paris BN 849, fol. 77b (Appendix 49). It is important to remark that the context is evidently influenced by Abulafian views, including the permutation of letters.

71. Presumably the patriarch Abraham, to whom *Sefer Yeẓirah* was ascribed.

72. I.e., the five vowels.

73. R. Shem Tov ben Shem Tov, *Sefer ha-ʾEmunot,* fol. 98b (see Appendix 50). Compare also fols. 26b–27a where an intermediary stage between cleaving and pronunciation of letters is indicated; the prophet conceives spiritual and subtle letters that become articulated, turning into vessels for the spiritual force (see Appendix 51). See also n. 120 below. The perception of the letters as talismans, capable of receiving and even attracting supernal influx, may be the result of the influence of Arabic sources; although no particular text discussing this view is known to me, it is disapprovingly mentioned by Ibn Khaldun in his *Muqqadimah—An Introduction to History,* trans. Franz Rosenthal (Princeton, 1958), vol. 3, p. 174: "It has been thought that this activity (i.e., letter magic) and the activity of people who work with talismans are one and the same thing. This is not so." It must be remarked that the talismanic magic described by Ibn Khaldun, *Muqqadimah,* pp. 166–76, deals mainly with "bringing down the spirituality of the spheres" (p. 165). In this context it is noteworthy that R. Shem Tov's views and Cordovero's views on *ruḥaniyyut* were quoted in *Shelah* I, fols. 16a–17a, 19b–20a and thus they became well-known to the early Hasidic masters, or authors active in their immediate surroundings. See e.g. the quotations of R. Barukh of Kossov, *ʿAmud ha-ʿAvodah,* fols. 113bc, 117c, 132a. This is a very important discussion of the talis-

manic linguistic, deeply informed by the Cordoverian school, and it can serve as an irrefutable example of the impact of the talismatic attitude to language on early Hasidic thought. In general, the impact of the *Shelah* on the spirituality of Hasidism is immense, as has been described in detail by Piekarz, in *The Beginning of Hasidism*. In this context I would like to draw attention to two traditions preserved in Yiddish, to the effect that the Besht was born in the same year when the second edition of the *Shelah* was printed in Amsterdam. This observation is very instructive, as it may betray an awareness on the part of the Hasidim as to the continuity, or the congeniality, between the *Shelah* and the Besht. See *Keter Shem Tov*. Additions, fol. 117ab. See also ibid., fol. 133b–134a, a question addressed to R. Shneor Zalmany of Liady, concerning the innovations of the Besht in comparison to *Reshit Ḥokhmah* and the *Shelah*! Thus, even in the circle of one of the most Lurianic among the Hasidic masters, the term of comparison was not Luria but the *mussar* books from the circle of Cordovero or his later followers. See also ibid., fol. 133a, where the student of the *Zohar* and the Kabbalah of Cordovero is mentioned. See also Kaidaner, *Sippurim Nora᾽im*, p. 112, on the profound acquaintance of the founder of Ḥabad with the *Shelah*.

74. The exact significance of the term *yedi῾ot* is not clear; this is not tantamount to the ten *Sefirot* or ten inner *Sefirot*. It seems that R. Shem Tov found the term in Kabbalistic material connected with the *Book of Speculation* literature.

75. R. Shem Tov ben Shem Tov, *Sefer ha-᾽Emunot*, fol. 104b (see Appendix 52). Also see ibid., fol. 105a (Appendix 53). Compare to *Sha῾arei Ẓedeq* from Abulafia's school (Appendix 54). Ms. British Library, Or. 10809 (Gaster 954), fols. 21b–22a (in print, p. 40). See also n. 48 and 58. See also below, chap. 6, par. 2.

76. R. Shem Tov ben Shem Tov, *Sefer ha-᾽Emunot*, fols. 20b, 22b, 59a, 104a, etc. R. Shem Tov overtly speaks about the *ruḥaniyyut* of the astral bodies, which may be pure or impure, i.e., holy or demonic.

77. See n. 70 above.

78. See e.g., R. Shelomo ben Ḥanokh Al-Qonstantini, *Megalleh ῾Amuqot*, Ms. Vatican 59, fols. 6a, 15b, 82a, 104a, 110a. On this text see Dov Schwartz, "The Land of Israel in the Fourteenth-Century Jewish Neoplatonic School," in *The Land of Israel in Medieval Jewish Thought*, ed. M. Ḥallamish and A. Ravitzki (Jerusalem, 1991), p. 141 (Hebrew).

79. Compare Alqabetz, *Pirqei he-Ḥakham*, chap. 16, ms. Mantua 66, fols. 55–56, who explicitly quotes R. Shem Tov's *Sefer ha-᾽Emunot*, fols. 26b–27a (see n. 73 above).

80. Alqabetz, Ms. Oxford-Bodleiana 1663, fol. 169b (Appendix 55).

81. See ibid., fol. 170b (Appendix 56). Compare these two citations to Horowitz, *Shelah* vol 1, fol. 5a. It follows that these views of Alqabetz could have also reached Hasidism as did the similar views of Cordovero.

82. See Ben-Shelomo, *The Mystical Theology*, p. 41, n. 80; Bracha Sack, *The Mystical Theology of Solomon Alkabez* (Ph.D. thesis, Brandeis, Waltham, 1977), pp. 13–4, passim (Hebrew). It is, however, important to remark that the opinion of the

scholars notwithstanding, it is quite possible that Cordovero was not influenced by Alqabetz, or at least not only by this Kabbalist; the latter apparently wrote the *Collectanaea of Introductory Theses* later, as it mentions his work *Berit ha-Levi,* and some of the material found in the second part of the work seems to be influenced by Lurianic motifs. See Idel, "The Magical and Theurgical Interpretation," p. 52, n. 121 and Scholem, *Kabbalah,* p. 73; see also Alqabetz, *Berit ha-Levi,* chap. 4.

83. I cannot adduce any hard evidence for the influence of Alemanno on Cordovero. However, such a possibility cannot be excluded; see n. 156. Alemanno's views and material, partially discussed above, bear evidence that the talismanic view of language was well known before the emergence of Safedian Kabbalah or Cordovero's knowledge of Abulafia's most important works; see Idel, *Studies,* pp. 127–28. It is also evident that Cordovero was well-acquainted with R. Shem Tov, *Sefer ha-ʾEmunot*; see e.g. Cordovero, *Pardes Rimmonim* 3, chap. 2; 1, fol. 12a.

84. Cordovero, *Pardes Rimmonim* 27, chap. 1; 2, fol. 59bc (see Appendix 57). The classification of the "path of the letters" as higher than the Zoharic type of Kabbalah fits the literary structure of *Pardes Rimmonim*; at the beginning Cordovero deals with the Sefirotic Kabbalah and only at the end does he discuss issues like the nature of the letters, Divine Names, permutation of letter, and so forth. Compare also Abulafia's view that his brand of Kabbalah is superior to that of the *Sefirot*; cf. Idel, "Defining Kabbalah," pp. 107–10. Compare also Alemanno's view that talismanic magic is the highest perfection, greater even than "Torah" and "Wisdom"; cf. Idel, "The Study Program," pp. 319–20. The first three stages of the study referred to above are parallel to Cordovero's other discussion on a similar issue in his *ʾOr ha-Ne ʿerav*; see Jacob Katz, *Halakhah ve-Kabbalah* (Jerusalem, 1984), pp. 56–57 (Hebrew). It is perhaps not superfluous to note that Cordovero's use of the phrase "creates worlds" is to a certain extent similar to that which occurs in R. Yiẓḥaq of Acre's quotation from R. Nathan, his master; see *Me ʾirat ʿEynayim,* pp. 222–23, where the mystical *ascensio mentis* ends with the transformation of the mystic into the "man of God" who is able to create worlds. R. Nathan's views were close to those of Abulafia; cf. Idel, *Studies,* p. 116–17; ibid., *Golem,* pp. 106–8. See also R. Menaḥem Naḥum of Chernobyl, *Me ʾor ʿEynayim,* p. 143.

85. Compare Cordovero's assertion that the content of the fourth division will be comprehended after resurrection (26, chaps. 1–2) to the statement of the introduction to *Pardes Rimmonim* 30 where, while discussing the combinatory techniques, Cordovero maintains that the content of this "gate" will be realized only after resurrection. See also his *Derishot,* p. 5. Cf. Cordovero's view that, above, the spiritual Torah consists of discrete letters: cf. *Shi ʿur Qomah,* fol. 63c (Appendix 58). Compare the ancient view of the letters that are inscribed upon the *Merkavah,* according to *ʾOtiyyot de R. ʿAqiba ʾ,* ed. Wertheimer, *Batei Midrashot,* vol. 2, p. 379; and n. 91, below.

86. *Pardes Rimmonim* 32, chap. 3; 2, fol. 79a (Appendix 59). On Cordovero's view on prayer in general see Sack, "Prayer," pp. 5–12. For some brief remarks on Cordovero's influence of Hasidism, concerning points other than those discussed here, see p. 8, n. 20–21; p. 10, n. 35, 11, 38. On the influence of the view quoted above on Hasidism, see Scholem, *Kabbalah,* p. 178, who considered it a Lurianic concept. However,

Tishby pointed out its Cordoverian source: see *Studies in Kabbalah,* p. 264, n. 24. Neither Scholem nor Tishby elaborated upon the magical implication of Cordovero's view, and its deep influence on other issues such as *Talmud, Torah, Ẓaddiq,* or *devequt.* Besides *Pardes Rimmonim,* this concept of *Kavvanah* was copied verbatim in Horowitz's *Sha^car ha-Shamayim,* p. 50 and thereby reached early Hasidism; see e.g. R. Meshullam Phoebus' *Yosher Divrei ʾEmet,* fol. 132a, where the author mentions both *Pardes Rimmonim* and *Shaʿar ha-Shamayim.* On R. Meshullam Phoebus' own view of mystical prayer see his *Yosher Divrei ʾEmet* no. 42; fol. 135b:

> You know that despite the fact that in my youth I had studied some *Kavvanot,* I do not intend them at all . . . Since the quintessence of the *Kavannah* is to break [your] heart, and love and fear and integrity . . . Should we reach them, we would easily be able to intend all the Kavvanot of R. Isaac Luria, which in fact were not promulgated except for persons like him, or slightly less than him, whose heart is pure . . . But we are impure from head to toe, without any integrity . . . and our hearts are not free of corporeal desires at all, a fortiori of the finer desires, since we enjoy and delight when we are praised and lauded, and we hate to be despised, and thus we are removed from God, Blessed be He. And we cannot intend our mind to Him at all, even [when praying] with the plain [meaning of the prayer]; how may we intend the most subline of the *kavvanot.* Therefore I chose to intend one single *kavvanah,* to direct my heart to God, Blessed be He, as much as possible, to the intention [i.e. meaning] of the words and sayings, as far as possible. At the same time, if I shall some time be able to intend, for a moment, as easy *kavvanah,* namely a certain [divine] name, without being bothered so as to turn away from the true *Kavvanah,* which I mentioned above, then it is fine. But when performing the acts of the commandments, like *Tefillim* and *Sukkah* and *Lulav* and *Shofar,* then it is good to intend to the *kavvanah* of the [divine] names, since no utterance is involved but an act alone. However, at [the time of] an utterance like prayer, there are many *kavvanot* that the heart has to intend to the utterance, that we almost cannot speak, except with great effort, how then can we pass from the plain [meaning] to the *kavvanah*? However, it is very good to study the *kavvanot* of all the prayers, since thereby [our] soul is [spiritually] awakened when it becomes aware what the impact [of *kavvanot*] is, namely that they perform a very great *Tikkun* above . . . All this I have written to make known what I have heard from the holy mouth of the Divine Master, Menaḥem Mendel of Premislany.

See also ibid., fol. 141b no. 55. On R. Meshullam Phoebus' attitude to Lurianic *kavvanot* see Krassen, "Devequt" and Faith, pp. 349–53.

87. Azulai, *Ḥesed le-ʾAvraham,* fol. 14a. I see no reason whatsoever for Scholem's statement that this view is an "analogy from the Lurianic school," cf. *Kabbalah,* p. 178. Regarding Azulai's influence on other issues occurring in *Toledot Yaʿaqov Yosef;* see Scholem, *Messianic Idea,* pp. 213, 223; Rapoport-Albert, "God and the Zaddik" p. 321 n. 71 and n. 88 below. See also R. Meir Margoliot, *Sod Yakhin u-Voʿaz,* p. 37; R. Jacob Joseph's *Ben Porat Yosef,* fol. 21a and R. Yeḥiel Mikhal of Zlotchov, *Mayyim Rabbim,* fols. 16a, 23b, 32b; R. Barukh of Kossov, *ʿAmud ha-*

ᶜ*Avodah,* fol. 212d; Heschel, *The Circle of Baal Shem Tov,* p. 108–9, 112; *Shivḥei ha-Besht,* ed. Rubinstein, p. 151; Ben Amos-Mintz, *In the Praise of the Baal Shem Tov,* pp. 103–4 where, interestingly enough, the Kabbalist, who mentions that he has written ten books, wonders why it is the Hasidic way of prayer that is making a great impression in the celestial academy. See also above, Introduction, n. 43. It should be emphasized that though Azulai was deeply influenced by Cordovero's magical view concerning the *kavvanah,* he was also well acquainted with the Lurianic *kavvanot,* and he compiled two compendia on this issue, which remained in manuscripts. See Liebes, "New Writings" p. 193. On the complex problem of the attitude of the Kabbalists to the two types of Kabbalah, see Tishby, *Studies in Kabbalah,* pp. 255–67, especially pp. 256–57, and Ronit Meroz, *Sefer ʾOr Ganuz by R. Abraham Azulai QS* 60 (1985): 310–24 (Hebrew).

88. *Toledot Yaᶜaqov Yosef,* fols. 3a, 6a–b. It should be mentioned that despite the acceptance of the Cordoverian definition of the mystical intention of prayer, this Hasidic master indicates that the *kavvanah* is the prerogative of the elite, while ordinary people are exempt from its performance. See ibid., fols. 51cd and 22ab. The elite is conceived as infusing the vitality and the spiritual force into the sounds of the prayer of the ordinary person. See Rapoport-Albert, "God and the Zaddik" pp. 303–9. On the emergence of the Hasidic elite see Shoḥat, "*ha-Ẓaddiq,*" p. 304–5.

89. Ibid., fol. 3a (see Appendix 60). Compare also to ibid., fols. 6a, 167ab. See however his *Ben Porat Yosef,* fol. 32d, where *Ḥesed le-ʾAvraham* is explicitly quoted, and also ibid., fols. 17c, 23cd where loosely parallel passages occur. Especially important is the fact that on fol. 23c he quotes the "Hasid R. Y[ehudah]," apparently R. Yehudah Leib of Pistin, in relation to prayer, as follows: "By the combinations of letters and words a vessel is produced to draw down the influx and blessing for [the people of] Israel." (On the combination of letters and prayer see below, n. 123.) Elsewhere, ibid., fol. 53b, he quotes R. Naḥman of Kossov, to the effect that speech generates a vessel to draw into it the influx. On this very important passage see above, chap. 3, n. 256. Therefore, the view of Cordovero, as presented by Azulai, was accepted not only by the Besht and his followers, but also by two important members of the circle of "pneumatics." Therefore, we may assume that this was one of the common features of the circle that generated the Hasidic movement. These views were paraphrased in R. Aharon of Zhitomir, *Toledot ʾAharon* II fol. 36b. See also a similar view in *ʾOr ha-ʾEmet,* fol. 39c in a passage to be quoted here below. See also chap. 2, n. 221. It should be mentioned that R. Zeʾev Wolf of Zhitomir claims that the view that the letters are vessels "is well known in the books." See *ʾOr ha-Meir,* fol. 14d.

90. The comparison of letters or sounds to the human body is influenced by Alqabetz (see n. 60 above) and Cordovero (see n. 92 below). See also the Great Maggid's view in *Maggid Devarav le-Yaᶜaqov,* p. 52 (Appendix 61) and *ʾOr ha-ʾEmet,* fol. 8c.

91. See *Pardes Rimmonim* XXVII, 2; II, fol. 60a (Appendix 62). For the image of letters as vessels, see R. Shem Tov ben Shem Tov, *Sefer ha-ʾEmunot,* fols. 27a, 59a, 98b, 104b and 105a, and see also n. 99 below. The latter Kabbalistic discussions of the image of body or vessel drawing down emanations stem from *Sefer ha-ʾEmunot,* fols. 59a, 98b. Compare also Cordovero's texts printed by Bracha Sack, "More on the

Metamorphosis of the Dictum 'God, Torah, and Israel Are One Unit'," *QS* 57 (1982): 184 (Hebrew). Compare this sentence to the monadic nature of letters discussed above, especially to the quotation referred to in notes 54, 86, and cf. *Pardes Rimmonim* XXX; II, fols. 68c–72a. It is worthwhile to remark that, according to Cordovero, not only the letters, i.e., the consonants, are endowed with spiritual force, but also the vowels, *nequddot;* see *Pardes Rimmonim* XXIX, chap. 5; II, fol. 68c: *ve-ruḥaniyyut ha-nequddot*. Interestingly enough, Cordovero tries to avoid the use of the term *ruḥaniyyut* in magical astral contexts; when dealing with the drawing downward of the supernal forces from the planets, he uses the term *Koaḥ*; see Cordovero, *Derishot* pp. 82, 84, 86; however, see ibid., pp. 37–38. According to Tishby-Dan, "Hasidism," col. 773, the source of the Hasidic view of the contraction of the Godhead into the letters of Torah and prayer is the Kabbalah of R. Yisrael Sarug. Compare, however, above chap. 2, par. 6.

92. This term occurs several times in Cordovero's works; see, above chap. 2, par. 5.

93. Jacob Joseph of Polonoy, *Toledot Ya ʿaqov Yosef,* fol. 62b (see Appendix 63). See n. 91, 98, 99. This view of letters *qua* vessels apparently influenced the Hasidic use of words such as "ark," *tevah.* See, especially, R. Moshe Ḥayyim Ephraim of Sudylkov, *Degel Maḥaneh ʾEfrayim,* p. 9, and R. Jacob Joseph's *Ben Porat Yosef,* fol. 19d (Appendix 64). This interpretation of the meaning of *tevah* is found also in the Great Maggid and his circles, and it reflects, therefore, an earlier source, apparently the Besht himself. See the quotation in the name of the Besht in *ʾOr ha- ʾEmet,* fol. 18b and that in the name of the Great Maggid in R. Levi Yiẓḥaq of Berdichev, *Qedushat Levi,* fol. 139a; *Ba ʿal Shem Tov* I, pp. 119–23. See also Idel, "Reification of Language," p. 73, n. 6.

94. *Toledot Ya ʿaqov Yosef,* fol. 62b (Appendix 65). Compare to ibid., fol. 3a discussed above par. 4. See also Schatz-Uffenheimer, *Quietistic Elements,* p. 111.

95. R. Elijah de Vidas, *Reshit Ḥokhmah,* Gate of Holiness, chap. 10; II, p. 247 (Appendix 66). This text was copied in *Shelah,* vol. 1, fol. 112b. I could not locate the work of Cordovero whence de Vida quoted this passage; however, it is obviously an authentic piece of Cordoverian Kabbalah. Cf., e.g., *ʾElimah Rabbati,* fol. 132d and n. 96 below. The cleaving to the spiritual force inherent within a form in this world is also Cordoverian: see his *ʾOr Yaqar* (Jerusalem, 1979), vol. 10, p. 7 (Appendix 67), and see also the passage from the same work in vol. 12, p. 147 cited below, Concluding Remarks, par. 3. It is highly interesting that Cordovero interprets Abulafia's technique of pronunciation of Divine Names in his own terms; the pronunciation is tantamount to the *kavvanah* of prayer. See also Vital's juxtaposition between prayers and pronunciation of names, though he refers to the angelic powers that are invoked; see *Sha ʿarei Qedushah,* p. 106, compare also n. 51 above and n. 123 below. See also below, chap. 5 n. 36. See also R. Barukh of Kossov, *ʿAmud ha- ʿAvodah,* fols. 46d–47a.

96. On the emanational structure as a chain, see below, Concluding Remarks, par. 3.

97. *Me ʾor ʿEynayim,* pp. 170–71 (see Appendix 68). Compare n. 105 below and R. Mordekhai of Chernobyl, *Liqqutei Torah,* fols. 5c, 10c, 19c, 25c, 29d, 30d and the quotation from R. Meir ha-Levi of Apta's *ʾOr le-Shamayim,* chap. 6, par. 4 below.

98. Compare Weiss, *Studies,* pp. 126–30; Schatz-Uffenheimer, *Quietistic Elements,* p. 96.

99. *Pardes Rimmonim* XXVII, chap. 2; II, fol. 59c (Appendix 69). See above, n. 91, 92. These sentences influenced R. Jacob Joseph of Polonoy; see n. 94, 95 above. See also Cordovero's *Commentary on Sefer Yeẓirah* (Jerusalem, 1989), p. 80.

100. *Pardes Rimmonim* XXX, chap. 3; II, fol. 69b (Appendix 70). See also chap. 2, par. 3 above and chap. 6, par. 2 below.

101. See also Idel, *Studies,* pp. 128–29.

102. Compare *Pardes Rimmonim,* 21, chap. 1; 1, fol. 96d (Appendix 71). Here the contemplation is apparently directed to written letters. Compare the Hasidic metaphor: just as a telescope enables one to see the remote stars, so the letters are instruments to see God: cf. *Shemu ͨah Tovah,* p. 73b, analyzed by Schatz-Uffenheimer, *Quietistic Elements,* pp. 97–98; ibid., "The Contemplative Prayer in Hasidism," pp. 213–14. However, even this text, which prima facie seems to refer unmistakably to written letters is, in my opinion, rather ambiguous; see Appendix 72. Compare also to R. Ḥayyim Ḥaike of Amdura, *Ḥayyim ve-Ḥesed,* fol. 7b and to R. Asher Ẓevi of Ostraha, *Ma ͨayan ha-Ḥokhmah,* fol. 89b, where the vision of the separate letters is transcended by an ecstatic state, where the letters vanished. This exalted state enables someone to draw down the influx, and this discussion is but another example of the mystico-magical model.

103. See R. Abraham Ḥayyim of Zloczow, *ͻOraḥ le-Ḥayyim,* fol. 98a (Appendix 73) and compare to *ͻOr Torah,* p. 30 (Appendix 74) and see also *ͻOr ha-Emet,* fols. 3bc, 14c, 17c and *Mayyim Rabbim,* fol. 29a. See Schatz-Uffenheimer, *Quietistic Elements,* p. 97; ibid., "The Contemplative Prayer in Hasidism," pp. 210–11, *Hasidism as Mysticism,* p. 169, where the passage is translated and briefly discussed. My translation and interpretation differ from the rendering given by this scholar. See also the version of this passage in *Maggid Devarav le-Ya ͨaqov,* pp. 13–14, 81, and in *Keter Shem Tov* II, fol. 56ab. In all these versions the pronounced letters are viewed as "palaces" of the Divine Presence, i.e., as quasi-talismanic utterances intended to capture the supernal force, and man is judged either according to his capacity to draw the spiritual force onto the profound sounds or by his success at cleaving to the spiritual force already dwelling there. Hence, neither an *ascensio mentis* through the supernal palaces during prayer is referred to (compare, Schatz-Uffenheimer's interpretation in the footnotes to her edition of *Maggid Devarav le-Ya ͨaqov,* pp. 13–14), nor a contemplation of written letters (compare Schatz, "Contemplative Prayer," p. 211, n. 2). Ignorance of the magical background of the concepts that reverberated in Hasidism has produced far-fetched interpretations of some Hasidic sources. See also Jean Canteins, *La Voie des lettres* (Paris, 1981), pp. 179–80, which compares Schatz's interpretation of the traditions from the Great Maggid's school, referring to the written letters, to Tantric and Sufi methods. Nevertheless, it should be mentioned that the term *Heikhal* could, in other Hasidic texts, still stand for a supernal palace: see e.g., Heschel, *The Circle of the Baal Shem Tov,* p. 94.

104. *Toledot Ya ͨaqov Yosef,* fol. 25a (Appendix 75). Compare the term *penimiut ruḥaniyyut* to the term *ha-ruḥaniyyut ha-penimi* in Cordovero's *Pardes Rimmonim*

XXXII, chap. 3; II, fol. 79a; Horowitz, *Sha ᶜar ha-Shamayim* p. 50. Compare also R. Menaḥem Naḥum of Chernobyl, *Me ᵓor ᶜEynayim*, p. 171, cited n. 98 above.

105. *Toledot Ya ᶜaqov Yosef*, fol. 25a–b.

106. Ibid., fol. 25a (Appendix 76). The terms *deviqah* and *ḥashiqah* occur in an overtly erotic context later on; see fol. 133c. Their direct source is de Vidas's *Reshit Ḥokhmah*, cf. Gedaliah Nigal, "The Sources of *devequt* in Early Hasidic Literature," *QS* 46 (1970–71), pp. 345–46 (Hebrew). See also the very interesting nexus between the issues of the spiritual force inherent in the letters, crucial for the magical model, and sexual relationship in R. Jacob Joseph's *Ben Porat Yosef*, fol. 33a. On the erotic symbolism of man's relation to the *Shekhinah* during prayer, see Jacobs, *Hasidic Prayer*, pp. 60–61, who refers to *Keter Shem Tov* and similar later sources: see *Toledot Ya ᶜaqov Yosef*, fol. 132c; Liebes, "A Treatise," (see above chap. 3, n. 223), pp. 177–78; and above chap. 3, par. 5.

107. The view that divestment of materiality is connected with an erotic experience occurs also in the name of the Great Maggid in R. Meshullam Phoebus of Zbarazh, *Yosher Divrei ᵓEmet*, fol. 17d (Appendix 77).

108. See Scholem, *On the Kabbalah*, pp. 55–56, 63–64. R. Jacob Joseph of Polonoy explicitly refers to the Zoharic parable in a very similar discussion in *Toledot Ya ᶜaqov Yosef*, fol. 133b–c. Furthermore, he identifies the twenty-two letters of the Hebrew alphabet with the *Shekhinah* (*Toledot Ya ᶜaqov Yosef*, fol. 6ab) in the context of Cordovero's definition of the *kavvanah* of prayer. Cf. Elliot Wolfson, "Female Imaging of the Torah: From Literary Metaphor to Religious Symbol," in *From Ancient Israel to Modern Judaism. Intellect in Quest of Understanding: Essays in Honor of Marvin Fox*, ed. J. Neusner, E. S. Frerichs and N. M. Sarna (Atlanta, 1989), vol. 2, pp. 302–5.

109. *Maggid Devarav le-Ya ᶜaqov*, p. 330 (Appendix 78).

110. Ibid., p. 335 (Appendix 79).

111. It is not clear if the divestment refers to the one who prays himself or to the utterances; both possibilities are corroborated by ibid., pp. 234–35. See also ibid., p. 26 where the text of the prayer was conceived as consisting, esoterically, of divine names.

112. *Toledot Ya ᶜaqov Yosef*, fol. 167b (Appendix 80). This view of the mental prayer as the highest level of prayer is obviously connected with Cordovero's statement that the *kavvanah* is higher than the utterances (see n. 120 below). See Cordovero, *Pardes Rimmonim* XXVII, chap. 2; II, fol. 59c (Appendix 81). See also Cordovero, *Derishot*, p. 84. Compare also to Abulafia's view of letters on these three levels; Idel, *Mystical Experience*, pp. 19–21. Moreover, compare to Cordovero's view discussed in Idel, "The Magical and Theurgic Interpretation," p. 53.

113. At least according to Cordovero's thought, the vocal expression is theoretically and explicitly superior to the written letters; see e.g. *Pardes Rimmonim* XXVII, 2; II, fol. 59cd (Appendix 82); ibid., 32, 3; 2, fol. 79a (Appendix 83). See also Cordovero's *Derishot*, p. 70 and his quotation adduced in n. 86 above. It is important to remark that here we can observe two stages: the drawing downward of the spiritual

force and afterward causing the ascent of the pronounced letters. The first stage was, as seen before, adopted by the early Hasidic masters, whereas the second appears only rarely; compare especially the view attributed to R. Jacob Isaac, the Seer of Lublin, which recommends the first stage when the time is short, whereas the second is to be used when there is no lack of time. Cf. Jacobs, *The Hasidic Prayer*, p. 79 and see n. 126 below. Compare to *Toledot Ya ͨaqov Yosef,* fol. 4d (Appendix 84), ibid., fol. 167a (Appendix 85). Compare also fol. 167b–c.

114. *ͻOr ha-Me ͻir,* fol. 83c (Appendix 86). This view recurs in many Hasidic texts.

115. *Ẓava ͨat ha-Ribash,* par. 40, in *Liqqutim Yeqarim,* fol. 5a (Appendix 87). Compare also *ͻOr ha-ͻEmet,* fol. 84a, *ͻOr ha-Me ͻir,* fol. 84a. See, however, Schatz-Uffenheimer, *Quietistic Elements,* p. 108.

116. Gries, *The Conduct Literature,* pp. 220–22. On techniques of pronouncing the names of God with closed eyes, see Idel, *Studies,* pp. 134–36.

117. *Liqqutei Yeqarim,* fol. 10a (Appendix 88).

118. Ibid., fol. 10b (Appendix 89). See also R. Barukh of Kossov, *ͨAmud ha-ͨAvodah,* fol. 132a.

119. Ibid., fol. 1b (Appendix 90). Therefore, "the whisper" is tantamount to "a low voice"; cf. ibid., fol. 16d (Appendix 91). Schatz-Uffenheimer, *Quietistic Elements,* p. 103 cited these passages in order to illustrate the "mental prayer" of Hasidism! See also her "Contemplative Prayer," pp. 223–25, *Hasidism as Mysticism,* p. 178, where she translates some of the texts she interprets as referring to spiritual prayer.

120. *ͻOr ha-ͻEmet,* fol. 65c (Appendix 92). See also R. Benjamin of Zalozitch, *ͻAhavat Dodim* (Jerusalem, 1978), fol. 61a.

121. Elijah ha-Kohen, *Midrash Talpiyot,* fol. 162c (Appendix 93). Compare immediately afterward with Appendix 94. See also n. 62 above. It seems that the term *mekhavvenim* refers to a crystallized form of prayer and its occurrence precedes the later eighteenth-century "Beit El" Kabbalists who were designated also as *mekhavvenim* as well as the Kabbalists of the Brody-Kloiz. See Weiss, *Studies,* pp. 97–98. See also the dialectics of *kavvanah* and impure forces in R. Ẓevi Hirsch of Zhydachov, *Peri Qodesh Hillulim* (Lemberg, 1802), fols. 1c–2b. This Hasidic master, who was deeply immersed in Lurianic Kabbalah, regards prayer with Lurianic *kavvanot* as lower than that of the *Ẓaddiq,* whose prayer is done in a state of *devequt.* However, this view does not abrogate the Lurianic *kavvanot.* See Liebes (n. 4 above), pp. 377–78. I wonder if the structural parallelism that Liebes proposed between the abrogation of the commandments by R. Wolf Eibeschuetz and the lower status of the *Kavvanot* that should not be used by the *Ẓaddiqim* is the result of a historical affinity.

122. Cordovero, *Pardes Rimmonim* XXVII, chap. 2; II, fol. 59c (Appendix 95). See Bracha Sack, "A Fragment of R. Moshe Cordovero's *Commentary on Ra ͨaya Meheimna*" *Kobetz al Yad* (Minora Manuscripta Hebraica) X (XX) (Jerusalem, 1982), pp. 270–71 (see Appendix 96). Compare also to de Vidas, *Reshit Ḥokhmah,* fol. 164c. Therefore, the ascent of the sounds of prayer are meant to cleave the prayer to God in

a way similar to that indicated by some Hasidic masters. See also Sack, "A Fragment," p. 270 n. 52.

123. Cordovero, *Pardes Rimmonim* XXVII, chap. 2; II, fol. 59d (Appendix 97). The reference to the "pronunciation of names" is obviously a reference to Abulafia's type of Kabbalah. The affinity between this technique of Abulafia and the *Kavvanah* of prayer is twofold: (a) both were, according to Cordovero, methods to draw downward the spiritual forces; (b) "the pronunciation of names" is described by Abulafia, in his *ʾOr ha-Sekhel* in terms very close to the situation of prayer: e.g., the usage of *Talit* and *Tefillin,* and catharsis of thought from alien thoughts, etc. The Cordoverian nexus between combinations of letters and *kavvanah* was paraphrased in Abraham Azulai's *Ḥesed le-ʾAvraham,* fol. 10a. On the "combinations of letters and prayer," see also the quotation of R. Jacob Joseph (n. 89 above), R. Abraham ha-Malakh, *Ḥesed le-Avraham,* fol. 12cd, one of his statements being quoted above chap. 1, n. 55, and compare to R. Shneor Zalman of Liady, printed in Mondshein, *Kerem CḤABAD* I, p. 95. Its earlier source seems to be an anonymous *Commentary on the Liturgy,* from the circle of Abraham Abulafia. See n. 60 above.

It is worth remarking that one of the earliest occurrences of the phrase *maḥashavot zarot* is to be found in *Shaʿarei Ẓedeq,* a work written under the influence of Abulafia; according to the anonymous Kabbalist (ms. Jerusalem, Heb. 8° 148, fol. 66a; in print, p. 24), a condition of the perfect performance of the Abulafian technique of permutation of letters is the annihilation of the "alien thoughts"; compare also Abulafia's *ʾOr ha-Sekhel,* and other Abulafian treatises, wherein the purification of thought is mentioned. Cf. Idel, *Mystical Experience,* p. 40. Therefore, one of the earliest appearances of the term "alien thoughts," well-known in contexts dealing with prayer, is explicitly connected to Abulafia's technique. This passage was copied word for word by Cordovero in *Pardes Rimmonim* XXI, chap. 1; I, fol. 97ab as *Sefer ha-Niqqud,* a mistake that can be easily understood: see Idel, *Abraham Abulafia,* p. 25.

124. R. Meshullam Phoebus of Zbarazh, *Yosher Divrei ʾEmet,* fol. 132a (Appendix 98). See also R. Abraham Yehoshuʾah Heschel of Apta, *ʾOhev Yisrael,* fol. 73a, compare n. 96 above. It should also be mentioned that elsewhere, R. Meshullam Phoebus quotes a definition of *Kavvanah* from R. Isaiah Horowitz's *Shaʿar ha-Shamayim* (ibid., fol. 26c), where the emphasis is upon the subduing of the human thought; the ultimate source for this view is the "father of Kabbalah," R. Yiẓḥaq Sagi Nahor, as he was cited in R. Ezra of Gerona's *Commentary on the Song of Songs*; the latter was adduced in R. Meir ibn Gabbai's *ʿAvodat ha-Qodesh* II, chap. 6, fol. 29a. See Idel, *Kabbalah: New Perspectives,* pp. 54, 298 n. 128.

125. The "longing" of man, as well as all other creatures, for God is a Hasidic commonplace: see e.g. *Maʾor va-Shemesh* II, fol. 3c, where he points out his source as R. Ḥayyim ben Attar's *ʾOr ha-Ḥayyim* on Gen. 2, 1, where, indeed, an interesting discussion of a cosmic desire to cleave to the light of God occurs. See also R. Yisrael of Ryzhin, *ʿIrin Qaddishin,* fol. 36d–37a. Compare also above chap. 2, par. 5 and n. 244.

126. *Maggid Devarav le-Yaʿaqov,* p. 324. It is easy to perceive the striking affinity of the terminology used by these two early masters of Hasidism; both prefer the term "vitality" *ḥiyyut,* though *ruḥaniyyut* occurs too; in the two texts the cleaving of thought

as a precondition, absent in Cordovero's text, is mentioned. However, the accepted, and correct, view that R. Meshullam Phoebus was influenced by the works of the Great Maggid though he also deviated from his thought (see e.g. Weiss, *Studies*, pp. 137–40) is corroborated by the comparison of the aforecited texts. R. Meshullam Phoebus' text explicitly points out its sources, and his terminology is closer to Cordovero than that of the Great Maggid. Moreover, the ascent of the pronounced letters, common to R. Meshullam Phoebus and Cordovero is absent in this passage of the Great Maggid, as well as in other similar contexts. See n. 114 above. I assume, therefore, that a text like that of R. Meshullam Phoebus, which stems from an earlier stage of Hasidism, i.e., the Besht himself, was in existence and influenced both texts adduced above. This conclusion does not contradict the fact that the Great Maggid is quoted several times by R. Meshullam Phoebus. On contracting God into human utterances see above, chap. 2, par. 6.

127. *Maggid Devarav le-Ya ʿaqov*, pp. 57–58 (Appendix 99). On the ascent of the letters and sounds see also Idel, "Reification of Language" pp. 66–69.

128. *ʾOr ha-ʾEmet*, fols. 8bc (Appendix 100).

129. *Shemu ʿah Tovah*, p. 72 (Appendix 101). Compare Schatz-Uffenheimer, *Quietistic Elements*, p. 109, who analyzes this passage in quite a different way. See also *Darkhei Ẓedeq*, fol. 7a.

130. Ben Amos-Mintz, *In the Praise of the Baal Shem Tov*, p. 51 (Appendix 102). See also pp. 52–53. Cf. Jacobs, *Hasidic Prayer*, p. 58, and Dubnow, *History of Hasidism*, p. 116, and Kaidaner, *Sippurim Nora ʾim*, p. 41. Eliach's assumption, that shouting during prayer has to be seen as influenced by a Russian sect, is therefore more doubtful: see "The Russian Sects," p. 74. See also *Sefer ha-Tanya, Liqqutei ʾAmarim*, chap. 30, fol. 38b, ibid., *ʾIggeret ha-Qodesh*, par. 22, fol. 134a–135b, and the texts adduced in Wilenski, *Hasidim and Mitnaggedim*, vol. 1, pp. 68, 125; vol 2, p. 293. See also the text from *Keter Shem Tov* (the actual source being *Maggid Devarav le-Ya ʿaqov*, pp. 85–86) translated and analyzed by Daniel Merkur, "The Induction of Mystical Union: Two Hasidic Teachings," *Studia Mystica* 14, 4 (1991): 71. See also the interesting formulation, in the name of the Besht and the Great Maggid, that the goal of the service "is to speak the speeches of Torah and prayer with all his strength, and then he will cleave to the light of the Infinite that dwells within the letters." R. Aharon of Zhitomir, *Toledot ʾAharon* II, fol. 20c. Compare also to chap. 5, par. 2, the quotations in the name of the Besht from R. Meir Margoliot and R. Aharon of Zhitomir. On the other hand, the same master maintains that by pronouncing the words of prayer and Torah with devotion, by "breaking his body," someone is able to bring down the influx and luminosity. Ibid., 2, fol. 48c. On loud prayer in Hasidism, see Wertheimer, *Law and Custom*, p. 106.

131. Jacobs, *Hasidic Prayer*, pp. 62–63; Wilensky, *Hasidim and Mitnaggedim* II, pp. 159, 173, 249.

132. Compare the positive attitude of the Besht toward the loud prayer of an ignoramus, found in a widespread legend. See Gedalyah Nigal, "A Primary Source of the Literature of Hasidic Stories—On the Book *Kether Shem Toc* and Its Sources," *Sinai* 79 (1976): 139–40, n. 18 (Hebrew).

133. On this theme see *ʾOr ha-ʾEmet,* fol. 15a, quoted above, chap. 2, par. 6.

134. Compare Idel, *Kabbalah: New Perspectives* pp. 67–68.

135. *ʾOr ha-ʾEmet,* fol. 39c.

136. *ʿOraḥ le-Ẓaddiq,* p. 70.

137. *Noʿam ʾElimelekh,* fol. 82cd (Appendix 103). See also ibid., fol. 109d. This interpretation of the verbal form *maggid* is based upon the understanding of the root *NGD* as signifying, through the influence of Aramaic, drawing. Interestingly enough, the noun *maggid* meant also preacher, and, on the other hand, an angelic mentor who reveals himself and reveals secrets. Do all these three meanings coexist when they refer to the same person? To put this question in a more concrete manner: is the preacher conceived of as being informed, while he preaches, by an angelic mentor, and drawing down, during his sermon, subtle entities, or spiritual forces from on high? It should be mentioned that the admired master of R. Elimelekh was none other than R. Dov Baer of Miedzyrec, better known as the Great Maggid! If these three meanings can be found together, it would strengthen our theory of the importance of the impact of talismatic magic on a crucial issue in Hasidism. For the time being, the single interpretation along the same lines is found in a text attributed to the Besht, and printed in R. Yehoshu'a Abraham ben Yisrael, *Geʾulat Yisrael,* fol. 1b. However, the Besht deals with the verb *higgid,* as a verb in the past tense, understood as drawing down, *hamshakhah,* while in *Noʿam ʾElimelekh* the verbal form as noun, *Maggid,* was dealt with. See also the quotation from *Shemuʿah Tovah,* chap. 3 beside n. 83. For a much earlier interpretation of the form *maggid* as drawing down, see the late thirteenth-century Kabbalist Todros ha-Levi Abulafia, *Sefer Shaʿar ha-Razim,* ed. M. Kushnir-Oron (Jerusalem, 1989), p. 57.

138. See below, Concluding Remarks, pars. 1–3.

139. An interesting formulation concerning prayer as a creative activity in sixteenth-century Kabbalah is found in Evans, *Rudolf II,* p. 239; though undocumented, it reflects Cordovero's general attitude quite remarkably: "The theory of prayer is a creative faculty in man, similar to the magical Neoplatonist world of atmospheres and Hermetic astrology." I would like to emphasize that congenial with the magical interpretation of the prayer in Hasidism, there is also a strong devotional aspect that was also emphasized by the first masters of Hasidism, but this issue, interesting in itself, must remain beyond the scope of the present analysis. In any case, several statements in the name of the Besht demonstrate that he regarded the moments of prayer as highly charged peaks of spiritual activity, which might even culminate in death. See e.g., the quotation in his name in R. Abraham of Radomsk, *Ḥesed le-ʾAvraham,* fol. 74c, where he mentions the death by cleaving to the speeches of the prayer." See also the parable in the name of the Besht quoted in *Toledot Yaʿaqov Yosef,* fol. 169b about the directness of the relationship between man and God during prayer and *Keter Shem Tov* I, fol. 21d, and *Baʿal Shem Tov* I, pp. 119–91.

NOTES TO CHAPTER 5

1. For more on this issue see below, Appendix A.

2. This archangel was also mentioned in connection to experiences of the Besht also in other instances, see *Ba ᶜal Shem Tov,* 2, p. 262.

3. Ben Amos-Mintz, *In Praise of the Baal Shem Tov,* p. 83. For the bibliography related to this text see ibid., pp. 323–24; see also Loewenthal, *Communicating the Infinite,* pp. 18–19, 217–18; Etckes, "Hasidism as Movement" p. 13, Dan, *The Hasidic Story,* pp. 127–28. For another version of the Besht's study of *Ma ᶜaseh Merkavah* with the Maggid, see Mondshein, *Shivḥei,* p. 278; Rubinstein, *Shiveḥei,* pp. 128–29, especially the content of n. 44 in the name of Isaac Alfasi. According to R. Shelomo of Lutzk, some other books were studied together by the Besht and the Great Maggid, none of them belonging to Lurianic Kabbalah; see his preface to *Maggid Devarav le-Ya ᶜaqov,* p. 2, where the divine names are also mentioned in this context. On the enthusiastic study of the Song of Songs by R. Barukh, the grandson of the Besht, which allegedly produced fire, see Jacobs, *Hasidic Prayer,* p. 97.

4. See Ben Amos-Mintz, *In Praise of the Baal Shem Tov* p. 323. On the Besht's ascents of the soul as constituting a continuation of the older *Heikhalot* practices, see Idel, *Kabbalah: New Perspectives,* pp. 94–96. It is possible, though I am not quite sure of this proposal, that the meaning of the peculiar position of the Great Maggid is that the Besht put him in the famous posture of the ancient Jewish mystics, namely with the head between the knees. See Idel, ibid., pp. 78–79.

5. See Ephraim E. Urbach, *The World of the Sages* (Jerusalem, 1988), pp. 486–513 (Hebrew); Martin Cohen, *The Shi ᶜur Qomah, Liturgy and Theurgy in Pre-Kabbalistic Jewish Mysticism* (Lanham, 1983, pp. 68–69. Although the mystical texts may have indeed been conceived, as Cohen proposes, of having theurgical effects when recited, it seems that the Besht envisioned the source of the revelatory experience to be not only in the special nature of the text but most especially in the initial psychological mood of the reader.

6. See Lawrence Fine, "Recitations of Mishnah as a Vehicle for Mystical Inspiration" *REJ,* vol. 116 (1982) pp. 183–99; Werblowsky, *Joseph Karo,* pp. 255–79.

7. See Werblowsky, *Joseph Karo* pp. 78–81, 265–66.

8. See Yaᶜari, "Two Editions," pp. 403–5; Mondshein, *Shiveḥei,* pp. 264–65; Rubinstein, *Shiveḥei,* pp. 340–41. Compare also R. Yiẓḥaq Aiziq Safrin of Komarno, *Heikhal ha-Berakhah,* 5, fol. 34b, *Ba ʾal Shem Tov,* 1, p. 12. See also the attempt of R. Naḥman of Braslav to transform the content of this book into mystical-ethical teachings, as described by Loewenthal in *Communicating the Infinite,* p. 285, n. 161, and see also below, Appendix B.

9. Angelology is a rather marginal topic in Hasidism, and it may well be that this statement reflects much earlier tradition. See Idel, "The Concept of the Torah," p. 41. It should be mentioned that extraordinary experiences related to the study of the Quran are mentioned in relatively early Muslim texts; see Ignaz Goldziher, "La Notion de la *Sakina* chez les Mahometans" *Revue de l'histoire des religions,* vol. 14 (1893) pp. 7–8.

10. It should be noticed that though in this version the studied book is Luria's *chef d'oeuvre,* the results of the special type of study are almost identical to that of the study

of the ancient text. I wonder whether it will not be pertinent to compare the above story to the confrontation between the Besht and R. Yiẓḥaq of Drohobicz regarding the use of the divine names, which ends with the success of the Besht; see above, chap. 2, par. 3. The Besht nevertheless mentions that "when he ventures the explanation of a passage in *Peri ʿEẓ Ḥayyim,* though I know a truer one, I am compelled to silence." (Cf. Heschel, *The Circle of the Baal Shem Tov,* p. 170.) The fact that this remark occurs immediately after the tale about the contest regarding the interdiction of using divine names may hint at a Beshtian interpretation of *Peri ʿEẓ Ḥayyim* that transforms this text into a continuum of angelic names, as in the case of *ʿEẓ Ḥayyim* in the above story.

11. The technical details of the transformation of the words of prayer into divine names, as part of the drawing down of the spiritual forces into the words can not be elaborated here. Although in the above-quoted texts the transformation of the studied texts changes them into a continuum of angelic names, while R. Jacob Joseph of Polonoy speaks about the transformation into divine names, there is a certain affinity between the two phenomena, an issue we shall take up elsewhere. For the time being see e.g., *Toledot Yaʿaqov Yosef,* fols. 3ab, 6c, 169a; R. Qalonimus Qalman Epstein, *Maʾor ve-Shemesh,* 1, fol. 3c; Meir ha-Levi of Apta, *ʾOr la-Shamayim,* fol. 89d. See also n. 23 below and chap. 2, n. 235. For another type of transformation of the text see the illuminating story regarding R. Meshullam Zushia of Hanipoli, who wondered during an attempt to study the Mishnah why not read the first word in the Mishnah, *me-ʾeimatai,* "from when" as if it stands for "out of awe." The awe of God was described as a characteristic of the spiritual life of this famous master. See R. Nathan Netaʿ ha-Kohen of Kalbiel, *Sefer Menorat Zahav* (Warsau, 1904) fol. 51b. See also chap. 3, n. 189.

12. See *Maggid Devarav le-Yaʿaqov,* pp. 234–35; see also *ʾOr Torah,* p. 47; *Maʾor va-Shemesh,* 2, fol. 21c.

13. *Taʿam.* For the use of this metaphor in order to describe the need for the experience in order to understand it, see the Sufi emphasis on tasting, *dhawq,* in Chittik, *The Sufi Path of Knowledge,* p. 474, s.v. tasting. See also the text of R. Zeʾev Wolf of Zhitomir quoted by Weiss, *Studies,* p. 111 and below Appendix A n. 69.

14. Compare this statement with the second version of the story of the encounter between the Besht and the Maggid quoted above, where Luria's text is perceived as a means to experience the *Merkavah.*

15. *Yosher Divrei ʾEmet,* fol. 122a; *Keter Shem Tov,* 1, fol. 31b; see Scholem, *The Messianic Idea,* p. 218; Tishby, "Les traces," pp. 452–53; Idel, *Kabbalah: New Perspectives,* p. 58; Krassen, *"Devequt" and Faith* p. 33. Part of this quote was cited by R. Ḥayyim of Volozhin, *Nefesh ha-Ḥayyim,* fol. 47d. See also Lamm, *Torah Lishmah* pp. 110–11, 125 n. 54 who refers to the Besht as the addressee of R. Ḥayyim's critique. See also Jacobs, *Jewish Mystical Testimonies,* pp. 4–5.

16. I would say that, despite the fact that the study of the Torah also includes, in ordinary nomenclature, the Oral Torah, in the Hasidic text it is not this corpus that is intended but more eminently the Written Torah.

17. See Idel, *Kabbalah: New Perspectives,* pp. 234–49.

18. *Yosher Divrei ʾEmet,* fol. 19c; see also Schatz-Uffenheimer, *Quietistic Elements,* p. 71 n. 61 and Krassen, *"Devequt" and Faith,* pp. 395–96. Compare also to the tradition adduced in the name of R. Aharon of Zhitomir, the student of R. Levi Yiẓḥaq, to the effect that the reading of the book of the *Zohar* should be done by *kavvanah,* because they are able to cause the cleaving between man and the Infinite. Quoted from *Sheʾerit Yisrael,* in *Liqqutei ʾAmarim,* fol. 29b. In fact, this is an extension of the Beshtian view regarding the reading of the Torah. See immediately below in this paragraph.

19. *Boẓinaʾ di-Nehoraʾ* p. 73.

20. p. 241.

21. *Pirqei ʾAvot* (Jerusalem, 1972), fol. 25b and compare also to the legend that states that the Besht was given the authority from above to do whatever he wishes with the letters of the Torah; cf. Kaidaner, *Sippurim Noraʾim,* p. 34. See also R. Menaḥem Mendel of Rimanov, introduction to his *ʾIlanaʾ de-Ḥayyei,* fol. 3ab, where he asserts that if someone studies the Torah for its sake, he is allowed to introduce his own thought into the Torah.

22. See e.g., *ʾOr ha-Meʾir,* fol. 190a. Compare to Cordovero's *Sefer ha-Gerushin,* p. 18, where he writes about the lights that are "enclothed" within the permutations of letters that occur during someone's study of the Torah.

23. See *Maggid Devarav le-Yaʿaqov,* pp. 26–27; the story on R. Aharon Aryeh of Premislany is quoted in R. Eliezer Zeʾev of Kretchinev, *Razaʾ de-ʿUvdaʾ, Shaʿar ha-ʾOtiyot,* p. 47. On the Torah as divine names see the lengthy discussion of the Great Maggid in *ʾOr Torah,* p. 115. See also n. 11 above. The interpretation of R. Aharon Aryeh is reminiscent of the famous pantheistic song of R. Levi Yiẓḥaq of Berdichev, *Dudele.*

24. R. Meir Ḥarif Margoliot of Ostrog, *Sod Yakhin u-Voʿaz,* pp. 41–42, quoting the Besht; *Midrash Ribash Tov* (1927), fol. 10a, Scholem, *The Messianic Idea,* pp. 221, 213, Weiss, *Studies,* p. 59, ibid., "Talmud Torah" pp. 162–67. Weiss has devoted a lengthy analysis to this text, coming to the conclusion that this quote, though authentic, was at least partially influenced by the writings of the other disciples of the Besht. See also above, chap. 2, par. 2, the text of R. Joseph Giqatilla on cleaving to the letters. A partial parallel to this text, again adduced in the name of the Besht, is found as a quotation from R. Menaḥem Mendel of Lubavitch, in R. Ḥayyim Liebersohn, *Ẓeror ha-Ḥayyim,* fol. 32bc: "The quintessence of *devequt* is [to cleave to] the vitality of the letters, in holiness and purity." See also ibid., fol. 29d, where the view of R. Menaḥem Mendel of Lubavitch is quoted to the effect that "the letters of the Torah are vessels, by means of which someone is able to cleave to God." On the need to concentrate all the spiritual faculties and link them to each other in order to cleave to God, see de Vidas, *Reshit Ḥokhmah,* Gate of Love, chap. 3; 1, p. 400, where he refers to Cordovero's *Pardes Rimmonim,* 32; but such a precise quote does not occur there. See also above, chap. 2 n. 337. Compare also *Toledot Yaʿaqov Yosef,* fol. 4a, and the important quote in the name of R. Elimelekh of Lisansk in R. Qalonimus Qalman Epstein, *Maʾor va-Shemesh,* 5, fol. 31b. Compare also to *Ben Porat Yosef,* fol. 21a; *Toledot Yaʿaqov Yosef* fol. 25a; R. Menaḥem Mendel of Rimanov, *ʾIlanaʾ de-Ḥayyei,* vol. 54c. For other views in

Hasidism on achieving a unitive experience by studying Torah, see Idel, *Kabbalah: New Perspectives,* pp. 244–46; R. Shneor Zalman of Liady, *Tanya,* chap. 5, ibid., *Liqqutei Torah* 3, fol. 5a. The more intellectualistic approach of Ḥabad to study and cleaving will not be dealt with here. See Gries, *The Conduct Literature,* pp. 133–34; Elliot Wolfson, "Female Imagining of the Torah: From Literary Metaphor to Religious Symbol," *From Ancient Israel to Modern Judaism, Intellect in Quest of Understanding, Essays in Honor of Marvin Fox,* eds., J. Neusner, E. S. Frerichs, N. M. Sarna (Atlanta, Georgia, 1989), vol. 2 pp. 302–5.

25. cf. *Avot,* chap. 6. Idel, "The Concept of Torah," p. 36 n. 38. For the importance of sound in the Hasidic view of language see above, chap. 4.

26. R. Yehoshuʿa Abraham ben Yisrael, *Geʾulat Yisrael,* 1, fol. 17c (Appendix 1). According to another Beshtian tradition, the divestment of corporeality facilitates the cleaving with the divine spark, the vitality found within the letters, which is divested of its corporeality. See *Maggid Devarav le-Yaʿaqov,* p. 45, quoted in *Keter Shem Tov,* 1, fol. 36c and in *Ner Miẓwah,* fol. 17a. Therefore, a spiritualization of man ensures in our case the encounter with the spiritual dimension of language, and with that of reality in general. Compare another tradition, also presented by R. Aharon of Zhitomir, *Toledot ʾAharon,* 2, fol. 20c also in the name of the Besht, as found in a "book" of the Great Maggid, where the divestment of corporeality follows the experience of cleaving to the letters, unlike this passage, where it precedes it. Also in this quotation, the mentioning of the divestment is not accompanied by a magical effect. I would therefore say that the two traditions quoted by R. Aharon of Zhitomir describe the mystical part of the mystico-magical model, while the magic implications are not mentioned there, but can be conceived of as complementary, as they may occur on a later step.

27. See Weiss, *Studies,* pp. 58–68; Schatz-Uffenheimer, *Quietistic Elements,* pp. 70–71, 157–67; Tishby, "Les traces," pp. 452–53 n. 62; Lamm, *Torah Lishmah,* pp. 190–273, Piekarz, *The Beginning of Hasidism,* pp. 346–56, Gedalyah Nigal, "The Doctrine of Hasidism in the Book *Maʾor va-Shemesh,*" *Sinai* vol. 75 (1974) pp. 167–68 (Hebrew).

28. Joseph Weiss, in "Talmud Torah," pp. 151–69, has concentrated upon this issue, but none of the texts he has adduced corroborates his interpretation, or at least his view that the main way of Hasidic meditation was through contemplation of letters of the open scroll of the Torah or prayerbook (ibid., pp. 155–56), which is still to be proven. The single series of texts where the contemplation of an open book is evident (ibid., p. 155 n. 12) does not deal with studying Torah at all, but with short glances for the purpose of pneumatic visions. Weiss himself was compelled to recognize that the Besht "really doesn't study at all." The rejection of the theory of contemplation of written letters will explain Weiss's own uneasiness (ibid., p. 169 n. 40) over the recognition that in *Shiveḥei ha-Besht* the contemplation is done by hearing the texts while they are read by another person! For the possibility that the letters of prayer serve as instruments to contemplate God, see above chap. 4, n. 102. Another mystical interpretation of the study of the Torah, done in order to reach an experience of annihilation within the divine, and not for the sake of knowledge, is evident in *Sefat ʾEmet,* 3, fol. 85b. This strongly mystical view awaits a separate analysis.

29. Cf. Vital, *Peri ᶜEẓ Ḥayyim,* fol. 83b. See already *Sefer ha-Bahir,* par. 196; Cordovero's *Commentary on Sabbaᵓ de Mishpatim,* Ms. Oxford 1811, fol. 1a; see also *Ben Porat Yosef,* fol. 39c. Compare R. Shabbatai of Rashkov, *Siddur ha-ᵓAri,* fol. 123ab. For a collection of Lurianic material on the study of the Torah, see *Shulhan ᶜArukh shel Rabbeinu Yiẓḥaq Luria* (Kapust, 1710) fol. 22ab. See already in R. Meir ibn Gabbai, *ᶜAvodat ha-Qodesh,* introduction, fol. 4a.

30. R. Jacob Joseph of Polonoy, *Ben Porat Yosef,* fol. 21a. His source seems to be R. Shabbatai of Rashkov, *Siddur ha-ᵓAri,* fol. 123b or Vital, *Peri ᶜEẓ Ḥayyim,* fol. 83c, or Luria's *Sefer ha-Kavvanot,* fol. 12b. For the view of *devequt* as intended to repair *ᵓAdam ᶜEliyon* see Idel, *Kabbalah: New Perspectives,* p. 57.

31. *Pardes Rimmonim,* 27, chap. 2; 2, fol. 59c (Appendix 2). Compare also Azulai's *Ḥesed le-ᵓAvraham,* fol. 10a.

32. *Pardes Rimmonim,* 27, chap. 2; 2 fol. 60a (Appendix 3). On the effect of the reading by the ignorants see Scholem, "Two Testimonies" p. 236; Piekarz, in *The Beginning of Hasidism,* pp. 358–59 has pointed out the Cordoverian source of the *Shelah* and of R. Barukh of Kossov's discussions, conspicuously influenced by this passage. See also the view adduced in the name of R. Menaḥem Mendel of Lubavitch in R. Ḥayyim Liebersohn, *Ẓeror ha-Ḥayyim,* fol. 31a: "The study and the prayer, despite the fact that they do not intend t the meaning of the words, because the letters are from the Torah, they [the words] are vessels to the dwelling of God." On the loud study, including the story of Kabbalah, see the view of R. Dov Baer of Lubavitch, in Jacobs, *On Ecstasy,* p. 165.

33. On the Oral Law as the secret meaning of the Written Torah, see Urbach, *The Sages,* p. 271; Idel, *Language, Torah and Hermeneutics* pp. 46–55.

34. *Pardes Rimmonim,* 27, chap. 2; 2, fol. 59d (Appendix 4). Although in the Kabbalistic texts both prayer and study of the Torah are implicitly presented as similar, because of their use of Hebrew letters, in Hasidism prayer is regarded as higher. See especially the quotation in the name of the Besht adduced by R. Menaḥem Mendel of Rimanov, *ᵓIlanaᵓ de-Ḥayyei,* fol. 56b, where the founder of Hasidism is reported to have asserted that not his study but his prayer induced the revelations he received.

35. See *Reshit Ḥokhmah,* Gate of Holiness, chap. 6; 2 p. 87 (Appendix 5).

36. See chap. 4, par. 5. Compare also Scholem, *The Messianic Idea,* p. 213.

37. *Commentary on Massekhet ᵓAvot,* fol. 2b. See already de Vida, *Reshit Ḥokhmah,* Gate of Holiness, chap. 6; 2, pp. 84–85, where the study of the Torah is described as drawing forth the influx. See also the very interesting passage in R. Shelomo Rocca, *Kavvanat Shelomo* fols. 78c–d, where persons are requested to draw down influx, light, knowledge, etc., by means of the letter that corresponds to him, when the scroll of the Torah is shown to the public in the synagogue.

38. See above chap. 2, par. 5.

39. *Ḥesed le-ᵓAvraham,* fol. 10b.

40. Idel, "Magical and Neoplatonic Interpretations," pp. 198–205. The view of the Torah as a talisman, found in Alemanno, has an interesting parallel in a discussion of R. Jacob Joseph of Polonoy, *Toledot Ya ʿaqov Yosef,* fol. 170a, where the Torah is conceived as a vessel, mediating between the world and God. This mesocosmic role is well known in Jewish mysticism, though without the talismanic function of the Torah. See Idel, *Kabbalah: New Perspectives,* p. 370 n. 122.

41. See also Moshe Idel, Preface, to R. Joseph Al-Ashqar's *Sefer Ẓafnat Pa ʿaneaḥ* (Jerusalem, 1991), pp. 43–44 (Hebrew).

42. Fol. 1a (Appendix 6); *ʾOr ha-ʾEmet,* fol. 83d. See Weiss, "Talmud Torah," p. 161; according to this text, divinity is already present in the letters, and what remains for the mystic, or the simple man is to contemplate it. See also R. Ḥayyim of Chernovitz, *Sidduro shel Shabbat,* fol. 80c. Compare this text to Alemanno's view on the performance of music: "The material music can operate the operations related to it given its proportions, because of the spiritual force (*ruḥaniyyut*) inherent in it, even if the performance of music is deficient, this is because of its proportions, the music will be able to operate its operations." Idel, "The Magical and Theurgic Interpretations," p. 39. See also the view of R. Ḥayyim of Volozhin, *Nefesh ha-Ḥayyim* fol. 48cd, where a concept of attracting the supernal light and vitality is conspicuous, apparently also influenced by the Cordoverean scheme.

43. In Hebrew, *ve-roʾeh,* can also be translated: "and he understands."

44. Piekarz, in *The Beginning of Hasidism,* pp. 355, 357–58 and n. 170, has correctly pointed out that Cordovero, via quotations in *ha-Shelah,* might be the source for Hasidic views, especially of the passage in *Liqqutei Yeqarim*; however, he did not analyze the importance of the question of utterance that occurs in this discussion. See also ibid., p. 359, where Piekarz pointed out that the Cordoverian tradition was known also to eighteenth-century non-Hasidic Kabbalists. For the view that the letters are the vessels of the light of the Torah see R. Menaḥem Mendel of Lubavitch, *Derekh Miẓwoteika,* fol. 75a. Interestingly enough, this master asserts that this is a Lurianic view.

45. See above chap. 4, n. 89 from *Toledot Ya ʿaqov Yosef,* fol. 3a.

46. *Na ʿaseh ʾaḥdut ʿImo*; on the term *ʾAḥdut* see above chap. 2, n. 235.

47. *ʾOr ha-ʾEmet,* fols. 15b–17a (Appendix 7) and chap. 2 par. 6; compare also to R. Aharon Kohen of Apta, *ʾOr ha-Ganuz,* fol. 30ab. On other aspects f this text and its context see Schatz-Uffenheimer, *Quietistic Elements,* p. 105. Compare *Yosher Divrei ʾEmet,* fol. 25d, see our discussion above, chap. 4 par. 3 on the saying that "each sound is an entire world." Very long and important discussions on the recitation of the sounds of the Torah and prayer, in relation to the term *Ruḥaniyyut* is found in R. Levi Yiẓḥaq of Berdichev, *Qedushat Levi,* fols. 139ab, 140d–141a and in R. Schneor Zalman of Liady's *Liqqutei Torah,* 3, fol. 76a, where the attracting of the revelation of the infinite light into the Torah is presented as the interpretation of the study of *Torah li-shemah.* See also Scholem, *The Messianic Idea,* pp. 211, 213.

48. On the identity between these three elements see Tishby, "*Qudsha*ʾ *Berikh Hu*ʾ." However, the view of the activity of Israel as a condition for the fulfillment of this identity is very rare. See also, Introduction, n. 10.

49. *Degel Maḥaneh* ʾ*Efrayim,* p. 103 (Appendix 8).

50. Ibid., p. 103 (Appendix 9). The cleaving in this passage explicitly refers to the Ten Commandments as they were pronounced at Sinai, namely to their oral status.

51. Compare the Lurianic view adduced by R. Meshullam Phoebus in the name of R. Menaḥem Mendel of Premislany, where the study of Torah is referred to by the term *qeri*ʾ*ah*—oral reading, which ends with the cleaving of the soul with her root: cf. Tishby, "Les traces," pp. 452–53, n. 62 (Hebrew version, p. 226, n. 61), who, however, does not mention the fact that "reading" is to be interpreted as an oral activity. See also the interesting story on the Seer of Lublin, who after studying a page of the Gemaraʾ, was fond of reciting it without thinking about the content, *beli* ʿ*iuun.* Cf. ʿ*Eser* ʾ*Orot,* fol. 46b, no. 30.

52. See *No*ʿ*am* ʾ*Elimelekh,* by R. Elimelekh of Lisansk, fols. 8a, 64b, 59b. See Gedalyah Nigal, "Study and Precepts in the Teaching of R. Elimelekh of Lisansk and His Disciples," *Tarbiẓ* 42 (1973) pp. 476–77 (Hebrew).

53. See e.g., R. Eliezer Lippa of Lisansk, ʾ*Oraḥ le-Ẓaddiq,* pp. 19, 32, 34, 82, 137, etc., where the phrases ʾ*Elohut, ruḥaniyyut, ḥiyyut ha-ruḥaniyyut* are mentioned in this context.

54. Cf. chap. 4, par. 5.

55. See above, chap. 3, par. 5.

56. *Toledot Ya*ʿ*aqov Yosef,* fol. 133c (Appendix 10). Compare also *Maggid Devarav le-Ya*ʿ*aqov,* pp. 26, 87; *Deḥel Mahaneh* ʾ*Efrayim,* p. 56; *Yismaḥ Lev,* p. 303.

57. 2, fol. 99b.

58. See also *Degel Maḥaneh* ʾ*Efrayim* pp. 175–76.

59. The Great Maggid is obviously influenced by the Cordoverian and Lurianic concepts of revelation of the supernal voice by its entering the material voice during prayer or study of the Torah; see e.g. Ḥayyim Vital's *Sefer ha-Gilgulim* (Vilna, 1886) fol. 60a, and Abraham Azulai's *Ḥesed le-*ʾ*Avraham,* fol. 11b. The latter is seemingly the direct source of the Great Maggid. See also Idel, *The Mystical Experience,* pp. 85–86 and compare to R. Shemuel Shmelke of Nikolsburg, *Divrei Shemuel,* p. 143.

60. ʾ*Or ha-*ʾ*Emet,* fols. 84d–85a (Appendix 11); see also ibid., fol. 83b and compare to the material adduced and discussed by Schatz-Uffenheimer, *Quietistic Elements,* pp. 119–21; *Hasidism as Mysticism,* pp. 201–3..

61. Compare this way of receiving knowledge of future events to the famous technique of the Besht of looking randomly in the Torah in order to answer questions: cf. Weiss, *Studies,* p. 59 and chap. 2, n. 185.

62. This view is already found in the text of R. Jacob Joseph of Polonoy, mentioned below, n. 63. See also R. Dov Baer of Lubavitch, *Be᾿urei ha-Zohar,* fol. 107a, where the deification of the Hebrew letters is formulated in the most explicit terms.

63. *Liqqutei Torah,* fol. 29d. A very similar passage occurs ibid., fol. 30d. See also the immanentistic view of the letters in *Toledot Ya῾aqov Yosef,* fol. 7a, quoted in chap. 2, par. 6. See also R. Qalonimus Qalman Epstein, *Ma᾿or va-Shemesh,* 1, fol. 3c and below, Concluding Remarks, par. 3.

64. See, however, the description of the Besht as contemplating the lights in the Torah; cf. n. 61 above.

65. See Idel, "The Concept of the Torah," pp. 52–54.

66. Ibid., pp. 49–52.

67. The view that each and every letter is a divine Name is discussed above, chap. 4 pars. 2–3.

68. *Degel Maḥaneh ᾿Efrayim,* pp. 119–20 (Appendix 12). Compare the interpretation of this verse in *Shemu῾ah Tovah,* p. 79. See also R. Shneor Zalman of Liady, *Torah ᾿Or,* fol. 1c, R. Aharon Kohen of Apta, *Ner Miẓwah,* fol. 30b and R. Yiẓḥaq Aiziq Safrin of Komarno, *Heikhal ha-Berakhah,* 5, fol. 41a.

69. *Li-shemah* turns into *le-hashem*; compare R. Ḥayyim of Chernovitz's interpretation of *li-shemah*; see *Sha῾ar ha-Tefillah,* Responsa, fol. 10b (Appendix 13). The author of *Degel Maḥaneh ᾿Efrayim* was among the authorities who approved the printing of R. Ḥayyim's book.

70. *᾿Oẓar ῾Eden Ganuz,* Ms. Oxford, 1580, fol. 172b; Idel, *Language, Torah and Hermeneutics,* pp. 106–7; and above, chap. 4, par. 3 and n. 43; Y. A. Vajda (ed.), *R. Judah ben Nissim ibn Malka's Commentary on the Book of Creation* (Ramat Gan, 1974), p. 53, and compare ibid., pp. 31–32, 41. See also chap. 4, n. 29.

71. Compare the transformation of the Torah during its mystical study into the divine names to a very similar phenomenon in Hasidic prayer, according to the Great Maggid, in *᾿Or ha-᾿Emet,* fol. 25bc (Appendix 14). It is probable that the higher efficiency of the letters, or words, seen as divine names, has something to do with a peculiar formulation of Cordovero's thought in *ha-Shelah,* 1, fol. 5a: see also Appendix 14. Compare the texts from R. Shelomo ha-Levi Alqabetz, Ms. Oxford 40, cited above, chap. 4, n. 80-81.

72. See Ms. Oxford 2239, fol. 124a (Appendix 15). This quotation appears in a *Collectanaea* of mystical quotes collected by R. Joseph Ḥamitz, which includes a large amount of Abulafian material. This quote may be part of a lost work of Abulafia that dealt with ways of interpreting the Torah. Surprisingly enough, R. Jacob Joseph also views the study of Torah for its own sake as the seventh way: *Toledot Ya῾aqov Yosef,* fol. 108d. See further in Appendix 16. The source of this seventh study is indeed Luria; and see Nigal (n. 52 above), p. 471. However, it is interesting to note that the link between the seventh way and *li-shemah* is R. Jacob Joseph᾿s.

73. Compare to the magical text discussed in Idel, "Magical and Neoplatonic Interpretation," pp. 199–200.

74. *Me ᵓor ᶜEinayim,* p. 171 (Appendix 17), and also there ibid., concerning Moshe being described as drawing down.

75. Ibid. (Appendix 18). On the phrase *Dibbur qadmon,* which recurs in this treatise and is a rather rare term, see Abraham Abulafia's passage analyzed in Idel, *The Mystical Experience,* pp. 83–84. See also the quote from *ᵓOr ha-ᵓEmet,* quoted above chap. 2, par. 6.

76. Ibid., fol. 56a (Appendix 19).

77. Ibid., fol. 56b (Appendix 20). Cf. ibid., fol. 3c.

78. Ibid., fol. 66b (Appendix 21).

79. Cf. *Yismaḥ Lev,* p. 297. According to the famous medieval definition of man, his essence is the power of speech; R. Menaḥem Naḥum interprets the medieval definition of man as a "thinking living being," as a reference to *medabber,* speaking, preferring speech rather than thought as the defining moment.

80. *Yeshu ᶜot.* This term recurs in Hasidic parlance in connection to remedies. See e.g., ibid., fol. 13d; *Darkhei Ẓedeq,* fol. 2a.

81. *Toledot Yiẓḥaq,* fol. 15a (Appendix 22).

82. Ibid.

83. See also ibid., fol. 14b again in the name of the Besht.

84. Ibid., fol. 14c (Appendix 23).

85. R. Asher Ẓevi of Ostraha, *Ma ᶜayan ha-Ḥokhmah,* fol. 42c. See also the Ḥabad version of this idea, cf. Loewenthal, *Communicating the Infinite,* pp. 59–60 and the corresponding footnotes (add also *Tanya, Liqqutei ᵓAmarim,* chap. 36 fol. 56a), R. Yehudah Arieh Leib of Gur, *Sefat ᵓEmet,* 3, fols. 7a, 72c, 84cd, 85b; 4, fol. 1c and many examples in quotes adduced in chap. 3.

86. Chap. 4, par. 4.

87. See however, chap. 2 n. 176.

88. See Idel, *Kabbalah: New Perspectives,* pp. 248–49.

89. Perhaps this is a view similar to the Avicennian theory to be referred to below, chap. 6 par 1. The expression "source of miracle" occurs also in *Sefat ᵓEmet,* 3, fol. 86a.

90. *Mayyim Rabbim,* fol. 42b, the editors quoting the various books of the Seer of Lublin, who repeatedly refers to the views of the Maggid of Zlotchov; see *Zikkaron Zot,* fol. 13c, *Zot Zikkaron,* fol. 19c; *Divrei ᵓEmet,* fol. 16c. Compare also to *Mayyim Rabbim,* fol. 23a.

91. See below, chap. 6, par. 1.

92. See above, chap. 4, par. 3. See also the view of R. Naḥman of Brazlav on the stories as vessels of a higher truth, as analyzed by Piekarz, *Studies in Braslav Hasidism,* pp. 112–13 and the view of R. Menaḥem Mendel of Rimanov, *ʾIlanaʾ de-Ḥayyei,* fols. 43d–44a, where the intention of the heart is able to change the meaning of the biblical text and attract the divine influx.

93. Compare to R. Abraham of Turisk, *Magen ʾAvraham* (Lublin, rpr. Brooklyn, 1985) 2, fol. 29cd. See also R. Messhullam Phoebus of Zbarazh, *Yosher Divrei ʾEmet,* fol. 140b where a Lurianic view, which does not use the talismatic notions, is quoted in the context dealing with reverberations of the primordial days in the post-creational aeon. See also the view, attributed to the Besht, that the events dictate the combinations of letters that express them in the Bible; see Scholem, *On the Kabbalah,* pp. 76–77. It means that if we repeat today the combination of letters that represent what happened in *illud tempus* the primordial event is reenacted.

94. Fol. 5a.

95. *ʾEreẓ Ḥayyim, Liqqutim Megillat Ester,* fol. 25cd. See also above, chap. 2, par. 3.

96. i.e. R. Israel of Ryzhin.

97. In Agnon's version, as transmitted by Scholem, the nature of this need is rather vague, as is its magical implication; in Wiesel's version, it is the necessity of saving the Jewish people from an imminent catastrophe.

98. The Besht.

99. It should be noted that our version does not mention the kindling of the candle, as in Agnon's story, where the fire in the woods is hardly understandable. It may well be that the motif of the fire is the result of a misunderstanding of the role of the candle in our version. I presume that the candle is a substitute for the soul of the son, according to the verse: "The spirit of man is the candle of God" (Prov. 20:27). The tree presumably stands for the tree of souls, while the link between the candle and the tree is accordingly an act of sympathetic magic, intended to strengthen the affinity between the son and his family. On the "tree of souls" in Kabbalah, see Scholem, *On the Mystical Shape,* pp. 95, 97–98. On the lighting of the candle as a symbol for an uninterrupted flow, see above, chap. 2, n. 312.

100. On the decline of the importance of Lurianic *kavvanot* in Hasidism, see above, chap. 4, par. 1. On the Besht's use of the *kavvanot* of the divine names see a tradition discussed by R. Menaḥem Mendel of Lubavitch, adduced in the additions to *Keter Shem Tov,* fol. 133b.

101. In the Hebrew version of R. Yisrael of Ryzhin, the word "*lehashʾyt*" may be a mistake, as noted by Piekarz, *Studies in Braslav Hasidism,* p. 103, the correct version being "*Vehashʾyt*" namely, "and [then] God helps." However, even if this correction is acceptable, the common interpretation that the storytelling is mainly directed toward man, thereby causing a certain result through the help of God, is not self-evident. Even according to the proposed correction, God may be the main aim of the narration, preserving the theurgical nature of this activity.

102. R. Yisrael of Ryzhin, *Knesset Israel,* fol. 12a. Another version of this legend was told by S. Y. Agnon to Scholem, *Major Trends,* pp. 349–50. However, the gist of Agnon's version, as well as Scholem's interpretation, differs from the above and from the interpretation proposed here. An important analysis of this study is found in Yoav Elstein, *Ma ʾaseh Ḥoshev, Studies in Hasidic Tales* (Tel Aviv, 1983) pp. 54–57; Assaf, *Rabbi Israel of Ruzhin,* p. 245. See also Elie Wiesel, *Celebration hassidique* (Paris, 1972), p. 172; Geoffrey Harmann, *The Fate of Reading and Other Essays* (Chicago and London, 1974), pp. 273–74; and n. 110 below. Crucial for the proper understanding of the story is R. Yisrael of Ryzhin's own distinction, already found earlier (see below n. 105) between two forms of activity: some of the *Ẓaddiqim* used Torah and prayer as the main agent of their acts when the world was in the state of *Gadelut,* while others used the telling of stories, because the world is in the state of *Qatenut.* While there is good reason to see the former type as earlier and the latter as later, the reason for the two types of activity is not the descent of the *Ẓaddiq* but of the populace. See *Razin de-ʿOraita ʾ,* no pagination.

103. On the important religious role of storytelling in Hasidism, see Piekarz, *The Beginning of Hasidism,* pp. 83–113, esp. pp. 102–3, where our story is referred to. See also Elstein, ibid., and Dan, *The Hasidic Story.* Compare especially to R. Yisrael of Ryzhin's *Knesset Yisrael,* fol. 16d, where storytelling is presented as tantamount to prayer.

104. R. Nathan in *Sippurei Ma ʿasiyot* of R. Naḥman of Braslav (New York, 1949) *haqdamah Rishonah,* p. 6. Adduced by Elstein, *Ma ʿaseh Ḥoshev,* p. 56 n. 30, in the context of the story of R. Yisrael of Ryzhin.

105. *Ma ʾor va-Shemesh,* 4, fol. 17c. The same list occurs again some lines later. On fol. 17d, he equates prayer to thought and constructs thereby the well-known medieval triad of deed, speech, and thought. However, the identification of prayer to thought reflects an attempt to fit the practice of *Ẓaddiqim* into the procrustean bed of medieval thought. On the Besht's view on speeches see also above chap. 3, n. 49. See also the view of R. Menaḥem Mendel of Lubavitch that it is possible to use the divine names either by deed, by speech, or by thought; see the passage quoted, in relation to the Besht, in the Yiddish additions to *Keter Shem Tov,* fol. 133b. Compare to another typology of magical activity of the *Ẓaddiqim* in R. Uzziel Meisel's *Tiferet ʿUzziel* (Warsau, 1863), fol. 28d, where he distinguishes between the righteous who are able to perform their deeds by means of speeches alone, and those who need a much more complex sequel of acts that include prayers, solitude, or mental concentration, etc. See also above, n. 102. Compare also the tradition of the Seer of Lublin adduced by R. Ẓevi Elimelekh of Dinov, *Benei Yisaskhar,* 1, fol. 20a, *ʾEser ʾOrot,* fol. 54a. On the distinction between miraculous achievements performed by speech alone, which are temporary, and those attained by prayer, which are lasting.

106. Rubinstein, *Shiveḥei ha-Besht,* p. 256; Ben Amos-Mintz, *In Praise of the Baal Shem Tov,* p. 199. On the mystical understandings of *Ma ʿaseh Merkavah* in Hasidism see Schatz-Uffenheimer, *Quietistic Elements,* p. 128; Loewenthal, *Communicating the Infinite,* pp. 59–60; Idel, "*Ma ʿaseh Merkavah.*"

107. *The Messianic Idea,* pp. 198–99. See also his *Sabbatai Ṣevi,* p. 206.

108. The closest statements are found in the book *Bahir,* par. 68, where mystical prayer is compared to contemplating the *Merkavah*; however, even this parallel is not close enough to constitute a significant source for the Hasidic view. A statement that seems more significant is found in R. Nathan Shapira of Cracow, *Megalleh ʿAmuqot* ed. Shalom Weiss (Benei Beraq, 1982) 1, p. 45, where each of the people of Israel is described as a "complete *Merkavah*" because of the divine Presence in their limbs.

109. On the soul of the righteous as the limb of the divine Presence, see also the quotes referred in chap. 4 n. 133. See also the important remark of Liebes on the possible sources of this view, "The Messiah of the Zohar," p. 162 n. 270. On the righteous as the *Merkavah* see Rashi on Genesis 17, 22; Azulai, *Ḥesed le-ʾAvraham,* fol. 13c (quoted by R. Jacob Joseph of Polonoy, *Ktoneth Passim,* p. 152); and above, chap. 3, n. 49 and below, chap. 6. See R. Joseph Moshe of Zalozich, *Berit ʾAbram,* fol. 42c, where he mentions the *Shelah,* as the source of the view of the *Ẓaddiqim* as a chariot. See also *Maʾor va-Shemesh,* 1, fol. 12b, apparently influenced by the passage from Horowitz's *Shaʿar ha-Shamayim,* quotd above, chap. 2, par. 6, and above n. 14, and below n. 111.

110. *Studies in Braslav Hasidism,* p. 107; Gries, *The Conduct Literature,* p. 141 n. 153. See also Buber's preface to *Tales of Hasidim, Early Masters* p. v who was able to capture, without using any parallels and technical terms, the gist of the storytelling, without however, emphasizing its magical aspects.

111. *Darkhei Ẓedeq,* fol. 6b, no. 40. See also ibid., fol. 5a, the tradition brought by the author in the name of his teacher, R. Elimelekh of Lisansk, to the effect that someone may think that he becomes the chariot of the *Shekhinah* by purifying his thought. This tradition is already found, as mentioned by the Hasidic master, in the influential seventeenth-century collection named *Shaʿarei Ẓiyon.* See also n. 109 and R. Pinḥas of Koretz's statement to the effect that by various good deeds man becomes the chariot of some angels. Cf. *Midrash Pinḥas,* fol. 20a. The most extreme mystical formulation is found in R. Barukh of Kossov's *ʿAmud ha-ʿAvodah,* fol. 238b, where the *Ẓaddiq*'s becoming the chariot of the *Shekhinah* is tantamount to being totally united with her. See also R. Eliezer Lippa of Lisansk, *ʾOraḥ le-Ẓaddiq,* p. 82.

112. The story is related by R. Moshe of Savaran, a student of R. Levi Yiẓḥaq of Berdichev; see Piekarz, *Studies in Braslav Hasidism,* p. 110 n. 62. See also above, chap. 3, par. 4.

113. On the pun *Ḥiyyut* and *Ḥayyei ha-Ḥayyim,* see above, chap. 3, n. 158 and R. Yehudah Leib of Gur, *Sefat ʿEmet,* 3, fol. 84c. The appellation "life of lives" for God is found already in *Shiʿur Qomah,* an ancient book from the *Heikhalot* literature, and probably also in Hermetic literature: see Grese, "Magic in Hellenistic Hermeticism," p. 53.

114. See *Sefer ha-Ḥayyim,* also called *Sefer Seggulot Yisrael* ed. Z. E. Sofer Fuchs (NP, 1905) fol. 55b. Compare also to the very interesting text of R. Naḥman of Braslav, about the drawing down of the interpretations by the interpreters; see Idel, *Kabbalah: New Perspectives,* p. 242.

115. See the very illuminating passage on fol. 10cd where the student of the Torah draws down the influx, or the *hamshakhah* by his delight in studying the Torah.

NOTES TO CHAPTER 6

1. The most important are Scholem, *On the Mystical Shape,* pp. 88–139; L. I. Niemirower, *Chassidismus und Zaddikismus* (Bukarest, 1913); Weiss, *Studies,* pp. 183–94; Schatz, "*Le-Mahuto*"; Elior, "Between *Yesh* and *Ayin*"; Green, "Typologies of Leadership," ibid., "*Ẓaddiq* as *Axis Mundi*"; Tishby-Dan, "Hasidism" pp. 779–83; Piekarz, "Devekuth," ibid., *Hasidism in Poland* pp. 44–47, 157–202; Weiss, *Studies in Braslav Hassidism,* pp. 153–54 n. 3; ibid., in Rubinstein, *Studies in Hasidism,* pp. 145–47; Gries, *The Book in Hasidism,* pp. 99–102; Louis Jacobs, *Holy Living—Saints and Saintliness in Judaism* (New Jersey and London, 1990); Mahler, *Hasidism and the Jewish Enlightenment,* pp. 245–70; Joel Orent, "The Transcendent Person," *Judaism,* vol. 9 (1960) pp. 235–52; Dan, *The Hasidic Story,* in the index p. 273 s.v. *Ẓaddiq,* Gedalyah Nigal, "On the Image of the Hasidic Ẓaddiq," *Molad,* vol. 35–36 (1975) pp. 176–82 (Hebrew); Jacobson, *La pensée hassidique,* pp. 161–78; Moshe Ḥallamish, "The Relation between Ẓaddiq and Community in the Doctrine of R. Shneor Zalman of Liady," *Society and History,* ed. J. Dan (Jerusalem, 1980) pp. 79–92 (Hebrew); Paul B. Fenton, "The Hierarchy of the Saints in Jewish and Islamic Mysticism," *Journal of the Muhyiddin Ibn ᶜArabi Society,* vol. 10 (1991) pp. 12–34. See also Katz, "Models" pp. 259–61. On the pre-Hasidic concepts of *Ẓaddiq* see, in addition to Scholem, ibid., also Tishby, *The Wisdom of the Zohar,* 2, pp. 655–702.

2. On this issue see below.

3. For a treatment of the Rabbinic views of *Ẓaddiq* see Urbach, *The Sages,* pp. 483–511, Rudolph Mach, *Der Zaddik in Talmud und Midrasch* (Leiden, 1967), Scholem, ibid., pp. 88–92; Jack N. Lightstone, "Magicians, Holy Men, and Rabbi: Patterns of the Sacred in the Late Antiquity" in ed. William Green, *Approaches to Ancient Judaism,* vol. 1 (1985) pp. 133–48; Jacob Neusner, *The Wonder-Working Lawyers of Talmudic Babylonia* (New York and London, 1987).

4. On this subject see Weiss, in ed. Rubinstein, *Studies in Hasidism,* pp. 125–34, 145–46; Mahler, *Hasidism and the Enlightenment,* pp. 251–62. It should be mentioned that Weiss, ibid., p. 146, strongly emphasizes that in the theory of the *Ẓaddiq* in the pneumatic circles that were congenial with the emergence of Hasidism, the magical element was totally absent! However, on p. 127 he himself adduces a quote in the name of R. Naḥman of Horodenka, cited by R. Jacob Joseph of Polonoy, *Ẓafnat Pa ᶜaneaḥ,* fol. 22a, to the effect that the prayer of the simple man is able to bring down material influx: *nimshakh shefa ᶜ*. In my opinion, the stark distinction between the earlier group of pneumatics and the later Hasidic views is untenable, beyond the material on the mystico-magical model in Kabbalah. See also above chap. 3, n. 267.

5. Scholem, *On the Mystical Shape,* pp. 124–26; ibid., *The Messianic Idea,* p. 197; ibid., *Major Trends,* p. 334; Weiss, in Rubinstein, ed. *Studies in Hasidism,* pp. 1238, 132; Liebes, "Ẓaddiq Yesod ᶜOlam"; ibid., "The Messiah of the Zohar," pp. 138–51 especially pp. 141–43 n. 211; Joseph Dan, *Jewish Mysticism and Jewish Ethics,* (Seattle and London, 1986) pp. 115, 117. Especially interesting is his declaration (p.

115) that "It is not difficult to discover the origin of this (*Ẓaddiq* as supplying sustenance) idea. It is a transformation of the Sabbatean theology of the Messiah." This is just one example how an uncritical reliance on Scholem, and a lack of attention to the magical sources, generate bizarre certainties. See also above chap. 3, n. 2.

6. "Les traces."

7. The general question of the influence of Sabbateanism on Hasidism is not our concern here. See more recently Etkes, "The Study of Hasidism," (introduction, n. 113). Rubinstein, in ed. Rubinstein, *Studies in Hasidism,* pp. 182–97.

8. *The Beginning of Hasidism,* pp. 299–302. It should be mentioned that another important source that could have been influential on Hasidism is the Maharal's concept of the righteous. See Sherwin, *The Mystical Theology,* pp. 164–66.

9. On the other, and in my opinion even more general, significance of Piekarz's findings for the definition of Judaism as religion, I hope to elaborate elsewhere. See his *Hasidism in Poland,* pp. 37ff, and his other studies mentioned on p. 39 n. 4.

10. Compare also above, chap. 5 par. 3 and Green, *Devotion and Commandment,* p. 16 and Idel, "*Be-ʾOr ha-Ḥayyim*" pp. 194–95.

11. *Beʾer Moshe,* fol. 28bc. The Neoplatonic explanation of the miracles was accepted by both Hasidim and Mitnaggedim. See the letter of R. Menaḥem Mendel of Shklov to R. Yehudah Leib de Butin, printed in Wilensky, *Hasidim and Mitnaggedim,* 1, pp. 315–16 or R. Barukh of Kossov, *ʿAmud ha-ʿAvodah,* fol. 199d.

12. See Dubnow, *The History of Hasidism,* pp. 217–18.

13. On the ide of a continuum see below Concluding Remarks, par. 3 and n. 35. See also Idel, "*Be-ʾOr ha-Ḥayyim*" pp. 194–96.

14. See ibid., pp. 194–96, 199–201.

15. Ibid., the author describes the commandment as it is in its source as "great and shining spiritual lights, which are infinite." This view is approximated already at the beginning of Kabbalah; see Idel, "*Be-ʾOr ha-Ḥayyim,*" p. 195.

16. See below n. 102 and above chap. 3 par. 3.

17. On *Ẓaddiqim* and magic in Hasidism, see Nigal, *Magic, Mysticism and Hasidism,* passim, Alfasi, "Supernal Apprehensions," Weiss, *Studies,* pp. 126–30; Mahler, *Hasidism and the Jewish Enlightenment* pp. 262–67. It should be mentioned that in a Yiddish version of a story of R. Naḥman of Braslav, a certain nexus between *Ẓaddiq* and sorcer, *mekashshef,* is mentioned. See Shmeruk, *Yiddish Literature,* p. 182 n. 30.

18. See chap. 3 pars. 3–6.

19. See above chap. 2 par. 3.

20. Ibid. The definition of man as a vessel, *Keli,* in relation to the supernal world appears already in R. Shem Tov ben Shem Tov, *Sefer ha-ʾEmunot,* fol. 55a (Appendix

1). Compare also to the anonymous Ashkenazi *Commentary on Shir ha-Yiḥud* discussed in Idel, "An Anonymous Commentary."

21. On the magician as a vessel and a channel see Georg Luck, *Arcana Mundi,* (Crucible, 1985) p. 3.

22. See, especially, the quote in Azulai's *ʾOr ha-Ḥamah,* 2, fol. 233c.

23. *ʾEreẓ Ḥayyim Liqqutim Shir ha-Shirim,* fols. 25c–26b.

24. See chap. 2, par. 7.

25. This term does not occur in the passage from Cordovero that inspired Azulai.

26. Fol. 21b. See also R. Abraham of Radomsk, *Ḥesed le-ʾAvraham* fol. 67b, where righteous woman are conceived as "houses" that receives the influx, and also as pipes.

27. See also R. Nathan-Netaʿ of Siniewa, *ʿOlat ha-Tamid,* 1, fol. 11b.

28. *Toledot Yaʿaqov Yosef,* fol. 66c. See Piekarz, "Devekuth" pp. 141.

29. Ibid., fol. 66c; see also Dresner, *The Zaddik,* p. 126. See also *Ẓafnat Paʿaneaḥ,* fol. 115c, where the Besht is quoted to the effect that the body is a vessel.

30. 2, fol. 218a; see also ibid., fol. 69a, and Cohen-Aloro, *Magic and Sorcery,* p. 104.

31. See *Ruth Rabba,* 4, 12.

32. See above, chap. 3, par. 2 on the nexus between humility and mystical achievement and Weiss, *Studies,* p. 85.

33. *Maggid Devarav le-Yaʿaqov,* p. 233 (Appendix 2). Compare to R. Jacob Joseph of Polonoy, *Toledot Yaʿaqov Yosef* fol. 169d (Appendix 3); see also his *Ẓafnat Paʿaneaḥ* fol. 15c; compare the Midrashic view of Moshe in *Mekhiltaʾ* on Exodus, 18, 19; Yehudah ha-Levi, *Kuzari* 4, 3, cf. Boaz Cohen, *Law and Tradition in Judaism* (New York, 1959) p. 24, n. 70.

34. Exodus 25, 8. See also beside n. 38 below.

35. *Ketubbot* fol. 111b.

36. This interpretation is an interesting approximation of the Rabbinic passages dealing with the impossibility of the achievement of *devequt* by the *vulgus,* but allowing such an attainment to the elite. See the important discussion of Sherwin, *The Mystical Theology,* pp. 124–27. On the study of the Torah for its own sake as the palace of the *Shekhinah,* see R. Yisrael of Kuznitz, *ʿAvodat Yisrael,* fol. 68c.

37. *Ẓafnat Paʿaneaḥ,* fol. 64d (Appendix 4); Dresner, *The Zaddik,* pp. 122–123, pp. 276–77. See also *Ẓafnat Paʿaneaḥ,* fol. 65a. According to an additional discussion, ibid., fol. 105c, the Besht was already maintaining this view. On the view of man as a temple in the context of astrological discussions, see Henry Corbin, "Rituel Sabéen et Exegese Ismailienne du rituel," *Eranos Jahrbuch,* vol. 19 (1951) pp. 194–97 n. 41; p.

214. The Arabic sources use the term *hayakal* when referring to man as the temple of the *ruḥaniyun,* the spiritual entities. It should be mentioned that in Arabic this term means both palace and body, and this double meaning was adopted by R. Yiẓḥaq of Acre in his *ʾOẓar Ḥayyim.* See e.g., Ms. Moscow-Guenzburg 775, fols. 94a, 181b and Idel, *Kabbalah: New Perspectives,* pp. 306–7 n. 69, 71. See also n. 26 above.

38. See n. 34 above.

39. *Yebamot,* fol. 63b–64a.

40. On the meaning of this word, *ʾot,* see also above, chap. 4 n. 45.

41. *Ẓafnat Paʿaneaḥ,* fol. 88b (Appendix 5); see also ibid., fol. 75cd. Compare also to R. Aharon of Zhitomir, *Toledot ʾAharon,* 2, fol. 47c and R. Yisrael Shalom Joseph of Buhush, *Peʾer Yisrael,* fols. 9b–10a. See also Cordovero's text printed by Sack, "The Attitude" (ch. 2, note 16), p. 74.

42. Ibid., fol. 31a (Appendix 6); Idel, *Kabbalah: New Perspectives,* p. 352 n. 366 and chap. 3, n. 246.

43. *Leẓamẓem.*

44. *Shemuʾah Tovah,* p. 73 (Appendix 7); see Schatz-Uffenheimer, *Quietistic Elements,* pp. 97–98. Earlier, the anonymous author from the Great Maggid's circle mentions the letters that are contemplated in the prayer's thought, whereas now he deals with the pronounced letters.

45. Cf. Isaiah 10:15; this metaphor was used to allude to the relations between the quintessence of the *Sefirot,* i.e. the lights, and the *Sefirot* qua vessels.

46. *Siddur ha-Geraʾ, ʾImrei Shefer,* fol. 5b (Appendix 8).

47. Ibid., fol. 6a (Appendix 9).

48. *Nefesh ha-Ḥayyim,* fol. 41c.

49. Ibid., fol. 48d (Appendix 10).

50. See Appendix 11.

51. See Idel, "Universalization and Integration," pp. 34–50.

52. *Sefer ha-Tanya,* chap. 41, fol. 57b (Appendix 12).

53. The exact performance of the Halakhic ritual is indispensable when viewed from a magical perspective: see already Alemanno's view, Idel, "The Magical and Neoplatonic Interpretations," p. 208; Idel, "The Epistle of R. Yiẓḥaq Pisa(?) in its Hebrew Versions," *Qovetz ʿal Yad,* vol. 10 (20) (Jerusalem, 1982), pp. 166–67 (Hebrew).

54. On the magical perception of the Temple see Idel, "The Magical and Neoplatonic Interpretations," pp. 208–10; Idel, "Magical Temples," p. 187.

55. Ms. Berlin, pp. 130–32.

56. See *An Autobiography,* p. 103; the content was quoted above chap. 1, par. 4; cf. also p. 95: "Originally, the Cabbalah was nothing but psychology, physics, morals, politics and such sciences," and p. 94, on the practical Kabbalah, "which teaches how to work upon nature at pleasure by means of those manifold names of God, which represent various modes of working upon, and relation to, natural objects. These second names are regarded, not as merely arbitrary, but as natural objects. These second names are regarded, not as merely arbitrary, but as natural signs." See also below n. 58, chap. 2, n. 184 and Concluding Remarks, par. 4.

57. The superiority of the magicians over the philosophers is pointed out by Alemanno: See Idel, "Magic Temples," p. 187; see also Pines, "On the Term *Ruḥaniyyut* and its Sources," pp. 531–34. Compare also to the similar distinction found in Iamblichus, *On the Mysteries of Egypt,* 2, 11 and the whole discussion of Georg Luck, "Theurgy and Forms of Worship in Neoplatonism," in Neusner et alia, eds., *Religion, Science, and Magic,* pp. 185–25, especially p. 186–87.

58. Ms. Berlin, p. 131 (Appendix 13); compare the two distinct attitudes to nature here, the knowledge of the ways of nature, and the ability to use this knowledge, to the definition of practical Kabbalah presented above, n. 56, which fits the second issue.

59. Compare chap. 4, n. 54, where Abraham Yagel defines the preparations of matters to receive spiritual force "natural magic" see Ruderman, *Kabbalah, Magic, and Science,* pp. 110–11.

60. See Ms. Berlin, p. 132 (Appendix 14).

61. The Besht was famous for his magical capacities; see also Maimon's *An Autobiography,* p. 165.

62. *Ḥesheq Shelomo,* Ms. Berlin, p. 145, printed in Idel, "The Magical and Theurgic Interpretation," p. 39, Cordovero's text, quoted anonymously, stems from his *Pardes Rimmonim,* 10, chap. 1; 1, fol. 59bc. See also above chap. 2, par. 3.

63. The white garments were used by Kabbalists as well as Hasidic masters, beginning with the Besht himself. Therefore, the assertion of Eliach, "The Russian Sects," p. 73, that the *khlysty* sect influenced the Hasidic wearing of white, this being of a non-Jewish nature, is very dubious. The use of the event of excommunication (Dubnow, *The History of Hasidism,* p. 121) to prove the alien origin is strange; the text quoted by Dubnow clearly evinces that the wearing of white clothes was not totally interdicted but only restricted to the famous scholars, *gedolei ʿolam.* On the magical significance of white garments, see also Abraham Azulai, *Ḥesed le-ʾAvraham,* fol. 29c–d who quotes from manuscript texts that report that white linen clothes have anti-demonic properties. For our purpose, namely the emphasis upon the magical understanding of the Hasidic thought, it is pertinent to mention a Hasidic story according to which the fact that someone feels the atmosphere of Shabbat during a regular day is explained as follows: "If you put on Sabbath clothes and Sabbath caps it is quite right that you have a feeling of Sabbath holiness. Because Sabbath clothes and caps have the power of drawing the light of the Sabbath down to the earth." Cf. Buber, *Tales of the Hasidim: The Early Masters,* p. 241, and Barbara Myerhoff, "Life Not Death in Venice: Its Second Life," in Victor W. Turner and Edward M. Brunner, eds., *The Anthro-*

pology of Experience (Urbana and Chicago, 1986), p. 265. This vision of the role of the clothes corroborates perfectly talismatic magic. See above chap. 2, n. 131.

64. *An Autobiography,* p. 168.

65. Ibid.

66. Ibid., p. 165.

67. Ibid., p. 166; see also Weiss, *Studies,* p. 71 who ascribes this passage to the Great Maggid himself. See also p. 91, n. 10 and Weiss's note in *Ẓion,* vol. 12 (1947) p. 97.

68. Weiss, *Studies,* ibid., rightly stressed the mystical facet of the description found in Maimon's *An Autobiography,* neglecting, however, the possible magical aspect.

69. See also n. 77, 78, and 79 below.

70. See Sack, "The Influence," p. 238 n. 46; ibid., "The Prayer" p. 10 and n. 35. "The Attitude" (ch. 2, note 16), p. 74. See also R. Jacob Joseph of Polonoy, *Ben Porat Yosef,* fol. 21a, where he quotes explicitly Azulai's *Ḥesed le-ʾAvraham, Liqqute Maharil,* fol. 7b; *Sidduro shel Shabbat,* fols. 41, 51d–52b, *Sefat ʾEmet,* 3 fol. 84d. This view is similar to some expressions found in earlier Kabbalah from the circle of R. Joseph Ashkenazi and David ben Yehudah he-Ḥasid. See Idel, "An Anonymous Commentary."

71. Shoḥat, "*ha-Ẓaddiq*" p. 302.

72. See also above chap. 3, par. 5.

73. On the different Kabbalistic understandings of this image see Idel, *Kabbalah: New Perspectives,* pp. 173–81.

74. On the descending of the influx as the result of the dwelling of the *Shekhinah* see chap. 2, par. 7 above.

75. *Ẓinorot kol ha-ʿolamot.*

76. *Nehenim.* This verb can be translated also as "taking delight in something."

77. Printed by Meir Benayahu, "R. Yehudah ben Moshe Albotini and His Book *Yesod Nishneh Torah,*" *Sinai,* vol. 36 (1955): 252 (Hebrew) Shoḥat, "*ha-Ẓaddiq*" p. 302. The double activity of the *Ẓaddiq,* above and below, is also mentioned among the Hasidic masters, though in a different way. In a passage quoted in the name of R. Levi Yiẓḥaq of Berdichev, R. Yehudah Leib of Zakilkov, a disciple of R. Elimelekh of Lisansk, mentions in his *Liqqutei Maharil,* fol. 45c, the following tradition: "When the *Ẓaddiq* is in the state of great expansion [of his consciousness, *Gadelut*] he operates above, in the supernal worlds very much, by means of *Yiḥudim* as is known. But when his consciousness is contracted [*Qatenut*] he operates here below, [bringing down] influxes, sustenance and remedy onto all the children of Israel." Prof. E. Wolfson has drawn my attention to an interesting parallel to this quote, found in R. Menaḥem Mendel of Premislany, *Darkei Yesharim* (Benei Beraq, 1981), p. 268.

78. See Idel, "The Theurgical and Magical Interpretation," p. 39. See also ibid., p. 50, the text of R. Yehudah Muscato, which describes the descent of the influx caused by human verbal activity, by means of pipes, *ẓinorot*.

79. Ms. New York, JTS MIC 1650, fol. 72ab.

80. Compare to Alemanno's text quoted in Idel, "Magical and Neoplatonic Interpretations," p. 198.

81. See *Talmud Yerushalmi, Sukkah,* 4, 6. For a transposition of this phrase on the human level see the anonymous Kabbalistic secrets, most probably authored by R. Joseph Angelet, Ms. Oxford, 1610, fols. 55b–56a. I hope to dedicate elsewhere a more elaborate study to the motif of transformation of the body into a transparent being in Kabbalah; see, for the time being, Idel, *Kabalah: New Perspectives,* p. 169; Elliot Wolfson, *Through a Speculum,* ch. 6 and notes 29 and 81 (forthcoming).

82. Ms. New York, JTS Mic 1650.

83. The Kabbalist that was described at length in the quote from Azulai.

84. *Bi-meqom ha-ẓinor ha-gadol.* See n. 86 below.

85. *Pardes Rimmonim,* 32, chap. 1; 2, fol. 78c. Copies also in the preface by R. Nathan Shapira of Jerusalem to Luria's *Peri ᶜEẓ Ḥayyim* and in his *Me ᵓorot Nathan.* Compare also the text of Cordovero, quoted above, chap. 2, end of par. 7. Apparently an elaboration on the concepts in this passage is found in R. Shelomo Rocca, *Kavvanat Shelomo,* fol. 78d, where the *Ẓaddiqim* sitting here below are described as drawing down the influx upon the supernal *Ẓaddiq* and then upon themselves. The language of this passage is interesting because this Kabbalist uses the phrase "upon us, the *Ẓaddiqim* who sit here below and their heart is [directed] above to draw down the influx," assuming that the magical activity of the *Ẓaddiq* is more than an abstract concept accepted from some sources. On the lower *Ẓaddiq* and his activity on high, which culminates with the drawing down of influx, see ibid., fol. 75cd. In general, the recurrence in this book more than in other texts, of the term *Ẓaddiq,* which appears in magical contexts, may be a sign of the surge of the importance of this concept. See also below, Appendix C, note 4.

86. This Tishby, *The Wisdom of the Zohar,* 2, pp. 298–99, 610–11, and his *Path of Faith and Heresy,* pp. 186–94; Liebes, "The Messiah of the Zohar," pp. 112–13 and especially n. 107; Elliot Wolfson, "Circumcision" (ch. 4, n. 24a). That in early Hasidic thought the *Ẓaddiq* was openly indentified with the *membrum virile* is evident in R. Jacob Joseph of Polonoy, *Ẓafnat Pa ᶜaneaḥ,* fol. 115d and Liebes, ibid., p. 113; Wolfson, "Walking as a Sacred Duty";

87. *Berakhot,* fol. 17a.

88. *Pardes Rimmonim,* 32, chap 1; 2, fol. 78c.

89. See Naḥmanides' *Commentary on Genesis* 1, 1, ed. Ch. D. Chavel (Jerusalem, 1959), vol. 1, p. 11.

90. This reading is already offered in the *Shelah,* and accepted by R. Jacob

Joseph of Polonoy; cf. Dresner, *The Zaddik,* pp. 125–28, 277–78, n. 33–34.

91. See Scholem, *On the Mystical Shape,* pp. 95–96; compare Green, "*Ẓaddiq* as *Axis Mundi,*" p. 333; Liebes, "The Messiah of the Zohar" pp. 138–41; Wolfson, "Walking as a Sacred Duty."

92. Cf. Piekarz, *The Beginning of Hasidism,* pp. 16–17.

93. p. 302.

94. *The Beginning of Hasidism,* pp. 15–16. Piekarz drew some very interesting parallels between the view of the Besht and some of his contemporaries concerning the interpretation of the *Berakhot* passage. In fact the affinity between the Hasidic interpretation of the *Berakhot* passage and that of the *Shelah* has already been advanced by R. Benjamin of Zalovitch, in his *ʾAhavat Dodim,* fol. 114a. On Joseph as a pipe see *Shelah,* 3, fol. 67a. See also his "Devekuth" p. 140 and Liebes, "The Messiah of the Zohar," pp. 120–21, n. 140.

95. This phrase already occurs in Cordovero in a similar context. See above, chap. 2, n. 152. Compare also to R. Aharon Kohen of Apta, *Ner Miẓwah,* fol. 5b on the mystic who transforms himself into "a pipe to the supernal well, and draws down the good influx upon himself and upon the entire world."

96. Fol. 30b. This text was referred by R. Jacob Joseph of Polonoy, *Toledot Yaʿaqov Yosef,* fol. 66c. See also his *Ben Porat Yosef,* fol. 21a, where he expressly refers to *Ḥesed le-ʾAvraham.* See Piekarz, "Devekuth" p. 141, *Hasidism in Poland,* p. 45.

97. See above, chap. 2, par. 7.

98. *Va-Yaqhel Moshe* (Zalkwo, 1741) fol. 10a.

99. See above chap. 4, par. 4.

100. *The Messianic Idea,* pp. 213, 233.

101. However, this is not always the view of R. Jacob Joseph. See, however above, n. 4. See also R. Menaḥem Naḥum of Chernobyl, in Green, *Upright Practices,* p. 100, where this Hasidic master also views the prayers and utterances of Israel as creating a path, *shevil,* for the divine influx and *Meʾor ʿEinayim* p. 109.

102. *ʾOr Torah,* p. 12; see also ibid., p. 13 "The *Ẓaddiqim* sustained and nourished the world" and the numerous discussions on pp. 28, 118, 148; cf. Green, "*Ẓaddiq* as *Axis Mundis,*" p. 338. According to other statements in the circle of R. Elimelekh, "The *Ẓaddiq* is like a channel, which draws liquids downward, since he, by the means of his good deeds, will draw good influxes downward on [the people of] Israel." (In his disciple, R. Yisrael of Kuznitz's *ʿAvodat Yisrael* fol. 70b.) Similar views occur in R. Elimelekh's *Noʿam ʾElimelekh.* See more on this subject in Schatz-Uffenheimer, *Quietistic Element,* pp. 114, 119, 120; and Elior, "Between *Yesh* and *Ayin,*" pp. 426–27, 448 n. 48. See however, the interesting discussion of R. Aharon Shemuel ha-Kohen, who introduces all the motifs of the drawing down the influx by becoming a path and a pipe, without mentioning the idea of the *Ẓaddiq.* Although close to the Great Maggid,

this author did not create a Hasidic community, and he seems to ignore the ideal of *Ẓaddiq* in the context of the talismanic model. See also above, chap. 3, par. 7.

103. See also *ʾOr Torah,* p. 13, where the author mentions that the whole influx, *kol ha-shefaʿ*, descends upon the *Ẓaddiq*. On the other hand, in a text very important for our discussion here, *Yad Yosef,* written by R. Joseph Zarfati at the beginning of the seventeenth century, and quoted by R. Jacob Joseph of Polonoy (see Piekarz, "Devekuth" pp. 140–41), the assumption is that the *Ẓaddiq* draws down the influx as a pipe, upon "all the people of his generation." It should be mentioned that the text of R. Joseph Zarfati, written before the *Shelah* and *Ḥesed le-ʾAvraham,* faithfully reflects Cordovero's terminology. Compare also the very important discussion of R. Eliahu ha-Itamari of Smyrna, in the wideread *Sefer Shevet Musar* ch. 39 (Jerusalem, ND) pp. 318–319. This book has been translated into Iddish and printed several times at the middle of the 18th century.

104. *Toledot Yaʿaqov Yosef,* fol. 65b. See Dresner, *The Zaddik,* p. 127. See also the opposite view, found in *Ben Porat Yosef,* fol. 18d, where the assumption is that by exercising an influence on the mundane world, the *Ẓaddiq* causes an abundance of the influx in the higher world. In other words, in some cases a magical activity also has a theurgical aspect.

105. See also *Degel Maḥaneh ʾEfrayim,* p. 5. See also above, chap. 5, par. 3.

106. *Toledot Yaʿaqov Yosef,* fol. 66c; this way of describing the righteous is very widespread in Hasidic literature, and it is impossible to exhaust the relevant passages. See e.g., Qalonimus Qalman Epstein, *Maʾor va-Shemesh* 1, fol. 21b.

107. On this topic, see below Concluding Remarks, par. 2.

108. In at least one case, the drawing down of the influx by the *Ẓaddiq* is conceived to be limited only to the children of Israel, and to exclude the idolaters. See R. Moshe Eliaqum Beriʾah, *Daʿat Moshe,* fol. 73a. See however, ibid., fol. 72c, and below Appendix C.

109. *ʾImrei Shefer,* fol. 2c. This is also the view of R. Jacob Ẓevi Yalish, *ʾEmet le-Yaʿaqov* (Lemberg, 1884) fol. 7d.

110. See R. Moshe Eliaqum Beriʾah, *Daʿat Moshe,* fol. 101b.

111. On this issue, see chap. 4., par. 5 above, and below, n. 116.

112. Compare R. Mordekhai of Chernobyl, *Liqqutei Torah,* fol. 19c.

113. *ʾor la-Shamayim,* fols. 98d–99a: see also ibid., fol. 89d, cited in chap. 3, par. 3 as well as ibid., where this Hasidic master recommends that one be united with the higher world but that it is necessary to become, at the same time, "pathways and degrees" in order to draw down the influx.

114. See ibid., in the name of the Seer of Lublin: "A man should be nil and nought in his eyes in order to arouse and draw down his influx from the attribute of Nought, and it is quintessential that the intention should not be for his sake." See also ibid., fol. 99b. Compare also to R. Yisrael, the Maggid of Kuznitz's view, quoted above n. 102

and that of his son, R. Moshe Eliqum Beri'ah, *Qehilat Moshe,* fol. 90d. It should be mentioned that more sources on the *Ẓaddiq* and Nought are found as we have seen in chap. 3. and in the rich material collected by Elior, "*Yesh ve-'Ayin.*" However, my purpose here is to detect the pre-Hasidic sources of some aspects of the Hasidic theory of the *Ẓaddiq,* especially in the magical model, and to show that this concept, and institution, is not the result of an attempt to resolve theological paradoxes of immanence and transcendence, *hitpashshetut* and *ẓimẓum,* as Orent (n. 1 above) and Elior, ibid., are inclined to propose, but the result of elaborations on sources that may be rather easily explored.

115. However, elsewhere in his book, R. Meir ha-Levi of Apta, following his masters, the Seer of Lublin, mentions the activistic drawing down of the influx. See e.g., ibid., fol. 99bc, and his own view ibid., fol. 97cd, where the transformation into a channel, *ẓinor,* is explicitly mentioned. A very activist attitude during the act of drawing down is expressed in an exceptionally illuminating passage of R. Moshe Eliaqum Beri'ah, *Qehilat Moshe,* fol. 101b, where he points out that while humility is necessary in order to attain the cleaving to God, a certain sense of greatness of oneself as a Jew, and therefore as a son of God, is necessary in order to draw down the influx.

116. On the mouth in some Hasidic texts see chap. 4, par. 5 and R. Barukh of Mezibush's *Boẓina' di-Nehora',* pp. 112–13. See also R. David of Zablatov, *Zemaḥ David* (Jerusalem, 1984) fol. 4b, where he speaks about the *Ẓaddiq* as a sage who is a pipe for his students. In this text wisdom, rather than influx, is drawn down through the human pipe. In this regard it is interesting that this nineteenth-century master emphasizes that by preventing knowledge from others, the sage is prone to lose it himself. See also R. Menaḥem Mendel of Kossov, *'Ahavat Shalom,* p. 269, where the cantor is portrayed, like the *Ẓaddiq,* as a channel. Prof. E. Wolfson has drawn my attention to the possible sexual implication of the "mouth" as a means of transmission, and the pipe-role. On the correspondence between the mouth and the *membrum virile,* see M. Idel, *Golem: Jewish Magical and Mystical Traditions on the Artificial Anthropoid* (Albany, 1990), pp. 13, 22, note 14.

117. *Qedushah.* See above, chap. 3, n. 81.

118. *BHT.* This is an acronym. Compare R. Yehudah ha-Levi's view of the synagogue, *Kuzari,* 1, par. 97 as analyzed by Pines, "On the Term *Ruḥayiyyut* and Its Sources," p. 530 and the similar view of R. Aharon Shemuel ha-Kohen, *Ve-Ẓivah ha-Kohen,* p. 150.

119. *'Olat Tamid* 2, fol. 8b.

120. The transition from the *Ẓaddiq* to the community of Israel is not so clear.

121. *'Olat Tamid* 2, fol. 8a; 1, fols. 49a and 57b, the last text is quoted above chap. 4, par. 2.

122. Ibid., 1 fol. 52b. Compare this text to a similar description of the soul in Azulai's *Ḥesed le-'Avraham,* fol. 13c.

123. See Alexander Altmann, "The Ladder of Ascension," *Studies in Mysticism and Religion presented to Gershom Scholem* (Jerusalem, 1967) pp. 1–32. See also above, chap. 3, n. 265.

124. Compare above chap. 3, par. 6.

125. "*Ẓaddiq* as *Axis Mundi*."

126. See *Ta ͨanit,* fol. 10a. Compare e.g. R. Ḥayyim of Chernovitz, *Be ͻer Mayyim Ḥayyim* 1, fol. 88cd, where the *Ẓaddiq* is described as distributing the influx he receives in accordance with the closeness to him of the recipients.

127. Cf. chap. 3, par. 1.

128. See the brief but wonderful autobiographical story of Martin Buber, *Hasidism and Modern Man,* pp. 64–69. It should be mentioned that the magical aspect of the model can be understood as expressing, in the way Wittgenstein would understand it, the sense of responsibility that is crucial for the Hasidic elite.

129. Compare also Heschel, *The Circle of the Baal Shem Tov,* p. 23.

130. See Weiss, *Studies,* pp. 19–20, 26; ibid., in Rubinstein, *Studies in Hasidism,* pp. 148–49; Rapoport-Albert, "The Hasidic Movement," p. 232–39; Elior, "Between *Yesh* and *Ayin,*" p. 404, Green, "*Ẓaddiq* as *Axis Mundi*" p. 339; Wolfson, "Walking as a Sacred Duty," par. 2. See the view of R. Moshe of Dolina, *Divrei Moshe,* fol. 38c. I suspect, though I do not have conclusive proof, that the assumption that someone has to elevate the sparks that belong to his soul by eating predates Hasidism, and already occurs in the circle of Luria's students. Especially important for this argument is a story quoted by R. Eliezer Ẓevi of Komarno, in the name of his father, who has read it in "holy books," to the effect that Luria told his disciple, R. Moshe Galanti, to eat in order to redeem the sparks he did not redeem in his former incarnation, when he abstained from eating because of his ascetic propensity. See his *Zeqan Beiti* (Jerusalem, 1973) p. 175. The anti-ascetic message of this story is also pertinent to the rejection of asceticism in Hasidism. However, for the time being I cannot locate this legend in earlier sources. See, nevertheless, the stories about the ritual eating of an animal into which the soul of a relative has transmigrated. See Moshe Idel, "Rabbi Yehudah Ḥalewah and His *Ẓafnat Pa ͨaneaḥ,*" *Shalem,* vol. 4 (1984) pp. 126–27 (Hebrew), and compare to Ruderman, *Kabbalah, Science, and Magic,* pp. 125–26. Compare also the story in *Shiveḥei,* ed. Rubinstein, pp. 312–13. On ritual eating, see Louis Jacobs (chap. 2, n. 265), and his "Eating as an Act of Worship in Hasidic Thought," in Sigfried Stein and Raphael Loewe, eds., *Studies in Religious and Intellectual History Presented to Alexander Altmann* (Alabama University, 1979) pp. 157–66; Ronit Meroz, "Selections from R. Ephrayim Penzieri: Luria's Sermon in Jerusalem and the ͻKavvanahͻ in Taking Food," *Lurianic Kabbalah,* eds. R. Elior and Y. Liebes (Jerusalem, 1992), pp. 211–245 (Hebrew).

131. See however, at the end of par. 3 above.

132. Cf. Maimon's description of the Great Maggid, *An Autobiography,* pp. 164–66.

133. *Spiritual and Demonic Magic,* pp. 82–83.

134. *Eros and Magic,* pp. 108–9.

NOTES TO CONCLUDING REMARKS

1. I have argued in several places that in Jewish mysticism, including Hasidism, expressions can be found that parallel expressions of *unio mystica* in other forms of religious mysticism. By analyzing the mystico-magical model, where the mystical is a means-experience, I do not intend to claim that in other cases we should also understand the experience of cleaving as a means-experience. On the contrary, it seems that many of the end-experiences of *devequt* seem to be closer to *unio mystica* than the means-experience.

2. On this issue see Weinstein-Bell, *Saints and Society,* pp. 239–40.

3. Haim Zafrani, *Kabbale, Vie Mystique et Magie* (Paris, 1986); Issachar Ben-Ami, *Saint Veneration Among the Jews in Morocco* (Jerusalem, 1984) (Hebrew).

4. Emile Dermenghem, *Vies des Saints musulmanes* (Paris, 1942).

5. See Ben Amos-Mintz, *In the Praise of the Baal Shem Tov,* pp. 12, 17, 22, 26, 27, 30, 34. On the solitude in the mysticism of the Great Maggid see Weiss, *Studies,* pp. 131–41.

6. In general, the question of mystics and responsibility was dealt with by Louis Dupré, "*Unio Mystica:* The State of the Experience," in Idel-McGinn, *Mystical Union,* pp. 14–16; Friedrich Heiler, "Contemplation in Christian Mysticism," in *Spiritual Disciplines,* ed. J. Campbell (Princeton, 1960), pp. 236–38.

7. Abraham Abulafia considered Judaism as the religion of devotion to the divine Name, particularly of those who accept has Kabbalah and implicitly are able to redeem themselves as individuals. See Moshe Idel, *Chapters in Ecstatic Kabbalah* (Jerusalem, 1990), pp. 67–69 (Hebrew).

8. This observation does not exclude the existence of learning groups, or people practicing mystical techniques around a central mystical figure, like Abulafia, for example.

9. "The Messiah of the *Zohar,*" pp. 128–38, 203–18 and his important article, "How the *Zohar* was Written," in *The Age of the Zohar,* ed. J. Dan, (Jerusalem, 1989), pp. 1–72 (Hebrew).

10. See Moshe Idel, "Inquiries in the Doctrine of *Sefer ha-Meshiv,*" *Sefunot* (NS) 2, 17, ed. Y. Hacker (Jerusalem, 1983): 246, 249 (Hebrew).

11. Given the fact that some medieval authors have explicitly defined their mystical experiences as messianic I see no reason not to grant to these expressions a messianic status even if they do not involve apocalyptic components. See above, introduction, par. 4. I hope to elaborate elsewhere on this point in a more detailed manner.

12. Adduced by Louis I. Newman, *The Hasidic Anthology* (New York, 1944), p. 262. For the reticence concerning wonders and miracles in the Ḥabad school, see Ada Rapoport-Albert, "Hagiography with Footnotes: Edifying Tales and the Writings of History of Hasidism," *History and Theory*, 27 (1988): pp. 155, 158.

13. *Zikhron Devarim* (Jerusalem, 1967), p. 149. See also R. Naftali of Ropshitz, *Ayalah Sheluḥah*, p. 9.

14. The extent to which this is also the case of the katabatic model (see above, chap. 3, par. 1), is an issue that must be checked in detail separately.

15. See above, chap. 2, par. 5.

16. See his "Devekuth."

17. See Ernst Cassirer, "Some Remarks on the Question of the Originality of the Renaissance," *Journal of the History of Ideas* 4 (1943): 29–38.

18. *Origin and Meaning*, p. 135; see also ibid., pp. 133–34, 179–80 and his *Teʾudah vi-Yiʾud* (Jerusalem, 1963), vol 1, p. 188 (Hebrew).

19. *Origin and Meaning*, pp. 133–34, "Interpreting Hasidism," p. 225.

20. See below, n. 27.

21. *A General Theory of Magic*, p. 23.

22. Ibid. Compare also to Walter Burket, *Greek Religion: Archaic and Classical*, tr. J. Raffan (Cambridge, Mass. 1985), p. 55: "acts which seek to achieve a given goal in an unclear but direct way are magical." Also here the unclear nature of the acts is part of their belonging to magic.

23. On the mystical attainment as generated by the drawing forth of *ʾAleph* into something, man for example, see Idel, *Kabbalah: New Perspectives*, p. 65. For more on this issue see chap. 3, n. 47.

24. *Taʾanug*. See above, chap. 3, par. 5.

25. *Maʾayan ha-Ḥokhmah*, fol. 38c (Appendix 1). See also above chap. 3 n. 220.

26. *A General Theory of Magic*, pp. 23–24, 50, 57.

27. Emile Durkheim, *The Elementary Forms of the Religious Life* (New York, The Free Press, 1965) p. 60; compare also to Burket, *The Greek Religion* (n. 22 above), p. 55.

28. Bartolome, quoted in Sullivan, *Icanchu's Drum*, p. 422. See also Gustav Mensching's interesting remark on the relationship between magic and communal life, as part of a coherent vision of reality; *Structures and Patterns* (chap. 2 n. 15 above), p. 10; see also Idel, *Kabbalah: New Perspectives*, p. 321, n. 137.

29. See above, Introduction, par. 5 and chap. 3, par. 2.

30. See Jacobs (above, chap. 2, n. 265). It should be mentioned that according to R. Yisrael of Ryzhin, each soul has a peculiar letter from the Torah that draws and

causes the emanation of vitality and illuminations to that soul. This is but an interesting formulation of the idea of the divine spark, explicated in linguistic terms. See *ʿIrin Qaddishin,* fol. 39a, to be compared to fol. 49d.

31. See Idel, *Kabbalah: New Perspectives,* pp. 64, 307, n. 85; "Universalization and Integration," pp. 28–29.

32. Compare to the phrase "mystical philology," coined by Charles Zika in order to describe Johannes Reuchlin's view of language, "Reuchlin's *De Verbo Mirifico* and the Magic Debate of the Late Fifteenth Century," *Journal of the Warburg and Courtauld Institutes* 39 (1976): 104–38 and Vickers, "Analogy and Identity," p. 106. See also Ruderman, *Kabbalah, Magic and Science,* p. 69. I hope to dedicate a separate study to talismatic linguistics, in which I shall elaborate upon some topics dealt with in this paragraph.

33. See Scholem, "The Name of God," Idel, "Reification of Language"; *Golem,* pp. 264–65 and "Jewish Kabbalah and Platonism in the Middle Ages and Renaissance," in Goodman, *Neoplatonism and Jewish Thought,* pp. 326–27, 330; "Infinities of the Torah," pp. 143–44, Wolfson, "Letter Symbolism."

34. Fols. 130c–133a. Compare to R. Shneor Zalman of Liady, *Torah ʾOr,* fol. 52b.

35. The metaphor of the emanational structure as a chain, *shalshelet,* occurs very frequently in Kabbalistic literature. Here we have a peculiar use of this metaphor: the emanational chain is not only the path of descent of divine power, but also the way of ascent of human influence. See R. Joseph Giqatilla, *Ginnat ʾEgoz* (Hanau, 1615), fol. 46b; ibid., *Shaʿarei ʾOrah* I, pp. 195, 199, but especially Moshe Cordovero's *Pardes Rimmonim* XXVII, chap. 2; 2, fol. 59c (Appendix 2), R. Shemuel Gallico's *ʿAsis Rimmonim,* fol. 69a, and it has influenced Vital's *Shaʿarei Qedushah,* p. 105, Azulai's *Ḥesed le-ʾAvraham,* fols. 9d–10a, 13d–14a; R. Jacob Kopel of Miedzyrec, *Qol Yaʿaqov,* fol. 1a, R. Barukh of Kossov, *ʿAmud ha-ʿAvodah,* fol. 47b, where the phrase *hevel ha-shishtalshelut* occurs; R. Zeʾev Wolf of Zhitomir, *ʾOr ha-Meʾir,* fol. 115a, R. Dov Baer of Lubavitch, in Jacobs, *On Ecstasy,* p. 102 and no. 2. This view of emanation, related to language, soul, and divinity, could contribute greatly to the understanding of the concept of the great chain of being. See also David Blumenthal, "Lovejoy's *Great Chain of Being* and the Jewish Tradition," in *Jacob's Ladder and the Tree of Life,* eds. P. and M. Kuntz (New York, 1986), pp. 179–90.

36. *ʾElimah Rabbati,* fol. 132d. Compare also to the view of *Keter* as the supernal mouth in *Tomer Devorah,* chap. 2, ed. Mopsik, p. 76.

37. "The will of the heart," apparently a symbol for *Binah,* the third *Sefirah.*

38. *ʾor Yaqar* 12 (Jerusalem, 1983): 147; see also Idel, "Reification of Language" pp. 49–52; 59–66.

39. Chap. 4, par. 5 and n. 95.

40. De Vidas' passage was quoted by Horowitz, *Shelah* I, fol. 172b, and see also Nathan of Gazza's *Derush ha-Menorah,* who gives to the chain motif a peculiar turn; Gershom Scholem (ed.), *Be-ʿIqevot Mashiaḥ* (Jerusalem, 1944), p. 106. Compare also

to R. Dov Baer of Miedzyrec's passage quoted from *ʾOr ha-ʾEmet* (chap. 4 before n. 96) and R. Meshullam Phoebus of Zbarazh's *Yosher Divrei ʾEmet,* fol. 132a, as well as R. Yisrael of Kuznitz's *ʿAvodat Israel,* fol. 77bc, R. Shneor Zalman of Liady, *Tanya ʾ ʾIggeret ha-Teshuvah,* chap. 5, fol. 95b where the interesting phrase *hevel ha-hamshakhah,* the cable of the drawing down, was coined, and R. Yisrael of Ryzhin, *ʿIrin Qaddishin Tanyyanaʾ,* fol. 8c. See also the quotation from Shelomo Maimon, chap. 5, n. 156. On the presence of the divine speech in every creature, as its vitality, see also Vital, *Liqqutei Torah,* fols. 96a–97a; Jacobs (above, chap. 6 n. 130), p. 158. Nevertheless, a perusal of the Lurianic corpus demonstrates that this Kabbalistic system was concerned with strong theurgical practices revolving around the various divine names, neglecting the more talismatic vision of the entire Hebrew language as a main tool of attracting the spiritual forces. See e.g., Vital, ibid., fols. 20b–21b. See also the identity between names and souls in the Safedian figure R. Joseph Ashkenazi, the "Tanna" of Safed; cf. Idel, *Golem,* pp. 70–71.

41. In fact, the core of the view is found already in *Shoḥer Tov,* a Midrash on the Psalms, and recent Hasidic writers had to offer a pretext for adducing this view in the name of the Besht. See the special issue of *Sefer Tanya* (Brooklyn, 1989), pp. 52–55. For another important quotation in the name of the Besht to the same effect, see R. Ḥayyim of Chernovitz, *Beʾer Mayyim Ḥayyim* I, fol. 8d.

42. *Maʾamarot.* According to rabbinic sources, in the first chapter of Genesis there are ten creative speeches. For the sources and reverberations of this view in Jewish mysticism see Idel, *Kabbalah: New Perspectives,* pp. 114ff.

43. See *Sefer Taynya,* ibid., fols. 76b–77a and the addition to *Keter Shem Tov,* fol. 84b. See also the quotations in the name of the Besht in *Toledot Yaʿaqov Yosef,* fol. 7a and in R. Yisrael of Kuznitz, *Sheʾerit Yisrael* (Lublin, 1895), fol. 66a, *Baʿal Shem Tov* I, p. 17, and n. 41 above. A part of the quotation occurs in *Maggid Devarav le-Yaʿaqov,* p. 66, but the name of the Besht is not mentioned. A very interesting parallel occurs in R. Meshullam Phoebus of Zbarazh, *Yosher Divrei ʾEmet,* fol. 25ab. See Krassen, *"Devequt" and Faith,* pp. 264–68. To a certain extent, the reduction of the vitality of all creatures to different forms of language assumes a "linguistic consanguinity of all these things," to paraphrase Ernst Cassirer. See his *Essay on Man* (New York, 1960) p. 108. Hasidism can be conceived as proposing a certain "law of metamorphosis" from one thing to another via language, a notion formulated again by Cassirer in the context of the primal thought.

44. *Qedushat Levi,* fol. 63d. Compare also to *Sefat ʾEmet* IV, fol. 1c.

45. See also Idel, *Golem,* pp. 57, 111.

46. See Idel, *Mystical Experience,* pp. 83–86.

47. *Noẓer Ḥesed,* p. 110.

48. Ibid. See also the text adduced in the name of R. Yisrael of Ryzhin in *Baʿal Shem Tov* I, pp. 17–18.

49. See above, chaps. 4, 5. Compare also to Buber's interesting assessment, formulated in the context of his view of Hasidism, to the effect that the "primitive" man is a "naive pan-sacramentalist," *Origin and Meaning,* pp. 167, 170–71.

50. See above, n. 35.

51. See Idel, *Language, Torah, and Hermeneutics,* pp. 11–13 and the pertinent notes, where Abulafia, the most Aristotelian among the Kabbalists, rejects this view insofar as the Hebrew language is concerned. The passage from Aristotle's *De Interpretatione* concerning language is conventional as understood by Averroes, was reinterpreted and neutralized by Abulafia; see Idel, ibid., pp. 12–13 and Vickers, "Analogy and Identity," p. 101. It should be noted that Abulafia's views on language were also known to Renaissance thinkers, having reached them through Flavius Mithridates's Latin translations of some of Abulafia's writings done for Pico della Mirandola, and absorbed by Pico in his own writings. See the important contribution of Chaim Wirszubski, *Pico della Mirandola's Encounter with Jewish Mysticism* (Cambridge, Jerusalem, 1989), where Abulafia's presence in Pico's thought was convincingly highlighted, along with his emphasis on the magical transformation of Kabbalah in the versions espoused by Mithridates and Pico.

52. For the contribution of the Hermetic magic of the Renaissance to later magical practices in various parts of Europe, see Thomas, *Religion and the Decline of Magic,* pp. 222–31; Evans, *Rudolf II,* and Charles B. Schmitt, "John Case on Art and Nature," in *Annals of Science* 33 (1976): 543–59. See also the collection of articles, *Presence d'Hermes Trismegiste,* published as part of the series *Cahiers de l'Hermeticisme* (Albin Michel, Paris, 1988), especially the studies of Antoine Faivre, pp. 13–56, 223–32. See also his contribution to *Hermeticism and the Renaissance* (n. 53 below), pp. 424–35.

53. See e.g. Brian Copenhaven, "Hermes Trismegistus, Proclus, and the Question of a Philosophy of Magic in the Renaissance," in eds. I. Merkel, A. Debus, *Hermeticism and the Renaissance* (Folger Books, Washington, 1988), pp. 79–110.

54. Charles Trinkaus, *In Our Likeness and Image* (London, 1970), vol. II, passim, Idel, "Hermeticism and Judaism," pp. 62–68.

55. See Francis Amelia Yates, *Giordano Bruno and the Hermetic Tradition* (Chicago, London, 1964), pp. 398–455. However, it should be emphasized that more recent researches, especially the two important books of R. J. W. Evans, have opened the way for a much better understanding of the repercussions of the Italian versions of the occult, including Kabbalah and Hermeticism, in the upper classes of central Europe, especially in Prague and Vienna, from the late sixteenth to the beginning of the eighteenth century. See his *Rudolf II* pp. 196–274 and *The Making of the Habsburg Monarchy, 1550–1700* (Claredon Press, Oxford, 1979), pp. 346–418. I would like to emphasize that I do not assume that Christian-educated magic, as Evans calls the Habsburgian fascination with astrology, alchemy, Hermeticism, and Kabbalah, influenced the Hasidic mystico-magical model. The reverberations of the occult within the highest classes, in the immediate vicinity of the areas where Hasidism emerged and flourished, shows that magic and a variety of occult preoccupations informed the worldview, and

sometimes financial investments, even of the Christian elite, in the period that immediately precedes the activity of the Besht. Indeed, a possible (though not probable) channel linking Polish and Ukrainian Hasidism to the occult interests of the Pragueian court are the writings of the Maharal, which certainly influenced Hasidism; however they do not reflect the occultic amalgam of the Rudolfine entourage. It should be remarked that Evans' characterization of Maharal's thought as "Cabbalist and Hermetic" seems to be more influenced by the intellectual ambiance of Prague than by the writings of this Rabbi. See *Rudolf II*, p. 241. I did not find significant Hermetical elements in his writings, and the impact of Kabbalah is only part of the more complex thought of this master. Likewise, Evans' suggestion that *Sefer Raziel*, which was translated into Czech, is related to Abraham Abulafia is not supported by the analysis of the various versions of this important magical book; see ibid., p. 238. The Czech version is but one of several European translations of a heterogenous collection of magical traditions that have nothing to do with ecstatic Kabbalah. See Francois Secret, "Sur quelques traductions du *Sefer Raziel*," *REJ* 128 (1969): 223–45; Idel, "The Magical and Neoplatonic Interpretations" pp. 193–94. I hope to elaborate on this magical treatise elsewhere.

56. See especially Vickers, "Analogy and Identity," and the bibliography adduced by him, pp. 96–97, 105–8, as well as his essay "On the Function of the Occult," in *Hermeticism and the Renaissance* (n. 53 above), pp. 265–92. See also Couliano, *Eros and Magic*, pp. 121–22 and the more critical approaches of Robert S. Westman and J. E. McGuire. *Hermeticism and the Scientific Revolution* (University of California Press, Los Angeles, 1977), and the review of Charles B. Schmitt, "Reappraisals in Renaissance Science," *History of Science* 16 (1978): 200–14.

57. See Raymond Klibansky, Erwin Panofsky and Fritz Sazl, *Saturne et al Melancholie* (Paris, 1989), pp. 389–432; Rudolf Wittkower, *Born under Saturn* (London, 1963). See also Moshe Idel, "The Anthropology of Yoḥanan Alemanno: Sources and Influences," *Topoi* 7 (1988): 208. It should be mentioned that the highly syncretistic attitude of the Renaissance culture is especially evident in its occultism, where Kabbalah, magic, philosophy, alchemy, and astrology were combined in different ways in different doses. Hasidism, however, despite the panoramic landscape I am advocating, is much more coherent: it excluded alchemy and confined astrology to the periphery.

58. I do not include in this context the legends of the satanic assemblies or cults, part of them the figment of the religious imagination; see Norman Cohn, *Europe's Inner Demons* (New York, 1977), Carlo Ginzburg, *Ecstasies, Deciphering the Witches' Sabbath* (New York, 1991) or the various esoteric groups like the Freemasons or the Rosicrucians, which cannot be considered as popular groups. Although some esoteric nuances can be discerned in the pneumatic groups that served as the starting point of Hasidism, the main trends of Hasidism from its very beginning do not stress esotericism. Even the elitism of some Hasidic masters, like R. Jacob Joseph of Polonoy and R. Israel of Ryzhin, is always colored by a concern for the life of their disciples.

59. See Vickers, "Analogy versus Identity" pp. 109–56.

60. Ibid., pp. 96–97.

61. See Vickers, "Analogy versus Identity," pp. 101–2; Idel, *Language, Torah, and Hermeneutics,* p. 143 n. 52. Besides the Christian Kabbalists of the Renaissance, it seems that it was only Jacob Boehme who attributed to language an ontological and creative status in Christian mysticism; see Wickers, ibid., pp. 107–8; Andrew Weeks, *Boehme, An Intellectual Biography of the Seventeenth-Century Philosopher and Mystic* (Albany, 1991), pp. 145, 188–91.

62. Trinkaus, *In Our Image and Likeness* (n. 54 above) vol. 2, p. 523.

63. See Idel, "The Study Program" pp. 326–27. See also above, chap. 2, n. 160. On the human body as able to link the different worlds, see e.g. R. Elimelekh of Lisansk, *No ᶜam ᵓElimelekh,* fol. 67d. As against this natural magic, which directs its efforts to change the course of nature in accordance with certain natural laws, see the more collective magic, found in Giordano Bruno, where a phenomenon closer to Hasidism occurs, according to the brilliant analysis of Couliano, *Eros and Magic,* pp. 87–106.

64. See above chap. 2, par. 3; chap. 4, par. 4.

65. It should be mentioned that the occult trends in Western Europe, especially those influenced by Kabbalah, were relatively more positively inclined toward Judaism, and sometimes even toward Jews, than the "scientific" mentalities. See Heiko Oberman, *The Roots of Anti-Semitism in the Age of the Renaissance and Reformation,* tr. J. I. Porter (Philadelphia, 1984).

66. See chap. 3, par. 4.

67. On this tension, see Schatz-Uffenheimer, *Quietistic Elements,* p. 76; *Hasidism as Mysticism,* p. 141; Green, *Tormented Master,* pp. 326–30; idem, "Discovery and Retreat," pp. 106ff, idem, *Devotion and Commandments,* pp. 23–24; Martin Buber, *The Legend of the Ba ᶜal Shem Tov,* tr. M. Friedman (London, 1978) p. 23.

68. See Chap. 3, par. 4.

69. *Quietistic Elements* p. 149; *Hasidism as Mysticism,* pp. 243–44.

70. See "Discovery and Retreat," pp. 110–11. See, however, his later mentioning of the thirteenth-century ecstatic Kabbalah in the context of the Hasidic concept of leader; see his "Typology of Leadership," pp. 146–47. See also Piekarz, *Hasidism in Poland,* pp. 37–49.

71. *Degel Maḥaneh Efrayim,* pp. 284–85.

72. See especially his mystical autobiography *Megillat Setarim,* ed. Naftali Ben Menaḥem (Jerusalem, 1944), a small part of it translated in Jacobs, *Jewish Mystical Testimonies,* pp. 239–44. See also above chap. 3, n. 111.

73. See e.g., Elazar Aziqri, *Milei de-Shemaya ᵓ,* ed. Mordechai Pachter (Jerusalem, 1991) (Hebrew), and his "The Life and Personality of R. Elazar Azikri according to his Mystical Diary," *Shalem* 3 (1981): 127–47 (Hebrew).

74. Repetitions of earlier formulae in the later generations can be considered as signs of conservatism without, however, implying at the same time a retreat from cultivating extreme experiences along the lines of the earlier masters.

75. Rold A. Knox, *Enthusiasm: A Chapter in the History of Religion* (Christian Classics, Westminster, Maryland, 1983), p. 1.

76. See Lewis, *Ecstatic Religion,* pp. 173–74.

77. See Idel, *Kabbalah: New Perspectives* pp. 59–73; "Universalization and Integration," pp. 33–48.

78. See above, chap. 3, n. 194.

79. Compare to my description of Abulafia's mysticism as nonascetic, in *Mystical Experience,* pp. 143–44.

80. See Schatz-Uffenheimer, *Quietistic Elements* pp. 101, 174, 175, 177.

81. Idel, "Defining Kabbalah," pp. 112–13.

82. *Quietistic Elements,* p. 18.

83. Ibid., p. 178. See also Weiss, *Studies,* pp. 69–94.

84. See especially R. Abraham Friedman, the Angel, in his *Ḥesed le-ʾAvraham.*

85. Cf. Idel, *The Mystical Experience,* pp. 179–80.

86. See Scholem, *Messianic Idea,* p. 218.

87. For the prominent role of Zoharic axiology in the ethical literature of the Safedian Kabbalist, see Pachter, "The Concept of Devekut," pp. 211–20.

88. See Hossein Ziai, "Beyond Philosophy: Suhrawardi's Illuminationist Path to Wisdom," in eds. F. E. Reynolds and D. Tracy, *Myth and Philosophy* (SUNY, Albany, 1990), p. 220.

89. See the series of studies edited by S. N. Eisenstadt, *The Origin and Diversity of Axial-Age Civilizations* (Albany, 1986).

notes to appendix a

1. See Scholem, *Devarim be-Go,* pp. 357–58; Elior, "The Affinity," Green, *Upright Practices,* pp. 10–14.

2. On this issue see Idel, *Kabbalah: New Perspectives,* pp. 146–53. Here I shall adduce some passages discussed there, together with some new evidence that is still in manuscript and not analyzed previously.

3. See Yehuda Liebes, "'Two Young Roes of a Doe,'" "The Secret Sermon of Isaac Luria before his Death," and Mordekhai Pachter, "*Katnut* (ʾSmallnessʾ) and *Gadlut* (ʾGreatnessʾ) in Lurianic Kabbalah," in *Lurianic Kabbalah,* ed. R. Elior and Y. Liebes (Jerusalem, 1992) pp. 113–70 and 171–210 respectively (Hebrew).

4. See chap. 5 par. 1.

5. On this issue, see Idel, *Kabbalah: New Perspectives,* pp. 151–53.

6. See chap. 1 n. 71.

7. Cf. Idel, *Kabbalah: New Perspectives,* pp. 151–53.

8. See Frank Talmage, "Apples of Gold: The Inner Meaning of Sacred Texts in Medieval Judaism," in Green, ed., *Jewish Spirituality* 2: 313–54, Marc Saperstein, *Decoding the Rabbis* (Cambridge, Mass., 1980), pp. 47–120.

9. For more on this issue see Idel, *Language, Torah, and Hermeneutics,* pp. 91–95, 122–24.

10. See *Kabbalah: New Perspectives,* pp. 137–41.

11. Ibid., p. 141–44.

12. "Some Psychological Aspects of the Kabbalah," in *God, the Self and Nothingness: Reflections Eastern and Western,* ed. Robert E. Carter (New York, 1990), pp. 19–43.

13. F. K. Burkitt, *Church and Gnosis,* (Cambridge, 1932) pp. 41–42; E. R. Dodds, *Pagan and Christian in an Age of Anxiety,* (New York and London, 1970), pp. 18–20. See also the important study of Hans Jonas, who conceived mysticism as looking for validation by means of philosophical worldviews, in "Myth and Mysticism: A Study of Objectivation and Interiorization in Religious Althought," *Journal of Religion* 49 (1969): 328–29; Idel, *Studies in Ecstatic Kabbalah,* pp. 2–3.

14. See Richard T. Wallis, "Nous as Experience," *The Significance of Neoplatonism,* ed. R. Baine Harris (Norkfold, 1976), pp. 122 and 143, n. 1, where a bibliography on the subject is provided.

15. See Idel, "Defining Kabbalah."

16. See Abulafia's attitude to the symbols for the *Sefirot* in the theosophical Kabbalah, see Idel, *Kabbalah: New Perspectives,* pp. 202–3.

17. See *Ve-Zot li-Yiḥudah,* p. 16, where Abulafia explicitly declares that this Kabbalah is superior to the Sefirotic one.

18. See Idel, *Kabbalah: New Perspectives,* p. 348, n. 315.

19. *Niẓḥono,* a term that refers to the *sefirah Neẓah.*

20. *ʿAẓmo ʿ*. The meaning of this term is not so clear.

21. *Kallato.*

22. *Ve-Zot li-Yiḥudah,* pp. 16–17, corrected according to ms., New York, JTS, 1887. For more on this text, see various notes in *Kabbalah: New Perspectives,* pp. 348–49.

23. See ibid., p. 349 n. 321.

24. *Sofer ha-Sefirot,* an appellation for the Infinite.

25. Compare below the next from *Ner ʾElohim.*

26. See Idel, *Kabbalah: New Perspectives* p. 350 n. 330.

27. This is an important example of the talismanic view of the letters, in our case those that form the divine names. See also above, chap. 4, n. 46, the text from Abulafia's *Gan Na ʿul.* Compare to the passage from Alemanno's *Collectanaea,* discussed in Idel, "Judaism and Hermeticism," pp. 68–69.

28. Ms. Milano-Ambrosiana LIII, fols. 155b–156a.

29. Compare a similar text in *Gan Na ʿul,* Ms British Library, OR. 13136, fol. 4b quoted in *Sefer ha-Peliy ʾah* I, fol. 73c.

30. See ibid., "There are in man three issues by means of which he receives all his apprehensions."

31. See also below the quote from *Gan Na ʿul.*

32. *Lehitboded.* See below, n. 36.

33. The question of the source of revelation and the awareness of its nature is an issue that recurs in Abulafia's ecstatic Kabbalah; see the important text printed by Scholem, *Major Trends,* p. 140.

34. On the three levels of letters see above, chap. 5, n. 105.

35. The view of letters as divine is rather rare in Abulafia's corpus.

36. *Hitbodedut.* See Idel, *Studies,* pp. 108–10.

37. On this metaphor see Idel, *The Mystical Experience,* pp. 180–84.

38. See *Kabbalah: New Perspectives,* p. 349, n. 319.

39. *Shemah ve- ʿaẓmah.*

40. *Nizkarim le-tovah;* probably by the Bridegroom, namely the Active Intellect or God.

41. Namely, the human and separate spiritual forces, which, prior to *devequt,* were divided. See below, n. 48.

42. I suppose these entities are the human spiritual forces and the corporeal forces; see the texts referred to in Idel, *Kabbalah: New Perspectives,* pp. 349, 351 n. 328, 347.

43. Ibid., p. 351, n. 348.

44. Ibid., pp. 307–8, n. 85.

45. This term, in original *nafsho,* seems to be an Arabism, introduced by the Tibbonian translations.

46. This view is characteristic of Abulafia's thought, which emphasizes centrality of the divine Name.

47. Ms. Sasson 56, fol. 33a. Compare also the quote from *Gan Na ᶜul,* adduced in *Sefer ha-Peliy ʾah* I, fol. 73c.

48. Abulafia has introduced the classical theosophical interpretation of the Rabbinic verb *qaẓẓeẓ* as a sin consisting of separating man from the divine powers in order to formulate his own view, which is palpably different. While for the Rabbinic and theosophical sources the separation is a cutting off of the supernal entities because of human sin or misunderstanding, in this text Abulafia speaks about the sin of separating man from the higher beings, namely the cutting off of man from the experience of union between soul, or intellect, and the spiritual entities, God or the Agent intellect. See also above, n. 41. A very similar understanding of this concept of separation is also found in the early Hasidic masters. See, e.g., the quote in the name of the Besht in *Ben Porat Yosef,* fol. 21ab, and copied in *Keter Shem Tov* I, fol. 4b, where the *qiẓẓuẓ bi-netiy ᶜot* is mentioned immediately after mentioning the cleaving of the human thought and soul to the root of the Torah and commandment, which apparently are identical in this text to the inner, spiritual dimension of the Torah. According to R. Jacob Joseph, this view of his master is based upon R. Abraham Azulai's *Ḥesed le- ʾAvraham,* fol. 10d, but this master does not mention the idea of the separation between the soul and its source as a sin. See also above, chap. 2, n. 228.

49. Abulafia, *Sefer Gan Na ᶜul,* Ms. British Library, OR. 13136, fol. 3a. I follow here the version of the manuscript. See the next note. For another quotation from this book, which formulates a similar view, see above, chap. 4, n. 46.

50. I, fol. 73a. Although the wording in the printed quotation of this passage differs slightly from the manuscripts, these varia do not affect the interpretation offered above, namely that the separation may affect the cleaving between the human faculty and the supernal realm, conceived as branches. See also n. 48. See also ibid., 2, fol. 1c, where it is written that "the ways of God are [also] in man but they are hidden just as He is hidden within the world."

51. *Moladetah.* On the symbolism of the tree, branches, and fruit in Abulafia's Kabbalah see *Gan Na ᶜul,* ms. British Museum OR. 13136, fol. 3ab, *Sefer ha-Peliy ʾah* I, fol. 73a.

52. *Sanhedrin* fol. 106b, and Rashi ad locum.

53. Ms. München 10, fol. 130b (Appendix 1).

54. MS. New York, JTS 1885, fols. 74b–75a. For more on this issue, see ibid., fol. 75ab, where a discussion reminiscent of that printed above from Abulafia's *Ve-Zot Li-Yihudah* appears.

55. See Moshe Idel, "An Anonymous Kabbalistic Commentary on Shir ha-Yiḥud" (forthcoming).

56. See ms. Vatican 274 fol. 170b (Appendix 2).

57. Compare above, chap. 2, n. 317.

58. Moshe Ḥallamish ed., *Kabbalistic Commentary of Rabbi Yoseph ben Shalom Ashkenazi on Genesis Rabbah* (Jerusalem, 1984), p. 151; for a comparison between the human soul and a tree, see ibid., p. 150. Compare also to his *Commentary to Sefer Yeẓirah,* fol. 24d.

59. *Commentary on Genesis Rabbah,* p. 152, to be compared to ibid., p. 150. See also Cordovero's *Pardes Rimmonim* XXXII, chap. 1; 2, fol. 78a where the term *Ẓinor nishmato* occurs. As I have shown in my article "Sefirot and Colors: A Neglected Responsum," in *Minḥah le-Sarah,* ed. D. Dimant, M. Idel, and S. Rosenberg (Jerusalem, 1994), pp. 1–14 (Hebrew). Cordovero was deeply influenced by the theories on colors from the circle of R. David ben Yehudah he-Ḥasid. For more on this issue see my monograph in preparation on Visualization of Colors.

60. *Studies in Ecstatic Kabbalah,* pp. 127, 160–61.

61. See 1, chap. 5; 1, fol. 4bc; 31, chap. 1; 2, fol. 72b.

62. See above chap. 3, par. 2.

63. See Yosha (chap. 2 n. 261) and Idel, "Differing Conceptions," pp. 155–57, 178–92.

64. *Major Trends,* p. 338, Piekarz, "Devekuth," Joseph Dan, "Hasidism: The Third Century" *Jewish Studies* 29 (1989) p. 2 (Hebrew).

65. *Ta ᶜanug.* See above, chap. 3, n. 246.

66. *Toledot Ya ᶜaqov Yosef,* fol. 86a.

67. See above, chap. 1, n. 17.

68. *ʾOr ha-ʾEmet,* fol. 36cd. See also Lamm, *Torah Lishmah,* p. 126, n. 62.

69. See above, chap. 5, n. 13.

70. See above, chap. 1, n. 20.

71. *Kabbalah: New Perspectives,* pp. 254–55.

72. Idel, "The Magical and Neoplatonic Interpretations"; ibid., "Differing Conceptions."

73. See Gershom Scholem, "*Shetar ha-hitqasherut shel talmidei ha-ʾAri,*" *Ẓion,* 5 (1940): 133–60 (Hebrew), *Major Trends,* pp. 256–57.

74. See Altmann (chap. 2 n. 249), pp. 23–33.

75. R. Hillel of Paritch, *Pelaḥ ha-Rimmon* (Brooklyn, 1957), vol. 2, p. 78 (Appendix 3). On the light and luminary, see ibid., pp. 77.

76. *Ba ᶜal Shem Tov,* 1, p. 18. See also another text adduced and analyzed by Elior, "The Affinity" pp. 107–8.

77. Ibid., 1, p. 26.

78. See Introduction, n. 84, chap. 2 n. 153, 176, 254; chap. 4, n. 126.

79. Cf. Idel, *Golem,* p. 318 s.v. Vitality.

80. See e.g., R. Menaḥem Mendel of Kossov, *ʾAhavat Shalom,* p. 11, where *ḥiyyut* and *hitlahavut* are mentioned together. See also R. Ḥayyim of Chernovitz, *ʾEreẓ Ḥayyim,* fol. 2c. Compare also to the Hasidic usage of the term *hitqashsherut,* above, chap. 4, n. 18. It should be mentioned that the phrase *ẓurah ḥiyyunit,* in the sense of the spiritual manifestation of the divine, occurring in R. Aharon Kohen of Apta's *Ner Miẓwah,* fol. 19a, seems to reflect the new status of the term *ḥiyyut* in Hasidic thought. Actually the vision of the *ẓurah ḥiyyunit* is tantamount to prophecy. In the Middle Ages, *ẓurah ḥiyyunit* would mean a lower form, the animal one.

81. *ʾAhavat Shalom,* p. 269.

82. Ibid., pp. 269–70. See also above chap. 2, n. 52.

83. See Clifford Geertz, *The Interpretation of Cultures* (Basic Books, Harper Collines, 1973) pp. 126–27.

notes to appendix b

1. See Wilensky, *Hasidism and Mitnaggedim,* 1, p. 317. This letter was written in 1805.

2. On this custom and its source in R. Moshe Ḥayyim Luzzatto's circle see Tishby, "Les traces," pp. 457–59. See also Weiss, *Studies,* pp. 80–81; on the use of the phrase *lomar Torah,* "to say Torah," to mean "preaching." see e.g. R. Yisrael Loebel, in Wilensky, *Hasidim and Mitnageddim,* vol. 2, p. 317, *No ʿam ʾElimelekh,* fol. 67c.

3. On the question of the language of these sermons there can be no dispute that, though printed in Hebrew, they were delivered in the vernacular Yiddish.

4. See the first statement of R. Nathan of Nemirov's introduction to *Liqqutei Tefillot.*

5. See above chap. 4, n. 22.

6. See *Liqqutei Moharan* I, fol. 33b; Green, *Tormented Master* pp. 319–20; Idel, "Universalization and Integration," p. 45.

7. See also the view of R. Naḥman's uncle, R. Moshe Ḥayyim Efrayim of Sudylkov, discussed in Idel, *Kabbalah: New Perspectives,* pp. 244–45.

8. See above, chap. 2, n. 33.

9. *ʿIrin Qaddishin,* fol. 49d (Appendix 1). On the notion of seventy facets of the Torah, see Wilhelm Bacher, "Seventy-Two Modes of Expositions" *JQR* 4 (1892): 509; Scholem, "On the Kabbalah," pp. 62–63, Idel, "Infinities of the Torah," p. 155 n. 31, Hananel Mack, "Seventy Aspects of the Torah: Concerning the Evolution of an Expression," in *Rabbi Mordechai Breuer Festschrift,* ed. Moshe bar Asher (Jerusalem, 1992), vol. 2, pp. 449–62 (Hebrew); Elliot Wolfson, "The Mystical Significance of Torah-Study in German Pietism," *JQR* 84 (1993) p. 77 n. 128 and for discussions of later

Kabbalists in Moshe Idel, see the preface to R. Joseph Alashqar's *Ẓafnat Paʿaneaḥ* (Jerusalem, 1991), pp. 41–43 (Hebrew).

10. See Moshe Idel, "On Symbolic Self-Interpretations in Thirteenth-Century Jewish Writings," *Hebrew University Studies in Literature and the Arts,* vol. 16 (1988), pp. 90–96.

11. *Genesis Rabba*ʾ XX, 12, p. 196. For the Cordoverian concept of the materialization of the Torah by its descent see Scholem, *On the Kabbalah,* pp. 71–72. See also the Beshtian view that there are teachers whose souls are from the world of unity, while others possess souls from *ʿOlam ha-Perud,* namely the world of separation. See *Keter Shem Tov,* I, fol. 4d and the view of R. Menaḥem Mendel of Kossov, *ʾAhavat Shalom,* p. 92, where the assumption is that R. Meir was able to become perfect, like Adam before sin, and this is why in his Torah, the version was written with *ʾAlef.*

12. See below, n. 18.

13. In Hebrew the word for "face," *Panim,* also means "facets."

14. On metoposcopy in Jewish mysticism, see Gershom Scholem, "Ein Fragment zur Physiognomik and Chiromantik aud der Tradition des spaetantiken juedischen Esoterik," in *Liber Amicorum, Studies in Honour of Professor Dr. C. J. Bleeker* (Leiden, 1969), pp. 175–93; Ithamar Gruenwald, "New Fragments from the Literature on *Hakarat Panim* and *Sidrei Sirtutim,*" *Tarbiẓ* 40 (1970): 301–19 (Hebrew); Schaefer, *Hekhalot-Studien,* pp. 84–95.

15. Fol. 24c (Appendix 2).

16. See Liebes, "The Messiah of the Zohar," pp. 208–15.

17. See Assaf, *Rabbi Israel of Ruzhin,* pp. 172–97, 212–48. Interesting as the issue of the *pidiyonot,* the money received by the *Ẓaddiq* for his advice or help to the Hasidim, may be in itself for a sociological understanding of Hasidism, we are concerned here mostly with the theoretical dimensions of magic. The more practical one should be investigated in itself.

18. The assumption is, according to numerous Kabbalistic and Hasidic sources, that every Jew has a share in the Torah. See e.g., Scholem, *On the Kabbalah,* pp. 65–66 and above chap. 4, n. 41, the view of R. Nathan Shapira of Cracow in *Megalleh ʾAmugot* and Lamm, *Torah Lishmah,* p. 132, n. 94.

19. See Maimon's and others' descriptions of the situation of the Great Maggid during his sermons as analyzed by Weiss, *Studies,* pp. 70–78.

20. See Assaf, *Rabbi Israel of Ruzhin,* pp. 127–28.

21. See ibid., p. 113.

22. On the discrepancy between the written literature and Hasidic life, see the caveats of Abraham Y. Heschel, *Kotzk* (chap. 3, n. 203), pp. 7–10, part of it translated in Dresner's introduction to Heschel, *The Circle of Baal Shem Tov,* p. 23, and his "Hasidism," in *Jewish Heritage* 14 (1972): 14–16; Heschel's introduction to Dresner, *Zaddik,* pp. 7–8; and Gries, *The Book in Early Hasidism,* p. 92.

23. On the issue of communication in Hasidism see Loewenthal, *Communicating the Infinite*, pp. 1–28.

24. See Idel, *Kabbalah: New Perspectives*, pp. 246–47.

25. See Yehuda Liebes, "How the Zohar was Written," in *The Age of the Zohar*, ed. Joseph Dan (Jerusalem, 1989), pp. 1–71 (Hebrew).

26. See Idel, *Golem*, p. 279.

27. Assaf, *Rabbi Israel of Ruzhin*, pp. 129–30.

NOTES TO APPENDIX C

1. Deuteronomy 11:26. The verse is interpreted here as addressed not to the whole nation, as in the Bible, but only to the elite (see n. 11 below). The Hasidic master exploits the singular form, which in the Bible is a way of speech. According to this reading, Moses actually gave, that is, he transmitted, to some individuals the power to bless or curse.

2. This was a well-known formulary in the Middle Ages. See above, chap. 1, n. 5.

3. *Derekh na-nevi ʾim*. On the phrase *derekh ha-nevu ʾah*, see Maimonides' *Mishneh Torah*, Hilkhot Yesodei Torah, VII, 6. I wonder whether the mention of the prophets has, nevertheless, something to do with the active induction of the divine presence onto the mystic, as we shall see immediately below. On the view in Hasidism that prophecy can be premeditatedly induced, see above, the quote from R. Aharon ha-Kohen of Apta's *ʿOr ha-Ganuz*, cited in chap. 2, par. 2, e, where the phrase "path of prophecy" also occurs. Written at approximately the same time, Epstein's view and that of R. Aharon of Apta demonstrate the resort to techniques in order to reach religious ideals. On the possibility that Epstein is presenting, via Cordovero, a view of Abulafia's dealing with the way of attaining a prophetic state, see above, chap. 2, beside n. 64.

4. This formulation shows that it is not a theurgical act that is intended but the attracting and distribution of power here below. The drawing down of the influx upon meritorious persons here below has been discussed above. See especially chap. 6, notes 85 and 103, where Cordoverian sources and Lurianic books influenced by them mention the concept of *Ẓaddiq* in this context.

5. *ʾanshei mofet* means literally "men of wonder." On the phenomenon of the magical righteous in the entourage of Epstein, see Mahler, *Hasidism and the Jewish Enlightenment*, pp. 262–67.

6. *kol ʾet ve-rega ʾ;* this expression occurs also in R. Elimelekh of Lisansk, *No ʾam ʾElimelekh* fol. 92c, where the awareness of the continuing performance of the commandments is described.

7. *noten da ʾato be-kol ʾet ve- rega ʾ lihiot +Elohut shoreh bo.* My translation opts for a more activist understanding of this sentence. The person actually induces the presence by his concentration of mind. Alternatively, one could assume that this statement deals only with the passive awareness of the divine Presence within man.

8. Literally, authorization of functioning as a rabbi, understood here as passing the capacity of blessing by putting the hands upon the mystagogue. The understanding of the term used for rabbinical ordination, as the act of transmitting the capacity to function as a wonder-maker, is very interesting, as it marks the difference in self-perception between the rabbinic and Hasidic elites.

9. *Ma᾽or va-Shemesh* V, fol. 14a. On this author, see Nigal's study mentioned above, chap. 5, n. 47. The restriction of the blessing here is reminiscent of another similar stand, discussed above, chap. 6, n. 108.

10. See, e.g., the introduction to *Sefer Berit Menuḥah,* spuriously attributed to R. Abraham of Granada (Jerusalem, 1959), fol. 21, and to Cordovero's *Pardes Rimmonim* XXI, chap. 1; I, fol. 96d. In Cordovero's discussion, the tradition has to do with the talismatic understanding of the divine names, which had already been received by the prophets. See also the quotation from Cordovero's *Derishot,* p. 76, introduced above (chap. 2, par. 3), where the transmission of the secrets of the Torah to the *Ẓaddiqim* is mentioned in the context of talismatic activity. On the question of genealogies of magical traditions, see Hans D. Betz, "The Formation of Authoritative Tradition in the Greek Magical Papyri," in ed. Ben F. Meyer and E. P. Sanders, *Jewish and Christian Self-Definition* (Fortress Press, Philadelphia, 1983), vol. 3, pp. 161–70. See also the following note.

11. *Ma᾽or va-Shemesh* V, fol. 14b, where he emphasizes that the recipients are *Yeḥidei sagullah.* Compare above, chap. 2, end of n. 201. See also R. Joseph Gikatilla's *Sha᾽arei ᾽Orah* I, pp. 58–60, where the transmission of the blessing in the Jewish elite is mentioned in the context of the knowledge of the divine Name and the drawing down of the divine influx. Gikatilla's mystico-magical model, as well as his own magical preoccupations, deserve a separate description that cannot be given here; see also ibid., p. 46. On the blessing of the perfect religious man, see the end of the passage from R. Yiẓḥaq of Acre, quoted above, chap. 2, par. 2. For the combination of the ecstatic approach, which became more esoteric in Hasidism, with the theurgical-magical approaches, which are considered more exoteric in Hasidism, see Idel, *Kabbalah: New Perspectives,* p. 17 and more recently Elior, "Between Divestment of Corporeality," p. 229.

12. See chap. 2, par. 3. On this point, as well as on my less dialectical and paradoxical vision of the relationship between mysticism and magic, my positions differ from that of Elior's ibid.

13. A shorter version of this text is quoted later on from *Ma᾽or va-Shemesh,* in the Holy Jew of Przysucha's *Beir Ya῾aqov* (Pietrkov, 1890), fol. 72bc.

14. Compare above, Concluding Remarks, par. 2.

15. See Elior, "Between *Yesh* and *᾽Ayin,*" "Between Divestment of Corporeality," and n. 5 above.

Bibliography

HEBREW PRIMARY SOURCES

ʾAhavat Shalom. R. Menaḥem Mendel of Kossov, *ʾAhavat Shalom* (rpr., Jerusalem, 1984).

ʿAmud ha-ʿAvodah. R. Barukh of Kossov, *ʿAmud ha-ʿAvodah* (Chernovitz, 1863).

ʿAsarah Maʾamarot. R. R. Menaḥem Azariah of Fano, *ʿAsarah Maʾamarot* (Frankfurt a/M, 1698).

ʿAvodat ha-Qodesh. R. Meir ibn Gabbai, *ʿAvodat ha-Qodesh* (rpr. Jerusalem, 1973).

ʿAvodat Yisrael. R. Yisrael of Kuznitz, *ʿAvodat Yisrael ha-Shalem*. (Munkacz, 1928).

ʾAyalah Sheluḥah. R. Naftali Ẓevi of Ropshitz, *ʾAyalah Sheluḥah*. (Budapest, 1943)

Baʿal Shem Tov. R. Shimeon Menaḥem Mendel Vodnik of Gavardshaw, *Baʿal Shem Tov* (Lodge, 1938).

Beʾer Mayyim Ḥayyim. R. Ḥayyim Turer of Chernovitz, *Beʾer Mayyim Ḥayyim* (Israel, ND), two volumes.

Beʾer Moshe. R. Moshe Eliaqum Beriah, *Sefer Beʾer Moshe* (rpr. Tel Aviv, ND).

Ben Porat Yosef. R. Jacob Joseph of Polonoy, *Ben Porat Yosef* (Pietrkov, 1884, rpr, 1971).

Benei Yisaskhar. R. Ẓevi Elimelekh of Dinov, *Sefer Benei Yisaskhar* (Benei Beraq, ND).

Berit Abram. R. Joseph Moshe of Jalovitch. *Berit Abram* (Brod, 1875).

Beʾurei ha-Zohar. D. Dov Baer of Lubavitch. *Beʾurei ha-Zohar* (Brooklyn, 1956).

Binat Moshe. R. Moshe Eliyaqim Beriʾah Shapira, *Binat Moshe* (Cracow, 1888).

Bozinaʾ di-Nehoraʾ. R. Barukh of Medziebuz, *Sefer Bozinaʾ di-Nehoraʾ ha-Shalem* (NP. 1985).

Daʿat Moshe. R. Moshe Eliaqum Beriʾah Shapira, *Daʿat Moshe* (rpr. Jerusalem, 1987).

Darkhei Ẓedeq. R. Zekhariah Mendal of Yaroslav. *Sefer Darkhei Ẓedeq* (Lvov, 1796).

Degel Maḥaneh ʾEfrayim. R. Moshe Ḥayyim Ephraim of Sudylkov. *Degel Maḥaneh ʾEfrayim* (Jerusalem, 1963).

Derekh Miẓwoteikha. R. Menaḥem Mendel Shneorsohn of Lubavitch, *Derekh Miẓwoteikha* (Brooklyn, 1984).

Derishot. R. Moshe Cordovero, *Derishot be-ʿInianei Malakhim*, printed as an appendix to Reuven Margoliot, *Malʾakhei ʿEliyon* (Jerusalem, 1945).

Dibrat Shelomo. R. Shelomo of Lutzk, *Sefer Dibrat Shelomo* (Zolkiew, 1848).

Divrei Moshe. R. Moshe of Dolina, *Divrei Moshe* (Zolkiew, 1865).

Divrei Shemuel. R. Shemuel Shmelke of Nikelsburg, *Divrei Shemuel* (Jerusalem, 1976).

Dudaʾim ba-Sadeh. R. Reuven Horowitz of Chernovitz, *Dudaʾim ba-Sadeh* (Lemberg, 1859).

ʾElimah Rabbati. R. Moshe Cordovero, *Sefer ʾElimah Rabbati* (Jerusalem, 1966).

ʿEser ʿAtarot. R. Yisrael ben R. Yiẓḥaq Simhah, *ʿEser ʾOrot* in his *Sefer Zekhut Yisrael* (rpr, Jerusalem, 1973).

Geʾulat Yisrael. R. Yehoshuʾa Abraham ben Yisrael, *Sefer Geʾulat Yisrael* (Amsterdam, 1821).

Giveʿat ha-Moreh. Shelomo Maimon, *Giveʿat ha-Moreh* eds. S. H. Bergman and N. Rotenstreich (Jerusalem, 1965).

Heikhal ha-Berakhah. R. Yiẓḥaq Aiziq Safrin of Komarno, *Heikhal ha-Berakhah* (Lemberg, 1869), 5 volumes.

Ḥesed le-ʾAvraham. R. Abraham Azulai, *Ḥesed le-ʾAvraham* (Lvov, 1863, rpr. Jerusalem, 1968).

Ḥesed le-ʾAvraham. R. Abraham Friedman, ha-Malakh. *Ḥesed le-ʾAvraham* (rpr. Jerusalem, 1973).

Ḥesed le-ʾAvraham. R. Abraham of Kalisk. *Ḥesed le-ʾAvraham* (rpr. Jerusalem, ND).

Ḥesed le-ʾAvraham. R. Abraham Yesakhar Beʿer ha-Kohen of Radomsk, *Ḥesed le-ʾAvraham* (Pietrkov, 1893).

ʾIlanaʾ de-Ḥayyei. R. Menaḥem Mendel of Rimanov, *ʾIlanaʾ de-Ḥayyei* (Pietrkov, 1908).

ʿIrin Qaddishin. R. Yisrael of Ryzhin, *ʾIrin Qaddishin* (rpr, Jerusalem, 1983).

ʿIrin Qaddishin Tanyyanaʾ. R. Yisrael of Ryzhin, *ʿIrin Qaddishin Tanyyanaʾ* (Barfeld, 1887).

Kavvanat Shelomo. R. Shelomo Rocca, *Sefer Kavvanat Shelomo* (Venice, 1670).

Keter Nehoraʾ. R. Aharon Kohen of Apta, *Sefer Keter Nehoraʾ,* a commentary on the Prayerbook (Jerusalem, 1975).

Keter Shem Tov. R. Yisrael Baʿal Shem Tov, *Keter Shem Tov* (Brooklyn, 1987), a collection of early Hasidic traditions compiled by R. Aharon Kohen of Apta, with additions from the Tanya.

Knesset Yisrael. R. Yisrael of Ryzhin, *Knesset Yisrael* (Warsaw, 1906).

Ktoneth Passim. R. Jacob Joseph of Polonoy. *Kotoneth Passim* ed. Gedalyah Nigal (Jerusalem, 1985).

Liqqutei ʾAmarim. Liqqutei ʾAmarim. An anonymous collection of Hasidic discussions reprinted in *Sefarim Qedoshim me-ha-ʾAri ha-Qadosh ve-Talmidav* (Brooklyn, 1983).

Liqqutei Maharil. R. Yehudah Leib of Zakilkov, *Liqqutei Maharil* (Lublin, 1899).

Liqqutei Mohoran. R. Naḥman of Braslav, *Liqqutei Moharan* (Benei Beraq, 1972).

Liqqutei Torah. R. Mordekhai of Chernobyl, *Liqqutei Torah* (1860, rpr. Benei Beraq, 1983).

Liqqutei Torah. R. Shneor Zalman of Liady, *Liqqutei Torah* (Brookline, 1979).

Liqqutei Torah. R. Ḥayyim Vital, *Liqqutei Torah, Taʿamei Miẓwot* (Vilna, 1880).

Liqqutim Ḥadashim. R. Yeḥiel Moshe of Jadislaw, *Sefer Liqqutim Ḥadashim* (Warsaw, 1899).

Liqqutim Yeqarim, Liqqutim Yeqarim (Jerusalem, 1981).

Maʿayan ha-Ḥokhmah. R. Asher Ẓevi of Ostraha, *Maʿayan ha-Ḥokhmah* (Podgorze, 1897).

Maggid Devarav le-Yaʿaqov. R. Dov Baer of Miedzyrec, *Maggid Devarav le-Yaʿaqov,* ed. Rivka Schatz-Uffenheimer (Jerusalem, 1976).

Ma᾽or va-Shemesh. R. Qalonimus Qalman Epstein, *Sefer Ma᾽or va-Shemesh* (Warsaw, 1902).

Messekhet ᾽Avot. R. Abraham Azulai, commentary on *Massekhet ᾽Avot* (rpr. Jerusalem, 1986).

Mayyim Rabbim. R. Yeḥiel Mikhal of Zlotchov. *Sefer Mayyim Rabbim* (Brooklyn, 1979).

Midrash Pinḥas. R. Pinḥas Shapira of Koretz (Warsaw, 1876).

Midrash Talpiyot. R. Eliahu ha-Kohen of Smyrna. *Midrash Talpiyot* (rpr. Jerusalem, 1963).

Mitpaḥat Sefarim. R. Jacob Emden, *Mitpaḥat Sefarim* (Lvov, 1871).

Nefesh ha-Ḥayyim. R. Ḥayyim of Volozhin, *Nefesh ha-Ḥayyim* (Vilna, 1874).

Ner Miẓwah. R. Aharon Kohen of Apta, *Ner Miẓwah* (Pietrkov, 1881).

Netiv Miẓwoteikha. R. Yiẓḥaq Aiziq Safrin of Komarno, *Netiv Miẓwoteikha* (Jerusalem, 1983).

No῾am ᾽Elimelekh. R. Elimelekh of Lisansk, *Sefer No῾am ᾽Elimelekh* (Jerusalem, 1960).

Noẓer Ḥesed. R. Yiẓḥaq Aiziq Safrin of Komarno, *Sefer Noẓer Ḥesed* (Jerusalem, 1982).

᾽Ohev Yisrael. R. Abraham Yehoshu῾a Heschel of Apta, *᾽Ohev Yisrael* (Zhitomir, 1863).

῾Olat Tamid. R. Nathan-Neta of Siniewa, *Siddur Tefillah, ῾Olat Tamid* (Permislany, 1895).

᾽Or ha-᾽Emet. R. Dov Baer of Miedzyrec, *Sefer ᾽Or ha-᾽Emet* (Zhitomir, rpr. Benei Beraq, 1967).

᾽Or ha-Ganuz. R. Aharon Kohen-Ẓedeq of Apta, *᾽Or ha-Ganuz la-Ẓaddiqim* (Zolkiew, 1800).

᾽Or ha-Ganuz. R. Yehudah Leib ha-Kohen of Hanipoly, *᾽Or ha-Ganuz* (Lemberg, rpr. Jerusalem, 1981).

᾽Or ha-Ḥamah. R. Abraham Azulai, *᾽Or ha-Ḥamah* (Premislany, 1896), 3 volumes.

᾽Or ha-Me᾽ir. R. Ze᾽ev Wolf of Zhitomir, *᾽Or ha-Me᾽ir* (Perizek, 1815).

᾽Or la-Shamayim. R. Meir ha-Levi of Apta, *᾽Or la-Shamayim* (Lublin, 1909).

᾽Or Torah. R. Dov Baer of Miedzyrec's collection of teachings. *Sefer ᾽Or Torah, Rimzei Torah* (Jerusalem, 1968).

᾽Oraḥ he-Ḥayyim. R. Abraham Ḥayyim of Zloczov, *᾽Oraḥ le-Ḥayyim* (Jerusalem, 1960).

᾽Oraḥ le-Ẓaddiq. R. Eliezer Lippa of Lisansk, *᾽Oraḥ he-Ẓaddiq* (Jerusalem, 1975).

Qedushat Levi. R. Levi Yiẓḥaq of Berdichev, *Qedushat Levi* (Jerusalem, 1972).

Qol Ya῾aqov. R. Jacob Kopel of Miedzyrec, *Siddur Qol Ya῾aqov* (Lemberg 1859).

Pardes Rimmonim. R. Moshe Cordovero, *Pardes Rimmonim,* ed. Muncakz (rpr. Jerusalem, 1962).

Pe᾽er Yisrael. R. Yisrael Shalom Joseph of Buhush, *Sefer Pe᾽er Yisrael* (Jerusalem, 1979).

Peri ῾Eẓ Ḥayyim. R. Ḥayyim Vital, *Peri ῾Eẓ Ḥayyim* (Dubrovno, 1848).

Peri ha-᾽Areẓ. R. Menaḥem Mendel of Vitebsk, *Sefer Peri ha-᾽Areẓ* (rpr. Jerusalem, 1969).

Raza᾽ de-῾Uvda᾽. R. Eliezer Ze᾽ev of Kretchniv, *Raza᾽ de-῾Uvda᾽* (Qiriat Ata, 1976).

Sefat ᵓEmet. R. Yehudah Arieh Lebi Alter of Gur, *Sefat ᵓEmet ᶜim Liqqutim* (Jerusalem, ND), five volumes.

Sefer ha-Berit. R. Pinḥas Eliahu Hurwitz, *Sefer ha-Berit* (Wilna, 1897).

Sefer ha-ᵓEmunot. R. Shem Tov ben Shem Tov, *Sefer ha-ᵓEmunot* (Ferrara, 1556).

Sefer ha-Gerushin. R. Moshe Cordovero, *Sefer ha-Gerushin* (Jerusalem, 1962).

Sefer ha-Kavvanot. R. Yiẓḥaq Luria, *Sefer ha-Kavvanot* (Koretz, 1784).

Sefer ha-Peliyᵓah. An anonymous fourteenth century Kabbalistic classic (Premislany, 1883).

Shaᶜar ha-Shamayim. R. Yeshaiah Horowitz, *Sefer Shaᶜar ha-Shamayim, Siddur ha-Shelah* (New York, 1954).

Shaᶜar ha-Tefillah. R. Ḥayyim Turer of Chernovitz, *Shaᶜar ha-Tefillah* (Jerusalem, 1968).

Shaᶜarei ᵓOraḥ. R. Joseph Giqatilla, *Shaᶜarei ᵓOraḥ,* ed. Joseph ben Shelomo (Jerusalem, 1970), 2 volumes.

Shaᶜarei Qedushah. R. Ḥayyim Vital, *Shaᶜarei Qedushah* (Benei Beraq, 1973).

Shem ha-Gedolim. R. Ḥayyim Joseph David Azulai, *Sifrei Shem ha-Gedolim va-ad le-Hakhamim* (Vilna, 1853, rpr. Jerusalem, 1970).

Shemuᶜah Tovah. R. Levi Yiẓḥaq of Berdichev, *Sefer Shemuᶜah Tovah* (Jerusalem, 1932).

Shiᶜur Qomah. R. Moshe Cordovero, *Sefer Shiᶜur Qomah* (Warsaw, 1883).

Siddur ha-ᵓAri. R. Shabbatai of Rashkov, *Siddur ha-ᵓAri* (Lemberg, 1866).

Sidduro shel Shabbat. R. Ḥayyim Turer of Chernovitz, *Sidduro shel Shabbat* (Jerusalem, 1960).

Sippurim Noraᵓim. Yaakow Kaidaner, *Sippurim Noraᵓim,* ed. Gedalyah Nigal (Jerusalem, 1992).

Sod Yakhin u-Voᶜaz. R. Meir Margoliot of Ostrog, *Sod Yakhin u-Voᶜaz* (Jerusalem, 1990).

Sullam ha-ᶜAliyah. R. Yehudah Albotini, *Sefer Sullam ha-ᶜAliyah,* ed. E. J. Porush (Jerusalem, 1989).

Tanya, R. Shneor Zalman of Liady, *Sefer ha-Tanya* (Brooklyn, 1966).

Tefillah la-Moshe. R. Moshe Cordovero, *Tefillah le-Moshe* (Premislany, 1892).

Toledot ᵓAharon. R. Aharon of Zhitomir, *Sefer Toledot ᵓAharon* (Lemberg, 1865).

Toledot Yaᶜaqov Yosef. R. Jacob Joseph of Polonoy, *Toledot Yaᶜaqov Yosef* (Koretz, 1780).

Toledot Yiẓḥaq. R. Yiẓḥaq of Neskhiz, *Sefer Toledot Yiẓḥaq* (Warsaw, 1868).

Ve-Ẓivah ha-Kohen, R. Aharon Shemuel ha-Kohen, *Sefer Ve-Ẓivah ha-Kohen* (Jerusalem, ND).

Ve-Zot li-Yihudah. Abulafia's epistle to R. Yehudah Salmon of Barcelona, printed by A. Jellinek, *Auswahl Kabbalistischen Mystik* (Leipzig, 1853) Erstes Heft, pp. 13–28.

Yesod ha-ᶜavodah. R. Barukh of Kossov, *Yesod ha-ᶜavodah* (Chernovitz, 1854).

Yosher Divrei ᵓEmet. R. Meshullam Phoebus of Zbarazh, *Yosher Divrei ᵓEmet* (printed together with Liqqutei Yeqarim).

Ẓafnat Paᶜaneaḥ. R. Jacob Joseph of Polonoy, *Ẓafnat Paᶜaneaḥ* (rpr. New York, 1976).

Ẓeror ha-Ḥayyim. R. Ḥayyim ben Yeshaiah Liebersohn of Chernobyl, *Ẓeror ha-Ḥayyim* (Bielgoria, 1913).

Zikkaron Zot. The seer of Lublin, *Zikkaron Zot* printed together with all the writings of this master in *Sefarim ha-Qedoshim mi-kol Talmidei ha-Besht ha-Qadosh* (Brooklyn, 1981), vol. 2.

Zohar Ḥai. R. Yiẓḥaq Aiziq Yeḥile Safrin of Komarno's *Commentary on the Zohar*, five volumes (Lemberg, rpr. Israel, 1971).

SECONDARY SOURCES

Alfasi, Yiẓḥaq. "*Supernatural Apprehensions and Miracles in Hasidism*." *In Sefer ha-Besht*, 112–28. Ed. Y. L. ha-Kohen Maimon. Jerusalem, 1960 (Hebrew).

Buber, Martin. *Hasidism and Modern Man*. Ed. M. Friedman. New York, 1966.

———. "Interpreting Hasidism." *Commentary* 36, no. 3 (September, 1963): 218–25.

———. *The Origin and Meaning of Hasidism*. Edited and translated by Maurice Freedman. Atlantic Highlands, NJ, 1988.

———. *Tales of the Hasidim, The Early Masters*. Translated by Olga Marx. New York, 1964.

Chittick, William C. *The Sufi Path of Knowledge: Ibn ʿArabi's Metaphysics of Imagination*. Albany, 1989.

Cohen-Alloro, Dorit. *Magic and Sorcery in the Zohar*. Ph.D. Dissertation, Hebrew University, 1989 (Hebrew).

Couliano, Ioan P. *Eros and Magic in the Renaissance*. Chicago and London, 1987.

Dan, Joseph. *The Hasidic Story: Its History and Development*. Jerusalem, 1975 (Hebrew).

Dubnow, Shimeon. *The History of Hasidism*. Tel Aviv, 1927 (Hebrew).

Eliach, Yaffa. "The Russian Dissenting Sects and Their Influence on Israel Baʾal Shem Tov, Founder of Hassidism." *PAAJR* 36 (1963): 57–83.

Elior, Rachel. "Between *Yesh* and *Ayin*: The Doctrine of the Zaddik in the Works of Jacob Isaac, the Seer of Lublin." In *Jewish History: Essays in Honour of Chimen Abramsky*, 393–45. London, 1988.

———. "ḤaBaD: The Contemplative Ascent to God." *Jewish Spirituality*, 157–205. A more elaborate Hebrew version of this study was printed in *Daat* 16 (1986): 133–77.

———. "Spiritual Renaissance and Social Change in the Beginnings of Hasidism." In Ḥallamish, *ʿAlei Shefer*, 29–40 (Hebrew).

———. "The Affinity between Kabbalah and Hasidism: Continuity or Change?" *Ninth World Congress of Jewish Studies, Division C*, 107–14. Jerusalem, 1986 (Hebrew).

———. *The Paradoxical Ascent*. Albany, 1993.

———. *The Theory of Divinity of Hasidut Ḥabad, Second Generation*. Jerusalem, 1982 (Hebrew).

———. "*Yesh* and *ʾAyin* as Fundamental Paradigms in Hasidic Althought." *Massuʾot: Prof. Ephrayim Gottlieb Memorial Volume*, 53–76. Edited by A. Goldreich and M. Oron. Jerusalem, 1994 (Hebrew).

Etkes, Emanuel. "Hasidism as a Movement: The First Stage." In *Hasidism: Continuity or Innovation?* 1–26. Ed. B. Safran. Cambridge, Mass., 1988.

Evans, R. J. W. *Rudolf II and His World, A Study in Intellectual History 1576–1612*. Oxford at the Claredon Press, 1984.

Fenton, Paul, trans. *Deux traites de mystique juive*. By Obadia and David Maimonide. Introduction by Paul Fenton. Lagrasse, 1987.

Goldreich, Amos., ed. *R. Yiẓḥaq of Acre's Me᾿irat ᶜEinayyim*. A critical edition with preface and commentary. Jerusalem, 1984. (All references to this work are to this edition.)

Goodman, Lenn E., ed. *Neoplatonism and Jewish Thought*. Albany, 1992.

Goetschel, Roland, ed. *Priére, Mystique et Judaïsme*. Paris, 1987.

Gottlieb, Efraim. *Studies in the Kabbalah Literature*. Ed. J. Hacker. Tel Aviv, 1976 (Hebrew).

Green, Arthur. *Devotion and Commandment: The Faith of Abraham in the Hasidic Imagination*. Cincinnati, 1989.

———. "Hasidism: Discovery and Retreat." In *The Other Side of God, A Polarity in World Religions*, 104–1130. Ed. Peter L. Berger. New York, 1981.

———, ed. *Jewish Spirituality*, 2 volumes. New York, 1986/1987.

———. *Menaḥem Naḥum of Chernobyl, Upright Practices. The Light of the Eyes*. New York, 1982.

———. *Tormented Master: A Life of Rabbi Naḥman of Bratslav*. Alabama, 1979.

———. "Typologies of Leadership and the Hasidic Ẓaddiq." In *Jewish Spirituality* by Arthur Green, Vol. 2, 127–56.

———. "*Ẓaddiq* as *Axis Mundi* in Later Judaism." *Journal of the American Academy of Religion* 45, 3 (1977): 327–47.

Grese, William C. "Magic in Hellenistic Hermeticism," *Hermeticism and the Renaissance*, 45–58. Ed. Ingrid Merkel and Allen G. Debus. Washington, London, Toronto, 1988.

Gries, Ze᾿ev. *Conduct Literature (Regimen Vitae): Its History and Place in the Life of the Beshtian Hasidism*. Jerusalem, 1989 (Hebrew).

Gries, Ze᾿ev. *The Book in Early Hasidism*. Hakkibutz Hameuchad, 1992 (Hebrew).

Ḥallamish, Moshe. *ᶜAlei Shefer Studies in the Literature of Jewish Thought Presented to Rabbi Dr. Alexandre Safran*. Ramat Gan 1990.

Halperin, David. *Faces of the Chariot*. Tuebingen, 1988.

Heiler, Friedrich. *Prayer, A study in the History and Psychology of Religion*. Translated by Samuel McComb. New York, 1958.

Heschel, Abraham J. *The Circle of the Ba ᶜal Shem Tov: Studies in Hasidism*. Ed. S. H. Dresner. Chicago and London, 1985.

Idel, Moshe. *Abraham Abulafia's Works and Doctrines*. Ph.D. Dissertation, Hebrew University, 1976 (Hebrew).

———. "'Be-᾿Or ha-Ḥayyim: An Observation on Kabbalistic Eschatology." In *Sanctity of Life and Martyrdom, Studies in Memory of Amir Yekutiel*, 191–212. Edited by I. M. Gafani and a. Ravitky. Jerusalem, 1992 (Hebrew).

———. "Defining Kabbalah: The Kabbalah of the Divine Names." In *Mystics of the Book: Themes, Topics and Typology*, 97–122. Ed. R. A. Herrera. Peter Lang, 1992.

———. "Differing Conceptions of Kabbalah in the Early Seventeenth Century." In *Jewish Thought in the Seventeenth Century*, 137–200. Ed. Isadore Twersky and Bernard D. Septimus. Cambridge, Mass., 1987.

———. "Hermeticism and Judaism." In *Hermeticism and the Renaissance,* 59–76. Ed. I. Merkel and A. Debus. Cranbury, New Jersey, 1988.

———. "Infinities of Torah in Kabbalah." In *Midrash and Literature,* 141–57. Ed. G. Hartmann and S. Budick. New Haven, 1986.

———. "Jewish Magic from the Renaissance Period to Early Hasidism." In *Religion, Science, and Magic,* 82–117. Ed. Neusner and alia.

———. "Ma᾽aseh Merkavah: A Case of Intercultural Interpretation." (Forthcoming).

———. "On the Concept of Ẓimẓum in Kabbalah and Its Research." In *Lurianic Kabbalah,* 59–112. Ed. R. Elior and Y. Liebes. Jerusalem, 1992 (Hebrew).

———. "Reification of Language in Jewish Mysticism." In *Mysticism and Language,* 42–79. Ed. S. Katz. New York, 1992.

———. "The Concept of the Torah in Heikhalot Literature and Its Metamorphoses in Kabbalah." *JSJT* 1 (1981): 23–84 (Hebrew).

———. *Kabbalah: New Perspectives.* New Haven, 1988.

———. "The Magical and Theurgical Interpretation of Music in Jewish Texts: Renaissance to Hasidism." *Yuval* 4 (1982): 33–63 (Hebrew).

———. "The Magical and Neoplatonic Interpretations of Kabbalah in the Renaissance." In *Jewish Thought in the Sixteenth Century,* 186–242. Ed. B. D. Cooperman, Cambridge, Mass., 1983.

———. "Sexual Metaphors and Praxis in the Kabbalah." In *The Jewish Family,* 179–224. Ed. D. Kraemer. New York, 1989.

———. *Studies in Ecstatic Kabbalah.* State University of New York Press, Albany, 1988.

———. *The Mystical Experience in Abraham Abulafia.* New York, 1987.

———. "Types of Redemptive Activities in the Middle Ages." In *Messianism and Eschatology,* 253–79. Ed. Z. Baras. Jerusalem, 1984 (Hebrew).

———, and B. McGinn, eds. *Mystical Union and Monotheistic Faith,* An Ecumenical Dialogue. New York, 1989.

Jacobs, Louis. *Hasidic Prayer.* New York, 1978.

———. *Jewish Mystical Testimonies.* New York, 1987.

———. *On Ecstasy: A Tract by Dobh Baer of Lubavitch* (Rossel Books, 1963).

Jacobson, Yoram. *La pensée hassidique.* Translated by C. Chalier. Paris, 1989.

Katz, Steven T. "Models, Modeling and Mystical Training." *Religion* 12 (1982): 247–75.

Krassen, Miles A. Devequt *and Faith in* Ẓaddiqim: *The Religious Tracts of Meshullam Feibush Heller of Zabarazh.* Ph.D. Dissertation, University of Philadelphia, 1990.

Lamm, Norman. *Torah Lishmah, Torah for the Torah's Sake in the Works of Rabbi Ḥayyim of Volozhin and His Contemporaries.* New York and New Jersey, 1989.

Lewis, Ioan M. *Ecstatic Religion: An Anthropological Study of Spirit Possession and Shamanism.* Penguin Books, 1971.

Liebes, Yehuda. "New Directions in the Study of Kabbalah." *Pe᾽amim* 50 (1992), pp. 150–70 (Hebrew).

———. "New Writings on Kabbalah from the Group of R. Yonathan Eibeschuetz." *JSJT* 5 (1986): 191–348 (Hebrew).

———. "Sefer Ẓaddik Yesod ᶜOlam: A Sabbatian Myth." *Daat* (1978): 73–120 (Hebrew).

———. "The Messiah of the *Zohar*." In *Messianic Idea of Israel,* 87–234. Jerusalem.

Loewenthal, Naftali. *Communicating the Infinite: The Emergence of the Ḥabad School.* Chicago, 1990.

———. "'Reason' and 'Beyond Reason' in Ḥabad Hasidism." In *ʾAlei Shefer, Studies in the Literature of Jewish Thought Presented to Rabbi Dr. Alexandre Safran,* 109–26. Ed. M. Ḥallamish. Bar-Ilan, 1990.

Mahler, Raphael. *Hasidism and the Jewish Enlightenment: Their Confrontation in Galicia and Poland in the First Half of the Nineteenth Century.* Translated by E. Orenstein. Philadelphia, 1985.

Maimon, Shelomo. *Shelomo Maimon, An Autobiography.* Translated by Clark Murray. London, 1888.

Marett, Robert R. *The Threshold of Religion.* London, 1914.

Matt, Daniel. "Ayin: The Concept of Nothingness in Jewish Mysticism." In *The Problem of Pure Consciousness, Mysticism and Philosophy,* 121–59. Ed. Robert K. C. Forman. New York, Oxford, 1990.

Mondshein, Yehoshuʿah. *Kerem CḤABAD* 4 (1992) two volumes.

———. *Sefer Migdal ʿOz.* Kevar Ḥabad, 1980.

———. *Shiveḥei Ha-Baal Shem Tov: A Facsimile of a Unique Manuscript.* Jerusalem, 1982.

Neumann, Erich Neumann. "Mystical Man." In *The Mystic Vision: Papers from the Eranos Yearbooks,* 375–415. Ed. Joseph Campbell, translated by R. Manhein. Princeton, 1982.

Neusner, Jacob, Frerichs, E. C., and McCracken Flesher, P. V., eds. *Religion, Science, and Magic: In Concert and In Conflict.* New York, Oxford, 1989.

Nigal, Gedalyah. *Magic, Mysticism, and Hasidism.* Tel Aviv, 1992 (Hebrew).

———. *Manhig ve-ʿEdah.* Jerusalem, 1962 (Hebrew).

Pachter, Mordechai. "The Concept of Devekut in the Homiletical Ethical Writings of 16th Century Safed." In *Studies in Medieval Jewish History and Literature,* vol. 2, 171–230. Ed. I. Twersky. Cambridge, Mass., 1984.

———. "Traces of the Influence of R. Elijah de Vidas's *Reshit Ḥokhma* upon the Writings of R. Jacob Joseph of Polonnoye." In *Studies in Jewish Mysticism, Philosophy, and Ethical Literature Presented to Isaiah Tishby,* 569–92. Ed. J. Dan and J. Hacker. Jerusalem, 1986 (Hebrew).

Piekarz, Mendel. *Ideological Trends of Hasidism in Poland During the Interwar Period and the Holocaust.* Jerusalem, 1990 (Hebrew).

———. *Studies in Braslav Hasidism.* Jerusalem, 1972 (Hebrew).

———. *The Beginning of Hasidism: Ideological Trends in Derush and Musar Literature.* Jerusalem, 1978 (Hebrew).

———. "The Devekuth as Reflecting the Socio-Religious Character of the Hasidic Movement." *Daat* 24 (1990): 127–44 (Hebrew).

Pines, Shelomo. "On the Term *Ruḥaniyyut* and Its Sources and on Judah Halevi's Doctrine." *Tarbiẓ* 57 (1988): 511–40 (Hebrew).

———. "Shiʿite Terms and Conceptions in Judah Halevi's Kuzari." *Jerusalem Studies in Arabic and Islam* 2 (1980): 165–251.

Rapoport-Albert, Ada. "God and the Ẓaddik as the Two Focal Points of Hasidic Worship." *History of Religions* 18 (1979): 296–325.

Rapoport-Albert, Ada. "The Hasidic Movement." *Ẓion* 55 (1990): 183–245 (Hebrew).
Ross, Tamar. "Rav Ḥayim of Volozhin and Rav Shneur Zalman of Liadi: Two Interpretations of the Doctrine of Ẓimẓum." *JSJT* 2 (1982): 153–69 (Hebrew).
Rubinstein, Avraham, ed. *Studies in Hasidism.* Jerusalem, 1977 (Hebrew).
———. *Shiveḥei Ha-Besht.* Jerusalem, 1991 (Hebrew).
Ruderman, David. *Kabbalah, Magic, and Science: The Cultural Universe of a Sixteenth-Century Jewish Physician.* Cambridge, Mass., 1988.
Sack, Bracha. "Prayer in the Althought of R. Moshe Cordovero." *Daat* 9 (1982): 5–12 (Hebrew).
———. "The Influence of R. Moshe Cordovero on Hasidism." *Eshel Be᾽er Sheva*ᶜ 3 (1986): 229–46 (Hebrew).
———. "The Influence of Cordovero on Seventeenth-Century Jewish Thought." In *Jewish Thought in the Seventeenth Century,* 365–79. Ed. I. Twersky and B. Septimus. Cambridge, Mass., 1987.
Safran, Bezalel. "Maharal and Early Hasidism." In *Hasidism: Continuity or Innovation?,* 47–144. Ed. B. Safran. Cambridge, 1988.
Schaefer, Peter. *Hekhalot Studien.* Tuebingen, 1988.
Schatz, Rivka. "Contemplative Prayer in Hasidism." In *Studies in Mysticism and Religion Presented to Gershom G. Scholem,* 209–26. Jerusalem, 1967.
———Schatz, Rivka. "The Besht's Commentary on Psalm 107: From Myth to the Rite of Descent to the Hell." *Tarbiẓ* 42 (1973): 154–84 (Hebrew).
Schatz-Uffenheimer, Rivka. *Quietistic Elements in Eighteenth-Century Hasidic Thought.* Jerusalem, 1968 (Hebrew).
———. *Hasidism as Mysticism.* Princeton and Jerusalem, 1993.
Scholem, Gershom. *Devarim be-Go.* Tel Aviv, 1976 (Hebrew).
———. *Kabbalah.* Jerusalem, 1974.
———. *Major Trends in Jewish Mysticism.* New York, 1967.
———. *The Messianic Idea in Judaism.* New York, 1972.
———. *On the Kabbalah and Its Symbolism.* New York, 1969.
———. *On the Mystical Shape of the Godhead.* New York, 1991.
———. *Origins of the Kabbalah.* Princeton, 1987.
———. *Researches in Sabbateanism.* Ed. Yehuda Liebes. Tel Aviv, 1991 (Hebrew).
———. *Sabbatai Ṣevi, the Mystical Messiah.* Translated by R. J. Z. Werblowsky. Princeton, 1973.
———. "The Name of God and the Linguistic of the Kabbala." *Diogenes* 79 (1972): 59–80 and 80: 164–94.
———. "Two First Testimonies on the Contrarities of Hasidism and the Besht." *Tarbiẓ* 20 (1950): 228–40 (Hebrew).
Schwartz, Dov. "Different Forms of Magic in Jewish Thought in Fourteenth-Century Spain." *PAAJR* 47 (1990/1991): 17–47 (Hebrew).
Sherwin, Byron. *The Mystical Theology and Social Dissent: The Life and Works of Judah Loew of Prague.* London and Toronto, 1982.
Shmeruk, Chone. *Yiddish Literature in Poland: Historical Studies and Perspectives.* Jerusalem, 1981 (Hebrew).
Shoḥot, Azriel. "Ha-Ẓaddiq in the Hasidic Doctrine." *Yaacob Gil Jubilee Volume,* 299–306. Jerusalem, 1979 (Hebrew).

Stace, W. T. *Mysticism and Philosophy*. New York, 1960.
Sullivan, Lawrence E. *Icanchu's Drum. An Orientation to Meaning in South American Religions*. New York, London, 1988.
Thomas Keith. *Religion and the Decline of Magic*. New York, 1971.
Tishby, Isaiah. "*Qudsha* ᵓ *Berikh Hu* ᵓ, ᵓOrayytaᵓ ve-Yisrael Kulla Had: The Source of the Dictum in R. Moshe Ḥayyim Luzzatto's Commentary on ᵓIdraᵓ Rabba." *QS* 50 (1975): 480–92, 668–74 (Hebrew).
———. *Studies in Kabbalah and Its Branches*. Jerusalem, 1982 (Hebrew).
———. "The Messianic Idea and Messianic Trends in the Growth of Hasidism." *Ẓion* 32 (1967): 1–45 (Hebrew).
———. *The Wisdom of the Zohar*, two volumes. Jerusalem, 1961 (Hebrew).
———. "Les traces de Rabbi Moise Haim Luzzato dans l'enseignement du Hassidism." *Hommage à Georges Vajda, Études d'histoire et de pensée juives*, 421–62. Ed. G. Nahon and Ch. Touati. Louivain, 1980; Hebrew version, *Ẓion* 43 (1978): 201–34.
———. *Paths of Faith and Heresy*. Ramat Gan, 1964 (Hebrew).
———, and Joseph Dan. "*Hasidut*." In *The Hebrew Encyclopedia* 17 (1988) cols. 769–822 (Hebrew).
Urbach, Ephraim E. *The Sages: Their Concepts and Beliefs*. Translated by I. Abrahams. Jerusalem, 1979, 2 volumes.
Vajda, Georges. *Le commentaire d'Ezra de Gerone sur le cantique des cantiques*. Paris, 1969.
Vickers, Brian. "Analogy Versus Identity: The Rejection of Occult Symbolism, 1580–1680." In *Occult and Scientific Mentalities in the Renaissance*, 95–163. Ed. B. Vickers. Cambridge, 1986.
Walker, Daniel P. *Spiritual and Demonic Magic from Fiano to Campanella*, London, 1958.
Weinstein, Donald and Rudolph M. Bell. *Saints and Society: Two Worlds of Western Christendom, 1000–1700*. Chicago and London, 1986.
Weiss, Joseph. *Studies in Braslav Hasidism*. Ed. Mendel Piekarz. Jerusalem, 1974.
———. *Studies in Eastern European Jewish Mysticism*. Ed. D. Goldstein. Oxford, 1985.
———. "Talmud-Torah le-Shitat R. Israel Besht." *Essays Presented to Chief Rabbi Israel Brodie Israel*, 151–69. London, 1967 (Hebrew part).
Werblowsky, R. J. Zwi. *Joseph Karo, Lawyer and Mystic*. Philadelphia, 1977.
Wertheim, Aharon. *Law and Custom in Chassidism*. Jerusalem, 1960 (Hebrew).
Wilensky, Mordecai. *Hasidim and Mitnageddim*. Jerusalem, 1970 (Hebrew), 2 volumes.
Wolfson, Elliot R. "Walking as a Sacred Duty: Theological Transformation of a Social Reality in Early Hasidism." Forthcoming.
———. "Letter Symbolism and Merkavah Imagery in the *Zohar*." In *ᶜAlei Shefer*, 195–236. Ed. Ḥallamish.
Yaᶜari, Abraham. "Two Basic Versions of 'Shiveḥei ha-Besht,'" *QS* 39 (1964): 249–72, 349–562 (Hebrew).

Appendix of Hebrew Quotes

1. ומכוון בכל עשיותיו כדי לעשות תענוג ליוצרו נמצא שממשיך בכל עשיותיו האלף שמרמז לאלופו של עולם אבל אם נוטל התענוג לעצמו לא כדי לעשות נחת רוח ליוצרו נמצא הוא מפריד אלף אלופו של עולם.

2. וכל אות ואות יש לה צורה רוחניות ומאור נכבד אצול מעצם הספי' משתלשל ממדרגה למדרגה כדרך השתלשלות הספירות. והנה האות היכל ומכון לרוחניות ההוא.ובהיות האדם מזכיר ומניע אות מאותיות, בהכרח יתעורר הרוחניות ההוא... והנה בהזכרת האדם התיבה ההיא הרומזת באותיות, בסבת תנועת הכחות ההם והכאתם זה בזה על ידי פטיש הנשמה, בזולת שיתעוררו הם בשרשם העליון לפעול הפעול' ההיא... וזהו סוד הזכרת השמות וכוונת התפלה.

APPENDIX A

1. וזאת המלחמה הנמצאת תוך הלב היא נוצרת מהספירה הראשונה. שהיא באדם מחשבה טובה ומחשבה רעה. וכשרש העץ והעלים יהיו הפירות. וכן תהיה גם כן מולדתה לטובה ולרעה ר"ל שיחכם המחשב לעשות בחכמה את שיעשהו טוב או רע. וכן תהיה הבינה והדעת טוב ורע שיהיה המבין מבין זה בין טוב לרע ומבדיל ביניהם ... והספירות מאצילות שפע ללב והשפע נחלק למינים רבים מהם טבעיים ומהם מקריים ומהם הכרחיים ומהם רצוניים ... ופי' רחמנא לבא בעי. הוא כאמרך הרחמן לב רחמן מבקש. רודף אחר מדותיו כעשן מהו רחום אף אתה היה רחום. וכן שאר המדות כולן.

2. דרך הבעש"ט והמגיד שהמשיכו בחי' התגלות אא"ס בריבוי אופני גילויים מבחי' ומבשרי אחזה שהוא מחיות הנפש בגוף הבא ונמשך בדרך העלם וגילוי משא"כ המקובלי' דברו בבחי' אור ומאור כו'.

APPENDIX B

1. סיפר אשר בין תלמידי המגיד הגדול ז"ל היה וויכח על תורה שאמר המגיד ז"ל. זה אומר כך אמר המגיד וזה אומר כך אמר המגיד. והשיב להם המגיד ז"ל אלו ואלו דברי אלקים חיים. כי הדיבורים שאמרתי כולל דברי כולם ע"כ דברי המגיד ז"ל. ואמר הוא ז"ל כי יש שבעין אנפין לאורייתא. ובאמת נמשכת התורה ממקום האחדות האמיתי. אמנם התורה במקור שרשה היא אחדות רק כשנמשכת לאלו העולמות נעשה שבעין אנפין לאורייתא ע"כ איתא בתורתו של רבי מאיר כתוב כתנות אור באלף כי רבי מאיר לקח את התורה ממקור שרשה. ע"כ נכתב אור באלף ואצלינו כתוב עור בעיין.

2. פעם אחת בליל חג השבועות ישב בשלחן ולא אמר תורה ולא דיבר אפי' דיבר אחד רק בכה מאוד ובליל ב' נהג ג"כ כמו בליל א' רק אחר ברהמ"ז אמר הלא המגיד זצ"ל כשאמר תורה על השלחן ואח"כ כשהלכו לביתם הי' חוזרים התלמודים בניהם את התורה זה אמר באופן זה שמעתי וזה אמר באופן אחר כי כל אחד ואחד שמע באופן אחר ואומר אני שאין זה חידוש כי יש ע' פנים לתורה וכל אחד ואחד באיזה פנים שהי' לו בהתורה באותו פנים שמע את התורה מהמגיד זצ"ל ואמר אבל כשמסתכלין היטב בהפנים אין צריכין לומר תורה כי הכרת פניהם ענתה בם וד"ל.

23. צריך שיה' בהלימוד הארה וחיות מהדביקות בו ית'. ועי"ז יתקיים הלימוד.

CHAPTER 6

1. כי האדם כמו כלי לעולם העליון.

2. אין הקב"ה שורה אלא במי שמקטין א"ע ע"כ נקרא הצדיק כל לשון כלי.

3. אין כלי מחזיק ברכה לישראל אלא השלום.

4. ושכנתי בתוכם, כי הצדיק נקרא היכל ה' ומקדש ה' שבו שוכן יה...וכאשר מדבק עצמו לת"ח, שבו שורה השכינה, ממילא דבוק בו ית' ממש.

5. ושכנתי בתוכם...בתלמידי חכמים שהם היכל ה' ולא בעצים ואבנים של המשכן...בתלמידי חכמים הראוים לכך וז"ש כי אות היא ביני וביניכם שעל ידו שורה שכינה בישראל.

6. ובאמת כששופע על הצדיק הרוחניות בתפלתו ותורתו, אין לך תענוג גדול מזה.

7. כי כח יש באותי' הללו לצמצם המעלות העליונות ולהמשיכם בתוכם וע"י האותי' הללו שורים על המדבר אותם.

8. נמצא בעת עשית המצוות, אנחנו כביכול כליו של הקב"ה ורצונו כביכול שורה על כליו. ואנחנו בידו כגרזן ביד החוצב בו...שרצונו שורה עלינו ואנחנו כליו.

9. בעת עשות האדם מצות ה', אז שורה עליו הרצון האלוקי שהם נקראים אורות דאצילות.

10. כי המצוה לית לה מגרמה שום חיות וקדושה ואור כלל, רק מצד קדושת אותיות התורה הכתובות בענין אותה המצוה.

11. אמנם עצמות האור מקבלת המצוה מאותיות התורה הכתובה בעניינה...ולא אמר ללומדיה או לעוסקיה אלא לעושיה.

12. לפני עסק התורה או המצוה כמו לפני לבישת טלית ותפילין וגם יתבונן איך שאור אין סוף ב"ה הסובב כל עלמין וממלא כל עלמין הוא רצון העליון הוא מלובש באותיו' וחכמת התורה או בציצית ותפילין אלו, ובקריאתו או בלבישתו הוא ממשיך אורו ית' עליו דהיינו על חלק אלוה ממעל שבתוך גופו ליכלל וליבטל באורו יתברך.

13. והנה כל אלה לא היו סכלים, רק חכמים גדולים שקטנם עבה ממתני הפלסופים, היו יודעים ומשיגים בדרכי הטבע...וכ"כ בדרכי ההבנות לקבל פעולות הטבע כפי הרצון המבוקש.

14. וכן לדעת המקובלים כל התורה והמצוות הם הכנות נאותות לקבל השפעות נצרכות בתכלית השלימות מבלי שיתערב עמהם איזה חסרון וע"ז סובבו כל המצוות התלויות בזמן ובמקום ובפעולות ידועות והם כלם מכוונות לעצמן בדקדוק גדול, אשר אם יחסר איזה ענין מהם א"א [אי אפשר] שתושלם הפעולה המבוקשת.

CONCLUDING REMARKS

סוד אלוה שבהם, שיעזור להם לדבר האותיות בכוונת אמת לשמה.

10. יש בעסק התורה ב' סוגיות או קשוטי הלכה זה חלק הנגלה מהתורה הנק' לבושי התורה...וכמו שהכלה אחר הקשוטין והלבושין הוא היחוד והזווג ואז ישתליל מלבושיה ודבק באשתו והיו לבשר אחד כך סוגי התורה, אחר הקשוטין והלבושין הוא היחוד ודביקו' בפנימיו' התורה...שהוא שמו ית' ממש.

11. כשמדבר, בדביקות בעולם העליון, ואין שום מחשבה זרה ובא לו מחשבה כמו בנביאות. בוודאי יהיה כך. והמחשבה הזאת בא מחמת הכרוזים שמכריזין למעלה על הדבר. ולפעמים ישמע כמו קול מדבר מחמת שידבק קול העליון בתפילתו וקוול תורתו, ישמע כמו קול אומר עתידות.

12. וכן שמעתי מן אא"ז זלה"ה...איך איפשר ליקח הקב"ה כביכול שישרה אצל האדם והיינו ע"י התורה שהיא שמותיו של הקב"ה והוא הקב"ה ממש...שהוא ושמו אחד...וכשלומד תורה לשם הקב"ה והוא לקיים מצותיו ולשמור ל"ת ומזכיר אותיות התורה שהן שמותיו של הקב"ה בזה הוא לוקח להקב"ה ממש...ושורה עליו השכינה כביכול כמ"ש בכל מקום אשר אזכיר את שמי, כשיזכיר שם של הקב"ה שהוא התורה הקדושה שכולה שמותיו אז אבוא אליך וברכתיך, נמצא בעוסקו בלימוד תורה לשמה, בזה הוא לוקח להשם כביכול וממשיך עליו השראת השכינה הקדושה.

13. כי למוד תורה לשמה היא ידיעת שמו הקדוש, המתיחד ע"י התורה.

14. כשמתפלל בפשוטה, אז התיבות אינם חיים. רק מחיה אותם למשל כשאומר ברוך אתה ה', אין חיות רק אח"כ כשמזכיר את השם. אבל כשמתפלל עד"ה [על דרך הסוד] אז כל התיבה שם בפ"ע, כי הוא עולם הדיבור.

15. שביעי...התורה שלמדה לשמה וסוד מלת לשמה שזכרו רבותינו בכל מקום תמיד. הוא שם המפורש.

16. שילמד בשנה השביעית לשמה...כי מבואר בכתבי האר"י זלה"ה שהי' למוד שש פנים בהלכה דרך פלפול להסיר קליפה שהוא בחוץ ולמוד שביעי למוד בפנימיות התורה.

17. שילמוד לשמה, לשם ה' המוצאות שהוא דבור הקדום.

18. להמשיך הדבור הקדום בחינת הה' לישראל בדרך כלל, כי כל זה הוא עיקר נתינת התורה, שבחי' הה' שהוא שמו ית' ממש, וחלק ה' נמשך ונשפע לתוך ב"י על ידי הדבור שנאצל מן דבור הקדום.

19. לשמור הדבור הנקבע בו כאמרו וע"י כן יהי' הדברו שלו היכל לאור א"ס ב"ה.

20. שלא יחלל הדברו הקדו' בפיו ככל היצא מפיו יעש' דנייינו[?] ככל היוצא מפיו של הבורא ב"ה כביעול, שהוא לכוונתו שידבק ע"י הדבור, בו ית'.

21. וע"י חדושין דאורייתא שמדבר הדבורים בדביקות גדול בשורשו, מעלה אותן נשמות שנבראו ע"י האותיות והדבורים וכו'.

22. ולהמשיך ברכות וישועות על ישראל. וממשיך קדושה ע"ע וזוכה להיות נקרא קדוש.

כי כלנו תלוים בך.

101. בדיבור יש קול ואות' ובשעת הדיבור הקול והדיבור ביחד נשמע, אבל הקול הוא הפנימיות והוא למעלה מהאותיו', אבל כשהמדבר חושב לדבר דברים חדשים שרוצה לחדש הדיבור, אזי מחשבתו אינו אלא בהאותי' של הדיבור ולא בקול ונגסר הדיבור מהקול והקול ישן. לכם אנו תוקעים בשופר והוא הקול בלא דיבור, ואנו מעוררים הקול העליון, שהש"י יחשוב שוב בהקול והוא ענין תקיעה, שיתקע המחשבה בהקול.

102. והיה מתפלל בזעקה גדולה והרב מגיד מישרים הגדול לא היה יכול לסבול כי היה חולה גדול ויצא מבהמ"ד.

103. ומעשה ידיו מגיד הרקיע דרקיע הוא לשון דקות ורוחניות כמ"ש וירקעו פחי הזהב והצדיקים נקראין מעשי ידיו של הקב"ה וזהו מעשה ידיו דהיינו הצדיק מגיד הוא לשון המשכה שהוא ממשיך דברים דקים ורוחניים במעשיו הקדושים שבורא עולמות בקדושתו.

CHAPTER 5

1. כי דרך האמת כן הוא שצריך בשעת עבודה להפשיט עצמו מגשמיות עוה"ז עד שיחשב בעיניו כאלו איננו בעוה"ז כלום ולומר האותיות בקול ודיבור פשטו ולדבק ולקשר מחשבתו בהאותיות הק' ולהבין פירוש המילות הק' ואז ממילא פתאו' יתלקח ויתלהב בו אש להבת שלהבת הבערת היראה והאהבה עילאין בעוז ועצום עד מאד. וזהו הדרך ישכון אור בעבודת הק' פנימה.

2. ובהיות האדם מזכיר ומניע אות מאותיות, בהכרח יתעורר הרוחניות ההוא...אלא גם במציאותם רצה לומר בכתיבתם, להם רוחניות שורה על האותיות ההם. וזה טעם קדושת ספר תורה.

3. אף על פי שלא ידע האדם כי אם קריאת התורה, ר"ל הפסוק לבד, בהכרח יקבל שכר על הקריאה ההיא ויהי' שכרו מרובה.

4. וקריאת המלו' העיקר צריך שיכוין בנשמתם ובמקורם וברוחניותם שהם פירושם...לזה צריך בהכרח שיתעסק בתורה שבעל פה, שהוא פירוש התורה והיא נשמת התורה, רוצה לומר מגלה רוחניותיה שהוא פירושיה וסודותיה.

5. שהלשון סולם לעליית התורה והתפלה.

6. ריב"ש אמר אדם שהוא קורא בתורה ורואה האורות של האותיות שבתור', אע"פ שאין מבין הטעמים כראוי, כיון שהוא קורא באהבה גדולה ובהתלהבות אין השי"ת מדקדק עמו, אף שאין אומרם כראוי.

7. הוא ית' צמצם את עצמו בתורה, מימלא כשמדבר ד"ת או תפילה, ידבר בכל כחו, כי בזה נעשה אחדות עמו ית', דכל כחו הוא באות, והוא ית' שורה באות.

8. כי אורייתא וקב"ה וישראל כולהו חד הוא, ואך ורק כשממשיכין סוד אלוה בתורה ע"י שלומדים התורה לשמה, אז יש בה כח אלוהות ונעשית סוד נביעו להחיות ולרפאות.

9. וע"י לימוד ועסק התורה לשמה יכול להחיות את נפשו ולתקן רמ"ח אבריו ושס"ה גידיו ודבק עצמו בשורשם ובשורש שורשם, שהוא התורה והוי"ה ב"ה...והכל הוא ע"י שעוסקים בתורה לשמה ולבקש מן האותיות ממש וכמו ששמעתי פירושו מן אא"ז [אדוני אבי זקני] זללה"ה פי' מן

90. צריך אדם ללמוד ולהרגיל א"ע שיתפלל אפי' הזמירות בקול נמוך ויצעק בלחש ויאמר הדיבורים בין בזמירות ובין בלימוד בכל כחו כדכתיב: (תהלים, לה, 10) כל עצמותי וגו' והצעקה שתהי' מחמת דביקות שתהיה בלחש.

91. וכן בתפלה יכול לעבוד עבודת התפלה להשי"ת שלא יהיה עבודתו שלא יעשה שום תנועה באיברים רק בפנימיות בנשמתו' יהי' בוער בלבו ויצעוק בלחש מחמת התלהבות.

92. ולפעמים יכול האדם לאמר התפלה באהבה ויראה והתלהבות גדול בלי שום תנועה ויהיה נראה לאדם אחר שהוא אומר אותן דברים בלי שום דחקות וזה יכול האדם לעשות כשהוא דבוק מאוד להשי"ת אז יכול האדם לעבוד אותו בנשמה לבד באהבה רבה גדולה וזה העבודה הוא יותר טובה והולכת במהירות יותר ומדביקות (!) להש"ת יותר מהתפלה שנראה בחוץ על האיברים ואין להקליפה אחיזה בזו התפלה שכולה היא בפנימיות.

93. שהשטן אינו מוציא זמנו כי אם להפיל הגדולים ארצה...לכן השלמים ביודעם מדת השטן שכך הוא מעולם לא היו מורין עצמם לעשות הכנות לכוונת תפלתם פן יראה השטן ויבוא לבלבל כוונתם, אך היו מכנים (צ"ל מכינים) עצמם במחשבת לבם שאין במחשבה גלוי מלתא לשטן וכשהיו עומדים להתפלל לא היו מורין עצמם בתנועות המכוונים.

94. צריך שלא להראות עצמם כאלו עומדים בכוונה.

95. ובהיות האדם מזכיר ומניע אות מהאותיות בהכרח יתעורר רוחניות ההוא והבל הפה ממנו יתהוו צורות קדושות ממנו יתעלו ויתקשרובשרשם שהם שרש האצילות.

96. ועל ידי העליה הזאת שהיא עולה להדבק בשורשה אין ספק שאותם האותיות עולות ובוקעות האויר ופותחות פתח ומדבקים את בעל העסק באלהות, ומשפיע בו ההבנה והדקות אשר לא היה בכחו להשכיל.

97. עוד יתהווה ממנה מהבל פיו, רוחניות ומציאו' יהי' כמו מלאך שיעלה ויתקשר בשרשו, שימהר להפעיל פעולתו בזריזות ומהירות וזהו סוד הזכרת השמות וכוונת התפלה.

98. ובהזכיר האדם האותיות, מנענע ההיות העליונה וכשמתדבק במחשבתו בתמימות להשי"ת, מחזיר החיות שנשתלשל ממחשבה העליונה עד שבאה לדיבור והושם בפה האדם והוא משתוקק בדברי התפלה להשי"ת, בזה מפריח האותיות לשרשם... אם יזכה שיוכל להמשיך רוחניות מלמעלה לדיבוריו להפריח האותיות למעלה כמ"ש בפרדס...

99. ופועה הוא לשון דבור, שהשופר מעלה את כל התפלות עולות ע"י הקול של שופר... ואנו מתפללין תפלת שחרית ואח"כ נשלח אותך, בעל התוקע, שתעורר את האבות והם יעלו את תפלתינו לפניו ית'... וכל תפלותינו יעלו על ידי תקיעותיך אלו ויתלבשו בזה הקול.

100. משל: לפני התקיעות מלך גדול מלך מפואר ששלח את בניו לצוד ציד ותעו הבנים מהדרך והיו צועקים אולי ישמע האב ולא נענו. ואמרו בלבם: אולי שכחנו את הלשון של אבינו לפיכך אינו שומע צעקתנו, בכן נצעק בקול בלא דיבור. ויעצו א"ע לשלוח את אחד לצעוק והזהיר אותו ראה והבן כי כלנו תלוים בך. כך הנמשל: הקב"ה שלח אותנו להעלות ניצוצות הקדושה ותעינו מאבינו. ואולי מפני ששכחנו הדיבור של אבינו, אין אנו יכולים להתפלל בדיבור, נשלח אותך בעל התוקע שתתעורר רחמים עלינו בקול בלא דיבור וראה והזהר

בכל היכל והיכל ומגרשין אותו מההיכל כשאינו ראוי זהו פרושו. ההיכלות נקרא הדבורים שהשכל שורה בהן והוא הולך מאות לאות ומתיבה לתיבה.

75. שקבלתי ממורי שעיקר עסק תורה ותפלה הוא שידבק א"ע אל פנימי' רוחני' אור א"ס שבתוך אותיות התורה והתפלה.

76. וכאשר שכב ודבק א"ע בדביק' וחשיקה אל אותיות התורה, נתפשט מהגשמיות.

77. אם תפשטו את עצמיכם מהגשמיות ותהיה (!) דבוקים בהשי"ת מאוד, ויהא הזווג שלכם לשמו ית' ויהיה מופשט מחומריות כל האפשר, אז תהיו גדולים מאוד, כיון שתהיו דבוקים בהשי"ת.

78. דיבורי התפילה... כשמסיח דעתו מכל וכל ונותן לבו לפני מי הוא עומד ומהות הדיבורים והצרופים והשמות והאורות שבתוכם, ומתדבק עמהם דבקות נפלא עד מאוד, אז נעשה עם הדבורים פנ"פ [פנים בפנים]...בסוד נפשט מהגשמיות.

79. ע"י תפלות ישראל נמשך השפע וחיות חדשים לאותיות וצירופים ודיבורים.

80. אומנם המתפלל שיזכה נדבק במחשבתו בו ית' ואין צריך הורדת השפע, אפשר דתפלה זו סגי במחשבה... שתפלה זו אין צריך כלי להוריד השפע.

81. האותיות הנכתבות הם גוף וכלי אל הנזכר בפה. ואות' הנז' בפה הם גשמיות בערך המחשביות שהם בלב.

82. ... רוחניות האותיות אפילו בכתיבתן לבד, כ"ש (כל שכן) בקריאתן, כ"ש בכוונתן, והענין האותיות הנכתבות הם גוף והיכל לאותיות הקבועות בפה. המשל בזה האותיות הנכתבות הם גשמיות והנקראות על פה הם רוחניות.

83. הבל פיו של אדם לא דבר רק הוא... אמנם היא רוחניות מתהווה מהבל פין של אדם. וצריך אל הרוחניות ההוא כח להפריח שאלותיו ולהעלות האותיות.

84. ע"י קול לימוד התורה הנק' ברית לדבק א"ע ע"י קול הדבור.

85. צריך דיבור בתפלה כי השי"ת יודע מחשבות ושמעתי תירץ כי צריך דיבור כדי לעשות כלי להמשיך השפע בתוכה (!) למטה.

86. הדביקות הוא כשאומר תיבה, הוא מאריך באותה תיבה הרבה, שמחמת דביקות אינו רוצה לפרוד עצמו מהתיבה ולכן מאריך באותה התיבה.

87. כשאדם במדרגה קטנה, אז טוב יותר להתפלל מתוך הסדור. שמכח שרואה האותיות מתפלל בכוונה. אבל כשהוא דבוק יותר בעולם העליון אז יותר טוב לסגור עיניו, כדי שלא יבטל אותו הראיה מלהיות דבוק בעולם העליון.

88. כשאני מדבק מחשבתי בבורא ית', אני מניח הפה לדבר מה שירצה כי אז אני מקשר הדיבורים בשורש העליון בבורא ית'.

89. והעיקר שילך תמיד בשמחה ובפרט בעת הדיבור, דבלא שמחה א"א להיות דבוק בבורא ית'.

הספירו' עם אור המהי' אותן.

61. ישראל עושין כלי מלת בפיהם.

62. כי האותיות הן היכלות וטירות לרוחניות והם כלים שואבים האצילות כדרך הגוף שהוא שואב הנשמה בתוכו... וקריאת המילות העיקר שיכוין בנשמתם ובמקורם וברוחניותם שהם פרושם.

63. ותירץ מוהר"ן שע"י הדבור נעשה כלים שבו יושפע שפע הברכה.

64. והנה כמו שהעולם אינו מתקיים כי אם על ידי שפע הרוחני שבתוכו... כך אותיות התורה והתפלה שנצטרכו לתיבות צריך להמשיך בתוך התיבה שפע רוחני הנקרא נח.

65. שיהי' הדיבור ע"י כלי הגוף... שיעשו כלים ע"י כלי הדיבור שבו ישפע שפע הברכה.

66. לאהבתו את האדם קבע בפיו האותיות האלה כדי שיוכל להדבק בבוראו, כי בהזכירו למטה אותיות אלו בתורתו או בתפלתו, מנענע ומעורר למטה השורשים העליונים והיינו מלת "קבע" שהיא כעין התוקע השלשלת ראשה א' במקום א' וראשה השני במקום אחר כי אע"פ שיהיה המקום ההוא רחוק בנענע האדם ראש השלשלת שבידו מנענע כל השלשלת... ובזה נבין מעלת הראשונים עליהם השלום שהיתה תפלתם נשמעת מיד, מפני שהיו נזהרים שלא לפגום כ"ב אותיות שהם ה' מוצאות הקבועות בפיהם.

67. ...ועיני גווניה אורותיה, משם יבא להשכיל פנימיות סתרי הסוד אשר ברוחניות הצורה ההיא (הכוונה ל"צורה אחת מהצורות הגשמיות") ויתדבק.

68. שאורות כ"ב אותיות התורה נקבעו בפה האדם בחי' דבור פנימי וקדוש מקדושתו ית'... אור שאין סוף שופע בה' המוצאות שנקבעו בפיו שג"כ אור הא"ס שופע בה' מוצאות האלו שהן נתינת התורה הכללית... וכשישמור מלטמא פיו אזי יהיה נקל לו לדבק את עצמו בעסקו בתורה ותפלה באותיות שנקבעו בפיו לדבק את עצמו לאור א"ס ב"ה השופע בתוך האותיות... שילמוד לשמה שהוא לשם ה' המוצאות שהוא דבור הקדום.

69. והנה האות היכל ומכון לרוחניות ההוא.

70. ופי' קצת קדמונים כי בצרוף וגלגול שם בן ע"ב או שאר השמות אחר התבודדות גדול, יתגלה לצדיק...קצת חלק הבת קול... מטעם שהוא מחבר הכחות ומיחדם...עד שיושפע עליו רוב השפע ובתנאי שיהיה העוסק בכך כלי המוכן לקבל הרוחניות.

71. והנביאים ע"ה היו משיגים דרך אותם האותיות, בהתבודדות גדול וזכות הנשמה הטהורה, אותו הרוחניות המתלבש באותיות.

72. כשאומר "גדול" ומסתכל על אותי' גימ"ל דלי"ת וי"ו למ"ד במחשבתו היטב... וע"י האותיות הללו שורים על המדבר אותם.

73. שמה שכתב בזהר שדנין את האדם בכל היכל, היינו הדבורים ואותיות התפלה הנקרא היכלות, שם דנין את האדם אם כדאי הוא לכנס באותיות התפלה ואם אינו כדאי, מגרשין אותו דהיינו ששולחין לו מחשבה זרה ודוחין אותו.

74. פי' ריב"ש זלה"ה אמר על מה דאיתא בזוה"ק שדנין אותו

47. ומבואר בספרי אבן לטיף כי יש רוחניות לאותיות במדרגת הצורות לחמרים.

48. וזהו סוד עולם האותיות כי הם צורות וחותמות לקבל השפעו' רוחניו' עליונות כמו החותמות המקבלו' השפעו' הכוכבי'.

49. כי אמר איכה נדע לעשות כל תמונה לרוחניות הספירות? והראה תנועת האותיות באותיות.

50. ומכח הצורות ההם היה נבנה דבור, וקול הדבור באותיות ההם היה דמיון גוף לאותיות הפנימיות רוחניות קדושות, שמות הבורא ודמיון הדולה ע"י כלי, מים העמוקים כן היה דולה ע"י צורתו באמצעות הקול ההוא פנימיות הידיעות... בנין האותיות שהם כלי הידיעות הפנימיות.

51. ...נמצא האותיות המפורסמות כלי לרוחניות והם כלים לצורות הפנימיות מושרשות בחכמת הנביא.

52. וכל ספר התורה כלו שמותיו ית'. והספורים ההם והמלות ההם כלים לענינים אלהיים וכל המעשים שארעו ונכתבו, הענין ההוא הוא כלי לידיעת העליון ית' ולכן באו אותיות התורה נפרדות, שאם נדבקה אות אחת לספר, פסול.

53. כשהאותיות התורה והנביאים הם כלים לחכמו' עליונו'... לפי שהאותיות נתנו נפרדות שכל אות מורה בענינו.

54. הבנת דבר מתוך דבר במעמקי סתרי התורה אשר היא כלולה מכל הצורות התחתונות והעליונות ולזה הראינוהו כלים עבים ודקים לפעול בהם במלאכת התורה ואמצעות החשק הרב אשר הוא סבה להתחדש בו רוח חדשה והיא רוח אלהים חיים.

55. וכל אותיות תורתנו הקדושה... הם בעצמם קדושה חמורה שהם כמו גופות והיכלות אל הרוחניות אשר בתוכם הבא מלמעלה, כדמיון הגוף אשר בתוכו הנפש הנשפע בתוכו מחלק חלוק ממעל וזה טעם אמירת הסופר הכותב ס"ת או תפילין: אני הכותב לשם קדושה וכו' כי בכוונה ההיא משפיע בגוף האותיות ההנה, הרוחניות הנ"ל מלמעלה.

56. כי בודאי אותיות השמות הם היכלות לאור ורוחניות זך ומבהיק ומזהיר ובהיר לאין תכלית... כי הספירות האלו אשר נאצלו יש להם רוחניות ונשמה לנשמה.

57. החלוקה הרביעית היא רוחניות האותיות ומציאותם וחבורם אלו באלו והתייחסם כי מי שירד לעומק הענין הזה יוכל לברוא עולמות... והחלוקה הרביעית אינה נמצאת כמעט ולכן לא באה בשם ותחתיה העמוד (!) השמות ופעולתם וצרופם מתוך הפסוקים.

58. אמנם למעלה הוא (התורה) האותיות, לא שמות ולא כנויים וברדתה למטה אל מקום השמות, נעשית כולה שמותיו של הקב"ה...

59. צריך המכוין להמשיך רוחניות מהמדרגות העליונות אל האותיות שהוא מזכיר כדי שיוכל להפריח האותיות ההם עד המדרגה העליונה ההיא, למהר שאלתו.

60. כי גוף האדם אינו רק בשר אדם [אולי צ"ל ודם] והנשמה שבתוכו היא האדם וכ' כך כל המצו+ת אפי' מצות התלויין בדבור כמו מצות תפלה ומצות עסק התורה וברכת הנהנין, הנה האותיות הן רק כלי ולבוש וצריך להמשיך בתוכו של האותיות בעת שמדבר בהם, רוחניות

27. בראש הפרשה מזכיר יהוה ואותיות של זה השם, כל אחת ואחת שם היא אם היתה לבדה נכתבת... ללמדך שכל אות ואות שם בפני עצמו הוא.

28. והנה רזיאל כוון להודיענו שמו יתע' לפי הדרך הנעלמת כדי להקריבנו אליו יתב' שמו, וחלק התיבות ושם לפעמים אות אחת כאלו היא תיבה גמורה להודיענו שכל אות עולם בפני עצמו אצל הקבלה. וצוה לרואי זה הכח המופלא האלהי להורות שמו ית'.

29. כל אות ואות ממנו לבדו עומד נפרד.

30. החבור הוא חבור אותיות רבות והשבתם אל אות אחת.

31. צריך לידע קריאתו בהזכרתו כי כל אות ואות צריך להזכיר בנשימה אחת, כמו שתצא רוחו מן המזכיר בקול רם.

32. סוד צב אות, שכל צבא סודו אות וכל אות סימן ורמז ליצירה.

33. כדי לקבל שפע החכמה וליצירה.

34. נגן בחרק הנמשך למטה ומושך כח העליון להדביקו בך.

35. צריך המתפלל להעביר כוונתו על ב' אלפא ביתות התחתוניות, להמשיך הברכה ממעין מקור חיים לשאר הספירות, על כל אות ואות מאותיות האלפא ביתות... ונתחייב המברך להניע ראשו כדי להורות המשכת הברכה ממעלה למטה.

36. כ"ב אותיות הם וכל אות ואות יש לו גוף ונשמה וכל י' ספירות בכל אות ואות, הרי כ"א פעמים י' ש"י עולמות.

37. ובדמות החלם הנמשך למעלה, נגן בחרק הנמשך למטה ומושך כח עליון.

38. אם יגזור הבורא יגזור להשפיע כח הצלחת זה הצרוף יתגלו לך מזלות וכוכבי לכת כחם וטבעם ופועל (!) בהם.

39. שעל ידי שמותיו הקדושי' וצרופי האותיות הפועלים, אמנם הוא הלכות יצירה, היינו סדר לדעת להכין החומרים במדה ובמשקל והיא חכמה הנקראת מאייה (!) טבעיית.

40. לעסוק בצרוף האותיות להמשיך בנו השכל האלהי.

41. בהסתכל באלהיות, ימשיכו מחשבותיו שפע מלמעלה וישכון בנפשו.

42. שאעפ"י שיעשה האדם בעצמו כל התנאים הצריכים להעשות כדי להמשיל רוח טהרה וקדושה על הנפש הוא לסייעתא דשמיא.

43. ולהלבישה רוחניות השכל.

44. ופורש מרוחניות האלהי כי הוא מורד ברוחניות האלהות.

45. רוחניות המציאות.

46. ...והם כ"ב אותיות פשוטות ורצה בו כי כל מה שברא מרוחניות המלאכים אל הנפשות החיצוניות יחקקו באלה הכ"ב מלות ויהיה לאדם דעה בעולם.

11. כשאנו רוצים שירחם עלינו הוא כביכול מצמם אלהות ית"ש בתיבות רחו"ם ר"ל באורות וכלים של אותיות אלו כידוע לי"ה וכן כל השמות וכנויים.והנה אנשי כנה"ג (כנסת הגדולה) ידוע איזה המשכות היות אלהות הנצרכים בכל עת ערב ובקר וצהריים, לכן תקנו כל כך שמות וכנויים ותיבות ואותיות לפי הנצרך כיד ה' עליהם השכיל.

12. ..ואעפ"י שאינו רואה שום דבר ואינו יודע לכוון כוונות, מכל מקום כשמשים כל ההיו' בהדבור, בדבור עושה נעשו יחודים למעלה כיון שעושה כפי שאפשר לו.

13. שכל תיבה בצורתה ממש היא העולה למעלה... לפעול פעולות ותיקוני' נפלאים.

14. בעת תפלתך ולמודך בכל דבור ודבור ומוצא תפתיך תבין וליחד, כי בכל אות ואו' יש עולם ונשמו' ואלקו' ועולים ומתקשרים ומתיחדי' זה בזה עם אלקו' ואח"כ מתקשרים ומתיחדים יחד האותי' ונעשים תיבה ומתיחדים יחוד גמור באלקו' ותכלל נשמ' עמהם.

15. בכל אות ואות מתה"ק נכללין כל אותיות התורה.

16. שכל אות ואות מן התורה כלולה בה התורה כולה ומה שהיה ומה שיהיה וממילא אין מקודם ומאוחר בתורה.

17. לפעמים אדם קורא פסוקי דזמרא ומתעורר אצלו קול לו, קול אליו, והוא מנשמתו שמשמחתו, בא בו קול גדול לעורר אהבת דודים, וזה לפעמים אף שאדם אינו יודע הכוונה, הנשמה של אדם יודעת ומשמחת אותו שמחת הנפש, וגם בק"ש האדם מביא על עצמו בכל אות ואות אור אל הנשמה , רמ"ח אבריו, וצריך לכוון בכל אות ואות כי רומז לעולמות עליונים כל אות בקדושה.

18. כי האותיות הם אורות ועולמות עליונים.

19. שים שלום: שים נגד פנינו ומחשבותינו האותיות בשלמות ובציור האורות.

20. וע"י התפלה אנו מורידין הקדושה מלמעלה, ולכך בתפלתו כל איש יכוון להוריד הקדושה מלמעלה ולהשפיע לנשמתו.

21. כשמדבר בדעת, ובדעת הדרים ימלאון, כי הוא משרה בהאותיות אלהות ית', וכשמביא בהם אלהות, אזי יש בהם הכל.

22. דע א"ת מי שיכניס הדעת באותיות שהם מא' ועד ת' ודעת הוא התחברות מלשון וידע אדם... ונקראים האותיות היכל ר"ל ה"י כ"ל שבה' מצאות מוצאות הפה שהוא הדבור נכלל הכל דהיינו הבורא יתברך הנק' כל שכולל הכל שהקב"ה שורה בהאותיות כשמדבר בדעת.

23 אמרו הקדמונים ז"ל שמך בך ובך שמך, כי אותיות שמו ית' הוא הוא כי אותיות פורחות ועומדות בו ית' כי האותיות לו כמו גוף והוא נשמה להם.

24. אילו עשרים ושתיים אותיות שהם עשרים ושנים שמות מאות אחת של תורה.

25. אמר ענפיאל השר: כל שהוא מבקש להתפלל תפלה זו ולהתבונן במעשה יוצרו, יזכור לו אות אחת מן האותיות הללו.

26. אפילו אות אחת משמו עושה צבא ככל שמו.

לכך, עד יערה עלינו רוח ממרום, ועתה אזלת יד בעו"ה, ולא יאמר ארבה לכוין ולא אסור מני דרך, כי יעשה בנפשו שקר. אף כי עתה נזדייפו כל כאר"י, גם ההעתקות מלאים שבושים וט"ס לרוב מאוד, כאשר ראיתי בעיני תפלה של האר"י ביד אחד מהמתחסדים, והיא מלאה שבושים קשים ולא קלי ולא מרגיש לכן אנשי לבב, שמעו לי אל תתאוו לעלות ולעוף השמים בלי אבר כי יפול הנופל ויביא עליו שבר... וטוב לכם מעט ביראת ה', רחמנא לבא באי, ובה' תשימו סבר.

2. ...ואלה עושים כנפיים לעוף השמים, ותמה על עצמך אם לפני מלך ב"ו (בשר ודם) יעשו כן, הלא ישליכום לארץ עד שאבריהם יתפרקו וכל גרמיהון הדיקו.

3. מעלת המכוון בתפלתו עשה יעשה לו כנפים לעוף השמים ותפלתו בוקעת עד למעלה...

4. שהסדורי' המה בכתבי יד ובאים מהעתק אל העתק והכונה או השם על התיבה, מאשה אל אחותה נעתק וניתן את של זה בזה ושל זה בזה וכבוד המקום מבוזה ומלאים טעיות כמעט בכל מלה, ואין כח ביד בעליהם להרים המכשילה, כי לא ידעו ולא יבינו בין טוב לרע אשר הכינו, ומוטב הי' להם שלא להתפלל כלל, ככל הגויים אשר סביבותיהם, מלהתפלל בסדורים אשר לפניהם.

5. ומיד כל א' וא' מכין לעצמו סדור הנכתב עם כונות המכונה להאר"י זלה"ה.

6. כי בודאי מי שלא הכניס צוארו בעבודה אפי' הוא ת"ח ואפי' יודע כל הכוונות, ידע נאמנה שעדיין לא טעי' טעם תפלה ואין רשומו ניכר ג"כ למעלה כי אינו יודע בין ימינו לשמאלו מה טיבה של הכוונה ובוודאי לא לזה כוונו אנשי כה"ג (כנסת הגדולה) כאשר הוא במיעוט הכרתו והשגתו, מדמה בנפשו וכונותיו שמכוין בהם כונת האר"י זלה"ה ולמה זה ביד כסיל ולב אין ואני ערב בדבר אם היה לו אפי' מעט מן המעט יראת שמים, אזי בודאי ירא בנפשו לחפש ולהסתכל בכוונות העומדי' ברומו של עול' והוא עומד עם ראשו ורובו למטה ואינו יודע אפי' תיבה אחת מכוונת האר"י זלה"ה... נדבר עוד מזה להוכיח אל פניהם' המדמי' בנפש' שגם להם יד ושם בין הגדולי' להתפלל מסדור האר"י זלה"ה לכוון כוונות וטוב להם אם יתפלל בפרוש המלות.

7. כמו שאמר המגיד להב"י באזהרה ב' ...להזהר מלחשוב בשעת תפלה בשום מחשבה, אפילו של תורה ומצוה כי אם בתיבות התפילה עצמם. דוק בדבריו, שלא אמר לכוון בכוונת התיבות כי באמת בעומק פנימיות כוונת התפילה אין אתנו יודע עד מה, כי גם מה שנתגלה לנו קצת כוונות התפלה מרבותינו הראשונים ז"ל קדישי עליונין ועד אחרון...האר"י ז"ל, אשר הפליא הגדיל לעשות כוונות נפלאים, אינם בערך אף כטפה מן הים כלל נגד פנימיות עומק כוונת אנשי כנה"ג מתקני התפלה.

8. כי עיקר ענין התפלה הוא להעלות ולמסור ולדבק נפשו למעלה.

9. להעלות ולדבק בתפלתו את נפשו למעלה.

10. המכוין בתפילתו בכל הכוונות הידועות לו, אינו מכוין רק אותן הכוונות הידועות לו. אבל כשאומר התיבה בהתקשרות גדול ונכלל בכל תיבה כל הכוונות מעצמן ומאליהן, שכל אות ואות הוא עולם שלם. וכשאומר התיבה בהתקשרות גדול בודאי מתעורר אותן העולמות העליונים ועושה פעולות גדולות בזה. לכן יראה האדם להתפלל בהתקשרות ובהתלהבות גדולה, בוודאי יעשה פעולות גדולות בעולמות העליונים כי כל אות ואות מעורר למעלה.

ר"ל משפיע ומקבל. ד"מ בחי' דכר הוא מה שדרכו להשפיע תמיד ע"י קדושתו וגודל הדביקות וטהרת המחשבה הוא משפיע תענוג רוחני באורות ועולמות ומדות עליונים. וגם יש אצלו בחי' נוק'. היינו שמקבל וממשיך שפע העולמות העליונים לתחתונים ולכל הכנ"י כל מיני הצטרכותם. וכל מיני חסדים טובים כמו בני חיי ומזוני ורפואה וכדומה. כי אותו בחי' דכר מה שגורם שפע למעלה. אותו השפע נתהפך לזר"ע ונעשה בחי' דכר לנוק' ... והצד של נוק' של הצדיק יהיה היכולת בידו לקבל שפע עליונה ולהמשיך ממעלה למטה כל מיני טובות אפילו בדברים גשמיים.

28. כי מלת זאת נקרא על בחי' נוקבא כידוע והנה כפי שאמרנו לעיל שעיקר העבדות יהי' רק על סיבת התענוג המגיע להבורא ב"ה ואז נקרא כביכול הבורא ב"ה בחי' מקבל וזהו מאת ה' היתה זאת דהיינו שהקב"ה כביכו"ל יהיה בבחינת נוקבא בחי' זאת הוא נפלאת בעינינו.

29. שיש ב' מיני עבודה מלמט הלמעלה בעבודת האדם בחי' רצוא ובחי' שוב. בחי' רצוא נק' חותם הבולט ובחי' שוב נק' חותם השוקע. ופי' בחי' רצוא היא אהבה ורשפי אש שבתשוקה והוא התגלות האהבה המסותרת ממטה למעלה הישראל לא"ס ב"ה ... כך על ידי בחי' אתעדל"ת שבבחי' רצוא שהוא בבחי' חותם בולט והוא בחי' יש מי שאוהב כו' עי"ז נמשך אתעדל"ע מלמעלה בחי' חותם שוקע והיינו שנמשך מזה התגלות והמשכת אורות בכלים ... העבודה הב' שמלמטה למעלה בבחי' שוב היינו ביטול הרצון בתכלית ונפשי כעפר יהא' בושת זהו בחי' חותם השוקע שמלמטה ועי"ז נמשך אתעדל"ע מלמעלה בחי' חותם בולט דהיינו התגלות אור א"ס שלא בהתלבשות כלל ... אכן ע"י בחי' אהבה וקיום מ"ע לא יוכלו להמשיך מלמעלה מהשתלשלות כי אהבה הוא ג"כ בבחי' יש וכלי לכן ממשיכים מלמעלה ג"כ התגלות אורות בכלים.

30. כשישראל עושין רצונו של מקום מוסיפין תענוג למעלה ... שישראל עושין תשובה ומחזירים הכל לשרשו ומוסיפין תענוג למעלה.

31. אמנם האין כלל לכל החכמות שהוא כח המוכן לקבל צורת וכשאדם רוצה להמשיך אליו חכמה יכול להמשיך משם חכמה וכן כל דבר ודבר שאדם רוצה רק שתלוי ברצון האדם אם עובד הבורא יכול להמשיך עליו.

32. ומשנה טבעו שהוא ביטול היש ומשנה מבחינת יש לאין ועי"ז ממשיך מבחי' מאין תמצא.

33. תכלית האדם בבואו לעולם השפל הזה הוא לסגל תורה ומצוה והוא סולם מוצב ארצה וראשו מגיע השמימה להמשיך ע"י עשייתו תורה ומצות שפע בכל העולמות ונותן כביכול כח בפמליא של מעלה.

CHAPTER 4

1. ובסמ"ח לא שמתי עיני בו כלל, מאחר שלפ"ד קבצו מכאר"י, אף את זאת אני אומר ומצוה לבני וי"ח (יוצאי חלצי) ותלמידי ואוהבי ורעי ושומעי הסרים למשמעתי הריני גוזר ואוסר עליכם להתפלל ע"פ מ"ח, גם לא מתוך סכ"י (ספר כתבי יד) שקוראים תפילה ע"פ כאר"י שסדרה ר"מ פאפרט ולא חלו בה ידי האר"י ולא רח"ו תלמידו פעל כל זאת אף ספר כונות האר"י לא נעשה לכוין דוקא כך בפועל רק על דבר הלמוד, ואם כאר"י תלמידיו יכלו לכוין בתפילתם על הדרך שלמד הוא ז"ל, מ"מ עכשיו קצרה דעת ב"א (בני אדם), ובלי ספק תתבלבל דעת במכוין בהם ויותר ממה שיחשוב להרויח יפסיד בודאי, על כן אני מזהיר ומתרה בב"א השומעים לקולי, שלא יבקשו לילך בגדולות ונפלאות מהם, הלואי יוכלו עמוד בכוונות כולליות שסדרתי בבית תפילתי קב ונקי ולא שאני נותן דופי בכאר"י, חלילה לי מה', אלא שאין הדור כדאי

19. אין אדם יכול להמשיך שפע כ"א ממקום שרש נשמתו לכן בזה הזמן לא שכיחי נשמות דאצילות ואין יכול להמשיך מאצילות לכן תקנתו שיקשור וידבק לנשמתו עם נשמת הצדיקים הידועים לו כפי מדרגת נשמתם מאצילות וזה כלל גדול בתורה ובמעש"ט ופדיון וכל המצות.

20. ועל ידי עשיות מצות ומע"ט מדבק א"ע ביש כי המצות הם יש וע"י עשיות המצות משפיע על עצמו שפע מהש"י.

21. הרוצה לחיות לא יחשוב עניני גופו כ"א תהיה מחשבתו בהבורא ב"ה דבוקה. וזה ימית עצמו יסתלק מעצמו ממילא הוא חי. כי הוא דבוק בחי החיים ... מי שהוא עני עי"ד שהוא דבוק בהבורא ב"ה. הוא ודאי חשוב. כי עבד מלך מלך. הוא כמת ונפטר ממיתה וחי בהם.

22. ולא שייך אז אפילו לקיים התורה. מרוב החשיקה ודביקות בבוראו יתברך. כדרך האב ובנו יחידו החביב עליו למאוד. כשלא היו בהתראות פנים יחד שנים רבות. ואחר כך תיכף בעת ראיית פנים זה לזה נעשה החיבוק והנשיקה בעזה כמות אהבה בכלות נפשם זה לזה. וכל שאר החושים נתבטלו אז מהם כבעת מיתה. ואהבה זו ראוי להיות לעם בני ישראל בחשיקה וחפיצה הזאת בהבורא ב"ה וב"ש. מאחר שהוא חלק מחלקיו. ואך כשיהיה תמיד בבחינה זו אין תורה. כי לא יוכל לקיים אז שום מצוה או לימוד התורה כי יצא מגדר אדם. ועל כן הטביע הוא יתברך להיות האדם נפסק ונופל מרוב אהבה זו. ואז יוכל לקיים את התורה ... ונפל מבחינת החכמה ...שהוא ביטול המציאות.

23. ממש אין ... ומעוררין שכל העולמות חוזרין לבחינות אין, ונעשה היחוד, כי כל בחינות יחוד וזיוג, הוא עליה עד בחינת אין סוף, והיו בטלין כל העולמות, והיו חוזרין לאין לגמרי, לבחינת אין סוף, אלא ששם בביטול זה, נכללין גם כן ישראל עם הקודש, והם בהכרח יש להם גוף וכלי וישות ואני הנצרך לעבודה, ולכן מושכין כל העולמות שלא יתבטלו לגמרי.

24. ישביע נפשו בשבועת האלה, או בשם הגדול והנורא, שבהיותו בעת המראה והמחזה שאז הוא איננו ברשותו, שלא תפרד נפשו ותלך לידבק במקורה, אלא שתחזור אל נדנה ואל גופה כבתחלה.

25. להיות ממש בטל במציאות בגודל הדביקות בהשי"ת ב"ה ... וכמו שבעיני ראיתי ממורי ורבותי ... ובפרט מאדמ"ו הרב הקדוש איש אלהים נורא מוהרר משולם זושע זצ"ל אשר כמה פעמים בהעלותו להתדבק בהבורא ב"ה וב"ש הי' מפשיט עצמו לגמרי מן העוה"ז עד היותו ממש קרוב להתבטל במציאות עד שהוכרח לנדר נדרים ונדבות שיתקיים נפשו בו.

26. כי העולמות לגבי קב"ה כנוקבא לגבי דכורא לקבל חיותם מן הקב"ה והקב"ה הוא בחינת דכר לכל העולמות שמשפיע להם חיות וחסד הנקרא דכר לכן כשאדם מתאוה לדבק בקב"ה בזה הוא מעלה בחי' מ"נ ונתעורר מלעילא בחינת מ"ד ונולד שפע וחיות לו ולכל העולמות לאפוקי כשמתאווה לתענוגי חמדת עוה"ז שהם עצמם בחינת נוקבא כי כולם צריכים לקבל חיות מאתו ית"ש וידוע [סוטה ג.] אין אדם עובר עבירה אא"כ וכו' ומסתלק ממנו הנשמה חלילה וחס אבל כשהנשמה אצל האדם אזי מתאוה לשורשה לקב"ה, וזהו שמרמז אשה כי תזריע היינו נשמה שהיא בחינת אשה ונוקבא לגבי קב"ה, כי תזריע היינו כשמתאווה לקב"ה ובזה היא מזרעת בחינת מ"נ בהתעוררות מלתתא לעילא אזי וילדה זכר כנ"ל שמתעורר חסד וחיים ושפע מלעילא לתתא בחינת מ"ד.

27. כי בכל דבר שבעולם צריך שימצא בו בחי' דכר ובחי' נוק'. ובפרט בעובד ה' צריך שימצא בו בחי' דכר ובחי' נוק' ...

10. כי יש אדם שעובד את הבורא ב"ה בשכלו שכל אנושי ויש אדם שהוא מסתכל על האי"ן כביכול וזהו א"א בשכל אנושי רק בעזר ה' ית' ... ובאמת זה האדם כשהוא במדריג' זו שיש לו עזר ה' להסתכל על האי"ן אז השכל שלו הוא בטל במציאות והוא כחרש שהשכל אנושי שלו הוא בטל במציאות ... ובאמת אח"כ כשאדם חוזר אל עצמות השכל אז הוא מלא שפע.

11. כשיגביה א"ע להקב"ה יכול להמשיך לעצמו החכמה. והנה כשהחכמה נמשך מהקב"ה אל האדם הוא נמשך השפעה דרך השמים והארץ שהוא דרך הצמצום. אבל כשהצדיק מקשר א"ע עם החכמה ומשפיע הרי השפע בא מיד אל האדם ואין ניכר הצמצום.

12. שזה העובד את הבורא במסירת נפש לא על ידי מצות ומע"ט הוא באין ממש וזה העובד את ה' במצות הוא עובד ע"י דבר היש כי המצות הם יש ולכן זה שעובד במסירות נפש דהוא באין אינו יכול להמשיך על עצמו שפע כי הוא אינו כלום רק שמדבק א"ע להשי"ת.

13. כשהצדיק מדבק עצמו בהאי"ן והוא בטל במציאות אז יעבוד את הבורא בבחי' כל הצדיקים כיון ששם אינו נראה כלל ח"ו שום חלוקות המדות ... כי יש צדיק אשר הוא מדבק עצמו בהאי"ן ואעפ"כ חוזר לעצמותו אח"כ אבל מרע"ה הסתכל תמיד בגדלות הבורא יתברך ולא חזר לעצמותו כלל כידוע כי משרע"ה היה תמיד דבוק באי"ן ובבחינה הזאת היה בטל במציאות ... כי כאשר מסתכל בהבורא ב"ה אז אין בו שום עצמותו מחמת שהיא בטל במציאות ... יסתכל באי"ן ויהיה בטל במציאות ... ומשה היה תמיד דבוק באי"ן.

14. יש שני מיני צדיקים יש צדיק שמקבל בהירות מהאותיות של תורה ותפלה ויש צדיק יותר גדול שמביא בהירות מלמעלה אל האותיות אעפ"י שהאותיות הם בעולם העליון אעפ"כ כשהצדיק הגדול מביא בהירות חדשה לעולם וזאת הבהירות אי אפשר לבוא להעולם רק על ידי התלבשות אותיות ... ובאמת כשבא הבהירות למטה פורחים האותיות למעלה והבהירות נשאר למטה ומדריגה של צדיק זה הוא מחמת שאומר הדיבורים בכל כוחו במסירת נפש ובכל רמ"ח אברים בא אל כל תיבה שמדבר בזה מביא בהירות.

15. כי בזה שכוונתו לעשות בהם נחת רוח לבורא והוא אינו כלום מדבק א"ע באין ועל ידי עשיות המצות ומע"ט מדבק א"ע ביש כי המצות הם יש וע"י עשות המצות משפיע על עצמו שפע מהש"י ולכן יש לפעמים אדם שמפרנס את עצמו ע"י מעשיו.

16. כי ידוע שצריך להצדיק להיות דבוק תמיד באין וזו ביטל במציאות מחמת גודל היראה ופחד מהבוב"ה ותיבת (והעי) הוא מל' עיי השדה וכשהצדיק הוא דבוק באין משם הוא מביא השפעות רצון וברכה לעולם כולו ... ר"ל שמקודם צריך להיות דבוק באין ... שהצדיק צריך להיות דבוק באין ולהיות בטל במציאות ואח"כ מביא כל הברכות לעולם.

17. יש ב' בחי' בעבודת ה'. הא' האהבה ברשפי אש בתגבורת מאד לצאת מן הגוף ... והוא בחינת אה"ר שאין כלי הלב מכילה אותה כי לא יכיל הלב ההתפעלות העצומה. לכן לא יוכל לעמוד בכלי גופו וחפץ לצאת מנרתקה חומר הגוף. והב' בחי' ההתפעלות המתיישב בכלי הלב ועיקר ענינה הוא בח' המשכח אלקות מלמעלמ"ט דוקא בכלים מכלים שונים בתומ"צ. וזהו ענין רצוא ושוב.

18. עבודת איש הישראל לבטל עצמו בכלות הנפש למקורא ושורשא ... ואח"כ להמשיך גילוי אלוקותו יתברך ... שזהו כלל העבודה להיות בבחינת גילוי.

בהתעוררותו ממדרגה למדרגה ומסבה לסבה עד שתגיע ותרצה ותראה לפני קונה, ותדבק במקורה במקור החיים, ואז ישפיע עליה משם שפע רב, ויהי הוא כלי ומקום ומכון להשפעה, וממנו יתחלק לכל העולם כנז' בזוהר פ' תרומה, עד שתדבק בו השכינה ... ואתם תהיו כסא לה ועליך יורק השפע כנז', כי אתה הוא במקום הצנור הגדול במקום צדיק יסוד עולם.

36. והנה כאשר האדם השלם יתרחק מתאות הגופניות ויתבודד בעצמו ויתיחד וידבק בו בהאל יתברך אז ישפיעו עליו שפע קדושה ויגלו אליו כל עניניו אשר הוא מבקש לדעת.

CHAPTER 3

1. ועולה מעולם לעולם ומייחדם ויכול לראות ממש בחוש עין השכל כל האורות העליונים ופשיטא שהעובד כזה מגיע לו גם כן תענוג גדול בכל רגע ורגע בלי הפסק כי שורש נשמתו דבוק למעלה.

2. וכביכול נכנס בקרבו ית' ממש וכשמתדבק הצדיק שנק' אחד בהבוב"ה שנקרא אחד אזי ב"פ אח"ד גי' כ"ו כמנין שם הוי' ב"ה ונעשה שלמות הוי"ה ... נכנס בתוך הויה ומדבק בו ית' ובזה יוכל להמשיך מאתו ית' השפעות טובות.

3. וכמ"ש בשם הבעש"ט ז"ל שלא יצטרך להתיישב א"ע באלוהות אלא יחשוב כאלו כולו גנוז באור אלוהות וז"ש והוא יושב פתח האוהל פי' הצדיק עושה יחוד עם א"ס שהוא פתח האוהל של כל העולמות.

4. צריך להוריד עצמו למדריגות התחתוניות ולהעלות בכח אתערותא דלתתא. ובחי' זה שהצדיק מוריד א"ע למדריגות תחתוניות נקרא עבודת האדמה רק שבחי' זו איננו יכול להיות אם לא מי שהוא אדם והוא בבחי' אתערותא דלעילא ... והוא בחי' אי"ן למעלה מהשגה ואז מביא כל ההשפעות טובות והברכה על זה העולם.

5. להיותו מחשיב עצמו לאין נגד המאציל, והוא משפיל ראשו להשגיח ולהשפיע בתחתונים, שכולם פונים לינק ממנו, וכן ראוי שהאדם יחשוב עצמו לאין נגד גדולתו יתברך, שאין לה סוף ותכלית.

6. וי"ל עד"ש בשם הבעש"ט ז"ל כי אדם צריך לחשוב עצמו שהוא אין כי הא"ס הוא א"ס ואין כלי יכול לסובלו משא"כ כשהוא אין ואם יקשה אדם ויאמר איך יכול אני לומר שאני אין ובאמת נראה לי שאני יש ולא אין ובאמת זה איננו כי הרי הכל הוא ממנו ית' נאצל ונברא ונוצר ונעשה כי אם יפסק מהם הרוחניות הרי הם כלא היו אך הקב"ה ברא הכל כדי להראות חסדו לברואיו ומדת החכמה.

7. מי שהוא אין הוא מזל ממשיך לישראל והוא מעורר עולם האחדות עליון הנקרא אין מפני העלמה ושם תלוים בני חיי ומזוני.

8. שמעתי אומרים בשם הרב מנעשכוז ... הצדיקים עושים לעצמם למדת שיהי' תמיד דבקים ומקושרים למעלה בעולמות העליונים ... שדהע"ה הי' תמיד דבוק ומקושר בעולמות העליונים הי' נעשה בריכה וצינור להמשיך שפע ממקור עליון לעולמים התחתונים.

9. ואז הוא תמיד דבוק וקשור בחי העולמות וצריך לחזק א"ע ולדבוק נפשו בצעלה ורצון הקודם אבל מכל מקום אף שהוא למטה בעולם המציאות צריך למהשיך לעצמו חיות ממקור החיים ושורש השרשים לתוך העולמות ... ונתדבק בעולם עליון בשורש התשובה שהוא למעלה מחיות העולמות ... אח"כ מדביקות עליון לתוך מציאת העולמות הורדת השפע למטה.

אלוהים.

27. לקבל מעט הבהירות להשיג אלקתו ית"ש ועשר ספירות דאצילות התלבשו א"ע בעשר ספירות דבריאה ועשר דבריא' בעשר דיצירה ועשר דיצירה בעשר דעשי' וע"י הצמצומים אלו יכולים בני אדם לקבל מעט השגה באלקותו מעט מעט מלמטה למעלה ולהסיר הצמצומים והמסכים בהדרגה מעט מעט עד שנהיה יכולים לקבל הבהירות גדול לדבק עצמינו בא"ס ב"ה בהדרגה וזהו הוא עיקר השכר שאנו מקבלים מאת הבורא עבור שבהא אותנו בעולם הגשמי בכמה וכמה אלפים צמצומים ומסכים שמכסים אלקותו ית"ש ואנחנו בכל כוחינו משברים המסכים והצמצומים כדי להשיג אלקותו ית"ש ולדבק בו.

28. הקב"ה צמצם כביכול א"ע בהתורה. וכשקורין לאדם בשמו מניח כל עסקיו ומשיב לזה שקורא אותו מחמת שהוא אסור בשמו כך כביכול הקב"ה צמצם את עצמו בתורה. והתורה היא שמו וכשקורין בתורה אז ממשיכים את השי"ת אלינו כי הוא ושמו אחדות גמור עמנו.

29. שצמצם עצמו בתוך האותיות התור' שבהם ברא העולם ... והצדיק העוסק בתור' לשמה בקדוש' הוא ממשיך את הבורא ב"ה ויתעל' בתוך האותיות של התור' כמו בשעת הבריא' ... שע"י אמרות הטהורו' שעסקו בתור' המשיך את הבורא אל תוך האותיות.

30. והנה כמו שיש כ"ב אותיות בדבור תורה ותפלה כך יש בכל עניני החומר והגשמי שבעולם ג"כ כ"ב אותיות שבהם נברא העולם ... רק שהאותיות מלובש בחומר עניני העולם בכמה כסויים ולבושי' וקליפי'. ובתוך האותיות שורה רוחניות הקב"ה הרי שכבודו ית' מלא כל הארץ וכל אשר בה לית אתר פנוי מני'.

31. כי האדם הוא כלול מכל הדברים הרוחניים ונשמתו השכלית היא העליונה על הכל ולכן באה התורה והמצוה להרחיק האדם ולהזהירו כי כל דרכי האדם מסורי' בידו ... וכמו שהצדיק השלם הוא קושר כתרים לקונו ע"י הדבקות שהוא מדביק נשמתו במקום מוצאו ומאציל הברכה כמדליק מנר לנר ומעמיד ומיישב ומוסיף כך הרשע עושה תמורתו.

32. וידוע כי הכחות הפנימיות והרוחות הנעלמות האנושיות הם תוך הגופים נחלקים ובעצם אמיתת כל כח וכח וכל רוח ורוח כשיותרו מקשריהם ירוצו אל מקורם הראשון שהוא אחד בלתי שום שנייות וכולל ריבויי עד א"ס וההתרה מגעת עד למעלה עד שמי שמזכיר שם אתאגא השם מתעלה ויושב בראש הכתר העליון והמחשבה שואבת משם ברכה משולשת ... נמצאת אומ' שמהזכרת השם שואב המזכיר הברכה מלמעלה ומורידה למטה.

33. וחיי צער תחיה בבית התבודדותך פן תגבר נפשך המתאוה על נפשך המשכלת שבזה תזכה להמשיך בנפשך המשכלת את שפע האלוהות ובתורה ר"ל בחכמת הצירוף ובכל תנאיו.

34. כל העולמות מתקשרים כאחד על ידי נפשו ורוחו ונשמתו, וגורם הארת המאציל מלך מלכי המלכים בכל העולמות, ואז הוא סוד נשיקין בכל העולמות, שיתקשרו ויוכללו אלו באלו, וכן נפשו ורוחו ונשמתו יאירו ויוכללו למעלה ויינקו רוב שפע ממקור כל הברכות.

35. האיש אשר חננו קונו ליכנס בפנימות החכמה הנסתרת וידע וישכיל כי באומרו ברך עלינו וכן רפאנו הכוונה בהם להמשיך ברכה ושפע בכל ברכה לספירה פלונית וברכת רפאנו לספירה פלונית כנודע אצלינו, הנה איש כזה עובד קב"ה ושכינתיה כבן וכעבד המשמש את רבו עבודה שלימה מאהבה בלי לקנות ממנו שום תועלת ולא פרס בעבודה ההיא ... כי החכם בטוב כוונתו כאשר יכוון בתפלתו, תתעלה נשמתו

ולא חויבנו להמשיכו אלא בה ... כאשר תהי' אותה ברכה על מצוה או פעולה ... אותה הפעולה הוא כלי ודלי שבו ישאבו מימי השפע.

17. וידוע בחכמת הכוכבים שכאשר יעשה אדם תמונה ידוע (!) מגשם ידוע שהוא מצב הכוכב הידוע וכמאמרם ז"ל אין לך עשב בארץ כו', ויעמידנו בכח הכוכב הנז' בהיותו במקום מעלתו ובית כבודו, אזי יושפע כח הכוכב ההוא על התמונה ההיא ותדבר ותעשה פעולות ידועות והם התרפים הנז' בס' הנביאים וכן בהכין האדם עצמו לזה עד"מ [על דרך משל] לקבל כח ורוחניות כוכב שבתי, צריך שילבש שחורים ויתע[טף] שחורים ויכסה המקום שעמד עליו בבגדים שחורים ויאכל דברים מגבירי השחורה המיוחסת לשבתי ... אזי ישפע על האדם ההוא כח ורוחניות הכוכב הנז' והוא ענין נבואת הבעל ונביאי האשרה והדומים להם ... וכן לדעת המקובלים כל התורה והמצות הם הכנות נאותות לקבל השפעות נצרכות בתכלית השלימות מבלי שיתערב עמהם איזה חסרון וע"ז סובבו כל המצוות התלויות בזמן ובמקום ובפעולות ידועות והם כלם מכוונות לעצמן בדקדוק גדול, אשר אם יחסר איזה ענין מהם א"א [אי אפשר] שתושלם הפעולה המבוקשת ... וכן בנין הבית, החצר וההיכל והדביר וכליו השולחן והמנורה והמזבחות והכיור וכנו ובגדי הכהונה למיניהם והקורבנות למחלקותיהם.

18. כי יש בשמות הצדיקי' הכנה גדול להשרות עליהם השפע האלהי כמו שכתוב בבצלאל ראה קראתי בשם ואח"כ ואמלא אותו רוח אלהים.

19. והציב לו תחתיהן אותיות אחרים שיומשך לו מהם חיות וקיום, והוא מדרגה גבוה מאוד שזכה אליה הבעש"ט.

20. וידיעה זו הכרחית הן לב"ש הן לדאקטר.

21. ... ולהתדבק באותיות הקדושים יוכל להבין מתוך האותיות ממש, אפילו עתידות ... שמאירה עיני המתדבק בהם בקדושה וטהרה כמו של אורים ותומים. ומילדותי מיום שהכרתי בדבקות האהבה עם מורי ידידי הרב מהור"ר ישראל תנצב"ה הנ"ל ידעתי נאמנה שזה היו הנהגותיו בקדושה ובטהרה בסוד חסידות ופרישות שאותיות תורתינו הקדושה הם כלם קדושים וכשאדם זוכה להתדבק עם אותיות בלומדו לשם שמים שיוכל להבין עתידות.

22. ולדבקה בו דבוק נפלא נקרא אחדות. ראוי להעלותו על לב בכל חלק וחלק מן השעה.

23. זהו טובתינו שנזכה אל היחוד ולהאיר באור התורה להכלל אור באור עד למעלה בבי' וחכ' שאין לידבק אלא ע"כ כי מכאן ולמעלה הוא ברצוא ושוב כדפי' וכל שאר הטובות אינם טובות כלל אלא השגה ידועה ודבקות ההוא היא הטובה העיקרית וכל שאר הטובות אינם אלא הכנה לטובה הזאת.

24. וכן הענין כי להיות הגוף דומה אל הרוחני לכן הוכרח כי אפילו שיה' הדבר רוחני יתדבק בגשמי לרוב תשוקתו אליו. והטעם מפני שהתחתוני' הם משכן לעליוני' וכמו שחשק המסובב לעלו' אל סבתו כן חשק הסבה שיהי' מסובבו קרוב אליו.

25. כל מקום שהצדיקים שם הקב"ה נמצא שם. והעד ע"ז בהיות ישי' במדבר היה המקדש עמהם ... א"כ הצדיקים הם המקדישים המקום מפני שהוא מתדבק בצדיקיו מצד התבודדותם בו ... כל מקום שהצדיקים שם כגון במשכן ... הוא נמצא שם.

26. אל האור הרוחניות והחיות הקודש השופע בכל ברכה מאור אלוהינו ית"ש להתדבק בו ולהמשיכו אליהם להתענג בדביקות אור

וזה שאמר לו שמואל הנביא לשאול ופגעת חבל נביאים ולפניהם נבל ותוף וחליל וכנור והמה מתנבאים פי' אותן בני הנביאים שלמדו א"ע תחלה לדבר ברוה"ק.

9. וכמ"ש בשם הבעש"ט ז"ל שלא יצטרך להתיישב א"ע באלוהות אלא יחשוב כאילו כולו גנוז באור אלוהות וז"ש והוא יושב פתח האוהל פי' הצדיק עושה יחוד עם א"ס שהוא פתח האוהל של כל העולמות.

10. והיא [שרה] היתה כן כוונתה בכל קשוטה והתייפותה רק לשמים כמקשט דיוקנא דמלכא פי' כיון שתפיסא לחיות עליון שהוא ניצוץ השכינה באדם א"כ אם מקשט אדם א"ע לרמוז לקישוט השכינה ויופי שלו הוא מזיו השכינה וכן יש לו לחשוב כשרואה אדם יפה ומקושט והרי האדם הוא בצלם אלהים א"כ יחשוב כאלו רואה יופי וקישוט דיוקנא דמלכא וכן היה כל כוונתה של שרה בקישוטה ויפיה וז"ש צאנה וראנה בנות ציון פי' צאנה מגשמיות וראנה ברוחניות הדבר כי הגשמיות של היופי הוא רק ציון וסימן ליופי של מעלה ששורה כאן ניצוץ של יופי מעולם התפארת וראוי לכוין שהיופי הזה הוא בטל כשרגא בטהירו ביופי ותפארת העליון.

11. ודע שהדבקות אור העליון לא יושג אלא מצד החשק והאהבה שהיא מעלה נפשיית ובזה תגבר נפש על החומר וידבק האדם בקונו וכל העולם תחת רגליו והוא מרומם על כל ופועל בעולם כרצונו מפני שהוא מקור שפע העליון מסיבתו אל סיבת העולם דהיינו היותר גובר על המלאכים הממונים על ענייני עולם וכולם כבישים תחת ידו לעשות רצונו כענין מי שאמר לשמן וידליק יאמר לחומץ וידליק והיינו שיחליף המלאכים ונתן כח השמן בחומץ וזה דבר קרוב מאד וטעם נכון אל הנסים.

12. ואין ספק שיש לגוונים מבוא אל פעולות הספירות והמשכת שפעם. ולסבה זו כאשר יצטרך הממשיך להמשיך שפע רחמים מהחסד יצייר נגדו שם הספירה בגוון הענין הנצרך אליו כפי גוון המדה אם חסד גמור ללובן גמור. ואם לא כ"כ יצייר לובן כסיד ההיכל וכיוצא בזה כמו שנבאר בשער הכוונה. וכן כאשר ירצה לפעול פעולה ויצטרך אל המשכת הדין אז יתלבש האדם ההוא בבגדים אדומים ויצייר צורת ההוויי' באודם, וכן לכל הפעולות וההמשכות ... ועד"ז ודאי לענין הקמיעין כאשר יעשה אדם קמיע' לחסד יצייר השם ההוא בלובן מזהיר כי אז תגדל פעולת השם ההוא.

13. וכאשר יצטרך חסד ורחמים יתעטף לבנים. ולנו בזה ראיות ברורות מהכהנים שהמשכתם מצד החסד ובגדיהם בגדי לבן להורות על השלום. וזה ענין כ"ג ביה"כ שהי' מעביר זהבים ולובש לבנים מפני שעבודת היום בבגדי לבן.

14. נמצא שפי' קצת מהקדמונים כי בצרוף וגלגול שם בן ע"ב או שאר השמות אחר התבודדות גדול יתגלה לצדיק הזכאי המשכיל בעניינם קצת מחלק הבת קול ר"ל רוח ה' ידבר בו ומלתו על לשונו מטעם שהוא מחבר הכחות ומיחדם ומחשקם איש אל אחיו כמער איש ולויות עד שיושפע עליו רוב השפע ובתנאי שיהי' העוסק בכך כלי המוכן לקבל הרוחניות וראוי לכך שאם לא כן יהפך לאכזר ונהפכו לו סורי הגפן נכרית.

15. הכל תלוי ברוחניות השפע הנשפע ע"י הצדיק ומעשיו הכשרים ... והיה העולם מתברך בזכותם מהרוחניות הנשפע בעולם בזכותם ... שכל העולמות והעניינים משועבדים לצדיק ... והכל תלוי בסוד התורה הנמסרת אליו.

16. והכוונה שהיא המשכת רוחניות ושפע מלמעלה מרום המדרגות עד המלכות שהיא הבריכה שבא קבוץ השפע ... משם נמשך אל התחתונים

תצדק בזה ידיעה והשגה אבל שמיעה או ראיה או הגדה וספור וכבר אפשר ללמוד ספורי הדברים עם תינוק דלא חכים ולא טפש שהוא בן חמש שנים.

19. והכת הב' היא כת המקובלים... החזיקו בחכמת הקבלה וחשבו בדעתם שכבר הגיעו בזה אל תכלית כוונתם והם מסתפקים בידיעת הדברים מבלי ציור הענינים כלל ויחשבו שידעו כל סודות המציאות וסדר בריאת העולם וסדר ההנהגה, וכל זה בדמיונות זרים קצת יביאו לשחוק וקצתם בהפך שראוי לבכות.

CHAPTER 2

1. שמעתי כמה פעמים מאאמו"ר זצ"ל שאמר שכך וכך יהי' בעולם בשנה זו ומאין הי' יודע. ובוודאי שכך לחשו לו משמים. וע"י שנמשכה לו ההאזנה מאוזן העליון ממש אל אזנו הגשמיית כנ"ל.

2. תדע בני ששמעתי צדיקים בעלי מופת בעלי רוה"ק בעלי גילוי אורות ועולמו' עליונים שצפו במרכבה כמו ר"ע וחבריו תלמידי אדונינו אלימלך הקדוש אור מופלא אדמו"ר ותלמידי רבינו יחיאל תלמידי מרן הריב"ש

3. כיון שהוא דבוק הרבה היטב בקדושה יכול להעלות דברי חול לקדושה ג"כ ע"י חכמת צירופי אותיות הנודעת להקדוש האלהי הבעש"ט זלה"ה ולתלמידיו בעלי רוה"ק ששתו מימיו מהם בעלמא דקשוט זי"ע ומהם בעוה"ז בחיים חיותם יהא רעוא מהשי"ת שיאריכו ימיהם ושנותיהם ויתקיימו בהם חכמי ישראל הם ובניהם כו'. ואין תימה בזה כי מוכרחים אנחנו להודות בזה שיש חכמה כזו כי הלא מצינו בגמרא כמה דברים באגדות שנראו דברים בטלים רק שהתנאים היו בעלי רוה"ק והיה להם חכמה זו בשלימות גדול ענין צירופי אותיות ודברו הכל ברוח קדשם והם סודות התורה והכל זכו מחמת דביקותם בקדושה עליונה מאד.

4. אבל בכדי להיות אחדות גמור עמו ית' צריך לצאת מן המדות כלל הנק' מלבושים כמאמר מדו בד קדש ילבש. ולבא למעלה מן המדות ע"י האותיות צרופי המדות עצמם.

5. אך ההתגלות הטוב בא על ידי תפילות וצרופי אותיות.

6. כי אותיות שם יהוה ית' הם אותיות כלם מושכלות ולא מורגשות והם המורות ענין הקיום וההווה וכל ההויה שבעולם וזהו סוד ואת הדבקים ביי' אלהיכם חיים כלכם היום כלומר אתם הדבקים באותיות ההויה הרי אתם קיימים לנצח נצחים.

7. ענין הנבואה דמה א"א ע"פ הרוב שיתנבא פתאם בלי הכנה וקדושה אך ע"י שמקדש עצמו האדם הרוצה להכין עצמו לנבואה בקדושה ובטהרה ובהתבודדות ובפרישות גדול מתענוגי עה"ז ומשמש בשמוש חכמים את רבו הנביא והתלמידים ההולכים בדרכי הנבואה נקראים בני הנביאים וכשמבין רבו הנביא שכבר תלמיד זה ראוי הוא לנבואה אזי מוסר לו רבו ענין הזכרת שמות הקדש שהם המפתחות לשערים עליונים.

8. כי אנשי קודש הראשונים היו מלמדין לעצמן לדבר ברוה"ק וזהו ענין בני הנביאים פי' שהנביאים היו מלמדין לתלמידיהם להיות כל דיבור שלהם בתורה ותפילה וזמירות שירות ותשבחות לדבר בדביקות ה' וכאלו מדברים ברוה"ק במחשבה באובנתא בטמירו בעין השכל ע"כ נקרא רוה"ק ל[שון] מחשבה עד שבאו למדריגה שהיו באמת נביאים ומתנבאים בניב שפתים ממש ברוה"ק כד"א כ"ד משמורות כולם מתנבאים ברוה"ק.

9. הזהר ניתן לנשמות שנכנסו בעולם הזה ויצאו ממנו...אבל מי שנכנס ולא יצא מגופניות בוודאי אין מבין כלל וכלל אפילו נקודה קטנה מן הזהר והכתבים ונדמים יודעים ולא יודעים.

10. שכל הזהר וכתבי האריז"ל הם לאנשים כמוהם די מדרהון עם בשרא לא איתוהי, אבל אנשים כמונו הרואים בזוהר וכתבי האריז"ל מתדמין לנו ענין אחר כלל שאין זה כלל כוונת לשון הזהר והאריז"ל.

11. ענין הנסתרות שבכל הזוהר וכתבי האריז"ל הכל בנווים על פי דבקות הבורא, למי שזוכה להתדבק ולהיות צופה במרכבה עליונה כמו האר"י זלה"ה.

12. וידוע לנו בברור גמור שהגאון החסיד נ"י אינו מאמין בקבלת האר"י ז"ל בכללה שהיא כולה מפי אליהו ז"ל רק מעט מזעיר מפי אליהו ז"ל והשאר מחוכמתו הגדולה ואין חיוב להאמין בה וכו' וגם הכתבים נשתבשו מאוד.

13. וכל דבריו דברי אלהים חיים ע"פ אליהו הנביא זכור לטוב וברשותו גלה מה שגלה.

14. הסתיר זה בכמה הסתרות כמו חידות ומשלים והתומים באלף עזקאן ואין מבין דבריהם אשר ע"כ רבים מהמקובלים האחרונים תפסו הדברים כמעט כפשוטן בהגשמה רבה השם יכפר בעדם.

15. כי לא כדורות הקדמונים והימים הראשונים שהיו באלף החמישי דורות הללו והימים האלה כי באותן אלף שנים היו שערי חוכמה זו סגורים ומסוגרים ולכן לא היו אז מקובלים אלא מעטים... לא כן באלף הששי הזה שנפתחו שערי אורה שערי רחמים כי הוא קרוב לעת קץ הימין ושמחה של מצוה ... ובפרט שנדפסו כל כתבי הקודש להאר"י לוריא ז"ל אשר פתח לנו שערי תורה שהיו סתומים וחתומים באלף עזקין מימות עולם.

16. כי זה השער לצאת בו מן הגלות, לעלות בשמחה לארצנו י"ר שיהיה זה במהרה בימינו.

17. כי כל אשר לא עיין בספרי הפלוסופים האלהים ובפרט בס' המורה להרמב"ם ז"ל להבין בענין הרחקת התארים והשנויים וההתפעלות ממנו ית', אין לו מבוא בשום אופן להכנס בחדרי הקבלה, השער הזה יה' סגור לא יפתח.

18. כי לדעתם יהיו מ"ב (מעשי בראשית) ומ"מ (מעשי מרכבה) סודות חכמת הקבלה... דע שאם כונת הרמב"ם ז"ל במ"ב ובמ"מ על הנמצא מבואר בס' הטבע והפלסופי' ולא יותר, אזי בודאי צדקו יחדיו המלעיגים עליו, אבל כיון שהוא אומר חכמת הטבע וחכמת האלהות הנה דעתו ז"ל כוללת כל מה שכבר נתבאר בס' ההו' עם כל מה שלא נתבאר עדיין, ר"ל כל מה שבכח שכל האדם להשיג, הנה אין מקום להלעיג עליו כלל... בדברי המקובלים ונאמר שבודאי האמת אתם ר"ל שמ"ב ומ"מ הם סודות יותר עמוקים ונפלאים מאשר חשבו חכמי הטבע הפלוסופים והם באמת סודות הקבלה אבל מה נעשה, הרי שלחן והרי בשר ואין לנו לאכול, כי דבריהם חתומים וסתומים, אין דרך להשגתם וכל דבריהם כדברי הס' החתום אשר יתנו אותו אל יודע ספר ואומר: לא אוכל כי חתום הוא והם כחלמא דלא מפשר ואם תשאלני ותאמרו וכי בשביל שלא השגת כלום מחכמת הקבלה אתה אומר אין דרך להשיגו והלא מצאנו וראינו בכל תפוצות ישראל למאות ולאלפים העוסקים בחכמת הקבלה, התשובה ע"ז גם לי לבב כמוהם בספורי הדברים ופרוש המלות כמותם, לא נופל אנוכי מהם בידיעה זו, אבל מה בצע בידיעתם שאבא ואמא מלבישים לאריך תחת זקנו... וכיוצא באלו הידיעות כי באמת לא

Appendix IV

Chapter 1

1. לא ידמה כל תלמיד בדעתו שיוכל ללמוד ס"ה (ספר הזהר) מפי ספרים בלבד, כי כמה הציצו ונפגעו כאשר שמענו גם ראינו בעו"ה (בעונותינו הרבים) בכת ...ש"ץ שר"י... וצריך שמירה מעולה ועצומה שלש להכשל בכתבי פלסתר חקקי און ומכתבי עמל של ש"ץ שר"י ותלמידיו הארורים אשר התערבו בי (!) ספרי המקובלים ביחוד כתבי האר"י נזדייפו מאוד על ידי המתועבים הללו... וקובעים עצמם כל ימיהם לעסוק בחכמת הנסתר לבדה, כאשר שמעתי נתפשט מנהג זה החדש במדינות מזרחיות שאין פונים ללמוד ידיעת קיום מצוות, רק לחפש בסתרה של תורה ע"י ס"ה (ספר הזהר) ובאר"י בלבד ובעו"ה היא היתה למכשול עון וגרמה פרצה עזה בישראל שע"י כך השליכו אחרי גוום שמירת התורה.

2. חכמת הקבלה מעוטה יפה ומקשטת האדם ורובה קשה, שהכרוך אחריה תבטלהו משאר החכמות היקרות כאשר קרה לכמה גדולים בה שלא היתה ידם תקיפה בגמרא ואיני מגלה ח"ו וד"ל.

3. כבר כתב הג' יעב"ץ בזה הלשון: כל דברי האר"י ז"ל בעץ החיים ושאר הספרים בענינים כאלה כלם אמת מצד ואינו אמת מצד. אמת כפי מה הבין אותם האר"י ז"ל והדומה לו ואינו אמת כלל כפי מה שאנו מבינם אותן כי כל האמור בכתבים וספרים הוא הנגלה של הקבלה וזה אינו אמת, אבל הנסתר של הקבלה הוא לבדו אמת וזה אי אפשר להכתב בשום ספר עכ"ל.

4. כל דברי האר"י ז"ל הם ככל דברי התורה שהם הפרד"ס, וכל מה שאמרנו הנה הוא רק בבחינת הפשט אך הסוד בזה הוא נעלם מאוד.

5. שאין דעתי מסכמת כלל להדפיס ספרי קבלה, והנסתרות לה' אלוקינו ואין דורשין במעשה מרכבה ברבים. והנותן דבר בדפוס הריהו כדורשו במקהלות, ושוה לכל נפש ראוי ובלתי ראוי. ובעוה"ר הן היו בעוכרינו יצאו מזה כמה תקלות ושתיקונם היה יפה מדיבורם. אבל הקונטריסים הנ"ל ראיתי שאין תופס בו השתלשלות האר"י ז"ל כתקוני עולמות ופרצופים אשר עליהם נאמר כבוד ה' הסתר דבר.

6. ונתגשם תורת אמת אשר נקרא קבלה ובאמת היא תורת אמת רק שנחשך ונתגשם עד למאוד בעונינו.

7. כאשר מבואר בהקדמה לסה"ק עץ חיים שהוא רק ראשי פרקים כמציץ מן החרכים ומגלה טפח ומכסה אלפים אמה, לא היה יכול עוד להרחיב הדבור בהרחקת ובהפשטת הגשמיות ממנו ית' ומה גם שלא היה לו מן הצורך כי גלה זאת רק לתלמידיו הקדושים שהיו כבר ממולאים חכמה ובינה יתרה ולמדו דעת מספריו הקדושי' של האלהי מוהרמ"ק זלה"ה.

8. ...בספר הפרדס ושאר ספריו הקדושים ולימד דעת את העם לידע ולהודיע ולהודע שהוא האל ית' מרוחק ונעלה מאוד ממדת הברואים ומזהיר ומשמר ומרחק מאוד מן ההגשמה ח"ו בחכמה זו, כי הם רק שכליים ואורות עליונים וחיות אלהות ית'.

Subject Index

Index of Works Cited

Author Index